ANTHROPOLOGICAL SERIES

NUMBER 6

BARRY C. KENT, GENERAL EDITOR

SUSQUEHANNA'S INDIANS

By BARRY C. KENT

— • —

COMMONWEALTH OF PENNSYLVANIA
THE PENNSYLVANIA HISTORICAL
AND MUSEUM COMMISSION
HARRISBURG, 1984

THE PENNSYLVANIA HISTORICAL AND MUSEUM COMMISSION

Preface

SUSQUEHANNA'S INDIANS tells part of the story of native Americans who lived along the streams and rivers of central Pennsylvania from about the fifteenth century A.D. until their eventual contacts with the Europeans. Some of the narrative is derived from contemporary historical accounts, but most of it is based on reconstructions from archeological discoveries.

Archeological interpretations of former cultures depend primarily upon examining and understanding the manufacture and/or use of preserved material things—artifacts—now buried in the places once occupied by ancient peoples. In the case of the Susquehanna's Indians the artifacts are things made and used by them as well as articles which they gradually acquired from the Europeans.

Through analogy, logic and some other fairly complex scientific methods, archeologists attempt to utilize artifacts, or what they imply, to more fully portray the way of life of those who left them. Descriptions of artifacts, and methods and results of analyses, are usually presented to other archeologists in technical reports so that they can evaluate the research and, perhaps, develop their own interpretations. However, in the long run archeology must be done for all those who want to understand our cultural heritage. Continued support for such work depends upon presenting final conclusions to the public in a manner that is understandable and which continues to stimulate a general curiosity about the past.

Much of this book is a description of artifacts, but its major goal is to explain, to as wide an audience as possible, how these things and their associations in the places where they were uncovered reveal something about the general culture and history of the Susquehanna's Indians.

ISBN 0-89271-024-1

Acknowledgments

LITERALLY hundreds of people have contributed, in one way or another, to this study. There are simply too many to list each by name. However, a number have given so extensively of their time, efforts and insights that they must be mentioned here.

For both sentimental and real reasons Henry Heisey heads the list of those to whom the writer is most indebted for help, guidance and encouragement in this undertaking. Henry, who lived on and farmed one of the most important of the Susquehannock sites, assisted with the excavation and interpretation of the site, while at the same time tolerating the inconveniences which our work there often caused him. Moreover, he has been a major participant in Susquehanna Valley Indian studies. Much of his research and many of his ideas are incorporated in this book.

Charles E. Hunter has been the greatest single contributor of time and energy. Charlie worked as a field director on several archeological excavations relative to this project; and in addition, he provided invaluable help in library, archival and museum research, plus extensive assistance with the details of manuscript, figure and bibliographic preparation.

Other than the writer's own institution, the Pennsylvania Power and Light Company of Allentown, Pennsylvania, has been the largest contributor of funds, for both fieldwork (in 1968, 1969, 1974 and 1978) and manuscript preparation (1981-1982). The assistance and cooperation of P.P.&L., particularly through their representative, Mr. Robert Zundel, are gratefully acknowledged.

Also on the list of the writer's mentors in the field of Susquehanna Valley archeology is John Witthoft, who has helped by generously sharing his extensive knowledge, and who, in fact, laid the foundations upon which most of the present interpretations are built. Ira F. Smith III, directed a good portion of the fieldwork for this study, and it was with him that the writer formulated many of the ideas expressed here. Others include: William A. Hunter, who provided invaluable leads in the area of historical research; Steve Warfel, who frequently served as field director and also critically reviewed much of the manuscript; and James T. Herbstritt, who also contributed in the field, read and commented upon portions of the manuscript, and assisted with much of the photography. Additional friends and colleagues who contributed in their own special ways include Fred Kinsey, Vance Packard, Charles Douts, Jr., Chuck Lucy, Art Futer, Gary Webster and Kurt Carr. Denise Grove typed or retyped most of the manuscript. Harold Myers, Associate Historian and publications editor for the Pennsylvania Historical and Museum Commission, edited the manuscript and made vast improvements in it.

During the course of the excavations many property owners put up with interruptions in their lives and landscapes, and to all of them goes a hearty thank you. But in particular, we must mention Mr. and Mrs. Lester Witmer, Mr. Leroy Funk and his brothers, and, especially, Mr. and Mrs. Scott Haverstick, all of Manor Township, Lancaster County, Pennsylvania.

Among those numerous contributors who must remain unnamed are over 50 field-crew members and other field directors, hundreds of field volunteers, dozens of college interns, and scores of volunteer laboratory assistants.

Finally, the author wishes to extend his gratitude to the administration of the Pennsylvania Historical and Museum Commission, which has largely financed and otherwise supported this work from beginning to publication.

Contents

List of Figures

List of Tables

Introduction

AT some remote time in the past, perhaps more than twelve thousand years ago, a single human being became the first person to see the Susquehanna River. In all likelihood he approached the main stem of the river from the west by following the downstream course of one of its tributaries. He did not call it Susquehanna, nor did he stand in great awe of its size and beauty. His people and their ancestors had seen and crossed many rivers in this new land.

Thousands of years would pass before the descendants of the discoverer of this river would come to know its many sources from Lake Otsego in New York to the head of Chesapeake Bay in Maryland.

These first occupants of Pennsylvania's longest river valley lived here at a time when the climate and vegetation were very different from today. The ragged front of the massive Wisconsin glacier stood not too far to the north in New York State; arctic plants grew in the numerous openings of spruce-fir forests. Mastodon, musk ox and herds of caribou grazed along the river's edge and in the clearings. These were some of the major food sources of the first human occupants along the Susquehanna. The paths of their wandering were made in pursuit of the most abundant of these resources. All that remains at the campsites of these tiny groups of people, to remind us of their existence, are a few of their carefully fashioned fluted spearpoints, knives, scrapers and other stone tools.

Nothing is known of their language, social organization, religion or their physical appearance; and we can only guess at the travails of their daily existence. Archeologists refer to them as the Paleo-Indians.

Artifacts of these first inhabitants of the New World are found widely scattered throughout North America. In some areas of the country, particularly in the southeastern United States, we can trace a gradual evolution of their stone tools into the succeeding Archaic period. Paleo-Indians living in the Northeast, including the Susquehanna Valley, seem to have followed the retreating Wisconsin glacier to the north. As the climate ameliorated and the environment returned to conditions like those we know today, the Susquehanna Valley, and eventually the entire country, was occupied by people of the Archaic culture.

This period endured throughout the Susquehanna Valley from perhaps 7000 B.C. to about the time of Christ. The period is characterized by its many different shapes of knives and spearpoints, which occur in great abundance on the terraces and flood plains along the Susquehanna.

Archaic peoples were hunters, fishermen and gatherers of wild-plant foods; and although the shapes of their stone tools changed as time went on, their basic economy did not. The next major cultural period, called the Early Woodland, is marked by the first use of pottery cooking vessels. Hunting and gathering were still the primary means of existence, but as time passed a food-getting revolution began to take place. This was the introduction of horticulture, and as it became more productive it led to enormous changes in the Indians' way of life. Larger and more permanent villages of people began to appear. Eventually these communities developed distinctive regional or tribal identities; and as is the way with human beings who fancy themselves as being unique and special, competition and conflict increased between the regions and tribes.

This was the stage onto which arrived the next and final source of culture change for the Indian—the Europeans. For about 50 years the Indian tribes of the Susquehanna Valley had only the merest hint of these strangers from another place. But by the middle of the sixteenth century the rumors were confirmed, at first by the shiny metal and glass objects which they received from other tribes closer to the ocean, and then by the tales of their own people who actually saw the great ships and the strange pale-skinned men whose bodies were covered with cloth and metal.

With the seventeenth century there began a number of historical accounts relative to the Susquehanna's Indians. In some respects the volume of primary and secondary resource material on this subject is almost staggering, especially if one takes into account the records of European and colonial events necessary to fully understand the background and nature of the interaction between whites and Indians. However, at the same time there is an enormous dearth of recorded information about so many aspects of the history and culture of these colonial-period Indians.

The people who, during the seventeenth century, became known as the Susquehannocks are historically the most important Indians of the Susquehanna River valley. Susquehannock culture history is in fact the major emphasis of the present volume; but again, we cannot hope to understand the Susquehannocks without examining the history and archeology of the other Indians who lived here and with whom they interacted.

Virtually all the important ethnohistoric data pertaining to colonial-period Indians of the Susquehanna Valley have been reported in other secondary literature. Undoubtedly some additional primary sources remain undiscovered in private hands, or are buried still in obscure archival repositories, but such documents will probably come to light only by accident. They now seem beyond the reach of most deliberate searches for new accounts.

Even though there has been a fair amount of historical and archeological research concerning these Indians, it is still apparent that a complete and orderly account of them has yet to be compiled. The present work is not an attempt to write a new history of the Susquehanna's Indians, at least not in the strict sense of that term. It would be difficult to find material not already covered by Hanna (1911) or Jennings (1967, 1968, 1978), upon whom we have relied heavily for much of the basic historical research. Rather, we have tried to undertake an updated and concise outline of the culture history of the Susquehanna's Indians, as interpreted through archeological investigations at many of their sixteenth- through eighteenth-century sites and, where possible, of the relation of these sequences to historical documentation.

The methods and final form of culture history, as the term is used by archeologists, are quite different from those of history as written by historians. Archeologists are frequently able to recover only certain remains of the tools (sometimes called material culture) of a society which they are studying. Consequently, much of their initial investigation is necessarily focused upon understanding the most basic aspect of an ancient culture or former way of life. Specifically this means determining how the excavated tools or artifacts reflect a society's particular form of technology (i.e., its characteristic or unique patterns of things and techniques by which it sustains life and attempts to make life more comfortable and secure). Once having demonstrated at least the general pattern of the technology of an archeologically investigated society, it is possible, through comparison with other ethnographically or historically better-known societies, to suggest something about the other aspects of its culture. These could include its patterns of social organization and, perhaps, even some notion of its ideologies. Tracing any and all of the demonstrable patterns of a culture and the changes in those patterns through time is what culture history means to an archeologist.

As implied here, archeologists must take advantage of any historical resources which may pertain to and enhance the understanding of the cultural remains which they unearth; however, it is most important that they exercise sufficient caution in the use of such records. Government proceedings, journals, letters, maps and other written accounts of the past are fraught with inaccuracies, uncertainties and sometimes propaganda or even lies. We have attempted to sift through these records with an open mind, recognizing the lure of events and statements which seem to fit or confirm the archeological sequences. Likewise, the results of archeological investigations must be used judiciously, for all too often, even though the "data may be good," the conclusions drawn from them can be fanciful and unscientific.

As previously stated, the primary purpose of this book is to interpret the culture of the Susquehannock Indians who formerly occupied the Susquehanna Valley of central and eastern Pennsylvania. In order to provide the reader with a basic framework for understanding and/or criticizing these interpretations, we first discuss the techniques which have been used for ordering (dating) the events of Susquehannock history and culture. This is followed by a very general summary of their cultural characteristics, and then a thumbnail sketch of the chronological and technological stages into which changing Susquehannock culture can be arranged. Next comes a more detailed fitting of the recorded historical material to the archeological records of all the various historic-period Indians of the Susquehanna Valley.

As a kind of appendix of the evidence, and so that the more casual reader need not struggle with the arduous details, we have separately presented the descriptions and analyses of the various categories of material culture or artifacts. Finally, there is a discussion of the methods and results of the archeological excavations of the sites. These include a variety of earlier investigations, plus the Susquehannock archeological research program which the Pennsylvania Historical and Museum Commission has been conducting since 1968.

All of these things, when considered together, provide the major references for our portrayal of the culture history of the Susquehanna's Indians.

Arranging the Culture History Of Susquehanna's Indians

DATING TECHNIQUES

BOTH history and archeology are concerned with discovering and ordering sequences of past events (or cultural patterns), the causes for their changes, and their impact on human ways of life. Knowing the approximate time, or when possible the precise date, at which various human events occurred is an important part of our ability to organize, understand and remember them. Sometimes it may appear that archeologists, in particular, are obsessed with discovering actual dates for things. Frequently this is possible when dealing with the era of written accounts and recorded dates; but in those vast periods of time before writing—the prehistoric era—such determinations are rarely possible.

Archeologists, of course, employ carbon 14 and other dating techniques which can produce approximate (more or less *absolute*) dates; but usually the results are expressed in brackets of hundreds or even thousands of years. More often, archeologists are only able to work out the *relative* chronology of human events; i.e., that one event occurred before another, with no proof of any actual (absolute) dates of occurrence.

Establishing the relative order, and where possible any absolute dates, of the changing cultural patterns of the Susquehanna's Indians is a necessary part of this book. It seems essential, therefore, at the beginning, to explain how unrecorded events or patterns of past cultures are discovered and then given some form of chronological ordering. The reader should be aware that any dates presented here, whether relative or absolute, are not infallible and that they should be continually subjected to criticism.

Archeology which has been done over the years concerning the Susquehanna's Indians has resulted in a basic or relative chronological ordering of many of their habitation sites and the artifacts found at those places. These arrangements have been accomplished through an archeological technique known as the "direct historical approach." This means working backward in time from some known date or cultural condition by tracing changes or differences in the technological remains (tools) at the various sites. This methodology involves several important anthropological assumptions. The first is that most of the technological products of a given culture will generally conform to specific patterns or customs for a certain length of time. Pottery, which will be dealt with in greater detail later on, is especially noteworthy in this regard. A majority of the pottery produced by a specific group at a particular moment in time will exhibit a uniformity of shape or decoration, in other words a type. In general we can say that, no matter where examples of the same type are found, they were probably all produced by one group of people at about the same time. Usually, however, a few persons at a given place and time will not conform to the commonly accepted or most popular type. Some will continue to make or use antique types. At the other end of this spectrum we may find certain individuals who have innovated or are making a new type. The most abundant type at a site can be considered the hallmark of that particular place and its time period. Stated in another way, anthropological studies have shown that a new type (an item of technology, a religious custom, actually any culture trait or behavioral pattern) will usually have a slow beginning, a somewhat later period of wide acceptance, and then a period of decline or decreased use.

Accordingly, when we find another site in which our hallmark type or trait is a minor occurrence or a small percentage of the total, a time difference between the two sites may be indicated. At this point these differences in the frequency of occurrence at the sites do not tell us which is earlier, for in neither of the sites can we necessarily determine which of the minor types are innovations and which are antiques.

We can more easily follow this discussion by using types of something specific, like pottery, and a diagram (or histogram as it is called in archeology) in which we have three separate sites and three different types of pottery which occur in differing (percentages of the total) amounts at each site; for example:

Sites	*Types and percentages of occurrence*		
	A	*B*	*C*
1	70%	30%	
2		10%	90%
3	10%	60%	30%

Given the above assumptions we can arrange these three sites in sequence based simply on the types which they share. In this case sites 1 and 3 both produce types A and B. Sites 2 and 3 share types B and C. Therefore, we can arrange them in order of their type relationships as 1—3—2. However, with the information given we still cannot tell if site 1 or site 2 is the earliest; site 3 is obviously chronologically in the middle. If we produce some additional archeological information about the sites, a chronological ordering may be possible. For example, if site 2 also yields European trade goods, but the others do not, then obviously the chronological ordering of the sites from latest to earliest should be 2—3—1. At this point we can also order the hallmark types from latest to earliest based upon the chronological position of the sites at which they are most abundant. Our diagram, rearranged in chronological order, would be as follows:

			Types	
		C	*B*	*A*
	sites	*latest*		*earliest*
latest	2	90%	10%	
	3	30%	60%	10%
earliest	1		30%	70%

Now we have a relative chronological ordering of habitation sites and some artifact types. However, we have no absolute dates for any of this, other than that one site existed during the historic (trade good) period. Occasionally, European manufactures are precisely datable; for example, coins, and sometimes other objects, bear the date of their manufacture. When such objects occur in an archeological site a more precise dating of the occupation of that place is clearly possible. Continued studies of the changes in form or style over time of European and colonial manufactures provide increasing potential for more accurate dating of the archeological sites at which they are recovered. In addition, historical documents will sometimes provide a definite date for an archeologically recognizable place.

The chronological ordering of the Susquehannock and other Indian sites which follows is based upon the above described dating procedures. Specific dates are derived from recent studies by the author, or those assigned by Witthoft and Kinsey (1959), based on their comparison of trade goods in Susquehannock sites with those chronologically ordered by Wray and Schoff (1953) for the Seneca sites of western New York. Trade-good dates and those implied by historical documents can be of real utility only if they are continually criticized and adjusted in the light of current work. A large portion of the present study is directed toward such updated refinements.

General Characteristics of Susquehannock Culture

As other studies have shown, and as we will point out in the present work, the Susquehannocks were culturally and linguistically very closely related to the Iroquois of New York State. Although the evidence is not always very positive, we can basically assume that the social organization, religious structures and technological capabilities of the Susquehannocks were more or less identical with those of the ethnographically and historically better-known Iroquois.

By simple comparison with Iroquis culture, we might propose that Susquehannock social organization also centered about establishing patterns of relationship through female (matrilineal) lines of descent. Membership in a group of relatives and all the benefits derived therefrom were determined by descent from one's mother and her female ancestors. Evidence for kin membership groups among the Susquehannocks is suggested by the "nation" or "family" affiliations given by those Susquehannocks who signed various treaties with the whites, particularly those with the Maryland colony as recorded in its Archives for 1661 and 1666 (Maryland Archives III: 417, 549).

Iroquois religion, and therefore, probably, Susquehannock religion, concerned itself with ways to alleviate individual and group frustrations. As Wallace (1970: 50) points out, the methods for doing so involved rituals of hope and thanksgiving, and rituals of fear and mourning. The former included various communal thanksgiving festivals and were concerned with the significance or interpretation of dreams. Ceremonies concerned with fear and mourning involved witchcraft, the masked dances and condolence rituals.

There is of course no way to be certain that these rituals were practiced in the same form by the Susquehannocks; but comparability in material culture between the two, especially in the artistic portrayals of animals, humans and mythical creatures, and in their concern for the dead suggest great similarity in religious forms.

It is not necessary to turn to Iroquois examples to uncover evidence of Susquehannock subsistence and technology. These are amply disclosed by the archeology at Susquehannock sites. Obviously the products of Susquehannock technology changed, to varying degrees, over the period of its existence. Another of the major concerns of the present work is the tracing of these changes.

In their most characteristic or typical form, the Susquehannocks can be described as a tribe of stone-age agriculturists who raised fairly large crops of corn, beans and squash on the fertile flood plains near their generally stockaded and well-situated villages of bark-covered longhouses. The middens and forgotten storage pits of their villages reveal that the women also gathered large quantities of wild-plant foods, seeds, nuts, insects, reptiles, mollusks, etc., while the men hunted and fished for virtually every mammal, major bird, and fish.

Environmental Setting

The environment of the Susquehanna River valley played a very influential role in the general character of Susquehannock and other native cultures which existed there. Naturalists usually consider environment as consisting of physical surroundings, which are made up of climate, hydrology,

Figure 1. The Susquehanna River looking south from Long Level in York County, before the construction of Safe Harbor dam.

geology, geography, etc., and the natural environment of plants and animals. Anthropologists include other cultures when discussing the environment of a particular group of human beings. Much of this book is concerned with the cultural environment of the Susquehannock Indians; that part of their surroundings changed rapidly and radically and with great impact on their way of life. Their physical and natural environment remained largely unchanged during this period, and thus once we have basically described it, we can consider it as a constant in terms of its effect upon changing Susquehannock culture.

The Susquehanna River valley cuts across a number of distinct physiographic and biotic zones. For that reason it is difficult to characterize its physical and natural environment succinctly.

The North Branch of the river has many tributary sources which emanate from the Appalachian Plateau Province of central New York. (See Fenneman 1938 for a fuller description of physiographic provinces.) From the point at Athens, Pennsylvania, where the North Branch crosses the Pennsylvania-New York boundary for the second time, and is joined by the Chemung, the river flows in a meandering but generally southeastern direction. Frequently these meanders are flanked on the outside of the bend by steep cliffs and on the inside by broad flood plains and second terraces composed of glacial till and alluvium. Here are found most of the Indian sites of this region. Aboriginal forest types in this portion of the Appalachian Plateau are described as hemlock—white pine—and northern hardwoods. Climate and basic faunal types are more like those of New York State and southeastern Canada. (See Braun 1964, and Dice 1943 concerning forest types and biotic provinces.)

As the river enters the Appalachian Mountain Section of the Ridge and Valley Province, at the mouth of the Lackawanna River and the upper end of the Wyoming Valley, it turns 90 degrees to flow in a southwest direction. From here the river no longer has any sharp meanders, but rather flows parallel to the ridge and valley topography. This province also marks the beginning of a new biotic zone. Here the forests were made up largely of oak, chestnut and hickory, with various conifers in the higher elevations. Animal species are those characteristically found in the so-called Carolinian Zone (Dice 1943). For our present purpose, we need not worry about the specifics since the same major species occurred throughout the Susquehanna Valley.

Indian sites of the various time periods in this area occur almost anywhere that there is a wide flat along the river, but a vast majority of sites are in the Wyoming Valley, centered around Wilkes-Barre. The North Branch continues its southwestward trend to Northumberland where it is joined by the West Branch. Here it turns almost due south.

Hundreds of tiny tributaries rising in the Appalachian Plateau of north central Pennsylvania enter the main stem of the West Branch of the Susquehanna along its eastward course. It emerges from the plateau at Lock Haven, collects the outflow of the Bald Eagle Creek, and continues along the scenic boundary of this province and the Appalachian Mountain Section on its way to join the North Branch.

Indian sites along the West Branch, in the Appalachian Mountain Section, occur on its several large islands and on the flood plains and higher terraces tucked between the river and the base of the ridges, or in the broader valley openings, usually at the confluences of smaller streams. Upstream from Lock Haven, in the Plateau, Late Woodland sites are often found on high ground quite removed from the river's edge.

From Northumberland southward to Harrisburg the Susquehanna cuts through or around the ends of 14 mountain ridges. Here the Indian sites are in the mouths of the cross-cut valleys and particularly on the lower-lying, frequently flooded large islands in the river. The giants of these, like the Isle of Que, Hoover, Clemson and Haldeman, are almost continuous sites.

At the downstream tip of Haldeman Island the Susquehanna is joined by the Juniata, and from that point the now often mile or more wide river makes its most spectacular slices through the Appalachian Mountains.

As it emerges from the gap in the Blue Mountain, just above Harrisburg, it reaches the Great Valley Section of the Ridge and Valley Province. The crossing of these two features—the Great Valley and the river—marks the largest intersection of prehistoric travel routes in Pennsylvania.

Near the mouth of the Swatara Creek, the Susquehanna enters the Triassic Lowland Section of the Piedmont Province. Here too, the sites occur frequently on the islands—notably Poplar, Hill, Shelley, Three Mile and Brunner. Terraces like those at Goldsboro, Bainbridge and Marietta also have numerous sites. Archaic and Early and Middle Woodland sites occur in all areas, but Late Woodland sites are comparatively infrequent on the islands.

The Piedmont Highland Section of the Piedmont Province begins at Chickies Creek. From here the river is rather continuously entrenched in the rolling terrain of the Piedmont Highlands. Small, usually basin-like openings occur along the river at Wrightsville, Columbia and Washington Boro. The latter of these might well be considered the Indian capital of Pennsylvania from Paleo-Indian times to the beginning of the eighteenth century. In aboriginal times the river must have been teeming with both anadromous and local species of fish, as well as freshwater mussels. The predominantly oak, chestnut and hickory forests provide abundant nuts and other wild-plant foods for man and numerous other animals, including such large species as elk, bear and deer. The fertile limestone and alluvial soils, the seemingly unique weather patterns, and the longer growing season make this basin one of today's richest agricultural areas in the northeastern United States. And so it must have been for the agriculturally based Shenks Ferry and later the Susquehannock Indians, for they played out practically their entire culture histories in this area.

Turkey Hill, at the downriver end of the Washington Boro basin, forces a narrowing of the river into the deep trench which it has carved through the balance of the Piedmont. At present, the only portion of this stretch of the river which retains some vestige of its unique, scenic, rocky and natural splendor is just below Holtwood Dam. Prior to the construction of the three hydroelectric dams in this part of the lower Susquehanna, its entire bottom was visibly choked with often massive outcrops of mica schist, sometimes catching soil and creating islands, or in other places exhibiting massive pleistocene potholes or causing waterfalls. These rocky conditions, while they created excellent fish trapping, also make it the least hospitable portion of the Susquehanna for canoe travel.

Here, practically the only, but very popular, places for Indian occupation were those portions of the river's high rocky islands which had captured some alluvial deposits. These also represent some of the Susquehanna's most significant deep, stratified Archaic sites.

Near Port Deposit, Maryland, the river crosses the so-called Fall

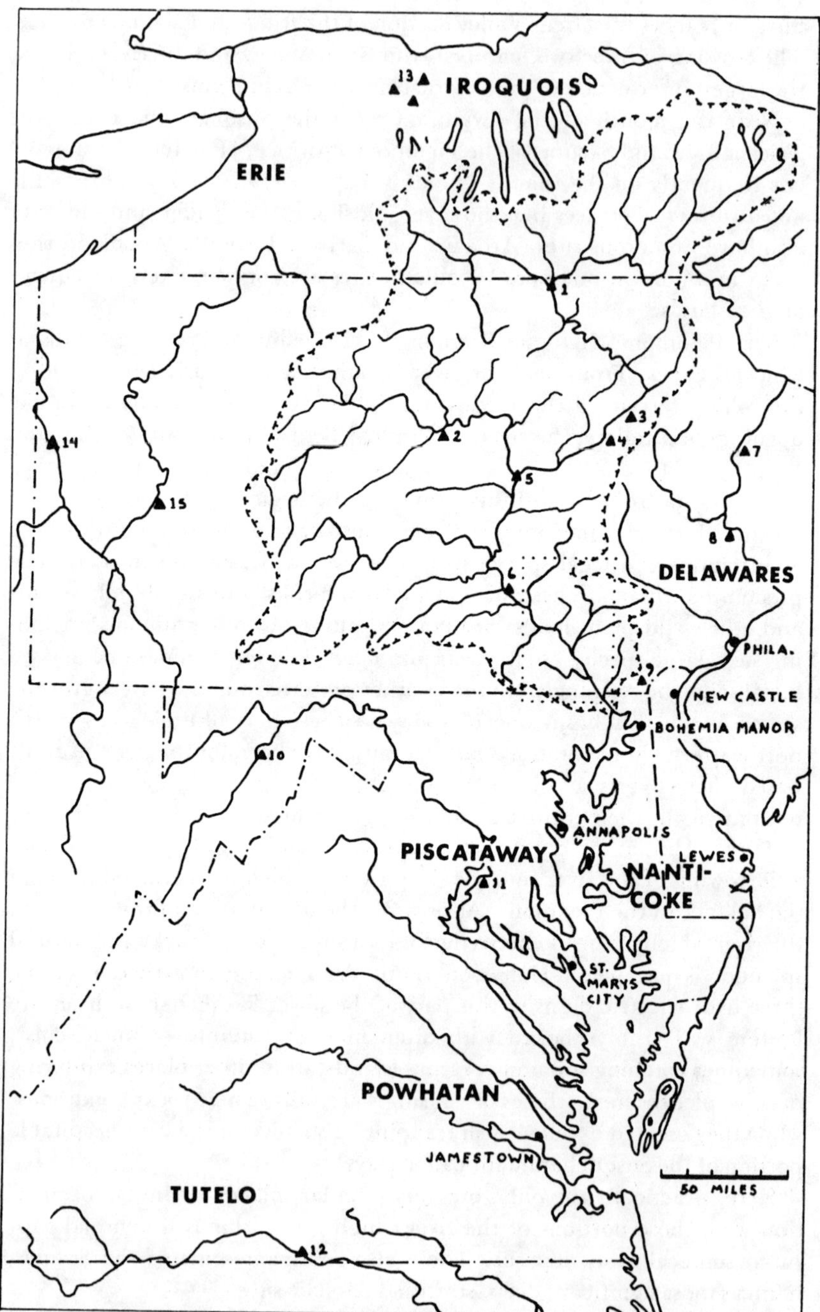

Figure 2. Map of the Susquehanna Valley and surrounding tribal areas (see opposite legend).

Line—that point which marks the head of tidal waters and the outer edge of the Piedmont physiographic province. Just a few miles further south, through the Coastal Plain, the Susquehanna ends in the Chesapeake Bay.

STAGES OF SUSQUEHANNOCK CULTURE HISTORY

Having touched briefly upon the chronometric methods, the general character of Susquehannock culture and its environmental setting, it seems prudent to proceed by giving the reader a general framework into which various distinguishable stages of Susquehannock culture can be divided. Technologies are the aspects of culture most discernible through archeology, and indeed, these aspects are most subject to change. As a result, the present stages are largely defined by recognizable differences in technology through time. When possible in later chapters, other aspects of Susquehannock culture will be added to this scenario.

The initial chronological ordering of Susquehannock sites in the lower Susquehanna Valley was largely worked out by Donald Cadzow (1936) as a result of his investigations of sites in Lancaster County, Pennsylvania. Cadzow and others before him (Hanna 1911; Landis 1929) recognized the archeological and historical interrelationships of the Susquehannocks and the Iroquois.

A refinement of Susquehannock archeological sequences and their cultural relationships with the Iroquois resulted from years of research on earlier notes and collections, and more current field work, by John Witthoft (1959a). His arrangements of Susquehannock culture history form the basis of our present-day archeological ordering of events.

To be certain, there is room for refinement and correction of Witthoft's sequences. To some extent these are reflected in the present thumbnail sketch. Others will be dealt with more fully in later chapters of this volume.

This brief introductory outline can be most concisely treated by reference to individual, or to groups of similar, habitation sites which, according to the methods of the direct historical approach to dating, or by virtue of trade good or document dates, fall into particular time periods. Generally, the unifying characteristics of a single site, or those which serve to relate a number of sites of a particular time span, are the technological as-

Figure 2, opposite. Inset: lower Susquehanna Valley (see Figure 3). Sites mentioned in the text: (1) Tioga Point (36Br3); (2) Quiggle (36Cn6); (3) Wyoming Valley; (4) Wapwallopen; (5) Shamokin; (6) Paxtang; (7) Minisink; (8) Overpeck (36Bu5); (9) Minguhanan (36Ch3); (10) Romney; (11) Accokeek Creek (Piscataway); (12) Occaneechee; (13) the Seneca towns; (14) the Kuskuskies; (15) Kittanning.

pects of the culture whose remains are found there. One of the most sensitive or diagnostic representatives of such technologies is pottery type.

Archeological investigations of the various Susquehannock sites have permitted the definition of seven technologically and/or chronologically distinct stages or periods of Susquehannock culture. All of the known major habitation sites can be placed in one or another of these seven stages. In addition, there are at least three other less well known time periods of apparently distinctive Susquehannock cultural dynamics, but for which we presently have either few or no identified archeological sites. These are treated below as arbitrary stages.

In order that we may conveniently discuss these periods, those which are not considered arbitrary have each been given a name which most readily calls to mind their identification in the previous literature. By and large this means using the name of the most important site of each period. Since we rarely know the name the Indians gave their town, we have had to assign our own designation—usually the name of the property owner at the time the site was first excavated. Hence the curious archeological practice of labeling an Indian site or period with a German or English surname.

Common Roots of Susquehannock and Iroquois Culture: The First Arbitrary Stage

In anthropological terms the stated (Witthoft 1959a: 19-21) relationships between the New York State Iroquois and the Susquehannocks would suggest either *divergence* or *convergence*. The former would imply a common ancestry, while the latter could indicate parallel development and diffusion (cultural exchange) between two entirely separate cultures. On the surface it might appear that a convergence and/or diffusion were/was in effect, since Susquehannock culture seemed to become increasingly like that of certain Iroquoian groups, particularly Seneca and Cayuga. On the other hand, it has been more difficult to recognize a divergence of Iroquois and Susquehannock from a common ancestor. This has been due to the paucity of indicative remains and the lack of work in this area. Actually we hope to demonstrate both divergence and a more or less continual diffusion between the two cultures.

Witthoft (1959a, and in MacNeish 1952: 55) was the first to point to their potential common roots, largely as manifest in the proto-Cayuga and Seneca pottery. A type known as Richmond Incised emerges from the myriad of earlier Owasco pottery forms which, although locally influenced and varied, underlie all of Iroquois ceramic development. The actual sequences from basic Owasco ceramics to recognizable tribal Iroquoian forms include a variety of horizon types, such as Oak Hill Corded, and then Chance Incised among the Oneida, Onondaga and Mohawk. In the

Seneca-Cayuga area similar developments take place, involving cord-impressed decorations on collared vessels, followed by incised decorations on increasingly higher collars, and finally various Cayuga and Seneca types. Richmond Incised would be one of the early incised types in that sequence.

Proto-Susquehannock Stage

Witthoft (1959a: 56-59) recognized another poorly known ceramic type which apparently developed out of Richmond Incised. He called the type Proto-Susquehannock, and as such *he felt* that it represented the earliest distinguishable Susquehannock material culture.

This is the second of our stages of Susquehannock culture and is in a large sense arbitrary, mainly because no single-component sites that produce this pottery have been found, and indeed because it is so poorly known in general. Nevertheless, the pottery does exist (see Lucy and Vanderpoel 1979), and stylistically it does seem to be leading into very distinctively Susquehannock pottery.

Proto-Susquehannock pottery had its inception sometime during the fifteenth or early sixteenth century. Because its presently known distribution is primarily in Bradford County, Pennsylvania, its transition from the earlier Richmond Incised may also have taken place there, or along the Chemung River toward the center of distribution for Richmond Incised in west central New York. Proto-Susquehannock, like Richmond Incised, is a grit-tempered ware. In Bradford County it occurs in small amounts on scattered sites, and occasionally it is found in apparent association with the immediately succeeding Susquehannock pottery type.

Early Schultz Stage and the Southward Migration

The third stage is also somewhat arbitrary, but certainly less so than the preceding stages. Again, it is based primarily upon a distinctive pottery type with a more or less limited geographical and chronological distribution. The pottery of this stage is *shell-tempered* and very similar to (but also distinguishable from) that of the later stage, which is called Schultz Incised. Thus the reason, albeit unimaginative, for calling the present stage *early* Schultz. Early Schultz Incised pottery is found at various small and scattered sites along the Susquehanna River in Bradford County, Pennsylvania, and in adjacent Tioga County, New York.

On the basis of its apparently very rare occurrence with scraps of European brass and perhaps a few glass beads, Witthoft (1959a), following Wray and Schoff (1953), suggested a date of about 1550 for this pottery type. More recent studies of early trade goods would suggest that their very earliest appearance on Indian sites of this general region in the northeastern United States could be as early as 1525 (Bradley 1979: 355-65).

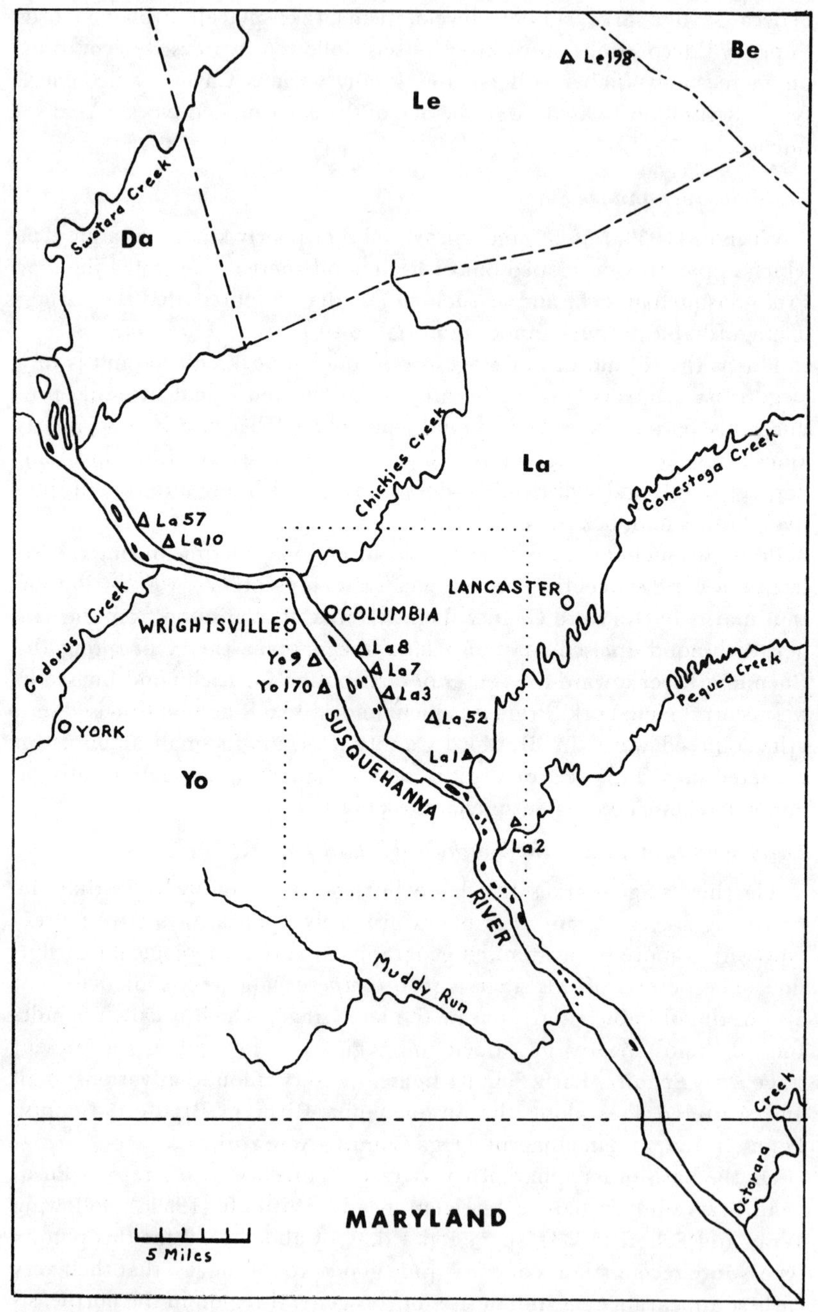

Figure 3. Map of the lower Susquehanna Valley (see opposite legend).

As we presently understand it, the settlement pattern of this period is one of various small, scattered sites along the upper reaches of the Susquehanna River. However, toward the end of this stage, sometime prior to 1575, the people responsible for the early Schultz Incised pottery began to abandon their small villages on the upper Susquehanna. Most of them eventually settled in Lancaster County on the lower Susquehanna, and that event marks the last phase of this stage. Where they settled between the upper Susquehanna and Lancaster County and how long it took them to move from one place to the other are something of a mystery. Eventually, and as it becomes better known, this period of migration will need to be considered a separate stage of Susquehannock culture history. We do find scattered pieces of early Schultz Incised pottery (and sometimes whole pots, see Wren 1914) along the way between the two areas, but nowhere have we found any clear evidence of the people having stayed very long; thus, for the moment, we will let this time of relocation stand as an arbitrary substage of the early Schultz period.

Early Schultz Incised pottery is, on one hand, unquestionably like classic Schultz Incised Susquehannock pottery; however, on the other hand, or more precisely at the other end of the time spectrum, it is far less like its presumed ancestor, Proto-Susquehannock; or so it might appear.

At this point a few words of explanation concerning the transition of Proto-Susquehannock pottery to early Schultz Incised seem in order. Later in this volume we explain more fully the theoretical transition of Proto-Susquehannock to early Schultz Incised. In essence, what we have proposed is that during the fifteenth and early sixteenth centuries, different ethnic groups of northern Pennsylvania and New York State were participating in what might be called a pan-proto-Iroquoian ceramic interaction sphere. Some of its participants in the area of Pennsylvania were the people at the Quiggle site and elsewhere on the West Branch of the Susquehanna River; the Wyoming Valley people at Wilkes-Barre; various groups in the upper Delaware; and the makers of Proto-Susquehannock pottery on the upper Susquehanna. Each of these ethnic groups may have made its own contribution to the interaction sphere, and each may have borrowed certain traits from the sphere.

We are proposing that the Proto-Susquehannocks borrowed the idea of shell-tempering their pottery from the people of the West Branch of the

Figure 3, opposite. Inset: Washington Boro area (see Figure 4). Site names: (36La1) Roberts; (36La2) Shenks Ferry; (36La3) Strickler; (36La7) Schultz; (36La8) Washington Boro Village; (36La10) Billmyer; (36La52) Conestoga Town; (36La57) Conoy Town; (36Le198) Tulpehocken; (36Yo9) Oscar Leibhart; (36Yo170) Byrd Leibhart.

Susquehanna. This, and other borrowings of design elements from less certain sources within the sphere, caused a transformation of Proto-Susquehannock to early Schultz Incised pottery. What we seem to be missing in order to positively prove this transition are examples of those probably very rare transitional pots.

The new pottery type—early Schultz Incised—was being made on the upper Susquehanna by at least 1550 A.D., and perhaps as early as 1525. By 1575, at the latest, the makers of this pottery had abandoned their scattered villages and moved south where they eventually coalesced in one large town. Throughout *most* of the period of their occupation of the upper Susquehanna, the early Schultz Susquehannocks maintained apparently amicable relations with their various Iroquoian neighbors to the north.

It seems logical to propose that their movement south and the coalition of their scattered villages may have been in response to eventual political and economic strife with the Iroquois. There is little or no good archeological evidence for such conflict between the two groups, but nevertheless, the possibility for such still exists. There is some evidence for hostilities between the early Schultz Susquehannocks and certain of their neighbors to the south, viz., the people of the Wyoming Valley, those of the West Branch of the Susquehanna, and particularly the Shenks Ferry people of the lower Susquehanna Valley.

None of these peoples survived as distinct cultures after 1575. Their demise is suspected to be the result of internecine warfare among themselves, followed by Susquehannock aggression during the period of their southward migration.

Table 1

TEN STAGES OF SUSQUEHANNOCK CULTURE HISTORY
WITH APPROXIMATE DATES

1.	Common roots with the Iroquois	-1450 A.D.
2.	Proto-Susquehannock	1450-1525
3.	Early Schultz and migration	1525-1575
4.	Schultz	1575-1600
5.	Washington Boro	1600-1625
6.	Transitional—Billmyer and Roberts	1625-1645
7.	Strickler	1645-1665
8.	Leibhart—defeat and turmoil	1665-1680
9.	The void	1680-1690
10.	Conestoga and the other Indians	1690-1763

Schultz Stage

One of the most complete sequences of trade materials for the eastern United States is that established by Wray and Schoff (1953, and Wray 1973) for the Seneca sites of western New York. A certain amount of refinement of this sequence and its dating is clearly possible. However, this basic chronological ordering is still widely accepted. By comparing the trade goods of the next period (Schultz stage) of Susquehannock cultural development with those of the Seneca sequence, Witthoft (1959a: 67) postulated a date of about 1575 for the beginning of the Schultz stage. More recent investigations have suggested only minor changes in this dating.

The Schultz stage occurs almost exclusively in the lower Susquehanna Valley, and specifically at the Schultz site south of Washington Boro in Lancaster County. Arrival of the Susquehannocks in the lower valley was shortly before 1575. The advance guard may have temporarily occupied small, as yet largely undiscovered hamlets, and/or lived with some of the indigenous Shenks Ferry people. Cadzow's (1936) evidence of remains of both cultures in the same storage pits at the Shenks Ferry site near Pequea points toward a brief co-habitation of the two groups. The sparse trade items found here, including a few strips of cut brass and a spiral brass earring, are very suggestive of the period between 1550 and 1575.

Despite the evidence for their occasional contemporaneous occupation of sites and the obvious interaction and blending of their ceramic arts, there is also evidence of violent contact between the Susquehannocks and Shenks Ferry people. The only known associations of trade goods with the Shenks Ferry are the above-mentioned items at the type site. Numerous fortified late-period Shenks Ferry villages are known from Lancaster County, but no trade goods are associated with any of them, thus suggesting the termination of most of them prior to 1575 and perhaps before 1550. If, as it appears, the Susquehannocks were responsible for the extinction of Shenks Ferry culture, they did so before the Shenks Ferry were able to actively enter the trade-good era. As we will see later, trade goods, at least to the Susquehannocks in the lower valley, became readily available after 1575.

Availability or, perhaps more accurately stated, better access to trade goods may have been a major reason why the Susquehannocks moved into the lower Susquehanna Valley. Competition for, and the actual Susquehannock denial of, those goods to other native peoples may have been the primary cause for conflicts which are implied by the archeological record.

Shenks Ferry culture, largely as traced through pottery changes, had its primary center of development in the lower Susquehanna Valley, beginning perhaps as early as 1300 A.D. It appears to have ancestral roots in the

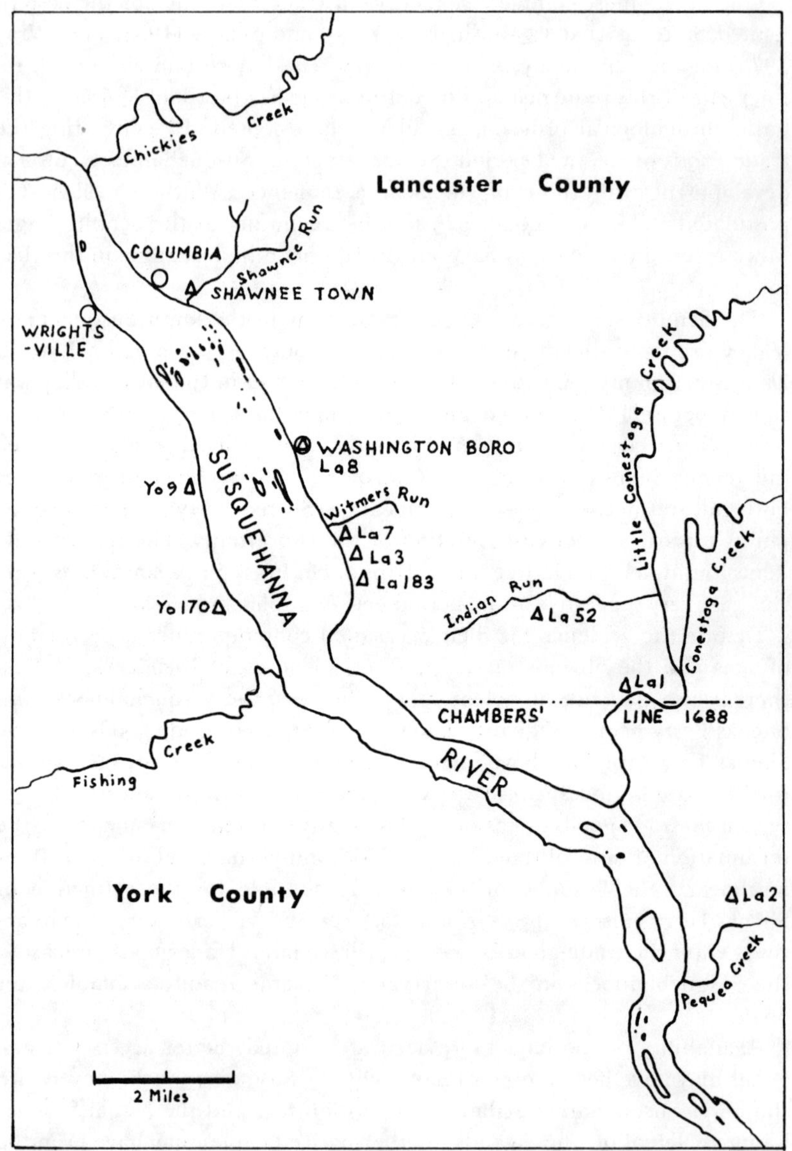

Figure 4. Archeological sites of the Washington Boro area. (See also Figure 3.) Note Chambers line.

Potomac Valley to the south. Following a period of development in the lower Susquehanna, its sites and pottery fanned out in a general northward direction for almost one hundred miles. Withdrawal during the fifteenth century to Lancaster County and into stockaded villages implies Shenks Ferry conflict with someone. Final disruption of their society and the disappearance of their villages in Lancaster County seem to coincide with the first Susquehannock incursions there between 1550 and 1575. However, as we shall see later, some of the Shenks Ferry people and a few of their culture traits survived.

There is no archeological or historical evidence for any major Susquehannock town at this time other than the one at the Schultz farm. The possibility for others must always be considered, since modern development and land use could easily eradicate such a site before anyone has bothered to record it. The Schultz site is twice as large as any of the preceeding Shenks Ferry sites. Population at the Schultz site increased (as several successive enlargements of the stockade suggest) to the point where it was overcrowded with as many as thirteen hundred people. When the soils and firewood around the village were depleted, it became necessary to construct a new town. As a guess, and for convenience, we propose that this occurred in 1600 A.D. An actual date, in any case, would be hard to pinpoint since, in all likelihood, there was a gradual move from one town to another.

Washington Boro Stage

The town of ca. 1600 was located in the present village of Washington Boro, Lancaster County—hence the name for this stage. This town was somewhat larger than Schultz, containing at its maximum perhaps seventeen hundred people. In its heyday it was probably the sole town of this stage, but again we admit that another undiscovered town may have existed. (These possibilities are more fully discussed in our chapter entitled "Other Susquehannock Sites.")

Almost certainly this was the place occupied by the Susquehannocks when Captain John Smith first met their embassy in 1608 at the head of Chesapeake Bay. Its geographical location coincides rather neatly with the position of the place marked *Susquesahanough* on Smith's map (1907: facing 396).

Once again pottery, now called Washington Boro Incised, is the most distinctive cultural trait. The type occurs primarily during this stage and is largely confined to Lancaster County, Pennsylvania. However, occasional pieces of it have been found as far away as New York Iroquois sites.

Transitional Stage: Billmyer and Roberts

Sometime during the latter portion of the occupation of the Washington Boro village site, or perhaps after its complete abandonment, around 1625 A.D., at least two new Susquehannock towns were established. Neither of these is well known. The first, called the Billmyer Quarry site, and largely destroyed by the quarry, is located just south of Bainbridge in Lancaster County. The scanty early collections from this site which still survive are barely sufficient to permit its assignment to a late phase of the Washington Boro period. A second and probably slightly later town was established at the Roberts site on the Conestoga Creek. The trade materials and pottery from this site indicate that it too is in a transitional period between the Washington Boro and subsequent Strickler stage. Also to be included here is the Frey-Haverstick cemetery, adjacent to the Washington Boro village site, and apparently a place where some Susquehannocks returned to bury their dead near the "old ones."

A possible third town of this period is suggested by the description of artifacts encountered in several burials at Columbia, Pennsylvania. *Hazard's Register* (1831) notes that in the *Columbia Spy* there appeared an account of the excavation of the graves of three Indians, and between the feet of one was, among other things, "an earthen vessel, at the spout of which was carved the figure of a human face." This is clearly a Washington Boro Incised vessel. Actually, the account is not clear on the precise location of these excavations, except that they were in the neighborhood of Columbia, and that this might actually include Washington Boro. It is conceivable that a Susquehannock town could be covered or, more realistically, destroyed by the streets and buildings of Columbia.

Strickler Stage

During the 1640's a new stage of Susquehannock culture was emerging. Politically speaking, it is marked by vacillating relationships with England's new Maryland colony, and by massive warfare with the Iroquois in competition for the fur trade. This period is designated the Strickler stage after the type site and its hallmark pottery—Strickler Cord-marked. Ceramics of the period are decoratively degenerate by comparison with earlier wares. Vessel forms are quite distinctive. Actually they have little or no added decoration, and they are almost entirely without the classic shell-tempering of Susquehannock pottery. With the exception of smoking pipes, most other native crafts also begin to deteriorate during this period—primarily as a result of the ready availability of European-made tools, utensils and decorative items.

The Strickler site, located only about five hundred yards south of the Schultz site, is the largest known Susquehannock village. This stockaded town encompasses over 10 acres. History implies and archeology confirms that on at least two of its corners it was protected by European-style bastions, and it appears to have been occupied until about 1665 A.D.

Leibhart Stage: Defeat and Turmoil

Two later Strickler-like sites occur almost directly across the Susquehanna River in York County. These are known as the Byrd (or Lower) Leibhart site and, less than a mile to the north, the Oscar (or Upper) Leibhart site. At least one of these two sites was occupied during the 1660's, probably during the gradual abandonment of the Strickler site. That same site should represent the place where Susquehannock power was brought to an end by wars with the Iroquois, and/or the political turmoil of 1673-1674. The other Leibhart site may represent a brief reoccupation of the area by scattered Susquehannocks who coalesced there in 1676.

After the removal of the Susquehannocks from one or the other of the Leibhart sites in 1674 at the hands of the Iroquois, and perhaps also due to efforts on the part of colonial Maryland, the lower Susquehanna Valley seems to have become a temporary void. The Susquehannocks scattered to various other areas. One remnant of them in 1675 took over an abandoned Piscataway Indian town on the Potomac River opposite the site of Mount Vernon. This was the proverbial move from the frying pan into the fire. Their presence at the Piscataway fort annoyed Virginia and Maryland settlers, who eventually laid siege to the fort. Some weeks later the besieged Susquehannocks slipped away from their attackers. From here they wandered about in what was then frontier Virginia. Unable to find asylum, they returned in 1676, according to several Maryland accounts, to their old fort or to a new fort, presumably near their fort. If indeed the Susquehannocks had built a new fort in 1676, it is most tempting to equate it with whichever is the latest of the Leibhart sites.

Distinguishing the chronological difference between these two sites is difficult. Many archeological samples have been collected from both. However, the artifacts are so similar that we cannot determine if one of them dates after 1676 or if they are strict contemporaries from prior to 1674. Later we make some guesses in this regard, and for now they stand as entirely that.

The Void of 1680 to 1690

Based upon a number of suggestive, but inconclusive documents and maps, it would appear that by about 1680 the Susquehannocks had once again abandoned their fort in the lower Susquehanna Valley. This would provide a terminal date for the latest of the Leibhart sites, and mark the beginning of another of our arbitrary stages. It is known that during this stage a hundred or more Susquehannock warriors, presumably with their families, were living in various Iroquois "castles" in New York. There are vague contemporary hints that some Susquehannocks may have been residing in places other than the Iroquois towns at this time. Even vaguer are the archeological indications of Susquehannock sites prior to 1690. Historical accounts do record passage of Iroquois and Susquehannock war, trading or negotiating parties through the Susquehanna Valley into Maryland.

Since most native crafts typical of the Strickler or Leibhart stages are not present after 1690, we can assume that they were lost in the 10-year period which preceded that date. Even with the void of archeological or historical data, we can postulate that this was an era of extreme culture change and overall social disruption for the Susquehannocks.

Conestoga Stage

Historic records mention a Susquehannock resettlement in the area of their ancient homeland by at least 1696. As will be shown later, there is some justification for beginning the final period of Susquehannock culture history about 1690. This is appropriately referred to as the Conestoga stage—the name of the place where they now resided, the name by which they as people were called, and the name of the town where they were to become extinct.

Actually, many of the people living at Conestoga were Seneca Indians. This nation (among others of the Iroquois) laid claim to the territory of the defeated Susquehannocks, and after 1690 some of them began to settle there with the Susquehannocks.

This town, or the Indian Farm as it was later called, consisted of a tract of land along Indian Run in Manor Township, Lancaster County. During most of the first half of the eighteenth century this was a very noteworthy Indian settlement. Many negotiations, treaties, and purchases were conducted there between the Pennsylvania Provincial government and various Indians. At the middle of the century the inevitable fate of the Conestogas might have been foretold. Their population had dwindled to a handful and their socio-economic condition was in a sorry state of decline. The final curtain of this last stage came abruptly in December, 1763, when the remaining indigent Conestogas were extinguished in the wake of the new and now dominant culture of the Americas.

Knowledge of these latter events is of course not based upon archeology. Rather, it is a part of the larger body of historical accounts of these people, which we will now attempt to correlate in fuller measure with the various stages of Susquehannock culture.

Evidence from History

A Background of Historic Events Relating to the Susquehannocks

THE history of European and Indian confrontation is one of conflict between a highly evolved civilization and an agglomeration of stone-age societies. By and large, the Europeans used the Indians so long as it was economically advantageous; then they eventually dispersed or destroyed them.

Although generally despising the sordid natives, the first colonists frequently found them useful as a means of securing victuals for their starving incipient settlements. Disappointed at the lack of precious metals, the explorers and settlers on the North Atlantic coast soon discovered a seemingly inexhaustible supply of furs for the hungry markets of Europe and Asia. Again the natives were tolerated, as long as they could supply furs; they could then be forced out of the way of the ever-widening land-grab.

The fur trade and the taking of Indian lands are the major factors influencing the course of seventeenth- and early eighteenth-century North American Indian history. Add to this the effects of fanatic religious proselytism, avarice, the inhumanity of man, the processes of acculturation, and a kind of cargo-cult effect, and we have a general picture of the impact and results of European contact on the native inhabitants of the New World.

Not to be outdone by the discoveries of Columbus for Spain, other European countries who could afford to do so soon sent their own explorers to the New World. Even before the end of the fifteenth century, English and Spanish ships laden with cheap trade goods had reached the east coast of North America. Both John Cabot of England and Amerigo Vespucci of Spain may have touched the Chesapeake area before the end of the century.

During the sixteenth century the French joined the list of discoverers. In 1524 Verrazano recorded a general description of Indians which he had seen along the Atlantic coast of present-day New York and New Jersey. Jacques Cartier sailed up the Saint Lawrence as far as the Indian town of Hochelaga (Montreal) in 1535.

Throughout the sixteenth century there were numerous European fishing fleets off the coast of North America. For example, in 1578 an Englishman recorded 50 English, 100 Spanish, 50 Portuguese, and 150 French and Breton fishing vessels in the vicinity of Newfoundland (Biggar 1901: 23-24).

These early ventures into the New World account for the first scraps of European materials in the Indian sites. Objects of brass and iron and glass beads were carried or traded from one Indian group to another, even to such remote spots as the upper Susquehanna Valley.

By the last quarter of the sixteenth century, England and Spain had unsuccessfully tried to establish settlements in the Virginias. Most notable was the ill-fated Roanoke colony, originally patented by Queen Elizabeth to Sir Walter Raleigh, and actually attempted by his associates in 1584.

The first relatively permanent settlement in this area was that led by Captain John Smith, the founder of Jamestown in 1607. Soon thereafter Champlain entered the Great Lakes region, and the famous Pilgrim fathers established their settlement at Plymouth in 1620. The great land-grab was on.

The First Description of the Susquehannocks

Captain John Smith (1907: 50-51), in the account of his travels, provides us with the first descriptions of the people whom he named the Susquehannocks. In 1608 (see McCary 1957a: 2) he met 60 of them near the mouth of the Susquehanna River. By that point in his circumnavigation of the Chesapeake he had seen many Indians, but he was obviously impressed with the Susquehannocks. Other than the Powhatan, with whom he had considerable dealings, the Susquehannocks are the only people he described in some detail. In addition to his well-known but inflated account about their enormous size, he also gives some details of their dress, weapons, speech and manners. As would be expected and as verified through archeology, the Susquehannocks of that time already had European objects. Smith (1907: 126) states that the Tockwhogh, a people living near the head of the bay on the east side, had "many hatchets, knives, and peeces of iron and brasse . . . which they reported to have from the Susquesahanockes." His reasons for being impressed with them are rather clearly stated in his account (Smith 1907: 50): "Those are the strangest people of all those countries, both in language and attire." Even at that time other Indians of the Chesapeake referred to them as a mighty people and the "mortall enemies" of the "Massawomeks" (Smith 1907: 226). Smith met a group of these Massawomek near the head of the bay. The Tockwhogh told him that the Massawomek and other people "inhabit upon a great water beyond the mountaines which we understand to be some great lake, or the river of Canada; and from the French to have their hatchets and Commodities by trade" (Smith 1907: 127). It might be assumed from this that the Massawomek were Iroquoian people, although other suggestions have been made.

Figure 5. The Susquehannock Indian and the river from John Smith's map of 1612.

In referring to the location of the Susquehannock town(s), Smith (1907: 126) states that "they inhabit upon the chiefe Spring of these foure branches of the Bayes head ["The Sasquehanough river we call Smiths falles," p. 127], two days Journey higher than our barge could pass for rocks." He also notes (Smith 1907: 51) that the Susquehannocks "can make neare 600 able men, and are pallisadoed in their Townes to defend them from the Massawomekes." If we were to employ a multiplier of ten persons per three warriors (see Mook 1944: 193-208, Feest 1973: 66-79; the ratio can be expressed as 1 per 3.33) the above figure would yield a total population *estimate* of two thousand persons.

Smith's map (McCary 1957a; Fite and Freeman 1969: 116) of the bay and its environs places a town, actually a "kings house," called *Sasquesahanough* on the east side of the "flu" (Lat. flumen = river) by the same name and spelling. Its position is pretty much in keeping with his description, i.e., two days' travel above Smiths Falls, and would be, in terms of comparative scale, somewhere in present-day Lancaster County.

It should be noted here that Smith apparently had no interpreter when he met the Susquehannocks, and could not converse with them. Of their language he says (Smith 1907: 50), "It may well beseeme their proportions, sounding as a voyce in a vault." This description probably reflects something of the tonal qualities of Iroquoian versus that of the Algonquian languages which he was accustomed to hearing.

A Name for Them

Smith's information about the Susquehannocks, and indeed the term by which he named them, came from his Algonquian-speaking informants. The word *Susquehannock* was not what these people called themselves. As is the case with many early historic-period Indian nations, it is difficult to be certain how they did refer to themselves.

Four basic names, each with various spellings, were used in reference to these people. The first, Susquehannock, was the Algonquian word for them used by the English throughout the seventeenth century. The Dutch and Swedes called them Minqua, the name given to them by the Lenni Lenape. French accounts of the seventeenth century use the Huron term for them—Andaste. After 1700, the few surviving people of this nation and the place where they lived became known as Conestoga.

Many Indian tribes have become popularly known by terms given to them by other Indians who were questioned about surrounding peoples by the Europeans. Frequently, Indians called their neighbors the human beings who occupied a particular place. Often the term *the real people* who lived at a certain named geographical location is what a nation or tribe called itself. When a tribe did not have amicable relations with certain neighboring groups, they might give the Europeans some derogatory term for them.

During the seventeenth century the Susquehannocks made little or no effort to inform the English or other Europeans with whom they dealt of their own proper name. They probably were not concerned with doing so.

In an account published in 1666, George Alsop (Hall, ed. 1910: 370) recorded that the "Susquehannocks" buried their dead

> within the wall or Palisado'd impalement of their City, or *Connadago* as they call it. Their houses are low and long, built with the Bark of Trees Arch-wise, standing thick and confusedly together. They are situated a hundred and odd miles distant from the Christian Plantations of Mary-Land, at the head of a River that runs into the Bay of Chæsapike, called by their own name The Susquehanock River. . . .

The unwary reader might equate Alsop's word *Connadago* with Conestoga, the name for the Susquehannocks as well as for the town which they occupied toward the end of the seventeenth century. General John S. Clark, as early as the 1880's (Murray, ed. 1931: 76), felt that Alsop's Connadago was a specific town name, but he also recognized its similarity to the Iroquois word *Canada*, meaning village or town. Mithun (n.d.) has confirmed this meaning for *connadago* by comparing it with a number of other Iroquoian forms of the word for town, most of which are phonetically very similar. In fact Alsop's orthography in this case was exceedingly good.

The word *Conestoga* was widely used during the eighteenth century to refer to the town in Lancaster County and the Susquehannock and Seneca Indians who occupied it. The earliest positive reference to this place, actually spelled Carristoga (perhaps as a misprinting), is in the account of John Stillman (variously spelled), as recorded in the *Maryland Archives* for 1697 (Maryland Archives XIX: 519-20). In the Pennsylvania documents of the British Public Records Office in London, there is a 1696 reference to this same place spelled *Quanestauga*.

The Herrman Map of 1670 (published in 1673, see Figure 7, and Fite and Freeman 1969: 150), which includes the Susquehanna River, marks a tributary stream with the name *Onestoga* in the same relative position as the modern Conestoga Creek. The phonetic and orthographic similarities of the two are quite apparent. Herrman also entered the word *Canoage* above the location of the "present Sassquahana Indian Fort" on the west side of the river. Hanna (1911: 53) felt that this word and its position on the map referred to the Conewago Falls, rather than to the fort. Other writers, however (Clark, see Murray 1931), have suggested that Canoage was the proper name of the fort.

The resolution of this problem may be in the phonetic similarity of *Canoage* and *Connadago*, but as orthographically compounded by Herrman, a Dutch (German) cartographer, and Alsop, an English writer. We

Table 2

VOCABULARY OF THE MINQUE LANGUAGE
[from Holm 1834: 158-59].

Itaeaetsin. A man.
Achonhaeffti. A woman.
Jase. Brother-in-law.
Generoo. Good friend.
Agaendeero. We are good friends.
Chanooro hiss. I make much of you.
Jihadaeaero. My particularly good friend.
Otzkaenna. Pious, good.
Zatzioore. To boil.
Orocguae. Flesh, meat.
Mnadra, Canadra. Bread.
Onaesta. Indian corn.
Oneegha, Caneega. Water.
Canequassa. Drink.
Tzátzie. Sit and stay.
Sischijro. Eat.
Naehhae. Yes.
Taesta. No.
Honon jaijvo. I am tired.
Hije. I.
Hiss. Thou.
Gaija? Have you?
Hijwe. Other things.
Tésta gaije. I have not.
Ahghoora, Zaband. Indian money as above described.
Skajaano. Valuable skins or furs, as sables, etc.
Sandergarjaago. Beaver.
Kanjooga, Ajung. Bear skin.
Hrwha. Elk's skin.
Sissw, Fox.
Skáirwha. Turkey.
Háque. Skin.
Kajunckekeháque. Black skin.
Kaatzie. Come here.
Zatznwri. Be quick.
Achòxa. Directly.
Avarúnsi. Thank you.
Katzha gaije? What have you got?
Kareenach. A knife.
Kareenach testa hije gaijw. I have a knife for you.
Naehhae hiss gaije kareenach. Yes, you have a knife.
Taesta Zwronchka. I don't understand.
Hije Zwroncka. But I understand.
Serwquacksi. You are bad.
Taesta, taesta. No, no.
AEnhoduraada? What will you?
Skaddenijnu? Will you sell or barter something.
Anhooda? What?
Katzera. Clothes.
Aanjooza. Linen, shirts.
Khaalis. Stockings.
Atackqua. Shoes.
Kahwroonta, Karwda. A gun.
Kazeequara. A sword.
Tinnijgo otthohwrha? How much money will you have for it?
Owntack. A pot, a kettle.
Kaatzie. A dish.
Karw̃w̃nta. A stone.
Chanoona. A tobacco pipe.
Ojeengqua. Tobacco.
Onùsse ojengua. Smoking tobacco.
Adwgen, hadoogan. An axe.
Uthsijsta. Fire.
Zaruncka kahwichw uthsüsta? Can you make fire?
Koona. Great, large.
Stunga. Little.
Tzidtze. A cat.
Abgarijw. A dog.
Testa sis chijerw. The dog does not bite.
Haagw. A deer.
Sarakaliw haago. To shoot deer.
Kassha schaeaenu. Give me that for nothing.
Chotsis chijrw. See here what I will give you.
Hie kakhto schaeaenu. I will give it you again.
Hoo. May be.
Hoona sattaande. Now I am going away.

NUMERALS.

Onskat,	1.	*Raiene schaaro,*	14.
Tiggene,	2.	*Wisck schaaro,*	15.
Axe,	3.	*Jaiack schaaro,*	16.
Raiène,	4.	*Tzadack schaaro,*	17.
Wisck,	5.	*Tickerom schaaro,*	18.
Jaiack,	6.	*Waderom schaaro,*	19.
Tzadack,	7.	*Tykeni d. washa,*	20.
Tickerom,	8.	*Washa ne washa,*	100.
Waderom,	9.	*Washa ne washa ònskat,*	101.
Wàsha,	10.	*Washa ne washa tiggene,*	102.
Onskat schaaro,	11.	*Washa ne washa axe,*	103.
Tiggene schaaro,	12.	*Washa ne washa rajene,*	104.
Axe schaaro,	13.	*&c.*	*&c.*

are suggesting that both words may equate to the Iroquoian word for town or village (*canada*).

A 1688 survey, known as the Chambers map (Pennsylvania State Archives, RG 26, no. 18; Figure 8; see Hanna 1911: 27n), also shows the Conestoga River, therein spelled *Conestogon R*. This map, together with that of Herrman, clearly indicates that the term *Conestoga* for a river (with various spellings) was in use by Indians of the lower Susquehanna prior to the establishment of Conestoga Town and at least as early as 1670.

Linguists have given various interpretations of the word *Conestoga*. Hodge (1910, part 1: 335), translating it as an Iroquois word, suggested that it meant "at the place [town?] of the immersed pole (see also Hodge 1910, part 2: 659).

Mithun (n.d.: 68) gives several variants of this translation. She feels that the noun root involved is probably *-nahst*, meaning rafter (lodge pole), incorporated into several possible verb roots. For example, *ka* + *nahst* + *oke*—"where the rafters are in the water."

Mithun has done considerable research on Iroquois languages. In fact, she has examined the small "Vocabulary of the Minque Language" recorded by John Campanius in the mid-seventeenth century (Holm 1834: 158-59) and concluded that it is Susquehannock. Her comparison of this vocabulary with similar words in other Iroquoian languages (including Cherokee, the Five Nations Tuscarora, and Huron) is extremely thorough. She does not seem to be bothered by the variability of seventeenth- and eighteenth-century orthography or the fact that contemporary chroniclers with different European language backgrounds heard and recorded different phonemes for Indian words. In spite of this criticism, we are inclined to agree with her analysis of the Campanius vocabulary (Table 2) as being Susquehannock, or Andaste as she calls it. Her conclusions, based on this study, are that Susquehannock as recorded by Campanius is clearly Iroquoian, but that it cannot be classified more closely with any one particular northern Iroquois sub-branch of that language, even though in some regards it does look more like Onondaga than any of the others.

The Iroquoian word *Conestoga*, or some form thereof, is clearly what the Seneca and Susquehannocks living at Conestoga Town during the eighteenth century called themselves. However, as indicated above, there are no primary documents to indicate what the seventeenth-century Susquehannocks called themselves.

The earliest recorded Iroquoian word or name for these people comes from the Jesuit records taken among the Huron during the 1630's. Clark (Murray 1931: 55) cites the following from *Jesuit Relations* for 1635 (See Thwaites 1959 VIII: 115):

> What rejoices me is that I have learned that this language (Huron) is common to some twelve other nations . . . namely . . . Sonontoerrhonons [Seneca], Onontaerrhonons [Onondagas], Ouioenrhonons [Cayugas], Onoiochrhonons [Oneidas], Agnierrhonons [Mohawk], Andastoerrhonons [our Susquehannocks], . . . whom we comprise all under the name Hiroquois. . . .

The most common spelling of the name as given to the Jesuits by the Huron was *Andaste*. Mithun (n.d.: 66) notes that the *-rho:no* suffix can be translated as *resident of*. Therefore, a translation of the Huron word *Andastoerrhonon* might be "residents of the place where the rafters are in water," and this is probably an untraceable idiom.

Somewhat later, when the Jesuits came among the Five Nation Iroquois, they recorded other, similar words for the Andaste, which presumably represent the slight variations in Iroquois language as spoken by each individual tribe. For example, the *Relation* for 1670, page 46 (see Murray, 1931: 73) recorded by Bruyas at Onneiout (Oneida?) gives *Andastogue*. The *Relation* of 1670, page 68 (Murray 1931: 73) gives the word *Gangastogue*. Another from 1672, page 20 (Murray 1931: 74) spells it *Gandastogue*.

Hodge (1912, part 1: 336) gives dozens of different spellings, such as *Canastogues* from documents of 1699. However, C-o-n-e-s-t-o-g-a spellings all seem to be basically eighteenth-century and of English records. The earliest similar spelling of which we are aware is that on the Chambers map of 1688, which gives *Conestogon* as the name of a tributary to the lower Susquehanna River.

Somewhere among the list of pronunciations and orthographies for *Andaste* through *Conestoga* must lie the actual word by which the Susquehannocks referred to themselves. In order to avoid interjecting any additional confusion into the chaotic history of these people, we will continue to refer to them by the misnomer Susquehannock. Most early historians recognized that the Susquehannocks and the Conestogas were essentially the same people. Few have thought that Susquehannock was their own name or that it was derived from any language other than seventeenth-century Chesapeake Bay area Algonquian.

In addition to the "place" Susquesahanough, Smith's map (1907: facing 396) includes four other names associated with "Kings howses" higher up the Susquehanna (viz., Attaock, Quadroque, Testnigh and Utchowig). A few later historians have taken these to be other Susquehannock towns, and several unsuccessful attempts (see Murray 1931: 30; Eshleman 1909: 12-13) have been made to correlate those towns and their presumed map locations with modern geography and archeologically known sites.

In the present archeological picture for the time of Smith's account, only one major Susquehannock town is clearly established. This is the Washington Boro site, occupied sometime between 1600 and 1625. Other possible sites of this period were probably only occupied at the latter end of this 25-year era.

Since no European on record, except perhaps Etienne Brulé, saw any of the supposed Susquehannock towns on Smith's map, and since no other Indian nations are clearly known here during that time, the significance of the places other than "Susquesahanough" must remain a mystery, at least so far as correlations with archeological locations are concerned. Part of the explanation may rest with Smith's informants, or with the lack of translators who could explain what the Susquehannocks were telling them about their territory. Words which Smith may have assumed to be town names could have been descriptions of natural or other features in the area, or perhaps even names of Susquehannock "kings" or chiefs.

Other Early Accounts

Historians have long puzzled over the people and location of the place which Étienne Brulé described to Champlain as Carantouan (Champlain 1632). In 1615 Champlain sent Brulé to Carantouan to secure forces to aid in his attack of an Onondaga fort. As the story goes, Brulé arrived at the Onondaga fort after Champlain had left. Consequently, Brulé found it necessary to return to Carantouan to await an escort which would enable him to rejoin Champlain. This he was not able to do until 1619. In the meantime Brulé traveled in the area of Carantouan, including a trip down what is supposed to have been the Susquehanna River (Murray 1931: 26) as far as the sea.

Clark (Murray 1931), more than anyone else, has fretted over the location of Carantouan. Eventually, and with dogmatic assertion, he stated that it was "located beyond any possible question on the hill near Waverly, on the east bank of the Chemung, just South of the State line" (Murray

1931: 22). The Carantouan were further identified as Andastes or Susquehannocks.

Subsequent archeological surveys at Spanish Hill (Moorehead 1918: 121; 1938: 68-69; Donehoo 1918: 130-34; Griffin 1931a) and elsewhere in the upper Susquehanna Valley (Witthoft 1959a: 29; Lucy 1959; Stewart 1973) have failed to locate any evidence of seventeenth-century Susquehannock towns. Susquehannock materials which have been found in this region all relate to the Proto-Susquehannock and early Schultz periods of the sixteenth century.

Here again, negative evidence from archeology leaves us in doubt as to the significance of the interpretations of the Brulé accounts, and for that matter, any reference to seventeenth-century Susquehannock towns north of Lancaster County.

The first English settlements after Jamestown in the Chesapeake Bay area, particularly the northern part, which have some bearing on Susquehannock history, were the trading posts established by William Claiborne about 1631 at Kent and Palmers Islands, the latter near the mouth of the Susquehanna River. Claiborne, who had been granted a trading commission by King Charles I, had high hopes of establishing a trade empire for himself, largely by capturing the Susquehannock fur trade. His venture and the conflicts it caused with Lord Baltimore's claim to Maryland are well known to students of early Maryland history.

Eventually, in 1638, Claiborne was evicted, at least temporarily, by Lord Baltimore, but in the interim before this he was responsible for much of the trade going to the Susquehannocks.

St. Marys was settled in 1634 (Johnson 1881: 15) and served as the seat of the Maryland colonial government throughout most of the seventeenth century. Soon after the establishment of St. Marys, other English towns and plantations began to spread around the bay environs of the new Maryland colony. These also became potential and actual sources for contact, trade and conflict with the Susquehannocks.

Even before this, the Dutch were conducting trade in the Delaware Bay, and in 1626 set up a trading post at Fort Nassau opposite the mouth of the Schuylkill (Weslager and Dunlap 1961: 58-59). Here they traded with the Lenni Lenape or Delaware Indians, but they also attracted the Susquehannocks who came down the Schuylkill with their furs.

In the early years of their trading venture, the Dutch were unsuccessful in establishing a settlement on the west side of the Delaware. We recall, for example, the ill-fated Swanendael settlement at Lewes, Delaware, whose inhabitants were massacred by Indians in 1632 (Weslager and Dunlap 1961: 11, 96).

When the Maryland colony was started in 1634, there were no European settlements on the west side of the Delaware River or its bay, and Lord Baltimore's grant included all of the Delmarva peninsula to the fortieth parallel.

The Dutch, however, continued to trade in the Delaware, but increasingly more with the Susquehannocks rather than the local Lenni Lenape. These people were in the process of being subdued and forced out of the fur trade by the Susquehannocks, who were anxious to secure the Dutch trade for themselves. As early as 1626, Isaack de Rasière reported to the Dutch Chamber of the West Indian Company that the Susquehannocks had gone to Manhattan in an attempt to open trade relations with the Dutch (Myers 1912: 24, 38; Jennings 1968: 17). This report also indicates that the Lenape were engaged in warfare with the Susquehannocks. The feuding continued until at least 1645, when Campanius (Holm 1834: 158) reports that the Lenape had become, in effect, tributary to the Susquehannocks.

In 1638 (Johnson 1911: 117) the Swedes also entered the fur trade on the Delaware. They erected Fort Christiana on the site of present-day Wilmington (Johnson 1911: 193). The Susquehannocks were now in a position to trade with English, Dutch and Swedes for the European manufactures to which they were becoming habituated. At the same time, the European nations were in considerable competition for the Indian trade, a factor which played an enormous role in seventeenth-century New World politics and warfare.

That same year (1638) Claiborne, in the heat of his feud with Lord Baltimore, returned to England. His absence may have shifted more of the Susquehannock trade to the Delaware. Hanna (1911: 36) suggests that during the course of his altercation with the Calverts, Claiborne attempted to incite the Susquehannocks against the settlers under Lord Baltimore's government. Apparently he was successful in this as Maryland eventually declared war on the Susquehannocks in 1642. Two expeditions against the Susquehannocks were undertaken in the following year. The first apparently routed the Indians; however, the second met with defeat, the Susquehannocks inflicting casualties and capturing 15 prisoners and two pieces of field artillery (Jennings 1968: 20; Maryland Archives III: 149).

Equating the Archeology and History of the Susquehannocks

From the time of John Smith's first encounter with the Susquehannocks in 1608, until about 1645, Susquehannock culture can be characterized within the previously described Washington Boro-Transitional archeological stages. Beginning about 1600, and perhaps until 1625, their major, and perhaps only, town was at Washington Boro. At some point during the third decade of this century the Washington Boro village was abandoned and one, or perhaps two, new towns replaced it. These are known as the

Billmyer Quarry and Roberts sites. Very little is known about either site, except that they produce materials more or less similar to those found at Washington Boro. On the basis of extant trade goods in various collections, the Roberts site would appear to be the latest.

During the latter portion of this period the Swedish missionary John Campanius (in a *Description of the Province of New Sweden*, published by his grandson Thomas Campanius Holm in 1834) indicates that the Mengwes had a fort, according to Hanna (1911: 45), in about the year 1645 "on a high mountain about twelve miles from New Sweden (now Wilmington)." Hanna (1911: 45) suggests that 12 Swedish miles would equal approximately 80 English miles. Campanius also said that

> the way to their land was very bad, being stony, full of sharp grey stones, with hills and morasses, so that the Swedes, when they went to them which happened generally, once or twice a year, had to walk in the water up to their armpits. They went thither with cloth, kettles, axes, hatchets, knives, mirrors, and coral beads. They live on a high mountain, very steep and difficult to climb, there they have a fort or square building surrounded with palisades in which they reside. There they have guns and small iron cannon. . . . (Holm 1834: 157-58)

It is difficult to correlate this third-hand description with the location of a known Susquehannock village. The distance given (80 English miles, and variously estimated by other writers) would easily take one to Lancaster County from Wilmington. The fact that the Swedes had to walk in water up to their armpits and climb a steep hill to reach the Susquehannock fort has caused some writers to locate it on the west side of the Susquehanna River. There are, however, no known sites of this early date on the west side of the river. The Roberts site, which almost certainly existed at this time, is on a small rise approximately 90 feet above the Conestoga Creek, and on the opposite side of the creek from Wilmington.

Plantagenet (1648) notes that the Swedes had actually sent soldiers to the Susquehannocks to teach them the "use of our arms and fights." He also implies (Plantagenet 1648) that sometime between his arrival in the New World about 1641 (Johnson 1911: 215) and the date of his publication (1648) the Susquehannocks had moved to another village: Their "new Town is also a rare, healthy, and rich place, with it a Crystall broad river, but some fals below hinder navigation." [1]

If such a shift of village location to a "new town" along a "crystall broad river" (almost certainly the Susquehanna) did occur during the 1640's, it was almost beyond question a shift to the Strickler site. Based largely upon the Plantagenet quote (see above), the year 1645 is hereby arbitrarily set as the beginning of the Strickler site and the Strickler period of Susquehannock culture history.

Another useful contemporary account of this period appears in the *Jesuit Relation* of 1647 (Thwaites 1959 XXXIII: 129):

> Andastoé is a country beyond the Neutral Nation, distant from the Huron country about one hundred and fifty leagues in a straight line to the Southeast, a quarter South, from the Huron country,—that is, Southward, a little toward the East; but the distance that has to be traveled to reach there is nearly two hundred leagues, owing to detours in the route. Those people speak the Huron language, and have always been the allies of our Hurons. They are very warlike, and in a single village they count thirteen hundred men capable of bearing arms.
>
> At the beginning of last year, 1647, two men of that Nation came here, deputed by their Captains to tell our Hurons that, if they lost courage and felt too weak to contend against their enemies, they should inform them, and send an Embassy to Andastoé for that object.

The reference to a "single village" at this time does not necessarily imply that only one existed in 1647. However, the reference to thirteen hundred men capable of bearing arms at that village (or an estimated [1300 × 3.3 =] 4,329 total population) implies the Strickler site, since this was the only known Susquehannock village of any period which could have accommodated that many people. Inasmuch as this population level was attained gradually over the preceding years, then prior to 1645 (our arbitrary date for the shift of towns) there must have been at least two villages. The Roberts site is simply not large enough, based upon our archeological understanding of its size, to have accommodated anywhere near the number of people suggested by the Jesuit accounts. This need not be a cause for concern—in fact quite the contrary, since we have already posited another town (the Billmyer Quarry site) that was a contemporary of the Roberts site. In other words, this population figure would seem to confirm the existence of the Strickler site by the year 1647, but also the co-existence of at least two smaller towns prior to the establishment of the Strickler site.

Throughout this period, the Swedish colony on the Delaware River was growing in strength and apparently wooing the Susquehannocks to increase their trade and military alliance. In an attempt to intercede in these arrangements, the Dutch built Fort Casimir (New Castle, Delaware) in

---

[1]Beauchamp Plantagenet was the pseudonym used by Sir Edmund Plowden (see Hanna 1911: 45; Johnson 1911: 399-401 for discussions of the relationship of these two names). The document referred to here was signed by Beauchamp Plantagenet December, 5, 1648, and is entitled *A Description of the Province of New Albion.* This work was subsequently reprinted in several places (see Scull, *The Evelyns in America,* 1881, which includes several other minor references to Susquehannocks by Robert Evelyn). The source of the present reference is in Peter Force's *Tracts and Other Papers* (Force 1836, reprinted 1947). Force's work is strangely paginated; the Plantagenet passage quoted here appears in Force, vol. II, section VII, page 28.

1651 (Myers 1912: 139). At this same time, the Dutch traders on the Hudson had a trade and treaty agreement with the Mohawk. Jennings (1968: 24-25) sees the 1651 Mohawk attack on the Susquehannocks as a rather indirect battle of the Dutch against their Swedish trade rivals on the Delaware. The Mohawks were not successful against the Susquehannocks. However, the Mohawk and particularly the Seneca were victorious in several encounters with other Indians over conflicts directly stemming from the fur trade. In 1649 the Seneca virtually destroyed the Huron (Hunt 1940: 87-95), and in 1654 they wreaked the same devastation upon the Erie Nation or Black Minqua of northwestern Pennsylvania and western New York (Hunt 1940: 101-102). These Iroquois successes may have been, at least in part, due to the superiority in arms which they achieved from Dutch support.

On July 5, 1652 (see Johnson 1881: 17-18; Maryland Archives III: 277-78), the Susquehannocks signed their first peace treaty with the English in Maryland. These articles of agreement gave to the English all the land on the west side of the Chesapeake Bay from the Patuxent River to Palmers Island, and from the Choptank River to the Elk River on the eastern side of the Bay. Signing for the Indians were the Susquehannock "Warr captains and councillors," Sawahegeh, Auroghtaregh, Scarhuhadig, Rutchchogah and Nathheldianch (Johnson 1881: 18; Maryland Archives III: 278n).

As Jennings (1968: 25) notes, this year also marked the beginning of the Anglo-Dutch War. In 1653 Governor Johann Printz, writing from the Printzhof, his home on Tinicum Island on the Delaware, recorded that "there is absolutely no profit any more in the fur-trade and especially now since the Arregahaga [Iroquois] and Susquahanoer (from whom the beaver come) began to make War upon each other" (Johnson 1911: 343). Taking advantage of the opportunities provided by the Anglo-Dutch War, the Swedes captured Fort Casimir at New Castle from the Dutch in 1654. Although they gained complete control of the Delaware Bay, it was short-lived. In 1655 the Dutch captured the Swedish forts, once again bringing the Delaware Bay under Dutch control.

Apparently the Dutch also found a diminished trade for furs in the Delaware Bay area, not only as a result of Iroquois-Susquehannock wars but also, probably, because certain fur-bearing animals were beginning to be over-harvested. To improve the trade, the Dutch tried to induce the Seneca to carry their furs, which they were still taking in abundance, to the Dutch posts on the Delaware. This was probably attractive to the Seneca for at least one reason—the Mohawk felt that they had the principal right to trade at Fort Orange on the Hudson. The difficulty with the Seneca carrying their furs to Dutch trading posts on the Delaware was that it meant they would have to pass through Susquehannock territory. Their efforts to do so at this time, with the encouragement and support of the Dutch, intensified the conflict among these Indian nations (see Jennings 1966, 1968).

In light of the growing tension between the Dutch on the Delaware and Lord Baltimore's English colony, the Susquehannocks, by virtue of their treaties, can be viewed as providing a frontier outpost to protect the northern borders of Maryland from Dutch-supported raids. Indeed, Lord Baltimore's people must have interpreted Dutch support of Seneca raids into the Susquehannock country as a Dutch effort to weaken the Maryland colony from the rear.

Maryland and Susquehannock relationships vacillated considerably over the years. Even after the treaty of 1652, the harmony of their coexistence depended upon the degree to which the English found the Susquehannocks useful as frontier defenders or trade partners. The relationship intensified greatly toward the end of the sixth decade of the century; and on May 16, 1661, Maryland signed a new and stronger treaty with the Susquehannocks (Maryland Archives III: 417).

One provision of the treaty called for Maryland to send men to the Susquehannock fort to aid in its defense against the Seneca. On May 18 of that year, the Maryland General Assembly issued orders to a Captain John Odber to proceed to the "Susquesahannough Forte" with fifty men. There he was to fortify himself for his own security either within or without the fort. He was instructed

> to demand the assistance of the Sasquesahannoughs to fetch tymber and other necessaryes for the fortificacon . . . and further to cause some Spurrs or flankers to be layd out for the Defence of the Indian Forte whome yow are upon all occasions to assist against the Assaults of their Ennemies (Maryland Archives III: 417a).

Furthermore, he was told to keep informed of the progress of the war between the Seneca and the Susquehannocks, and if he found the latter lacking in it, to press them to a vigorous prosecution of it. He was also to keep an eye on the Dutch who might come to the Susquehannock fort, and to inform the council of their actions and any other attempted treaties with the Susquehannocks (Maryland Archives IV: 417-18; Hanna 1911: 43-44).

Hanna (1911: 44) points out that, according to the Maryland records, Captain Odber failed to carry out his orders, at least in 1661.

It has previously been suggested that the Strickler site had been occupied during a period which would almost certainly include the year 1661. The 1968-1969 excavations at the Strickler site disclosed flankers or bastions at two corners of the fort. These appear to be of European influence, if not construction, and suggest that someone, if not Captain Odber, assisted the Susquehannocks who were living at the Strickler site about 1661 in laying out these structures.

As mentioned above, the records show a number of raids were made into the Susquehannock country during the 1650's and 1660's by the Iroquois, and particularly by the Seneca. A major attack on the Susquehannock fort by the Seneca came in 1663. This event is recounted secondarily, from Indian informants, by Jerome Lalemont in the *Jesuit Relations* for 1662-1663 (Thwaites 1959 XLVIII: 77):

> Raising, accordingly, an army of eight hundred men, they embarked on Lake Ontario toward the beginning of last April, and directed their course toward the extremity of that beautiful Lake, to a great river, very much like our Saint Lawrence, leading without rapids and without falls to the very gates of the village of Andastogué.

As Hanna (1911: 46) points out, this description was probably inaccurate and certainly secondhand. From the description it would appear that the Susquehannock fort was above the Great Conewago Falls in the year 1663. In point of fact no major historic Susquehannock sites are known from above the falls.

Lalemont (Thwaites 1959 XLVIII: 77) goes on to say that the Iroquois

> saw that this village was defended on one side by the stream [the river], on whose banks it was situated, and on the opposite by a double curtain of large trees, flanked by two bastions erected in the European manner, and even supplied with some pieces of Artillery.

The Susquehannocks were successful in the defense of their town and the Iroquois returned in humiliation. According to the Iroquois account as related by Lalemont, they were unsuccessful because of the European-style fortifications and because the Susquehannocks would not engage them in open battle outside the fort.

Hanna (1911: 46-47) cites two Dutch accounts which also refer to the attack on the Susquehannock fort in 1663. These present a considerably different picture of the Iroquois defeat. One of these letters, written by William Beeckman in New Amstel (New Castle, Delaware) on June 6, 1663, to Director-General Peter Stuyvesant at New Amsterdam, states that a report from two Minqua who had arrived at New Amstel a few days earlier indicated that the Minqua (Susquehannocks) had made a sally in force and driven the Seneca away.

None of these accounts provides any precise information on the location of the besieged Susquehannock fort. However, the Strickler site is the only known village of this period located close enough to the river to serve as part of the defenses of the fort. In addition to this clue, Lalemont also mentioned the European-style bastions, which clearly existed at the Strickler site.

In 1666 George Alsop (Hall 1910: 370-71) published a brief account of

Figure 6. Diorama of a Susquehannock village in the Anthropology Gallery of the William Penn Memorial Museum.

the Susquehannocks, which provides some potentially useful information about them:

> When any among them depart this life, they give him no other intombment, then to set him upright upon his breech in a hole dug in the Earth some five foot long, and three foot deep, covered over with the Bark of Trees Arch-wise, with his face Du-West, only leaving a hole half a foot square open. They dress him in the same Equipage and Gallantry that he used to be trim'd in when he was alive, and so bury him (if a Soldier) with his Bows, Arrows, and Target, together with all the rest of his implements and weapons of War, with a Kettle of Broth, and Corn standing before him, lest he should meet with bad quarters in his way. His Kinred and Relations follow him to the Grave, sheath'd in Bear skins for close mourning. . . .
>
> * * * *
>
> They bury all within the wall or Palisado'd impalement of their City, or *Connadago* as they call it. Their houses are low and long, built with the Bark of Trees Arch-wise, standing thick and confusedly together. They are situated a hundred and odd miles distant from the Christian Plantations of Mary-Land, at the head of

> a River that runs into the Bay of Chæsapike, called by their own name The Susquehanock River, where they remain and inhabit most part of the Summer time, and seldom remove far from it, unless it be to subdue any Forreign Rebellion.
>
> About November the best Hunters draw off to several remote places of the Woods, where they know the Deer, Bear, and Elke useth; there they build them several Cottages, which they call their Winter-quarter, where they remain for the space of three months, untill they have killed up a sufficiency of Provisions to supply their Families with in the Summer.
>
> The Women are the Butchers, Cooks, and Tillers of the ground, the Men think it below the honour of a Masculine, to stoop to any thing but that which their Gun, or Bow and Arrows can command. The Men kill the several Beasts which they meet withall in the Woods, and the Women are the Pack horses to fetch it in upon their backs, fleying and dressing the hydes, (as well as the flesh for provision) to make them fit for Trading, and which are brought down to the English at several seasons in the year, to truck and dispose of them for course Blankets, Guns, Powder, and Lead, Beads, small Looking-glasses, Knives, and Razors.
>
> I never observed all the while I was amongst these naked Indians, that ever the Women wore the Breeches, or dared either in look or action predominate over the Men. They are very constant to their Wives; and let this be spoken to their Heathenish praise, that did they not alter their bodies by their dyings, paintings, and cutting themselves, marring those Excellencies that Nature bestowed upon them in their original conceptions and birth, there would be as amiable beauties amongst them, as any Alexandria could afford, when Mark Anthony and Cleopatra dwelt there together. Their Marriages are short and authentique; for after 'tis resolv'd upon by both parties, the Woman sends her intended Husband a Kettle of boyl'd Venison, or Bear; and he returns in lieu thereof Beaver or Otter Skins, and so their Nuptial Rites are concluded without other Ceremony.

Alsop provided descriptions of various other aspects of Susquehannock culture. Most recent historians, however, have taken these to be rather fanciful or fictitious. The purpose here is not to defend or refute his descriptions, but rather to point out certain possible causes for some of his remarks.

He describes their burials as being made in a hole some five feet long and three feet deep. This agrees rather well with the archeological data from most Susquehannock sites. He also says that the interments were made with the individual sitting "upright upon his breech." Objects were placed before him in the grave and the hole was "covered over with the Bark of trees Arch-wise."

The notion that Indians were buried sitting up is a popular folk tale in certain areas. No properly reported Susquehannock burial has ever exhibited this posture. Alsop implies, however, that the grave was not immediately filled with earth. A body placed in a sitting position might therefore eventually decay and collapse into a kind of flexed position after which the grave could have been filled. The archeological evidence for this is extremely scanty, but such collapse could, perhaps, account for the occasionally observed jammed-in or crowded position of a skeleton at one end of a sufficiently large pit.

The Alsop account also says that the bodies were placed so that they faced west, and that the burials were made within the "Palisado'd impalement of their City, or *Connadago* as they call it." Most Susquehannock burials occur outside the palisades and with the face looking east. Exceptions do occur: at the Strickler site, for example, at least a dozen burials were found inside the stockade, and two of these were facing west!

The Connadago (town) referred to by Alsop in 1666 was probably the Strickler site. This was the date of his publication, and his actual visit to the site, if any, obviously took place sometime prior to this.

In 1664 England effected a complete conquest of New Netherland. At that point England controlled all of the coastal colonies from present Maine to the Carolinas. As Jennings (1968: 29) points out, this should have brought peace to the Indian tribes—the source of conflict had been removed. There was no more competition among European nations for control of the colonies and the fur trade.

This condition was, however, short-lived. The French of course were still in Canada, and the bickering among the English provincial governments continued. France was again bent on destroying the Iroquois because of their interference with the French fur trade in Canada.

In 1666 the Anglo-Dutch war was revived and France now allied herself with the Dutch. That same year the Susquehannocks, adding to the confused melee of events, attacked and destroyed an Onondaga war party (Jennings 1968: 30). Susquehannock harassment of the Iroquois continued, and in view of this they must have found it prudent to renew their treaty with Maryland, which happened on June 29, 1666 (Hanna 1911: 47; Maryland Archives III: 549-50).

Augustine Herrman, in 1673, published a map of Virginia and Maryland which shows "the present Sassquahana Indian Fort" on the west side of the Susquehanna River (Hanna 1911: facing 54; Fite and Freeman 1969: 150). Herrman positioned this fort precisely on *his* line of the fortieth parallel.

It is now known that two Susquehannock sites of this approximate period existed on the west side of the river. The Lower, or Byrd, Leibhart site is about a mile and a half south of the fortieth parallel, and the Upper, or Oscar, Leibhart site is less than a mile south of the parallel.

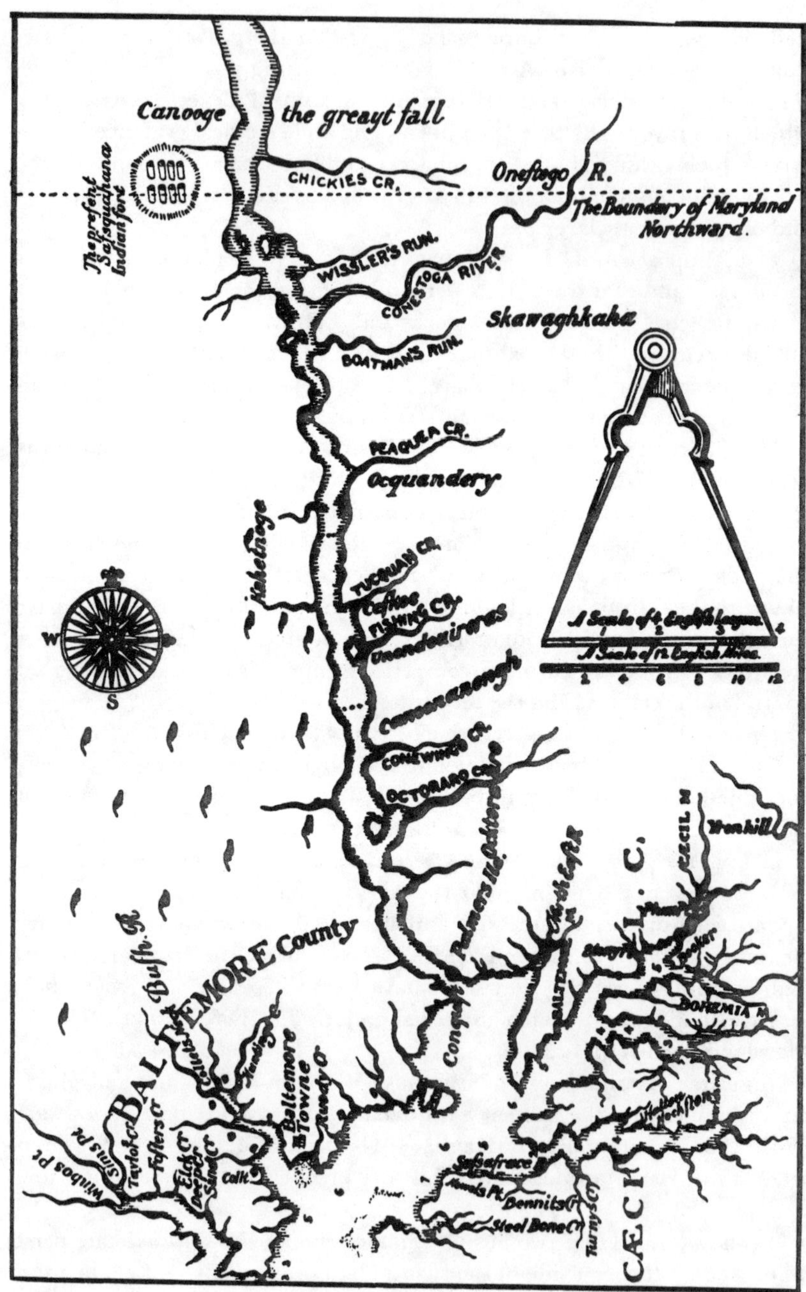

Figure 7. Herrman map of 1673 (after Landis 1910, with modern stream names).

The legend on the Herrman map indicated that he gathered the cartographic information prior to 1670. The tributaries of the Susquehanna marked on his map coincide well enough with the modern map to suggest that he actually visited the area. (Landis 1910: 94)

Both Leibhart sites are equally prominent, and it is unlikely that only one would have been noticed if both were extant when the cartographic data were collected. The caption on his map, i.e., "the Present Sassquahana Indian fort," implies that this was *now* the place of the fort, as though its location had recently changed. Herrman began the surveys for his map in 1660 (Landis 1910: 93), but there is no way to know in what year, prior to its completion in 1670, the Susquehanna River and the new fort were surveyed. It was previously suggested that the Seneca attack of 1663 occurred at the Strickler site. If this is indeed correct, the new fort on the west side of the river must have been built during the next seven years. We have arbitrarily picked the year 1665.

If there was only one occupied fort on the west side of the river at the time his survey was made, the second archeologically known site (one of the Leibhart sites) must have been built after 1670, or whenever the cartographer last visited the area.

Archeological evidence (printed elsewhere in this volume) would seem to suggest that the Byrd Leibhart site is the later of two sites. This would mean that the Oscar Leibhart site was the fort shown on the Herrman map.

During the early 1670's Susquehannock population seems to have been severely reduced as a result of disease and continued warfare. The *Jesuit Relations* for 1671 (Thwaites 1959: 57; see also Murray 1931: 74) indicates that the Andastogue (Susquehannocks) could count but three hundred warriors. The same account tells how a war party of Seneca and Cayuga warriors was routed by a group of Susquehannock boys.

The Iroquois were also weakened by disease and desultory warfare. In July, 1673, the Iroquois met with Count Frontenac to urge the French to support them in their continuing war with the Susquehannocks, who were their sole enemies at that time. These representatives of the Five Nations reported to Frontenac that the "Andastoguez" were well fortified in their fort "with men and Cannon" (not canoes, as indicated in O'Callahan 1855 IX: 110; see Margry 1876 I: 229; Hanna 1911: 47).

Hanna (1911: 48; see Margry 1876 I: 240-41) cites a letter written by La Salle to Count Frontenac on August 10, 1763, in which La Salle reports that several French traders had joined the Iroquois and had gone to war against the Andastoguez. This is an additional, albeit minor, historical confirmation of actual warfare between the Iroquois and the Susquehannocks at this time.

It has generally been assumed by most historians that this war of the summer of 1673, and extending perhaps into 1674, was that responsible for the final defeat of the Susquehannocks. The outcome of that war is indicated by the brief statement in the *Jesuit Relations* for 1675 (Thwaites 1959 LIX: 251):

> . . . since the Sonnontouans [Iroquois] have utterly defeated the Andastogués, their ancient and most redoubtable foes, their insolence knows no bounds; they talk of nothing but renewing the war against our allies, and even against the French. . . .

Jennings (1968: 31-34) views the removal of the Susquehannocks from their homeland during the period 1673-1675 as a political maneuver on the part of Lord Baltimore's Maryland government, rather than as a result of any defeat by the Iroquois. According to Jennings, Maryland feared that the Dutch, who were again at war with England (1672-1674), and once again in control of Manhattan, would incite and support the Iroquois against the English in Maryland. Perhaps they did support them in a war against the Susquehannocks.

As an attempt to forestall such action, Maryland sought to secure a peace treaty with the Iroquois. However, as Jennings points out, the ongoing Iroquois-Susquehannock feud stood in the way. Jennings feels that this was overcome by removing the Susquehannocks to Maryland at the *invitation* or *coercion* of Lord Baltimore.

Jennings, however, provides no suggestion as to how Maryland managed to accomplish or enforce this transplant. He declines to accept the traditional, although perhaps tenuous, theory involving a war in which the Iroquois defeated the Susquehannocks. His major reason for this stems from the stated weakness of the Iroquois in their July, 1673, plea to Frontenac. Apparently, Jennings gives no credence to the previously cited 1675 Jesuit account concerning the Seneca defeat of the Susquehannocks.

Furthermore, Jennings admits that there are no records of any invitation or ultimatum from Lord Baltimore. Rather, he implies that such records were deliberately not kept. A major inconsistency in this theory lies in the fact that Maryland did not really want the Susquehannocks.

Tooker (1982) has recently discussed at length Jennings' position concerning the Susquehannock removal from their homelands during the period 1673-1675. Tooker concludes in favor of the traditional history—the removal of the Susquehannocks was actually a result of their military defeat at the hands of the Iroquois.

In June, 1674 (Maryland Archives II: 378), the Maryland Assembly voted for a peace with the Seneca (Iroquois in general). At the same time realizing that this might bring war with the Susquehannocks, the Maryland government made provisions for such war "even without the province" if that should become necessary. This shift in alliance may also be indicative of a defeat of the Susquehannocks. They apparently were no longer an effective buffer against the Iroquois. These actions of the Assembly imply, however, that the Susquehannocks were still there and capable of making trouble for the Maryland colony.

By February, 1675, some Susquehannocks were reported living at the Patuxent River in Maryland (Hanna 1911: 48). Ostensibly the Susquehannocks had come into Maryland to seek protection from the Seneca, but some officials feared that they actually had a secret alliance with the Seneca and had come into Maryland to discover the strength of the province. That same month the Susquehannock Chief Harignera and several others came before the Assembly to ask where they could live within the province. After much uncertainty and debate it was decided that the Susquehannocks should move above the falls of the Potomac (Maryland Archives II: 429).

The Susquehannocks failed to move that far up the Potomac, for in the summer of 1675 they were living at an abandoned Piscataway Indian fort opposite present-day Mount Vernon. Archeological work at the Piscataway site (Stephenson et al. 1963) has clearly established their presence here.

That summer a white man was murdered by Indians on the Virginia side of the Potomac, possibly by Seneca or other Indians, but not clearly by the Susquehannocks. The latter, however, were blamed for the incident. A Virginia militia retaliated by killing some Susquehannocks, and additional killings followed on both sides (Washburn 1957: 21).

A major offensive against the Susquehannocks at the Piscataway fort was organized by Virginia and Maryland. In September this force appeared before the fort and asked the defenders to send out their chief, Harignera, to meet with them. Harignera was apparently dead, but several other chiefs did emerge from the fort, only to be subsequently murdered by the provincial forces. The events which followed and the sporadic siege of the fort during the ensuing six weeks are recorded in several contemporary documents. These have been well summarized by a number of later historians (Streeter 1857; Hanna 1911: 49-52; Washburn 1957: 21-24; Ferguson 1941).

An exciting discovery was made by Professor T. J. Wertenbaker in 1910 regarding the fort at Piscataway. While working with documents in the British Public Records Office in London, Professor Wertenbaker found a map of the "Suskahana fort" apparently made at the time of the siege (see Kellock 1962: inside front cover; and Ferguson 1941: 1-9). The contemporary drawing of the fort is amazingly like the postmold plan uncovered archeologically and mapped by Ferguson (1941; see also Stephenson et al. 1963).

Finally, during the night, some 75 starving Susquehannock men plus women and children slipped by the sleeping forces surrounding the fort (Hanna 1911: 51; Maryland Archives V: 134, give a slightly different account). From there they headed southward toward the Roanoke River on the Carolina border, where they took refuge near the Occaneechee Indians. During this period a number of other killings were committed by the Indians.

This was also the time of King Philip's War in New England. Governor Berkeley of Virginia feared that the New England Indian uprising was also influencing the Indian troubles in Virginia and there was widespread concern over a general Indian movement against the English. The Governor also feared the loss of Virginia's Indian trade. His vacillating responses with regard to these problems prompted the rash actions of Nathaniel Bacon, who took matters in his own hands and eventually effected a major rebellion against the Virginia government (Washburn 1957).

Bacon was not successful against the Susquehannocks, largely because he could not find them. But he needed an Indian victory to bolster his image, and in lieu of the Susquehannocks, he attacked the friendly Occaneechee in May, 1676.

The scattered Susquehannocks roaming the back country of Virginia and Maryland, having found life difficult, to say the least, began to return to the Susquehanna Valley.

In a letter dated August 6, 1676, Maryland's Deputy Governor Notley reported to the Governor of Virginia that

> the Susquehannough Indians have resided at their old fort, about sixty miles above Palmers Island for so many months that they now have corn fit to roast.
>
> That they shortly expect the remainder of their troops, and as many of the western Indians near or beyond the mountains as they have been able to persuade to come and live with them. We are further informed that by means of colonel Andrews the Governor of New York, a peace was made last summer between them and their old enemies, the Cinigos, so that now they are at ease, and out of our reach. (Maryland Archives XV: 122)

The Susquehannocks' New Fort

Apparently the Susquehannocks *were* widely scattered in 1676. Those who planted corn ready for roasting in August, 1676, at their old fort (the Oscar Leibhart site?) could hardly have been those pursued by Bacon on the Roanoke River the previous May.

Maryland continued its historically difficult to follow pattern of uncertain peace and enmity toward the Susquehannocks. Shortly after the Susquehannocks were reported to have returned to their old fort in 1676, Deputy Governor Notley of Maryland met (August 17, 1676) with the chiefs of the Piscataway and Mattawoman Indians to ask if they would be willing to make peace with the Susquehannocks. The chiefs did not want peace at that time. The Council then asked "whether they will march with the English to the new ffort they [the Susquehannocks] have built, or otherwise pursue the Susquehanoughs" (Hanna 1911: 53; Maryland Archives XV: 126). The chiefs replied that they were ready to march against the Susquehannocks; however, a few months later they agreed to make peace with them.

The historical reference to the Susquehannocks' *new* fort, apparently near their old fort on the Susquehanna, is especially interesting in light of the archeology of this period. It is most tempting to equate their new fort with the Lower (Byrd) Leibhart site. Unfortunately there are no trade goods from this site which would permit the tight dating necessary to place it after 1676. Archeological and historical data relative to this site are suggestive but do not provide conclusive support for such dating.

It was previously stated that the Upper (Oscar) Leibhart site appears to be slightly earlier and that it was probably the one extant site at the time of the Herrman map just prior to 1670. This is the most likely place from which the Susquehannocks were dispersed between 1673 and 1674.

In spite of Jennings' (1968) admonitions to the contrary, the present writer gives credence to the Jesuit (Thwaites 1959 LIX: 251) account which implies an Iroquois defeat of the Susquehannocks in 1673-1674. However, this need not have been a complete rout of the Susquehannock force at the Oscar Leibhart site, but rather a serious enough loss for the Susquehannocks to have caused them trepidation about staying there much longer. Gradually the fort may have been abandoned, some of its occupants going into Maryland and eventually to the Piscataway fort. Other Susquehannocks may have gone elsewhere – to the Lenni Lenape on the Delaware, and perhaps to the west.

The previously mentioned Susquehannocks ("seventy-five Indians, with them their women, children, etc."), who slipped away from the Piscataway fort late in 1675 (Hanna 1911: 51), would seem to represent a population of about (according to our formula: 3.3 x number of warriors) 250 persons. The number of Indians who died at the Piscataway fort during the siege is not recorded.

Stephenson et al. (1963: 80-81) report two ossuaries from within the fort which contained appropriate trade goods and a total of 53 burials. These may or may not all be Susquehannock interments. Ossuaries are not a Susquehannock burial form, but some of the recovered material, and one pipe in particular (Stephenson et al. 1963 XXII: Figure A), is definitely Susquehannock. Probably no more than this number of Susquehannocks were killed at the Piscataway fort. Some of the material and the interments may well pertain to the historic Piscataway Indians who occupied the place prior to its use by the Susquehannocks.

If the Piscataway fort was the only place occupied by the Susquehannocks after leaving their fort (Oscar Leibhart site) in 1673-1674, then we could count their total population in the autumn of 1675 (after the siege of the Piscataway fort) at about 250 people. Prior to this the most current population estimate for them is that in the Jesuit account of 1671 (Thwaites 1959 LVI: 57; Hanna 1911: 47), which gives three hundred warriors (or about one thousand persons). This would mean a reduction in population over a period of four years of more than seven hundred people. Intuitively this seems like too large and too severe a loss, even if the Iroquois had inflicted heavy damages in the wars of 1673-1674. Jennings (1968) of course would not allow such a battle. Presumably, he would attribute this drastic population decline to other causes—disease perhaps; or, as suggested elsewhere, maybe only a portion of the Susquehannocks went to Piscataway.

If the "new fort" of the Susquehannocks in 1676 was in fact the Byrd Leibhart site, it would seem that some sort of reconciliation of the historically and the archeologically *implied* population figures for the Susquehannocks is in order. Our population estimates for the better-known Strickler site (see Table 22) work out to about one person per 190 feet of area inside the stockade. Using these same figures for the 3.75-acre (163,000 sq. ft.) Byrd Leibhart site would suggest a population of nine hundred people.

In the pages which follow we have *arbitrarily* proposed a four-year occupation for the Byrd Leibhart site. To some extent the number of interments reported for this site—approximately two hundred—supports a population estimate of about nine hundred people over a period of four years. Details of this prediction are more fully discussed in the chapter on the Byrd Leibhart site.

Several very large questions loom over such remarks. Was this actually the new fort of the Susquehannocks after 1676? Did they live there for only four years? Were there as many as nine hundred of them in spite of historical implications to the contrary? And why did history apparently ignore their presence here?

More than anything else, it is the frustration caused by the lack of clear-cut references to Susquehannocks in the lower Susquehanna Valley after 1677, and until 1690, which has prompted the following, perhaps overwrought, interpretation of the history and archeology of this period.

An absolute terminal date for their occupation of the "new fort" on the west side of the lower Susquehanna (Byrd Leibhart site) is implied by the actions of William Penn (or his representatives), who visited the Susquehanna River in 1683 (Klein and Hoogenboom 1973: 24) seeking Indians from whom lands there could be purchased for the new Province of Pennsylvania. Apparently no Susquehannocks were in residence on the Susquehanna in 1683, for, although Penn did buy the "quiet lands" extending to that river, his deeds, dated September 10, 1683, and October 18, 1683, are signed by Lenni Lenape Indians, not Susquehannocks (Pennsylvania Archives, 1st Series I: 67). The Indian signers, Kekelappan and Machaloha, have been identified as Lenni Lenape, in name at least, by William A. Hunter (see Jennings 1968: 47, n. 128).

Further difficulties are imposed upon the interpretation of the Susquehannocks' fort by the account in the *Maryland Archives* (XV: 175; see Hanna 1911: 67), which says that on June 13, 1678, one Jacob Young was instructed to go to the *Old* Susquehannock Fort and treat with the great men of the Sinnequos Nation regarding a rumor that the Susquehannock Indians, living among the Seneca ("Susquehannoughs now amongst them"), had instigated a war upon the Piscataway Indians. The question is, why meet the Seneca at what would appear to be a vacant "Old Susquehannock Fort"? Evidently the Susquehannocks' fort or castle, whether vacant or not, was an important point of reference during this period. Other contemporary accounts of it are given below.

One of these, regarding the Susquehannocks' last (prior to 1683) village, is recorded on a map published in the *Livingston Indian Records, 1666-1723* (Leder 1956: facing 70). Much of what is recorded in the *Livingston Records* concerns efforts on the part of Maryland and Virginia officials to have the Iroquois and Susquehannocks among them cease their raiding and killing of Maryland settlers and "Marylands Indians" (primarily Piscataway). Included with these records is a map dated September 7, 1683, made at Albany from information supplied by two Cayuga Indians and a Susquehannock who was then living with the Onondaga. The map gives the travel distance in days from the various "castles" of the Five Nations to the "Susquehannes Castle" on the west side of the Susquehanna River below the great falls (at Three Mile Island).

Explanations accompanying the map do not say that there were any Susquehannocks living in the "castle" at that time (1683); nor do they say that they were not. However, a map published by John Thornton of London, presumably in 1681 (Pennsylvania Archives, MG 11, #150) shows on the west side of the Susquehanna a "Sesquehana Fort Demolished." This map is clearly based upon the earlier Herrman map which it corrects and/or updates, including the change from Herrman's "The Present Sasquahana Indian Fort" to the then (1681) more accurate "Sesquahana Fort *Demolished.*" If we accept the date (1681) attributed to this map by Albert Cook Myers in a footnote appended to its margin in 1923 (Pennsylvania Ar-

Table 3

A LIST OF NAMES OF SUSQUEHANNOCK CHIEFS AND QUEENS

Name	*Identification*	*Source*
Sawahegeh Aurotaurogh Scarhuhadigh Ruthcuhogah Wathetdianeh		July 5, 1652 treaty with Maryland, see Hanna 1911: 43
Dahedaghesa	of the Great Torripine (Terrapin) family	
Sarangararo	wolf family	May 16, 1667 treaty with Maryland, see Hanna 1911: 43-44
Waskanecqua	of Ohongeoguena Nation	
Kagoragaho	of Unquhiett Nation	
Saraqundett	of Kaiguarioga-haga Nation	
Uwhanhierelera	of Usququ-haga (Snake?) Nation	
Wadonhago	Sconondi-haga (Deer?) Nation	
Civility (Harignera)	mentioned on July 28, 1663	Hanna 1911: 47
Wastahunda-Hariquera	of the Terrapin family	June 29, 1666 treaty, Hanna 1911: 47
Goswein-querackque	fox family	
Harignera	dead at Piscataway Fort, 1675	Hanna 1911: 50
Mitatsimit	1639	
Quaclickhe	1647	Hanna 1911: 59
Aquarichque	1647	
Jonnay Tonnahoorn Pimadaase Connowa Rocquaes	witnesses to deed of July 19, 1655	Hanna 1911: 59
Connoodaghtoh Widaagh (alias Oretyagh) Koqueeash Andaggy-Junkquagh (or Ojunco)	Treaty of 1701	Hanna 1911: 77-8
Kyanharre	conference of 1694	Hanna 1911: 77-8
Queen Conguegos	Connoodaghtoh's widow 1710	Hanna 1911: 77-8
Sotayriote	at conference of 1714-15-16	Hanna 1911: 80
Taghuttalesse, Togatolessa, Tago-drancey, Togod-hessah, or Civility	1710-12-13-14, 1718; in 1718 "the present chief known as Captain Civility"	Hanna 1911: 80
Oneshanayan		Hanna 1911: 81
Tawenna	1700-01	Hanna 1911: 81
Cantowa (a queen)	1719	Hanna 1911: 81
Tiorhaasexy	a chief who speaks Oneida language; at 1744 Lancaster conference, according to Hanna	Hanna 1911: 81
Sohais or Shahaise	signed treaty of 1701; the chief in 1758, murdered in 1763: It seems impossible he could have signed in 1701.	Hanna 1911: 81

chives, MG 11 #150), we have an indication that the Susquehannocks had abandoned the area by that time. Similarly this would imply that the Livingston map of 1683 *did* refer to a vacant Susquehannock castle or fort; and indeed that there were no Susquehannocks there from whom Penn could have purchased the land.

The recording of the "Susquehannes Castle" in 1683, even though probably vacant, further underscores its contemporary significance and forecasts the important role it was to have slightly later in history, particularly in the Penn-Calvert debates over the boundary line between Pennsylvania and Maryland. We might note parenthetically here that it would have been to Penn's advantage not to note a Susquehannock village in the area of the Lower Leibhart site (almost at the present-day fortieth parallel), since the "Sasquehannah Fort" was considered by Lord Baltimore in 1680 to be the boundary between the two provinces. In June, 1680, Lord Baltimore's agent wrote:

> It is desired, that if the Grant pass unto Mr. *Penn*, of the Lands petitioned for by him, in *America*, that it may be expressed to be Land that shall lie *North* of *Sasquahannah Fort*, and *North* of all Lands in a direct Line between the said Fort and *Delaware* River; and also *North* of all Lands upon a direct Line *Westward* from the said Fort; for that Fort is the Boundary of *Maryland*, *Northward*. (Pennsylvania Archives, 8th series I: xiii-xiv)

If in fact the Susquehannocks were no longer living at the Byrd Leibhart site (or elsewhere on the lower Susquehanna Valley) in 1681, we might arbitrarily set the date of their exodus at 1680. The reader will note that we use this arbitrarily derived date elsewhere in this volume for the termination of both the Byrd Leibhart site and the primary occupation of the area by the Susquehannocks. This date would allow for approximately four years of settlement at the Byrd Leibhart site (1676-1680).

Clearly the Susquehannocks were in this general area, and presumably at Byrd Leibhart's in 1676 (cf. the Notley letter, Maryland Archives V: 152-54) and in 1677 (Coursey letter to Notley, Maryland Archives V: 246-48), which indicates that the Iroquois party returning home with the Susquehannocks from Shackamaxon (Philadelphia) stopped off at the Susquehanna River when they picked up 30 more of the chief warriors of the Susquehannocks (Jennings 1968: 40; Maryland Archives V: 246-48).

Susquehannocks among the Delaware and Iroquois

The geographical position of those Susquehannocks who were living among the Lenni Lenape in 1676 and 1677, plus the complexion of continental and colonial politics at the time, continued to cast the Susquehannocks in a role as pawns, this time in a game of political chess involving

New York and Maryland. Susquehannock involvement in this power politics has been extensively treated by Jennings (1968), and therefore need only be summarized here. Jennings concerns himself only with those Susquehannocks living on the Delaware among the Lenni Lenape. Nothing is said about those settled at or near the "new fort" on the Susquehanna.

Maryland had always wanted control of the Delaware, but was never really able to effect this. After the Dutch surrender in 1664, the Delaware Bay was placed under the control of New York. In 1672 the Dutch reconquered New York and the Delaware Bay, but only to lose them again to an English fleet in 1674. The Delaware Bay once more came under the jurisdiction of the English in New York.

Maryland was still intent upon seizing the Delaware Bay for itself. The presence of "hostile" Susquehannocks there would provide it with an excuse for invading the Delaware area. Ostensibly this would have been to punish the Susquehannocks there, but covertly it would give Maryland an opportunity to seize land along the Delaware. As Jennings (1968: 38) puts it, Governor Andros of New York must have gotten wind of this. He followed up with various measures to remove the Susquehannocks from the Delaware. Their removal to New York would have provided additional trade resources for his government, and made any invasion of the Delaware Bay by Maryland "naked aggression," which "could be dealt with as such, both on the premises and in England" (Jennings 1968: 38).

Andros was himself unsuccessful in removing the Susquehannocks, but eventually he managed to have the Iroquois attending the March, 1677, Shackamaxon (a Lenni Lenape village at present-day Philadelphia) conference bring some of them into New York. Apparently the Iroquois were delighted to be able to augment their population and fighting forces, even to the point that the various tribes bickered over the distribution of the Susquehannocks.

Jennings (1968: 40) feels that although the Iroquois may have exerted some pressure on the Susquehannocks at Shackamaxon, the latter made their own decision to join the Iroquois. Not all of them did so; at least some of them remained among the Lenni Lenape (Hanna 1911: 57; Maryland Archives XV: 175). According to Jennings (1968: 40), this removal of the Susquehannocks was later interpreted in some quarters as a capture of the Susquehannocks resulting from an Iroquois conquest (the war of 1673-1674), and therefore contributed to what he (Jennings 1968) considers the "Iroquois conquest myth." Jennings, as was noted above, places no credence in a Susquehannock-Iroquois war of 1673-1674; rather, he feels that it eventually became politically useful for the provincial government of New York to have pretended such.

For a while, at least, after the conference at Shackamaxon (1677), there is a diminished number of references to the Susquehannocks. When they do occur it is largely with reference to the rather desultory warfare in the late 1670's and early 1680's that the Iroquois, and the Susquehannocks who were living with them and perhaps elsewhere, were waging upon the outlying settlers of Maryland (and Virginia) and Maryland's Indians—the Piscataway and Mattawoman (Jennings 1968: 45). Major contemporary accounts include the letters of Maryland's Colonel Coursey and his dealing with Iroquois and New York officials at Albany (see Jennings 1968 for various citations in *New York Colonial Documents* and the *Maryland Archives*), and the *Livingston Indian Records* (Leder 1956). These contain several accounts of the numbers of Susquehannocks living among the various Iroquoian tribes.

Another account (Maryland Archives XV: 383) for the year 1681, in a report to the Governor of Maryland, notes that there were one hundred fighting men of the Susquehannocks (330 people?) living among the Five Nations (see Hanna 1911: 58).

Whether or not all of the Susquehannocks had moved into New York State after 1677 is still a moot point with the present writer. That their numbers should be so carefully assessed among the Iroquois villages, while at the same time there is no mention of them in the lower Susquehanna Valley during this period, seems to contradict the writer's argument for their occupation of the Lower Leibhart site until about 1680. Clearly they (and the Iroquois) were a nuisance to the Maryland colony, and should have warranted enumeration wherever they lived.

Can it be that our postulated nine hundred Susquehannocks lived at the Lower Leibhart site for as long as four years and within 60 miles of the Maryland frontier, and yet received no official (or any other) mention of their presence or of the exodus of about 1680? History generally does not confirm any of this, while archeology leaves us with a very real village which most conveniently fits into this time period.

A void of Indian settlement in the lower Susquehanna does seem quite real after at least 1680. It was shortly after this time that William Penn began to purchase "the quiet land" as far west as the Susquehanna River (Pennsylvania Archives, 1st series I: 67). Much to the consternation of Lord Baltimore, he bought (from the Lenni Lenape) land extending to the head of the Chesapeake. Again, this implies that there were no Susquehannocks living there from whom he could more legally have made such purchases.

New York, it must be noted, was also interested in this territory. For a time, at least, Governor Dongan of New York managed to forestall Penn's claims to the lower Susquehanna by obtaining from the Iroquois a grant for the Susquehannock land which they had conquered. Jennings (1968:

49) states that herein lies the reason for, and the origin of, the "Iroquois conquest myth." In any event, Penn did eventually purchase New York's "fraudulent" deed to the Susquehanna Valley. From then on his disputes over its ownership were primarily with the Calverts of Maryland.

The Susquehannocks Return to Their Homeland from Various Places

For the next 10 years (after 1680) there are scattered accounts of Iroquois (primarily Seneca) and Susquehannocks coming into or through the lower Susquehanna for purposes of trade and what often appears as mischief. Increased activity here on the part of the Seneca can probably be traced, among other things, to destruction of their villages by the French army under the Marquis de Denonville in 1687 (Thwaites 1959 LXIII: 271-75). One thing is certain: the Seneca, more than any other of the Iroquois, were anxious to take advantage of the trade outlets already established in the Susquehannocks' territory. The renewed efforts of the French against them in 1687 must have intensified this desire.

Perhaps, as suggested below, a vanguard of Susquehannocks, probably in small groups, had already returned prior to 1690 to the lower Susquehanna, possibly to their Old Fort at Byrd Leibhart's, but perhaps also to other less conspicuous places. Small, poorly known sites which produce a few glass beads of the period, like the one at Creswell Station south of the Strickler site, may well be such sites. Others that may have existed could be as unnoticed (or unreported) today by collectors as they were unrecorded by Europeans during the seventeenth century.

Another very curious, but potentially significant, historical reference to a Susquehannock town during this period is recorded in the Pennsylvania Bureau of Land Records, Old Rights, D-81 0.98.* On March 9, 1689, the Surveyor General for Pennsylvania was issued a warrant to survey 500 acres for William Markham, and a contiguous 500 acres for Jacob Pellison, in Philadelphia County:

> Beginning at a corner tree standing at the North West end of the *Susquehannah Indian Town* thence N.E. by a line of trees 963 perches, thence S.E. by a line of trees 600 perches, thence S.W. by the Mannor of Gilberts 633 perches to a corner tree of the same *standing by the Schuylkil,* thence up the several courses thereof to the place of beginning.

Since the location of the Proprietary Manor of Gilberts along the Schuylkill River (in present-day Montgomery County) can be fairly well established, it is also possible to fix the approximate location of the Susquehannock Indian town mentioned in the warrant description. It should be somewhere in the vicinity of present-day Royersford.

---

*The author would like to acknowledge William A. Hunter for pointing out this document.

A Susquehannock town here is historically unexpected and unpredictable. Perhaps the warrant description is in error: could the survey have been meant to say Schuylkill Indian (Delaware) town? Or, could this be a remnant group of those Susquehannocks who joined the Lenni Lenape in 1676, and who perhaps never left the area? Oddly enough, there is a hint of just such a situation in a letter written June 25, 1696, describing the results of a meeting between Captain Lasse Cock with 15 "Skoolkill" Indians and the Susquehanna Indians at "Quanistagua" (Conestoga Town in Lancaster County). The letter describes the speech given by one of the "Skoolkill Indians," Alamayon, to the Susquehannocks:

> We are very glad you [the Susquehannocks] sent us [the Skoolkill Indians] a messenger to acquaint us of ye Dangers you were in wee are come to assist you in what wee can you are our *cousens still* tho' you *live a little ffurther ffrom us then you did*. . . . (British Public Records Office C.O. 5/1233 [Pennsylvania Material 1689-1707] F.O. 353/59 357/60, Microfilm Collections of the Bureau of Archives and History, Pennsylvania Historical and Museum Commission)*

This document demonstrates a very close, friendly relationship between the Schuylkill (Delaware) Indians and the Susquehannocks in 1696. It also shows that the Susquehannocks formerly lived much closer to the Schuylkill Indians—perhaps, as suggested by the 1689 warrant survey, on the Schuylkill River!

Seneca Among the Susquehannocks

On May 30, 1690, the trader and interpreter Jacob Young (various spellings) sent a letter reporting Indian affairs at the head of Chesapeake Bay to John Coode, the Commander-in-Chief of Maryland:

> There is att my house 14 Cemockoes [Senecas]. . . . these Cenockoes came from their own country about the last of Aprill last past, their intent is to settle among the Susquahanough Indians here, upon the Susquahanough River for there is some of every ffort of the Cenockoes come down to them and they tell me th[a]t their great men will be downe very shortly. (Maryland Archives VIII: 181)

This account clearly points to an extant Susquehannock settlement somewhere in the lower Susquehanna Valley in the spring of 1690. Although it does not identify the place of residence as Conestoga, we are proposing here that this was the place alluded to by the Young account, and that 1690 be arbitrarily set as the founding date of that settlement.

Three years later, on April 11, 1693, Colonel Casparus Herman (the son of Augustine Herrman) and Jacob Young, brought a number of Susquehannocks before the Maryland Council where they stated that

*The author is indebted to William A. Hunter for this reference.

> being reduced to a small number & as it were newly grown up they desire the Favour of the Govr and Councill that they may have liberty to Come & settle upon their own Land at the Susquehannoh Fort & to be taken & treated as Friends. . . .

The reply of the Council was that

> their Fort as they call it falling within the Limits of another Government as Pensilvania, this Governmt can take no cognizance thereof. . . .

Later, the Council decided that the Susquehannocks

> may Continue at their Fort, & if they are Inclined to enter into a League with us there may some of their great men come down to confirm the same. . . . (Hanna 1911: 58-59; Maryland Archives VIII: 518).

Here again we see an example of what might be considered vagaries of historical accounts. The 1690 account above says the Susquehannocks are already in the lower Susquehanna. Then, three years later, it appears that they are just then asking the Maryland government for permission to settle there. At first, Maryland says it has no authority to sanction the relocation, and then shortly thereafter it permits such, even though their (new) settlement falls within the limits of Pennsylvania.

As a point of clarification here it should be noted that the Maryland records frequently used the name Seneca to refer to any or all of the Five Nations of the Iroquois. However, in the accounts cited above, by Jacob Young, the term *Cenockes* clearly means the Seneca Nation. Largely as a result of encouragement by the governors of New York, most of the Iroquois, and particularly the Cayuga, claimed (Hunter 1959: 16) ownership of Susquehannock lands. Actually, only the Seneca showed any real interest or readiness to move into the Susquehanna area, and many of them did shortly after 1690.

At this point in the Indian history of the lower Susquehanna Valley, a number of other Indian groups come onto the scene. Beside the Susquehannocks and Seneca, the Indian tribes of greatest historical importance who settled there were the Shawnee and Conoy. The history and archeology of these latter two will be dealt with separately below. For the present we will continue to follow the course of events relating to the Susquehannocks, or the Conestogas as they were soon to be known.

THE CONESTOGAS

Previously, it was proposed that, even though there was no specific mention of an Indian town called Conestoga, we would arbitrarily set the founding of that place in 1690. That being the case, we can assume that the two Susquehannock Indians, Widaagh and Kyanharra, who attended the conference held at Philadelphia on July 6, 1694, were from Conestoga.

Also in attendance at this meeting with Lt. Gov. William Markham were six Delawares.

The earliest recorded account of an actual town of Conestoga (spelled *Quanistagua*) is in the previously cited draught of a 1696 letter relating the visit to that place by Captain Lasse Cock and 15 Delaware or Schuylkill Indians (see British Public Records Office C.O. 5/1233 [Pennsylvania Material 1689-1707] F.O. 353/59 357/60, Microfilm Collections of the Bureau of Archives and History, Pennsylvania Historical and Museum Commission).

Next mention of the place is that by the trader John Hans Tillman (variously spelled Stillman, Tilghman, Steelman, etc.) in the *Maryland Archives* for June, 1697 (Manyland Archives XIX: 519-20). He reports,

> at Carristauga [perhaps a printer's error for Conistauga], the Susquehanna & Seneca Indians have about forty lusty young men besides woemen & children [a total population of 132 persons] . . . the Shevanor [Shawnee] Indians being about thirty men besides woemen & children live within foure miles of Caristauga lower downe. . . .

This particular account is given in fuller form below, as it relates to the nearby Shawnee and Delaware towns of this period.

A year later (July 1, 1698) Tillman again appeared before the Maryland Council to give additional depositions relating to the Indians. There he stated that the "Susquehannahs are about Fifty men live two miles further up [from the Shawnee town] at Caristaugua [*sic*] & Came from the Seneques." He further states that the "Susquehannahs . . . live about thirty Miles above Octerara Creek" (Maryland Archives XXIII: 444).

Much of this testimony concerning the Susquehannocks given at this time by Tillman and other deponents relates to the lengthy dispute between William Penn (and his successors) and the Calverts over the boundary between Pennsylvania and Maryland.

Disagreement over the line, which was not settled until many years later, centered around the location of the "Sasquehanna Fort" which was to mark the boundary (Pennsylvania Archives, 8th series I: xiii-xiv). During the course of the debates, Pennsylvania officials produced a number of traders who testified that an ancient Susquehannock site existed at the mouth of the Octoraro Creek. These statements have led a number of later historians to place a Susquehannock town in the vicinity of the Octoraro. However, recent surveys have failed to produce (as did Penn's witnesses) any substantial evidence that a Susquehannock site ever existed in this area.

William Penn was most cunning in his dealings with other provincial governments, especially when it came to laying the boundaries for his own colony. At the same time, Penn was noted for his fairness in purchasing land from the Indians.

It is not our intention here to dwell upon the Penn-Calvert boundary disputes, so we can leave the issue for now. Later on, however, we will find it useful to pick up, once again, the threads of this discussion as it relates to the historical confusion between a Conoy Indian town called Conejehola and a Maryland patent for lands called Canhodah in present York County, Pennsylvania.

In 1700 Penn obtained from the Indians of Conestoga a deed for all of the "lands, which are or formerly were the Right of the People or Nation called the Susquehannagh Indians." (Pennsylvania Archives, 1st series I: 133)

It is interesting to note that Penn had already (1694) purchased the Susquehannock land claimed by the Iroquois from Governor Dongan of New York for the sum of £100 (Landis 1924: 136). Jennings (1968: 50) suggests that Penn visited Conestoga Town at the time the September, 1700, deed was secured. Other historians, e.g., Eshleman (1909: 159-62), argue that Penn did not visit Conestoga until June, 1701. The following quote from the *Maryland Archives* (XXV: 404, from the proceedings of the council on March 2, 1722; see also Colonial Records II: 252-53, 244) should be of interest to those who question Penn's visit to Conestoga:

> . . . in the year 1700 when Mr. Penn was travelling from Below Annapolis to visit the Indians at Conestogoe being out of respect to his Character waited upon by divers Gentlemen Magistrates and others of the Northern parts of Maryland these Gentlemen made a Stop in the Ford of Octararoe River telling Mr. Penn they had now accompanied him into his own Province and therefore desired to take their Leave but he answered he hoped they had been already in Pennsylvania long before they came to that place, all which expressions can be very well attested by witnesses still Living who were in that Company[.]

By 1701 the name Conestoga Town begins to appear frequently in the Pennsylvania records. In April of that year representatives of Conestoga and other local Indians traveled to Philadelphia to confirm the September, 1700, sale and to sign the famous treaty permitting them to use the land they were living upon in peace, so long as they obeyed all the English conditions set forth therein (Colonial Records II: 15). That same year, Indians from Conestoga traveled to Philadelphia to say goodbye to Penn prior to his departure for England (Colonial Records II: 46).

Origins of the word *Conestoga* have previously been discussed. It was suggested that some form of this word is what the Susquehannocks actually called themselves. Similar words for the present-day Conestoga Creek appear on the Herrman map of 1670 and the Chambers survey of 1688. In the early years of the eighteenth century, Conestoga was the place, near the Conestoga Creek, where the Susquehannocks and Senecas lived. Initially it was important to be able to distinguish the separate groups of people occupying the town, but eventually the Susquehannock population was largely absorbed by the Seneca. Later the Seneca residents lost their political, and to some extent, their social ties with their tribesmen in western New York. Thus it became largely a matter of convenience, so far as the officials and settlers of Pennsylvania were concerned, to refer to the occupants of Conestoga Town as Conestogas.

Conestoga rapidly became an important town. First of all it was a major trading center for the Seneca, Susquehannocks and other local Indians. James Logan, Penn's Provincial secretary, worked actively to keep this trade in the hands of Pennsylvania-licensed traders, and, as Jennings (1966) points out, under his own control for personal financial gain.

Secondly, Conestoga was also a convenient place for negotiations between the Pennsylvania Proprietaries and the various Indians of the lower Susquehanna. Numerous peace treaties and land purchases were concluded there.

The volume of trade conducted here is to a large extent reflected by the large number of traders who were licensed by Logan to trade in and about Conestoga Town during the first three or four decades of the eighteenth century (see Hanna 1911 II: 326-43). The first deeds for land in the Conestoga area were all to Indian traders.

In 1720 the French established a trading post on the Niagara which provided the Seneca with a closer-to-home trade outlet. Their interests in the Pennsylvania trade continued for at least another 10 years, but it was on the decline (Hunter 1959: 17).

By the 1740's, depletion of fur-bearing animals and the westward migration of the settlers with its consequent displacement of the Indians caused the traders to leave the Conestoga area. The remnant Indian population of Conestoga, although becoming increasingly impoverished, continued to stay. These people were Conestogas more than anything else. This was their home, protected as it was by the government of Pennsylvania, and there they would remain.

In its heyday, Conestoga was visited by many of the most important people of Pennsylvania. After William Penn's visit in 1700, his secretary, James Logan, went to the site in 1705, 1720, 1721, and 1722 (Hanna 1911 II: 40, 151, 153, 164, 208; II: 347). Governor Evans traveled to Conestoga in 1707 and 1708 (Hanna 1911 I: 37, 134, 151, 161, 172-73), as did the minister Thomas Chalkley in 1706 (Hanna 1911 I: 78); Governor Gookin in 1711 (Hanna 1911 I: 165), Governor Keith in 1717 and 1721 (Hanna 1911 I: 100, 153), and Governor Gordon in 1728 (Hanna 1911 I: 183, 299). Including the retinue of these noted visitors, and the other lesser-known individuals who traveled to Conestoga to trade, proselytize, negotiate, cheat or kill, literally hundreds of white people came to this town.

With so many visitors to Conestoga, it is surprising that so little was recorded about the place. None of the official records in the archives or any of the surveyed collections of private correspondance of the period gives any real insight into the nature of life at Conestoga or, in fact, its precise location. The way to Conestoga was well known during the eighteenth century, and evidently no one saw much need to record it.

The location of the Conestoga tract is recorded in a survey map of 1717. In that year the Pennsylvania land commissioners, including James Logan, ordered the Surveyor General, Jacob Taylor, to survey the land about Conestoga Town. This land was to be held as one of William Penn's many proprietary manors, and it was known as the Conestoga Manor (Brackbill 1938: 22). The survey map (Pennsylvania Archives, 3d series IV: map 11) shows that the tract contained sixteen thousand acres, and also gives the general location of the Conestoga Indian town within the manor. Later eighteenth-century deeds pertaining to the "Indian reservation" describe it as 414 1/3 acres of land which

> was leased or licensed to some Indian families, who by virtue of the said proprietor's [Penn] license lived and maintained themselves on the said land until they were destroyed. (Lancaster County Deed Book B-B:28; see McGee 1924: 139)

In addition to the recorded treaties, land purchases and official journeys to Conestoga, there is a good deal of material relating to the activities of Indian traders in the vicinity. Again, these records are of interest from a historical point of view insofar as the early settlement of Lancaster County is concerned. However, they provide very little in the way of information about the culture of the Conestogas.

During the first four decades of occupation at Conestoga, a number of "chiefs" and "queens" are mentioned in the accounts. The most frequently occurring name is Captain Civility (Tagodrancy or Tagotalessa, and others). Hanna (1911: 80-81) and Sipe (1927: 79-87) discuss him and many others at some length. Captain Civility should not be confused with a seventeenth-century Susquehannock known as Civility or Harignera. There is some evidence (Colonial Records III: 133) that Captain Civility was a true Susquehannock.

Most of the prominent historical figures of Conestoga were Seneca. It also appears that Seneca was the language spoken there. Witthoft (n.d.a: 16) feels that the change in language from Susquehannock to Seneca was complete by about 1740. According to Witthoft, most of what is known about Conestoga linguistics is based on an unpublished vocabulary in the collections of the American Philosophical Society. This vocabulary, taken from a Conestoga named Bill Sock, was written in 1757. In Witthoft's (n.d.a: 17) opinion, the vocabulary is entirely Seneca.

One feature about the site which is repeatedly mentioned is that the Indians lived in cabins. To some extent this may reflect the manner in which eighteenth-century observers perceived Indian houses. It is known, however, that many Indians of the eighteenth century had adopted a form of colonial-style log cabin construction. It is thought by some that such log cabins were in use at Conestoga Town. This may have been the case during the later years at Conestoga.

During the excavations at Conestoga in 1972, three separate postmold patterns were uncovered, which represent rectangular structures (averaging about 15 feet by 45 feet) with upright-post construction. It is unlikely that any horizontal log structure built by the Indians would have had footer trenches for foundations, and none was found at the site.

One thing which is clear, by inference from contemporary accounts and from archeology, is that the Conestogas were becoming increasingly Europeanized or acculturated. Their demand for and dependence upon the trade is evidence of this. Many of the treaties, for example, include lists of the items given to the Indians to consummate the agreements. A standard list of things exchanged with Indians for furs is found in the inventory of Martin Chartier's home and trading post (in present-day Washington Boro) after his death in 1718. A portion of this inventory is here reproduced (from the Logan Papers X: 110, Historical Society of Pennsylvania, and printed in the Lancaster County Historical Society *Papers*, XXIX(10): 130-33, 1925):

	£ s d
In the Store:	
To 1 pr of plow Irons and Swingle Tree Tackle.	-15
To 4 Sadles and pads.	-15
To one Ketle and 2 Iron Wedges	- 7
To 1 handsaw 1 adds 1 drawing Knife and 2 Augers	-10
To 2 horse Collars	- 7
To 8 baggs and 3 busl. Sumr Wheat .	2- 3
To a pr of brass Stilliers.	- 5
To 2 Cask. Salt abot 3 bushl	- 9
To 2 Sickles Some rope and black oak and othr Lumb	-10-
In ye Celler:	
To 2D wt. of Tobacco	1- 5-
To Some Cork and a Grindstone	-14-
To Some Tallow	11-
In the House:	
To 1 frying pan and 1 brass Skillt. . . .	8-
To 1 frow and one Axe	6- 6

To one Iron pott and hangers	6-
To one pewter bason	9-
To 2 Juggs 1 Candlestick 1 Tin quart .	2- 6
To 1 file 1 Chissell and 2 Door bands .	2
To ye building and Improvements on plantation	30
To a Small Cart	-10-
In the upr Store:	
To 1 pcs red Duffels qt 47 yds at 5s. . .	11-15
To 1 pcs. blew Ditto 46½ yds 5	11-12- 5
To 1 pce red Strowd 23:/yds at 8s . . .	9- 8
To a pce blew Strowd 23½ yds—8s . .	9- 8
To a pce red half Thicks 32 yds at 2s 10d	4-10- 8
To 3 half barl Gunpowdr at 7:10	11- 5-
To 1 doz. large looking Glases	" -18-
To 16½ 11½ 12¾ yds Strowd 40½ yds in all at 8s	16- 4
To 10 Strowds in 20 yds at 8.	8
To 4¾ & 3 yds—is 7¾ yds Strowd—8	3- 2
To 1 pce red half Thicks 32 yds & 12½ yds blew is 44½ yds 2:10 . .	6- 6- 1
To 4 blankets at 12s	2- 8-
To Duffel Conts is 6 yds at 5s	1-10-
	233- 7- 3

(End first page of M.S.)

	£ s d
Brought over	£233- 7- 3
To 22½ yds blew Duffel at 5s	5-12- 6
To 32½ yds red Ditto—5	8- 2- 6
To 6 brass Kettles wd 43 les @ 3s 4d. .	7- 3- 4
To 15¾ yds Garlix at 20d	1- 6- 3
To 4 drawing Knives at 2s 4d	- 9- 4
To 10½ yds Dowlas at 2s.	1- 1
To 1 doz & 8 Hatchets @ 22/	1-16- 8
To 10 box Handled Knives at 6d	- 5-
To 1 doz. Clasp ditto.	- 7-
To 13 Screw boxes at 1½d.	- 1- 7½
To 22½ lb Shott @ 3d	- 5- 7½
To 306½ lb Lead @ 3d.	3-16- 7½
To 9½ lb Small beads @ 2/6	1- 3- 4¼
To 3 C flints—216 or 2/6	- 7- 6
To 9 Steels—2d1/4	- 1- 8
To doz 1 awls @ 216 or 2/6	- 5- 2½
To 9 dutch Knives @ 5d	- 3- 9
To 8 bath metle vings 5d	- 3- 4
To 2½ lbs heads 3/.	- 7- 6
To 3 doz buttons at 4d.	- 1-
To ½ gross Threed	- 6-

To a pr blew Stockings	- 2- 8
To 2¼ yds ozenbrugs—1/	- 2- 3
To 28 lb powdr at—1/8	2- 2-
To 2 Small brass Kettles	-10-
Brought from ye Shawnes Towne:	
To 5 Shirts at 716 (or 7/6)	1-17- 6
To 1 old gun	1-“ -
To 5 bone handd Knives @ 6d.	- 2- 6
To 8 Jews Harpes @ 3½d	- 2- 4x
To 5 Rasars at 1/	- 5-
To 9 doz & 2 belts at /2d	-18- 4
To 6 doz & 3 awkes blades at 18d	- 9- 4½
To 18 yds red ribbon—3d	- 4- 6
To 19¾ yd greene ditto—3d	- 4-11¼
To 1 lb. wt beads	- 3-
To 32 Shirts at Thos. Baldwins @ 8/12	- “-
To 214 fall Deer wt 831 lb at 15d in Towne.	51-18- 9
To 6 Sumr Ditto 12 lb—20d	1-
To 9 drest wt 15 lb @ 3/9	2-16- 3
To 34 or 32 bear at 8s	12-16-
To 2 Elks 6s	-12-
To 2 fishers—5	-10-
To 2 Otters—3/6	- 7-
To 8 foxes Catts and Woulfs 2s	-16-
	358-11-10¾
(End of 2nd page of M.S.)	
Brought over	£358-11-10¾
To 70 or 65 raccowns @ 16d	- 3- 5
To 12 full Deer wt 52 lb at 15d.	- 3- 5
To 1 Elke	- 6-
To 1 large Cubb bear	- 3-
	£366-12- 6¾

The Within goods was appraised
by us May the 7th 1718
Jno Cartlidge
his
James I H Hendricks
mark

No. 113, Chartier: Martin 1718 3 154.

Examples of most of the non-perishable items mentioned in this inventory, and many that were not, were recovered at Conestoga Town during the 1972 excavation. Some of these items were not put to the use intended by their white manufacturers. For example, many utilitarian pieces were used instead as ornaments.

Conestogas, like other eastern Indians of the period, were in a state of flux. These were indigent farmers and hunters caught between the old world of the Indians and the rapidly changing world of eighteenth-century colonial America. They were not a part of either sphere. On the one hand, the cherished old ways were difficult or impossible to adapt to their present way of life. On the other hand they could not belong to, nor were they wanted in, the world of the whites.

We might view the economy, and to some extent the technology, of these Indians as being somewhat like that of the poorest of the European immigrants to the frontiers of the New World. In this respect both groups were attempting to adapt to new situations in essentially the same manner. However, the social and ideological differences were insurmountable for the Indian. His eventual option, other than extermination, was to fully adopt white culture at its lowest level.

By the time of the great Lancaster treaty of 1744, Conestoga had declined as a place of importance. In fact it is uncertain what the representation from Conestoga was at this pan-Indian treaty. Some of the "principal men" of Conestoga were there, but their names are not mentioned (Pennsylvania Archives, 1st series I: 656-57).

There were also a number of beggars from Conestoga in Lancaster during treaty sessions (Eshleman 1909: 343-47). This is rather indicative of the condition of the Conestoga at this period, and in the nearly 20 years which followed. The population was dwindling and the condition of the inhabitants was continually deteriorating. If we may use as a source Eshleman's (1909) diminishing accounts of events at Conestoga, very little happened there after 1744. The most frequent references are to their need for clothing and other basic necessities of life.

Brackbill (1938: 46) points out that several Indians at Conestoga, most notably Bill Sock, were spies giving information on the movements of Provincial troops to the Seneca, Shawnee and Delawares on the western frontier. However, most of the hapless Conestogas were innocent old men, women and children.

Not until 1763 does Conestoga again become a place of historical note. On December 14 of that year six Conestogas were brutally murdered at the Indian town. Although it was not known immediately, the massacre was committed by a group from the Harrisburg area called the Paxton Boys. This infamous group, apparently incensed by Indian atrocities resulting from Pontiac's rebellion on the western frontier, had decided to seek retribution by killing some Indians themselves. Incapable of confronting any warlike Indians, they found it convenient to attack the Conestogas.

At the time of the first massacre a number of the Indians were away from the town selling brooms, or on other business. In order to protect these survivors from further attempts, the Provincial Council ordered that they be taken under protective custody by the magistry at Lancaster, and there to be placed in the workhouse.

Not satisfied with their first efforts, the Paxton Boys returned on December 27. Largely unopposed, they broke open the doors of the workhouse and killed all 14 of the Indians who were being held there under "protection."

In the *Colonial Records* (IX: 101-103) there appears a list of the possessions held by the Indians at the time of the massacre, together with a list of the names of the victims. Among the items listed were several letters, two wampum belts and two peace treaties, one of which was their 1701 agreement with William Penn.

The six Indians killed at Conestoga during the first massacre were buried in a common grave near their cabins after the coroner's inquest. There are several conflicting statements by local historians as to where those murdered at the workhouse were finally interred. Witthoft (n.d.a: 8-10), who had undertaken some research concerning this matter, concludes in favor of a location previously suggested by Eshleman (1909: 391). This place, in Eshleman's time, was known as Martin's Hall, and was located on East Chestnut Street in Lancaster. Witthoft (n.d.a: 9) found a record pertaining to the removal of Indian graves in 1880 from the rear of 131 East Chestnut Street (the Martin's Hall location). He also found that this location was a farm cemetery, in use as early as 1750, but that it was later (the 1840's) swallowed by Lancaster. According to Witthoft (n.d.a: 9) this place was referred to in the early nineteenth century as the "Indian burial ground." He goes on to state,

> Lancaster had no potters' field, and the Indians, not being members of any Christian sect, would not have been placed in a church cemetery. The Indians were buried by the Jailor, Felix Donnally and a bill was submitted to the Sherriff, John Hay: since their interment was a matter of official concern it should have been in a cemetery under very proper circumstances. The Nissley Cemetery [as it was known in the eighteenth century] would have been the likeliest place. . . . This cemetery was partially destroyed by a railroad cut in 1833 and the remainder of the plot dug away in 1880 when the tracks were relocated. This excavation has since been refilled, and the site of the cemetery is now the Moose parking lot in the rear of 111 and 113 East Chestnut Street. (Witthoft n.d.a)

Two Indians from Conestoga survived the massacres. These two were given a letter from Governor John Penn guaranteeing them safety. The letter, dated August 17, 1764 (eight months after the massacre), and addressed to "whom it may concern," states that

> the Bearers Michael and Mary his wife are friendly Indians who formerly resided with other Indians . . . in Conestoga Manor, and have for upwards of fifteen months last past lived with Christian Hershey, at his plantation in Warwick Township, Lancaster County. . . . (Eshleman 1909: 386-87; see also Pennsylvania Archives, Series, 2d: 739)

This letter appeared in the Lancaster *New Era*, a newspaper, on September 11, 1907. It was part of the announcement of the Hershey family reunion, which was held at the old Hershey homestead. The article also noted that the graves of these two Indians, Michael and Mary, were found at that time "in a lonely spot in one of the back pastures of this homestead" (Eshleman 1909: 386-87).

The Conestoga Indians have become a part of the legends and traditions of Lancaster County. However, no event relating to these people was so well remembered as the infamous massacre.

Shortly after the massacre, the Paxton Boys claimed, by right of conquest, the Indian farm and erected two cabins there. However, by order of the Governor, they were removed from the land and it was returned to the possession of the Penn proprietors (Landis 1924: 138).

A letter written by Thomas Barton in 1770 (Landis 1924: 138) describes the "Indian farm." It mentions that there were no houses or barns on the farm except for the two cabins erected by the "Paxton people." Landis (1924: 138) says that

> this appears to contradict Rupp's [1844: 356] statement that Isaac Kuhn's house was the last Indian cabin, but it does not as the Kuhn's cabin was not located on the 414 acre Indian farm or reservations but . . . was on the John Cartledge tract [to the south]. That site was doubtless the scene of the Massacre.

One of the last significant official incidents relating to Conestoga occurred in 1775, when eight Cayuga Indians came to Philadelphia to exercise their claims to the land at Conestoga. One of these Cayuga claimed to be a brother of the old Seneca, Sohaes, who was murdered at the first massacre. The Cayuga said that the land now belonged to the relatives of Sohaes and that they had come to sell it. After some deliberation the Council reported back to the Indians, saying that the Governor had purchased the 500-acre tract at the 1768 Fort Stanwix treaty from the Cayuga Chief Togaiato, and that he paid him $500 in goods for the land. The Governor said that he was not anxious to pay for the land twice. However, in order to preserve peace and friendship, he agreed to pay them an additional $300 in full satisfaction of all the claims of Sohaes' family. This the Indians gladly accepted, and signed a receipt on the back of the deed transacted at the Fort Stanwix treaty (Eshleman 1909: 389).

In 1780 John Penn, the proprietor of the tract, and grandson of William Penn, sold this land to John Musser of Lancaster (Magee 1924: 139). From this sale and deed the successive owners and subsequent partitions can be traced through the Lancaster County court records (Magee 1924: 142-43).

The boundaries of the Indian farm are recorded in the survey, and in the Penn to Musser deeds of 1780, 1784 and 1786 (Magee 1924: 139). Based upon these descriptions, Landis (1924: facing 133) produced a rough map of the present (1924) farms with the boundaries of the 1780 survey of the tract superimposed. On this map he locates three Indian towns, including where he thought the 1763 cabins had been located, which he places outside the tract. One of the places indicated on his map is clearly the Conestoga site excavated in 1972. Landis obviously knew this site, and his collection from there, now in the Hershey Museum, includes appropriate material. Surface surveys at his third location have produced only prehistoric materials, primarily Shenks Ferry pottery and Archaic points. Landis probably mistook similar finds of his own as the remains of another Conestoga-period site.

It seems reasonable to suppose that the Conestogas lived at more than one location within the tract during the 70 or more years that it was occupied. Earlier Susquehannock sites and Seneca sites, for example (Wray and Schoff 1953), had an occupation span of about 10 to 20 years. This was due largely to the depletion of local wood supplies and soil fertility. At first glance we might expect the same to apply to Conestoga. However, it must be remembered that the Conestogas were no longer living in quite the same manner as their ancestors: this was a highly acculturated group. In the later years of Conestoga, at least, agriculture and hunting must have diminished, due to the availability of foods from nearby traders, farmers and the city of Lancaster. Hunting decreased due to diminishing quantities of game and fur-bearing animals.

It must also be remembered that the Conestogas were not nearly as numerous as their predecessors, who occupied the big towns along the Susquehanna. Consequently, the conditions of their town would deteriorate less rapidly and they could have occupied it for a longer period.

Landis (1924), as previously noted, suggested that the Conestoga site of 1763 was outside the tract, and that no Indian cabins were still standing within the tract. He knew the location of at least one Conestoga site within the tract. The location of that site had been largely forgotten since Landis' time, until Witthoft (n.d.a) rediscovered it in 1950. This is the same site which the Pennsylvania Historical and Museum Commission excavated in 1972. Results of that work, which are more fully discussed in a later chapter, suggest that this town may have been occupied by the Conestogas until about 1740. Subsequent sites and the place of the massacre are uncertain.

Conoy

Probably the most significant, and certainly the shortest, history of the Conoy Indians is the account of his people by the Conoy Chief Old Sack in a letter (written for him by Thomas Cookson, the Chief Burgess of Lancaster) to Governor Thomas of Pennsylvania in 1743.

> The Governor laid before the Board the following Letter, which was wrote by Mr. Cookson at the Instance of the Conoy Indians:
>
> "May it please your Honour—
>
> "The Indians of the Conoy Town, on the East side Sasquehanna, in the beginning of April Last sent me a Message, signifying their having some thing to Communicate to your Honour by me, and desired me to be at Home the 11th of the same Month, on which Day they came down to the Number of 14. I invited them into my House, and after some time Old Sack (who is the Chief of that Town) spoke to the following purpose: 'We desire you to acquaint our Brother the Governor, that our fforefathers came from Piscatua to an Island in Potowmeck, and from thence down to Philadelphia in Old Proprietor Penn's Time, in Order to shew their ffriendship to the Proprietor; That after their return they brought down all their Brothers from Potowmeck to Conejoholo, on the East side Sasquehannah, and built a town there.
>
> " 'That the Indians of the six Nations told 'em there was Land enough, they might chuse their place of Settlement any where about Sasquehannah.
>
> " 'That accordingly they thought fit to remove higher up Sasquehannah to the Conoy Town, where they now live; And on their first settling, the Indians of the six Nations came down & made their ffire, and all the great Men declared the fire of their Kindling in token of their approbation of their settling there; But that now the Lands all around them being settled by white People, their hunting is spoiled And they have been long advised by the six Nations to leave the place and go higher up the River and settle either at the Mouth of Conodogwinnet, Chiniotta, or up at Shamokin.
>
> " 'That now they are come to a Resolution to remove up to Shamokin; And, therefore, according to their Custom, they desire to acquaint their Brother, the Governor, therewith, that he may know certainly where to find them upon any occasion; that they will be down at Philadelphia in one Year, and then they hope the Governor or some Gentlemen of Philadelphia will give them something for their old ffields.' And in order to satisfy your Honour that this Message was sent down at their instance, they desired the String of Wampum herewith sent to be delivered. (Colonial Records: IV: 656-57)

Numerous other historical references to the Piscataway Indians of Maryland, who later became known as the Ganowese or Conoy, appear in the contemporary documents of Maryland and Virginia. These have been well summarized by Alice Ferguson (see Ferguson and Stewart 1940; Ferguson and Ferguson 1960; and Stephenson et al. 1963). Our purpose here is to briefly summarize the relationship of these accounts to the archeology of the Piscataway.

The first historical reference to the Piscataway are those of Captain John Smith (see Tyler 1907), who visited the town of "Moyaone" on the Potomac River below the mouth of Piscataway Creek, opposite present-day Mount Vernon, Virginia. Archeological investigations at the presumed site of Moyaone (Stephenson et al. 1963) have uncovered numerous periods of successive occupation of the site. No artifacts of European provenience have been recovered during the extensive investigations there. However, there is convincing evidence of several burnings of the town, which are also indicated by contemporary accounts. The first of these was brought about in 1623 by Governor Wyatt of Virginia in retribution for the Indian murders of English traders. A second burning of the town, in about 1630 by northern Indians, is implied in the narrative written by the fur trader Henry Fleet (see Ferguson and Ferguson 1960; Neill 1876 for a reprint of Fleet's narrative). Following this second burning the Piscataway moved to a second location—the Piscataway fort on the south bank of the Piscataway Creek, according to Ferguson and Stewart (1940). Glass beads from this site, and particularly the jettons described by Ferguson and Stewart (1940: 13), clearly suggest that it was occupied between about 1630 and 1640. It was almost certainly at this place that Leonard Calvert in 1634 obtained permission from the Piscataway "emperor" to begin settlement of the Maryland colony—that first settlement being at St. Marys. It follows then that this was the place visited by the Jesuit Father Andrew White, who provided excellent (ethnohistoric) observations of the Piscataway Indians (see Hall 1910: 43-45).

Unquestionably the Piscataway empire of this period included a number of separate towns (see Ferguson and Ferguson 1960: 5, for a map of the "Piscataway Empire"). One of these towns, occupied subsequent to that on the south bank of Piscataway Creek, was presumably that at the mouth of the creek in the area known as Mockley Point. It was this "abandoned Piscataway fort" in which the Susquehannocks fortified themselves in 1675 against the Maryland and Virginia militias.

Shortly after the removal of the Susquehannocks from the old Piscataway fort, the Piscataway themselves moved (June, 1680) to a place called Zachiah Fort in the Zachiah Swamp, east of Port Tobacco, Maryland. (See Maryland Archives XV: 303.)

Susquehannock and Iroquois animosity toward Maryland's friendly Indians, primarily the Piscataway and Mattawoman, greatly intensified during the period following the defeat of the Susquehannocks. Susquehannocks and Seneca apparently attacked the Zachiah fort in 1681 (Ferguson and Ferguson 1960: 41). In 1682 and again in 1685 (Maryland Archives XV: 303), the Iroquois and Piscataway entered into peace agreements. Now at ease with the Iroquois and Susquehannocks, their only major problems were with the whites of Maryland, who no longer needed them as trade partners or as buffers against the northern Indians.

In 1697 (Maryland Archives XIX: 520) the Piscataways, who were then generally known by the name given them by the Iroquois—Ganowese, or the Anglicized form, Conoy—had moved into the back country of Virginia. Two years later they moved to Conoy Island in the Potomac near Point of Rocks, Maryland (see Ferguson and Ferguson 1960: 43). Their presence here has been archeologically confirmed by work done there under the direction of Robert Schuyler (personal communication 1972). A general summary of the history of the Piscataway during the latter part of the seventeenth century can also be found in Semmes (1937), *Captains and Mariners of Early Maryland.*

In 1701 (Pennsylvania Archives, 1st series I: 144-46) the Ganowese were represented at a meeting in Philadelphia with William Penn. In the agreements reached there, the Ganowese were promised peace and permission to settle within the bounds of Penn's Province. Some of the Ganowese remained for a time at Conoy Island, where they were seen, according to Count Christoph von Graffenried (see Landis 1933: 119) as late as 1711. However, sometime soon after the 1701 treaty with William Penn and at the recommendation of the Iroquois (Wallace 1964: 107), the Ganowese began to move into the lower Susquehanna Valley.

A number of Ganowese were definitely in the area of Conestoga by at least October, 1705, when James Logan visited there. In his report to the Provincial Council, he said that after a successful meeting with the Indians at Conestoga, "he . . . made a Journey among the Ganawese, settled some miles above Conestogoe at a Place called Connejaghera, *above the fort*, and had conferences with them" (Colonial Records 1838: II, 255). Logan gives no indication of having crossed the Susquehanna to reach Connejaghera, hardly a task to go unmentioned. This is almost certainly the same place which Old Sack, in the letter written for him in 1743, referred to as "Conejoholo, on East side Sasquehanna."

Hanna (1911: 151) equates, and probably rightly so, the fort mentioned by Logan with the "Fort Demolished" of the Chambers Survey of 1688 (Figure 8). This "Fort Demolished" has elsewhere (see under Strickler site excavations) been fairly well established as the remains of the palisades at the Strickler site. Connejaghera, being above this fort, would be in the vicinity of Washington Boro, as suggested by Hanna (1911: 151), or at Columbia, as implied by Landis (1933: 120-21). Both authors suggest that

Connejaghera and Dekanoagah, mentioned by Evans in 1707, are the same place.

According to Lt. Governor Evans (Colonial Records II: 255), Dekanoagah was on the Susquehanna about nine miles from Pequehan. If, as we have suggested, Pequehan was near the mouth of the Pequea, nine miles in a straight line would take one to Washington Boro. The distance to Columbia would be about 12 miles.

Some historians, including most notably George Donehoo (1928: 33-34) and David Landis (1933), have interpreted several 1730 references to this area, referred to by the Indians as Conejoholo, to mean that it was on the west side of the Susquehanna River, or as Landis (1933: 120) postulates, on both sides, and that Conoy Indians lived there.

As a footnote to the history of this area on the west side of the river, we have included the following remarks concerning Conejoholo, Connejaghera, and a creek in York County called Canadochly. Wallace (1964: 107) suggests that the latter name is taken by some other historians to be a survival of the word *Conejoholo*.

Recently, while tracing land deeds for the area about the two Leibhart sites in York County, which includes the lower reaches of Canadochly Creek, the writer found the following Maryland patent to

> Stephen Onion of Cecil County [Maryland] . . . bearing date 2d of Dec 1729 . . . a parcel of land called Conhodah . . . beginning at the West end of a West line . . . of land laid out for Thomas Bond . . . and is on the west side of Susquehannah River and *opposite the river to a tract of land called by the Indians Conejohah* and also at the West end of a west line of one hundred perches length of a tract of land laid out for Thomas Cresap of Cecil County called Pleasant Garden. (Hall of Records Commission, Annapolis, Maryland, Vol. PL#8 folio 93-94; see also York County, Pa., Deed Book G114, 1776; see also Kent et al. 1981: G)

This patent description clearly places Conejohah (Conejoholo) on the east side of the Susquehanna and clearly distinguishes that place from Onion's warrant name for his tract, "Conhodah." A connected draft of all the Patent Lands which adjoined Onion's tract enables their placement on the modern topographic map. The point of beginning "opposite the River to . . . Conejohah" is directly across the river from Washington Boro, and therefore confirms the location of Conejoholo at that place in Lancaster County, Pennsylvania. This connected draft also confirms the location of Thomas Cresap's tract as including the Byrd Leibhart site. Onion's Conhodah encompassed the Oscar Leibhart site. The map plotting of the connected drafts also shows modern Canadochly Creek flowing through the southwest portion of Onion's tract. The relationship of Onion's tract name—Conhodah—and modern Canadochly Creek are most apparent, but the word *Conhodah* hardly appears to be a derivative of *Conejoholo.* However, *Canhodah* is strikingly similar to the Iroquois word for village or town—*Canada, kaná:takow,* etc. (see Mithun n.d.: 6). It would appear then that this area, or perhaps Canadochly Creek, was originally given the Iroquois name for town, and that Stephen Onion used this to designate his patented land. We know of course that there were two Indian towns here during the last quarter of the seventeenth century—Oscar and Bryd Leibhart's.

In all probability the Indians living in this area around 1730 recognized one or both of the Leibhart sites as old Indian towns, and in fact probably knew that they were old Susquehannock town sites. The Penn-Calvert debates over the border line between their respective provinces also have significance in this regard, since it was agreed that the line should be drawn at the old Susquehannock fort. Penn argued that the fort was at the mouth of the Octoraro Creek, but the Calverts wanted to use the Indian town mentioned on Herrman's map (1670) at the fortieth parallel.

During the 1730's the Calverts were issuing patents in this area and to the north based upon the location of Herrman's fort. Consequently, it was most prudent of Mr. Onion, a Marylander, to call his patented tract Indian Town ("Conhodah"). We are tempted to equate this word with the name on Herrman's map—"Canoage"—which we have previously suggested may also mean *town.* However, this line of reasoning, even if correct, does not necessarily mean that Canoage was the Oscar Leibhart site, which was within Onion's patent. Both Leibhart sites in the early eighteenth century would have been equally conspicuous fort ruins, so that either one or both could have been called Conhodah. It has previously been noted that the present writer favors the Byrd Leibhart site, i.e., that on Cresap's tract, as the last or latest Conhodah of the Susquehannocks.

Having resolved, we hope, the issue of where the Conejoholo of the Old Sack history and the Connejaghera of Logan's 1705 journey were located, we can continue our history of the Conoy Indians. Our conclusion is that they came from Conoy Island to Conejoholo, somewhere at Washington Boro, about 1701, and that their next place of residence was not on the west side of the river, but rather at the place we now call Conoy Town, on Conoy Creek below present-day Bainbridge in Lancaster County.

According to Landis (1933: 122), the earliest reference to Conoy Town is a statement in the *Colonial Records* (III: 79) to the effect that, on May 20, 1719, a marauding party of Five Nations Indians stopped at the "Connoy Town, under the Govmt. of Pensilvania." In July, 1722, a council was held at the "Conay Town" in the "Township of Donnegall, bounded by the River Sasquahanna," where there were "present the Chiefs of the Conestogoes, Sawanies & Conays, together with seven Chief men of the Nanticock Indians, who are upon their Journey going to the five Nations" (Colonial Records III: 198).

Based upon these records and in the absence of any earlier mention of Conoy Town, most historians have suggested that it was occupied about 1718 (Landis 1933: 123; Hanna 1911: 151; and Wallace 1964: 108). The reference to the council held at Conoy Town in 1722 also serves to establish its location. Archeologically, the location of Conoy Town has been known for at least a hundred years. S. S. Haldeman, who was born in 1812 at Locust Grove, located at the center of the site, collected numerous trade goods there. Later collectors referred to the village site along Conoy Creek (36La57) as the "bead patch." This village and one of its attending cemeteries (36La40) were the scene of the Museum's excavations in 1970, which are reported in a later chapter.

Historians have used the date of Old Sack's letter (1743; Colonial Records IV: 657), in which he indicates to the Governor of Pennsylvania that his people are going to have to move, as the terminal date for Conoy Town.

There is surprisingly little mention of Conoy Town in the archives pertaining to the 1720's and 1730's. The Conoy are mentioned along with other Indians of the area insofar as they were all an occasional matter of concern to the Provincial government. Meetings between government officials and the Indians in the lower Susquehanna Valley almost always took place at Conestoga Town, the locus of Iroquoian influence in the area.

The Conoy, by themselves, seem to have caused very little disturbance and to have taken no part in any activities which warranted mention in the records of the Assembly. Nor does it appear that they were a matter of much concern to the numerous local settlers who, by 1740, completely surrounded them. The settlers of the area included numerous Indian traders (Hanna 1911: 161-81). Based on archeological evidence, the Conoy must have had considerable contact and exchange with the traders, but there is little mention of this in any preserved accounts.

By 1743, the Conoy obviously felt the pressure of the white society crowding in around them, as indicated in Old Sack's letter to Governor Thomas. Accordingly, and again at the suggestion of the Iroquois, they decided to move further up the river. Old Sack indicated that they might settle either at the mouth of the Conodoguinet or of the "Chiniotta" (Juniata), or at Shamokin.

The town of Conodoguinet, at the mouth of the creek of the same name (opposite Harrisburg), was occupied by unknown Indian groups by at least 1737 (Kent et al. 1981; Donehoo 1928). Whether the Conoy also lived there is not recorded. Nor does there seem to be any historical evidence that the Conoy moved to Shamokin. However, their settlement at the region around the mouth of the Juniata River ("Chiniotta") is recorded in a 1760 Patent Survey of Haldeman Island, which clearly notes an "Old Conoy Town" Division of Land Records, Survey Book D-113-39, also B-23-112). Further confirmation of this appears in the account of the July 1, 1749, council at Philadelphia, which states that the Conoy had left Conoy Town to "live among other Nations at Juniata" (Colonial Records 1851 V: 390).

During the 1740's and before, there may have been a number of Indian towns in this vicinity. The Taylor map of 1727 (see Hanna 1911: opposite 192) locates three separate Indian towns in the general area of "cheniaty" (Juniata).

Weslager (1948: 57-59) cites a number of accounts from this period which demonstrate that the Nanticoke Indians were one of the other nations living at the mouth of the Juniata. Prior to this time we have seen a number of mentions of the Nanticoke and Conoy together. Weslager (1948: 31-36) has discussed the occasional political ties of these two tribes even during the seventeenth century. Later, in the eighteenth century, Conoy and Nanticoke folk who had moved into New York State essentially merged into one nation. It may well be that the merger had its beginnings in the co-settlement of the two tribes at Juniata.

The missionary David Brainerd (Styles 1821: 235-38) visited the Indians at "Juneauta island" in 1745 and recorded a number of ethnographic observations about them:

> In the evening they met together, near an hundred of them, and danced around a large fire, having prepared ten fat deer for the sacrifice. . . .
>
> The Indians of this island can, many of them, understand the English language considerably well, having formerly lived in some part of Maryland, among or near the white people; but are very drunken, vicious and profane, although not so savage as those who have less acquaintance with the English. Their customs, in various respects, differ from those of the other Indians up this river. They do not bury their dead in a common form, but let their flesh consume above the ground, in close cribs made for that purpose. At the end of a year, or sometimes a longer space of time they take the bones when the flesh is all consumed, and wash and scrape them, and afterwards bury them with some ceremony. Their method of charming or conjuring over the sick seems somewhat different from that of the other Indians, though in substance the same. . . .
>
> It seems chiefly to consist in their "striking their hands over the diseased," repeatedly stroaking them, "and calling upon their god;" except the spurting of water like a mist, and some other frantic ceremonies common to the other conjurations which I have already mentioned.

> When I was in this region in May last, I had an opportunity of learning many of the notions and customs of the Indians, as well as observing many of their practices. I then traveled more than one hundred and thirty miles upon the river, above the English settlements; and in that journey met with individuals of seven or eight distinct tribes, speaking as many different languages. But of all the sights I ever saw among them, or indeed anywhere else, none appeared so frightful, or so near akin to what is usually imagined of *infernal powers*, none ever excited such images of terror in my mind as the appearance of one who was a devout and zealous reformer, or rather restorer of what he supposed was the ancient religion of the Indians. He made his appearance in his *pontifical garb*, which was a coat of *bearskins*, dressed with the hair on, and hanging down to his toes; a pair of bear-skin stockings, with a great *wooden* face painted, the one-half black, the other half tawny, about the color of an Indian's skin, with an extravagant mouth, cut very much awry; the face fastened to a bear-skin cap, which was drawn over his head. He advanced towards me with the instrument in his hand which he used for music in his idolatrous worship; which was a dry tortoise-shell with some corn in it, and the neck of it drawn on to a piece of wood, which made a very convenient handle. . . .
>
> * * * *
>
> He had a house consecrated to religious uses; with diverse images cut out upon the several parts of it: I went in, and found the ground beat almost as hard as a rock with their frequent dancing.

This zealous reformer, as Brainerd called him, was a revivalist who was attempting to bring back the old religion to those of his group who had fallen from it. Brainerd does not identify these people other than to say that they formerly lived in Maryland. We can assume that they were either Conoy or Nanticoke, or both. Much of the dance and the accoutrements of the dancer, described by Brainerd, have curious Iroquoian similarities, e.g., the wooden face masks and the turtle rattle, etc.

By 1750, at the latest, the town(s) at the mouth of the Juniata was completely abandoned. The Conoy now lived with various other Indians along the Susquehanna, but primarily with the Nanticoke. One of these places was the Town of Nanticoke, in the Wyoming Valley at present-day Nanticoke, which was occupied from 1747 to 1753 (Weslager 1948: 61, fn. 7). Afterward, both groups lived in the refugee Indian town (or area of a collection of towns) called Otsiningo on the Chenango River in Broome County, New York (see Elliot 1977: 93-105 for a full discussion of the Indian settlements at Otsiningo).

Not all of the Conoy (or the Nanticoke) followed this linear progression of movements from one town to the next. Some, for example, moved from Maryland directly to Otsiningo; some never left Maryland. But this kind of movement, based upon the whims or actions of individuals or small groups, is difficult to trace and insignificant for the present history. Those who finally arrived at Otsiningo in 1753, or later, soon became "one Nation" with the Nanticoke (Wallace 1964: 108).

In 1779, faced with the impending threat of General Sullivan's army sent by Washington to burn and destroy the towns of the Iroquois, Otsiningo was abandoned. In a census taken at Fort Niagara of the refugee groups who fled there as a result of Sullivan's march, there are recorded 120 Nanticoke and 30 Conoy (Weslager 1948: 86).

On December 8, 1978, Philip Sheridan Proctor, also known as Turkey Tayac, a Piscataway Indian dreamer of the old ways and a friend to many, died at the Veterans Hospital in Washington. Almost a year later his remains were reburied at the edge of Ossuary 2 at the Accokeek Creek site, the ancient residence of his people in Piscataway National Park, southern Prince Georges County, Maryland (personal communications, Tyler Bastian).

SHAWNEE

Among the historic-period Indians living in Pennsylvania, the Algonquian-speaking Shawnee, although not the most poorly known, are certainly one of the most elusive groups. A number of Shawnee bands lived at various places in Pennsylvania during the seventeenth and eighteenth centuries. Their apparent proclivity for moving frequently and fragmenting into new bands makes them difficult to follow historically, and a real challenge to trace archeologically.

Although we are now inclined to dismiss them as cartographic errors, there are, curiously, at least four early- to mid-seventeenth-century sources which locate the Sauwanoo (various spellings) in what would appear to be southeastern Pennsylvania (Hanna 1911: 119). The word *shawŭn* (see Hodge 1910: Pt. 2, 530) means *southern* in certain Algonquian languages, and may therefore account for the appearance of similar words on certain early maps of this area. Early French sources place them in various locations throughout the Mississippi and Ohio drainages. Still other sources mention them in the southeastern United States (Callendar 1978: 623-35).

Archeological indications of the prehistoric backgrounds for Shawnee are not at all certain. They have frequently been identified with the Fort Ancient cultures of the Ohio Valley (Callender 1978: 630; Griffin 1943; Witthoft and Hunter 1955). Our first positive record of Shawnee moving toward eastern Pennsylvania is found in a late seventeenth-century account in the Archives of the State of Maryland. In August, 1692 (Hanna 1911: 126; Maryland Archives III: 341-50), a meeting of the Maryland Council was held at St. Marys to hear various reports about a group of strange Indians and a Frenchman who had come into the colony. The Maryland authorities were concerned that these Indians might be Seneca and that the Frenchman might be a spy. Accordingly, they took the Frenchman into custody. During their questioning of the supposed spy, it was discovered that he had left Canada about 1684. He had been living with the strange Indians at a fort called St. Louis, and when the Indians left there in 1690 he followed them.

The Frenchman was subsequently released, but questioned again on several occasions. In February, 1693 (Hanna 1911: 127), it was reported to the Maryland Governor that these Indians were living on Bohemia Manor, the land of Colonel Casparus Herman, son of the cartographer and statesman, Augustine Herrman, on the south bank of the lower Elk River in Cecil County, Maryland. In a deposition given to the Maryland Council on April 11, 1693 (Hanna 1911: 128), the name of the Frenchman is given as "Martin Shortive." Some Susquehannock Indians questioned at the same time stated that they knew these Indians as the "Stabbernowles."

Hanna (1911: 130-31) indicates that the name for these Indians appears in the Maryland records from 1696 to 1700 as *Chanhannan*, *Shevanoe*, *Shavanole*, *Shevanor* and *Shavanolls*, all of which are synonyms (or varying orthographies) for *Shawnee*.

In June, 1697, Captain John Hans Tillman (see under *Conestoga*) gave a report to the Joint Session of the Maryland Council and Assembly regarding the Susquehannocks and other Indians at the head of the Chesapeake Bay. The statements, as recorded on June 1, 1697, are as follows:

> Came vp accordingly M[r] Speaker attended with the whole house Cap[t] John Hance Tillman being called to the Conference came accordingly
>
> He is required to give an account what he has done in pursuance of the late order of Council given him in charge, who sayes that according to the said Order he went to the Susquehannah & other Indians at the head of the bay That the Delaware King, and Chanhannan king would have come along with him but that their greate men were gone abroad a hunting, and because he vnderstood the rest were willing to come downe about a month hence he did not bring them with him
>
> Reports that at Carristauga, the Susquehanna & Seneca Indians have about forty lusty young men besides woemen & children That the Shevanor Indians being about thirty men besides woemen & children live within foure miles of Caristauga lower downe & submit themselves & pay tribute to the Susquehannahs & Senecars
>
> That the Delaware Indians live at Minguannan about nine mile from the head of Elke river & fifteen mile from Christeen & Thirty mile from Susquahanah river & are about Three hundred red men & are tributary to the Senecars and Susquehannahs fifty

> of them living at Minguhanan & the rest vpon Brandy wine and vpland Creekes.
>
> That the Susquehanahs Delawares, Shevanoes, doe take themselves to be & are inclinable to be vnder this province because of their hunting within the same betwixt Susquehanah & Potomoke. (Maryland Archives XIX: 519-20)

A statement identical to the third paragraph quoted above appears on page 565 of the same volume of the *Archives*.

The following year (on July 1, 1698) Tillman was again questioned by the Maryland Council:

> Cap[t] Iohn Hans Tilman an Indian Trader att the head of the Bay being asked Concerned the Indians that live there what Nations they are, he says they are Chauhannauks Susquehannahs & Delaware that the Chauhannauks are about forty men & live at a Town fifty miles of his house the Susquehannahs are about Fifty men live two miles further up at Caristaugua & Came from the Seneques
>
> That the Delawares live at white Clay Creek are about forty men
>
> Captain Hans being Asked whether the Susquehannahs live in this Province says they live about thirty Miles above Octerara Creek. (Maryland Archives XXIII: 444)

Tillman here provided some additional information regarding the location of *Caristaugua* (Conestoga) and thereby the location of *Chauhannauk* (Shevanoe, etc., or Shawnee). Thirty miles from the mouth of the Octerara Creek (Octoraro), would take one to present-day Washington Boro. However, 30 miles *via* the river and/or Indian trails would probably be very close to the actual distance to Conestoga. It should be noted here that Tillman's population figures for both the *Susquehannahs* and the *Chauhannauck* are ten men more than stated in his report of the previous year. He also states that Caristauga (a misprinting of Conestoga) is two miles farther up from the Chauhannauk. In his depositions taken in 1697 (Maryland Archives XIX: 519-20, 565), he said that the Shevanor lived within "*foure*" miles of Caristauga "lower downe." From the evidence presented here and elsewhere in the historic accounts, there should be no doubt that the Shevanor, Chauhannauk and Shawnee are the same people.

The precise date of their movement to the town below Conestoga cannot be firmly established. The Pennsylvania records are of no help in this regard, for not even the town of Conestoga is mentioned until 1696. In terms of the Maryland records, however, the date can be fixed somewhere between 1693 and 1697. We have arbitrarily set 1695 as the date for the founding of what will later be identified as their town of Pequehan.

A band of Shawnee, apparently some of those who were in Maryland, appear during the 1690's at various places along the middle and upper Delaware, particularly in the vicinity of present-day Shawnee Island and above the Water Gap at a place which they called Pechoquealin (Hanna 1911: 137-45). This was the country of the Minisink Delawares. Many of the Shawnee remained in this area until about 1728; their settlement among these Delawares marks the beginning of a long period of close interaction between these two peoples.

Local traditions (see Rupp 1844: 42) also refer to several Shawnee towns in Chester County. One of them was supposedly located along the Octoraro in the vicinity of Steelville, West Fallowfield Township. This may coincide with the place mentioned in the account (cited below) of Governor Evans' 1707 trip to Conestoga. On the second morning after leaving New Castle they stopped at "Otteraroe" (Colonial Records 1838 II: 402).

In William Penn's 1701 treaty with the Indians of the lower Susquehanna appears the first major reference in the Pennsylvania records to the Shawnee living near Conestoga (Proud 1797: 428-32). Wopaththa (alias Opessah), king of the lower Susquehanna Shawanese, represented his people at the signing of the treaty in Philadelphia.

Thereafter, the Shawnee of this area are frequently mentioned but primarily with reference to the Conestogas. The first recorded visit to Opessah's Town was made by Lt. Gov. John Evans of Pennsylvania in June of 1707:

> The Govr., with Msrs. John ffrench, Wm. Tonge, Mitchel Bezaillion, ________ Grey, & four servants, sett out from Newcastle the 27th of June, and ye next morning arrived at Otteraroe, where the Govr. was presented with some skins by the Indians, and the same night we arrived at Pequehan, being received at Martines [Martin Shartive of the Maryland accounts, or Chartier as he is known in Pennsylvania records] by O Pessah and some Indian Chiefs, who conducted us to the Town, at our Entrance into which place we were saluted by the Indians with a Volley of small arms. On Munday we went to Dekanoagah, upon the Sasquehannagh, being about nine miles Distance from Pequehan. Sometime after our Coming here a meeting was held of the Shawanois, Senoqois and Canoise Indians, and the Nantikoke Indians from the 7 following Towns, vizt., Matcheattochousie, Matchcouchtin, Witichquaom, Natahquois, Teahquois, Byengeahtein, & Pohecommoati. . . . (Colonial Records 1838: II, 402)

Rupp (1844: 46) in quoting from this account added, after the words "we arrived at Pequehan," the words "*at the mouth of Pequae Creek.*" According to Landis (1919: 73), Rupp was the first historian to indicate this as the location of Pequehan. None of the colonial records gives this or any other clear-cut location for Pequehan. Landis took exception to the Rupp location and presented (Landis 1919) evidence which he felt placed Pequehan on the Dr. Hiestand farm along Conestoga Creek in Manor Township,

Lancaster County. This site is presently known as the Roberts site (36La1). Cadzow (1936: 39-43) excavated several pits at the Robert site in 1931. The Museum conducted excavations here in 1971, during which time seven Susquehannock graves were excavated. The other major collections known from the site include those of John Stone, Columbia, Pennsylvania, which is not catalogued but which includes some Susquehannock material; and the D. H. Landis collection at the Hershey Museum, most of which is also Susquehannock.

Based upon the materials recovered by the Museum in 1971, the major occupation of the site is Susquehannock, and should date to somewhere between 1630 and 1645. Other minor components of the site include Archaic, Early Woodland and Shenks Ferry.

The Landis collection at Hershey includes one string of 90 wire-wound, early eighteenth-century beads (catalogue no. L-829/1) from the Heistand farm. Unfortunately Landis (1919: 74) lists two Heistand farms; one is the present Roberts site, and the other includes a tract of land on the Conestoga site, which of course does produce beads of this type.

Landis had two primary lines of evidence for placing Pequehan at the Roberts site. First, it produced "Indian trade articles" which, prior to 1919, he had not found near the mouth of Pequea Creek. His primary evidence was based upon the statements (quoted above; Maryland Archives XIX: 519) of John Hans Tillman, in which he said that the Shawnee lived within four miles of Conestoga, lower down. Landis (1919: 72) felt that at the time of Tillman's statement (1697), Conestoga was at the H. G. Witmer farm (the present Strickler site, 36La3). Four miles "lower down" from the Strickler site would take one to about the Roberts site. However, as we have already shown, there are no Conestoga-period trade goods at the Strickler site.

Some years later, and after having done more field work and archival research, Landis (1933: 129) did admit to a Shawnee settlement near the mouth of the Pequea:

> The Shawnee first settled on the Colonel French tract, in what is now southeastern [?] Conestoga Township, Lancaster County. This Indian site is on the present Frank Warfel farm, north of Colemanville. Martin Chartier and his band of Shawanese were located here about 1697, though for a short time, as is proven by the very limited number of Indian trader articles found there. From there they moved to Pequehan, north of the Conestoga Creek, north of Safe Harbor, on the present properties of Earl Hoover, Walter E. Herr, Reuben Longsbury [*sic*], and Charles Roberts.

Landis still felt that Pequehan was at the Roberts site, and as additional evidence he cites a letter from Secretary James Logan to Surveyor General

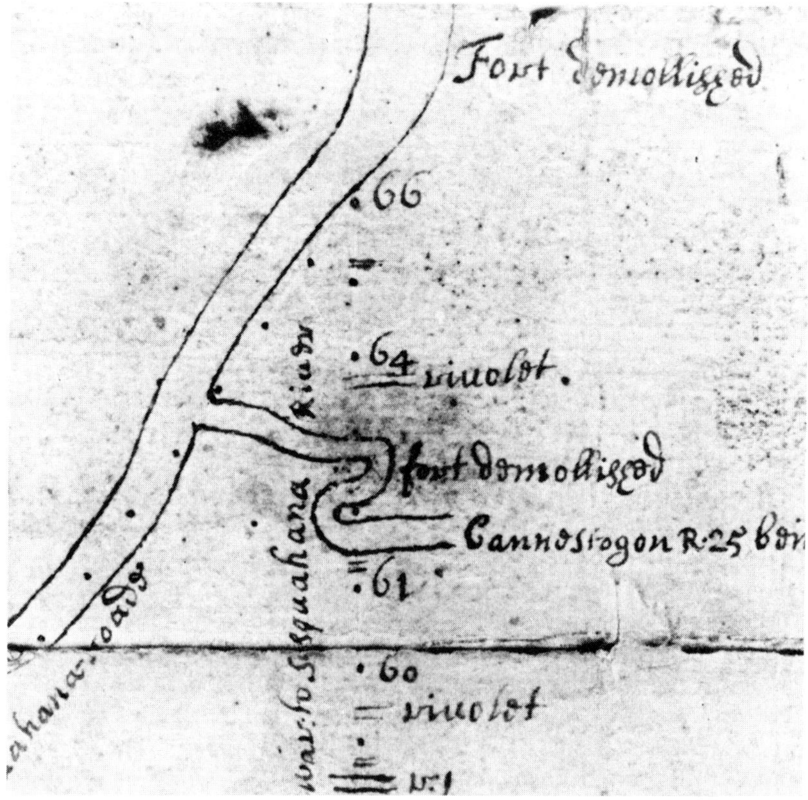

Figure 8. Western end of the Chambers survey of 1688 showing two "fort demolished" locations: the Roberts site on the "Cannostogon," and the Strickler site on the "Sasquahana" above the end of the line.

Isaac Taylor, dated December 18, 1714, in which application was made for a grant of land to Robert Hodgson and James Hendricks, which included the "Old Indian Fields" (Landis 1933: 128). This grant included the Reuben Longsberry property (and the Roberts site), and of course provided Landis with an approximate terminal date for his Pequehan, *viz.*, sometime prior to 1714. We submit that this "Old Indian Field" might have been the clearing, probably now well grown over, where the Roberts Susquehannock site of ca. 1630-1645 had stood. A rough draft of the Chambers map of 1688 (see Figure 8) shows a "Fort Demolished" at this location.

The Colonel French tract, granted in 1717, which included the "Sawannah Old ffields on Pequea Creek" (Pennsylvania Archives, 2d series

XIX: 625), had previously misled Landis and some other historians because, in the same reference (page 625), there is mention of an illegal survey by a Marylander "involving a considerable tract of Land near the *head* of Pequea Creek in this Province, including within the same the Old Sawannah town." The land granted to Colonel French, near the mouth of Pequea Creek, was assigned largely in the interest of "preventing the incroachm'ts of Maryland on the lands of this Province."

The description of this warrant, in Survey Book D-80, page 263, at the Division of Land Records in Harrisburg, mentions that the 500-acre tract includes the "Indian fields of Old Great Suwanah Town." The survey map does not mention the Indian town, but it is accurate enough to show that it includes the present Warfel farm discussed by Landis (1933: 129).

All of this is extremely suggestive of the location of Pequehan. However, an examination of the Landis collection and catalogue turned up no artifacts which would indicate a late seventeenth-century site in that area. Likewise, an interview with the present owner of the Warfel farm, and a surface survey of the property in 1975, failed to produce any evidence. These negative results do not mean that the site was not in that area; more intensive testing and survey work would certainly be in order.

In view of the scanty evidence presented here, it might be reasonable to suppose that the Shawnee town of Pequehan visited by Lt. Gov. John Evans in 1707, and the place referred to by Tillman, was near the mouth of Pequea Creek, perhaps a half mile upstream from the mouth, or possibly on Grubb Creek, which flows through the Warfel property. The abandonment of this town, although not recorded in history, was certainly before its designation as "Sawannah Old ffields" in 1717.

According to Magee (1925: 97), Martin Chartier settled at present Washington Boro about 1710-1711. He died there in 1718 (see the inventory of his estate reproduced above under Conestoga). A warrant was issued in 1717 (Pennsylvania Archives, 2d series XIX: 625) to "lay out to Peter Chartier 300 acres of land where his father is settled on the Susquehanna River." The location of this land and the approximate position of Chartier's cabin are shown on the 1717 survey of Isaac Taylor (Pennsylvania Archives, 3d series IV: Map 11).

It seems reasonable to suppose that some of the Shawnee at Pequehan may have moved with Chartier to Washington Boro, and that they continued to live there with his son Peter. Hanna (1911: 153) notes that Opessa was no longer king of his people, and that he had left them about 1711. Sometime thereafter, he took up residence in Maryland at a place known as late as 1725 as Opessa's Town, presently Old Town, on the Potomac. Opessa's leaving suggests that the community of Pequehan was breaking up (again) at about this time. Its occupants may have moved to several new locations. The archeological and historical records offer only minor confirmation of this.

Surface surveys of the area of Chartier's cabin at Washington Boro (along Shuman's Run) in 1975 produced no clear artifactual evidence of its location, nor of any contemporary Indian town. Occasional glass trade beads and other objects of the proper time period have been found at scattered locations in the Washington Boro area, but we cannot be certain just what they mean. In no one spot are they abundant enough to indicate a town of this period. It is unlikely, in this most hunted of all archeological areas, that such a concentration has been overlooked. But this area never ceases to produce astounding discoveries, and an eighteenth-century Indian town may yet be discovered there—we know that Chartier's trading post was there somewhere.

It should be remembered that Lt. Governor Evans, in 1707, mentioned going nine miles from Pequehan to Dekanoagah, a town apparently of mixed population, possibly including Shawnee. This place could have been at Washington Boro, if in fact Governor Evans started his trip near the mouth of Pequea Creek. Secretary James Logan went from Conestoga town to "Connejaghera" in 1705, which Hanna (1911: 151) and others felt was also at Washington Boro (see a more detailed discussion of Connejaghera under Conoy). One or the other (or both of these places) could have been what attracted Chartier to set up his trading post at Washington Boro.

The fragmentation of Shawnee bands among new places of residence, which we have already observed, could and did lead to numerous contemporary settlements. David Landis (1910: 152) suggested that Dekanoagh was at the site of present-day Columbia. This is a question which may never be resolved, but without doubt there was a Shawnee town at Columbia.

The Taylor survey (1726) of the Columbia area, by which its earliest land patents were established, shows a "Shawanah Town" apparently bordering present Shawnee Run (Taylor Papers 2736, Historical Society of Pennsylvania; see also Ellis and Evans 1883: 542).

Several early accounts of archeological discoveries in Columbia mention objects which may be from the first two decades of the eighteenth century:

> While in Columbia, our genial friend, Mr. F. X. Ziegler, socially entertained us for a short time, during which he exhibited the relics he obtained while the workmen were making excavations for the foundations of the new roundhouse, two or three years ago, and upon which, we are compelled to confess, we gazed with something of a covetous desire; for we have for years been longing to make Lancaster city the depository of historical, archaeological and scientific objects; and we are altogether unable to comprehend why a county with such a vast population,

> such vast wealth, and such vast resources, should not possess at its centre a vast museum of its historical, artificial, natural, and scientific productions; and posterity will often regret that such an institution was not founded in our day.
>
> The relics referred to probably once belonged to an Indian chief who had been Christianized, or to a Jesuit missionary, and consist of the remains of two guns, or perhaps muskets, and one pistol, in a very corroded condition, part of the iron being oxidized almost into its original elements. Of the gun-stock not a vestige remains, but the barrels with the breeches attached, two corroded locks, one of which contains in place a well defined flint, and some brass mountings, all in a tolerable state of preservation—sufficient to be easily recognized. Indeed, the brass mountings, the guard, shoulder-plate and escutcheon are in a remarkably good state of preservation. Also, a brass crucifix and two brass medals, the inscriptions upon which cannot be made out, a steel or iron paint box, about the size of a common tobacco-box; very much corroded. With these were also found a steel knife blade and an iron tomahawk. Also, a glass bottle, or flask, containing a small quantity of a dark colored liquid, and about twenty white, opaque, apparently glass beads, a good imitation of laminated agate or chalcedony. The box contained a small quantity of a bright red pigment, when it was first opened. Along with these were also found some human bones. Judging from the character of the brass mountings and other indications, Mr. Z is of opinion that the fire-arms are French, and very probably he is right in his conjectures. (Undocumented nineteenth-century newspaper clipping, see WPMM files)

Prowell (1907: 32), the noted York County historian, mentions a find of his own which may relate to the Shawnee there:

> The grave or burial ground of this village was located at the foot of what is now Locust street. When excavations were made for the Philadelphia and Reading railroad depot the writer was able to secure a fine specimen of shell and skull bead from one of the graves.

Another reference to the Shawnee town at Columbia is found in the survey of Governor Keith's Newberry tract in York County. According to the return of the survey by Taylor and Steele (dated 1722), the tract began at the mouth of White Oak Branch (now Kreutz Creek, Hellam Township) and "opposite [across the Susquehanna from] to the Sawanna Indian Town" (Prowell 1907 I: 21). The mouth of Kreutz Creek is directly west and across the river from the mouth of Shawnee Run.

Several locations within present-day Columbia are implied by these accounts. They could represent different occupations at different times. On the other hand, Kent et al. (1981: 4) suggest that the individual habitations of a single named town (or area) are often scattered over many acres, even miles, and in some cases on both sides of a river.

Prowell (1907 I: 23) also tells us that there are two drafts of the Newbery tract survey:

> The draft in the Department of Internal Affairs [Pennsylvania Division of Land Records, see Survey Book B23-231, 1722] identifies the habitation of John Grist and Captain Beaver, an Indian. The draft in the York Court [found by Prowell in the garret of the York County Court House] fixes Captain Beaver's place about where the Pennsylvania Railroad Station now stands at Wrightsville, and a number of wigwams, called Indian huts, are located on the same draft further up the river at the site of the present iron furnace and extending toward the high hill opposite Chickies Rock.

Archeological evidence for an early eighteenth-century Indian settlement at Wrightsville can also be found in some local records. The Attreus Wanner collection, part of which is at Indian Steps Museum, includes a few eighteenth-century beads and a broken catlinite pipe found at Wrightsville.

Hayden (1884: 228-29) cites the following article from the *Columbia Spy* in 1835:

> A brass medal has been left at this office, which, together with several articles and a human skull, were dug up a few days since in Wrightsville, York county, Penn'a. It bears on one side a head, with the inscription, "*George King of Great Britain*," and on the other an Indian with his bow and arrow in the act of shooting a deer. It appears to be worn as an ornament in the nose or ears. There were found also two others of similar description—a brass kettle—a string of white beads, one and a half yards in length—some red paint and twenty-five rings, one of which was dated 1716.

Whether or not these historical records pertain to a Shawnee town at Wrightsville is uncertain, but again it is clear that some Indians were there about the year 1720.

According to Brackbill (1938: 29; see also Pennsylvania Division of Land Records Survey Book A6-210), Peter Chartier established a trading cabin at the Shawnee town of his mother's people opposite Paxtang, near the mouth of the Yellow Breeches Creek at present New Cumberland. At that time the Yellow Breeches was known as Shawana Creek. Peter Chartier and his band of Shawnee may have lived at a number of places in the Cumberland Valley (as implied by Durant and Richard 1886: 41-42), but most of them moved to the upper Ohio Valley by about 1730.

The Shawnee living on the Ohio were too far away from English interests and subject to French enticements. Realizing the danger of this, the Pennsylvania Provincial authorities made an effort to have the Shawnee return to the Susquehanna Valley. In 1731 the commissioners sent Peter Chartier a letter informing him that a tract of land had been laid out

> between Conegogwainet [Conodoguinet] and Shaawna [Yellow Breeches] creeks five or six miles back from the River, in order to accommodate the Shaawna Indians or such others as may think fit to settle there (see Pennsylvania Archives, 3d series IV: no. 34; also Division of Land Records, Patent Books B-B-2-47, B-B-4-18).

A warrant survey dated 1737 (Pennsylvania Division of Land Records, Survey Book A1-238; see also Kent et al. 1981) shows an Indian town north of the mouth of the Conodoguinet Creek, opposite Harrisburg, in present-day West Fairview. Conrad Weiser, Pennsylvania's most noted ambassador to the Indians, mentions a town in 1743 called Canadaqueany at the mouth of this same creek (Colonial Records IV: 667). It is unclear, however, which Indians were living there—the Shawnee who had moved to the Ohio River never returned to the lands set aside for them by the Proprietors at Canadaqueany.

Thus far there is no good archeological evidence of any Shawnee towns in this area of the Cumberland Valley. A burial, perhaps relating to the Shawnee settlement, was removed some years ago during the excavation for a gasoline tank near the mouth of the Yellow Breeches Creek.

Hanna (1911: 151) felt that there were also Shawnee living at Peixtan (Harrisburg), largely because he thought that this was a Shawnee name derived from the word *piqua* or Pequeas town. This town, situated somewhere between the mouth of Paxtang Creek and Harrisburg, was undoubtedly comprised of a mixed population. At least one Shawnee chief, Paxinosa, is said to have come from there (Hanna 1911: 187). We do know that there were also Delawares there. The famous Delaware Chief Sassoonan (or Allumapees), a former resident of the Schuylkill Valley, was living at "Peshtang" in 1709, as recorded in the minutes of an Indian conference held that year in Philadelphia (Colonial Records II: 489). Sassoonan was still residing at Paxtang in 1718, when he and six other Indians acknowledged that they had formerly released to William Penn all of the land below the South Mountain from the Susquehanna to the Delaware. Shortly after 1718 Sassoonan moved up to Shamokin.

The earliest reference to an Indian village at Paxtang is that fascinating narrative of Governor Evans' trip to that place in 1707, where he went to arrest the French trader, Nicole Godin (Colonial Records II: 402).

Paxtang was an important trading center well into the 1730's, and most of the major Indian traders of the first four decades of the century are mentioned in connection with this place. Most notable of these was John Harris. Documents in the Division of Land Records record a survey at *Pexton* for Joseph Turner in 1733; later that year (1734, new style) it was surveyed to John Harris (Survey Book A6-210; Daniel et al. 1948). Harris died and was buried at Paxtang in 1748. His grave is along the Susquehanna

River just opposite the house built by his son, which is now the headquarters of the Dauphin County Historical Society. Presumably this site was within the old Indian town of Peixtan; unfortunately there are no archeological finds which might serve to confirm its precise location. We note again that the actual Indian habitations here could have been widely scattered throughout a town-region called Peixtan.

Not all of the Shawnee had moved directly west from the Peixtan-Conataqueany region in the years just before 1730. Hanna (1911: 161) suggests that between about 1735 and 1745 there were Shawnee towns on Haldemans Island in the Susquehanna River above the mouth of the Juniata and on the west shore of the river adjacent to that island. His evidence for this statement is not documented. Other contemporary accounts mention both Nanticoke and Conoy Indians here (see the chapter on Conoy), but provide no clear reference to Shawnees. Hanna (1911: facing 192) does illustrate a map which shows four Indian towns in this general vicinity, but again there is no indication of the ethnic composition of these towns. Nor is there very much archeological confirmation of these towns. A few appropriate artifacts, like the pipe tomahawk described by Witthoft et al. (1953: plate 3, Figure 13) from Duncans Island, give only a brief hint of the eighteenth-century Indian occupation of this general area.

The map illustrated by Hanna (1911: facing 192) is of considerable importance to our discussion as it locates nine Indian towns from Harrisburg up to about Chillisquaque Creek. The original survey map from which this one was copied was made by Isaac Taylor, according to Hanna (1911: facing 192) about 1727 or 1728. Egle (1883: 18), who previously published the map, erroneously assigned it a date of 1701.

The southernmost town on the map (above Swatara Creek) is almost certainly Peixtan. The four near the mouth of the Juniata have been mentioned above. On the east bank at the Forks of the Susquehanna is a place called Mikquar Town, later to become known as Shamokin Indian Town. Two towns are shown a short distance up the West Branch with the words "Chinasky or Shamokin" written between them (for an explanation of this situation, see Delaware Indians at Shamokin). Still farther up the West Branch is one more town, which was probably the Shawnee town of Chillisquaque.

Various historical accounts refer to a Shawnee town of Chillisquaque at the mouth of the stream in Northumberland County which now bears this name. No precise date for the earliest settlement there can be established from the records. A letter written by chiefs of the Shawnee at Allegheny to Governor Gordon of Pennsylvania in 1731 (see Hanna 1911: 189-90) would seem to fix the date of their removal from Shallyschohking (Chillisquaque) at three years prior to the date of the letter (i.e., 1728). Conrad Weiser, in

1737 (Hanna 1911: 191), speaks of having been ferried across the Chillisquaque Creek by an old Shawnee who was apparently still a resident at the old town.

Local collectors have found a few artifacts appropriate to the first quarter of the eighteenth century at the mouth of the Chillisquaque, and these probably represent the Shawnee occupation of that place.

Going further west along the West Branch of the Susquehanna, via the historic records, we find mention of at least two other Shawnee towns. Conaserage, at present Muncy in Lycoming County, apparently had a small Shawnee community in 1755 when it was visited by Conrad Weiser (see Donehoo 1928: 18; Kent et al. 1981). Accounts also indicate that the Shawnee settled for a short time on Great Island at Lock Haven (Donehoo 1928: 12; Kent et al. 1981).

On the North Branch of the Susquehanna River, Wallace (1965: 73) locates an old Shawnee town near the mouth of Fishing Creek in Columbia County. This Old Town is also indicated on Scull's map of 1759. No other mention of the nationality of this town has been found.

Wallace (1964: 122) implies that some Shawnee bands had moved into the Wyoming Valley (Shawnee Flats, below Plymouth) by 1701. The evidence for this is not at all clear. However, the *Colonial Records* (III: 309, 330, 506) show that the Shawnee Chief Kakowatchey, living at Pechoquealin on the upper Delaware, moved with his people to Shawnee Flats in 1728. Kakowatchey and many of his people left Shawnee Flats in 1743 or 1744 for Logstown on the Ohio River near present Ambridge, Pennsylvania (Hanna 1911: 187). As mentioned above, Paxinosa, a Shawnee who, according to Hanna (1911: 187), was a former resident of Peixtan, became the new chief of those who stayed along the Susquehanna (see Colonial Records VI: 35; VII: 52, 108; VIII: 126; Pennsylvania Archives II: 33).

The Shawnee at Shawnee Flats in the Wyoming Valley were visited by the Moravian missionary Count Zinzendorf in 1742 (see J. Martin Mack's recollections in Reichel 1870: 100-105). Count Zinzendorf's stay here, according to Mack's narrative, was most uncomfortable for he was not well received by the Shawnee. The account refers to Indians at the nearby Upper Town, presumably the Delaware Indian town of Wyoming, where there were also a few Mohican Indians.

John Martin Mack, also a Moravian, journeyed to the Shawnee Town in the Wyoming Valley in 1744, at which time he reported that there were but six or seven Indian *cabins* left standing, the rest having been pulled to pieces (Hanna 1911: 187). Apparently the Shawnee settlement there experienced something of a revitalization around 1748 under the leadership of Paxinosa (Hanna 1911: 187; Wallace 1964: 123); but finally, about

1756, Paxinosa and his people moved up to Otsiningo (near Binghamton, in Broome County, New York).

Once again we see a great confusion of movements by the Shawnee, in and out of their towns, to new places, to towns with multi-ethnic compositions, etc. Their town in the Wyoming Valley was their last major place of residence in eastern Pennsylvania, and few if any families lingered anywhere along the Susquehanna after 1758.

Their Old Town at Shawnee Flats is located on the survey map of the "Manor of Sunbury" (Pennsylvania Archives, 3d series IV: no. 67; see also Pennsylvania Division of Land Records Survey Book B-B-4-19). Archeological confirmation of this town is reported by Christopher Wren (1912: 198-204), who described three extended burials in stone-lined graves found during the 1905 excavation of a cellar hole on the south side of Bead Street in Plymouth, Pennsylvania. Associated with one of the burials were about two hundred faceted, blue glass beads, about one hundred brass finger rings, a possible kaolin pipe, and two "long-necked glass bottles." The name of this street, and indeed the name of this general area of Plymouth — Bead Hill — is derived from the numerous glass beads found there, and is clearly an artifact of the former Shawnee town at this place.

From here the history (and archeology) of the Shawnee shifts primarily to the Ohio Valley, where as readers of Daniel Boone's biographers or Simon Kenton's (Eckert 1967) or the continued works of Charles Hanna (1911) know, much of the story of the Shawnee had still to be played out. But this is obviously beyond the scope of the present work, and far from the Susquehanna.

DELAWARE

Delaware, the English name for the river and bay upon which the Lenni Lenape Indians once lived, has become a synonym for this group of people (see Wallace 1949: 7). Their own name for themselves, Lenni Lenape, translates as "a male of our kind," or more literally as the "real people" (see Brinton 1885: 35). Based largely upon the accounts of eighteenth-century Moravian missionaries, it would appear that the Lenni Lenape were divided into three named geographical groupings. The Unalactigo were the most poorly known, but are generally thought to have occupied southern New Jersey. More recently, Hunter (1978) has suggested that this term, Unalactigo, applied only to an eighteenth-century grouping of the Lenni Lenape. Unamis occupied the Delaware River and its tributaries from about the head of the bay to the Water Gap. On the upper Delaware, above the Water Gap, were the somewhat distantly related peoples called the Munsee or Minisink.

Heckewelder (1819) erroneously equated the three clan names of the Delawares, Turtle, Turkey and Wolf, with three geographical divisions. Numerous subsequent historians and anthropologists have disproved Heckewelder's assertions in this matter. Authorities on Delaware Indian ethnography and history are numerous; to name only a few, there are Becker (1976, 1980), Hanna (1911), Hunter (1978), Kinietz (1948), Kinsey et al. (1972), Kraft (1974), Newcomb (1956), Speck (1931 and numerous others), Wallace, A. (1949), and Weslager (1972, 1976). The list of contemporary chroniclers of Delaware life in the seventeenth and eighteenth centuries is equally impressive; there are, for example, DeLaet, Danckaerts, DeVries, Heckewelder, Campanius Holm, Lindeström, Van der Donck, Zeisberger, Zinzendorf and others (see Goddard 1978 for detailed references).

Without question the Delawares are Pennsylvania's (and New Jersey's) historically best-known aboriginal group. Regrettably they also have the distinction of being one of the State's most poorly known archeological cultures.

By the latter part of the eighteenth century, the Delawares left Pennsylvania, and no distinct community of them existed here again. Delaware Indians today live primarily in Oklahoma and at various places in Ontario. Their old culture is largely a thing of the past, or of the ethnographies. The language will probably cease with the few speakers of the present generation.

The Lenape are generally considered to stem from a more widely distributed Algonquian-speaking Late Woodland culture which flourished in the Middle Atlantic coastal plain from Manhattan Island to southern New Jersey. Its western boundaries were the headwaters of the west tributaries of the Delaware River. Unfortunately for Delaware Indian archeology, this region has become one of the most populous and heavily developed in the nation. The dearth of archeological data about these people is probably due both to their particular settlement pattern and to the fact that early and continued urbanization and industrialization of the lower Delaware Valley megalopolis have erased most of their archeological remains.

The Philadelphia area, if we can judge from Lindeström's 1654 map of New Sweden (Johnson 1925), was the major center of the Unami Delaware Indian population. We can surmise that the precontact-period Lenni Lenape culture of this area was typified by what Witthoft (n.d.d; see also Black 1954: 292-348) has called the Overpeck phase of Late Woodland culture in the lower Delaware Valley. The fate of its characteristic pottery, Overpeck Incised, and its other technological traits cannot be traced yet with certainty into the contact period. Contact with European cultures and the trade items resulting therefrom should date to as early as 1525. For whatever reasons, sites in this area dating from 1525 to about 1650 seem almost non-existent. Perhaps the one exception to this, and a minor one, is the Overpeck site, located along the Delaware River below Kintnersville, Pennsylvania. In addition to some "trade vessels" of more-or-less datable Susquehannock pottery (early Schultz Incised), this site has produced a very few early trade items, including brass beads, a brass earring, part of an iron axe, and some other less convincing metal objects (Forks of the Delaware, Chapter 14, 1980: 20-21, 45). Cross (1941) reports upon a few sites along the lower Delaware in New Jersey that have also produced European trade materials, but these all seem to be post-1650. Becker (1980) has also discussed this frustrating paucity of sites (and trade goods) from the period of first contact to the middle of the seventeenth century. Even after that date, and until the eighteenth-century exodus of the Delawares from their homeland, there are incredibly few identified sites and artifacts.

Curiously, in the upper Delaware Valley above the Water Gap, where urbanization and industrial development have occurred much more slowly, the shift from protohistoric Munsee to historic Munsee Delaware culture is also difficult to trace archeologically. This is not due to the lack of archeological investigations (cf. the long-term Tocks Island project, Kinsey et al. 1972). Again, the few exceptions to this almost total lack of historic-period Indian sites are after 1650 A.D. The portion of the Bell-Philhower site at Montague, New Jersey, presumably the Indian town of Minisink, which was excavated by Heye and Pepper (1915), produced materials which do not appear to date prior to about 1660 (see also Marchiando in Kinsey et al. 1972: 131-58). Similarly, the small assortment of trade items found by Kraft (in Kinsey et al. 1972: 50-54) at the Miller Field site along the Delaware River, about 12 miles south of the Bell-Philhower site in New Jersey, are also of the second half of the seventeenth century. (See also Kraft 1974: 46-50.)

Available evidence suggests that Delaware communities were typically rather small, breaking down in periods of decreased food availability into even smaller foraging groups. Sites which exemplify the temporary habitats of these smallest food-gathering social units are those like the two rock shelters discussed by Butler (1947: 246-55) along Darby Creek in Delaware County, Pennsylvania.

Their seasonal round probably involved agglomerations of clan- or lineage-related folk who lived on the major flats at the confluences of the Delaware River and its various tributaries during fishing seasons and at times essential to agriculture. During periods of lesser food abundance along the Delaware, smaller groups of nuclear or extended families would have hunted and collected from small camps in more favorable areas up to the headwaters of the various tributaries. Judging by the number of riverine hamlets discovered archeologically for the upper Delaware area, and those shown on Lindeström's map of the lower Delaware, it would appear that the Delawares were fairly populous in pre- to early-contact times. Kroeber (1939: 140) probably overestimates their total population of eight thousand. Goddard (1978: 214) gives some even higher estimates.

It is not our purpose here to describe in detail the material culture of the Delawares. However, in connection with the discussion of their settlement pattern, a few notes concerning their housing seem in order. A longhouse, perhaps 20 feet by 60 feet with rounded ends and one door on a long side, is implied by the archeology of the few Munsee sites which have been studied (Kraft 1974: 43-44). This general house form is largely confirmed by contemporary descriptions, most notably the 1679-1680 account by Jasper Danckaerts and Peter Sluyter (Murphy, 1867: 124-27; also in Smith 1950: 104-105), which describes a longhouse of closely related Algonquian-speaking peoples on Long Island, New York.

> We went from thence to her habitation, where we found the whole troop together, consisting of seven or eight families, and twenty or twenty-two persons, I should think. Their house was low and long, about sixty feet long and fourteen or fifteen feet wide. The bottom was earth, the sides and roof were made of reed and the bark of chestnut trees; the posts, or columns, were limbs of trees stuck in the ground, and all fastened together. The top, or ridge of the roof was open about half a foot wide, from one end to the other, in order to let the smoke escape, in place of a chimney. On the sides, or walls, of the house, the roof was so low that you could hardly stand under it. The entrances, or doors, which were at both ends, were so small and low that they had to stoop down and squeeze themselves to get through them. The doors were made of reed or flat bark. In the whole building there was no lime, stone, iron or lead. They build their fire in the middle of the floor, according to the number of families which live in it, so that from one end to the other each of them boils its own pot, and eats when it likes, not only the families by themselves, but each Indian alone, according as he is hungry, at all hours, morning, noon and night. By each fire are the cooking utensils, consisting of a pot, a bowl, or calabash, and a spoon also made of a calabash. These are all that relate to cooking. They lie upon mats with their feet towards the fire, on each side of it. They do not sit much upon anything raised up, but, for the most part, sit on the ground or squat on their ankles. . . . All who live in one house are generally of one stock or descent, as father and mother with their offspring.

During those periods when the Delawares scattered into back-country camp sites, their housing, when other than a rock shelter, may have taken the form of a circular or dome-shaped, bark-covered hut, generally referred to by the Algonquian word wigwam. This same form of housing may also have been employed in their larger, more permanent hamlets, for it was described in several contemporary accounts (see Newcomb 1956: 24-25). Nowhere do we find archeological evidence that their hamlets or towns along the river, or in the back country, were stockaded. A possible exception to this may be the historical account (see Ritchie 1949: 156) which implied that the Minisink town of 1663 was palisaded as protection against Iroquois raids. Goddard (1978: 219) also infers historical evidence for a few stockaded Delaware towns. By and large such inferences seem to be drawn from the "fanciful" depiction of a stockaded town thought to be at the location of Minisink on the Adrian Van der Donck map of 1656 (Van der Donck 1841). Extensive archeology at the location of Minisink (Bell-Philhower site, cf. Kinsey et al. 1972) has failed to produce any evidence of a stockade. Historically the Delawares who inhabited the Delaware River and its tributaries in the seventeenth century seem to have maintained a role of neutrality and general non-involvement, or even submissivenesss, in the warfare which was so rampant among other Indians of this period.

Their lesser entanglements in the internecine warfare of the seventeenth century may be a result of their fragmented settlement pattern and reduced political structure. This does not say that the Delawares were considered harmless by neighboring tribes or by the Europeans. However, it is difficult to mount successful military actions against peoples who frequently live in small, hard-to-find groups. Consequently, it would appear that they found it unnecessary to protect themselves behind palisade defenses.

These conditions also make their places of settlement more difficult to find archeologically, and that, coupled with the rapid destruction of the land surfaces upon which they once lived, has placed them in what is almost an archeological void.

Dutch explorers and traders were the first Europeans to settle in the Delaware Valley. Fort Nassau was established at Gloucester, New Jersey, in 1626, and the Dutch, in 1631, built another small fort in Lewes, Delaware. They found the Lenni Lenape scattered in small communities in many of the most favorable areas along the Delaware.

Unquestionably these Delaware Indians were passing through many of the stages of acculturation experienced by the Susquehannocks. In the technological sphere of their culture, the most dramatic changes would have been in shifts from bows to guns, stone to iron, and ceramics to brass kettles. These changes plus the physical presence of persons from another, more dominant and advanced culture ultimately brought on other massive and disruptive changes in the social and ideological aspects of the culture.

By and large the relationship of Europeans with the Delawares was fairly amicable, certainly so by comparison with Indian-white relations in many other areas.

On the heels of the Dutch settlements, the Swedes (1638) established Fort Christiana at present Wilmington. Peter Minuit bought Indian lands from there to present Trenton on both sides of the river. For a time, at least, the Indians continued to occupy the region, but they gradually moved away as they came to understand what it meant in European law to sell their land.

Although they had no great love for the Lenni Lenape, the Swedes seem to have gotten on better with them than did the Dutch. It might be noted here that someone, though not necessarily the Lenni Lenape, burned the Dutch settlement at Lewes within a year of its building.

After 1630 the history and the culture changes of the Delawares are directly tied to the economic and political history of the European occupation of the area. This is essentially the history of the international competition for control of Indian lands and the fur trade.

Largely because of their geographic position with respect to other Indians and to the sources of fur-bearing animals, the Delawares never played a very important role in the fur trade. They were not strong enough, nor well enough organized politically, to act as middlemen in the trade. Consequently they were forced to assume a role secondary to the Susquehannocks and other Iroquois. On the other hand, they were occupants of what was to become some of the most valuable real estate in the New World. Their history, then, is largely characterized by a lack of control of the fur trade and the growing efforts of the Europeans to remove them from the lower Delaware Valley.

Fortunately for the Delawares, removal from this area took place through numerous land purchases of varying degrees of legality, rather than through military annihilation as suffered by many Indian nations. Contemporary accounts (e.g., Robert Evelyn in 1634; see Brinton 1885: 41) and the 1654 map by Lindeström (Johnson 1925) indicate the locations of numerous Lenni Lenape settlements in the lower Delaware Valley. A few of these, like Shackamaxon, where as previously mentioned the Iroquois, Susquehannocks and Delawares held a conference, were still in use in 1677 or later. When William Penn arrived (1682) in the area (Philadelphia), the Delaware Indians had already begun to pull back from the river to places higher up the tributaries. It was not long before many of the Indians must have found it impossible to include the flats along the Delaware River in their seasonal round. Because of the European towns developing on the lower Delaware, the Indians were forced to withdraw into northern New Jersey, including the Raritan Valley, and north and westward along the west-side tributaries of the Delaware River. This must have represented a drastic departure from their customary settlement pattern and ecology, but one which marked the beginning of their new way of life.

Some Lenape of this period felt enough of the ill effects of acculturation or culture contact to move far away from the Europeans. Many, however, stayed on the fringe of the colonial settlements.

The governors of both New York and Maryland were still interested in making good their claims to southeastern Pennsylvania. Much of the territory was claimed by one or the other by reason of old charters or older conquests of the Dutch or Swedes. William Penn was quick to purchase, or repurchase, from the Indians, in a more honest manner, what would eventually comprise all of southeastern Pennsylvania. Establishment of clear title to these lands was necessary to thwart the efforts of the neighboring provincial governors to annex portions of Penn's colony.

Penn also reserved for exclusive Indian use certain tracts of land on the fringe—quickly engulfed usually—of his proprietary patents. The 500-acre Okehocking tract in Chester County, established in 1703, can be considered one of Pennsylvania's first Indian "reservations" (see Becker 1975: 24-61).

Okehocking and similar Indian tracts, as set aside by the Proprietaries, were the Indians' to use so long as they continued to occupy them. Delaware settlement patterns, as we have seen, involved seasonal movement and, consequently, the abandonment of some tracts during certain times of the year. It did not require very many of these seasonal abandonments for some white man to apply for and get title to the land.

The situation on the Brandywine Creek in Chester County, Pennsylvania, is perhaps the best-documented example of Delaware removal during this period of turmoil and culture change. In aboriginal times, the Brandywine drainage was probably a roughly defined territory of a band of Delaware people—perhaps a hundred or so. Depending upon the season and ecological factors, these people might settle anywhere within this drainage area. Obviously, the number of people living together at any one location was greatly influenced by food resources.

Similar groups occupied, and carried out the same lifeways on, most of the major tributaries of the Delaware River. We have previously cited references to the Okehocking Delaware on Ridley Creek (Becker 1975), and to the Delawares living upon the Schuylkill River. Another group of them is documented on White Clay Creek, Chester County, in the Warrant Survey (BB3-19) of 1699. An additional reference to this place, called Minquannan, appears in the previously quoted 1697 deposition by John Hans Tillman (Maryland Archives XIX: 519-20): "The Delaware Indians . . . are about three hundred red men . . . fifty of them living at Minquahanan and the rest upon Brandywine and Vpland Creeks." The following year (1698) Tillman reported "that the Delawares living at White Clay Creek (Minquannan) are about forty men" (Maryland Archives XXIII: 444).

History (Du Ponceau 1834: 79; Becker 1980: 22) records a named Lenni Lenape settlement called Hopokahocking (Hopohaching) at the mouth of the Brandywine Creek (present Wilmington). It represents one of many named localities used by the Brandywine Delawares during the course of their seasonal movements. By at least 1650, Swedish and other European settlements of this area were large enough to make Hopokahocking unsuited for use by the Delawares. Another named town, somewhat further up the Brandywine, was Queonemysing (on the Pennsylvania side of the Big Bend of the creek). A survey map in the Pennsylvania Division of Land Records (BB 65-155) shows that this tract, "including ye Indian town," was purchased by one George Harlan in 1701 (see also Weslager 1976: 143-44).

Archeological testing at Queonemysing (36De6) by the Pennsylvania Historical and Museum Commission in 1978 (see Becker 1978b) recovered a small quantity of colonial ceramics and glass, which may signify the actual location of this town in the Big Bend. The Indian occupation of this place ceased no later than its purchase in 1701 by Harlan; its beginnings can only be guessed at. Queonemysing may have been an ancient stopping place in the seasonal round of the protohistoric Brandywine Delawares. But, sometime after the abandonment of Hopokahocking as a major residence of the Brandywine Delawares, Queonemysing may have become a more permanent hamlet—perhaps the center for a new pattern of seasonal movements.

Their next major line of retreat would appear to be some 12 miles higher up the Brandywine near Northbrook in Newlin Township, Chester County. Graves excavated here over the past one hundred years (Weslager 1976: 126-36) have produced trade goods (e.g., kaolin pipes and wire-wound beads) typical of the first two decades of the eighteenth century. The land on which this site was located had been purchased from the Proprietors by 1724 (Weslager 1976: 69-70), and again the Delawares found it necessary to remove higher up the creek.

By this time many Delaware Indians from the Brandywine Valley and elsewhere had completely abandoned their native territories. Governor Evans (Colonial Records 1838 II: 404-405), during his trip to the Susquehanna River in 1707, found Indians, some of whom may have been Delawares, living at Peixtan (near present-day Harrisburg). Two years later, Sassoonan, a chief of the Schuylkill Delawares, was known to be living at Peixtan (Hanna 1911: 104).

Still, some of the Delawares persisted in staying *near* their old territories. Their latest settlement, high up the Brandywine, was at the Montgomery site (36Ch60) in Wallace Township, Chester County. Excavations of a small cemetery here (Weslager 1967: 112-15; and Becker 1978a) produced glass beads, kaolin pipes and other trade goods of the 1720 to 1740 period.

The village for this cemetery, probably a number of widely scattered and inconspicuous house sites, has not yet been located. Evidence from the graves, i.e., material items recovered, suggests that these folk were quite impoverished and highly dependent upon, in fact habituated to, the material culture of the colonial settlers.

During this period (ca. 1725), quite a number of the Delaware hamlets were scattered throughout the secluded headwaters of other tributaries to the Delaware River. The contents of several Delaware graves from a site of this period, located just west of Kutztown in Berks County, Pennsylvania, are in the Deisher collection at the William Penn Memorial Museum, Harrisburg (Cat. No. D.843-D.857, 36Bk450). These include wire-wound beads, four kaolin pipes (all marked *E.R.*), brass thimbles, a flintlock cock, and a few other odds and ends. Additional objects from this site are mentioned in Brunner (1897: 113-14).

Historical records and a few objects in the Farver collection at the William Penn Memorial Museum (Le198/1) indicate that a similar site existed along the Tulpehocken Creek near Myerstown, in Lebanon County. This is almost certainly the town of "Turpyhocken," mentioned in the narrative of Governor Evans' 1707 trip (Colonial Records II: 405) and the place called "Talpahockin" on the 1723 Warrant Survey of the area (Pennsylvania Division of Land Records/BB23-96).

Some Delaware Indians of this period had completely abandoned eastern Pennsylvania. According to Hanna (1911: 183), a number of them had already moved to the town of Kittanning on the Allegheny River by 1724, and to Aliquippa at McKees Rocks (near Pittsburgh) and Kuskuski near New Castle, Pennsylvania, by about 1731.

Many of the Delawares at this time had moved to the place called Shamokin on the Susquehanna. In 1732 Sassoonan, the Schuylkill chief, together with other chiefs then residing in Shamokin, conveyed to the Penns (the Proprietors) all of the land along the Schuylkill between Lechay Hill (South Mountain) and Kittochtinny Hills (Blue Mountain) from the branches of the Susquehanna. This opened the way for white settlement in the upper Schuylkill Valley (south of the Blue Mountain) and the Tulpehocken Valley.

This, coupled with the effects of the infamous Walking Purchase of 1737 (see Wallace 1949: 18-30), brought about the final exodus of the Delawares from southeastern Pennsylvania. Those few who remained in the area of the Forks of the Delaware in eastern Pennsylvania were told by the Iroquois (in 1742) to move either to Shamokin or up to the Wyoming Valley. Move they did, or at least most of them; some went to Shamokin, some went a little higher up the North Branch of the Susquehanna, and others, along with the Minisink Delawares, settled the town of Wyoming (see 1768

Survey of the Manor of Stoke, Pennsylvania, *Pennsylvania Archives,* 3d series IV, no. 66; also Kent et al. 1981: 7) at present-day Wilkes-Barre and opposite the Shawnee town at Plymouth (see also Donehoo 1928: 259-63, discussion of Wyoming; and Colonial Records IV: 579-80).

As indicated elsewhere in this volume, the Iroquois claimed ownership of the Susquehanna Valley; but in order to hold it against the whites they found it useful to invite other Indians to settle there, the only price being political homage to the Iroquois. Their treatment of the Delawares sometimes seems heavy-handed, as it is related by a few historians. Wallace (1949) gives a rather softer interpretation of the statements that the Iroquois had made women of the Delawares. As part of what were actually their light-handed efforts to control the various Indians in the Susquehanna Valley, the Iroquois sent an overlord (perhaps mediator is a better word) to live among the Susquehanna Indians. The first of these vice-regents was Shickellamy, a Cayuga who was sent to the Susquehanna (West Branch) about 1728 and who after 1737 lived with various other Indian nations at Shamokin (see Wallace 1964: 178). For a period of some 15 years, until its abandonment in 1756, Shamokin was the veritable Indian capital of Pennsylvania, albeit often a rather dismal place. Because of its historical importance, a brief digression concerning it seems in order here.

Based largely upon evidence suggested by the Isaac Taylor map of 1727, Hanna (1911: 193-96) concluded that Shamokin (perhaps synonymous with Chenasky or Otzinachse), when first settled by Indians, was somewhere along the West Branch of the Susquehanna between present-day Warrior Run and Chillisquaque Creek in Northumberland County. Later, but before 1737, Shamokin was located at present-day Sunbury. Conrad Weiser visited Shamokin in that year and he recorded in his Journal of March 4, 1737: "We reached Shamokinna but did not find a living soul at home who could assist us in crossing the Susquehanna River" (see Wallace 1945: 77-78). The following day Weiser did manage to cross the river (from Shamokin to present-day Northumberland). On the 8th of March he arrived at the place near present-day Milton on the West Branch of the Susquehanna where "Shikelimo" (Shickellamy) was then living. Shickellamy moved to Shamokin (at Sunbury) shortly thereafter. (See Hanna 1911: 196-97.) In 1745, the missionary David Brainerd visited "Shaumoking" (Shamokin) and recorded that it

> lies partly on the east side of the river [Sunbury] partly on the west [Northumberland] and partly on a large island in it [Packers Island], and contains upwards of fifty houses and near three hundred persons but of three different tribes of Indians, speaking three languages wholly *unintelligible* to each other. About one half of its inhabitants are Delawares, the others called Senekas and Tutelas [Tutelo]. . . . [Styles 1821: 128-29]

Sassoonan, also known as Olumpaies or Allumapees, who was chief of the Delawares at Shamokin, died there in 1747. On Tuesday, December 6, 1748, in the presence of his daughter and other family members and the Moravian missionary David Zeisberger, Schickellamy died in his house at Shamokin. His daughter, with the help of one Henry Fry, made a coffin for him in which were placed two blankets, a loaf of bread, a tobacco pipe, tobacco, flint and tinder, etc. (Wallace 1945: 274, 596).

Between 1858 and 1863, a Mr. M. Hendricks exhumed approximately 25 Indian burials from an area about one block north of the site of Fort Augusta in Sunbury. A general list of articles recovered is printed in Meginness (1889: 59). One of the interments, in a wooden coffin, contained numerous glass beads, brass rings, bracelets, an iron tobacco box containing some tobacco, a fishing line, needle, several coins, a George I medal (Figure 84), knife, musket barrel, iron tomahawk, white clay pipe, and a green glass bottle (see Wallace 1945: 596-97 and Carter 1931 III: 52).

A monument to Shickellamy, illustrated in Sipe (1929: facing 134), was erected over the site in 1915 by the Daughters of the American Revolution and the Pennsylvania Historical Commission.

Recent (1978-1979) excavations by the Pennsylvania Historical and Museum Commission and members of the Northumberland County Historical Society in an area immediately north of Fort Augusta produced a variety of objects, including beads, coins, iron tools, worked brass, pipes (including a calumet), and other objects which may relate to a specific part of the Indian town of Shamokin. Mixed with these objects are difficult-to-sort artifacts relating to the (1756-1794) military occupation of Fort Augusta. These excavations also produced what would appear to be the footer for a blacksmith's forge. Surrounding this stone feature were large quantities of wrought iron (worked and unworked), melted brass, and clinkers, which support the interpretation of this feature as a forge (Nichols 1980).

In 1747 the Moravian missionaries at Shamokin built a blacksmith's shop within a few paces of Shickellamy's house (Carter 1937: 52-72).

As Wallace (1945: 274) puts it, with the death of Shickellamy a lamp went out that left the Indians living in the dark at numerous places along the North and West branches of the Susquehanna and at various towns in the upper Ohio Valley (see Kent et al. 1981). After Shamokin, Wyoming at Wilkes-Barre was the most important of their towns on the Susquehanna. The history of Wyoming is well treated by Wallace (1949) in his treatise on Teedyuscung, the most notable resident of that place. The city of Wilkes-Barre has long since destroyed any archeological evidence of "Wyoming," as marked on the survey map of the Manor of Stoke (Division of Land Records Survey Book BB417). However, isolated finds of eighteenth-century trade items, such as that reported by Kent (1970), or the cemetery reported by Miner (1845: 26-27), may represent portions of the more widely dispersed settlements of Wyoming.

Discoveries of various more-or-less datable eighteenth-century objects have been made at many places along the West and North branches of the Susquehanna. Occasionally these can be associated with a known town site, but more often than not they seem to represent an isolated burial or house site of some unidentified eighteenth-century Indian.

Another Delaware site at which we can relate a certain amount of history and archeology is the place called Wapwallopen, opposite the new nuclear power plant in Luzerne County. Our friend David Brainerd also traveled here to spread his message to the Indians. In his Journal for October 5, 1744 (Styles 1821: 85-86) he says, "We arrived at Susquahannah river, at a place called Opeholhaupung; found there twelve Indian houses." Donehoo (1928: 248) identifies Opeholhaupung as a variant spelling of Wapwallopen. Records for the year 1748 in the Moravian Archives at Bethlehem, Pennsylvania (Fliegel 1970: 879), label Wapwallopen a "Delaware town." Other Moravian records indicate that most of the Indians who resided here had been Christianized. In 1752 it was noted that this was a place where the Nanticoke stopped on their "homeward journey."

Objects of eighteenth-century origin were found at a site north of present-day Wapwallopen in 1936 by Eugene Gardner, who directed WPA excavations at a place then known as the Smith Farm site (Gardner 1939: 23-26). Several pits were excavated by Gardner (1939: 23-26) which contained glass, kaolin pipe fragments, redware, and other colonial ceramics, and one George III half-penny dated 1774. Gardner erroneously, and without any documentary support, interpreted the site as a Nanticoke town from "about 1730 to the late 1790's."

In 1978 the Pennsylvania Historical and Museum Commission, with the aid of a grant from the Pennsylvania Power and Light Company, undertook additional excavations at this location, now known as the Knouse site (36Lu43). Twenty-two burials and a number of other features were discovered. Some of the burials were in coffins, attesting to Christian influence. None of these interments was accompanied by very abundant grave furnishings, but the items recovered, including kaolin pipes, seed and wire-wound beads, brass rings, bracelets, a vanity box, religious medals, etc., all pertain to a period from about 1740 to 1760 (see a more detailed description under site reports; also see McIntyre 1979).

It is known from the Brainerd account (Styles 1821: 85-86) that the place was occupied by 12 households of Indians at least as early as 1744. If we can trust the archeological record, it would appear that a few Indians may have resided there long enough to have lost an English coin dated 1774.

In the darkness that hung over Shamokin following the deaths of Sassoonan, and particularly Shickellamy, all Delaware individuals were forced to make decisions about their futures: some stayed at Shamokin for a few more years, some moved up the North Branch to small hamlets like Wapwallopen, but many migrated westward. Teedyuscung became the leader of most of those who stayed along the Susquehanna, until he was burned to death in his cabin at Wyoming in 1763.

Missionizing efforts on the part of the Moravian church, centered at Bethlehem, Pennsylvania, from about 1740 onward, generated numerous Indian converts to Christianity. Most of these baptized folk, generally known as "Moravian Indians," attached themselves to the various Moravian settlements or Moravian Indian towns. Many Delaware Indians are buried in the Moravian cemeteries at Bethlehem. From 1746 to 1756 there were many living at the Moravian Indian town of Gnadenhuetten, at present Lehighton on the Lehigh River in Carbon County, Pennsylvania.

In the years leading up to the beginning of the French and Indian War (formally begun in 1756), the Indians at Gnadenhuetten also found themselves in the dark as to their future—should they be Christians or Indians? Teedyuscung led many of them to Wyoming in 1754, and here most of them stayed throughout the French and Indian War (Wallace 1949: 47, 77).

By and large the Delawares at Wyoming and upriver remained neutral throughout the war. Those Delawares who, with the Shawnee and others, played a really hostile role in the war, were in the upper Ohio Valley in towns such as Kittanning (Armstrong County, burned by the English in 1756), Shingas Town (Beaver County), Mohulbucteetam (Armstrong County), Custaloga's Town (Crawford County), Shenango (Mercer County), and the Kuskuskies (Lawrence County).

General John Forbes' successful expedition against the French at Fort Duquesne, located at the forks of the Ohio in 1758, brought a temporary halt to Indian hostilities in Pennsylvania. Termination of the war between France and England in February, 1763, did not mean the end of Indian wars in Pennsylvania. Such promises as were made to the Indians at the close of the war were generally not kept. Once again, the Indians attacked the frontier, this time (May, 1763) in unison under the Ottawa Chief Pontiac, at all the major western forts. Until August of that year, the frontier was literally on fire. Colonel Henry Bouquet's defeat of the Indians that month at the Battle of Bushy Run (Westmoreland County, Pennsylvania), and his expedition against them the following year in the Ohio Country, brought an end to Pontiac's War. Once again there was a halt to Pennsylvania's Indian wars, at least until the American Revolution.

Many Indians left Pennsylvania after Pontiac's War. In 1763 the Moravians established another mission town for those Indians still residing on the Susquehanna. This place, called Friedenshuetten, near the mouth of the Wyalusing Creek in Bradford County, was the scene of archeological investigations in 1972 (Delaney 1973). Very little was recovered archeologically, but there was sufficient evidence to determine the precise location of Friedenshuetten.

The Pennsylvania Historical and Museum Commission marker near the site summarizes concisely the history of this last major residence of Delaware Indians in the eastern part of the State:

> FRIEDENSHUETTEN
> Moravian mission founded at Wyalusing Indian town, 1763, by Zeisberger, who built a model Indian town. Abandoned in 1772, when pastors Ettwein and Roth led some 200 Indians to the mission of Friedensstadt on the Beaver River.

OTHER INDIANS OF THE SUSQUEHANNA VALLEY

Other Indians, in addition to those already discussed, temporarily inhabited the Susquehanna Valley during the eighteenth century. For the most part, their minor impact upon the history of the valley is underscored by the paucity of contemporary accounts concerning them. In many cases their sojourn in the valley is known to us only through warrant surveys or other records. It is this unfortunate lack of adequate documentation which necessitates our discussing them all under one seemingly undignified chapter heading.

The best known of these Indians are the Nanticoke, Algonquian-speaking peoples who formerly resided in Eastern Shore Maryland. Others include the Tutelo, Siouan speakers from southcentral Virginia; and the Tuscarora, Iroquoian speakers from North Carolina. Even less well known are the Saponi, relatives of the Tutelo; the Algonquian-speaking Mahigan and Mohegan of New England; and, on a very few occasions, the Twightwee (or Miami, or Naked Indians) from the Ohio Valley area.

Historians have frequently disagreed as to why or how the Iroquois Indians laid claim to the Susquehannocks' territory in the Susquehanna Valley. However, most historians do agree that their claim began about 1675, when the Susquehannocks temporarily removed from the valley. As we have seen, after 1675 the Susquehannocks became, in effect, minions of the Iroquois, most specifically of the Seneca. Regardless of why this happened, it is nevertheless true that the Iroquois were able to show title to the Susquehanna Valley, at least in the sense that many original land purchases there, by the Pennsylvania Proprietaries, were negotiated with the Iroquois.

One reason for Iroquois claims to the Susquehanna Valley was to stay, at least temporarily, the movements of white settlement in the direction of Iroquoia. Another, perhaps more pragmatic, reason was that the Iroquois had discovered the European concept that land is power and wealth, and that indeed it could be exchanged for handsome returns.

As is often the case, the maintenance of territorial claims required at least a show of occupancy. The Iroquois managed a token occupancy through towns like Conestoga, and a few other small settlements higher on the North and West branches of the Susquehanna. They greatly increased the display of their presence by encouraging other Indian nations to settle in "their" Susquehanna Valley. Many of these people were former enemies of the Iroquois; but now they were refugees, fleeing the encroachment of the whites in their old homelands. The only price for lands to settle upon in the Susquehanna Valley was political homage to the Iroquois. In some cases, as a show of their hegemony, the Iroquois would send a vice-regent to live among the resettled refugees. Shickellamy, who lived with the Seneca, Delawares, Tutelo and Saponi at Shamokin, was the best known of these Iroquoian viceroys.

Almost 50 eighteenth-century Indian towns are known from the historical records for the Susquehanna Valley (see Kent et al. 1981). Fewer than a dozen of these have been verified archeologically, and none of the latter can clearly be attributed to any of our so-called "other Indians."

A few sites, which from their artifactual content are clearly eighteenth century, have been discovered archeologically, but we cannot assign any ethnic or tribal affiliations. Notable examples of these are the County Park site (36La96; see Kinsey and Custer 1982), the site of the Sarf cache find at Wilkes-Barre (Kent 1970), or the several sites in the Williamsport area (see Turnbaugh 1975: 242-46).

In a few cases ethnic origins of sites have been suggested by researchers, but have not been confirmed. For example Bender (1929) has postulated that Cocalico, in Lancaster County, and Tulpehocken, in Lebanon County, were Nanticoke towns (for locations see Kent et al. 1981).

If we judge by the number of pages written about them, the Nanticokes are the best known of our "other" eighteenth-century Indian residents of the Susquehanna Valley. The first mention of them in this area appears in Governor John Evans' 1707 account of the Indians whom he met at Dekanoagah. They included Nanticoke from the seven following towns: Matcheattochousie, Matchcoushtin, Witichquaom, Natahquois, Teahquois, Byerengeahtein and Pohecommoati (Colonial Records 1838 II: 402). It has never been established whether these were scattered Nanticoke towns in the vicinity of Washington Boro (Dekanoagah), or were seven places of residence in Eastern Shore Maryland; the latter seems more likely.

Weslager (1948: 58) has traced some of the documentary history of the

Nanticoke in Pennsylvania, and he found that their first identifiable settlement in the Susquehanna Valley was with the Conoy Indians on a site at the mouth of the Juniata River in the year 1742-1743 (see also Kent et al. 1981). By 1747 (Weslager 1948: 61) many Nanticoke had moved up to Nanticoke Town at the lower end of the Wyoming Valley in Luzerne County. They remained there only until 1753, at which time the Iroquois gave them permission to settle at Otsiningo on the Chenango River, near present-day Binghamton, New York (Weslager 1948: 61-62; see also Feest 1978: 240-52).

A brief history of the Tutelo (usually classified with the Saponi) is recounted by Claude E. Schaeffer (in Speck 1942: v-xvii). Conrad Weiser (see Wallace 1981: 116) found them in 1744 at Shamokin, where they were also mentioned the following year by David Brainerd (in Styles 1821) in his account of the town and its Delaware, Seneca, and "Tutelas" (and presumably Saponi) inhabitants. After 1748 some of the Tutelo and Saponi settled at a town called Skogari (Oskohary) at the mouth of Catawissa Creek in Columbia County (see Schaeffer in Speck 1942: xiii; Wallace 1981: 116). By about 1753 many of them had moved to Tioga Point or to the nearby Tutelo Town at the junction of Tutelo Creek and the Chemung River opposite Athens, Pennsylvania. Some may have stayed in the Tutelo Town area until the opening of the American Revolution. Most had previously (1771) moved towards the Cayuga settlements in New York State (Schaeffer in Speck 1942: xiv).

The Tuscarora were one of the most notable groups of Indian travelers through eastern Pennsylvania, but their settlements in this State were few and short-lived: by about 1710 (Hanna 1911: 81) these people had begun moving northward from North Carolina to join the Iroquois. Some Tuscarora were present at a conference held at Conestoga Town in June, 1710 (Hanna 1911: 84). In 1722 they were officially admitted as the sixth nation of the Iroquois (see Landy 1978: 518-24).

The Tuscarora left their name in many of the places which they traversed in Pennsylvania. However, according to Donehoo (1928: 237-40), the only sites which they were known to have occupied for any length of time were along the Susquehanna River in Susquehanna County at places called Ingaren and Tuscarora Town. These villages were destroyed by General Sullivan's army in 1779. Hanna (1911: 85-87) argues that the Tuscarora also had towns elsewhere in Pennsylvania, particularly in the Tuscarora Valley, and names one as being at Aughwick in Huntingdon County. Donehoo (1928: 238) disagreed with this, saying that Aughwick was a Delaware town.

The history of the coming and going of other Indians in the Susquehanna Valley, such as the Miami, who came on several occasions in war parties, the Mohegan, the Mahican, and surely some others, is little known, and they are seldom mentioned on old maps and in the colonial records.

Mahican Indians originally resided in an area basically in eastern New York, east of the Hudson River. These folk had very strong cultural and linguistic ties with the Munsee of the upper Delaware Valley. In fact, the archeological connections of these two groups seem thus far to have been largely ignored or underestimated. A good current discussion of the culture and history of the Mahican is provided by Brasser (1978: 198-212).

Heckewelder (1819: 78) seems to have been confused about the differences between the Mahican of the Hudson Valley and the Mohegans of eastern Connecticut, perhaps not so difficult to do given the similarity of their names and languages. However, as later researchers have shown, they were separate peoples (see Salwen 1978: 160-76).

Mahican and Mohegan experienced the same cultural breakdown suffered by other Indians of the East Coast during the seventeenth and eighteenth centuries. Many from both groups moved towards Iroquoia to escape pressures from whites. Some of these people joined the Delawares, with whom many became baptized Christians at the hands of the Moravian missionaries.

It is primarily in the various and copious records of the Moravians that we find occasional mention of Mahican and Mohegan among the Delaware towns and in the so-called Moravian Indian settlements (see Fliegel 1970). Specific examples include Mahican at the Indian town of Wyoming (Zeisberger in Reichel 1870) and Mohegan at Tioga (Donehoo 1928: 227).

More of the abstruse history of the other Indians of the Susquehanna Valley can be found in the laudable two-volume set entitled *The Wilderness Trail*, by Charles Hanna (1911). In a significant effort to preserve widely scattered accounts of the locations of towns occupied by seventeenth- and eighteenth-century Indians, George P. Donehoo (1928) published *A History of the Indian Villages and Place Names in Pennsylvania*. Important additions to the study of those Indians were made by Paul Wallace in his *Indians in Pennsylvania* (1964, with subsequent editions) and *Indian Paths of Pennsylvania* (1965). Some of the research by these earlier historians has been recently collated and presented together with *A Map of 18th Century Indian Towns in Pennsylvania* (Kent, Rice and Ota 1981).

For the really serious student, the most satisfactory understanding of the culture history of all the Indians dealt with in the present volume requires a first-hand examination of the archeological studies of them, together with the pertinent primary documents and major secondary works. We have already touched upon most of the primary and secondary historical sources, and our bibliography should lead the more inquisitive reader to other background material. However, our primary goal in this part of the book has been to summarize, for the more casual reader, the highlights of the history and way of life of these fascinating peoples of the past. What follows is a more detailed, and perhaps more cumbersome, account of the archeological resources for this story of the *Susquehanna's Indians*.

Evidence from Artifacts—Native Objects

MATERIAL CULTURE OF THE SUSQUEHANNA'S INDIANS: INTRODUCTION

MATERIAL culture—the tangible products or objects of a society's way of life—constitutes the major portion of that which is recovered by archeological excavation. It is not inappropriate therefore that much of this volume should be devoted to describing these things and the contexts in which they were found. One of our first concerns is to organize the various and numerous bits and pieces of archeologically recovered material culture into types in order to have meaningful or distinguishable groups of things to describe. But more than that, our purpose is to study these things to discern their functions, their changing forms, and the reasons for those changes. At an even higher plane of inquiry, we must exercise a concern for an anthropological understanding of the whole culture whose remains we have uncovered. This means using the evidence from the material culture and less tangible data as means for understanding the total fabric of, and the changes in, that culture, or at least as much of it as can reasonably be reconstructed from these remains. That which is reconstructed in this manner is usually called a culture history.

Discussions of the technological remains or the material culture of the Susquehanna's Indians which follow here are organized into two major categories. The first of these includes those things which are native-made products. The second consists of European-made items recovered from Indian sites. Subcategories for each of these two groups are based primarily upon the raw materials of which the various types of items were made. This arrangement is for convenience of analysis and organization of the descriptions.

CULTURE HISTORY OF THE SUSQUEHANNA'S INDIANS AS TRACED THROUGH NATIVE CERAMICS

Among all the artifacts collected by archeologists, pottery has generally proved to be the most instructive. Clay, which can easily be formed into various shapes, decorated and fired to create useful ceramic containers, provides an excellent medium for individual artistic expression. Yet in almost every society, individual artistic expressions on ceramics are executed within certain customary boundaries. That is to say, in almost any given society and during a particular time period, the majority of the ceramics which are produced will exhibit certain uniform characteristics. In subsequent time periods, these characteristics or styles may change, but for a while at least some persons may continue to follow the older, more traditional styles.

For all of these reasons, pottery provides a major means for tracing the cultural developments of the societies which produced it. Recognizing this, archeologists have seized upon ancient fragments of pottery in a manner which is often difficult for the layman to understand. Complex and often torturous harangues by archeologists about attributes, types, etc., which may or may not serve to relate various groups of pottery, are necessary to sort out the essential features which enable us to trace their ancestry.

Once the specific pottery type(s) of some historically known society has (have) been identified, it may be possible to discover the prehistoric antecedents of that society by backtracking its pottery through other sites and time periods.

Such has been the case with the Susquehannocks. Archeologists and historians have eventually come to recognize that "Fort Demolished" near Washington Boro (the Strickler site, see Figure 8), as mentioned on late seventeenth-century maps, was a Susquehannock town. After having examined the pottery from this town, and by comparing it and its occurrence or quantity at other towns, it soon becomes possible to trace the relative sequence of the towns and all other remains which they produce.

This direct historic approach to Susquehannock archeology through ceramic analysis has been the major means for understanding the culture history of these people. Most of the backtracking of Susquehannock pottery and sites has already been done. Our purpose here is to review the pottery sequences and to refine them and their implications for Susquehannock culture history in light of more recent studies. But, since the basic sequences have already been worked out, it will not be necessary for us to follow the pottery back in time. Our overall approach will be to trace Susquehannock and related pottery forward from its earliest-known point of origin.

The History of Susquehannock Pottery Studies

D. H. Landis (1910) was probably the first person to actually identify in print a number of archeological sites as being Susquehannock. However, the earliest published illustration of pottery thought to be Susquehannock was that by Holmes (1903: pl. CXLIV). He illustrates eight sherds of what we now call Washington Boro Incised, from a village site at Bainbridge,

Pennsylvania (probably the Billmyer Quarry site). He notes (Holmes 1903: 165) that "the people to whom this earthenware belonged were *possibly* the Susquehannocks of John Smith." He goes on to describe it briefly, noting its shell-tempering, heavy overhanging collars, and rudely modeled faces.

Landis provided Charles Hanna with a photograph of objects from Susquehannock (and other) sites which included one Susquehannock pot (Hanna 1911: facing 42). Christopher Wren (1914) illustrated a number of unidentified pots which can now be labeled Susquehannock.

Alanson B. Skinner, in 1917, wrote the first description of pottery positively identified as Susquehannock (actually called Andaste pottery). However, his article was not published until 1938 (Moorehead 1938: 45-67). Skinner was a member of Moorehead's 1916 Susquehanna River expedition, and the sample upon which he based his description was primarily from Bradford County, Pennsylvania. Many of those pots which he identified as Andaste (or Susquehannock) are now known to be other Iroquoian forms, but those which he described as having shell-tempering were definitely Susquehannock.

James B. Griffin (Cadzow 1936) provided the first detailed description of the Susquehannock pottery types which are now called Washington Boro Incised and Schultz Incised.

Even though Holmes (1903) was not certain which if any of the pottery he examined from the Susquehanna Valley was of Susquehannock origin, he did recognize that most of it showed very definite relationships to Iroquois pottery of New York State. Skinner, and later Griffin, confirmed this Iroquois-Susquehannock pottery association. With but few exceptions, this theory of Iroquois-Susquehannock relationships has gone unchallenged ever since.

MacNeish (1952: 55) paid lip service to this association by including a two-paragraph chapter on "Susquehanna Pottery" in his *Iroquois Pottery Types*, but at that time neither he nor anyone else was quite prepared to discuss the detailed culture-history relationships of the two. The first major effort in this regard came with publication of the *Susquehannock Miscellany* by Witthoft and Kinsey in 1959.

An Ancestry for Susquehannock Pottery

Witthoft (in Witthoft and Kinsey 1959) was solely responsible for the first proposed ancestry of the Susquehannocks. In essence his theory is that the development of Susquehannock pottery is parallel to that of eastern Iroquois (Mohawk, Oneida and Onondaga), or to that of Munsee Incised in the upper Delaware Valley. He also felt that, during the early phases of this development, Susquehannock and Cayuga were one and the same.

The common ancestry for all these parallel developments lies in the Owasco ceramic tradition, with its various forms. Out of this base arises what Lenig (1965) has called the Oak Hill Horizon, with its various corded-collar forms; then the Chance Horizon, with its various incised forms; and ultimately the various specific tribal potteries. The most important stylistic bond in all these developments, from the point of view of the present analysis, is the Chance Horizon. In the eastern Iroquoian area the major pottery types comprising the Chance Horizon are Chance Incised, Deowongo Incised, and Durfee Underlined, which lead into early colonial types, perhaps best typified by Garoga Incised (Lenig 1965). Comparable Chance Horizon forms occur in the upper Delaware Valley, where they lead to a pre- and early-colonial type known as Munsee Incised. Similar developments, albeit with localized variations, took place in the Wyoming Valley of Pennsylvania. However, here the local, evolving expressions of the Chance Horizon are terminated and are followed by a nearly complete void in pre-colonial times.

The parallel for the Chance Horizon in the area of developing Seneca-Cayuga-Susquehannock culture in southern New York and Bradford County, Pennsylvania, is somewhat less like those of eastern Iroquois, but still recognizable as such. It involves increasingly higher collars, as primarily expressed in the precolonial type known as Richmond Incised (MacNeish 1952: 51).

From this apparently common ancestral form the lines of development seem to diverge slightly. On the one hand, that leading to colonial-period Cayuga (and Seneca) passes through Cayuga Horizontal, Ithaca Linear and others (MacNeish 1952: 135, 141; Ritchie 1954: 51, 58). On the other hand, the very close parallel line of development for Susquehannock, as seen in the upper Susquehanna Valley, involves an infrequently encountered type which Witthoft (Witthoft and Kinsey 1959: 56; see also Lucy 1959, 1979) designated as Proto-Susquehannock.

Over the years, there has been some disagreement concerning the precise stages in the development of Cayuga-Seneca and early Susquehannock (Lenig 1965: 77). Most critics would probably find the present, admittedly generalized, outline far too simplistic.

One thing is certain, however. Throughout Iroquoia and in adjacent areas of parallel or related pottery development, such as the upper Delaware, the Wyoming Valley, and the upper Susquehanna, there was a basic, common theme of pottery decoration, involving increasingly higher collars, added to which was a great deal of exchange of local decorative ideas by all participants in the theme. It is foolishly centric to assume that all of these developments were the result of a one-way, outward spread of ideas from somewhere in New York State.

Figure 9. Schultz Incised pots. Front: from the Overpeck site (approximately 11 inches high). Courtesy *Pennsylvania Archaeologist* 50(3): 28. Back: from Sheshequin, Bradford County (seven inches high; see Wren 1914: pl. 13).

All of the pottery types thus far discussed are grit-tempered wares. The first truly distinctive Susquehannock pottery type to emerge from this sphere of development, now called Schultz Incised by Witthoft (Witthoft and Kinsey 1959: 42-51) was a shell-tempered ware. Except for this very apparent difference, one is often hard put to distinguish between certain Schultz Incised vessels and Cayuga Horizontal or Ithaca Linear.

The earliest occurrences of classic Schultz Incised are in Bradford County, Pennsylvania, and Tioga County, New York. Some trade goods have been found in graves which have also produced this early Schultz Incised pottery, viz., Engelbert (Stewart 1973; Dunbar and Ruhl 1974), Upper Queen Esther's Flats, and Murray Gardens (Skinner in Moorehead 1938: 64-65).

Based upon the type and quantity of these trade goods (primarily brass scrap and glass beads), and as compared with those of the Seneca sequence (Wray and Schoff 1953), Witthoft (Witthoft and Kinsey 1959) suggested a date of about 1550 for the first appearance of Schultz Incised in the upper

Figure 10. Top: Richmond Incised (36Br3, Vanderpoel collection). Bottom: Proto-Susquehannock (36Br50).

Susquehanna Valley. Bradley (1979: 379) would push this date back about 25 years.

This addition of crushed, roasted river mussel shell to their paste by certain potters of the upper Susquehanna Valley, whose finished products were otherwise very similar to that of their relatives, the Cayuga (and the Seneca), seems to mark the divergence of the Susquehannock from the Cayuga in particular, and the rest of Iroquoia in general. Witthoft (Witthoft and Kinsey 1959: 39) suggested that this new influence, viz., shell-tempering, was perhaps derived from contemporary western Pennsylvania cultures. Impressive confirmation of this came about a dozen years later with Stewart's (1973) publication of two shell-tempered Monongahela and one shell-tempered, Fort Ancient-like vessels from the Engelbert cemetery site.

We have implied here, as did Witthoft (Witthoft and Kinsey 1959), that Schultz Incised Susquehannock pottery grew out of Proto-Susquehannock, which in turn grew out of Richmond Incised. In point of fact this specific line of development is not at all clear. The addition of shell-tempering to the paste of Proto-Susquehannock does not produce Schultz Incised. We have previously suggested that shell-tempering is the only major difference between Schultz Incised on the one hand and Cayuga Horizontal and Ithaca Linear on the other. If the divergence really did come with the addition of shell-tempering to whatever pottery was the parent of all three of these, Proto-Susquehannock might also have to be considered somewhere in the line of development to all three. Proto-Susquehannock is very poorly known—because there are so few examples. Nevertheless, it certainly does exist in Bradford County, Pennsylvania. Chronologically, and to a great extent stylistically, it is in the right place to be in the parentage of the later Seneca-Cayuga-Susquehannock forms. In terms of published examples, Richmond Incised is almost as poorly known. Some of the illustrated examples, as well as specimens of both types at the Rochester Museum and Science Center, do suggest a very close relationship between Richmond Incised and Proto-Susquehannock. Lucy (1979: 7) illustrates one pot from Bradford County which he considers a sort of blend or transition between the two types. But again, the leap from either or both of these to Schultz Incised or Cayuga Horizontal or Ithaca Linear is not easy. Something still seems to be missing.

Ritchie (1954: 58, plate 28, no. 1) illustrates a Richmond Incised vessel from the Seneca Dutch Hollow site (ca. 1590-1615) which, if it were actually typical of earlier forms of Richmond Incised, could very neatly serve as the parent for Schultz Incised and its Cayuga-Seneca counterparts. Except for its lack of shell temper and horizontal lines below the lip, it is virtually a Schultz Incised pot, and it is what we would expect our missing immediate

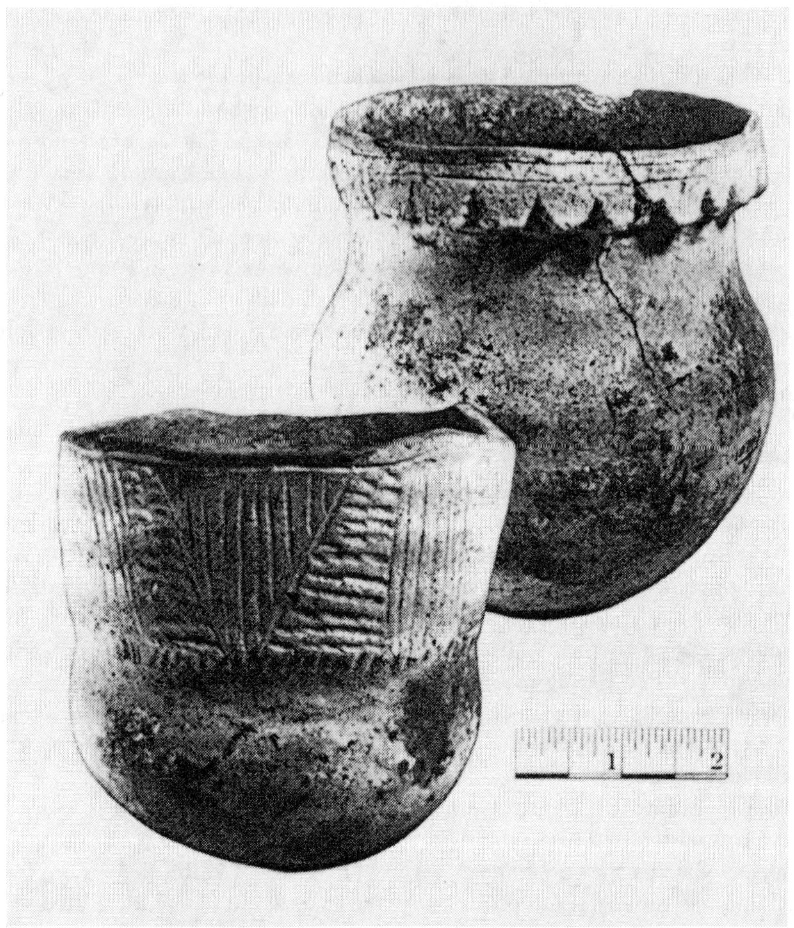

Figure 11. Related Iroquoian pottery types. Front: Ithaca Linear from the Warren site. Back: Genoa Frilled from the Dutch Hollow site. Courtesy Rochester Museum and Science Center.

parent type to look like. This particular example, of course, was found at a site which is too late to fill this position (apparently it is a mistyped Ithaca Linear pot).

Obviously the origin for Schultz Incised and its cousins, Cayuga Horizontal and Ithaca Linear, is somewhere in northern Pennsylvania and south central New York. Clearly they are an outgrowth of the more classic Richmond Mills forms as evolved and modified by the blending of a number of different stylistic sources. It simply appears that the specific transitional pots have not yet been found.

Movements and Interactions as Seen Through Ceramics

Sometime before 1575 the Susquehannocks of the upper valley began to abandon their scattered hamlets and move southward. Thinly scattered examples of their "early" Schultz Incised pottery found along the Susquehanna mark the path of their journey to Lancaster County. An even thinner scattering of this pottery occurs along the Delaware River at least as far south as the Overpeck site in Bucks County, Pennsylvania (Figure 13), and at the Abbott Farm site in New Jersey (Cross 1956: plate 41).

Reasons for this southward migration, and the split from Cayuga, are usually explained as the result of political and economic pressures on the Susquehannock by the Iroquois. We can offer no more plausible reason for their movement, but move they did. They may have been reaching out for European contacts in the Delaware and Chesapeake bays. There are no associations of trade goods with Susquehannock pottery anywhere north of Lancaster County after 1575. By that date all or most of the scattered Susquehannock communities had coalesced in one very large palisaded town in Lancaster County—the Schultz site.

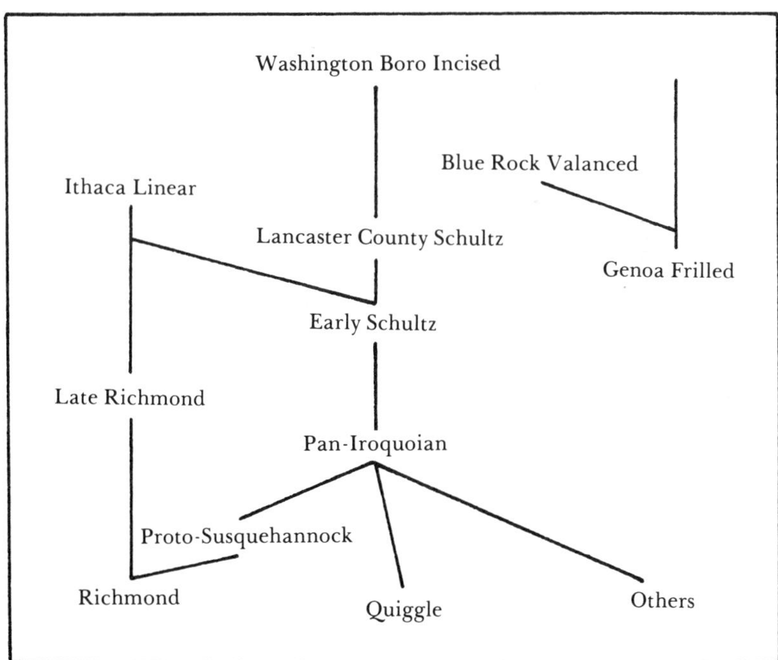

Figure 12. Diagram of pottery-type interrelations.

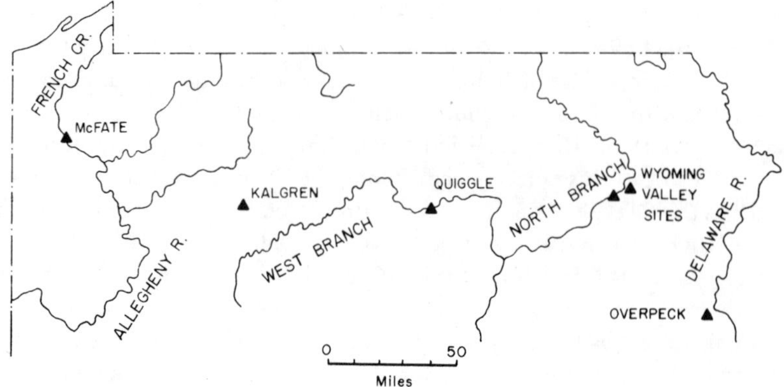

Figure 13. Map showing the locations of sites with McFate-Quiggle pottery.

Other Early Susquehanna Valley Ceramics

Witthoft (1959: 24-26) alludes to various conquests by the Susquehannocks of local Susquehanna Valley people, particularly those of the Shenks Ferry culture, as they moved southward. One such place, he suggested (Witthoft 1959: 26), was the Quiggle site, along the West Branch of the Susquehanna in Clinton County. Here, he said, Schultz Incised pottery intruded into the pits of the local Shenks Ferry occupants.

More recent, and rather extensive, excavations at the Quiggle site (Smith 1976, 1981b) turned up very little evidence of Shenks Ferry pottery, but instead a rather sizable stockaded village which produced incised, high-collared, shell-tempered wares resembling early Schultz Incised in some ways, but apparently antecedent thereto. No trade goods occurred at Quiggle, thus suggesting that it dates prior to 1525.

As a result of the larger pottery samples from the Quiggle site, which Smith's (1976, 1981b) work made available, he and others began to look elsewhere for its relationships. It quickly became evident that, in terms of other known samples, its closest ties were not with Susquehannock, but rather with the Kalgren site in Clearfield County (James Herbstritt, personal communication) and particularly the McFate site in Crawford County (Schoff n.d.).

Ceramics from the Quiggle site are not precisely like those from McFate. For one thing, there are more plain, cord-marked vessels in the sample from McFate. Interestingly, some of these plain vessels have their closest parallels in the Chautauqua Cord-marked pottery of southwestern New York (Guthe 1958: 56-57). Others in this plain series are derived from the Monongahela pottery types of southwestern Pennsylvania.

Even though the total assemblage of pottery from Quiggle and from McFate varies slightly, there is nevertheless a very positive relationship between the two, particularly when we consider the shell-tempered vessels with incipient collars and incised decorations. This type, which has previously been labeled McFate Incised (Mayer-Oakes 1955: 204; see also Murphy 1973), is a hallmark of the culture area that includes such stockaded sites as McFate, the Elk County earthworks (Smith and Herbstritt 1976), Kalgren and its neighbors in Clearfield County, and in our opinion all those sites along the West Branch of the Susquehanna, at least as far east as the Quiggle site, which produce pottery of this sort.

This general type (shell-tempered pottery from McFate, Kalgren, Quiggle, etc.) overlaps to varying degrees into adjacent culture areas. For example, it occurs as a minority type at both the Schacht and Parker sites in the Wyoming Valley (Smith 1973). A probable pot of this type was found in a rock shelter near Bear Creek Reservoir in Luzerne County (see WPMM files). Related forms have been found at the Sheep Rock Shelter in Huntingdon County, at the Mohr and Locust Grove sites in Lancaster County, and as a very curious occurrence (and somewhat variant form) as far east as the Overpeck site in Bucks County (see Forks of the Delaware, Chapter 14, 1980: Fig. 21, B and C).

Again, we recognize that there are certain differences between the examples of this incised type as manifested at the McFate site on the one end of its major distribution and at Quiggle, etc., on the eastern end. Treatment of the vessel lips is one noticeable area of difference; surfaces of the vessels and collar size and shape also vary somewhat. However, at this point, it would appear that these differences are not sufficient to warrant giving them separate type names. Indeed, we have opted to underscore the interrelationships of these ceramics by referring to them with the hyphenated names of the two major sites at either end of their primary area of occurrence, viz., McFate-Quiggle. Perhaps in the future, when all of the characteristics of this pottery are fully identified, it may prove useful to establish more specific variants of the type, e.g., McFate Incised—variety Quiggle, etc. For the present this seems unnecessary.

All of this still leaves us with the question concerning the relationship, if any, of this pottery with the Schultz Incised of the North Branch, and later with that in Lancaster County. Witthoft's earlier assertion (in Witthoft and Kinsey 1959: 26-27) that Quiggle shell-tempered pottery was Susquehannock is now clearly in error, and indeed there may be very little relationship between them. For quite some time this misidentification of shell-tempered pottery at Quiggle (Witthoft *ibid*), Sheep Rock (Michels and Smith 1967: 483-86) and in the Wyoming Valley (Smith 1973) as Susquehannock has clouded our understanding of the ancestry and development

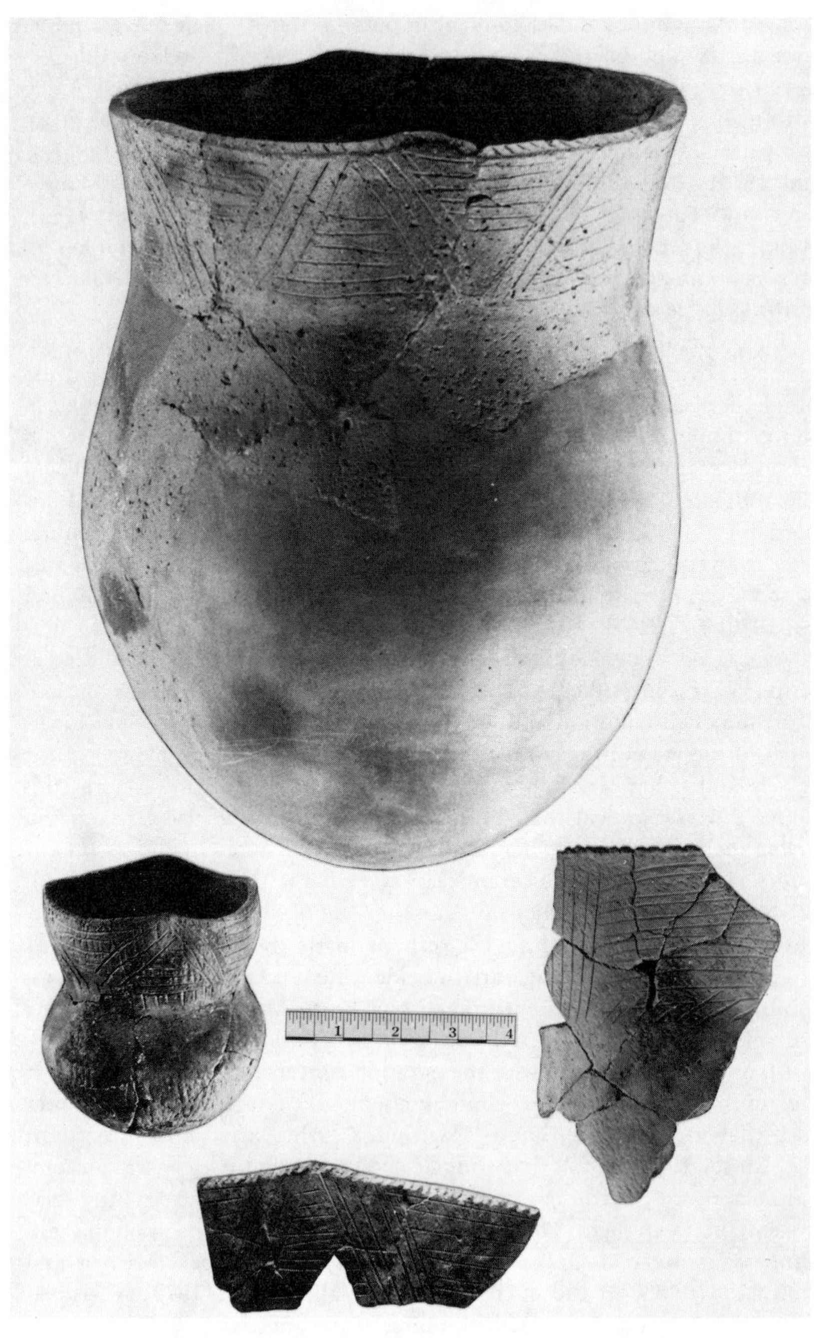
1
2
3
4

of Susquehannock. At the same time it totally obscured the existence of McFate influence in central and eastern Pennsylvania.

Another difference (in addition to pottery) between the Quiggle site and early Susquehannock is evident in the settlement patterns of the two. Quiggle, like Kalgren and McFate, had circular arrangements of houses inside a stockade, with external ditches. Each of these also has the curious keyhole structures (Smith 1976). None of these traits appears in early North Branch Susquehannock.

In light of these new discoveries we need not, and should not, look to McFate-Quiggle pottery as an ancestor for Susquehannock. We already have, in the upper Susquehanna at about the same time as Quiggle, a good ancestral form for Schultz Incised and the Cayuga-Seneca parallels, namely Richmond Incised-Proto-Susquehannock. All that is really necessary to transform these into Schultz Incised is the addition of shell temper and some minor changes in design.

The potters of Quiggle and elsewhere could have provided some of these influences, and that is what we are proposing. Obviously if McFate-Quiggle Incised pottery from the Quiggle site, or elsewhere, was a source of influence upon evolving Proto-Susquehannock in the upper Susquehanna, then the two peoples must have come in contact with one another at some place and time. It is quite possible that we will never be able to pinpoint any major physical (ceramic or otherwise) evidence for such contact, but that need not detract from the theory. We do have several Monongahela-like vessels from the early Schultz Engelbert site, and these vessels are actually quite similar to minority forms found at Quiggle, Kalgren or McFate.

We suggest that the makers of McFate-Quiggle Incised were participants in that sphere of ceramic interaction which all of Iroquoia and its other neighbors were caught up in. Part of this interaction and exchange of ideas was apparently the by-product of aggression. The stockaded villages of the Quiggle-Kalgren-McFate peoples and those folk residing in the Wyoming Valley at the Parker and Schacht sites (see Smith 1973) clearly indicate that they were in conflict with someone, perhaps with each other, probably with the Shenks Ferry to the sourth, and also with the proto-Iroquioans to the north.

Of all the participants of this melee, only the Iroquoians were successful against the others—for it is only they whose progeny survived well into the

Figure 14, opposite. McFate-Quiggle Incised pottery. Top: restored vessel from the McFate site (36Cwl). Middle left: pot from the Kalgren site (36Cd7). Middle right: sherd from the Quiggle site (36Cn6). Bottom: sherd from a rock-shelter in eastern Pennsylvania (36Mg19).

Figure 15. McFate-Quiggle-like pot from the Schultz-Funk site (La9/116).

historic period. No village of the people who made McFate-Quiggle pottery nor any of the Wyoming Valley ceramic complex has been found with associated trade goods. Only one site—Shenks Ferry in Lancaster County—has produced any evidence of the Shenks Ferry people in association with trade goods. Based on this it would appear that they barely made it into the historic period before their demise as a distinct cultural entity.

Pottery made by one group of people and found in the villages of some other group would, generally, seem to be good evidence of at least overlapping or partial contemporaniety of those peoples. This condition may be the result of either peaceful or aggressive interaction between the groups. We find, for example, a fair amount of McFate-Quiggle pottery at both the Schacht and Parker sites in the Wyoming Valley (see Smith 1973); very little pottery from the latter sites was found at Quiggle or elsewhere in the West Branch. We find some Shenks Ferry pottery at Kalgren and a little of it at Quiggle. At the Mohr site in Lancaster County, a small but conspicuous amount of shell-tempered McFate-Quiggle and Monongahela-like pottery was found in association with a new Shenks Ferry pottery type (later described as Lancaster Incised). At the Kalgren site there were a few, but again conspicuous, occurrences of this new Shenks Ferry type, together with an unusual assortment of types from other areas (James Herbstritt: personal communication).

None of the sites discussed above, except the Shenks Ferry type site and Overpeck, has produced any confirmed Susquehannock sherds. To be certain, there are shell-tempered sherds in these other sites; but in our opinion, these are all either Monongahela or McFate-Quiggle, not Susquehannock.

It was toward the end of this period of ceramic exchanges that Quiggle and its related sites in the West Branch and the Wyoming Valley sites ceased to be inhabited. We have not yet found these folk removed in any numbers to other locations and it appears, therefore, that they suffered extermination. Perhaps this was due to warfare with the Shenks Ferry, who do seem to have survived a while longer, at least in the lower Susquehanna Valley.

However, we might consider other possible causes of this postulated extermination. It could have happened as late as 1525, just prior to the introduction of trade goods to residents of the Wyoming Valley or the West Branch. But by that time another circumstance of European origin may have been introduced to the area, viz., European diseases. This could well have caused the extermination of peoples throughout the West Branch and the Wyoming Valley. Why it would not have affected early Susquehannocks living at that time on the upper reaches of the North Branch or the Shenks Ferry people who had withdrawn to the lower Susquehanna is a difficult question.

Perhaps the spread of such epidemics played a role in the eventual southward movement of the Susquehannocks. There is no positive evidence, however, that when they did move they met and destroyed indigenous folk in the Wyoming Valley or in the West Branch. The only thing which is clear is that after the Susquehannocks passed through or by these areas, there no longer were other peoples living there. Those who remained after 1550 would surely have acquired some trade goods and these would have been found in the archeological record—and they were not.

At least a few makers of the McFate-Quiggle pottery type seem to have survived long enough to come into direct contact with the Susquehannocks during the period of their southward migration.

What appears to be McFate-Quiggle shell-tempered pottery has been found at the Overpeck site along the Delaware River in Bucks County, Pennsylvania (see Forks of the Delaware Chapter 1980: Figure 21, A, B, C). Heretofore, these too had been misidentified as Schultz Incised Susquehannock vessels. Some quantity of actual Schultz Incised (cf., ibid: Figure 21, D; Figure 22, E) has been found at Overpeck, suggesting a contemporaniety of the two pottery types. Additional evidence of Susquehannock and McFate-Quiggle interfacing was discovered at the Schultz site in Lancaster County. A single vessel from a grave which included trade goods in the main Susquehannock cemetery is, in our opinion, a fairly good example of the type which we have been calling McFate-Quiggle (Figure 15).

These examples of rather apparent contact between the two cultures certainly do not prove that the Susquehannocks were responsible for the termination of McFate-Quiggle society. However, it does suggest that the Schultz site, dating to probably no earlier than 1575 A.D., did overlap, ever so slightly, with the end of the McFate-Quiggle ceramic tradition.

To summarize briefly, we have suggested that the people of the West Branch Valley (and adjacent areas) who made shell-tempered pottery were not genetically ancestral to the Susquehannocks on the upper North Branch of the Susquehanna. Rather, these inhabitants of the Quiggle and other similar sites were eastern relations of the McFate (and to a lesser extent Monogahela) peoples of western Pennsylvania. Furthermore, they may well have been in conflict with the Shenks Ferry and Wyoming Valley folk. Finally, we note that there is a certain resemblance of their shell-tempered pottery to that of early Schultz Incised. Unfortunately, this resemblance has caused numerous misinterpretations of the role of the Quiggle site in the early events of Susquehannock culture history. In our opinion, these similarities between McFate-Quiggle pottery and early Susquehannock are the result of the unconscious participation of both groups in the pan-Iroquoian ceramic interaction sphere. The contribution of the potters at Quiggle to this pool of ideas was, seemingly, the shell-tempering of ceramics and, perhaps, certain elements in design.

Shenks Ferry Ceramics

As we have seen, the Shenks Ferry people also played an important role in the fifteenth- and early sixteenth-century Indian history of the Susquehanna Valley. Their archeological culture was first clearly identified and labeled by Witthoft (in Witthoft and Farver 1951). Cadzow had earlier excavated some of their ceramics at several sites in Lancaster County, including the type site, but he identified them only as Algonquian in the Algonquian vs. Iroquois dichotomy of his day. Continued studies of the Shenks Ferry, particularly by Heisey and Witmer (1964), Kinsey and Graybill (1971), and Heisey (1971), have gone a long way toward improving our understanding of the culture history of these people.

Earliest recognizable remains of Shenks Ferry culture date to perhaps the fourteenth century, and they are best identified in association with

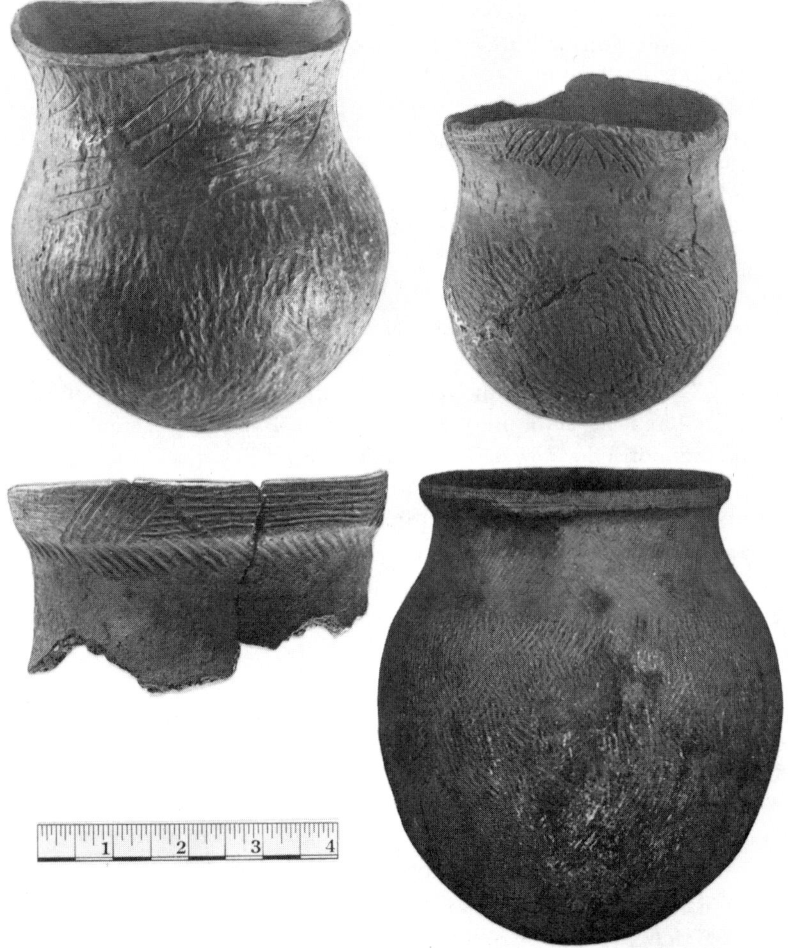

Figure 16. Shenks Ferry pottery types. Top left: Cord-marked, Miller site (36Le2). Top right: Incised (36Le2). Lower left: Incised, Shenks Ferry site (36La2). Lower right: Stewart phase, Bald Eagle Valley (not to scale—10 1/2 inches high), courtesy *Pennsylvania Archaeologist*, 51 (1-2): 8.

their pottery—Shenks Ferry Cord-marked and Shenks Ferry Incised. Both types, but most noticeably the latter, are scattered throughout much of the Susquehanna drainage system. However, without question, the majority of their sites and artifacts are found in the lower Susquehanna Valley in Lebanon, Cumberland, York and, particularly, Lancaster County.

Origins of Shenks Ferry are not at all clear. Shenks Ferry Cord-marked pottery and, to a lesser extent, Shenks Ferry Incised wares show some potential relationships to contemporary or earlier types of the Virginia-Maryland piedmont area (see Clark 1980). It is apparently not derived from any preceding indigenous cultures in Pennsylvania, nor does it have any good ancestral relationships in New York. Smith (1981b) has proposed a Clemsons Island ancestry (see Kent et al. 1971: 329-419 for a description of this culture) for Shenks Ferry, but the evidence for this is presently not very convincing.

Whatever its point of origin, this culture seems to have moved into the lower Susquehanna Valley around 1300 A.D. It flourished here, due largely to the extremely rich agricultural soils of the area, and because there were apparently no other societies with which it had to compete. From here certain groups of Shenks Ferry people expanded up the Susquehanna to about Wilkes-Barre.

Advance north of this point was largely blocked by the native cultures which inhabited the Wyoming Valley at Wilkes-Barre. Some small excursions further north do show up in the archeology of Bradford County (Lucy 1959: Plate III), but these do not represent major occupations.

Shenks Ferry peoples also moved into the West Branch of the Susquehanna. Initially their westward spread through this valley seemed unimpeded, suggesting that no other groups were living there at that time. The exception may be the Clemsons Island culture, but an actual face-to-face contact or contemporaniety between Shenks Ferry and Clemsons Island peoples is not yet clearly demonstrated. At the least, small groups of Shenks Ferry peoples eventually traveled as far as the headwaters of the western tributaries of the Susquehanna and the Juniata rivers. At the divide between the Susquehanna and the upper Ohio drainage, they almost certainly had some contact with the native peoples of western Pennsylvania. These could have included the Monongahela folk of southwestern Pennsylvania as well as the McFate people of the upper Allegheny.

Witthoft (1954) labeled the Shenks Ferry sites in the West Branch Valley the Stewart complex of that culture. These people produced pottery vessels which often had smaller collars then those in the lower Susquehanna Valley. By and large the design motifs were the same, albeit more compressed on the diminutive Stewart-phase collars. Stewart-phase pottery and other aspects of that culture were contemporary with and quite like those of the so-called conservative, Shenks Ferry Incised or Blue Rock phase (Heisey 1971) of the lower Susquehanna. Most Blue Rock-phase sites were small and widely scattered. As yet there is no evidence that any of them was stockaded. However, some of the Stewart-phase people of the West Branch did eventually find it necessary to protect themselves in more concentrated and palisaded villages. Bressler (1980) has reported two such towns, at Bull Run and Wolf Creek near Williamsport (see also Witthoft 1954: 29).

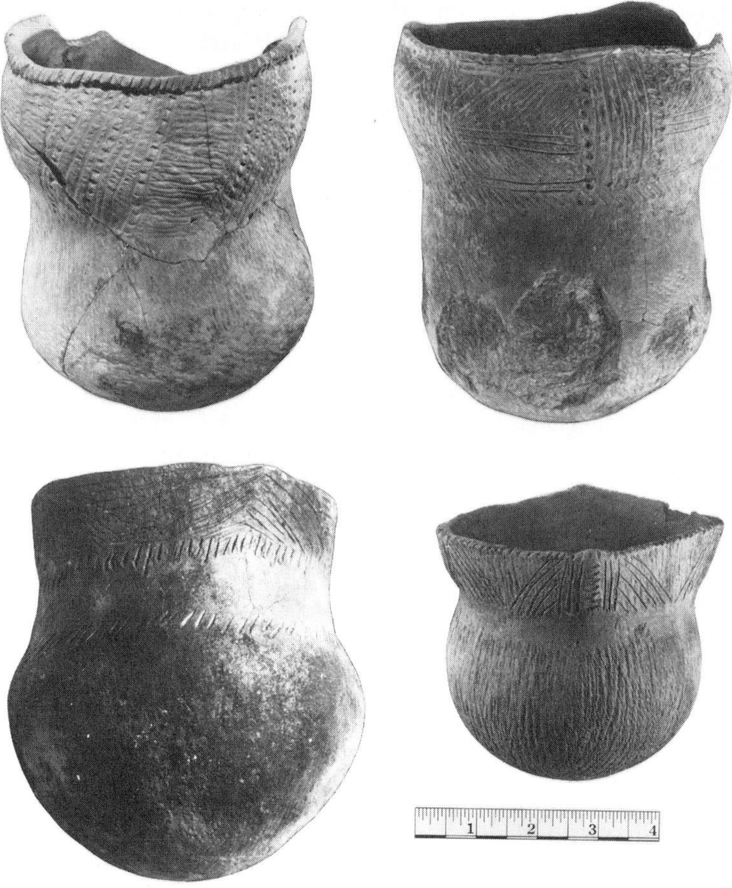

Figure 17. Shenks Ferry pottery types. Top left: Funk Incised from a Susquehannock grave at the Schultz site (36La7). Top right: Funk Incised, Shenks Ferry grave (36La7). Lower left: Lancaster Incised, Mohr site (36La39), courtesy Department of Anthropology, Temple University. Lower right: Lancaster Incised, Douglass farm, Washington Boro.

These defenses could well have been in response to aggressive actions of McFate peoples, who eventually began to move eastward along the West Branch. Ultimately these West Branch Valley McFate peoples (as evinced by the presence of their pottery) reached the Schacht and Parker sites of the Wyoming Valley in some numbers (see Smith 1973: 39). Their primary eastern-most village appears to be that at the Quiggle site in Clinton County along the West Branch some 20 miles west of Williamsport.

It is at about the time of the establishment of the Quiggle site, toward the end of the fifteenth century, that we see a withdrawal or termination of Shenks Ferry occupation of the West Branch Valley. Following this, the only known Shenks Ferry sites are in Lancaster County on the lower Susquehanna. These sites are distinguished by a new pottery type—Lancaster Incised—and for the first time in the lower Susquehanna some of the Shenks Ferry sites were stockaded.

Older patterns of seasonal satellite hunting and fishing stations continued in the lower Susquehanna, but it is obvious that at this time there was a concentration of people into primary villages with a new emphasis on defense of those places. Heisey (1971: 58) has referred to the new pottery type of this period as a transitional form which incorporated much of traditional (Blue Rock) Shenks Ferry Incised with various new design motifs. It was John Witthoft (Witthoft and Farver 1951) who first recognized this new type and labeled it Lancaster Incised.

Witthoft felt that Lancaster Incised represents an acculturation response of Shenks Ferry potters who had come in contact with early Susquehannock wares. Within a fairly short time a new pottery type emerged on the Lancaster County Shenks Ferry sites. This one Witthoft (in Witthoft and Farver 1951) called Funk Incised, and he felt that it represented even stronger Susquehannock acculturation forces and actual Shenks Ferry attempts to mimic Susquehannock pottery.

There are a great number of sites in Lancaster County where Lancaster Incised and, particularly, Funk Incised pottery were made. Very few of these sites have any evidence of direct contact with the Susquehannocks. Only one of these, the Shenks Ferry-type site found by Cadzow, has associated trade goods. In light of this, it would appear that all Lancaster Incised sites and most Funk Incised sites predate 1550, or even 1525. These factors have caused others to question or doubt the impact of Susquehannock pottery on Lancaster and/or Funk Incised, since both of these may precede Susquehannock.

Recognizing this, Heisey (1971: 62) suggested that Lancaster and Funk Incised pottery result from Shenks Ferry participation in the pan-Iroquois sphere of ceramic influence and that these types are in a sense (or para) Iroquoian, but not wholly the result of Susquehannock influence.

Our own examination of this situation finds Shenks Ferry people of at least the Lancaster Incised period in contact with (and probably in conflict with) two other groups of people, neither of which was the Susquehannocks. These were the makers of McFate pottery, at the Quiggle site (and elsewhere), and the people of the Wyoming Valley pottery complex at Wilkes-Barre. Virtually all of the things which make Lancaster Incised pottery different from the preceding Blue Rock or Stewart phases occur on the McFate pottery at the Quiggle site. Similarly, most of the things which give Funk Incised its peculiar characteristics (notched lips, globular bodies, excurvate high collars, and plats of incised lines often outlined with rows of punctates) occur at either the Quiggle site or, to a lesser extent, in the sites of the Wyoming Valley Complex. In our opinion these are the sources which influenced the changes in Shenks Ferry pottery as first manifested in Lancaster Incised and as later elaborated upon in Funk Incised.

Few Lancaster Incised and hardly any Funk Incised pots are exact, or even good copies of pots from the McFate-Quiggle complex; nor should we expect them to be, given our theory of borrowed ideas, for borrowing was exactly what they were doing. Very few cultures involved in acculturation borrow and reuse in exactly the same manner everything to which they are exposed; for they are adopting and adapting selected new ideas to their own way of life—not taking on a whole new culture. Nor should the notion that Shenks Ferry and the Quiggle, etc., folk were antagonists negate this borrowing of ideas—warfare usually acts to intensify such exchanges.

Kinsey and Graybill (1971) have recorded an almost incredible number of Lancaster-Funk-phase sites in Lancaster County. At least four of these have been partially excavated and are known to be stockaded (Mohr, Locust Grove, Murry and Funk). They (Kinsey and Graybill 1971: 35) list 38 sites, indicating an impressive population concentration in a relatively confined area. Many of these sites must represent seasonal or special food-collection stations. Several of the larger, more permanent villages were probably occupied contemporaneously. None of them shows any evidence of occupation after 1575, and as previously noted only the Shenks Ferry-type site near Pequea produced trade goods. The cause of their termination before the acquisition of any quantity of trade goods was in all probability the result of their defeat by the Susquehannocks, who began to arrive in Lancaster County between 1550 and 1575.

Not all of this contact between the Shenks Ferry and Susquehannocks was one of kill or be killed. Members of the two societies did live together. At the Shenks Ferry site there were Susquehannock sherds in pits which also produced fragments of Funk Incised vessels. The date of their co-habitation of this site is pretty well fixed between about 1550 A.D. and 1575 A.D. by the presence of several brass scraps in the pits and the finding of one

Figure 18. Pots with Shenks Ferry, Susquehannock and McFate-Quiggle influence, Shenks Ferry site (36La2).

spiral brass earring in an extended interment of what was, almost certainly, a Shenks Ferry individual.

Several pots from the Shenks Ferry site have been interpreted as hybridizations, involving Susquehannock potters and Shenks Ferry paste, or the reverse of this situation (see Smith 1970: Figure 3; see also Kent and Packard 1969, concerning the Erb Rockshelter). These situations, if indeed correctly interpreted, would further verify face-to-face contact of persons of Shenks Ferry and Susquehannock backgrounds. Neither of the vessels illustrated by Smith (1970; Figure 3, 2–3) as Susquehannock motifs on Shenks Ferry paste falls within the established range of design elements for Schultz Incised. One of them (Figure 18) is more like (but not typical of) certain forms seen in the McFate-Quiggle ceramic complex. All of these examples, and several others not shown here, do seem to imply experimentation and exchanges of ideas between groups—but just who was influencing whom and why is not clear.

The Schultz site, where the Susquehannocks, about 1575, built what was apparently their first large town, with a stockade, partially overlaps the stockaded village known as the Funk site, the type site for Funk Incised pottery. The resulting confusion of pits, which was revealed by early archeology at this site (Cadzow 1936), led Witthoft to postulate a captive village of Shenks Ferry people next to the Susquehannock stockade. Subsequent archeology here (Smith 1977) showed that the two villages were separate in time (if not in space) by perhaps 25 years or more.

Archeology at the Schultz site has demonstrated that some Shenks Ferry people were living there with the Susquehannocks. In all likelihood most of these captives or adoptees at the Schultz site more or less became Susquehannocks. A few women, however, continued to make the old-style pottery—Funk Incised—as is made evident by the occasional placement of vessels of this type in Susquehannock graves. For the next 50 years at least, the influence of these Shenks Ferry potters remained a minor but discernible underlying current in the mainstream of Susquehannock pottery. Occasional hybrid forms—very curious admixtures of Susquehannock traits with those of Shenks Ferry—occur as late as the Frey-Haverstick and Roberts sites.

Characteristics of Susquehannock Pottery

Smith (1981a) constructed a list of Schultz Incised traits to which he has compared other shell-tempered potteries. These include: (1) top of the collar bounded by one or two lines of horizontal incising or punctations; (2) broad, shallow incising; (3) triangular, diamond, or rectangular plats combined to form numerous geometric patterns; (4) enclosed right triangular plats filled with elliptical punch marks, short lines of incising, or parallel horizontal incisings; and (5) smoothed collars onto which incising was applied. He notes that what we have here called McFate-Quiggle Incised pottery, from the Quiggle site, by and large has none of these traits.

Early Schultz in the upper Susquehanna much more frequently exhibits some or all five of the traits. Ithaca Linear, as illustrated in the literature, also shows all of these traits. But of even greater interest is the fact that Proto-Susquehannock (although not always on one vessel, but as an overall group or type) also exhibits four of the traits. Perhaps the most significant trait in this regard, and that which Proto-Susquehannock lacks, is that concerning the right triangles, usually on one or both sides of parallel vertical lines under the castellations, which are filled with elliptical punch marks, short lines of incising, or horizontal lines. Proto-Susquehannock never seems to have this. These, perhaps more than anything else, constitute the single most noticeable characteristic of Schultz Incised (and, for that matter, Ithaca Linear).

In spite of all the ceramic trait differences, the overall appearance of McFate-Quiggle pottery is still more like Schultz Incised than is Proto-Susquehannock. The necks of most Proto-Susquehannock vessels are much more apparent, i.e., sharply defined, than on Schultz or McFate-Quiggle.

However, a few modifications of Proto-Susquehannock, viz., the necks, the addition of shell temper, and the use of elliptical punch marks would transform it into Schultz Incised. Again we are suggesting that McFate-Quiggle did not become early Schultz, but rather that it contributed certain ideas which the makers of Proto-Susquehannock adapted or adopted, and which resulted in early Schultz. Quiggle is rejected as a direct ancestor because certain of its other cultural traits (viz., keyhole structures, palisades with external ditches, lack of longhouses) do not show up with early Schultz or classic Schultz. Again, what we seem to be missing are the probably very rare transitional pots between Proto-Susquehannock and early Schultz.

Following the development of early Schultz Incised in the upper Susquehanna, there are four major types of Susquehannock pottery. Each of these is rather neatly associated with a new time period and a new site. Witthoft and Kinsey (1959) and Heisey and Witmer (1962) have rather extensively described the various traits which characterize each of these types. For that reason we have elected not to relist the detailed type descriptions, but rather to provide complete photographs for each type. (Figures 19, 21, 24)

Schultz Incised is clearly the predominant pottery type at the Schultz site. Kinsey (in Witthoft and Kinsey 1959: 95) reports about 61% of the sherd sample from the village area excavated by Cadzow (1936) as being Schultz Incised. Fifteen per cent was recorded as "Low Collar." This type

Figure 19. Susquehannock pottery types. Top left and right: Schultz Incised. Lower left: Schultz Incised. Lower right: Blue Rock Valanced.

Figure 20. Atypical vessel forms from the Susquehannock cemetery at the Schultz-Funk (36La9) site, showing probable western New York influence.

was later redefined by Heisey and Witmer (1962: 111), who dubbed it Blue Rock Valanced. The remaining 19% of the sample was a type called Washington Boro Incised.

More recently excavated samples from the village and two of its cemeteries suggest a considerably lower percentage of the type Washington Boro Incised. Nevertheless, it was present at the Schultz site and therefore clearly had its beginning there. Sufficient transitional pots exist to show that Washington Boro Incised evolved from Schultz Incised. The third type at the Schultz site, Blue Rock Valanced, has no antecedents whatsoever in Susquehannock tradition. It appears for the first time at the Schultz site, as if out of nowhere—unless we look to the Seneca and Cayuga relatives of the Susquehannocks. Its relationship to Genoa Frilled (MacNeish 1952: 50-51) of the Seneca sequence is especially undeniable. The only real difference is that Genoa Frilled is made with a grit-tempered paste.

A small amount of Genoa Frilled was reported from the Richmond Mills site (MacNeish 1952: 39), which has since produced a few trade goods typical of the first half of the sixteenth century. If these trade goods also apply to the Genoa Frilled material from the site, the type is clearly earlier than Blue Rock Valanced at the Schultz site—and logically the source of it. The presence of Blue Rock Valanced (or shell-tempered Genoa Frilled) at the Schultz site may well represent an influx of Seneca or Cayuga potters—perhaps as captives of the Susquehannocks.

We have already noted the remarkable similarity between Schultz Incised and Ithaca Linear. Again, the major difference is in the temper. Schultz Incised seems rather securely dated to at least 1550, if not earlier at the Engelbert site. Thus far Ithaca Linear in the Cayuga or Seneca areas does not appear to be so early. The amount of Ithaca Linear on Cayuga or Seneca sites does not seem well established in the literature; however, on no

Cayuga or Seneca site does it appear to be nearly as predominant as is Schultz Incised at the Schultz site.

We might reassert our earlier suggestion that Ithaca Linear is derived from Schultz Incised, and that its presence on Seneca and Cayuga sites may represent their having taken Susquehannock captives.

Whatever the conditions under which these ceramic technologies were exchanged between Susquehannock and Cayuga-Seneca—either friendly or aggressive—the fact remains that the exchanges did occur.

Washington Boro Incised reaches its peak of popularity at the next site

Figure 21. Washington Boro Incised pots, from the Washington Boro village and its cemetery sites.

in the Susquehannock sequence. This is the Washington Boro village site, occupied from about 1600 to 1625. Here Washington Boro Incised comprised about 70% of the ceramic sample. Although Kinsey's chart (in Witthoft and Kinsey 1959: 95) would suggest otherwise, the actual percentage of Blue Rock Valanced for the total Washington Boro village and cemetery complex is more like 10 to 15% of the sample. We also note a certain degree of grafting of Washington Boro Incised design elements onto the collars of Blue Rock Valanced.

The actual percentages of these types at the Washington Boro site vary considerably, depending upon whether we are looking at samples from the village or one of four known cemeteries. As Kinsey's chart (1959: 95) shows, about 27% of the pottery from the village site (the Eschelman site) is Schultz Incised. However, the amount of Schultz Incised used as burial offerings is considerably less. The old-style pottery, viz., Schultz Incised, while still being rather widely used as cooking ware, was much less popular as an item to accompany the dead. Washington Boro Incised vessels, whether funerary pots or utilitarian cookware, rarely exceeded 14 inches in height and 12 inches in diameter. Schultz Incised pots, on the other hand, were frequently this size or larger. The largest in the WPMM collections measures over 21 inches in height and about 16 inches in diameter.

The next type of pottery in the sequence was just beginning to make its appearance at Washington Boro. This is Strickler Cord-marked, which technologically seems to represent a deterioration in certain aspects of Susquehannock ceramic arts.

Following the occupation of the Washington Boro village, it would appear that two new towns were established. At least there are two sites which produced trade goods and pottery of the sort we would expect after about 1630. These are the Roberts and Billmyer Quarry sites, neither of which is well known. The small ceramic samples from both sites are predominantly Washington Boro Incised, but the trade goods are more like those from Strickler—thus their placement in the interim between Washington Boro and Strickler. The available sample from the Roberts site consists of only seven pots. Two of these are represented by sherds excavated by Cadzow (1936) from one pit. One is Washington Boro Incised, the other is Strickler Cord-marked. Another restored pot recovered by Cadzow is also Strickler Cord-marked. Of the remaining four complete pots recovered during limited excavations in 1971, two are very debased forms of Washington Boro Incised, one is a Seneca pot (Figure 22), and the other is an unusual nondescript cord-marked vessel.

Our sample from the Frey-Haverstick site, which as suggested elsewhere is largely contemporaneous with the early occupation of Roberts, is somewhat larger and perhaps more instructive. It consists of 22 pots, 12 (55%)

Figure 22. Atypical forms from Susquehannock graves at the Roberts site (36La1). Left: shows Seneca influence.

of which are Washington Boro Incised, four (18%) Blue Rock Valanced, two Schultz Incised (9%), and four Shenks Ferry-Susquehannock hybrids (18%). There were no recorded examples of Strickler Cord-marked pottery.

As we have indicated elsewhere, the Frey-Haverstick Susquehannock cemetery, although close to the Washington Boro village site, was not strictly contemporary with the town; rather it seems to be the cemetery for those perhaps more tradition-oriented Susquehannocks who wanted to bury their dead near the old town, and who had not yet adopted the new style of pottery, Strickler Cord-marked.

Strickler Cord-marked is the last pottery type in the Susquehannock sequence. It just begins to appear in the last years of settlement at the Washington Boro village, and it reaches its zenith at the Strickler and Upper and Lower Leibhart sites. Blue Rock Valanced pottery does not occur at these sites, and Schultz Incised is only vaguely present as debased forms or as antiques. Washington Boro Incised accounts for about 25% of the ceramic sample from the village area at Strickler and about 15% from the cemeteries. These percentages, based on 127 vessels from the Funk-Strickler cemetery, support the figures given by Kinsey (1959: 95); however, the more recent data from the village show that Washington Boro Incised was somewhat more popular than the cemetery samples would suggest.

The more recent data from the Lower (Byrd) Leibhart site show approximately the same distribution of Washington Boro Incised and Strickler Cord-marked from the village, i.e., 21% vs. 78%. Washington Boro Incised is much less abundant in the cemetery sample (about 7%), but not, as Kinsey (1959: 95) indicated, totally absent.

Kinsey (1959: 88-90) described two basic varieties of Strickler Cord-marked: rounded collar and flared rim, and an intermediate form with narrow, thickened collars. In our opinion this latter form, although rare

Table 4

WASHINGTON BORO INCISED AND STRICKLER CORD-MARKED

	Washington Boro Incised	*collared*	*flared*	*rounded*	*total*
Yol70*	3	2	25	15	45
(%)	(6.7)	(4.4)	(55.6)	(33.3)	(100.0)
La3	11	4	74	27	116
(%)	(9.5)	(3.4)	(63.8)	(23.3)	(100.0)
La4	60	3	9	1	73
(%)	(82.2)	(4.1)	(12.3)	(1.4)	(100.0)
Total	74	9	108	43	234
(%)	(31.6)	(3.8)	(46.2)	(18.4)	(100.0)

*Includes counts from the G. Keller collection.

(never more than about 10% of any one Strickler Cord-marked sample), should constitute a third variety.

Kinsey (1959: 88) notes that the temper of Strickler Cord-marked is crushed mussel shell in small proportions—about 5%. Our observations suggest that a majority of this pottery has no apparent aplastic whatsoever.

The vast majority of Strickler Cord-marked in its three vessel forms have no incised decoration, and vessels are entirely covered with marks from the cord-wrapped paddle. Exceptions which occur on a few vessels include punctates, small notches and simple incised designs. The latter are exceedingly rare, and may in fact be foreign pots.

This type is usually described as being the product of ceramic degeneration brought on by acculturation and the increasing availability of the more functional brass kettles. In fact, Strickler Cord-marked exhibits a complete departure from the elaborate incised designs of the preceding types; it does appear to represent a degeneration in pottery decoration techniques. However, a majority of Strickler Cord-marked examples, even though made in very simple or basic forms, are in fact technologically fairly good pottery. The type is usually quite symmetrical in outline—generally more so than the preceding types—and overall it is slightly harder and more durable than other Susquehannock types. This latter factor may be a condition of the decrease or absence of shell-tempering.

As a group, Strickler Cord-marked pots are noticeably smaller than the preceding types. Miniature pots and paint cups are more abundant than before. Much of the Strickler Cord-marked pottery found placed in graves appears to have been made for just that purpose. Pottery found in refuse or storage pits in Strickler-period towns is not nearly as abundant as in the earlier sites. The pottery from such pits, presumably utilitarian cookware, also appears to represent much smaller pots than those made at Washington Boro or Schultz.

Reasons for this decrease in vessel sizes are probably several. First of all, most Strickler Cord-marked pottery was made to be used as burial furniture, and the size of the meal which it contained need not have been large. In common parlance, it was the thought that counted, and not the quantity of food which accompanied the dead. During the Strickler period it is

Figure 23. Hybrid forms showing McFate-Quiggle, Shenks Ferry and Susquehannock interrelations. Top left: Keller cemetery (36La4, 1.258). Top right: Frey-Haverstick (36La6). Lower left: Roberts (36La1). Lower right: (36La6).

unlikely that very much cooking was done in pottery vessels. They were of course useful as household containers. Rarely do they show the charred cooking residue found on the brass kettles or seen on many of the pots from the middens and refuse pits of the earlier sites. By Strickler times, brass kettles had clearly become the most efficient way to cook; clay pots were reduced to use as containers and grave offerings. If this is not true and these pots were frequently used for cooking, then we are looking at a switch from the large family-group pots of Washington Boro times to individual meals prepared in much smaller pots—a situation which seems most unlikely.

The evolution of Schultz Incised to Washington Boro Incised is fairly easy to follow. A number of good transitional pieces exist which suggest the gradual crossover from one to the other. However, the antecedents for Strickler Cord-marked are not nearly so apparent. On the surface, at least, Strickler Cord-marked would seem to represent a sharp and strict departure from the traditional high-collared and elaborately incised Susquehannock pottery. To account for this we might posit any number of causal factors. We have already mentioned possible degeneration as a result of acculturation, or availability of brass kettles. Anthropologists often attribute such rapid and radical changes in cultural traditions to new outside influences. None of these factors, by itself, seems to account for the obvious ceramic changes which occurred. Rather, it may be that all of them came into play in bringing about these shifts.

The distribution of the three forms of Strickler Cord-marked pottery by sites (Table 5) does little to suggest any chronological ordering of these forms. By plotting the distribution of Strickler Cord-marked without reference to the other types which occur at the sites, there is a hint that the thickened-collar forms may be more abundant in the earlier sites, and that the rounded-collar forms may have a greater popularity in the later sites (Table 5). The early placement of thickened-collar forms is not apparent in Table 4, which includes Washington Boro Incised in the sample.

Table 5

STRICKLER CORD-MARKED

	collared	*flared*	*rounded*	*total*
Yol70	2	25	15	42
(%)	(4.8)	(59.5)	(35.7)	(100.0)
La3	4	74	27	105
(%)	(3.8)	(70.5)	(25.7)	(100.0)
Wash. Boro	3	9	1	13
(%)	(23.1)	(69.2)	(7.7)	(100.0)
Total	9	108	43	160
(%)	(5.6)	(67.5)	(26.9)	(100.0)

Figure 24. Varieties of Strickler Cord-marked pottery from the Strickler site (36La3). Top left: Flaired rim. Top right: rounded collar. Lower left: rounded collar with applied "ladders." Lower right: thickened collar.

With the large sample of Susquehannock pottery available in the WPMM collections (over three hundred complete or restored vessels), it is possible to lay out a sequence of pots which shows a trend from Blue Rock Valanced into forms with diminished lobes and collars which approximate or actually become the thickened-collar form of Strickler Cord-marked. This latter form was produced by adding a band or strip of clay to a vessel with a flared collar. Pinching this strip around the base of the now-formed collar produces the diminutive lobes which characterize this form of Strickler Cord-marked. By not adding (and pinching) this strip of clay, the potter had produced what we have called the flared-rim variety of Strickler Cord-marked.

Some Blue Rock Valanced vessels, in addition to their lobes, have three or four encircling lines roughly incised above the lobes around the top portion of their collars. Several pots from Washington Boro have these same simple, encircling lines, but no thickened collars and no lobes—thus they become flared-rim vessels with encircling incised lines.

Several of these simple, flared-rim vessel forms were also found at the Schultz site. The only difference in these is that they have nicks or gashes across the lips of the rims. As such, they are probably foreign pots, perhaps from western New York. In any event, it is doubtful that these have anything to do with the development of Strickler Cord-marked.

This form, with only cord-marked surfaces, also occurred on Monongahela sites, Fort Ancient (Madisonville), much earlier Shenks Ferry, and in limited numbers at Lancaster phase Shenks Ferry sites in Bainbridge. These latter pot forms, including shell temper (as described by Kent 1974), are incredibly like Strickler Cord-marked. However, their chronological separation by over one hundred years makes any relationship between them impossible—or so it would seem.

Several Fort Ancient (Madisonville phase, see Hooton 1920) shell-tempered, flared-rim vessels, both with and without strap handles, have been found on Susquehannock sites, particularly at the Byrd Leibhart site. This documents contacts between the Susquehannocks and peoples of the upper Ohio Valley, and may therefore be one source of influence for this pot form.

The fact that the flared-rim form is so simplistic might well suggest that no major outside influence was necessary for it to be made by the Susquehannocks and become the predominant form after 1650. The fact remains that they were caught up in a trend to simplify pottery by dropping incised decorations and producing very basic forms. The relationship between this and the thickened-collar form is unquestionable. All that is necessary is to delete the thin strip of clay to thicken the collar, and presto—we have the flared-rim form. If the thickened-collar form is derived from Blue Rock Valanced by simplifying and diminishing the lobes, we have the developmental sequence for these two forms of Strickler Cord-marked.

At least 60% of the flared-rim forms have three or four castellations. About half of the pots with castellations have them bent outward (Figure 24) or down, almost against the wall of the vessel, to form lugs. One might get the impression that these were intended to mimic either the castellations of the Washington Boro Incised pots, or, when bent outward or downward, to call to mind the face effigies of Washington Boro Incised or the lobes of Blue Rock Valanced.

The rounded-collar forms of Strickler Cord-marked are equally difficult, and yet not impossible, to derive from earlier Susquehannock forms. Some vessel forms of Washington Boro Incised seem to foreshadow the shape of this Strickler Cord-marked variety. Those Washington Boro Incised vessels which do so, exhibit very poorly incised decorations, and generally they are from post-Washington Boro village sites, such as Roberts or Strickler. Most of the Washington Boro Incised pottery from the Leibhart sites is quite degenerate in form and design motifs.

Leaving the cord-wrapped paddle impressions on the vessels of this shape, while deleting the traditional incised designs and lessening or eliminating the shell temper, describes in essence the manufacture of a rounded-collar Strickler Cord-marked pot. However, the sequence of cultural events which led to this change is hardly so simple to reconstruct.

The pottery vessel form which looks most like this variety of Strickler Cord-marked is Funk Incised of the Shenks Ferry sequence. Here, too, the chronological gap between the two would seem to negate any relationship, for very little pure Funk Incised was made after 1600 A.D.

Without question, Shenks Ferry potters were adopted by the Susquehannocks. Hybrid pots of Shenks Ferry designs on Susquehannock paste, and vice versa, particularly at the Shenks Ferry site, are good evidence of their interaction. Funk Incised vessels in Susquehannock burials (at Schultz, and at least one example at the Keller cemetery at Washington Boro, catalogue number 1258) provide further evidence. Even though we can point to only one Funk Incised vessel in association with post-Schultz Susquehannock burials, a number of pots exhibit a curious admixture of Susquehannock and Shenks Ferry ceramic ideas.

At the Frey-Haverstick site, two side-by-side burials disclosed an array of such pots. One of them (La6/120) produced trade beads, an axe, a hoe, a Washington Boro Incised vessel, and a Blue Rock Valanced vessel inside of which was a shell-tempered pot of Washington Boro Incised form, but with Shenks Ferry-like incised decorations. The second burial (La6/121), a few inches to the east and with the same orientation, produced three shell-tempered pots with very definite Shenks Ferry-like decorations. The burial also included lumps of red ochre, a seldom-encountered trait for Shenks Ferry. One of these pots (La6/121) has a form very much like that of the rounded-collar Strickler Cord-marked.

Two of the pots found at the Roberts site (Lal/4, Lal/8) show very crude attempts to produce Washington Boro Incised motifs, as though they were done by very inept potters or by someone with a somewhat different template for pottery decoration. Both pots have very small amounts of shell-tempering, but the pottery has a very gritty feel, like Shenks Ferry paste. Both also exhibit a tendency toward the rounded-collar form.

All of this would seem to confirm that within the Susquehannock communities there were adopted Shenks Ferry people and their descendants, albeit heavily intermarried and inbred with Susquehannocks, and that some of them maintained certain of the old Shenks Ferry customs regarding the making and decorating of pottery. These old ideas seem to have survived more as an underlying current that surfaces for us today in a few strange pots which are cumbersome mixtures of Shenks Ferry and the dominant Susquehannock.

When we add to this picture all of the other adoptees—certainly various Iroquois, various Algonquian, and probably some Monongahela and Fort Ancient folk, each with its own heritage of ethnic ceramic traditions—it is not surprising that the changes in "Susquehannock" pottery during the seventeenth century were curiously complex.

It is neither impossible nor unlikely that a few "Susquehannocks" of the mid-seventeenth century who had some Shenks Ferry ancestry would strive (perhaps unconsciously) to produce a pottery form which in some crude way reflected their heritage. Without real good evidence for doing so, we are suggesting that rounded-collar Strickler Cord-marked, although partially derived from Washington Boro Incised, represents a resurgence of ceramic traditions among those Susquehannocks who had a bit of Shenks Ferry in them.

Another curious feature of the rounded-collar Strickler Cord-marked is that about 30% of the vessels have applied vertical strips of clay which have been gashed horizontally, giving them a ladder-like appearance. These ladders appear under castellations, and these castellations, like those on the flared-rim pots, are either vertical or are flared outward. A few ladder-like motifs appear as incising under the castellations on a very small percentage of Schultz Incised vessels. And, at the Schultz site, there was at least one vessel, otherwise very like the pottery from the Quiggle site, which had the applied strip ladders (La9/116).

Our guess is that the ladders on the rounded-collar, Strickler Cord-marked vessels are very stylized representations of full-figure effigies which appear on some Washington Boro Incised pots. When the full bodies appear as applied strips of clay, they are invariably decorated with horizontal gashes.

Perhaps we have gone too far in attempting to trace the relationships of the various types of Susquehannock pottery. When so many combinations of design elements occur, we can pretty much see or not see what we want in terms of tracing the changes. We can say, without question, that it is all "Susquehannock" pottery with various infusions from other tribal groups. The combinations and recombinations brought about by the processes of evolution (or simple style change) and diffusion are usually apparent, but always difficult to account for.

Sometime between the defeat and dispersal of the Susquehannocks in 1675 and their resettling at Conestoga in 1690, the art of pottery-making and the need for it were lost.

Native Pipes of Clay

Similarities between the material culture of the Susquehannocks and the Iroquois are most pronounced in the comparison of their antler combs and clay smoking pipes. Specimens in both categories from Iroquois and Susquehannock sites are often identical and virtually inseparable without provenience (see Rutsch 1973 for numerous illustrations and a discussion of Iroquois pipes).

The evolution of Susquehannock and Iroquois combs and pipes is one and the same until about the beginning of the seventeenth century. After 1600 a separate but parallel evolution begins. Differences do not really become apparent until about 1650 and after.

In essence, this pipe evolution grows from an Owasco base. The earliest recognizable Iroquoian-Susquehannock forms are the so-called trumpet pipes. Most of these are plain, i.e., without any incised or impressed designs. Chronologically the ring bowls are next in the sequence, but these are not clearly an outgrowth or evolution from the trumpet pipes. If anything, the two forms have a common evolutionary base in the preceding Owasco forms—from which they may have developed separately.

A few large, rather clumsy ring bowl pipes occurred at the Schultz site, and this is probably their earliest appearance. Ring bowls were outnumbered by trumpets at Schultz by more than two to one. However, by Washington Boro times they occurred in equal numbers. No trumpet pipes have been found in sites later than Washington Boro, but the ring bowls continue, with diminishing popularity, into the Strickler period.

A possible third (but minor) type at the Schultz site is illustrated in Figure 25a (La7/463). Its antecedents, and indeed the successor of this form, are not at all apparent in the local sequences. It may have its roots in earlier Shenks Ferry pipes, or it may be a variant (without the flaring mouth) of the trumpet pipe. Except for its near right angle between stem and bowl, it might also be thought to bear a relationship to certain pipes of the Maryland and Virginia tidewater area.

Effigy pipes, that is, variously formed bowls (but most frequently a ring bowl) which incorporate, or have attached, animal, geometric or human figures, are next in the sequence. At least two such pipes are known from the Schultz site, one of which (Figure 26) had a well-fashioned, clay owls' head extending from the bowl. Effigy forms are only slightly more common at Washington Boro, but, toward the end of this period and in the interim between Washington Boro and Strickler—namely at Haverstick—

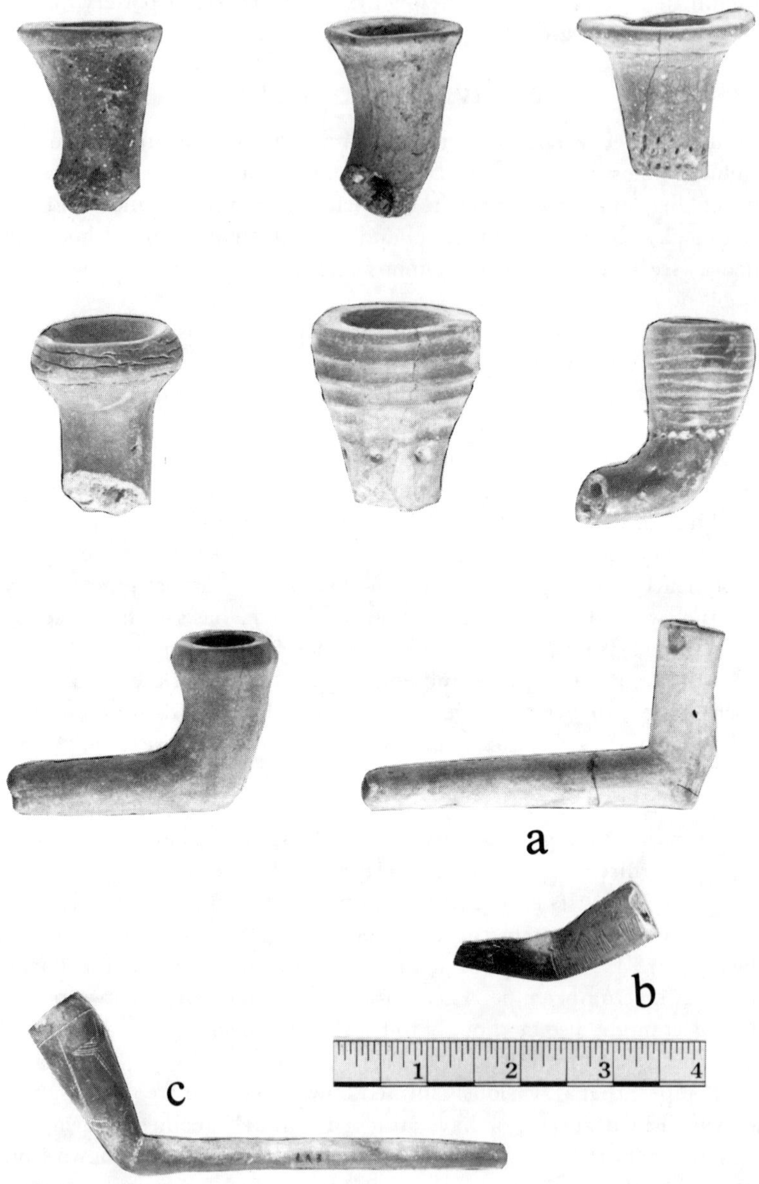

Figure 25. Smoking pipes. Top: trumpets. Second row: ring-bowls. Third row: miscellaneous (36La7). a, b and c (see text).

some very fine effigy pipes were produced (Figure 26). Such pipes proliferate at Strickler and their variety also increases. Bird forms are the most common. Effigy forms have been found at both Leibhart sites, but they are much fewer; in fact, those which have been found are probably antique carry-overs from Strickler.

The latest pipe form in the Susquehannock sequence is the tulip bowl (Figure 27). Its earliest occurrence is at the Roberts site, and probably also at Billmyer. These pipes became the rage at Strickler—where they comprised 70% of the sample. Plain tulip bowls are by far the most common (65% of the tulip bowls are plain). At least ten of the tulip pipes from the sample at Strickler, and several from the Leibhart sites, were painted, either completely in red, or with dark (probably black) spiraling bands on the stems. Surfaces of the tulip pipes are generally quite smooth, and usually light tan or yellow in color. They are not burnished like the ring bowl and many effigy pipes, which often have a dark brown surface color. It seems likely that many more of the tulip types were painted, but that the colors have not survived.

Tulip bowl pipes evolve from the ring bowls. On the earlier end of the ring bowl spectrum, the bowls are heavy, with rather wide, clumsy rings. On the later end, the bowls become more tulip-like, with much finer rings. These later ones are not easily separated from those which we have designated tulip bowls. This fact is in itself evidence for the evolution of tulip bowls from ring bowls.

Tulip bowls, and a few with horizontal incised bands (late ring bowl-tulip transitional pieces), continued to be made at the Leibhart sites, but in numbers fewer than at Strickler. At the Lower Leibhart site the ratio of all native pipes to kaolin pipes is roughly two to one, as compared to a ratio of ten to one at Strickler.

One typical tulip pipe was found at the Piscataway fort and is in fact the only real archeological evidence for identifying the Susquehannock occupation of that site in 1676 (Stephenson et al. 1963: 137-38).

It is most interesting to note that although the ring bowls, and particularly the specific forms of effigy pipes as found on both Seneca and Susquehannock sites, are virtually indistinguishable (compare Rutsch 1973: 178-221), the tulip bowl pipes do not occur on Seneca sites except as very rare transported pieces from the Susquehannocks. Ring bowl pipes and various effigy forms seem to be more abundant and are earlier in the Seneca sequence, and they continue throughout the period when tulip bowls were most popular among the Susquehannocks.

During the 1931 excavations at the Strickler site cemetery (southeast cemetery), Cadzow recovered a single example of what is sometimes called a "Tidewater" pipe (Figure 25c). This pipe form clearly has its center of distribution in the tidewater areas of Maryland and Virginia. Chronologically, most of them seem to pertain to the second half of the seventeenth century. However, a date of 1550 or earlier is definitely implied by the discovery of one of this type (Figure 25b) in a Shenks Ferry pit at the Schultz-Funk site (cat. #La9/146).

A common characteristic of this pipe type is its very fine "watchwheel" or "roulette dentate" impressions, usually on the bowls of the pipes. The most frequent designs, which are filled and sometimes outlined with the

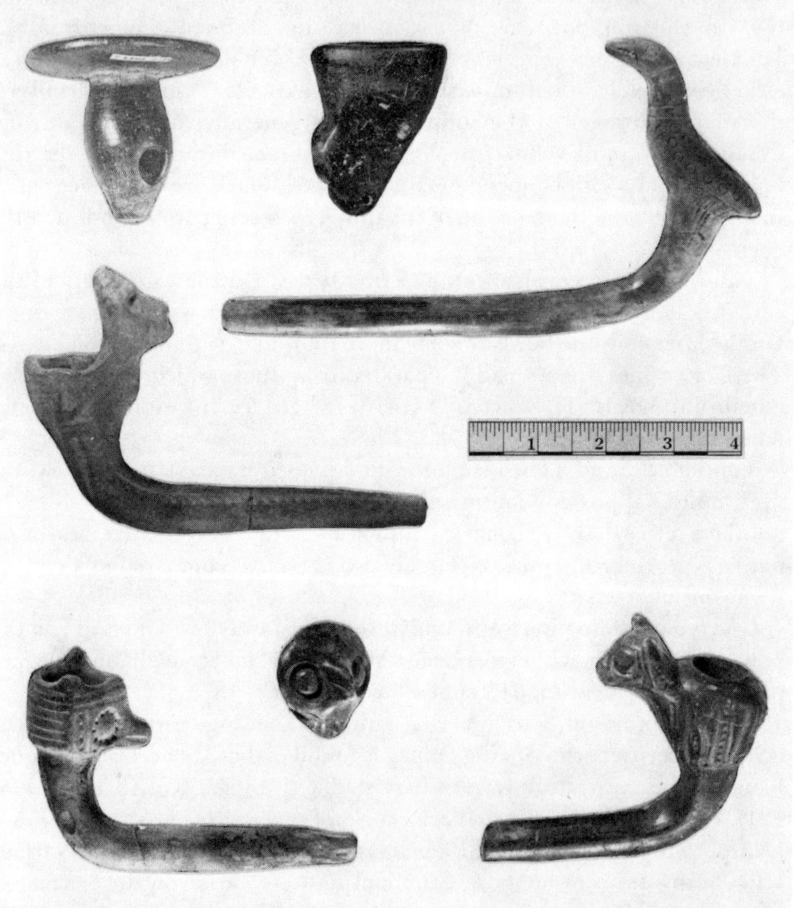

Figure 26. Susquehannock smoking pipes. Top left to right: steatite disc calumet, Strickler (36La3, Futer collection); steatite vasiform, Keller site (36La4); clay bird (36La3). Second row: clay human form, Frey-Haverstick (36La6). Bottom left to right: clay bird (36La6); clay owl, Schultz (36La7); clay bear with brass eyes, Byrd Leibhart (36Yo170).

Figure 27. Tulip-bowl clay smoking pipes. Note painted stems, left and fourth specimen from left, all from the Strickler site (36La3). Right side: Seneca pipe form from Conestoga Town (36La52).

dentate impressions, are running-deer and geometric patterns, including a frequent "star shape" (see Blaker 1963: 27-29; Mitchell 1976: 83-92; and Henry 1979: 14-37). The "star shape" appears on the very early example cited above from the Schultz-Funk site.

The great quantities of these pipes from certain seventeenth-century colonial sites in Maryland and Virginia have led some researchers (cf. Henry 1979) to further investigate the possibility that certain categories of these pipes were of colonial manufacture.

Many of these so-called terra-cotta (Henry 1979) or brown clay (Mitchell 1976) pipes from these sites show rather definite European styling and decorative design. However, many also exhibit very Indian-oriented designs, e.g., the various running-deer and geometric patterns. All of this *might* suggest that both Indian and colonial manufacturers are represented in the "Tidewater" pipes.

The specimen from the Strickler site (Figure 25c) has on its bowl two running deer. Both its overall shape and the details of its decoration make it unlike any other Susquehannock pipe with rouletted designs. This design

a
1
2
3
4

technique was employed on a limited number of Susquehannock pipes, particularly at Strickler (Figure 27). Some of these have rather atypical Susquehannock bowl forms. Generally the rouletting on them is not as fine (individual imprints are not as close or small) as that on the "Tidewater" pipes; nor are the designs often very similar. However, the fact that certain Susquehannocks did employ this design technique suggests a borrowing and therefore a relationship of some sort with the pipes of the Tidewater area.

During the 20 years following the Leibhart sites, the manufacture of locally made native pipes stops completely. No such pipes were found at Conestoga Town.

Nine non-local, native-made pipes were recovered at Conestoga Town in 1972. One of these (Figure 27) is ceramic. We have not seen this particular form on any Susquehannock sites, but it is definitely a Seneca pipe form which appears at the Boughton Hill site (1670-1687) and continues to Hooten site times (1710-1730). A very similar clay pipe, found at Lock Haven, is in the Stewart collection (see also Holmes 1903: Plate CLVI). In the same grave at Conestoga Town which produced this clay pipe, there was also an unusual calumet form of dense, rather hard, grey stone (Figure 31). This pipe has a vertically drilled hole through the heel which protrudes beyond the bowl. It also has incised zig-zag lines on the top and two sides of the stem. The remaining stone pipes from Conestoga will be discussed later.

Native Pipes of Stone

Other than an occasional Adena tubular pipe or various Middle Woodland forms, little evidence of stone pipes in the Susquehanna Valley prior to Susquehannock times has been found. The earliest Susquehannock stone pipes come from the Schultz site, and the few which do occur here are all made of steatite. The execution of the steatite pipes from the Schultz site is quite crude. It is not until the Washington Boro period that we see any really well-carved pipes of this stone. Birds, animals, and human faces appear as protrusions (usually on the fronts) of the bowls.

The greatest variety of forms and number of steatite pipes occur at the Strickler site. Figures 26, 29 show some of the most unusual steatite pipes from this site. A platform pipe is in the Heisey collection at Franklin and

Figure 28, opposite. Smoking pipes with human forms. Top left: clay, front of bowl, Schacht (36Lu1). Top right: replica, Wermuth (36Lu2). Second row left: stone, Warren County. Right: steatite with three human faces, Wyoming Valley. (a) Front and side view of a steatite pipe from Strickler (36La3).

Marshall College, and was found in the southeast cemetery. One pipe in Figure 29 was incised to receive pewter inlays. It and the human form (Figure 28) are in the William Penn Memorial Museum collections from the northeast cemetery. An interesting feature of this human-form pipe (found in a child burial) is the anus that is drilled through to the bowl. By placing a finger over the lit bowl and blowing out, the smoker could have expelled smoke through this orifice. Another pipe in Figure 26 is in the Art Futer collection and is also from the northeast cemetery. This is a vasiform pipe surmounted by a disc and is quite similar to the western Great Lakes area

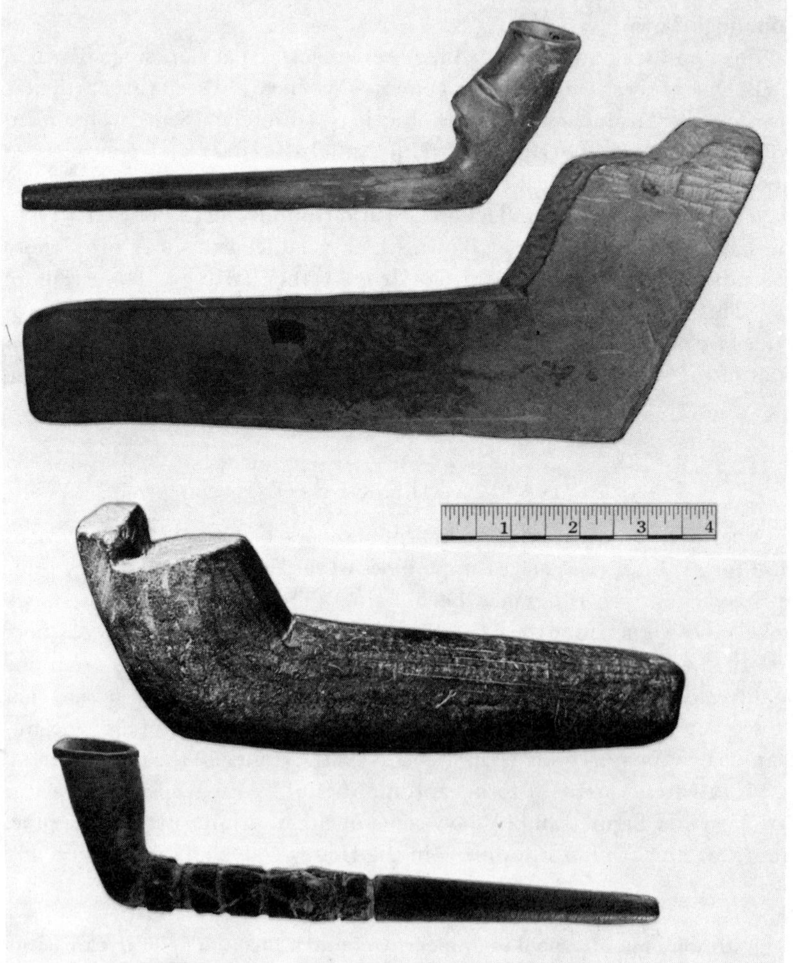

Figure 29. Steatite pipes and blanks from Susquehannock sites. Top to bottom: (36La3); blank (36La3); (36La4); inlaid with pewter (36La3).

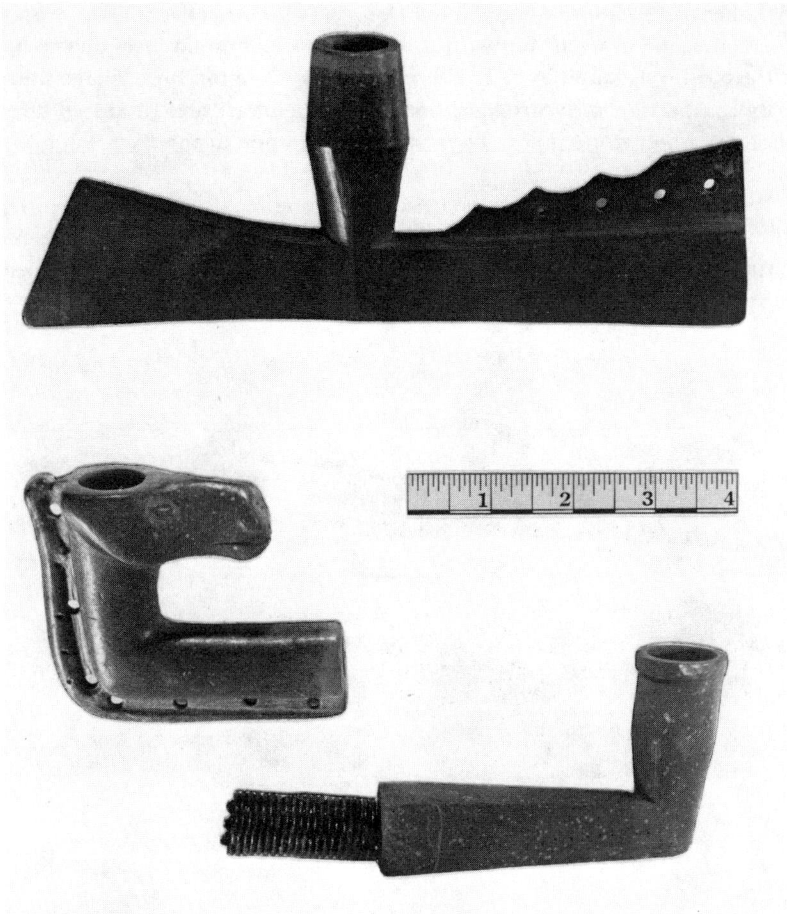

Figure 30. Catlinite pipes from Conestoga Town (36La52). Bottom: brass coil around wooden stem.

disc calumet, and as such is a rather early example of this pipe form. This specimen appears to be made of steatite-related serpentine. The Futer collection also includes a steatite vasiform pipe with a small drill hole through its base (see Kinsey 1958: Figure E). Vase shapes (and variants thereof) are not common on Susquehannock sites. A curious, rather vase-shaped pipe was found by Cadzow at the Keller cemetery associated with the Washington Boro village site. This specimen (Figure 26) has two exceedingly similar relatives at the Oscar Leibhart site. One of these, when found, had a brass chain attached to a hole in its base (Kinsey 1958: Figure I). This pipe, and the other like it, are presently in the Donald Leibhart collection. A pipe of this same general form, but with three protruding human faces on the lip of the bowl, was found by S. S. Farver at the Washington Boro village site.

By comparison with Strickler, both of the Leibhart sites produced considerably fewer stone pipes. They are least common at the Byrd Leibhart site.

We have previously mentioned two of the non-local, native-made pipes from Conestoga. The remaining seven specimens are exceedingly fine examples of western Great Lakes area catlinite calumets. These are described

Figure 31. Calumet pipes. Top two rows: catlinite forms from Conestoga Town (36La52). Third row left: catlinite from Strickler (36La3). Right: slate from Wapwallopen (36Lu43). Bottom: grey slate from Conestoga Town.

under Catlinite, and are illustrated in Figures 30, 31 with a very early catlinite calumet found at the Strickler site. Fragments of what are probably two separate catlinite pipes are in a private collection from the site of the Shawnee town at the mouth of Chillisquaque Creek in Northumberland County. Another broken calumet of catlinite was found in Wrightsville and is now in the Wanner collection at the Indian Steps Museum in York County, Pennsylvania. In 1978 a grey slate calumet was excavated at the site of Wapwallopen in Luzerne County (Figure 31).

No native-made pipes were found during the William Penn Memorial Museum excavations at Conoy Town. However, the Museum's collection does include a hard, grey shale Micmac pipe found by S. S. Farver on the surface of the village area (Witthoft, Schoff and Wray 1953: Plate 2, no. 19). Micmac pipes are not very common in the Susquehanna Valley, but some have been found in the vicinity of Lock Haven and elsewhere on the West Branch, and may have been associated with mid-eighteenth-century Delaware and Shawnee sites (Witthoft, Schoff and Wray 1953). A broken Micmac pipe was found near the site of Fort Augusta (Shamokin?) during the 1978 excavations there by the Northumberland County Historical Society.

Witthoft (et al. 1953: 90) has concluded that the Micmac pipe, although it had certain of its roots in the earlier vasiform pipes, was otherwise a derivative ("diffuse copy") of the Plains calumet.

In summary, we can trace a general evolution of Susquehannock pipes growing out of earlier Iroquoian and Owasco ceramic forms. Smoking had a very modest beginning among the early northern Pennsylvania Susquehannocks, and even at the Schultz site after 1575, it was still not a widespread habit. Trumpet and ring bowl forms were the most common shapes at this time, but a few steatite and even some antler and, probably, wooden pipes were in use. By the time (1600) the Susquehannocks settled at the Washington Boro village, smoking was becoming more popular. Ring bowls were the favored form, but the variety of steatite pipes was increasing and their quality improving. No kaolin pipes appear yet, but various forms of brass pipes do occur. By the time of the Strickler site (1645) the habit was widespread among the Susquehannocks; and if we can judge by grave associations, women and children, as well as men, were addicted to tobacco. The tulip bowl, which evolved out of the ring bowl, was the most abundant form. But here too we see a great deal of individualized pipe designs, not only in clay but also in steatite and other stones. Kaolin pipes were quite available, and by the period of the Leibhart sites, they were as abundant as the native tulip bowls.

Native-made pipes, at least locally produced ones, stop very abruptly with the end of Susquehannock political and military power in 1675. After that date we find only kaolin pipes and ones imported from midwestern Indian cultures. The catlinite calumets were the most outstanding of these. They were buried with, and presumably used by, both males and females of all ages. In addition, the calumets had been an important part of a pan-Indian ceremonialism, which was frequently displayed at various meetings between whites and Indians. The calumet was smoked to encourage honor and truth among the speakers, and wampum belts were given in confirmation of these truths.

Lithic Tools

Lithics, as a category of raw materials used by the Indians, is presented here as rather a miscellany. Several classes of stone objects which occur on historic-period sites are discussed elsewhere, e.g., stone pipes and native gunflints.

Triangular projectile points with isosceles to equilateral outlines are the most common worked-stone objects on Susquehannock sites of the sixteenth and most of the seventeenth centuries. As indicated elsewhere, in the lower valley they were most commonly fashioned from local quartz, but were closely followed in frequency by various cherts, most of which were also derived from local sources. Triangular points of other stones, such as jasper, chalcedony, rhyolite, quartzite and others, are quite rare anywhere in the Susquehanna Valley. In the North and West branches of the Susquehanna, triangular points were most commonly made of chert.

On the mid- to late-seventeenth-century Susquehannock sites, all of which are in the lower valley, native gunflints become the most numerous worked-stone items.

For those sites which were occupied prior to the introduction of European metals, one might expect that chipped-stone knives would be one of the next most common items. In point of fact, stone knives of any descrip-

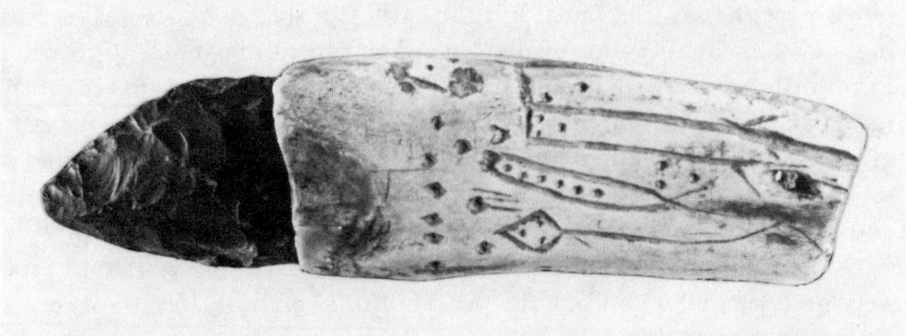

Figure 32. Flint knife and decorated bone handle (4 3/4 inches long) from the Sheep Rock Shelter (36Hul).

Figure 33. Bone and antler tools from Susquehannock sites. Top: harpoon. Left to right: three flaking tools; two fishhooks; three miniature war clubs, Keller (36La4).

tion are quite rare at all Susquehannock sites. Those stone tools which are generally classed as knives are more or less ovate in outline. Three or four bone handles for such knives have been found at several sites. One of these, from the Sheep Rock Shelter, was found in close proximity to an ovate knife which seems to fit very well in this decorated handle (Figure 32). But again, and most surprisingly, both the bone handles and the ovate knives are exceedingly rare on Susquehannock sites.

Other items, such as flakes (which show the proper evidence), or splits from pebbles (teshoas), or even triangular points used as knives, are also rare, all of which leaves us in the dark as to what these people were using for the daily chores of cutting, butchering, etc. Abundant, sharp, chert and quartz flakes with no obvious evidence of use, could have served as "pick-up" tools for short-term cutting, and perhaps therein lies the answer to the question about the knives of the early Susquehannock sites. From 1650 onward there were certainly enough iron knives available so that everyone had at least one.

The scraper, another stone tool which we would expect to be quite important, is also rather rare. Those which have been identified as such are quite crude, being little more than utilized chunks of quartz or chert, or occasionally a rough bifacial form.

Figure 34. Stone tools. Top: notched disks (hoes?). Bottom left to right: milling stone; hoe; two celts, Schultz (36La7).

Following projectile points in order of abundance in the pre-contact sites are the so-called netsinkers. Those from Susquehannock sites, particularly in the lower valley, are not the classic small, flat pebble with two notches. Instead they are more often flat (sometimes laterally chipped) stones with irregular outlines, and they often weigh several pounds. It has been suggested that some of these may have been used as hoes. Higher up the Susquehanna Valley, more of the "classic" netsinkers are found, but since the Susquehannock sites there often occur as parts of multicomponent sites, it is difficult to determine how many of the netsinkers were made by Susquehannocks, or by earlier Owasco or other folk.

A category of stone tools referred to as hoes is the next in order of abundance. We have indicated elsewhere that the chipped-stone disks commonly referred to as "pot lids" may have been used as hoes. Generally these are made of whatever stone having tabular fractures was available locally—schist, shale, sandstone, etc. Usually these average four inches in diameter and about three-eighths inch in thickness. They were chipped and pounded into circular forms, and the majority of them have two opposing lateral notches. Some of these seem too small to have been hafted for use as hoes, but the larger ones could certainly have been so employed.

Some of them, although not the majority, show wear and striations on both faces, which could have resulted from chopping and digging soft alluvial soils. All of them were apparently made by chipping and pounding or grinding the circumferences. Those which show chipped, but not ground, edges may also reflect their use for chopping soil. Broken ones are always more abundant than whole specimens. Another curious note concerning them is that they are sometimes found in pits where they were intentionally stacked like pancakes—perhaps a half dozen or more in a stack.

Also included in the category of hoes are various notched stones, which were more obviously used as hoes. However, these irregular forms are not at all common on Susquehannock sites.

Milling stones and mill slabs are the next categories for consideration. The ratio of milling stones to slabs for Susquehannock sites preceding Strickler averages about five to one. From Strickler times on the milling slabs are far less common. By the beginning of the eighteenth century the milling stones and slabs are practically non-existent. A number of milling stones were recovered from the Strickler site, but interestingly the majority of these were found in graves, and very few were found in the village pits here or at the Lower Leibhart site. The lack of milling slabs at these sites and the fact that most of the grinders at Strickler were grave offerings (heirlooms perhaps?) suggest that even as early as about 1650 this tool set was going out of use.

The slabs are simply flat, water-worn rocks, recognized as grinding slabs because of dished-out surfaces caused by the abrasion of the millstone. Probably they were employed for crushing or otherwise processing a variety of foodstuffs, but most certainly for producing meal from nuts and corn. They were probably also used for cracking bones to extract marrow. The most likely replacement for this tool set is the wooden pestle and mortar combination. Readily available iron axes, gouges, etc., from Strickler times on would have rendered the wooden mortar and pestle rather easy to make, and would perhaps have led to its rapid replacement of the stone equivalents for crushing and grinding foodstuffs. Lindström wrote in 1691 (see Johnson 1925: 25) that the Delawares did not use the quern (stone mortar), but rather made their mortars and pestles of wood.

Some pestles do occur on the earlier (pre-Strickler) Susquehannock sites, but they are usually rather short (6 to 10 inches). Occasionally the larger stone pestles, measuring up to 24 inches or more, are found on Susquehannock sites. These, however, are known from positive Archaic-period contexts, and we suggest that the few found on Susquehannock sites are antiques which they picked up on Archaic sites.

The milling stones (Figure 34) used by the Susquehannocks are of various descriptions: Some are single- or bi-pitted stones used largely around their circumferences, and perhaps represent another reuse of an antique tool. The most common grinders show the greatest use on the flat surfaces of the cobble, made frequently of granite or dense sandstone.

Celts were practically a universal tool, although they do occur at different times throughout the world. In Pennsylvania they seem to have developed out of Archaic-period adzes; by Early Woodland times they take an overall appearance which changes little through the entire sequence to early contact times. Those used by the Susquehannocks were made of a variety of dense, relatively hard siltstones and other fine-grained stones. Usually they have the characteristic tapered poll to facilitate hafting through self-wedging. Their sizes vary from a few inches to over 10 inches in length. Frequently they are polished over the entire surface.

By experiment we know that they certainly can be used for felling trees, but the tremendous superiority of iron axes for this purpose made the celt one of the first tools to be replaced by European equivalents. They simply were not used after the Washington Boro period.

Those stone tools of the sort usually called sinew stones, because of the numerous striations on them, were rather common at the Parker site. The actual use of these peculiar tools is unknown. They do not occur, except as antiques or readapted tools, at the later Susquehannock sites.

Hone stones, usually abraded flat pebbles, are, besides gunflints, the only stone tools of native manufacture to increase in numbers through the Susquehannock sequence. This is obviously in response to the need for these tools to sharpen their growing assortment of iron knives, axes, etc. We can only imagine the delight of the first Indian to discover the marvelously sharp edge he could bring to an iron axe with his sandstone hone.

Lithic Ornaments and Amulets

Among the remains of the Susquehannocks are certain decorated items which we can generally classify as objects of specific raw materials which have been carved, molded or painted in geometric, zoomorphic or anthropomorphic forms, and which can be worn, carried or used for various purposes. This definition would exclude petroglyphs, i.e., designs or shapes carved or pecked into bedrock, which are therefore not portable, but which might otherwise fit the definition. It is very likely that the purposes for carving petroglyphs and the purposes for decorating certain portable objects overlapped.

Parenthetically, we note that there were a number of petroglyphs in the lower Susquehanna Valley, the most notable and only extant ones being those in the Susquehanna River opposite the mouth of the Conestoga (see Cadzow 1934). The chronological position and ethnic provenience of these remain a mystery (Figure 35).

Figure 35. Donald Cadzow inspecting petroglyphs at Little Indian Rock (36La185) near Safe Harbor dam.

Our present definition of decorative objects could include both decorated tools and other items without apparent function that were worn as adornments or otherwise used for art's sake. For example, we could include within the definition decorated clay or stone smoking pipes, pottery vessels, wooden bowls, ladles, antler combs, and bone and stone tools, as well as clay, stone, wood, shell, antler or bone beads, ornamental pendants, amulets, etc.

All this begs the question—should we consider in one category, for purposes of description and analysis, such items as the carved-bone knife handle from the Sheep Rock Shelter, a wooden owl decorated with brass staples from the Strickler site, and a steatite masquette from Washington Boro?

The decoration of certain of these items may be purely for art or adornment, with no other function or symbolism intended. This, however, is a very difficult judgment to make for archeological specimens. Because we know that many ethnographically studied peoples ascribe symbolic or religious connotations to much of their artwork, we have a tendency to do the same for any archeologically recovered primitive art, whether it be on a tool or in the form of a purely decorative item. As anthropologists, it seems incumbent upon us to attempt some interpretation of the philosophical or religious underpinnings of the art forms which we recover archeologically. This is tantamount to one of our successors trying to explain the philosophy behind an oil on canvas rendering of a soup can. Nevertheless, we surge ahead with our guesses. Naturally, a certain amount of this sort of thing can be done, especially if we have ethnohistoric data on religion, mythology or folklore as they relate to material objects and art.

George Hamell (1979) has made some progress in this area concerning the interpretation of Seneca archeological art, particularly decorations on pipes and combs, in light of ethnographic records of Iroquois mythology.

Inasmuch as certain classes of objects, such as pipes, tools or even combs, may or may not have decorations added, we have found it useful to describe them, first, according to the raw material of which they are made; and second, according to basic functions or forms. For that reason we will here deal with decorated stone objects which can be worn, or used or carried for decorative or religious purposes, but which have no other function. In terms of artifacts recovered from sites of the Susquehanna's Indians, and most specifically the Susquehannocks, such items would be those things which have generally been called amulets or effigies. The examples at hand fall into three major categories: human forms, generally masquettes; wolf- or dog-like creatures; and turtles, bears, owls, and even rarer animal forms.

Actually, the only clear representation of a bear is one made of catlinite from Conestoga Town. Since we have decided to deal with catlinite as a separate descriptive category, the bear is excluded from the present consideration. The primary raw material of which the present class of decorative stone objects is made is steatite (or soapstone). The nearest sources for this material are the ancient Transitional-period quarry sites in the vicinity of Christiana in southern Lancaster County. Other lithic materials which might be included here are shales, slates, serpentine (a relative of steatite), coal, and indeed, any stone other than catlinite.

We note that these same basic forms—human heads (sometimes entire bodies), wolves, turtles, and bears—also appear in artistic renderings on antler combs, pipes, pottery vessels and wooden ladles. Some of these other media also include decorative forms which do not occur in stone. Several creatures appear on clay or stone pipes which are not found on stone ornaments, e.g., lizards, snakes, geometric forms, and birds.

Our point here, again, is that all of these various representations and their symbolic or religious significance might well be discussed under one heading; however, descriptively it is more convenient to deal with larger basic categories of the media in which the representations appear. For that

Figure 36. Stone masquettes, effigies and coal beads from Susquehannock sites.

reason, combs, whether decorated or not, pipes, pots, etc., are described and discussed according to the raw materials of which they are made.

We may note here, so that we need not repeat it too often, that many of these representations, such as human faces, wolves, turtles, etc., regardless of the item on which they are portrayed, may have very similar symbolic purposes, or so we might guess.

Human figures are very prevalent in Iroquois (and probably, therefore, in Susquehannock) culture, folklore, mythology, religion or what have you. Those which are represented in the types of stone included in this category are generally very stylized and often rather crude. A few are very carefully and realistically executed. Most of the masquettes (and the turtles and wolves of this group) have either drilled holes or knobs from which they could be suspended on necklaces.

The use of the human-form stone amulets (and perhaps also the turtles, wolves, etc.) is very likely to have had magico-religious undertones for the Susquehannocks. This perhaps gratuitous statement is not based entirely on intuition, but rather on possible ethnographic precedents for such usages among their Iroquoian relatives. Iroquois religion is rife with beliefs in, or manipulation of, human and animal mythological creatures. Primary concerns, as in all religions, are control (or at least explanation) of the unexplainable: sickness, death, bad luck and other imponderables. Parker (1923) and Beauchamp (1922), among many others, have collected some of the numerous folk tales and legends which make up Iroquois religion. Among others on this subject is Jesse Cornplanter (1938), who, in his *Legends of the Longhouse*, has described the small (ca. one inch high), carved false faces ("charm masks") which were to be worn around the neck *in* a small leather bag (or on a necklace), and whose purpose it was to be protectors or guardian spirits bringing good fortune to the wearer (Cornplanter 1938: 204-16). He also shows in a diagram (Cornplanter 1938: 205) the placement of "Sacred Tobacco" at the back, apparently in a hollow, of the masquette. We note that a number of the Susquehannock masquettes, and some of the wolf heads and turtles, have hollow backs (masks), or undersides in the case of others.

Cornplanter (1938: 201) notes that the charm mask was blessed with the sacred tobacco. Smoke from sacred tobacco was essential in Iroquois myth as a means for attracting the attention of the appropriate spirits when one was in need of their special protection or services. Perhaps the hollows carved into certain of the Susquehannock stone amulets served also as repositories for sacred tobacco; or more likely, they could be used as receptacles for a small amount of burning tobacco so that the wafts of smoke could call up the services of the spirit represented by the image.

Wallace (1969: 79) feels that the false-face masks and the important ceremonies of which they were a part go far back into Iroquois history. He notes their similarity to archeologically recovered masquettes. Clearly, some of those from Susquehannock sites, particularly those several carefully carved catlinite examples from Conestoga Town, are miniature copies of the contorted false-face masks. Wallace states (1969: 80) that the false-face masks loved tobacco, and that, in addition to being baptized in the smoke of the council fire, they must also have a small bag of tobacco tied inside the mask. They required careful attention, for they gave much to the people who believed in them.

The extension of these same religious and psychotherapeutic values to the stone masquettes and other amulets, including those in other materials, is of course a guess on the part of outside observers.

It may well be that certain types of these amulets had greater religious significance and power than some others (if indeed any of them really relate to religion or psychotherapy). Some may have become so highly stylized that they carried only minimal symbolism. For example, human forms on combs may not have been as "powerful" as human-form stone effigies.

The probability that effigies or amulets also had social significance, particularly as totemic reflections of clan membership, should also be considered. For example, a wolf figure on stone might imply one's affiliation with the wolf clan. This of course is also exceedingly difficult to document.

The importance of these emblems or amulets was recognized by Europeans who, at least during the eighteenth century, copied certain forms in silver, pewter and even shell for trade to the Indians. Some metallic copies, including cast pewter, lead, some silver, and particularly cut brass, were made by Indians.

A majority of the lithic ornaments in this category, viz., amulets, effigies or items of purely decorative nature, which are attributable to the Susquehannocks, have been found at the Washington Boro site or one of its attending cemeteries. The largest single collection of these was gathered by Gerald B. Fenstermaker of Lancaster. Most of the Fenstermaker collection of masquettes is now at the Denver Museum of Natural History (some of these specimens are illustrated by Carter 1973: 23). A lesser number of Fenstermaker specimens were purchased by the Pennsylvania State Museum, and some of these are shown in Figure 36. These objects were considerably less frequent at the Strickler site, and we know only one from the Byrd Leibhart site.

Simple stone beads are not an important artifact at any Susquehannock site. Two discoidal steatite beads were found at the Schultz site. Also found here were two miniature boatstone-like beads, a crude steatite turtle, and one of red shale. A human face of this latter stone, about a dozen and a half coal beads (Figure 36), two nondescript steatite pendants mentioned by Cadzow (1936: 197), and 16 discoidal-shaped catlinite beads (also described under catlinite) complete the rather sparse inventory of such items from the Schultz site.

CATLINITE

Indians, like most peoples, exhibit a desire for bright, colorful or exotic materials. This is especially true with regard to raw materials from which ornaments can be fashioned. Exchanges of such items are the basis for most trade among primitive societies. Among the Indians of the Susque-

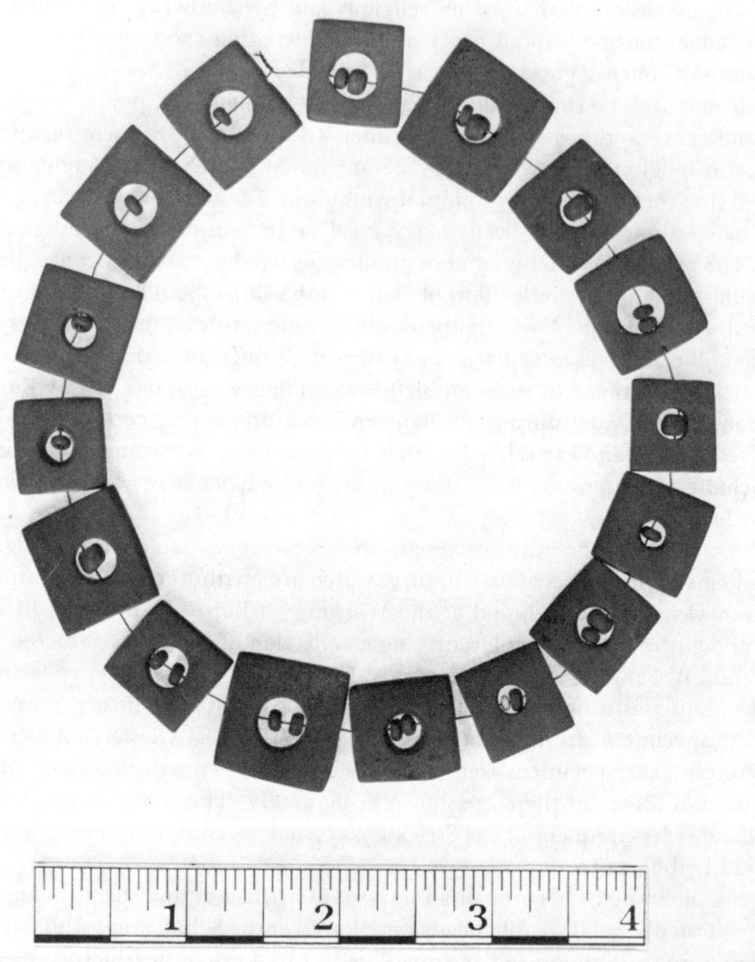

Figure 37. Actual necklace of catlinite squares and glass beads, Conoy cemetery (36La40).

hanna Valley, the most distant material which they received through the native trade networks was catlinite, which probably came from Minnesota.

Kinsey (1981) has employed a scratch-plate technique and Munsell color hues in an effort to identify more specific quarry origins for varying color shades of catlinite. He notes that there are at least 12 known quarry sites for catlinite, including (in addition to Minnesota) localities in Wisconsin. Based upon his reseach on samples and color hues from the various quarries, Kinsey feels that a majority of the abundant catlinite objects found on

Seneca sites in western New York were made of stone collected from quarries in Wisconsin. On the other hand, he finds that specimens from lower Susquehanna Valley sites are derived from both Wisconsin localities and from the "true" catlinite sources in extreme southwestern Minnesota. It is his suggestion (Kinsey 1981) that Minnesota catlinite in the lower Susquehanna Valley sites may have come there *via* trade from the Ohio Country, whereas the Wisconsin catlinite may have reached this area as a result of trade with the Seneca.

The diffusion of catlinite—probably finished objects rather than raw material—into the Eastern Woodlands, particularly during the eighteenth century, may have come in tandem with the use of the Plains calumet (catlinite) pipe. According to Turnbaugh (1979), the calumet pipe (most properly made of catlinite) was the major symbol of a spreading nativistic or revivalist movement among many eighteenth-century Indians. An alternative theory regarding the eastward spread of the calumet pipe (and presumably other Plains-manufactured ornaments of catlinite) is set forth by Blakeslee (1981). He has presented evidence for the calumet pipe ceremony prior to 1634 on the Great Plains. However, he proposed that the eventual eastward spread of the pipe and certain aspects of the ceremony surrounding its smoking were a result of alliances for trade and warfare between various Indian nations.

We note here that there are hints of the esteem in which this stone was held by Indians (namely Susquehannocks) in eastern Pennsylvania long before any of the causal factors (cited above) for the spread of the calumet had come into play.

From the Schultz site, occupied from about 1575 to 1600, at least 16 thick discoidal catlinite beads have been recovered. In addition, there were also two red-shale pendants—one a human face, the other a turtle. These are not catlinite, but rather it would appear that the local red shales were selected to mimic catlinite. Such pendants of catlinite do occur elsewhere, and they are known from later sites in the Susquehanna Valley. As further evidence of the desirability of catlinite at Schultz, there are three European red glass beads (Type 2bbl in the Kidds' 1970 classification) which had their blue and white stripes ground off to make them appear as catlinite. The colors of these are so remarkably close to catlinite that they cannot be separated without scratching the beads.

Catlinite beads are rare or almost non-existant at the Washington Boro and Strickler sites. However, at Strickler there is an increase (at least a half dozen specimens) in the grinding of *2bbl* beads to produce imitation catlinite.

The only really startling piece of catlinite from Strickler is a calumet pipe recovered from a grave in 1974 (catalogue number La3/505). This

Figure 38. Catlinite decorative objects from Conoy cemetery (36La40) and Conestoga Town (36La52).

pipe (Figure 31) was found with an adult and in association with three other Strickler-period, native-made pipes, two Strickler pots, and other objects typical of the period. It is not, therefore, an intrusive or later grave. The pipe is important because it represents one of the two earliest known (so far as we are aware) Plains-type, prowled calumet pipes in the East. The other pipe was found at the Dann site, a Seneca cemetery in western New York, which is dated almost the same as the Strickler site (Witthoft et al. 1953: 91). Catlinite in other objects is apparently somewhat more abundant on Seneca sites during this period (Wray and Schoff 1953: 62), largely because of their proximity to the Great Lakes and the western tribes. We have already mentioned the considerable interaction between the Seneca and Susquehannocks. This pipe from the Strickler site may well have come to the Susquehannocks by way of the Seneca. The WPMM collections from the Byrd Leibhart site include but one poorly formed triangular pendant of catlinite.

Hundreds of catlinite ornaments were recovered at Conestoga and Conoy Town. By far the most common forms are the longitudinally drilled triangles ranging in length from one-half to two inches. Some have concave sides, but most are straight-sided; some have beveled surfaces, although most are flat on both faces. A number have geometric patterns incised on them. Generally these were strung on necklaces and frequently they were separated by one or more glass beads. Next in order of abundance are the squares of catlinite with circular cut-out centers, ranging from three-sixteenths to about one inch square. These are also drilled longitudinally. The drill holes are from the outside to the center, cut out on two opposing sides of the square. These were also necklace adornments, and in some cases a glass bead was placed on the string inside the center cut-out of the squares. One such necklace was found intact at Conoy Town (Figure 37).

Long, thin (usually square in cross-section) rectangles are the next most common catlinite objects. These range in length from one to five inches (those from Conestoga Town were all over three inches long). Like the long shell "hair pipes," they are amazingly well drilled through their length. The shorter varieties, primarily from Conoy Town, sometimes having rounded edges, are rectangular in cross-section, and may taper from one end to the other. One circular piece from Conestoga, about one inch in diameter, with a circular center cut-out, has two longitudinal holes.

There are also six effigies in catlinite from Conestoga. One of these is a bear, and five are human faces or masquettes. Two of these are a very similar pair, looking like miniature false-face masks, and they are not drilled for suspension (Figure 38). Another, which is drilled, is a very neatly carved false face (Figure 38). A fourth piece is also drilled, and the remaining specimen is in the collection of the owners of the site (see also the discussion of Susquehannock masquettes made of other stones).

Catlinite ornaments and beads of the previously described shapes have been reported from eighteenth-century sites elsewhere in the Susquehanna Valley, including the Park site (36La96) near Lancaster (Kinsey and Custer 1982), and Wapwallopen (36Lu43), as described by McIntyre (1979). The Zakucia collection from Kuskuski (36Lr11) near New Castle (WPMM files) includes a small catlinite turtle.

Seven catlinite pipes were recovered at Conestoga Town. Four of these are traditional prowl-shaped Plains calumets (Figure 31). Of the remaining pipes, two are prowlless (Figure 30), and the last is a magnificent horse head with a lizard mane (Figure 30). Each of these may originally have been interred with its customarily decorated, long wooden stem. Blakeslee (1981: 759) suggests that it was actually the long stem of the pipe to which the term calumet was first applied.

One of the prowlless Conestoga pipes has with it a preserved section of its stem. This resulted from the preservation afforded the distal end of the stem (at the point where it was inserted into the bowl) by a brass coil wrapped around it (Figure 30).

Those specimens which have more than one perforation in their "dorsal fins" may have had feathers or other ornaments suspended from them. One of the prowlless forms had a white glass seed bead forced into one of its fin holes. On those pipes with only one fin hole, the function of the hole was probably to hold a cord which served to tie the stem and bowl together.

Our old friend Sassoonan, chief of the Schuylkill Delawares, along with 13 other Delaware Indians, attended a conference with the Governor at Philadelphia in 1712, where it was recorded that he, the Governor, and the other Indians in the party smoked a "calumet, with a stone head, a wooden or cane shaft and feathers fixt to it like wings, with other ornaments" (Minutes of the Provincial Council of Pennsylvania 1838 II: 571-74).

Two of the pipes found at Conestoga Town were buried at the head of an adolescent; another was also buried with a child. At least one was with an adult female, and the others accompanied adult males.

Another catlinite pipe was reported to the author by Mr. Reeves Goehring of Columbia, Pennsylvania, who claims that it was a local find and was from an old collection from near Millersville. Given the circumstances, this pipe may have been found at Conestoga Town.

The previously mentioned (see Native Pipes of Stone) fragments of catlinite pipes from Wrightsville, Pennsylvania, and the mouth of Chillisquaque Creek, may very well indicate Shawnee use of these pipes. We have already noted their use by the Delaware Indians as early as 1712.

Additional finds of catlinite pipes are reported by Witthoft, Schoff and Wray (1953) for the West Branch of the Susquehanna, but none of these can be given accurate provenience. Several other unsubstantiated finds of such pipes are reported by a local collector who purchased them from the Dr. Shipman collection, which was purportedly obtained from local excavations at Sunbury (Shamokin?) and elsewhere along the Susquehanna.

It is our general impression that the several forms of the catlinite calumet pipes and the five or six other basic categories of objects are more or less universal to the area in which quantities of catlinite were traded or diffused. All of the forms found in the lower Susquehanna Valley sites also occur in the Seneca sites of western New York. However, the relative paucity of reports of catlinite objects from the "core area" (the Great Lakes region) seems to suggest some minor differences in specific items and in the quality of workmanship compared to the Seneca or Susquehannock areas. For example, none of the triangles illustrated by Cleland (1971: 44-45) from the Lasanen site in Michigan, nor any of those depicted by Quimby (1966), is as well made as the best of those from Conestoga, Conoy or various Seneca sites. This must be a factor of the sample of reported specimens which have been reviewed here. We do note that there are several forms reported by Cleland (1971: 42-43), for example, which do not occur in the lower Susquehanna Valley. These include a four-pointed "star-shaped" object and beaver effigies.

Sites in the Great Lakes region naturally produce a certain amount of broken, unfinished or rejected items of catlinite representing the manufacture of those items at those places. No such pieces, implying local manufacture, have been found in lower Susquehanna Valley sites. One minor exception may be the Iroquoian-like false-face effigies—these probably represent local work.

In conclusion, a limited survey of the literature might give one the false impression that Seneca-Susquehannock catlinite objects are generally better made than many of those found on sites in the Great Lakes area. It is our contention, however, that a vast majority, if not all, of the Seneca-Susquehannock catlinite was in fact made at various places in the Great Lakes region, nearer to the quarry sources, and eventually was traded or otherwise carried eastward.

SHELL OBJECTS

Shell beads and pendants were made and used by Indians for a long time—as far back as Archaic times. By the time the first Europeans arrived, there was a widespread native use of shell beads and pendants. During the sixteenth century the so-called discoidal wampum, or drilled discs, of shell were popular. Larger beads in more or less tubular shapes were made from conch columns, but these were not nearly as common as the disc-shell beads. Occasionally sixteenth-century sites produce a much smaller tubular-shell bead which can be considered the forerunner of the later conventional wampum. Generally these are made of white shells, but at least one lavender wampum bead is known from the Schultz site (Heisey and Witmer 1962: 115). At least a half-dozen wampum-like white-shell beads were recovered from the Schultz site in 1974. These are not quite as delicate, nor are the holes as small, as later wampum. Shell beads of this size (about one-fourth inch), with about three-thirty-seconds-inch drill holes, do not seem to appear in the archeological record before the sixteenth century. The techniques for producing such fine holes in these beads, like those in the later conventional wampum, involved drilling from both ends.

One wonders whence came the impetus for shell beads of this type. Tubular glass beads of European manufacture, in a variety of colors, were fairly common at this time. Over four hundred such beads (including 167 white ones which look very much like wampum) were recovered from the Schultz site in 1974. Is it possible that the Indians copied, in shell, this bead which the Europeans were already making? It seems unlikely that, at this date, the European glass industry was making particular shapes just to suit the Indians' fancy.

The first true shell wampum in the Susquehanna Valley sequence appears at the Washington Boro cemetery known as the Keller site. Here, in 1932, Cadzow excavated (Burial #10, catalogue number 756—Cadzow 1936: Plate 34, page 82, mistakenly shows it with Strickler site artifacts) a fragmentary wampum belt of brass and white-shell wampum on native-made, two-strand cordage. The shell beads are three-sixteenths inch in length with drill holes of one-sixteenth inch or less. Except for this specimen, wampum was still scarce at Washington Boro.

As early as the 1630's, however (Woodward 1933: 14), there were colonial documents which spelled out the monetary equivalents of wampum as a means of exchange among both Indians and colonials (see Becker 1975). Because of its value, the colonial manufacture of wampum had become, by the second half of the seventeenth century, fairly large. Much of the wampum found in Indian sites after that date was of colonial manufacture, but unquestionably, the Indians were making some of it themselves.

Wampum has a startling increase of occurrence at the Strickler site, and here for the first time we see both lavender and white in quantity. Most of the wampum at Strickler was on strings (necklaces), some was used on bracelets, and there is some evidence of its actual use in belts.

At the Byrd Leibhart site wampum was more numerous than glass beads, and it occurred on necklaces, bracelets and belts.

Glass and wampum beads occur in about equal amounts at both Conoy and Conestoga. At both sites there is a definite increase in the number of belts. In a few instances, particularly at Conoy Town, fragments of belts were actually recoverable, but unfortunately no large patterns were discernible. Geometric patterns are definitely in evidence.

Wampum began to decline as a medium of economic exchange during the eighteenth century, but it increased in importance as a mnemonic device to consummate or commemorate treaties and agreements. Obviously

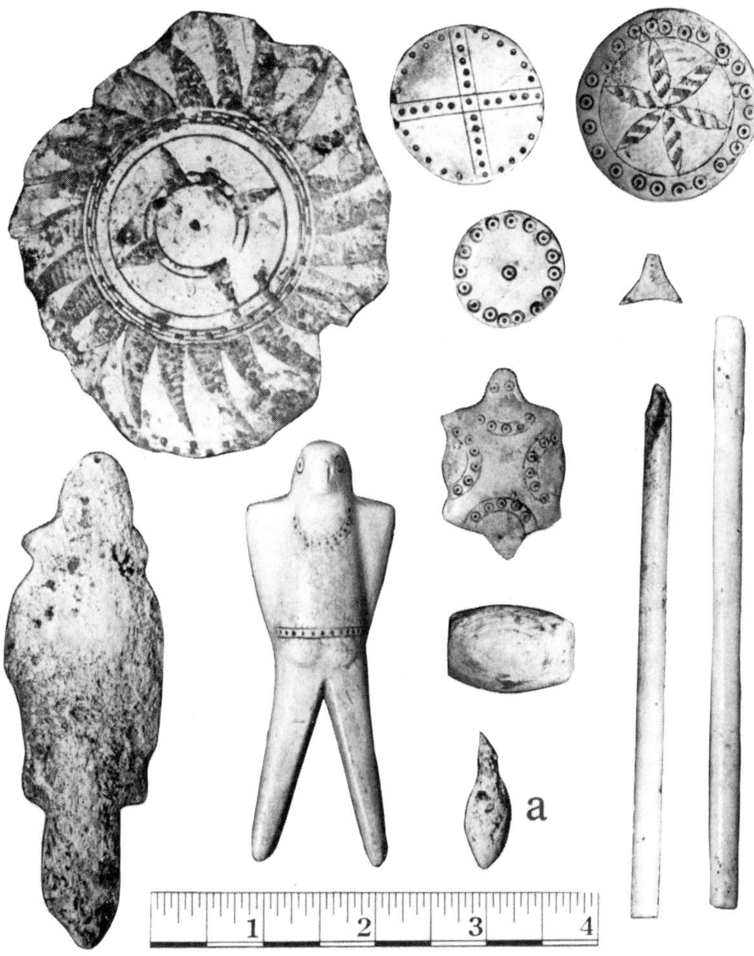

Figure 39. Shell decorative objects. Note long "hair pipes" and "Geese" form (a).

it was also an important burial offering and continued to be so as long as the Indians lived in the Susquehanna Valley.

Large circular sections of conch-shell walls are found as early as Washington Boro. In the later sites these are often engraved. Discoidal shell beads diminish in popularity through the seventeenth century and are seldom seen in eighteenth-century sites. Large shell beads of various shapes, most noticeably in barrel and spherical form, have their greatest occurrence on eighteenth-century sites.

Pendants and runtees first appear in number at Strickler. Most common of the early pendants are the so-called "geese," crescents, and owls. There are at least three beavers in the Keller collection from 36Yo170. Runtees or discs, usually with two longitudinal drill holes, are known from seventeenth-century sites, particularly at Byrd Leibhart's. They occur somewhat more frequently at Conestoga (and less so at Conoy), and many of them were engraved with geometric designs. These designs, like those illustrated by Kent (1970), have a decided European flavor, suggesting that they were made by the colonial wampum manufacturers. Longitudinally drilled beavers, triangles, fishes and occasional birds also appear in the eighteenth-century sites.

Perhaps most notable of the shell objects from Conoy and Conestoga are the so-called "hair-pipes." These are long (up to five inches), and thin (usually not more than one-fourth inch in diameter), with drill holes (about one-eighth inch) through the length of the tube. These were also highly polished. The evidence from the ground does not clearly suggest their use. Generally they were found stacked (parallel) together in caches. In several cases they were associated with skulls, which might imply their use as hair- or head-covering ornaments.

Among the Plains Indians of the nineteenth century, long beads of this sort, made of various materials, were worn in parallel arrangements on the chest. Their use in this fashion is not evident for the archeologically recovered samples described here. Long thin shell beads definitely have a seventeenth-century ancestry. Two and perhaps three shell beads of two or more inches in length were recovered at the Frey-Haverstick site, which, as previously indicated, dates from the 1630's.

Bone and Antler

Bone and antler are raw materials that were used extensively for the manufacture of tools and ornaments by Indians of all times prior to the introduction of European tools. Since these are perishable materials, it is only the ravages of time which make them appear to be more abundant in Late Woodland and historic-period contexts.

For purposes of the present material classifications, bone will be thought of as including turtle shells, teeth and any other used portion of the skeleton of any animal species. Although it may not be entirely proper, antler, for present purposes, will be thought of as including horn and claws.

Both bone and antler can be sawed, cut, polished, engraved and drilled with the stone tools available to American Indians prior to historic contact. In post-contact times, the acquisition of European tools by the Indians did not greatly extend the range of things which could be made of bone or antler, but it did decrease the time required to produce certain items.

Things made of these materials fall into two basic categories. One includes tools or components of tools, the other, things which are ornamental. Obviously there may be some overlapping here, e.g., ornamented tools.

Bone is considerably softer and less dense than antler, and is therefore more easily and more quickly worked. The archeological example of various stages in the manufacture of an antler comb, shown in Figure 40, serves to illustrate most of the basic processes for working either antler or bone. In aboriginal times a saw made from a slab of sandstone was used to first sever an antler and then split it into longitudinal sections. Stone knives, gravers, drills and chisels (sharp but heavy edges of chert, etc.) were then used in various stages of carving and cutting-out. A final step may have involved polishing with grit, water and leather, or very fine-grained stone slabs. Antler spoons may have been steamed to form the bowl.

The list of bone and antler tools found on Susquehannock sites includes turtle-shell cups and rattles, fishhooks, awls of various shapes, knife and other handles or components, pressure-flaking tools, chisels (usually beaver teeth), harpoons, some conical arrow points, occasional smoking pipes of antler, scraping tools, hoe blades, spoons (of antler), needles (with

Figure 40. Stages in carving an antler comb.

notches, rather than eyes), and a few other miscellaneous nondescript items.

All of the above items have been found at the Schultz site. Without question, most, if not all, of these also occurred on the earlier Susquehannock sites (on the North Branch of the Susquehanna). However, because of the paucity of archeology at such sites, we cannot document very many of these tools (see Crannell 1970; Stewart 1973: 11).

With no apparent exceptions, all of the bone or antler-tool types indicated for the Schultz site also occur at Washington Boro. Because of the small size of the Roberts and Billmyer site collections, it is not possible to demonstrate a gradual decline for bone and antler Susquehannock tools. At the Strickler site they are practically gone. The handful of awls, the four or five antler punches or flaking tools, and the few turtle-shell cups recovered here may actually have been antique tools at Strickler. Even fewer bone tools were found at the Leibhart sites, and by the time of Conestoga Town, bone tools were just not being made.

Decorative items from Susquehannock sites include various drilled or notched teeth (generally the vestigial elk canine, or bear or wolf canines); a few bird-bone beads and some longer tubes of unknown use; antler effigies of humans, animals and other miniatures; and a wide variety of antler combs.

The teeth and bird-bone beads are probably just that—purely and simply decorative objects for suspension on necklaces, or for sewing on clothing. Bear canines which are not drilled or notched for suspension are quite common, and their frequent inclusion in burial caches suggests that they may have had some special use or symbolism.

We have previously (in the section on lithic ornaments and amulets) suggested the possibility that the various caricatures incorporated into the designs of antler combs may have had religious or mythological, or even clan significance. At the same time, we should remind the reader that these interpretations are speculative, and that the creatures represented on combs (and other amulets) may be nothing more than attractive things of nature which the carver was attempting to reproduce for art's sake. Combs were clearly used for decorative purposes, for when they are recovered from a grave they are frequently in such a position as to suggest that they were worn in the hair.

Wray (1964) has discussed the significance of the bird in Seneca culture and he notes that, among other objects (pipes, woodcarvings, etc.), it was used extensively in the designs of comb handles.

Combs have considerable antiquity in North American Indian culture, particularly in New York State. Without question, Susquehannock combs have the same ancestry as the rest of those in Iroquoia. As Wray (1963: 36) notes, this can readily be carried back to at least the Point Peninsula culture of Middle Woodland times, and these are probably directly tied to the even earlier combs of the Frontenac Island phase of the Archaic period in New York State.

For the most part, Susquehannock combs cannot be distinguished from those made by the Seneca. Combs found elsewhere in Iroquoia have not generally been well published, but in the few cases where they have been illustrated (cf. Pratt 1976: 219-20, Oneida; Beauchamp 1902: plates 16-20, various tribes), we can see other close similarities.

Wray (1963: 45) also suggests that the particular carved figures *may* represent popular legends, myths or *perhaps* clan affiliations. Wray (1963: 45) notes that, of the eight totemic clan symbols of the Seneca, only the turtle fails to appear on a comb. One turtle comb has been found at the Schultz site (Figure 41). Various other birds, bears, possible wolves, and geometric forms appear on Susquehannock combs. The largest category of figures is human, of which a single carving may include one to four individuals. Many of these show details of dress and, particularly, hair style. Some have a single hair bob or vertical shaft extending upward from the top center of the head (Figure 41). A feature of Susquehannock combs which may be unique to that tribe is the "horned" human (Figure 41). Cadzow (1936: 123) suggested a relationship between combs with this feature and the "horned devils" referred to by Captain John Smith.

Some combs have no creatures carved on them at all. Occasionally, the comb has only a simple handle (see Cadzow 1936: 118). Many antler effigies, animal or human, occur at the Schultz and Washington Boro sites. Most of these are broken from combs, but some are complete human or animal carvings which were never a part of anything else.

It seems hard to escape allusions to the religious, mythological or social symbolism of the carved combs. Our tendency is to read into them various meanings which stem from our own culturally conditioned perceptions. For example, we see in the holding of hands a symbol of peace and agreement. Whether or not it meant that to a Susquehannock is very difficult to tell. Some Susquehannock combs may have been intended to portray mesages other than religious or mythological. The comb illustrated in Figure 42, from Conestoga, shows a white man and what is apparently an Indian in a posture of hand-holding. *Perhaps* this reflects some implied or anticipated agreement between the two.

The earliest Susquehannock combs are those from the North Branch of the Susquehanna in the vicinity of Tioga Point. In particular, a number are reported from the Murray Garden site at Athens (Murray 1908, 1921; Wright 1885). A more recent discovery of an antler comb in this area is the three-tined example from the Englebert site in nearby Tioga County, New York (Elliot and Lipe 1970; Stewart 1973: 11).

Figure 41. Antler combs. Top left to right: Strickler (36La3); Schultz (36La7); Byrd Leibhart (36Yo170). Bottom left to right: Washington Boro village (36La8); Conestoga Town (36La52); (36La7); (36La8).

Miscellaneous combs are reported from various sites farther down the Susquehanna River, which *may* pertain to the southward movements of the Susquehannocks. However, the first large occurrence of such items is at the Schultz site. Here, combs have been found in both the village pits (Cadzow 1931) and in the cemeteries associated with the town (Heisey and Witmer 1962: 107; Smith and Graybill 1977). The artistry and general quality of workmanship on the Schultz-site combs are quite good. The frequency with which combs occur, and their quality, is undiminished at the Washington Boro village site (Cadzow 1936; Witthoft and Kinsey 1959: 151-53). At both sites combs were more common in the village garbage pits than they were in the burials.

Several fragmentary combs were found at the Frey-Haverstick site, including a European-made bone "cootie comb." None has been reported at the Roberts or the Billmyer site. Three or four combs have been found in garbage pits at the Strickler site (Figure 41), but we have few records of any from the hundreds of graves excavated here. The paucity of combs from Strickler is perhaps not so striking when we see that they are equally uncommon at the Oscar Leibhart site—the village occupied after Strickler. However, this paucity is made most noteworthy when we discover that there are at least ten combs, apparently all from graves, at the Byrd Leibhart site. Five of these were in the George Keller collection, two are at the York County Historical Society, and one, found by Byrd Leibhart, is in a private collection (see also Kinsey 1977: 117). This would almost suggest a resurgence in the art of comb making, at least as compared with the two previous sites. This trend more or less continued at Conestoga Town, where at least five combs of mediocre to excellent quality (Figure 42) have been found. Four "cootie" combs were also found there. The native-made comb form illustrated by that in Figure 41a is apparently an eighteenth-century development. At least one other like this was found at Shamokin (collections of the Fort Augusta Museum, Sunbury, Pennsylvania). All of the other Conestoga combs seem to represent a continuation of a Susquehannock-Seneca tradition of comb making, which we first see in the sixteenth century.

Items Made of Other Organic Materials

This category includes miscellaneous perishable materials not described elsewhere in this volume. By and large it consists of things which can be classified as botanical. For the sake of convenience, this chapter also deals with the few extant artifacts made of leather that have been found in archeological sites in the Susquehanna drainage area.

Artifacts made of organic materials are also frequently referred to under the heading of perishable objects—for that term describes what normally

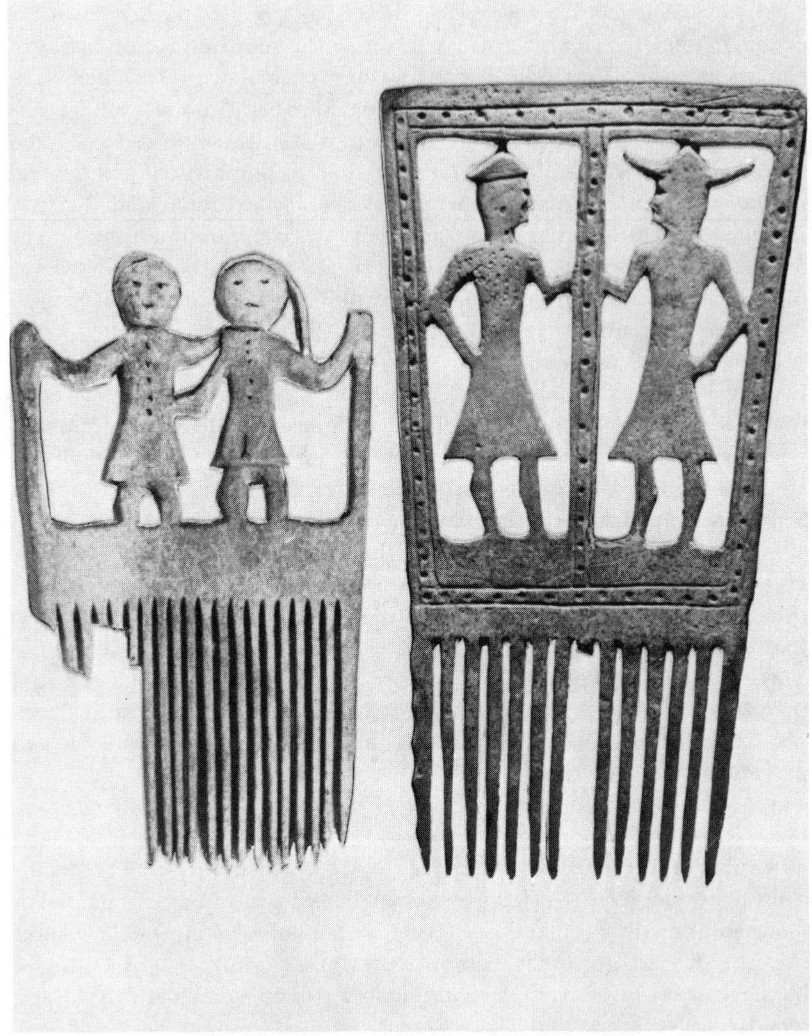

Figure 42. Antler combs from private collections. Left: Byrd Leibhart (36Yo170). Right: Conestoga Town, 4 3/4 inches high (36La52).

happens to them. When such items are preserved in an archeological context it is generally for one of four reasons.

Two of these preservation processes involve the object being held in a uniform environment of either (1) constant wetness or (2) constant dryness. A third mechanism for such preservation involves incomplete combustion, which results in the charring of an object. Charcoal is extremely stable,

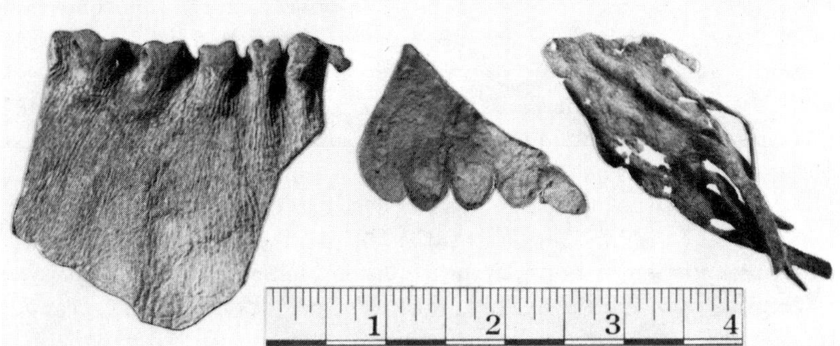

Figure 43. Leather from the Late Woodland level at the Sheep Rock Shelter (36Hul). Left to right: bag with drawstring closure; decorative edge; fringed edge.

and when the amount of charring is just right it can retain or preserve the shape of an organic object. The fourth process is a chemical preservation resulting from the coating or impregnation of a porous organic substance with copper sulfate. This compound is readily produced by the action of organic acids and ground water on brass or copper (Wray 1964: 20). The normally rapid course of organic decay is often retarded when an object is buried in contact with one of these metals. Brass kettles are the best source

Figure 44. Cordage and woven fabrics. Top left to right: four pieces of cordage from the Sheep Rock Shelter (36Hul); wooden strips held with cordage, Schultz-Funk (36La9); coarse cloth (36Hul). Bottom left to right: herringbone weave, European (?), Strickler (36La3); coarse cloth, Keller (36La4).

of copper sulfate (or verdegris, as it is commonly called), and objects in them or next to them are frequently spared the ravages of time. Iron oxides also occasionally contribute to the preservation of organic materials. The process would seem to be similar to fossilization, for a veritable cast of such things as fabrics is sometimes found on the surface of the rusted iron box or other objects of this metal.

Raw materials dealt with in this category can include trees and the various parts thereof; an enormous variety of plants and their various parts; and, as mentioned, skins (or leather) of birds and animals.

Trees can provide the building materials for stockades, houses, canoes, racks, traps, containers, tools, ornaments, clothes, etc. Things made of plants include arrow shafts, knives, fibers for cordage and fabrics, matting, bedding, etc. Animal skins were, of course, extensively used for containers, clothing, house coverings, tying materials and tool components.

Objects from Susquehannock or other Indian sites in the Susquehanna drainage which have been preserved as a result of desication are primarily derived from dry rock shelters. The most outstanding examples of such materials in Pennsylvania are from the Sheep Rock Shelter in Huntingdon County (Michaels and Smith 1967: 303-76). Dried objects from this site (Figures 43-45) include a wide variety of plant-fiber cordage, an elm-bark basket, a stirring or canoe paddle, arrow parts, hearth-and-hardwood shafts for friction fire-making sets, other miscellaneous tool parts, and several fragments of leather clothing and moccasins (see Willey 1974).

Several dugout canoes have been recovered from lakes in the Susquehanna drainage area. The specimen in the William Penn Memorial Museum's collections from Mud Pond in Luzerne County has been radiocarbon dated to 1250 A.D. Although not from our study area, the celt handle (Figure 45) in the Museum's Ross Pier Wright collection, from a bog in Chautauqua County, New York, is worthy of mention here.

The Museum's best example of a charred artifact is also not from the Susquehanna Valley. Shown in Figure 47 is a rare example of a cord-wrapped potter's paddle. This specimen was recovered at the Late Woodland-period McFate site in Crawford County, Pennsylvania.

Objects preserved by contact with brass or copper are quite numerous from Susquehannock and other Indian sites. These are important because they enable us to study artifacts of which we otherwise might not have even

Figure 45, opposite. Celts and wooden handles. Top left to right: celt handle, Chautauqua County, New York; replica of the celt; steatite celt smoking pipe (not to scale, length of pipe 4 1/2 inches) from Rock Hill, Lancaster County, Pennsylvania, Landis collection (L.322), Hershey Museum. Lower left: wooden canoe or stirring paddle, Sheep Rock Shelter (36Hul).

1
2
3
4

conceived. The list of such items includes cordage, arrow parts, wooden combs, smoking pipes, matting, basketry, fabrics (coarse-woven European cloth), wooden (and gourd) spoons or ladles, a few purely decorative or ornamental wood carvings, gunstock parts, and miscellaneous unidentified objects.

Wooden smoking pipes are not at all common in Susquehannock sites, but a few pieces are known from the Strickler site. The brass pipes, like the one from Frey-Haverstick or the identical one from the Ibaugh cemetery at Washington Boro (Witthoft and Kinsey 1959: 118, 144), and a piece reported by Heisey and Witmer (1962: 105) from the Schultz Site cemetery may have been liners for wooden pipes. Hamell (1979) has described some very elaborate wooden pipes from Seneca sites.

Perhaps the finest single medium for artistic expression for the Susquehannocks was in the carved wooden handles of their ladles or spoons. Wooden spoons are in evidence at the Schultz site and definitely are a part of the inventories for every Susquehannock site up to and including Conestoga Town. These carvings show remarkable details of animals and, particularly, human beings, including dress and hair styles. The most outstanding example is that in a private collection from Conestoga Town (Figure 48), which portrays a seated male with the classic Iroquoian hair roach.

Bows and Arrows

Arrowheads are without question the most widely known archeological artifacts. In common parlance the term is variously used to label chipped-stone arrow tips, spearheads and knives.

The bow and arrow is generally considered to have had its first use in North America during the Late Woodland period. If this is indeed the case, then the first true arrowhead must be the ubiquitous triangular point of the Late Woodland. Some have suggested that the bow and arrow was introduced to American Indians by Viking explorers, who carried this weapon with them to the New World. The Indians and Eskimos of eastern Canada and perhaps the natives of New England would have seen Viking bows and arrows as early as the tenth century A.D.—about the beginning of the Late Woodland period.

There are, however, some who suggest that the bow and arrow was an independent invention of Middle Woodland times and that the smaller varieties of corner-notched points of this period were arrow, rather than spear, points.

Answers to the questions concerning the first use of the bow and arrow by native North Americans are beyond the scope of the present research. Archeologists are well aware of the enormous quantity of written material

Figure 46. Bark basket lashed with cordage, from the Late Woodland levels of the Sheep Rock Shelter (36Hul); approximate height 14 inches.

about arrowheads (and other projectile points). These are by far the most numerous among the fashioned artifactual remains of our native American cultures. In a sense, then, it is somewhat surprising that so little has been written about the shafts which held these projectile points, and the devices by which they were propelled. Obviously, this is primarily due to the paucity of preserved wooden parts from these tools. There are a few surviving ethnohistoric specimens in various museums, but they are not widely known. In addition, there are some archeological fragments, particularly of arrows, which are also important.

There are no surviving bows or parts thereof from any Susquehanna Valley site. In view of the number of wooden objects preserved in graves by contact with pieces of brass, one might expect to find at least a portion of a bow. A local collector reported that he followed what he thought was the stain of a bow in a grave which he excavated at the Byrd Leibhart site.

The Susquehannock Indian on the upper right corner of Smith's 1612 map of Virginia is holding a bow in his right hand. As McCary (1957) notes, this figure is a clever copy of De Bry's engraving of "A weroans, or Chieftain, of Virginia," a figure originally drawn by John White (see Lorant 1946: 231). The engraver of the Smith map, William Hole, clearly had access to Smith's description of the Susquehannocks, for he has attired the

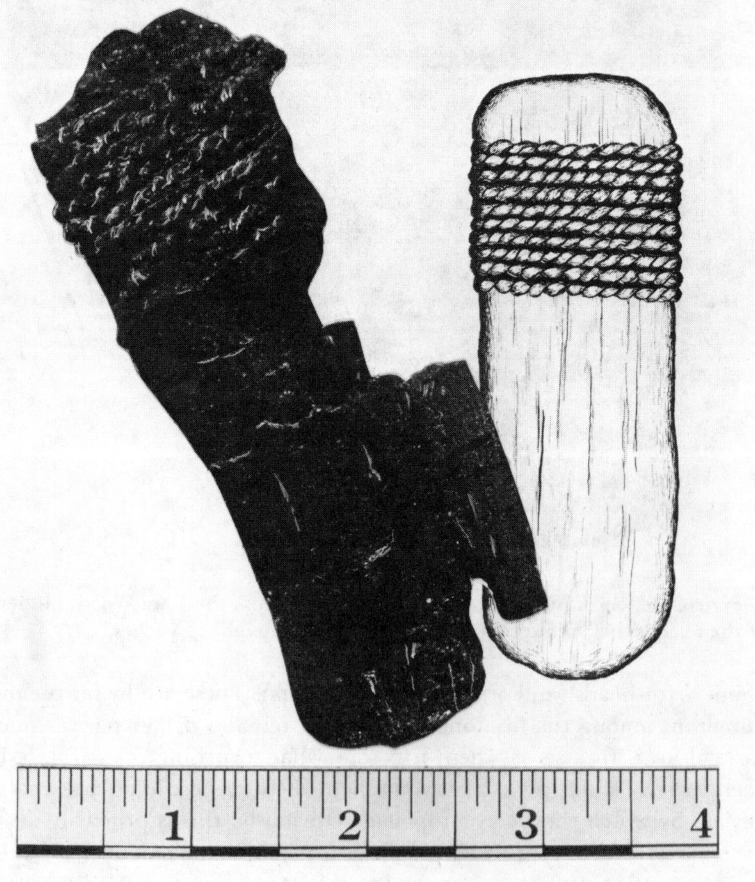

Figure 47. Charred cord-wrapped potter's paddle from the McFate site (36Cw1), with reconstructed drawing.

Figure 48. Wooden spoons from Susquehannock sites. Top right: male figure with hair roach, Conestoga Town (36La52).

figure according to that account. From this we can conclude that the Indian on the Smith map is not based on a first-hand sketch of a Susquehannock, but rather is the re-dressing of a Virginia Indian according to a written account. We note that the bow held by the "Susquehannock" is longer than the figure is tall—just as was that held by the Weroan in White's original sketch. With regard to their principal weapon, Smith (1907: 51) notes that their bows and arrows were commensurate in size with their large physical stature, the "arrows were five quarters yard long headed with splinters of a white crystall like stone in the form of a heart an inch broad and an inch and a half or more long." He goes on to say that these were worn at the back in a wolf's skin quiver.

Herein lies the only contemporary description of Susquehannock bows and arrows. The few surviving examples of seventeenth-century eastern Indian bows would suggest that they were commonly as long as a man was tall (but so was the English longbow). We have already noted the two contemporary engravings of such bows. In addition, there is one specimen known as the "Sudbury Bow," attributed to the Wampanoag of Massachusetts and reportedly taken from an Indian in 1660. The bow, now on exhibit at the Peabody Museum in Cambridge, Massachusetts, is, according to authorities there, made of ash and measures 66¾ inches in length (Figure 49).

The Ashmolean Museum at Oxford, England, has three Virginia bows in the Tredescant collection, which was acquired before 1656, when the first catalogue of the collection was printed. These are reportedly made of ash (McCary 1957: 40) and their measurements range from approximately five feet three inches to five feet nine inches.

Lindeström (Johnson 1925: facing 195) gives no detailed description of Delaware bows or arrows. Two bows are illustrated, but they appear to be rather short and with recurved ends. This is a rather simple, fanciful illustration and the bows are probably generalized from European forms.

Rev. John Campanius, in his history of New Sweden, written between 1643 and 1648, says of the Delaware bows that they were made "with limb of a tree, of above a man's length, and their bow-strings out of the Sinews of Animal" (Holm 1834: 129).

Beauchamp (1905: 122-23) mentions that there are no accurate descriptions of seventeenth-century Iroquois bows; however, he does note that, in all of Champlain's illustrations, the native bow is shown as quite long.

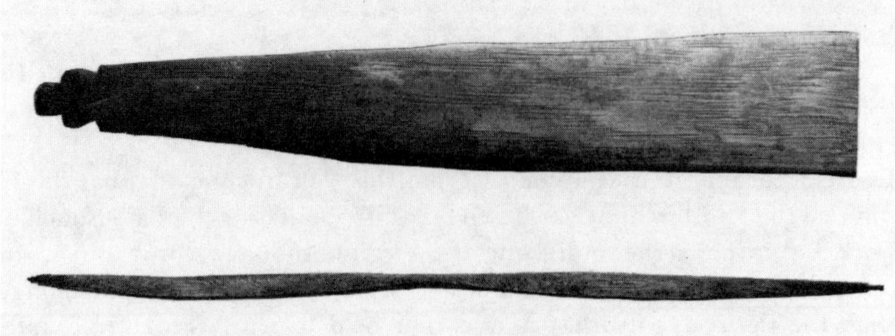

Figure 49. Bow (and enlargement of one end) taken from an Indian at Sudbury, Massachusetts in 1660, attributed to the Wampanoag. Courtesy Peabody Museum, Harvard University.

From these accounts we can rather reasonably assume that the Susquehannock bow was generally as long as a man was tall. Susquehannock graves frequently contain caches of arrowheads. In some cases they were clearly just that — a bag or other container of arrowheads without shafts. However, in other instances these groups of points are all that remains of a quiver of arrows. We might assume, therefore, that a bow would also have been placed in such graves. Susquehannock interments were, typically, of the body in the flexed position, and the average length of such graves is about 65 inches, or generally long enough to contain a bow of the size described above, especially if the bow was placed across the corners. Some graves with quivers of arrows were definitely too small to contain such a bow, no matter how it was placed. In other cases the graves were of sufficient length to contain a bow laid next to the body.

As noted previously, Smith (1907: 51) said that Susquehannock arrows were five quarters of a yard (45 inches) long. He also states, with regard to other Indians of Virginia, that "his arrow-head he maketh quickly, with a little bone [flaker], of any splinter of stone or glass." Bone flakers were common at both Schultz and Washington Boro, but less so at Strickler and later sites.

McCary (1957: 41) gives a quote from Percy concerning seventeenth-century Virginia arrows:

> One of our gentlemen having a target [shield] which hee trusted in, thinking it would beare out a slight shot, hee set it up against a tree, willing one of the Savages to shoot: who tooke from his backe an arrow of an elle [45 inches] long, drew it strongly in his bowe, shoots the target a foote thorow, or better: which was strange, being that a pistoll could not pierce it. Wee Seeing the force of his bow, after wards set him up a steel target: he shot again, and burst his arrow to pieces.

There is evidence from contemporary accounts that both solid-shaft and composite reed arrows were used by Indians of the Middle Atlantic coast area (McCary 1957: 40). Campanius (Holm 1834: 129) states that

> they make their arrows out of a reed a yard and a half long, and at one end, they fix in a piece of hard wood about a quarter's length; at the end of which they make a hole to fix in the head of the arrow, which is made of black flint stone, or of hard bone or horn, or the teeth of large fishes or animals, which they fasten in with fish glue in such a manner, that the water cannot penetrate: at the other end of the arrow they put feathers.

We could reasonably suspect that Campanius' description of the Delaware arrows might also apply to those made by the Susquehannocks. In fact, there are sufficient archeologically recovered fragments of local sixteenth-century arrows to enable us to more or less reconstruct a complete specimen. Two nock ends of arrows were recovered from the dry levels of the Sheep Rock Shelter (Michaels and Smith 1967: 353) (Figure 50). These were in fairly certain association with sixteenth-century McFate-Quiggle pottery. The nocks in both specimens are cut out, and one is reinforced forward of the nock with a fine wrapping of sinew or fiber, covered with glue. Willey (1974: 189) suggests that both specimens have been formed from a twig or branch. In our opinion the uncharred nock, with the fiber wrapping, is a plant stem with a pithy core. This piece also has a small section of feather underneath the wrapping. Another portion of shaft with wrappings (separated by about one and a half inches) over pieces of feather was found in the same levels. Unfortunately it is not possible to determine whether two or three feathers were attached to this shaft. This also appears to be a plant stem with a soft core. Another portion of arrow shaft from these dry levels is decorated with three zig-zag, red pigment-filled lines, or "lightning grooves" like those commonly seen on Plains arrows. This piece, although rather harder and more wood-like (possibly cane) on its exterior, also has a soft center. A number of possible hardwood foreshafts were also recovered at the Sheep Rock. The most convincing of these is split at one

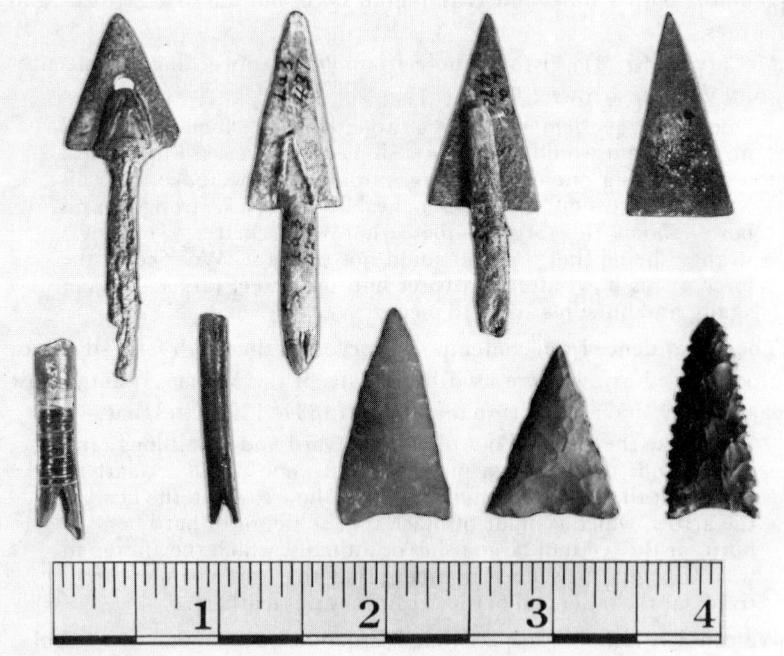

Figure 50. Arrow parts. Top: brass arrowheads with preserved foreshafts and bindings, and typical brass arrowhead shapes from Susquehannock sites. Bottom left to right: arrow nocks from the Sheep Rock Shelter (36Hu1) and typical forms of Susquehannock stone triangular points.

end to receive the projectile point, and has a long taper at the other end for insertion into a hollow mainshaft.

At least two dozen arrow foreshafts with attached brass triangular points have been found in the lower Susquehanna Valley. There were several in private collections from the Byrd Leibhart site, and we know of 14 such points from two separate graves at the Strickler site (one in the northeast and one in the southeast cemetery). A quiver containing hafted brass points was found at Conestoga Town.

These points, and the methods of hafting, fall into two categories. All of the brass points from Conestoga have a small hole drilled through their centers. The lashings of these (either sinew or plant fiber) are wrapped around the shaft just below the point, and also pass through the hole in the point, as shown in Figure 50. All of these would appear to be on hardwood foreshafts which were split to receive the projectile. In shape, these points approach being equilateral triangles (generally the base is a little shorter than the two sides). The two sides of the points are slightly beveled to sharpen them.

In addition to a few strays, including a few Archaic points, there was only one other grave at Conestoga which contained triangular points. This was a cache of 26 points found by the owners of the property. At least 12 of these were of a western New York chert. These were isosceles triangles with markedly excurvate sides, and they are without question similar to ones from the Seneca sites of the last half of the seventeenth century, as seen in the Wray collection at the Rochester Museum.

At the Leibhart sites brass arrowheads outnumber stone points by about two to one. Brass triangles with holes in them are rather uncommon at this site. In a sample of about 50 points, only three had the center hole. We note also that these tend more toward an isosceles form than those from Conestoga.

Triangular points from Strickler are about equally divided between brass and stone. Here too the common outline is isosceles. Stone triangular points with serrated edges, although uncommon everywhere, are comparatively more abundant at Strickler.

The Museum's collection from Strickler includes six hafted brass points. Three of these have the central hole, and the points were secured in the same manner as those from Conestoga. The difference here is that the points are more isosceles in shape, and that the wrappings are of a fine two-strand twisted cord, possibly of flax and therefore of European manufacture. One of these shafts is clearly cut to a taper at its proximal end, implying that it was part of a composite arrow with a hollow mainshaft. Three specimens were slightly beveled to sharpen their edges. The other three hafted points have neither beveled edges nor center holes. They are wrapped with an untwisted fiber, and only around the shaft at the base of the point.

Brass triangular points were exceedingly rare at Washington Boro. The ratio of brass to stone triangular points is perhaps 1 to 200. No brass points were found at the Schultz site.

A few odd-shaped brass points have been recovered from Susquehannock sites. Several pentagonal shapes have been found by private collectors, and a tanged, somewhat bifurcate-base brass point was found at the Eschelman portion of the Washington Boro site.

Stone triangular points from both Washington Boro and Schultz definitely tend more toward equilateral outlines, as compared to those at Strickler and Leibhart. Quartz is the favored lithic material at both Schultz and Washington Boro (Schultz 48%, Washington Boro 76%). Cherts are the next most common at these sites (Schultz 47%, Washington Boro 21%). A small percentage (perhaps 5%) of these cherts are Onondaga. However, this does not necessarily mean that the points or the raw material were transported from New York. Glacial pebbles of Onondaga chert can be found in the till of the Susquehanna River, and, in fact, caches of such pebbles have been found at both the Schultz and Washington Boro sites.

Jasper and other more exotic stones are about equally uncommon at all Susquehannock sites where chipped-stone triangular points were in use. Two triangular points chipped from green bottle glass were recovered by Art Futer from a grave in the northeast cemetery at Strickler.

Conical antler points are not clearly associated with any Susquehannock complex. They do occur at some sites, such as Schultz, but it is very likely that they relate to the Shenks Ferry occupations at such sites. It is possible that a few conical brass points were used by the Susquehannocks, but these could easily be mistaken for brass jinglers, which were quite abundant at all periods.

As to the uses of arrows, little needs to be said. Several pieces of animal bone with embedded triangular points have been found in the refuse pits at both the Schultz and Washington Boro village sites. All Susquehannock sites have produced burials in which some of the human remains have had associated projectile points, but few which were actually embedded in parts of the skeletons. There are, interestingly enough, a number of Shenks Ferry skeletons with embedded points.

In summary, we can postulate that the Susquehannock bow, made of various woods, was generally as long as a man was tall. Their arrows can be somewhat more positively reconstructed. Ethnohistoric evidence would suggest that they were usually over a yard long, to perhaps as much as 48 inches. Both solid and composite shafts were used. The latter, made of plant stems or cane, had cut nocks with reinforcing wrapping just ahead of the nock. Shafts were fletched with at least two feathers just forward of the nock wrappings and extending along the shaft for at least two inches. Shafts were decorated, in some cases, with incised "lightning grooves" filled with red pigments and probably extending from the feathers to the ends of the mainshafts. It is reasonable to suppose, although we have no archeological or ethnohistoric evidence, that the distal end of a reed, cane or plant-stem mainshaft also had a reinforcement wrapping covered with glue. Hardwood foreshafts (of various woods) were tapered at their proximal ends for insertion into the hollow mainshaft, and split at the distal ends to receive the projectile points. The longest foreshaft from the Sheep Rock Shelter appears to have been split twice, with the intervening section removed in order to better receive the point. Judging from the specimens at hand, foreshafts may have ranged from about three to nine inches in length. The largest of these are about one-fourth inch in diameter, while the largest mainshaft (the decorated piece from Sheep Rock) is about three-eighths inch in diameter.

Since none of the hafted brass points has wrappings which pass over the lateral edges of the points, we might assume that stone points were tied to the foreshaft in this manner. That is, they were wrapped with fiber, cord or sinew, around the shaft only, to create a vise grip of the split shaft on the point (like those brass points without center holes described above). We see no clear evidence of any pitch or glue having been applied to the haft wrappings. This was done by many native-American groups, but perhaps among the Susquehannocks the concern was that the point stayed on the shaft only until it penetrated its target.

As indicated elsewhere, most Indians were gone from the Susquehanna Valley after about 1755. The exceptions include those few people at Conestoga, the Delawares and some Shawnee in the Wyoming Valley, and various groups of Moravian Indians. Historical and archeological evidence for this period clearly points to the continuing use of the bow and arrow, although much less frequently than in earlier times.

No excavated Indian sites of the post-1755 era in the Susquehanna Valley have produced arrowheads. However, sites of this period in western Pennsylvania, e.g., Kuskuski (36Lr11) and Mohulbucteetam (36Ar12), have produced some brass arrowheads. The sample from 36Ar12 includes six isosceles triangles with central holes, and 14 which have no holes; three of the points are pentagonal in shape, and have central holes. The latter form also occurs at Kuskuski, and it is known from various eighteenth-century Iroquois sites.

Food

One of the primary concerns of many anthropologists and archeologists is the discovery of precisely how a particular society (or culture) adapted to its environment. In essence, this means determining the specific techniques or procedures a culture used to exploit or cope with various aspects of the environment (meaning physical, natural and other cultural surroundings) in which it existed in order to provide a way of life for its members.

For most archeologists the major adaptive factor in a given way of life is how its members fed themselves. That is, what food resources were utilized (and which were not) and how were they secured?

Adaptation of a culture to its environment also means the customs or rules it follows in extracting and utilizing *all* the things from nature which it has found necessary or useful to provide for its way of life. It is obvious, however, that the primary and most basic consideration of any culture is the nourishment of the individual bodies of its members. All else—tools, clothing, housing, beliefs, other cultures, even sex—is secondary in order of importance. At times other things may seem of the utmost concern, but only when individuals are not hungry.

We have looked at most of the native technology (and the raw materials for building it) of the Susquehannock Indians. In doing so we have seen how it was used to exploit the environment in which these people lived for the purpose of securing food and making life more secure and comfortable. We have also seen how certain aspects of their technology changed over time in response to changes in their surroundings, primarily changes brought about by interaction with other societies. What remains for us is to enumerate those various items in nature which were eaten by the Susquehannocks in order to sustain life and culture. The particular things which they ate, or did not eat, and the way in which foods were secured and processed were all part of the pattern of culture which was Susquehannock.

Archeological techniques for recovering food remains or evidence thereof are quite simple. They involve the excavation of macro and micro eatables from areas in which food may have been processed, discarded, expelled as waste, or given as a funeral offering. The difficult part is in identifying what the food items actually are. Macro food stuffs would include easily seen evidence of fish, birds, reptiles, shellfish, mammals and plant parts. Micro remains, usually recovered through water screening or flotation, although smaller, can represent the same categories of things listed above, but these may be even more difficult to recognize.

The archeological and ethnohistorical evidence about the food-getting technologies of the Susquehannocks clearly shows them to have been hunters and gatherers of a wide range of wild foods—including both plants and animals—as well as farmers of certain domesticated plants. This combination of technologies, although not unusual throughout the world, enables us to generally characterize certain basic features of Susquehannock culture with respect to other cultures of other places.

It is not our intention here to engulf the general reader in a lengthy description of the techniques for recovering or analyzing evidence of various food sources utilized by the Susquehannocks. Instead, the various identified food items have simply been listed in order of the frequency of their use and importance to these people. It is possible to demonstrate that the quantities consumed or the importance of certain food resources changed over time (see Table 6). It should be realized that these changes can be both the cause and effect of changes in other aspects of Susquehannock culture during the period of its existence.

Table 6

OBSERVED MEAT (LBS.) CONTRIBUTIONS BY ALTERNATE PREY IN SUSQUEHANNOCK VILLAGES (after Webster 1983: Tables 24-25).

Prey	*Schultz*	*Washington Boro*	*Strickler*	*Byrd Leibhart*
Bear	810 (.15)	4455 (.18)	1080 (.26)	135 (.16)
Beaver	120 (.023)	390 (.016)	150 (.036)	30 (.035)
Bobcat	30 (.000)	75 (.003)	30 (.007)	0 (0)
Deer	3010 (.573)	12740 (.506)	2310 (.559)	350 (.413)
Dog	50 (.01)	210 (.008)	50 (.012)	10 (.012)
Elk	789 (.15)	5523 (.219)	263 (.064)	263 (.311)
Fish	118 (.022)	729 (.029)	98 (.024)	36 (.043)
Fowl	36 (.007)	172 (.007)	11 (.003)	6 (.007)
Fox	15 (.003)	30 (.001)	10 (.002)	5 (.006)
Lion	0 (0)	120 (.005)	0 (0)	0 (0)
Marmot	5 (.001)	14 (.005)	9 (.002)	0 (0)
Muskrat	2 (.0004)	8 (.0003)	4 (.001)	0 (0)
Other	8 (.002)	39 (.002)	7 (.002)	0 (0)
Pecan	10 (.002)	44 (.002)	10 (.002)	0 (0)
Rabbit	2 (.0003)	6 (.0002)	3 (.001)	2 (.002)
Raccoon	120 (.023)	352 (.014)	24 (.006)	8 (.009)
Skunk	8 (.002)	8 (.0003)	4 (.001)	0 (0)
Squirrel	8 (.002)	38 (.002)	5 (.001)	0 (0)
Waterfowl	32 (.006)	79 (.003)	25 (.006)	2 (.002)
Wolf	60 (.011)	120 (.005)	30 (.007)	0 (0)
Aquatic Reptile/ Amphibian	18 (.004)	22 (.001)	8 (.002)	1 (.001)
Total	5250 (1.00)	25174 (1.00)	4130 (1.00)	847 (1.00)

Chi-Square = 1186.482, DF = 60, Prob. = .0001

Notes: Prey categories included in analyses.

Fish	(suckers, catfish, eel, gar, small bass, sea bass, walleye, shad)
Aquatic Reptiles/ Amphibians	(musk turtle, map turtle, bullfrog, frog, snapping turtle)
Waterfowl	(loon, grebe, gull, heron, egret, swan, geese, duck)
Pecan	(otter, fisher)
Squirrel	(gray squirrel, fox squirrel, flying squirrel)
Fowl	(grouse, quail, turkey)
Other	(eagle, hawk, vulture, owl, crow, raven, grackle, flicker)

From other sources of information we might have predicted that corn (Zea maize) was the single most important food item. Indeed, if we count individual kernels of corn preserved in brass kettles or by charring, it is by far the most abundant individual food source. The numbers of recovered pumpkin and/or squash seeds would indicate that they were the next most abundant of the domesticated plant foods. Beans occur, but with an unexpectedly low frequency at all of the sites studied. Various wild or perhaps semi-domesticated plant foods, such as nuts, berries, seeds, tubers, roots, plant stems and leaves, also served as food sources. However, the degree of their importance as either substitute foods in times of shortage of major foods or as dietary varients is not presently well understood.

Again, if we judge by individual occurrences of food items, fresh-water mussels, as represented by the shells, would be the second most frequently used food. Actually, however, this is probably a reflection of the relative ease with which the shells were preserved, rather than their de facto importance in general subsistence.

Deer bones are by far the most numerous indicators of mammal food resources, and probably second only to corn in overall importance. Fish remains (represented by scales, vertebrae and sometimes jaw parts) of all species are the next most abundant.

Other animal species, both those that are larger than the deer (including elk and bear) and those numerous forms which are smaller, follow in various orders of succession depending upon sites and samples collected. Table 6 reflects some of these changes in frequency (see also Guilday, Parmalee, and Tanner 1962).

There is sufficient breadth in the food-remain sample from all Susquehannock sites from all time periods to indicate some variety of diet beyond that created or imposed by seasonal availability of food. Nevertheless, it seems clear that the most frequent meal consisted of corn and/or venison, undoubtedly prepared in a variety of ways, but most frequently boiled in the soup pots.

Certainly, there were periods of food shortage because of the vagaries of storage methods, season, climate, warfare, crop failure, game shortage, etc., but what foods may have been substituted or what degree of starvation may have occurred at such times is uncertain. Other than during the siege which the Susquehannocks suffered at the Piscataway fort in 1675, and at various times at Conestoga after about 1740, there is little historical evidence that they suffered any extended periods of starvation. Archeological evidence for such is similarly hard to find and even more difficult to prove. It is very possible that certain major cultural changes which the Susquehannocks underwent may have been attended, if not entirely caused, by severe food shortages.

As more things of European manufacture became available, including new tools for hunting, fishing, trapping and farming, there were probably also some new food commodities. Indians of the seventeenth century definitely received and consumed Euopean-made wines and liquor. During the eighteenth century it is clear that they traded for such items as sugar, flour, molasses, salt-pork, dried beef, etc. The subsistence and dietary patterns of the Susquehannocks were definitely changing, but in terms of their basic techniques for adapting to their environment they remained farmers and hunters to the end.

Physical Susquehannock

Diet has a great deal to do with the general physical condition of a specific population of human beings, as do genetics and total environment. Diet, or the amount and nature of food consumed by a population, is actually a reflection of the adaptation of that group to its environment, i.e., its ecology. Genetics is also related to, or at least influenced by environment. In the very broadest sense then, we really consider environment and human adaptation to it when studying the cause of the physical condition of a given population.

The impacts or effects on the body of what can best be termed ecology are most easily seen and recorded in living human populations. However, for ancient societies where examination of the living is obviously not possible, physical anthropologists or osteologists are still able to discern certain things about the physical condition of such populations by studying their skeletal remains. Stature, gender, age, an inkling of health and disease, certain racial features or genetic ties, and even some notion of demographic conditions or changes can be determined through careful examination of archeologically recovered skeletal remains. All of these things reflect, or relate to, the adaptation of a group of people (or a population) to its environment. Herein lie the primary reasons for exposing and studying ancient human skeletons.

Physical anthropologists have pretty well demonstrated that certain language and/or racial (actually genetically interrelated) groups of American Indians can be characterized by certain metric indices of the skull (or cranium), for example, breadth of skull divided by length, height of skull divided by length, etc. The former of these, known as the cranial index, describes head shape from long and narrow to round. Most Susquehannock skulls yield a cranial index of about 76.0, which places them between these extremes, or in the category known as mesocranial.

Little progress has been made toward characterizing Susquehannocks with regard to other cranial indices, or additional discrete attributes, and unfortunately the opportunities to do so have been rapidly diminished.

During the past 30 years, changes in the amount and type of fertilizers used on the soils in which the Susquehannocks are buried have drastically increased the rate of decomposition of their skeletal remains. In a vast majority of graves excavated in recent years, only the teeth caps are preserved, whereas excavations in those same areas 30 or 40 years ago frequently exposed full skeletons.

A grave in which human remains consist of nothing but teeth caps can reveal little more than the approximate age of an individual. Other, more useful anthropometric observations are generally impossible. However, a composite picture assembled from the Susquehannock graves excavated and recorded over the past four decades allows us at least a minimum understanding of their skeletal population.

In addition to being basically mesocranial, we note an average height of about five feet, four inches, generally good health, an average life span of about 25 years, a fairly equal distribution between the sexes, remarkably few dental caries, and a notable paucity of bone injuries, abnormalities and diseases.

We should remember that these describe average conditions, and that there are exceptions. For example, some individuals were decidedly taller than five feet, four inches. However, there is little archeological corroboration for the statements by Captain John Smith, who in 1608 reported of the Susquehannocks that "such great and well proportioned men are seldome seene, for they seemed like Giants to the English, yea and to the neighbors" (Smith 1907: 50). Very few Susquehannock skeletons measuring over five feet, ten inches (based upon measurements of the femurs or other long bones) have been recorded; and it is unlikely that men of that height would have seemed *unusually* large even to the normally short seventeenth-century Englishmen. On the other hand, the 60-man Susquehannock embassage assembled to confront Smith might well have comprised persons well above average height and bodily proportion. These individuals simply have not yet shown up in the archeological record.

Distributions of males and females, as represented in the skeletal populations recorded for various Susquehannock sites, differ somewhat; but overall they are about even, with females having a slight edge. Heisey and Witmer (1962: 104) recorded 68% females and 32% males (n = 19) at the Blue Rock cemetery of the Schultz site. Combined samples from Frey-Haverstick (36La6) gave 57% females and 43% males (n = 14). The 1974 sample from the Strickler site (36La3) yielded a count of 56% females vs. 44% males (n = 23). Data recorded in 1970 at the Byrd Leibhart site (36Yo170) showed 58% females and 42% males (n = 17). Conestoga Town, on the other hand, excavated in 1972, produced a sample of 44% females and 56% males (n = 23). Overall percentages for this total sample are 56% female and 44% male. Variations in the distribution of sexes for ancient populations can be subjected to a number of interpretations, not the least of which may be misidentification of sex, particularly since *relative* gracility (or robustness) is often the major determining criterion in field identification.

Average age of a skeletal population is obviously affected by infant and adolescent mortality rates, and the ability of the observers to accurately age the remains. Unfortunately, average age in this case is not a reflection of average life expectancy of those who reached adulthood. A reasonable guess for this more interesting figure might be 35; but the samples of carefully aged adults are simply too small to substantiate any such claims. Table 7 shows the distribution of ages in three gross age classes. Obviously there were some arbitrary assignments for individuals who approached the margins of any class.

Table 7
DISTRIBUTION OF AGE GROUPS

Site	*Adults (21+)*	*Adolescents (3-20)*	*Infants (0-2)*	*Total*
36La6	74%	19%	7%	27
36La3	75%	17%	8%	156
36Yo170	63%	29%	8%	48
36La52	66%	25%	9%	64

Tooth decay, although infrequent, was present, particularly in adult individuals. Those few adults who did have noticeable cavities rarely had more than two or three. In at least a few cases, however, the severity of the caries was such that it may have been the cause of death. A fair number of instances of missing teeth were noted among adults. Wear on all teeth, but particularly molars, was noticeable in most adults, and in fact formed a major criterion for determining the age of adult individuals. We note parenthetically that the Susquehannocks, like most American Indians, typically displayed shovel-shaped upper incisors.

Bone trauma was even more infrequent in all examined samples. There were a few cases of healed broken bones and at least two examples of unhealed fractures, which likely were the cause of death, or associated with it. Both projectile points and musket balls have frequently been found in areas which could have been within the body of buried individuals, but only a few projectiles were discovered actually embedded in the bone of a Susquehannock skeleton (see for example La9/66).

Evidence of artificial deformation of the cranium or post cranial skeleton is largely non-existent among the Susquehannocks. A few skulls show occipital (back) and/or frontal flattening, but these do not seem to have been the result of intentional practices. In fact, some of these conditions as observed in the field may be post-mortem, due to decay and soil pressure.

Other palaeopathologies, such as infections, deficiency diseases and degenerative changes, are present to what would appear to be a very minor degree. Their precise diagnosis must await analysis of extant laboratory samples by expert physical anthropologists.

The apparent paucity of bone diseases, more than average stature, and the low degree of bone trauma and dental caries may or may not be indicative of the general health of the Susquehannocks. Other sources of archeological and ethnohistoric data suggest that from about 1550 to perhaps 1660, their population was growing—an indication of a more than successful biological adaptation to environment. However, from about 1660 onward, Susquehannock population exhibits a rather steady decline. Without question, the Susquehannocks of the latter period were exposed to a vastly changed environment—one brought about by the proximity of other (particularly European) cultures. Their declining population during this period is evidence of their obviously less than successful adaptation to these changes. More simply stated, the Susquehannocks were suffering from a death rate greater than their birth rate. As we have stated in the previous chapter, this was not obviously a result of starvation. There may well have been an increase in the number, duration or severity of temporary food shortages. But again, these alone do not seem to account for the demographic changes of the late seventeenth and first half of the eighteenth centuries. Social, psychological, even political factors of insufficient adaptation were very much involved in and responsible for what was happening. Of paramount significance was their biological and genetic inability to develop resistance to newly introduced diseases.

Obvious signs of such conditions in skeletal populations are the lesions or scars from nutritional deficiency or epidemic diseases which affect bone surfaces. We have said that observed examples of such were not numerous. New strains of influenza and probably smallpox, which do not scar the bone, plus warfare, adoption and migration all combined to decrease Susquehannock population.

Evidence like mass burials or an increased number of graves, which would indicate a rapid increase in the death rate, caused by war or epidemic, is not apparent in *most* of the archeological record for this period.

It seems fairly obvious from historical and archeological hindsight that their population was, for the most part, slowly, but steadily, declining through this period. Whether the Susquehannocks themselves recognized this is of little historical importance. What is significant is that they did not or could not do anything about it, and this describes, in a nutshell, their adaptation (or lack of it) to their changing environment.

Description of actual Susquehannock burial practices and changes thereof, additional thoughts on demography, and some other paleopathological observations are presented in the site reports (particularly the Strickler site report).

Current objections and philosophies of native Americans, and present ethical practice by anthropologists, neither warrant nor condone the future disturbance of Indian remains, except in cases where they would otherwise be destroyed without any notice or scientific record.

European Objects

Items Made of Brass

GLASS beads and items of brass are the earliest trade materials to occur, and the most numerous at all periods of Susquehannock culture. The earliest brass objects are spirals, or the so-called Basque earrings. One such specimen was recovered from a burial at the Shenks Ferry site, and therefore probably dates from before 1575.

Items of this sort, including brass scraps, were being received by coastal Indians from European fishermen as early as 1525, if not before (Bradley 1979: 355-82). By the time the Susquehannocks were settled at their Schultz site location (ca. 1575), brass scraps and some ornaments were becoming considerably more abundant, at least by comparison with scattered Susquehannock hamlets in Bradford County, where such items are very rare. Sources for the trade materials at Schultz must still have been the coastal Indians who received them from fishermen, since there were as yet no European settlements north of Spain's New World empire.

Strips and bent fragments of brass, semispherical discs of brass, and coils were the most common items. One small brass kettle has been found at the Schultz site. Kettles were the primary source of brass being used at this time, and the Indians were probably those who were responsible for cutting and fashioning those items (excluding the spiral earring) which are found. Kettles were just not being used as such. It is doubtful that very many whole kettles ever reached the Schultz Susquehannocks, having already been cut apart by the coastal peoples. The bright yellow metal was too attractive and too easily worked into baubles. Cooking was better done in the traditional clay pots.

When the Washington Boro site was settled (ca. 1600), the quantity of brass being used by the Indians had at least quadrupled. Many more ornaments were being fashioned, including jinglers of both sheet and corrugated brass, various cut-out shapes, the earlier-mentioned discs, and even a few triangular arrow points. Among the inventory of unmodified European manufactures are at least one conventional bell, numerous hawkbells, a brass spoon (described later), and no fewer than four whole kettles.

Sites of the succeeding period (Billmyer, Frey-Haverstick, and Roberts) produce increasingly large amounts of brass bells, kettles and arrowheads. A decrease is apparent in the number of Indian-made ornaments, such as pendants.

Figure 51. Early brass objects, primarily cut from brass kettles, found at the Schultz and Washington Boro sites. Note "Basque" earring (spiral, center of Figure).

By the time they had moved to the Strickler site, ornaments cut from brass were very rare, and jinglers declined in popularity. Brass arrowheads now outnumbered stone triangular points. Jesuit and secular rings appeared for the first time. Whole brass kettles were very common, occurring in about the same numbers as the native pots. Kettles of this period varied in size from five inches in diameter to 17 inches. By far the greatest number of kettles were about nine inches in diameter and five inches deep.

Kettle bails are of both brass and iron, but the latter are more common. Lugs vary in form, including folded sheets of brass and more ornamental hammered loops (Figure 55). Both lug forms sometimes occur on one kettle, suggesting Indian repairs. Holes in kettles were frequently repaired with a patch of brass that was riveted to the walls or bottom. Kettles often exhibit concentric rings or lines on their bottoms (when they survive), and parallel encircling rings on their walls. These are the marks made by spinning the kettles in order to form them. A few kettles have incised designs on their inside bottoms – apparently Indian work.

Brass hawkbells and conventional bell shapes were still very popular during Strickler times. One very large bell (Figure 53) was in a grave at the Strickler site.

Conjoined brass spirals and brass snuff or vanity boxes, usually ovoid in outline, are also fairly abundant at this site. The boxes often contain beads, strike-a-light sets, plum-pit dice, or other trinkets. Some of the lids of these boxes bear European inscriptions or other decorations; one has a ship engraved upon it.

The list of items also includes brass chains (for necklaces), tubular beads and bracelets. The latter ornaments are made of both rods and strips of the metal.

Brass kettles, Jesuit rings, a candlestick, arrowheads, bracelets, thim-

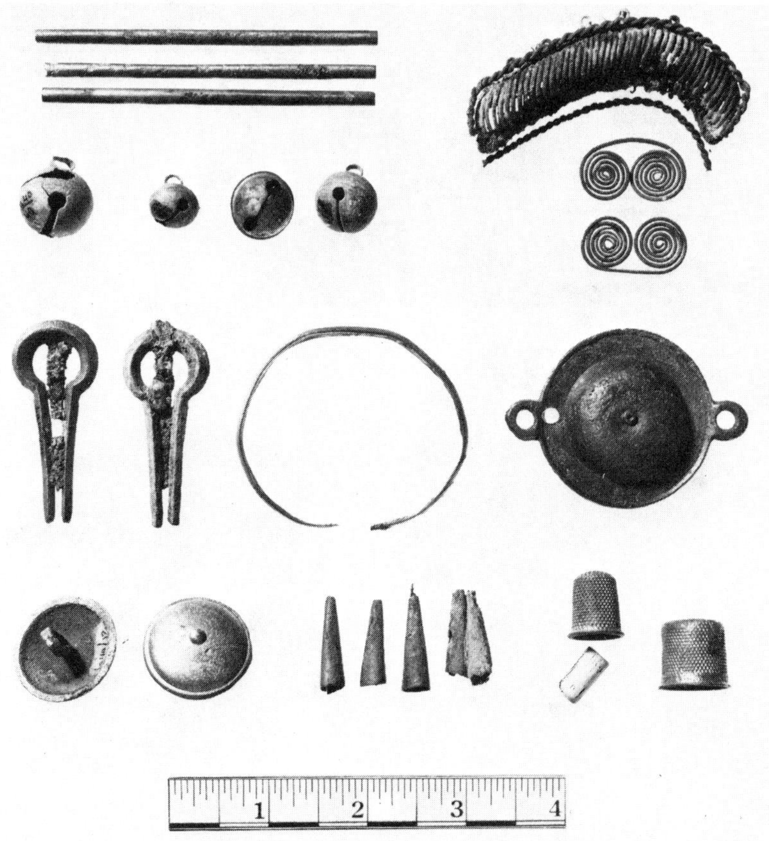

Figure 52. Brass objects from graves at Conestoga Town (36La52) and Conoy cemetery (36La40), including from top left to right: tubes, coils, hawk bells, Jews harps, bracelet, part of a horse briddle, buttons, conical jinglers, and thimbles.

Figure 53. Brass bell and tobacco or vanity boxes. Lower left: note 1634 date.

bles, bells, etc., were all found at the Oscar Leibhart site, but again, their frequency cannot be determined from available data.

The same general range of items occurred at the Byrd Leibhart site. However, it was possible to see that brass kettles, for example, were not as numerous as at Strickler. There was roughly a one-to-five ratio of kettles to native-made pots at Byrd Leibhart's. Triangular brass arrowheads now outnumbered stone points by almost four to one.

This diminishing use of kettles, guns, glass beads, iron axes and certain other European items at the Byrd Leibhart site (and evidently at the Oscar Leibhart site) is, as previously suggested, a reflection of the declining military and economic status of the Susquehannocks and consequently their reduced trade relations.

In 1978 the William Penn Memorial Museum purchased, at the auction of the George Keller collection, a number of items from the Byrd Leibhart site. Among them was a heavily encrusted brass vanity or snuff case. Upon cleaning the object by electrolysis, it was discovered that the straight sides of the box (it is oval in outline from the top view) contained a panel of baroque designs in relief, including flowers, Tudor roses and two birds. The lid of the case had a raised relief bust of a man and the following inscription of raised letters: "Freder. Henr. D.G. Princeps, AVRIAC. Com. Nass." (Frederick Henry by Grace of God, Prince of Orange, Count of Nassau). Opposite the right shoulder of the prince is the date 1634. Similar lids for such boxes have been found at Oneida sites and elsewhere in New York State. One of these from the Dann site appears to be identical to the specimen described here, including the 1634 date (see Pratt 1976: 232): a commemorative medal with the same inscription, but dated 1631, is illustrated in Betts 1972: 16). Obviously this specimen was antique by the time it was placed in a grave at Byrd Leibhart's. It is the only "signed" Dutch trade item that we know of from a Susquehannock site.

By the time the Susquehannocks and Seneca had established the town of Conestoga, the use of brass kettles was once again increasing. Now they were a matter of absolute necessity and every family had them. The simple reason for this is that they were readily available from numerous traders, and the Indians no longer made any of their own pottery cooking vessels.

Brass kettles at Conestoga occurred with a frequency of one per every one and a half graves. Their size, shape and lugs are essentially the same as those of the preceding periods. Some as small as three inches in diameter were found at Conestoga, but the larger ones were less abundant.

Jinglers, thimbles, chains, brass tubular beads, strip bracelets and bells were still fairly common. The collection includes 78 bells, of which 69 are hawk bells like those from earlier sites. Five of them were conventional or flared bells. For the first time in the sequence we see the cast "rumblers" or sleigh bells, of which six were recovered. At least three of these bore the initials W.K. or K.W. One bell was marked W.G., which Noël Hume (1976: 58-59) attributes to the Wells Foundry, Aldbourne, Wiltshire, England, which produced bells from 1694 to the first quarter of the nineteenth century. Several bells still had preserved strips of leather thong attached to their hangers.

Conestoga Town produced at least 11 snuff or vanity boxes. Two of these were brass, the remainder were made of iron. Most of them contained trinkets such as beads, catlinite objects, jettons, coins, buttons and at least one thimble. A number of the boxes had woven cloth, preserved by oxides, adhering to their outer surfaces. These materials were probably pieces of garments or blankets with which the boxes were in contact.

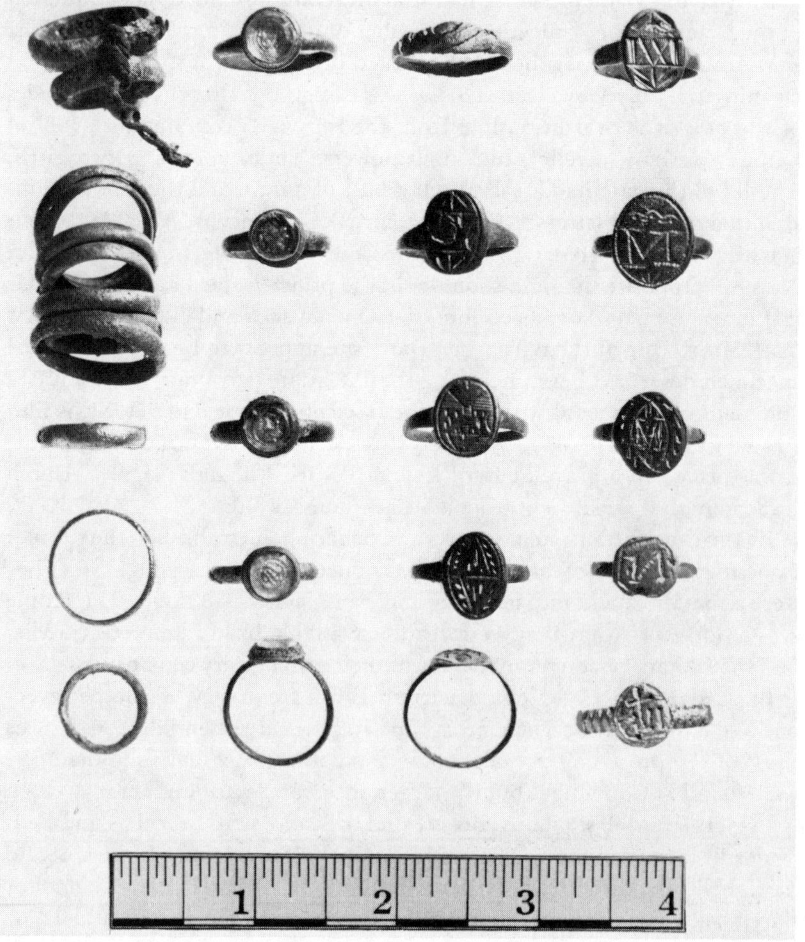

Figure 54. Brass rings. Lower right: note Jesuit ring.

Figure 55. Brass kettles, note size and lug variations. Top left to right: Conestoga Town (36La52, Witmer collection); Conoy cemetery (36La40). Bottom left to right: (36La40); unusual round-bottom kettle, Strickler (36La3, Futer collection).

Coils of brass wire, ranging in diameter (of the coil) from one-eighth inch to one and one-half inch, also appear for the first time at Conestoga. Their uses consisted of hair and ear ornaments, necklaces and pipestem decorations. A number of them were wrapped around wooden dowels and quite possibly served as hair pullers or a kind of tweezers.

Excavations at Conestoga Town produced 272 finger rings, many of which were worn as decorations elsewhere on the body as, for example, necklaces. Plain wedding-band types, one-eighth to three-sixteenths inch wide, were the most common, being represented by 188 specimens. Twelve additional rings of this type have designs on the outside of the bands. An undetermined number, because of corrosion, had inscriptions such as "true love" on the inside of the band. Twenty-one rings had clear or colored paste settings, and six of these had designs under the settings. Bezels of several outlines occur on 35 rings from Conestoga. These contain various initials, religious figures, hearts and other decorations. Cleland (1972: 202-10) feels that many of these forms have evolved from the earlier and more classically Jesuit rings, i.e., those marked IHS, with a cross above the H. Only three IHS rings were found at Conestoga—or somewhat less than 1% occurrence. By contrast, at least 50% of the (26) rings from Strickler bear the IHS mark.

Graves at Conoy Town were also loaded with trinkets, but surprisingly, there were very few utilitarian trade goods buried with the dead. Only two brass kettles were found in 71 graves. Likewise axes, knives and guns were much less frequent. There is every reason to believe that the Conoy had these commodities, particularly brass kettles, in some quantity. The lack of their placement in the graves may be a sign of their impoverished state, but it may also be a reflection of the difference in burial customs between the Conoy and Conestoga. Brass trinkets and their quality at Conoy are quite similar to those at Conestoga. We note almost the same (about 1%) proportion of IHS rings to other types at Conoy Town.

This preponderance of brass items, particularly at Conestoga Town, is not a reflection of the wealth of its inhabitants; perhaps more than anything it is a product of the town's place in both history and geography. Until about 1725 it was pretty much at the edge of Pennsylvania's frontier, and yet close enough to serve as a convenient place of contact for whites and Indians. Throughout the first quarter of the eighteenth century, Conestoga Town was the focal point for a very brisk trade as well as numerous land-sale negotiations with many Indians. Proprietary land buyers, and numerous traders, with the backing of shrewd Philadelphia merchants, could transport large quantities of small inexpensive goods to Conestoga Town, where they were very profitably exchanged for land, furs or hides (principally deerskins). Similarly, the Indians could easily travel to Philadelphia for such exchanges.

The Indians' fascination with, but more accurately their now total dependence upon, cheap European-made (or colonial) baubles as well as utilitarian items often made them an easy mark for unscrupulous land speculators or fur traders. Such gross inequities in the market place are precisely what history has taught us to expect when one culture comes to enjoy, but cannot itself produce, the better products of another. One of the things which can bring a halt to such profitable, but perhaps morally objectionable, markets is that the technologically inferior group may simply run out of goods that the other wants. This is precisely what happened to the Susquehanna's Indians—they soon sold off all of their lands and killed off most of the fur-bearing animals. Now they would either be absorbed by the whites or flee beyond the frontier.

Much of this book is concerned with the impact of these culture contacts and interactions. Other than the few written words about these matters, the items of brass and the other yet to be described "trade goods" are all that we have to remind us of these historical and cultural events.

Beads

European-made beads have become our most important class of trade objects for dating historic-period Indian sites. The bead types were not presented to American archeologists as precisely datable objects which could be used to determine the age of the Indian sites at which they were encountered. In fact, quite the opposite is true. The chronology of trade beads as we now know it is largely the result of American archeologists having found them in otherwise datable contexts. As the temporal sequences of the various bead types are worked out and refined, the beads themselves become very useful chronometers for other sites in which no more precisely dated objects are found.

Beads have become very important as dating fossils for two reasons: First, they were the most numerous items traded to the Indians; and second, the various styles generally came and went very rapidly among both the manufacturers of beads and the users.

During the past several decades archeologists began to seriously describe glass trade beads, thus generating a growing body of information about their chronologies and numerous types, particularly in the New World. Kinsey (1960: 91), for example, published a typology of beads and their numbers from the Ibaugh cemetery, which is associated with the Washington Boro site. Shortly thereafter, Heisey and Witmer (1962: 117) provided descriptions of additional types from the Schultz, Washington Boro and Strickler sites. Smith and Graybill (1977) presented a typology for a more recent and much larger collection from the Schultz site, including black and white drawings of 65 varieties of glass trade beads.

Peter Pratt (1961) published, in a very limited edition, color photographs of beads from dated central New York Iroquois sites. Thus far this has been one of the more useful tools for dating the wide range of bead types in the northeastern United States. Its drawbacks, like those of other typologies, are in accurately comparing the colors and structures of one's own sample with those illustrated and/or described by Pratt. In addition, there are also certain problems of sample size, so that it is not always possible to determine at which site (or time period) a particular bead type was most abundant, and thereby most closely dated.

Realizing these impediments to the development of good bead type chronologies, the present writer nevertheless endeavored to produce yet another scheme to organize the growing bead sample from Susquehanna Valley sites. This system, employing a numbered "type board" of actual specimens, based on criteria of color, layering, embedding and shape, was found useful for classifying the samples at hand. However, this clearly was still not the answer to the need for a universal typology, primarily because of the absence of any standardized description of the colors, and the lack of adequate color photographs or illustrations which could be distributed to other researchers.

This problem was largely solved with the publication of Kidd's and Kidd's (1970) "Classification System for Glass Beads," wherein they meticulously describe the various construction features of beads and present generally recognizable color illustrations which can be used to standardize the color designations.

The Kidds made no effort to determine the distributions of their types at any dated sites. Consequently, it remained for others to apply the Kidds' typology to dated sequences wherever they might occur. Until the Rochester Museum and Science Center Bead Conference in 1982, there were very few formal efforts in this regard.

Prior to the publication of the Kidds' (1970) classification system, the present writer had already counted datable samples of over seventy-five thousand beads in more than 150 type groups. Ultimately the sample was increased to over one hundred ten thousand beads derived from 13 sites covering a time span from about 1575 to 1760 A.D. Realizing the widespread applicability of the Kidds' system, the present sample was converted to their type numbers. For economy of space in our early application of the Kidds' typology, their Roman numerals were transposed to Arabic. Unfortunately, but in order to avoid reproducing charts and tables, that transposition has been retained here.

Distributions of the various types are expressed in terms of their percentage of occurrence in the total from each site (Table 8). This chart shows the distribution of all the types at each of the various sites, as well as their distributions through time. It will be noted that a few beads in this sample are not found in the Kidd typology. However, for the most part, these are single or very minor occurrences. Any bead which occurs with a frequency of less than 1% at a particular site is simply indicated as being present (x). Although no description of the types in the earlier Susquehanna Valley (Kent) scheme is provided here, the comparison of the two type-numbering systems is shown in Table 8 and Figure 56 to emphasize certain minor differences in the recognition of types.

For the reader who may not have Kidd's and Kidd's (1970) classification close at hand, we have provided a color plate (Figure 57) of the hallmark, or most popular, beads, together with a chronological arrangement and their percentage distribution at each site (Figure 56, a dot indicates less than 1% occurrence).

The researcher who is comparing his own bead collection with this sequence should obviously consider his total sample as it may compare to Table 8. A few of the hallmark types which appear in Figure 56 seem to occur at only one or two sites of close time periods. These should be considered the most important in cross-dating other samples. As a word of caution concerning infrequently occurring types, we should note that Indians, particularly during the eighteenth century, occasionally looted earlier sites to secure beads; and of course, there is always the possibility that the beads may have been heirlooms. Small samples from a site, therefore, should be considered very carefully in this regard. The geographic extent of the applicability of these cross-correlations is uncertain; for example, they may not apply well in the southeastern United States, where various blue beads were widely selected above all others.

Certain hallmarks and/or combinations of types seem to be of paramount utility for purposes of comparative dating. For example, 2a15, a white oval-shaped bead, is the most abundant type at the Schultz site, and occurs almost exclusively at that site. The so-called flush-eyes (4g1), although scarce everywhere, are also most frequently encountered at the Schultz site. Blue beads of the type 2a53, although found at both earlier and later sites, can be considered a hallmark of the period from 1600 to 1630, when they are the most common type from a particular site. Straw beads, especially red ones, and to a lesser extent blue, black and white ones, definitely have their greatest occurrence at sites dating 1630 to 1670. Sites after 1670 produce fewer straw beads and increasing numbers of pea-size, round, solid red (2a1) or solid black (2a6) examples.

Wire-wound beads (Kidd and Kidd 1970: 62), which clearly exhibit that manufacturing technique, probably do not occur on Indian sites before about 1690. These beads are quite characteristic of sites from the first three or four decades of the eighteenth century. Although not necessarily the most common of the wire-wound beads, the very large spherical whites, the so-called raspberry, and the blue-faceted ones are generally the most outstanding and easily recognized of this period. By at least 1750 small, shiny white seed beads (4a13) become the predominant type.

Susquehannock sites dating to before 1575 in Bradford County, Pennsylvania, and at nearby Engelbert site in New York have produced very few glass beads. Those which we have seen were so badly deteriorated that their type could not be identified. Probably fewer than 1% of the Susquehannock graves from this area or time period include beads as burial offerings. At the Schultz site, after 1575, at least 30% of the graves contained beads. These were in positions which would suggest that they were used on necklaces, were sewn on clothing at the waist, and were rarely used on clothing covering other parts of the body. Also at Schultz we find that, occasionally, beads were scattered through the fill of the grave as it was being closed. There were a few examples of this at Washington Boro, less evidence of such practices at Strickler, and a reoccurrence at both Byrd Leibhart's and at Conestoga Town.

FIGURE 56 DISTRIBUTION OF THE MOS

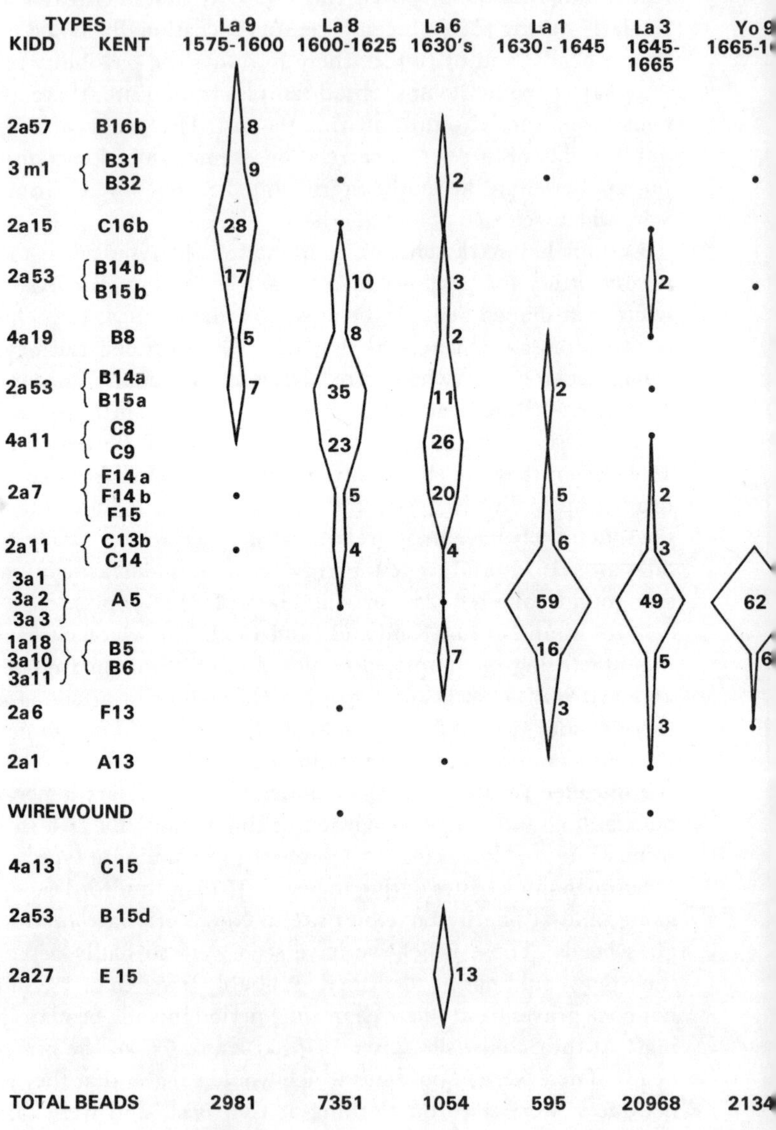
TYPES
KIDD
KENT
La 9 1575-1600
La 8 1600-1625
La 6 1630's
La 1 1630 - 1645
La 3 1645-1665
Yo 9 1665-1
2a57 B16b
3 m1 B31 B32
2a15 C16b
2a53 B14b B15b
4a19 B8
2a53 B14a B15a
4a11 C8 C9
2a7 F14 a F14 b F15
2a11 C13b C14
3a1 3a 2 3a 3 A 5
1a18 3a10 3a11 B5 B6
2a6 F13
2a1 A13
WIREWOUND
4a13 C15
2a53 B 15d
2a27 E 15
8
9
28
17
5
7
10
8
35
23
5
4
2
3
2
11
26
20
4
7
13
2
5
6
59
16
3
2
2
3
49
5
3
62
6
TOTAL BEADS
2981
7351
1054
595
20968
2134

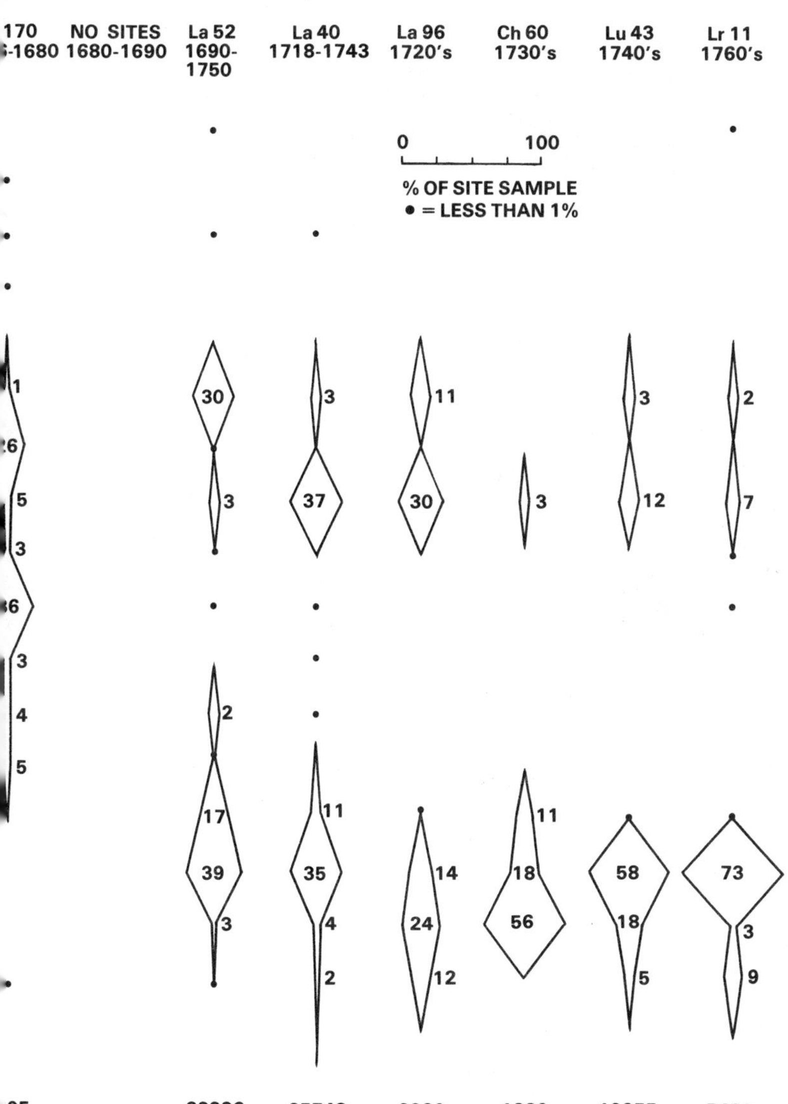
OPULAR BEAD TYPES
170 -1680
NO SITES 1680-1690
La 52 1690-1750
La 40 1718-1743
La 96 1720's
Ch 60 1730's
Lu 43 1740's
Lr 11 1760's
0 100
% OF SITE SAMPLE
• = LESS THAN 1%
1
6
5
3
6
3
4
5
30
3
3
37
11
30
3
3
12
2
7
2
17
39
3
11
35
4
2
14
24
12
11
18
56
58
18
5
73
3
9
05
23336
25748
2329
1889
13355
5483

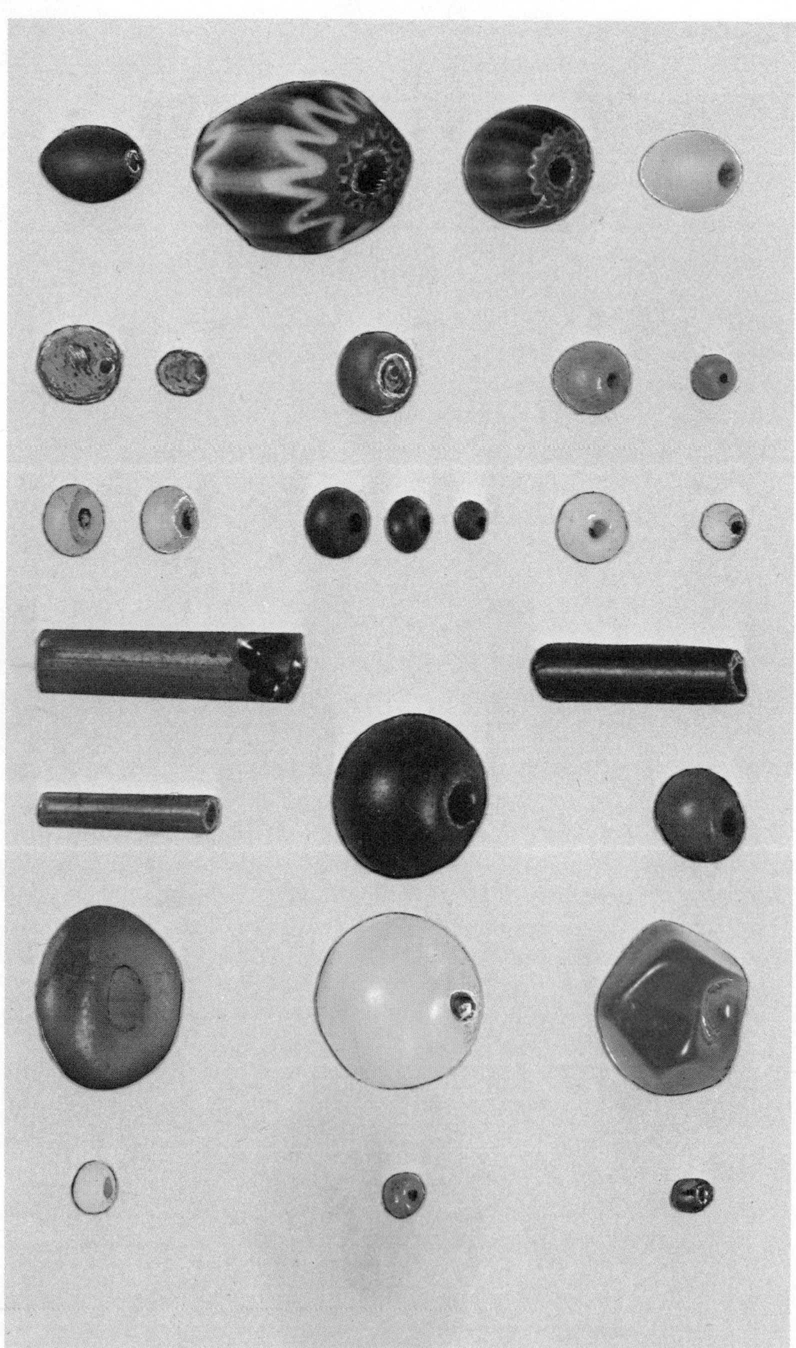

In general, the percentage of graves containing beads increases through time. At least 85% of them at Conestoga Town included beads. There is occasional evidence of beads in the hair or on bands worn on the head, particularly at the Strickler site. Necklaces were a consistently popular way to use beads. By at least the time of the Roberts site (ca. 1640) straw beads were being used to make bracelets in wampum-belt fashion, with geometric patterns created by using two or more differently colored beads (Figure 97). Bracelets of this sort continued to be made right up through the period of Conestoga. At Strickler there would seem to be an increase in the use of beads that were sewn onto shirts, but it is admittedly difficult to differentiate these from long necklaces. Occasionally, graves from this site produce a container of beads—usually an iron or brass vanity or snuff box, or sometimes what must have been a leather pouch.

For whatever reason, glass beads were less common (as compared to Strickler) at both Leibhart sites, and particularly at Byrd Leibhart's. This latter site shows an increase in the number of graves in which beads were haphazardly thrown into the grave fill, although, in most cases, the number of beads was only a dozen or so.

Beads were enormously popular at both Conestoga Town and Conoy Town. The total sample from our excavations at these two sites is in excess of sixty thousand beads. At Conestoga Town beads were used for decorating clothing, bags, and some hair or head ornaments. Necklaces and bracelets were exceedingly common. Here too, beads were scattered throughout the fill of some graves, and often they were to be found in caches contained in pouches or iron boxes.

All of the interments at the Conoy Town cemetery (36La40) were bundle burials, wrapped probably in cloth or sacks. In all likelihood there was little use of bead-decorated clothing. The majority of the beads recovered here were either on belts or necklaces. These were placed both on and under (rarely next to) the bone bundles. In many cases the necklaces, and occasionally a belt, could be uncovered as they were actually strung if they were found on the floor of the grave. Unfortunately, most of the necklaces so recovered were composed of one color. In the few exceptions where necklaces of more than one color were found, there was no ordered arrangement or sequence of different-colored beads. Rather, the colors seem to have been strung at random.

Figure 57, opposite. Most popular glass bead types (after Kent, see Figure 56). Top row left to right: B16b, B31, B32, C16b. Second row: B14b, B15b, B8, B14a, B15a. Third row: C8, C9, F14a, F14b, F15, C13b, C14. Fourth row: A5, B6. Fifth row: B5, F13, A13. Sixth row: three typical wirewound forms (D30 [Kidds' type W1d1], C28 [Kidds' type W1b5], B29a [Kidds' type W2C11]). Bottom Row: C15, B15d, E15. All beads shown twice actual size.

Table 8
DISTRIBUTION OF GLASS-BEAD TYPES

Kidd	*Kent*	*La9*	*La8*	*La6*	*La1*	*La3*	*Yo9*	*170*	*La52*	*La40*	*La96*	*Ch60*	*Lu43*	*Lr11*
1a1	A11a		x	2.7		x		x		x				
1a2	F11	x	x		x	12.6		3.4		x				1.5
1a4	C11	5.6				x				x				
"	C11b								x					
1a5	C6													1.7
1a7	D11					x		x						x
1a8	(29)	2.3												
1a12	B11b	x												
1a18	B5					2.7		3.1		x				
1a19	B11a	4.4	x			1.0			1.0	1.5	x			x
1a21	A11b	x				x								
1b3	F23					5.4	x	x		x				
1b4	F22c					2.2	7.6							
1b5	F23b					1.4								
1b7	C27a					x								
1b8	B27	x												
1b9	C24a			x		x	x							
1b14							4.0							
1bb1	A18	x		x						x				
1c'1	A1					x	x	x						
1c1	A2					x				x				
1c'2	E2					x		x	x	x				
1c'3	B2				x	x		x						
1e'2	E11a					x								
1f6	A29								x					
1f7	B29c								x					
2a1	A13			x		x		4.7	x					
2a2	A15					x								x
2a3	A16							x						
2a6	F12									x				
"	F13		x		3.4	3.2	x	3.8	1.8	x				
"	(70)	1.0		x		x								

Kidd	*Kent*	*La9*	*La8*	*La6*	*La1*	*La3*	*Yo9*	*Yo 170*	*La52*	*La40*	*La96*	*Ch60*	*Lu43*	*Lr11*
2a7	F14a	x	4.8	x		1.5		4.6	x	x				
"	F14b			19.5		x			1.0	35.7				
"	F15				5.0				1.9	1.3	30.1	3.5	12.3	7.3
2a8	F16b	x		x										
2a11	C13b		4.2	1.1				1.9						
"	C14	x		2.7	6.0	2.5		1.1	x					x
2a13	C13			x		x				x				
2a15	C16b	28.0	x			x		x	x	x				
"	C16c					x			x					
2a18a	C16a					x	x		x					x
"	C16d								x			x		
2a19	D15			x		x			5.5	3.2			2.8	
2a19a	D16	x		x		x								
2a21	C12		x											
2a27	E14								x					
"	E15			13.3				x	x	1.5	11.6		4.5	9.2
2a28	E13									x				
2a39a	B12								x	x		x		
2a48	B14c	x	3.2	x										
2a52	B13a	x	5.2	2.4	1.3	x		x		x				x
2a53	B14a	3.6	33.0	11.0	2.5	x			19.4	x				
"	B14b	7.6	8.8	x		x	x	x	x	x		x		
"	B15a		1.6	x				1.5	11.0	3.2	10.8		3.2	2.3
"	B15b	9.8	1.1	3.2		1.5								
"	B15d								2.7	3.9	23.7	56.3	18.3	2.5
2a54	B16a							x		x				
2a55	B13b	x	x							x	x	x		
2a56			2.5			x								
2a57	B16b	8.1							x					x
2a60	(4)	1.3												
"	(47)	x										x		
2b'7	C26	x							x					
2b10	F22b						x							
2b11	F22a	x			x	x								
2b15	F26	x						x						

Kidd	*Kent*	*La9*	*La8*	*La6*	*La1*	*La3*	*Yo9*	*Yo 170*	*La52*	*La40*	*La96*	*Ch60*	*Lu43*	*Lr11*
2b19	G22a									x				
"	G22b	x								x				
2b39	C24b		x											
2b52a	E26		x											
2b53	E22a									x				
2b56	B22a		x	x										
2b59	B23	x												
2b61	(55)	x												
2b68	B22c								x		x			
"	B22d								x	x				
2b72	B25									x				
2bb1	A19a	x				x	x	x						
	(59)	x												
2bb2	A19b		x	x										
2bb13	C27c					x			x	x				
2bb24	B26									x				
2bb27	B26b	1.4												
2g3	(64)	x												
2g4	(38)	x												
2g6	G36		x											
2h1	B34				x			x						
2j3	F37									x				
2j5	F38					x		x	x	x	4.8			
3a1 ⎫														
3a2 ⎬	A5		x	x	59.0	49.4	62.0	36.4	x	x				x
3a3 ⎭														
3a8	C5					4.7	2.0	5.3		x				
3a10 ⎫	B6			7.2	16.0	2.2	5.5	x		x				
3a11 ⎭														
3a12	(17)	x												
3b10	B20	x	x											
3bb8	(12)	x												
3c1			x											
3c'3	B1		x			x								

Kidd	Kent	La9	La8	La6	La1	La3	Yo9	Yo 170	La52	La40	La96	Ch60	Lu43	Lr11
3e1	A3					x								
3e'1	A4					x								
3bb5	A17					x	4.0	x	x	x				
3k3	B33		x											
3m1	B31	2.3			x		x							
"	B32	6.9	x	1.6				x						
4a2	A7					x		x		x				
4a3	A8	x	x	x	x	x		x	x	x		x		
4a5	A10					x		3.7	x	x	2.6			
4a6	A9	x	2.5	2.0	2.5	1.2	11.0		x	1.2		10.2		
4a11	C8		18.8	25.6		x		25.9						
"	C9		4.1							x				
4a13	C15								38.6	34.8	14.1	17.8	57.9	73.0
4a19	B8	5.3	8.3	1.8		x								
4b5	A22		x											
4b13	C23		x	x			x	x						
4b16	C27b		x			1.0		x						
4b31	B21b		x											
4b33	B21a	1.3	x	x	2.5	x		x						
4bb4	A21b								x					
4bb8		x												
4g1	B35	x												
4k6	E32	x							x					
4nn4	C31		x					x						
4nn5	G31	x												
"	G32	1.2												
W1b4	B28								x	x		x		
W1b5	C28								3.2	2.6			x	
"	G28a												x	
"	G28b								1.5	x	x			
W1b5a	C30									x				
W1b7	D28								x	x	x	1.6	x	
W1b9	E28								x	x				

Kidd	*Kent*	*La9*	*La8*	*La6*	*La1*	*La3*	*Yo9*	*Yo 170*	*La52*	*La40*	*La96*	*Ch60*	*Lu43*	*Lr11*
W1b14	A28									x				
W1c12	F16									x				x
W1d1	D30								1.0	x	x	5.0		
W1d5	G30									x	x			
W2a1	D40					x								
W2a3	E40					x								
W2c1	F29									x				
W2c2	C29								x	x	x			
"	G29a								x	x		2.1	x	
"	G29b								x					
W2c5	D29								x	x		x	x	
W2c11	B29a								x			1.8	x	
W2c12	B29b								5.3	4.7				x
W2c13	B40								x					
W2d2	B37									x				
W2d8	E37									x				
W2d6	B38								x	x	x			
W2e5	E38		x											
W2f2	A41									x				x
Total beads:		2981	7351	1054	595	20968	2134	3505	23336	25748	2329	1889	13355	5483

Total beads: 110,728

Parenthesized numbers in column two are type numbers assigned by Smith and Graybill 1977: 57-59.

x ′ = presence less than 1.0 per cent.

Temporal ranges of occupations:

La9	1575-1600	La52	1690-1750
La8	1600-1625	La40	1718-1743
La6	1630's	La96	1720's
La1	1630-1645	Ch60	1730's
La3	1645-1665	Lu43	1740's
Yo9	1665-1674	Lr11	1760's
Yo170	1676-1680		

It would sometimes appear that Indians had an exceeding fascination with shiny, colorful ornaments, but so do many people in our own society. Indians often used beads and other ornaments in association with certain things of religious or mythological significance, but so do we. Frequently, Indians placed high exchange values on small baubles, but so do we. Certain colors of beads or other things were associated with particular Indian rituals, celebrations or mourning, but so it is for many of us.

Some might say that these similarities are contrived, or perhaps fortuitous; others might feel that they are rooted in some innate sense of all mankind. Reasons for symbolism are among the darkest mysteries upon which anthropology attempts to throw some light. Perhaps, for those who care, someday there will be answers. For the present, our more mundane concern has been largely with the chronometric significance of glass beads and other such things of the Susquehanna's Indians.

Glass

One shoulder fragment of a thin green-glass case bottle was found amidst a cache of other objects in grave number La1/8 at the Roberts site. This is the earliest site in the sequence to have produced any recorded glass bottles or vessels. A circular glass mirror from the inside of a vanity case was found at Frey-Haverstick, and this represents the earliest recorded mirror in the sequence. Mirrors from later sites are very infrequent until we reach Conestoga Town and Conoy, where such objects, usually rectangular in outline, are rather common. A number of these had molded wooden frames preserved around them, and one specimen from Conestoga was set into a carved board.

Strickler was the next site in the sequence to produce glass bottles. At least two dozen more or less complete, thin-walled, green-glass case bottles are represented in various collections from this site. Thirty-five separate pits from the village area, excavated in 1968 and 1969, produced fragments of such bottles. All of the extant whole specimens have approximately the same dimensions. They are generally seven to eight inches high, about three inches square at the shoulders, and taper slightly toward the base. Sides are straight to barely concave, and the bases have small pontil marks with very small kick-ups. All of them have everted lips. Illustrated in Figure 58 are two bottles found by Cadzow in 1931 at the southwestern cemetery, and one recovered in 1974 from the northeast cemetery. These latter excavations also produced the Susquehanna Valley's earliest-known fragment of a squat bottle. Actually the example is a seal from such a bottle, chipped around its margins by an Indian to remove its sharp edges. The seal bears the raised initials B. M. over a still (Figure 59). McKearin and McKearin (1941) have suggested that squat bottles may date as early as 1630. Noël Hume (1961: 93; 1976: 61) feels that in England their first appearance is likely to have been around 1650. According to him (1961: 98), the earliest dated seal on such a bottle is 1652.

Cadzow (1936) also recovered, from the southwest cemetery (36La3), a clear drinking glass, possibly of Dutch origin (Figure 61).

Byrd Leibhart's was the only other seventeenth-century site in the Susquehanna Valley to produce any evidence of squat bottles. One whole example was found here by Leibhart and is now in a private collection (Figure 59). Its form is identical to that illustrated in Noël Hume (1976: 63) for the 1650's.

At least two complete case bottles from Byrd Leibhart's are known from private collections. One was found by Leibhart and Graham in the northeast cemetery, and is now on exhibit at the York County Historical Society. Fragments from at least a dozen additional case bottles can be accounted for in the Museum's collection from burials and pits at the site and in various private collections.

Witthoft (n.d.c) mentions having seen two case bottles in the Oscar Leibhart collection from the site on his property.

It would appear that case bottles were declining in popularity during the

Figure 58. Dark green glass case bottles, Strickler site (36La3).

period of the two Leibhart sites, as compared to their rather frequent occurrence at Strickler. No green case bottles or fragments thereof were found at Conestoga or Conoy towns.

English globular bottle forms changed after about 1675, and although there are no known Susquehannock sites of this period (between Leibhart and Conestoga), we have illustrated (Figure 59) a typical globular bottle of that period which was found during the excavations at William Penn's home (Pennsbury Manor) on the Delaware River.

Bottles from the Conestoga site include three of very similar form, all of about a four-ounce capacity (Figure 59a). One of these contains a viscous yellow substance which may be bear grease or other tallow. The glass in them is a very pale green, and their kick-ups are rather low. Noël Hume (1976: 72-73) refers to them as pharmaceutical bottles, dating to the first two decades of the eighteenth century. Other pharmaceutical vials of about the same time period are shown in Figure 59.

Two complete globular-bodied bottles from the site show a tendency toward straight rather than round sides. Fragments from two additional squat bottles were also recovered. A globular bottle with two flattened sides (so that it has an oval outline in cross-section) was also found here, but its neck had previously been broken and removed by plowing. The intact squat bottles from the site are similar in form to those which Noël Hume (1976: 64) dates between 1700 and 1730.

A clear-glass cruet (Figure 60) was also found here, but the most outstanding bottle from the site is a clear-glass case bottle with its original pewter cap, which is decorated with red, white, blue and yellow enameled flowers. This bottle is probably of north central European origin (Figure 60).

Three bottles have been found at Conoy Town. The earliest of these is similar in form to the three from Conestoga Town described above (Figure 59a) except that it has about twice the capacity and its metal is much clearer, with only a tint of green. Another bottle from the site has a seal with the initials I.B. and the date 1716 (Figure 59).

During earlier excavations at the Conoy village, Witthoft found a broken bottle in a refuse pit (Figure 59). This almost certainly relates to the last years of Conoy occupation here, as it is similar to forms which Noël Hume (1976: 65-66) dates to the 1740 to 1750 period.

Wineglass stems are the remaining category of glass objects from Susquehanna Valley sites. One hollow and twisted green-glass stem and base was found in a grave at the northeast cemetery at Strickler. Actually it was recovered in three pieces. The base was broken prior to burial and the top of the stem, just below the bowl, was purposely chipped to remove sharp edges (Figure 61). This came from the same grave which produced the B.M. bottle seal.

a

Figure 60. Enameled glass bottle and clear glass cruet, Conestoga Town (36La52).

The only other examples of wineglass stems come from Conestoga Town. Five stems were found, and on all of them, where the original break was not clean, rough edges had been chipped away. Their use was probably ornamental. We can probably add to this group a glass stopper (Figure 61). All of the stems from Conestoga fall into types which Noël Hume (1976: 191) dates to between 1690 and 1740.

Figure 59, opposite. Glass bottles in chronological order. Top left to right: Byrd Leibhart (36Yo170); Pennsbury Manor; Market Street, Philadelphia. Second row: Conestoga Town (36La52); Conoy cemetery (36La40); Conoy Town (36La57). Bottom left: four small pharmaceutical bottles from Conestoga Town; enlargement of seal from Conoy cemetery bottle (above); enlargement of an Indian-chipped bottle seal from Strickler (36La3).

Figure 61. Glass. Chipped wineglass stems and a stopper, Conestoga Town (36La52); drinking glass, Strickler (36La3). Lower right: chipped wineglass stem (36La3).

Glass bottles, mirrors, and wineglass stems, like beads and other trinkets, were regarded by the Indians with a certain amount of curiosity and fascination. Most of these things also had value to them as ornamentation or, in the case of bottles, as containers for liquids. It is doubtful that very many bottles reached the Indian towns full of their original spiritous contents, especially during the seventeenth century. It is more likely that the contents of wine and liquor bottles would have been consumed near whatever trade center the Indians acquired them. That they were "very fond of Strong Liquors" is well documented in seventeenth- and eighteenth-century accounts. Wine and liquor which were transported to the Indian town were more likely to have been carried in wooden casks. Bottles were too clumsy and fragile as containers for the beverages to make the trip from the Chesapeake or Delaware trade centers. Any bottles which did survive the trip probably reached the villages empty, carried in the hands of an Indian with a hangover. Once in the village, bottles would certainly have been useful as containers for water, or for the redistribution of wine and liquor from casks, for storing grease and tallow, and for use as burial offerings.

We can estimate, for example, that the total number of wine and liquor containers, both glass and ceramic, at the Strickler site would exceed several hundred. This is not a measure of the drunkenness of the Susquehannocks—two or three hundred liters of wine or liquor does not reflect much of a party for three thousand people over a period of fifteen or more years. Judging again from the contemporary accounts, drunkenness was a problem for the Indians, but its worst effects were probably more often manifest at the white man's towns and trade centers than in the Indian villages. Not until the eighteenth century was there very much trading conducted at the Indians' towns, and the amount of alcohol carried to them would have been quickly and violently consumed.

The utilitarian value of bottles as receptacles was never as essential to the Indian as were the white man's cooking pots, knives, axes and guns. But clearly, the Indians' lust for alcoholic drink was the impetus for many trips to the traders' stores, and for their encouragement of traders to convey their goods to the Indian towns.

IRON

Items made of iron were the single most useful category of trade goods to the Indians of the seventeenth and eighteenth centuries. Some iron objects found at Susquehanna Valley sites can hardly be viewed as having great functional importance to the Indians, e.g., padlocks, door keys, scrap, firetongs, broken or worn-out gun parts, or jews harps.

Other things of iron, such as scissors, awls, claw hammers, chisels, saws, vises, files, fishhooks, pins, needles, containers, ladles, tweezers, tongs, cannonballs (and a few reported cannons), nails, screwdrivers, armour, swords, strike-a-lights, drawknives and wrenches, all of which have been found at their sites, were obviously useful to the Indians, but not essential. Many of these are shown in Figure 63.

Four types of iron tools were exceedingly useful to the Indians, and these rather quickly replaced their native-made equivalents, to the point where they became virtual necessities of life.

Knives are the first of these, and the earliest to appear in the sequence.

The advantage of a steel or iron knife over the native-made stone knife is quite obvious.

Following closely in the order of introduction to the Indians is the iron axe. It too had an obvious advantage over its native equivalent. Next in order of appearance is the iron hoe blade (and adzes used primarily as hoes). These were a significant improvement over native digging sticks and stone hoes, both for horticultural purposes and for digging holes.

Guns and related accoutrements (bullet molds, black powder, flints, lead and tools for minor repairs) constitute the fourth and most important tool type. As previously indicated, in another chapter, guns first appeared on the scene about 1630 and by 1700 had almost completely replaced the bow and arrow.

Iron knives and a few daggers first occurred at the Schultz site. All of the knives in the present sample have flat (simple extension of the blade as opposed to rattail) tangs. Most of the daggers from this site are worked (faceted) on only one side, being flat on the other. These must have been mass-produced in Europe and carried by common folk much as the switchblade is today.

There is some evidence that a few rapier blades were secured by Susquehannocks at the Schultz site, but these were cut and refashioned into knives by the natives.

Knives and daggers greatly increase in numbers at Washington Boro. Here we see both flat- and rattail-tanged knives with bone handles. Also, there is an increase in the number of rapier blades that were cut up to make knives. One knife of better than common quality was found here. It has a carved or incised ivory handle.

A few knives, particularly those with rattail tangs, were set in Indian-made hafts of antler. The specimen illustrated in Figure 64 is from Frey-Haverstick. Also found at this site was a cast-bronze knife handle (a Scottish piper) without a blade. Similar knives, although not the same casting, were found by Futer (1959) at the Strickler site (Figure 64).

Knives were certainly present at the Roberts site, but the sample is not large enough to determine if there was any increase in popularity as compared to Washington Boro. The sample from Strickler, however, is large enough to make this determination. Iron knives at Strickler were enormously more abundant; in fact they are practically countless. Daggers are less common at this time period, and few if any rapier blades were cut up to make knives; rather they were used as swords. Rattail tangs are slightly more common than flat-tanged knives. Actually, several distinct types of both basic forms are observable. Following Hagerty's (1963: 93-114) typology, we find his types G and H in the rattail category, and his types D, E and K in the flat-tang varieties. An example of the bone handle for the rat-

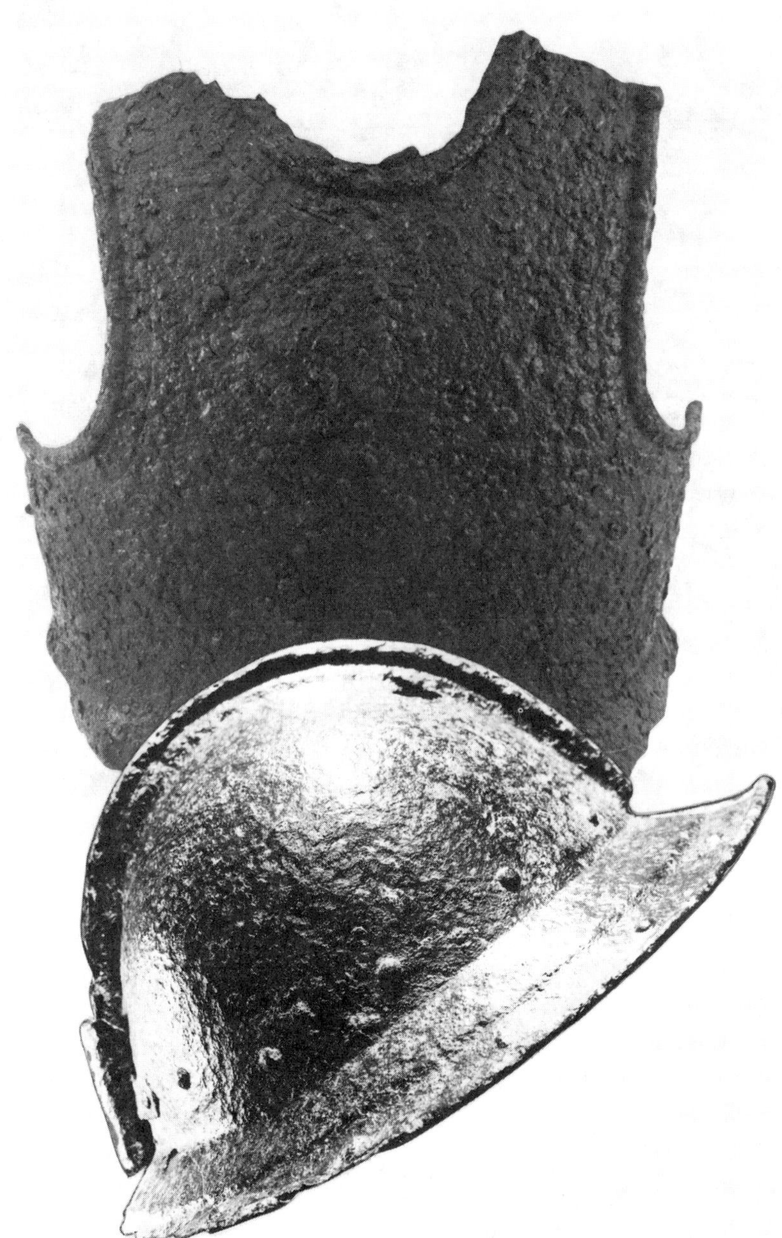

Figure 62. Armor from graves. Breastplate (36La3); and helmet (36La6), courtesy Historical Society of Pennsylvania, Philadelphia.

Figure 63. A 1930's newspaper photograph of the Leibhart and Graham collection from the Byrd Leibhart site (36Yo170).

tail forms is shown in Figure 64. Most of these, however, probably had wooden handles, which accounts for their paucity. Several minor variations of bone handles are noted (Figure 64) for the flat-tanged knives. Decorations on these are commonly small "compass-work" circles.

The two tang forms at Byrd Leibhart's occur with about equal frequency. In the Museum's 1970 collection there are eleven rattail forms and nine flat tangs.

Clasp knives became the rage at Conestoga Town. At least 50 of them, of various sizes and shapes, were found here, as opposed to straight knives of which there were only 25 (Figure 64).

Knives were greatly diminished in numbers at Conoy Town, at least as grave offerings. The sample includes four clasp knives and one wooden-handled rattail-tanged knife.

Graves from Kuskuskies, near New Castle, Pennsylvania (1760's; see Kent et al. 1981) produced very few knives of any sort. They were definitely in use by the people at Kuskuskies, and so we must assume that their choice for not placing them in graves was a culturally determined custom.

Axes are the next major category of iron tools which were of great importance to the Indians. They first appear at Schultz and have a steady increase of popularity right through the sequence to Conestoga Town. Interestingly, they were not placed in any graves at Conoy Town, nor were they associated with any known eighteenth-century Delaware graves. Again, the axes were present among these folk, but it was definitely not their custom to bury such items with their dead.

Iron of any sort, and particularly in the form of axes, was very precious to the Indians of the earliest contact-period sites. Several examples of sawed iron axes have been recovered from Schultz (Figure 66). This work was done with sandstone saws to the point where the metal in the cut was thin enough to permit the piece to be broken off. The purpose was to make several iron celt blades out of one large axe (Figure 66). Not all of the axes were so parsimoniously used by the Susquehannocks at Schultz. A few iron axes were reduced to celts at Washington Boro, but within a few years of the first settlement here, axes were sufficiently abundant, and the laborious practice of sawing them into smaller pieces was no longer necessary.

The form and size of iron axes changed considerably over the two hundred-year period covered by the sample at hand. Figure 65 illustrates the changes in form as viewed from the tops and sides of the axes. Until the last quarter of the seventeenth century, the lateral profile of the axes was largely unchanged. A majority of them have a downward-curving blade. Differences which are discernible involve the shape of the eye and the weight of the axes. In general, the shape of the eye becomes more rounded, and the weight decreases through time. These data are summarized in Table 9.

No touch marks have been found on any of the 24 axes from Conestoga Town. They occurred most commonly at Strickler (six out of 22 had touch marks), and most are in the form of a cross. Generally there is only one mark, and only on one side. However, at least one specimen from Strickler has three individual cross-touch marks clustered together on one side of the blade.

All of the axes in the sample have eyes which taper from top to bottom. This is necessary to keep the head on the handle during use. The earlier axes probably had their handles inserted from the bottom of the eye, and then a wedge (usually wood, but a few nails have survived) was driven into the top in order to swell the handle to fit the taper. Many of the axes from Conestoga Town, particularly those with round eyes, were top-loaded with tapered wooden handles. These axes also have longer but thinner blades

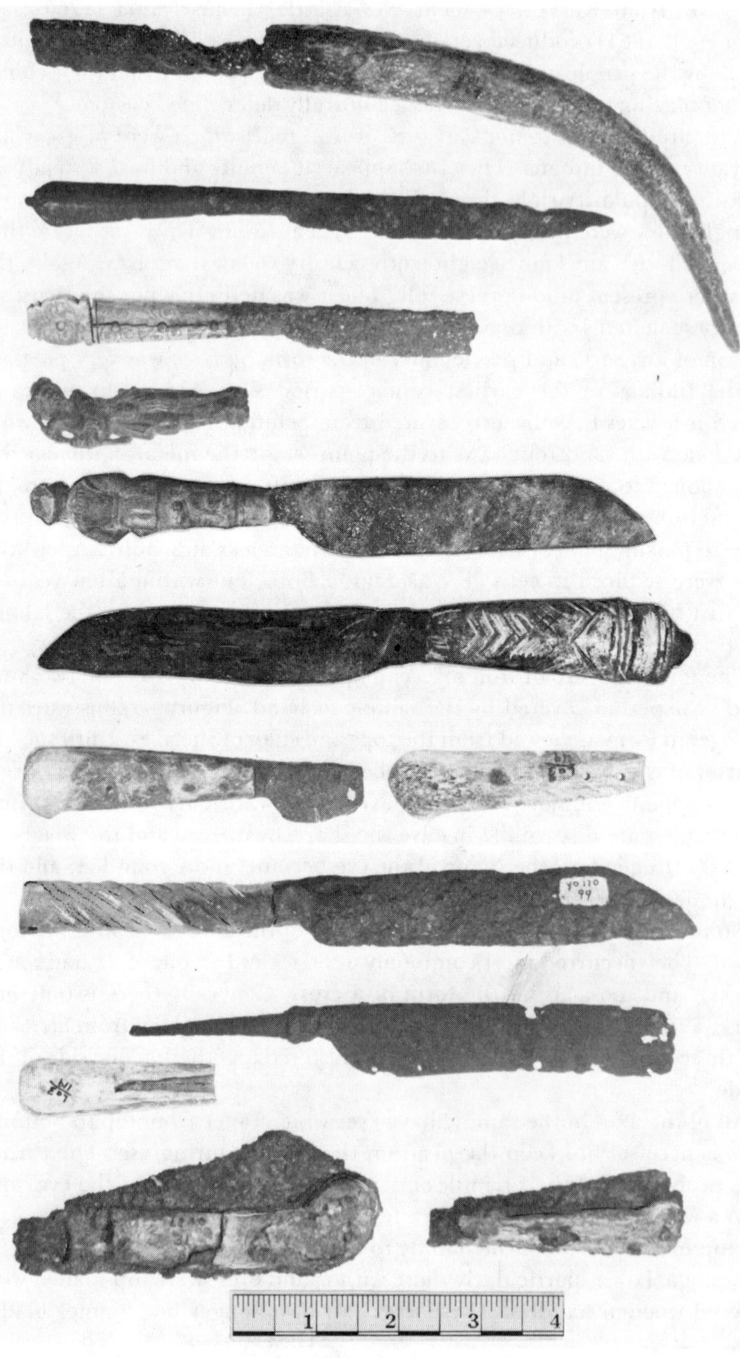
1 2 3 4

generally, and they are either straight or curve upward. All of these are features which are essential to a good throwing axe or tomahawk. They are still perfectly suited to chopping, albeit to somewhat lighter work than that performed by the earlier axes; but undoubtedly many of them were also thrown. The George Keller collection, presumably from the Lower Leibhart site, included one six-inch-long spike-back tomahawk with a punched oval eye. If it was indeed found here, it is one of the earliest dated examples of this type of tomahawk.

Small hatchets first occur at Strickler, and in fact four of them from this site are the smallest in the total sample (Figure 65). Strickler has produced the greatest variety of axes; Futer (in Witthoft and Kinsey 1959: Figure 23) illustrates three of these uncommon forms. These are described as an English axe, a lath hatchet, and a "gooseneck" axe.

Small axes, i.e., forms with smaller than average eyes, occur at Schultz (one example) and Washington Boro (at least three examples). Even though these have relatively short blades, they are probably more accurately classed as small axes, since in every case their blade length is a result of extensive resharpening.

Spark tests on those axes whose blades are not greatly worn down show that most of them have a steel bit welded into their wrought-iron blades.

Table 9

AVERAGE CHARACTERISTICS OF IRON AXES

Site	*Eye length-width ratio*	*eye height*	*weight*	*sample size*
Schultz	2.1-1	2 ⅛″	940 g.	3
Washington Boro	1.95-1	2 1/16″	862 g.	13
Strickler	1.6-1	1 ⅞″	761 g.	22
Conestoga Town	1.2-1	1 11/16″	543 g.	24

We have previously noted that the total absence of axes in graves at Conoy Town was a cultural preference. However, we know that this was not the case with the Susquehannocks. Their paucity in graves at Byrd Leibhart's can probably be explained in terms of their great value and the difficult times into which the Susquehannocks living there had fallen. It is curious to note that this site has the greatest occurrence (as compared with

Figure 64, opposite. Iron knives arranged in approximate chronological order. From top (earliest) to bottom: blade in antler handle (36La6); forged dagger (36La7); incised handle (36La4); cast-bronze bagpiper knife handle (36La6); bagpiper knife (rear view) (36La3, Futer collection); flat-tang knife with carved handle (36La3, Futer collection); two typical shapes for flat-tang knife handles (36La3); spiral, carved knife handle (36Yo170); handle and rat-tail knife (36La3); two clasp knives (36La40).

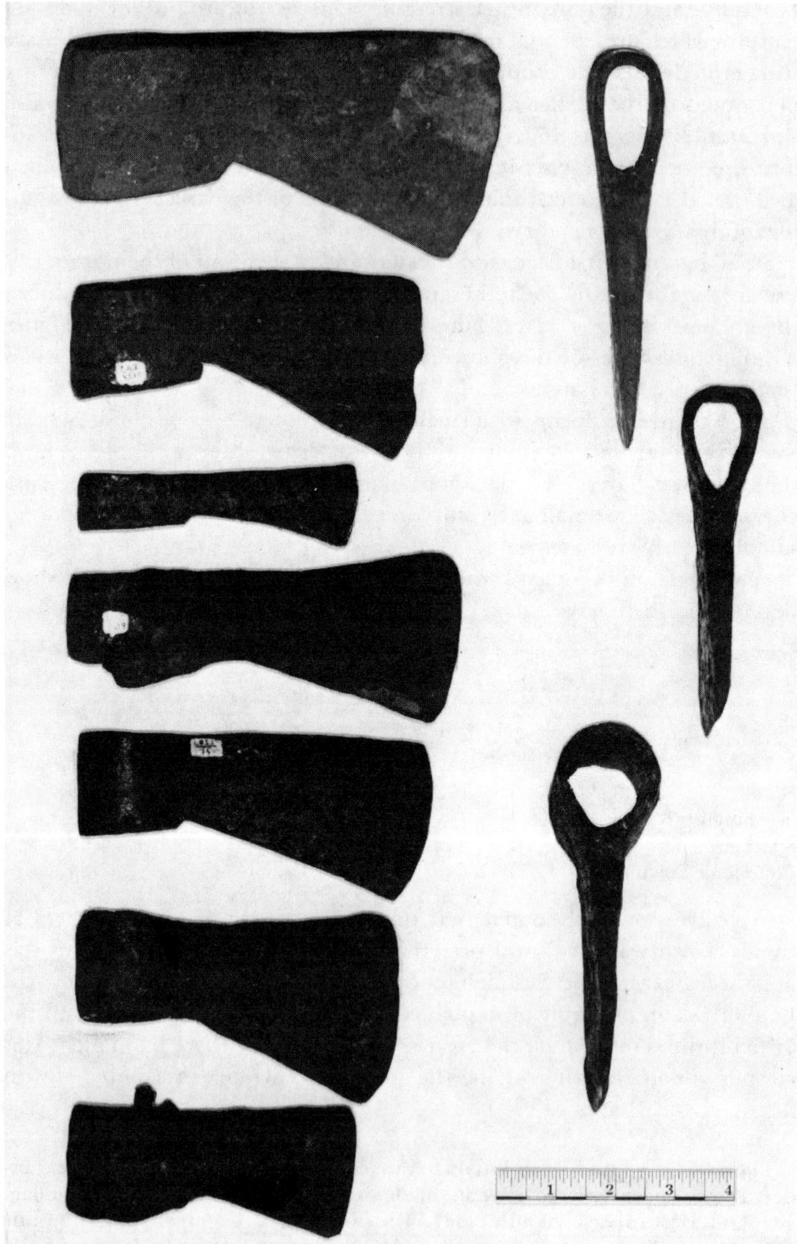

Figure 65. Shapes of iron axes from early (top) to latest (bottom).

all other sites) of iron hoes per grave. Perhaps this was an offering made in place of valuable axes.

Iron hoes fall into two basic categories of form—those that were hoes, and those that were probably adzes, but used as hoes. Illustrations of early hoes and adzes are not at all numerous, and for this reason our characterization of the functions of samples at hand may be entirely whimsical. They are differentiated here solely on the basis of their eye shapes. Those with round eyes, and there are several varieties, were without question made to be used as hoes. Those with square eyes are called adzes because of their similarity to identified eighteenth- and nineteenth-century adzes.

The illustration volumes of Diderot's *Encyclopedia* (Diderot 1959), under agricultural tools and carpenter's tools, depicts a hoe and an adze, both of which have round eyes. A specimen in the PHMC collections at Pennsbury Manor is identified as a seventeenth-century adze; it too has a round eye.

The 1816 "Key" to the manufactories of Sheffield (Smith 1816) illustrates a variety of hoes and adzes. All of the hoes (Figures 330-38 and 364-68 therein) have round eyes, while all but one of the adzes have square eyes (Figures 240-48).

Our archeological sample of these tools consists of over 40 specimens, of which only 25% have round eyes. The remaining 30 or more have square, or more commonly, slightly rectangular eyes. The latter average about one by one and one-half inches and the eyes are generally tapered. Blades on the round-eye hoes range up to seven inches in width, while those with square eyes are not usually more than four and one-half inches wide. Those with square or rectangular eyes generally show more blade curvature than those with round eyes.

Because of their great width, the round-eye forms could hardly have served as anything but hoes. On the other hand, the square-eye forms may well have been made to be used as adzes. Figure 63 of the Leibhart collection, does show one ships carpenter's adze (left side of photo) with a hammer poll. This is without question an adze, and shows very little wear on its cutting edge, suggesting that this one was not used as a hoe. The manufacturer's intended function of these tools is a moot question. However, it is not so with regard to their use by Indians. They had little or no use for adzes as such, but plenty of need for an iron tool which could be used to dig holes or work their agricultural fields. Almost every specimen in the present collection, both round- and square-eye forms, shows excessive wear from soil abrasion. This is further borne out by the fact that they frequently occur in graves where they were discarded after they were employed to open the pit.

In most cases the hoes show uneven wear on their cutting edges, i.e., either the left side or the right is more severely worn. This may be a function of left- or right-handedness.

Hoes reached the greatest number and popularity as grave offerings during the period of the Strickler and Byrd Leibhart sites: we can account for at least 37 hoes from the three major collections from the Lower Leibhart site. The proportion of round- to square-eye forms is fairly constant from their first appearance at Schultz on to the eighteenth century. The round-eye forms exhibit several minor variations of form, while the only really discernible difference in the square-eye forms is in size. But none of these

Figure 66. Iron axes from the Schultz site (36La7) showing steps employed by the Indians to saw an axe into stock for making a celt.

Figure 67. Shapes of iron hoes.

variations is clearly a function of time, i.e., there seems to be no very evident change in form for at least 150 years.

Stone hoes with the expected kind of wear, which are found in the Susquehanna Valley, are generally associated with Shenks Ferry sites (Figure 36). So-called pot lids, usually with two opposing lateral notches, but sometimes without, occur on Owasco and Wyoming Valley Complex sites and at Quiggle, Schultz and Washington Boro. It is our suggestion that these were the stone hoes of early Susquehannock culture. An argument against this notion is that many of these disks do not show (although some do) the kind of wear or polish on their faces which would result from extensive use in digging and chopping soil. Their circumferences or edges do show battering and grinding, but this could be either the result of efforts to shape a flat stone into a disk, or the result of using it as a hoe.

There is also some minor evidence for the use of elk scapulae as hoes. However, the paucity of such bones with appropriate wear patterns implies that this was not a common raw material for making hoes. Digging sticks, probably with fire-hardened tips, were almost certainly used by the Susquehannocks, but the sticks themselves are not apparent in the archeological record. Occasionally the impression of a pointed digging stick can be seen in the bottom or sides of a pit or burial.

Although we cannot positively assert that "pot lid" disks were used by the Susquehannocks as hoes, we do note that their occurrence on Susquehannock sites decreases as iron hoes increase. Fewer examples were found at the Washington Boro village than at Schultz; and none was found at Strickler, where iron hoes have their greatest occurrence (see Table 19).

Sizes of iron hoes were probably insignificant to the Indians: in fact we have suggested that they also used other tools, viz., adzes, for this purpose. Such distinctions were made by the English—one of the primary suppliers of such goods to the Susquehannocks. Captain John Smith (1624: 316) gives a list of things which were necessary for persons going to Virginia, in which he includes the following for a family of six:

5 broad hoes at 2s. a peece
5 narrow hoes at 16d. a peece
2 broad axes at 3s. 8d. a peece
5 felling axes at 18d. a peece

Other items which he lists are "saws, hammers, shovels, spades, augers, chissels, percers stocked, gimblets, hatchets, frowes, handbills, grindstones, nails and pickaxes."

Most of the tools mentioned in this list are well represented by those recovered from Susquehannock sites. Conspicuously absent from this list are shovels and spades. We know of no examples of such tools from Susquehannock or other sites in the valley. Undoubtedly some few of these did reach the Susquehannocks, but they certainly were not very important items of white-Indian commerce.

GUNS AND GUNFLINTS

Frey-Haverstick

The earliest site in the sequence which has produced guns or gun parts in any quantity was Frey-Haverstick. As previously mentioned, the stoneware jug bearing the date 1630 establishes the approximate date for this cemetery.

In 1971 two flintlock pistols were recovered from one grave (La6/94). Only one of these pistols was more or less intact. The other had been disassembled and included a barrel measuring nine inches, but obviously broken short of the muzzle. The section of this barrel which survives is full-octagon, and has an approximate .55-caliber bore. A barrel hanger is dovetailed into the bottom flat six inches from the breech end. Hardware found in direct association with the barrel includes a frizzen and an iron trigger guard.

The second pistol was somewhat more complete at the time of its interment. Its barrel is 19 inches long and is about .50 caliber. The associated lock is relatively small, measuring five inches in length and one inch in height. The cock or hammer, with a native gunflint still in its jaws, has a doglock-type notch cut into its posterior side. However, the lock functioned as a conventional flintlock, since its unbridled tumbler with vertically operating sear had both half- and full-cock notches. The only part of this lock which was missing, thereby rendering it inoperable, was the mainspring. A screw which once held the mainspring against the plate was still in place.

One short, round, brass ferrule, containing a section of ramrod, was against the underside of the barrel. This would suggest that the gun was in its stock when it was buried. Three .55-caliber lead balls and two dozen pieces of lead shot were also found in this grave.

Another grave (La6/100) at the site produced a similar-type lock, but larger, which was fully operable. Associated items included an iron trigger guard, a second cock and a frizzen spring.

A third grave (La6/99) contained a cache of gun parts consisting of two fragmentary cocks (without doglock notches), two snaphance batteries, a mainspring, a flintlock pan, a snaphance pan with exterior circular guard, and a brass forearm cap. Also included was one .50-caliber lead ball and one small (one and one-half inches in diameter) iron cannon ball.

A double burial (La6/116) excavated here in 1975 produced a rather large cache of gun parts, but no barrels. A single flintlock with a bulge in the plate beneath the pan was found at the feet of one of the individuals. This lock, whose outline resembles that of a wheel-lock plate, was fully operable. At the feet of the second individual, and apparently in a small wooden chest, was the major cache of gun parts. Among the items were three locks. Two of these had the bulging plates mentioned above (see Mayer 1943: 22), presumably dating from about 1630-1650. One was fully operable, consisting of a vertically operating sear, unbridled tumbler with half- and full-cock positions, and without any projection from the pan to support the frizzen. The other lock consisted of only the plate, with pan and frizzen still attached.

The third lock in this cache was an unusual, at least from an American Indian site, miguelet or "Mediterranean" snaphance lock (Lenk 1965: plates 5 and 6). The shape and operation of its frizzen-pan cover are essentially like those of the flintlock; but there the similarities cease. On the miguelet the mainspring is on the outside of the plate and works directly against the foot of the cock. The half- and full-cock positions are held by spring-mounted sears on the inside of the plate, with the foot of the cock held by pins that pass through the plate (Figure 68). Held (1970: 74-75) illustrates and describes, in careful detail, the action of this type of lock.

Other items in the cache include a pan cover for the so-called Netherlands snaphance (Lenk 1965: plate 7), two pans with circular guards for

the snaphance, one battery, two sears to open the pan covers, one horizontally operating sear, and three cocks possibly used in this type lock. The latter have axles attached to the hammer, and the tumbler was secured by a pin through the axle.

In addition there were six mainsprings, one sear spring, one frizzen spring, one vertically operating sear, two top-jaws for cocks, one pan, one broken lock plate, one cock with a posterior notch, and one iron trigger guard.

Roberts Site

Two gunlocks were found in 1971 at the Roberts site, which, as previously indicated, has approximately the same dates as the Frey-Haverstick site. Both pieces (La1/7 and La1/8) are conventional flintlock mechanisms. The cocks of each have slightly different shapes, but their plates are of similar form. The plates have the previously described bulge below the pan.

These locks were in separate graves and neither was part of a complete gun. Both were associated with a separate frizzen. Landis' (n.d.) catalogue mentions a brass pistol barrel from the Roberts site.

Strickler Site

More guns have been found at the Strickler site than at all of the other Susquehannock sites combined. At least 40 more or less complete guns have been recovered from burials here. A large number of gun parts have also been found both in burials and in pits within the village.

Art Futer (Witthoft and Kinsey 1959) recovered a spanner wrench and the wheel for a wheel lock from graves which he excavated at the site. His collection also includes eight doglocks and nine flintlocks. Witthoft (1966: 14-15) describes, in great detail, an unusual "Jacobean lock" from the Futer collection (Figure 68). The horizontal operating sear mechanism of this doglock occurs in only one other specimen in the WPMM collections. Also included are 13 locks collected by Cadzow in 1931 and six collected in 1968-1969 and 1974. With regard to the so-called English doglocks, Lenk (1965: 21) notes that a distinction must be made between those on which the cock is secured in the manner of the Dutch snaphance (i.e., like that illustrated by Witthoft 1966: 15, in which a pin from the sear

Figure 68, opposite. Gun parts. Top (earliest): wheel from wheel lock, and spanner (36La3). Second row left to right: Miguelet lock (36La6); snaphance parts (36La6). Third row: flintlock with bulge in plate (36La1); doglock (36La3). Fourth row: conventional flintlock and poorly reassembled lock (36La3). Bottom: cocks, frizzens, and homemade brass trigger (36Yo170, York County Historical Society).

passes through the plate to engage a notch in the cock), and those in which a posterior notch on the cock and "dog" catch on the outside of the plate to secure the hammer at half-cock. Lenk (1965: 21) would date the former to about 1620, whereas the latter, in which the hooked catch engages the heel of the cock, dates from the middle of the seventeenth century. The functioning of these locks is illustrated by Peterson (1956: 23).

None of the examined locks from the Strickler site, except that described by Witthoft (1966: 14-15), had any sort of frizzen bridle or reinforcement.

The range of lock plate and cock sizes and forms is shown in Figure 68. The WPMM collection includes three pistol barrels ranging in length from only five inches to over 24 inches. The three fowler barrels collected in 1974 range from 39 to 48 inches in length. Bore sizes on these guns, although difficult to determine accurately because of their rusted condition, average about .55 caliber. One hundred and twenty-one musket balls from the 1974 excavations were measured; the resulting range was .50 to .68 caliber, with an average of .56 caliber. A number of graves also produced lead shot.

Additional gun-related grave offerings include triggers, mainsprings, frizzens, cocks, ferrules, lock plates and trigger guards. Only a few butt plates have been found with complete guns, and all of those in the WPMM collections are simple forms cut from rather thin sheet brass. These fold only a short distance over the combs, and the few complete examples are cut off straight, rather than ending in any sort of decorative finial. Only one cast-brass trigger guard was recovered. The others, in sheet brass or iron, are all typical seventeenth-century shapes. Ferrules and forearm caps are likewise very simple bent pieces of sheet brass.

The majority of guns at the Strickler site are conventional flintlocks, with a lesser number of doglocks. Snaphances are represented by only a few parts, including pans with circular guards and the batteries. Almost without question some matchlock guns were in use by the Susquehannocks, but so far as we are aware no part of such a lock has ever been found on any Susquehannock sites.

Figure 69, opposite. Gun hardware. All specimens are brass and from Conestoga Town (36La52) unless otherwise indicated. Top row: trigger guard, bottom view. Second row: trigger guard, side view. Third row: iron trigger guard. Fourth row: trigger guard (36La3). Fifth row left to right: serpentine side plate; forearm cap with preserved stock (36La3). Sixth row left to right: side plate; ramrod pipe with preserved rod and stock. Seventh row left to right: side plate; rear ramrod pipe. Bottom row left to right: simple butt plate with preserved stock (36La3); simple butt plate; elaborate butt plate finial; touchhole pick; two thumbpiece escutcheons.

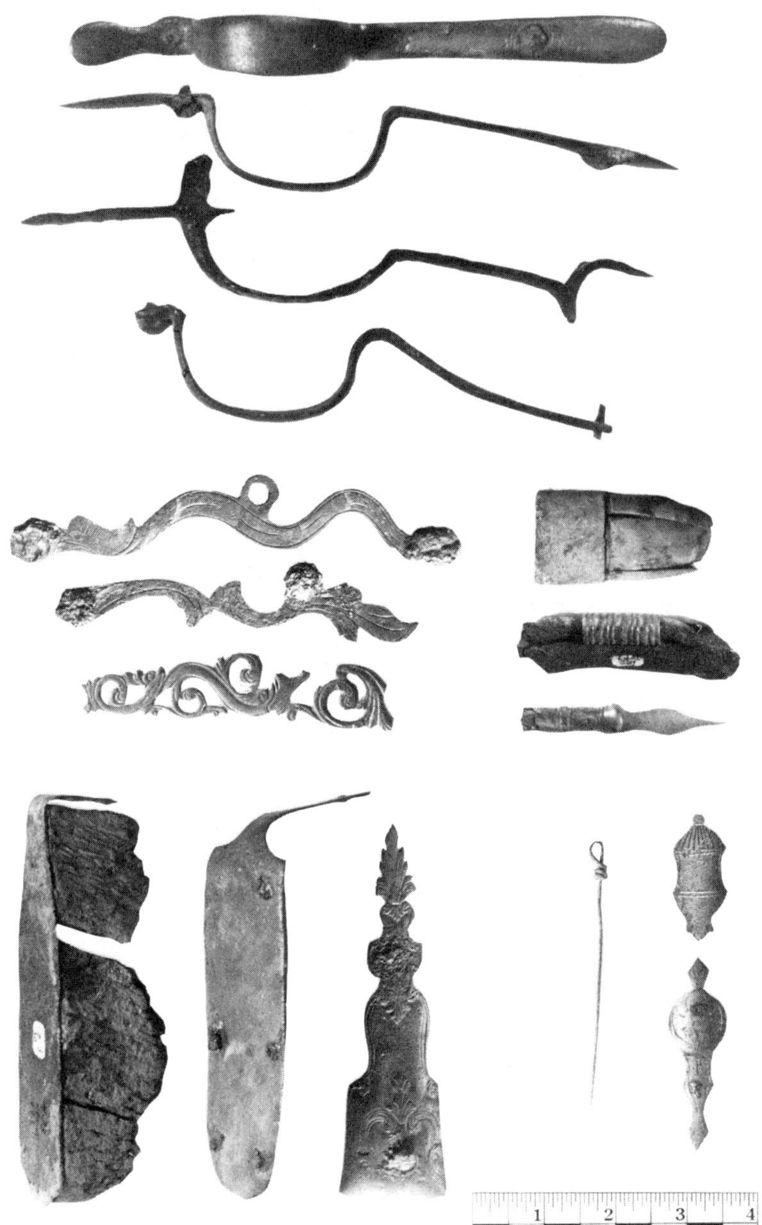
1
2
3
4

Oscar Leibhart Site

Landis' (n.d.) notes on the Upper Leibhart site mention one flintlock gun with a 46-inch barrel and about two dozen miscellaneous gun parts. The Oscar Leibhart collection (photos in the WPMM) includes one octagonal pistol barrel approximately eight inches in length, and a number of musket balls. According to sketchy notes (WPMM files), Donald Leibhart recovered at least three long guns and parts of two others from the 105 graves which he excavated here. Although our knowledge of this site and collections from it is very limited, one gets the impression that guns were less frequently used as burial furniture than at the Strickler site.

Byrd Leibhart Site

Very few complete guns have been found at this site: Table 19 implies an even lower percentage per grave than at the Upper Leibhart site. None was found in the 35 graves excavated by the WPMM in 1970. Landis (n.d.) lists only three among the 90 graves excavated by Leibhart and Graham in the 1930's.

In spite of the paucity of whole guns from this site, it has produced more gun parts per grave than any other Susquehannock site. In the photograph of the Leibhart-Graham collection (see Figure 63), there are at least a hundred gun parts. Also included was a gunsmith's tool kit, as discussed in Landis' notes; plus numerous bullet molds, some broken gun barrels, and a few cannon balls. Approximately half of the gun parts shown in the photograph are now in the possession of Mr. Reeves Goehring of Marietta, Pennsylvania.

Part of the Graham portion of this collection is now on display at the York County Historical Society, and it includes one short barrel (apparently a broken fowler barrel), a cast-brass trigger guard similar to that from the Strickler site, a cock, bullet mold, and an incomplete wheel lock. The remainder of the Graham collection is in storage at the York County Historical Society. These specimens were cleaned and catalogued while on loan at the William Penn Memorial Museum in 1981. They were assigned the numbers Yo170/A-DDDD. Presented here is an inventory of the parts, many of which are in a remarkable state of preservation (see also Figures 68).

Inventory of gun parts from the Byrd Leibhart site
at the York County Historical Society

11 vertically operating sears

23 frizzens, three of which have neatly faceted fronts, i.e., side opposite the striking face, plus a decorative semi-circular file cut on the angle of the frizzen; all others have flat or rounded fronts.

10 cocks without top jaws or top jaw screws; one has a posterior notch for the safety dog, one has a groove on the under side (Yo170/115A) to receive a laterally moving sear arm. In top view the lower

jaws are generally rounded, but in three examples they are expanding to a squared-off lead edge.
1 cock with bifacial gunflint still intact
2 top jaws, one rounded in top view, one squared
2 lock plates; neither has a maker's stamp, but both are in a relatively good state of preservation.
4 mainsprings
1 frizzen spring
3 flash pans: all have neatly filed faceted edges on their undersides
7 tumblers, each with full, half and rest notches
1 breech plug (thread size: ⅝" x 11")
1 spanner wrench
1 worm for cleaning barrels
2 bullet molds, 1 approximately .50 caliber

The Wallace surface collection from this site includes a lock plate with bottom bulge, and a battery from a snaphance.

During the 1970 excavations at this site, it was noted that the Indians had a distinct tendency to place pairs of gun parts in the graves of many of their deceased. Frequently two cocks, two mainsprings, two frizzens, or two triggers, etc., were found in individual graves. Several pieces of gun barrels were found in 1970, one of which had been hammered at one end to make a chisel or prying tool.

Conestoga Town

Nine complete flintlocks were found at Conestoga. Here for the first time we see a few guns of some quality. Four of these guns showed refinements in their hardware which would indicate that they were not ordinary trade guns. These included such features as engraved butt plates, openwork and engraved side plates, thumb plates and fancy ramrod pipes. One of these was a Jaeger with all iron hardware and a full octagonal .55-caliber, 35-inch rifled barrel with a flared muzzle. Its iron butt plate had a notch to receive its sliding, wooden patch-box cover.

All but one of the better-made guns had bridled tumblers. None of the ordinary guns had such refinements, and none of the nine guns had a projection from the pan to reinforce the frizzen. At least two of the ordinary trade guns appear to have external dog safety catches.

Bore sizes for these guns ranged between .50 and .60 caliber. With the already noted exception of the Jaeger, all of the guns were smooth-bores with rather light barrels averaging 49 inches in length (range 41 to 59 inches). Again, with the exception of the Jaeger, the barrels appear to be tapered, octagonal to round. Two of the guns may have had completely round barrels; they were too badly rusted for the observer to be certain. Most of them had brass rear sights and several had brass front sights.

The five ordinary trade guns had almost identical butt plates of sheet brass. Their locks varied in size, as did their barrels. Four of them had serpentine side plates with varying qualities of engraving. Their trigger guards were similar in shape, four of them being of cast brass and one of iron; only their terminal ends varied in shape. These guns had both plain and cordoned ramrod pipes. All of the triggers which could be studied had a reverse curl at the bottom.

It would appear that all of the guns from Conestoga were in working condition when they were buried. Only two graves produced miscellaneous gun parts and these consisted of one frizzen, one hammer and a brass serpentine side plate.

Conoy Town

Two pistols were found in graves at Conoy Town. One of these was in an excellent state of preservation, including much of its wooden stock. Missing portions of the stock, up to the rear entry pipe, were restored with wax. All of the fittings on this gun were of iron. The second pistol also had all iron hardware, but there was no butt cap. No miscellaneous gun parts were found at this site.

GUNFLINTS

The distribution of gunflints coincides with those sites at which guns or gun parts have been reported. Witthoft's (1966) typology of gunflints (with modifications as suggested by Kent (1983) is used here to describe the specimens recovered from the sites.

Kent (1983) has proposed that the earliest European gunflint was simply a chunk (or sometimes a deliberate chip) of flint of the right size and shape.

These, or any other gunflint types, were secured in the jaws of spring-activated mechanical devices, the various forms of which we have called snaphance, miquelet, or conventional flintlock engines. Their purpose, when triggered, was to rapidly produce sparks by the action of the flint being scraped against a piece of hardened steel. These white-hot sparks would fall into and immediately ignite the priming powder held in a pan against the touchhole of a gun barrel, in order to explode its main charge.

As indicated by Kent (1983), the presumed earliest, or "chip gunflints," are very difficult to identify, inasmuch as they are just that—chips. They are, of course, chips of European flint; but chips, particularly of English flint, are quite common on Susquehannock sites. Four or five small flat flakes (of just the right size) with some edge wear or battering were recovered from the Strickler site. These *could* very well have served as gunflints, and perhaps they are examples of the first type of European gunflints to arrive with the earliest trade guns.

Another departure which Kent (1983) has made from Witthoft's typology is that he feels that all of the so-called bifacial or Abbevillian gunflints of the Witthoft typology were made in North America by Indians. Witthoft's theory is that those made of European flint were produced in Europe, and those chipped from local cherts, jaspers, quartz or other less suitable stones were made by Indians. Kent (1983), on the other hand, has proposed that all of the bifacial gunflints were manufactured by Indians, and that those made of European flint (primarily from English sources) are derived from colonial ships' ballast heaps, from which the Indians collected these stones.

Fragments of European flint which occur on Susquehannock sites represent several categories, including what are simply smashed, unused chunks; various briefly used pieces; and some extensively battered chips of the stone (Table 10).

About half of the European (English) flint, particularly as seen at Strickler and Byrd Leibhart, can be considered unused waste material resulting from the fracture or rough smashing of nodules of ballast flint. However, *waste material* is a misnomer in this case, since little of the stone was actually thrown away. Instead, it was placed in piles or in bags as grave offerings. Most of the worked (or more properly, used) flakes or waste flint recovered from these sites also came from grave caches. Even some of the tiniest chips show nibbled edges. The source or cause of this nibbling or edge use is almost certainly a result of striking the stones against a piece of hardened steel (strike-a-light) to produce sparks which could be caught in tinder and blown into a flame.

We have noted that a fair quantity of native stones, chert, jasper, and some quartz also found as caches in graves show similar edge use, and probably for the same reasons. Naturally, there are many unused fragments or chips of native stones in these sites, and obviously there is no point to our tabulating them here with similar pieces of European flint.

Because of the uncertainties surrounding their positive identification, no

Figure 70. Gunflint types. Left to right: chip; native biface; wedge-shaped (gunspall); French; English.

effort was made in Table 10 to specifically identify chips which may have served as gunflints; but almost surely the category—used chips or chunks of European stone (meaning pieces of flint with edge wear or use)—includes some chips which actually served as gunflints. The distinction between chip and chunk is tantamount to that between a flake (a broad, thin piece of flint) and a thick angular lump of the stone which might result from crushing a larger block of flint.

TABLE 10

DISTRIBUTION OF CHIPS AND CHUNKS OF FLINT

Sites	*used chips or chunks of native stone*	*used chips or chunks of European stone*	*unused chips or chunks of European stone*
La1	1	1	
La6	5	1	7
La3	100's	43	28
Yo170	20	42	34

The earliest sites in the Susquehannock sequence at which guns have been found have produced only those gunflints which Witthoft (1966) has defined as bifacially chipped (of the "Abbevillian-like" technology of flint knapping). Specimens recovered from the sites are made of both transported English ballast flints and local cherts, jasper and quartz (the latter are very uncommon). These gunflints are characteristically square or slightly rectangular in outline, and are usually almost completely flaked over both faces. In most samples about 40% of the bifacial gunflints, whether of European or native stone, have rounded outlines, or at least severely battered corners. This would imply the frequent turning of square bifacial gunflints in the gunlock to improve their sparking capability (the edge needs to be ragged or sharp), or their heavy use against the strike-a-light steel in fire-making. We acknowledge the possibility that some Indians may have intentionally produced rounded bifacial gunflints. A few do appear to be chipped, rather than battered into a rounded outline.

It is our contention (Kent 1983) that the extra effort of the Susquehannocks to secure the English ballast flint from the Chesapeake and Delaware Bay harbors into which it was being dumped shows that the Susquehannocks recognized its superiority over native stone for producing sparks from steel.

The 1970 excavations at the Roberts site (La1) produced one bifacial gunflint of local chert and one of quartz. Our own experiment with the latter type of stone suggests that it makes a very poor gunflint.

Nine bifacial gunflints were found at the Frey-Haverstick site. Two of these are made of Onondaga chert from New York State (or perhaps from more locally derived till). One may be a European flint (English), and the remainder are local lower Susquehanna Valley cherts.

Hundreds of native-made bifacial gunflints of both European and native stones have been found in the village and in the cemeteries at the Strickler site. For the cemetery-derived samples we note a ratio of about one gunflint for every three graves.

Two gunflints of the next type in Witthoft's (1966) series were found at the northeast cemetery of the Strickler site in 1974. Witthoft employed three terms in discussing this type, including Clactonian, which more or less describes its flint-working technology in European archeological terms; wedge-shaped, which describes its appearance in cross section; and Dutch gunflint, after what he (Witthoft 1966: 26) thought was the primary country of origin for this type. Other writers, following Hamilton (1960: 73-79), have called this type gunspalls. Subsequent researchers, viz., White (1975), and particularly De Lotbiniere (1980), have clearly shown that this type was also made in great quantities in England. They make their first appearance, as Witthoft (1966) and De Lotbiniere (1980) suggest, about 1650. From evidence shown in Table 11, it would appear that the wedge-shaped (*our* preferred name for them) gunflints did not become popular (abundant) in Susquehanna Valley Indian sites until after 1700. Actually, this is a reflection of the paucity of Susquehannock sites during the last quarter of the seventeenth century. If we look at Seneca sites for this period (see Kent 1983), we find that the wedge-shaped gunflints begin to increase in use on Indian sites in the period between 1675 and 1687.

Table 11

DISTRIBUTION OF GUNFLINT TYPES

	---*Bifacial gunflints*---			
Sites	*native stones*	*European stones*	*wedge-shaped gunflints*	*French blade gunflints*
36 La1	2			
36La6	8	1		
36La3	58	73	2	6
36Yo9	17	1(?)	1	3(?)
36Yo170	22	27	4	1
36La52	1	1	89	10
36La40,57			6	
36Lu43			4	1
36Nb71			26	6
36Lr11			21	5
Valley Forge*			54	86

*Included to show the trend at the time of the American Revolution. See also Kent 1983: Tables 1 and 2.

At the Strickler site the ratio of bifacial gunflints of native manufacture to European-made wedge-shaped forms is about 70 to 1.

The Art Futer collection from the Strickler site (northeast cemetery) includes several of Witthoft's (1966) next gunflint type. These are the prismatic (or trapezoidal) blade forms made of a blonde or beeswax-colored, fine-grained French flint.

The six specimens of French gunflints in the Futer collection from the Strickler site all appear to have come from typical Susquehannock graves of that period and are therefore not intrusive, nor later. As such they represent one of, if not the earliest, dated (1645-1665) samples of this type. Hamilton (1980: 142) mentions a sample of French gunflints in a Canadian site, with rare closed terminal provenience attributable to 1663. Witthoft (1966) and Kent (1983) have shown that this type does not attain any real popularity in North America until about 1740.

Bifacial gunflints are present at the Oscar Leibhart site, but, although a number of them have been found there over the years by various collectors, no accurate count of these or other types is possible. The Joseph Wallace collection at Craley, Pennsylania, includes at least 60 bifacial gunflints of both native and European stones, which were collected from the surfaces of both the Oscar and Byrd Leibhart sites. Kinsey recovered three such gunflints and one probable wedge-shaped form from the longhouse which he excavated in 1956 at the Oscar Leibhart site (Kinsey 1957).

Witthoft (1966: 23) reports three French-blade gunflints from the Donald Leibhart collection from the Oscar Leibhart site. However, in recent discussions with Donald Leibhart we were unable to confirm this discovery.

Twenty-four bifacial gunflints, primarily of local stones, and two definite wedge-shaped forms were found at the Byrd Leibhart site in 1970. The York County Historical Society collection includes several more of the bifacial and at least two more of the wedge-shaped gunflints. The ratio of bifacial to wedge-shaped gunflints for the Byrd Leibhart site is about 14 to 1, as compared to the 70 to 1 for the earlier Strickler site.

A single-blade gunflint made in the French manner, but of the relatively unusual dark or black French flint, was found (1970) in a grave at Byrd Leibhart's, which also contained an Ohio Valley-style (Fort Ancient?) pot and an extended skeleton.

At Conestoga Town, settled after 1690, there were 101 gunflints from 69 graves (although not every grave produced gunflints). Eighty-nine of these were wedge-shaped. Only two bifacial forms were found, and both of these are rather large and were probably used in flint and steel fire-starting sets. The remaining 10 gunflints at this site were blade forms of the beeswax-colored French stone. Almost one half of the gunflints found at Conestoga exhibited some very hard use against a strike-a-light steel. This can show up as the partial bifacial flaking of either a wedge-shaped or a blade gunflint. It may be both the result of extra-hard pounding against the fire steel and/or efforts to resharpen or rejuvenate the edges of gunflints by striking them at a more obtuse angle against a strike-a-light steel.

The ratio of bifacial to wedge-shaped gunflints had, by the period of Conestoga Town, shifted to about 1 to 45, as opposed to 14 to 1 at the previous site. As we see, the French blade gunflints were also beginning to increase in popularity or availability.

The sample of gunflints from Conoy Town is too small to give any accurate reflection of the distribution of types at that time. By way of comparison, though, we may note that the Kuskuski site (1760) produced wedge-shaped and blade flints in a ratio of three to one, while at Conestoga the ratio was nine to one. By the time of the American Revolution the French blades had generally replaced the wedge-shaped forms, at least in military sites. To our knowledge, no eighteenth-century Indian site in Pennsylvania has thus far produced any examples of the type which Witthoft (1966) has called the English black gunflint. In fact, this type is rare on any Pennsylvania archeological site. During the nineteenth century it becomes the major form in the world's gunflint commerce.

Conclusions

Guns were obviously a major item of equipment carried by Europeans coming to North America. Peterson (1956: 317-35) has published a sample inventory, taken from contemporary records, of arms brought to or used in the New World from 1540 to the late eighteenth century.

Contact between Indians of eastern North America and Europeans is in evidence at least as early as 1525, by virtue of the occasional trade goods found in the sites of this period. History records even earlier contacts. Those sixteenth-century Indians along the Atlantic coast who met European explorers and fishermen undoubtedly saw guns, and some experienced their operation. A few must have managed to secure guns. However, no significant quantities of guns got into Indian hands until well into the seventeenth century.

There is no evidence of the use of any guns at the Schultz site. The Washington Boro site overlaps the settlement at Jamestown by as much as 20 years, and yet there is practically no archeological evidence, from either the cemeteries or the village, of these Susquehannocks having had any guns. The only exception is an iron trigger guard from a grave which Cadzow (1936; catalogue number 1158) excavated at the Keller cemetery. In the catalogue the specimen is described as a spoon, and it may have been used as such; but it is obviously a trigger guard.

Matchlocks, wheel locks, snaphances, even doglocks are rare—almost non-existent in Indian sites of any period. But again, some of these surely were acquired by the Susquehannocks prior to 1625. After this date and coincidental with the invention of the conventional flintlock, we begin to see increasing evidence of their possession of guns.

The historical impact of guns among the Indians has been widely treated (*e.g.*, by Hamilton 1960, 1980; Russell 1957; Hunt 1940; Jennings 1978; and others) and need not be reviewed here at any length. Jennings (1978) in particular ascribes a great deal of importance to the role of the gun among the Indians and its effect upon the course of seventeenth-century events. Obviously it was a major factor in the intercourse of trade between Indians and whites. Those Indians who had guns in quantity were those in control of the trade. Parenthetically, they were in control of their neighbors and generally a force to be reckoned with by the Europeans.

Advantages and disadvantages of the gun, as compared to the bow and arrow at this period, have also been widely argued, but history has shown that the gun quickly became the more formidable weapon of war. Among the Indians of the lower Susquehanna Valley, the gun's replacement of the bow and arrow was nearly complete by the beginning of the eighteenth century.

In the middle of the seventeenth century the Susquehannocks living at the Strickler site were at the peak of their population, political impact, and control of the trade and their Indian neighbors. These facts are evident both in the historical accounts and through archeology. The number of guns which they possessed is in itself a good indication of the height of their power. They clearly had more guns (including cannon) than at any other point in their history.

The Susquehannocks, and many other Indians for that matter, were accustomed to disposing of goods rather lavishly with their dead. The placement of iron tools, and particularly guns, in the graves of the dead would have been an extravagant waste for the seventeenth-century European settler. But for the Susquehannocks it had become an important ritual and custom to furnish their deceased relatives with items useful in life. Generally they made the best offering they could afford or that circumstances would allow. We note a certain amount of prudence in this regard, as frequently guns and tools from the graves are pretty well worn out.

Even in less prosperous or more desperate times the practice of burying guns with certain individuals continued. However, the offering often became a token, as for example, a completely useless gun, or various parts of a gun.

Heisey and Witmer (1962) have noted that the Susquehannocks often appeared to have more faith in the magic of the grave-offered gun than in its functional capabilities. On several occasions guns have been found which had their barrels bent to conform to the shape of the normally short grave pit.

The Susquehannocks knew how to take guns apart—no great feat, unless we consider the apparent lack of appropriate tools. Screwdrivers, at least in the form we know today, are very rare. This is not, however, a difficult tool to make. Almost any suitable-sized strap or rod of iron could have been filed into the proper shape. Files were fairly common tools, at least at Strickler and the Leibhart sites. Apparently seventeenth-century screwdrivers were chisel-shaped. Chisels are fairly common on these sites and some of them could have served as screwdrivers to remove screw-fastened parts on guns.

Once a gunlock had been disassembled by an Indian, it is very doubtful that he could have effected very many repairs. Guns of the period were not easily fixed with replacement parts from other guns. There were no standard sizes. Hammers, frizzens, springs and sears are the most likely parts to become broken or worn out. Replacement parts from other guns would invariably require filing, if not drilling, tapping or forge-shaping. Some of the necessary tools have been found in Susquehannock graves: an enormous cache of blacksmith's tools was found in one grave at the Byrd Leibhart site (Landis n.d.). But that the owners of such tools knew how to use them, especially for major gun repairs, is certainly questionable. Some gunlocks (Figure 68) were very badly reassembled. At the same time the enormous number of gun parts from some of the sites certainly implies that these Indians could take them apart, probably undertake a few minor repairs, and put them back together.

An operable gunlock, as found by itself in a grave, could represent more than just a token offering of a gun. Although it would have been rather clumsy, the gunlock could have been used as a flint and steel set for starting fires. A frizzen could also serve as the steel in a strike-a-light set. Frequently they are found in a cache of strike-a-light flints.

On the other hand, pans, springs, cocks, lock plates, broken barrels, ferrules, butt plates, nose caps, triggers and trigger guards, all of which occur as separate or paired items in graves, had little or no functional value except as fortuitous replacement parts. They were largely tokens or curios.

Flint and steel sets, including gunlocks probably, and certainly frizzens, together with several types of conventional strike-a-light steels (Figure 71) were fairly frequent grave offerings. Flints for strike-a-light sets are the most numerous lithic items in seventeenth-century Susquehannock sites after 1625. Regular gunflints, of both native and European stones, particularly those which were highly worn, were used in this manner. However, the majority of the flints used against the strike-a-light steel were simply spalls of various stones. The most common, and empirically the most effective, stones for this purpose are, oddly enough, flakes of grey and black English flint. The source of this material was the ballast piles of the Chesa-

Figure 71. Shapes of steel strike-a-lites.

peake and Delaware harbors. These same flint nodules can still be collected today where they were dumped from the holds of seventeenth-century ships.

Conestoga Town produced a relatively high ratio of guns per graves. All of these guns were functional pieces, and some were of rather high quality. This should not be taken as an index of wealth or military strength; the Conestogas had neither.

Some of the pieces, as indicated earlier, can be considered Indian trade guns, as they were probably made specifically for that purpose. They are not unlike later eighteenth- and nineteenth-century English and American-made "Indian trade guns." It is interesting to note the long survival of the serpentine or dragon side plates, similar trigger guards, and the simple, sheet-brass butt plates (see Hamilton 1968 for illustrations of these later forms).

Many collectors would refer to those better-made guns at Conestoga as also being Indian trade guns. It is our opinion, however, that they were not made specifically for that purpose. Rather, they would seem to be the ordinary or slightly above average guns of colonial use. These long, slender fowlers show too much individuality and too much attention in the design and decoration of their fittings to have been produced specifically for the Indian market.

Gun offerings were still an important part of Susquehannock (and Seneca) funerary practices, and when appropriate and economically feasible they were buried with the deceased. Probably every adult male living at Conestoga owned a gun, and perhaps his attachment to it had some bearing on whether or not it was buried with him. The fact that most, if not all, men had guns is again not a reflection of their wealth, but rather a result of the times and cultural changes. Guns had very nearly replaced the bow and arrow as a weapon and hunting tool for all of the Susquehanna's eighteenth-century Indians.

EUROPEAN CERAMICS

No European ceramics of any sort have been found at either the Schultz or Washington Boro sites. The earliest site in the Susquehanna Valley to have produced such items is the Frey-Haverstick Susquehannock cemetery. As we have previously indicated, this site is spatially associated within the Washington Boro village, but it appears to have been used just after the village was abandoned, probably by families who wanted to bury their dead near the old ones. One of these pieces from Frey-Haverstick is an Indian-worked delft disc (Figure 72) with a central drill hole. This piece was glazed with a cream-colored slip and then decorated with stripes and other designs in blue, brown and yellow. Other delft discs, both drilled and undrilled, have been found at Strickler and Byrd Leibhart. A second ceramic item from Frey-Haverstick is represented by eight sherds of soft-paste earthenware (buff colored), to which a partial cream-color glaze was applied. This vessel had a tapered bottom on a pedestal base. The glaze

Figure 72. Delft disks cut by Indians. Left to right: (36Yo170); (36La3); (36La6).

was apparently applied only on the top half of the vessel, but some of it ran in streaks down over the bottom half. The third and most important piece from this site is a salt glaze, cream-colored stoneware jug (Figure 73). This jug was recovered from a very shallow grave and a portion of the piece was lost when the topsoil was bulldozed from the site. As restored (Figure 73) the jug contains three seals bearing the arms of the city of Amsterdam, surmounted by the date 1630. Decoration on the vessel consists of horizontal encircling rows of cordoned rings covered in three bands with a glaze of cobalt blue. This same blue was also applied to the periphery of the seals. We know of at least four other examples of this same jug shape, all of which are about the same size and have the same seal with the arms of Amsterdam. The only difference is that none of the other seals has a date. Cox (1944: 419, Figure 619) illustrates one of these. Another, with grey instead of cream-colored glaze, was found at the Byrd Leibhart site and is now in a private collection (Figure 73). A third example, in a private collection, was found at an Iroquois site in central New York, and a fourth was found at the Seneca site of Boughton Hill (Rochester Museum and Science Center *Newsletter* 1975 XII: no. 1).

Figure 73. Two salt-glazed stoneware jugs. Left: (36La6). Center: enlargement of seal from 36La6. Right: similar jug without date (36Yo170, private collection).

Figure 74. Blue on grey stoneware *krug* (north of 36La6, Landis collection, Hershey Museum).

About two hundred yards north of the Frey-Haverstick cemetery, at the site of the modern Church of God cemetery, some additional Susquehannock graves were encountered. In all likelihood these are strict contemporaries of those at Frey-Haverstick, but the reason for their distant separation is something of a puzzle. During the excavation for the interment of Mrs. Caroline Markley, the grave-diggers found a large sheet of perforated

Figure 75. European ceramics from the Strickler site (36La3). Top: soft-paste earthenware with red and green glaze. Middle left: unglazed soft-paste mug (New World product?). Middle right: tin-glazed apothecary jar (Futer collection). Bottom left: blue on grey salt-glazed stoneware mug (Futer collection). Right: brown salt-glazed stoneware "Grenzhausen" jug (Futer collection).

brass, a small brass kettle, a small Washington Boro Incised pot, and a superb paneled Rhenish *krug* (Figure 74). These specimens are in the D. H. Landis collection at the Hershey Museum. This blue-on-grey stoneware mug probably dates from the first quarter of the seventeenth century.

By the time the Susquehannocks were well-settled at the Strickler site, the quantity of European ceramics available to them had greatly increased. Sherds recovered from pits on the village area represent at least 13 delft vessels, most of which were probably pharmaceutical jars; seven blue-on-grey salt-glazed stoneware jugs or mugs; eight brown salt-glazed stoneware jugs, of which both Grenzhausen jugs and bellarmines are represented; and 12 soft-paste earthenware jugs with red- and brown-glazed surfaces, and at least one green-glazed. This latter category, the redwares, would seem to represent primarily plates or shallow bowls, and these probably relate to the North Devon potteries described by Watkins (1960: 15-59).

Ceramics from the graves at Strickler include a number of additional soft-paste, tin-glazed (delft) items, among which is one very small cup from the southeast cemetery and the handle for a mug from the northeast cemetery. Art Futer's collection from the latter cemetery includes one delft pharmaceutical jar (Figure 75), a blue-on-grey stoneware mug (Figure 75), and a so-called Grenzhausen jug of brown, salt-glazed stoneware. A jug, almost identical to this one, was found by the owners of this site. In 1974 the Museum field crew recovered a pedestal-based bowl with two handles, made of soft-paste earthenware and glazed red on the outside and green on the inside (Figure 75). At this same time the crew also found an unglazed soft-paste mug, which we suggest may be the product of a New World, perhaps Virginia, pottery (Figure 75).

At least two complete bellarmine or *bartmann* jugs have been found at Strickler. One, excavated during the 1880's, was reportedly purchased from a local collector by E. A. Barber for the Philadelphia Museum of Art (Barber 1907).

Cadzow (1936: 64, 91) found a rather unusually shaped, squat bellarmine in the southwest cemetery (Figure 76). Witthoft (n.d.c) reported seeing a bellarmine jug in the Oscar Leibhart collection from the site on his property, but the location of this jug is not now known. Other than this we are not aware of any European ceramics from the Upper Leibhart site, although some others must have been found. The Byrd Leibhart site has produced the largest number of whole or nearly complete specimens of European ceramics. At least five such pieces were found by Leibhart and Graham, all of which appear in the newspaper photograph (Figure 63) taken in 1933. The first of these was in a cigar box under the table at the right side. Since then, the specimen has changed hands a number of times,

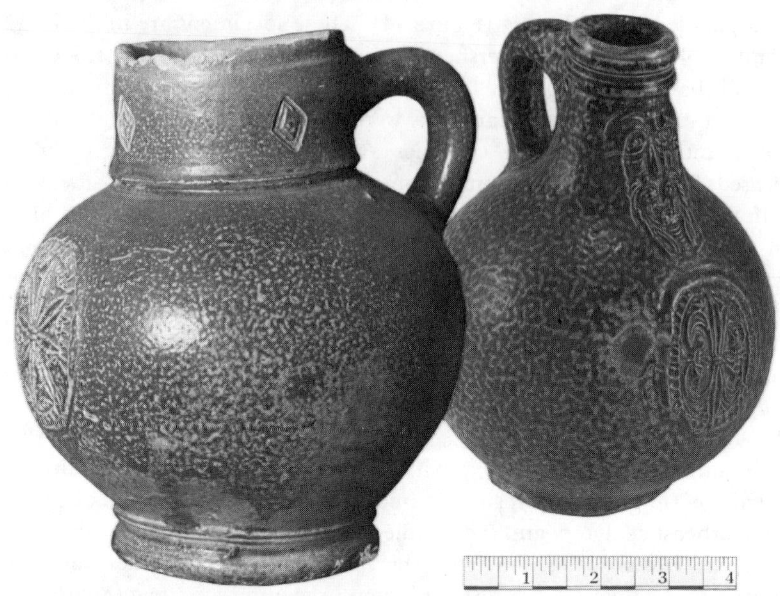

Figure 76. Brown salt-glazed stoneware vessels. Left: (36Yo170, York County Historical Society collection). Right: bellarmine (36La3).

and in 1972 it was purchased by the Museum and restored. It is a magnificent pitcher-jug (*Kannen*) with a lion's head pouring spout. Its body is a grey, salt-glazed stoneware to which numerous sprig-molded decorations have been applied. The triangles and the cordoned rings are covered with cobalt blue, and the large 11-point star is filled with a brownish-purple manganese (Figure 77). An almost identical jug in a private collection bears the date 1661.

Also in this photograph is the previously mentioned jug, which is similar (but undated) to that from the Frey-Haverstick site (Figure 63). The mug (*Krug*) to the right of the case bottle is of brown, salt-glazed stoneware, and is now on exhibit at the York County Historical Society (Figure 76). To the right of this last-mentioned mug is a delft jar whose present whereabouts is unknown.

Toward the left of the table is a small redware mug. Its whereabouts is also unknown, but in the 1930's a better photograph was taken by Gerald B. Fenstermaker of it and two other vessels, then owned by Byrd Leibhart (see Figure 78). A mug similar in form to this one, but which is not decorated with incisions, was found at the site by George Keller and sold at auction in 1978 (Kodachrome slide A.23.80, collections of the William Penn

Figure 77. Blue-on-grey salt-glazed stoneware *kannen* (36Yo170).

Figure 78. Soft-paste earthenware vessels from the Byrd Leibhart site (36Yo170). Delft salt in foreground is about four inches in diameter and was found in 1970.

Museum). The pot to the right of the Fenstermaker plate (Figure 78) is also an enigma. It would appear to be soft-paste, glazed earthenware, possibly of sixteenth-century origin. The redware mug to the top left of Figure 79 is in a private collection in Lancaster.

In 1970 the Museum's field crew recovered three additional pieces of European wares. One of these is the bottom of a bellarmine jug, another is a broken "Grenzhausen" jug, and the third is a blue-on-white delft salt (Figure 78). Sherds from the village pits represent additional salt-glazed stoneware and redware vessels.

European- and/or American-made ceramics from Conestoga Town consist primarily of redwares. Only one fragment of stoneware was found on the surface. Numerous fragments of redware were recovered from the surface and from the fill of the grave pits. Intact specimens of redware consist of two cups, one of which is quite similar to those from Byrd Leibhart's, while the other has a dark brown and very shiny glaze; a small dish or saucer with a black and very glossy glaze; and three miniature jugs (Figure 79). A shallow infant's grave, partially cut away by plowing, produced a broken, yellow-glazed earthenware mug with brown manganese (combware) decoration. Combware is generally thought to have first come into production about 1710.

No ceramics of any sort were found in the graves at Conoy Town. Fragments of redware were abundant in the village area as they generally are at other eighteenth-century Indian sites in the Susquehanna Valley.

Figure 79. Redware containers. Top left: (36Yo170). Others: (36La52).

European Clay Pipes

Frey-Haverstick (36La6) was the earliest site in the sequence to produce European-made clay pipes. Three pink- or tan-colored, gritty clay pipes were found in one grave at this site. All three could well have been made in the same mould (Figure 80). Although one has a broken stem, it shows extensive teeth wear at the end of its short stem, and was obviously used. The stems on the intact specimens measure about four and three-eighths inches from the front of the heel; and the stem-hole diameter of all three pieces is 11/64 inch, which, by the way, gives the ridiculously early date of 1511, using the Binford (1962) formula. Just below the mouth of each of these pipes is a moulded or impressed band of chevrons or triangles which completely encircles the bowls. Henry (1979) suggests that these tan-colored pipes, as found in Maryland (specifically at St. Marys City), may be colonial manufactures. Their large stem holes (bores) do rather suggest something at variance with normal continental manufacturing techniques. We note, however, as Oswald (1975: 11) does, that the clay in certain areas of England and in other European countries frequently fired to a reddish, tan or yellowish color.

No European clay pipes of any other form are known from the Frey-Haverstick site. Two pipes which are very similar to these tan varieties were found at the Strickler site (36La3).

Following Frey-Haverstick in the sequence, or possibly contemporaneous with it, is the Roberts site (36La1). One kaolin (or as it is now sometimes called, ball clay) pipe is known from this site.

Table 19 suggests a decline in the use of kaolin pipes at Strickler, at least as buried offerings. We note, however, a tremendous increase in the use of native-made pipes at Strickler, as compared to those sites which precede it. Actually, the number of kaolin pipes owned and smoked by the Strickler Susquehannocks was definitely on the increase as compared to the earlier sites. At least 30 kaolin pipes, represented by stem and bowl fragments, were recovered from the village area at Strickler, and at least that many more occur in various private collections. The Museum's collection from graves at Strickler includes eight kaolin pipes.

Not very many of the pipes from Strickler bear any makers' marks. *E. B.*, in raised letters on a flattened, very diminutive heel, appears on at least seven pipes from this site. One *E. B.* pipe from Strickler has the mark, an apparently identical stamp, on a protruding heel.

We know of only three other examples (one of each type) of initialed pipes from Strickler. One of these is marked on the heel with *I. H.* under a possible crown. Another, in a private collection, is marked *I. D.*; the third is marked *P. E.* Oswald (1975: 138, 153-54) lists at least nine *I. H.* makers in London and Bristol during the early to mid-seventeenth century. We should also note that the possible crown on this pipe has similarities to the Dutch examples illustrated by Oswald (1975: 117). Bradley and DeAngelo (1981: 121) mention a Dutch maker with these initials—Jan Hendricxse, who worked, at least, in 1658. Identification of the *I. D.* pipes is perhaps less elusive—Oswald (1975: 135, 152) lists three English pipe makers with these initials, all of whom worked before 1664.

The *P. E.* pipe is in the Henry Heisey collection in the North Museum at Franklin and Marshall College. Heisey excavated this specimen from a grave in the southeast cemetery at Strickler. According to Oswald (1975: 182), these initials pertain to Philip Edwards of Bristol, who worked between 1649 and ca. 1680. Edwards was a known exporter to America.

Kaolin pipes have a great potential as an aid in dating sites. We now have a fairly useful typology of forms (Oswald 1975). There is also the pipestem-dating formula (Harrington 1954; Binford 1962a; etc.). In addition, the dates of manufacture are known for hundreds of British pipe makers who signed their pipes (Oswald 1975). We hope that in the future there will be similar lists for makers in other European countries, particularly those in the Netherlands.

The bowl-form typology can provide, in many cases, 30- to 40-year time-brackets for particular pipes. The stem-hole formula can theoretically produce (although this is subject to much doubt and criticism) specific mean dates for a group of pipes from a particular site. Makers' marks provide the most reliable dates, but unfortunately we rarely encounter seventeenth-century pipes for which the maker can be unequivocally identified. Such is the case for the *E. B.* pipes from Strickler and elsewhere. In addition, this unheeled type does not appear in the Oswald (1975) typology. There are at least four English pipe makers with the initials *E. B.* who were working during the third quarter of the seventeenth century (Oswald 1975; Omwake 1959: 132). One of these men, Edward Biggs of Henley, was working as early as 1653 (Omwake 1959: 132). The others all seem too late to have been responsible for these pipes at Strickler. Omwake (1959: 132-33), in fact, suggested that these *E. B.* pipes might be of Dutch manufacture. More recent research (Bradley and DeAngelo 1981: 15) strongly suggests that these *E. B.* pipes were made by Edward Bird, who lived in Amsterdam from 1630 until his death in 1665.

Pipes bearing the *E. B.* mark occur at both the Oscar Leibhart (36Yo9) site (Omwake 1959) and at Byrd Leibhart (36Yo170). At the latter site, from which there is a fairly large sample of pipes, it is clear that the *E. B.* pipes are much less common than they are at Strickler. In the sample of 53 pipes from various collections known to have come from the Byrd Leibhart site, only two have *E. B.* marks. One of these is on a protruding heel, the other on one of the heelless variety.

Other marked pipes from the Byrd Leibhart site include one with a rosette on the heel; two with the initials *D. V.* on their heels; and two with the letters *L. E.* and a decorative scroll stamped on the backs (facing the smoker) of their bowls. Only one maker with the initials *D. V.* appears on Oswald's list of British pipe makers. This person was Daniel Usner (Usher) of London, who signed the oath of allegience ca. 1696 as a journeyman. This does not tell us the duration of his working period as a pipe maker, but it is doubtful that he was making signed pipes before 1680 (or even 1690). Consequently, these *D. V.* pipes are at this point of little use in fixing more precise dates for this site. The *L. E.* pipes, on the other hand, are quite important in this regard. These two pipes came to the Museum from the George Keller collection and were probably excavated from the southwestern cemetery at this site. Almost without question, these were made by Lluellin Evans of Bristol, a known exporter to the West Indies and America who, according to Oswald (1975: 152), was working between 1661 and 1688. These dates rather nicely bracket those which we have proposed for the occupation of this site.

According to Oswald (1975: 40), pipes without a base or spur (heel) are most commonly found in America. These spurless export forms otherwise generally duplicate the types which do have the spur or base. His typology shows that the types without spurs begin about 1660.

In the sample from Strickler (16 bowls), only one is without a flattened base or spur. We have already noted that the *E. B.* pipes generally have no projecting base at the heel, but that they do have a flattened area on which the stamp was impressed, and so they are counted as pipes which have a base.

The sample from the Byrd Leibhart site shows a marked difference in the percentage of pipes which do not have a base or spur. In a sample of 33 bowls, 15 (or 45.5%) are without bases or spurs. In terms of their outlines, these baseless pipes equate most closely with Oswald's (1975: 41) Types 25 and 26, to which he assigns an overall date of 1660 to 1710. Actually, many of them would seem to fall between the characteristics of his Types 25 and 26.

Approximately 50% of these baseless pipes have rouletting below the mouth of the bowl; the others are plain. Pipes with bases from this site fall primarily into Oswald's (1975: 39) Types 5 and 6. All of these have rouletting.

Some of the pipes from the Byrd Leibhart site were anachronisms when they were buried. For the most part, however, we feel that kaolin pipes used as grave furniture were generally fairly current with their period of manufacture, probably more so than any other kind of trade item, except glass beads.

The heelless kaolin pipes changed very little in the 30 or 40 years following the close of the Leibhart sites. Unfortunately we do not find them again anywhere in the Susquehanna Valley until Conestoga Town was settled, about 1690. Kaolin pipes without bases or spurs from Conestoga show three major differences as compared to those from Byrd Leibhart's. A line across the mouth of the bowl is parallel to the stem, the stems are slightly thinner, and rouletting below the mouth of the bowl does not seem to occur.

Oswald's (1975: 40) statement about pipes without bases or spurs being most commonly exported to America seems to be verified by the sample from Conestoga. Only six pipes (16.2%) in this sample of 37 had spurs or bases.

Eighteenth-century pipes with makers' marks can be identified far more readily than those of the preceding century. The probable mark identifications of the pipes from Conestoga are listed below, with page references to Oswald (1975). Italicized names are known exporters to America.

Table 12

PIPES WITH MAKERS' MARKS FROM CONESTOGA TOWN (36La52)

Catalogue number	*Initials*	*Name*	*Date*	*City*	*Page*
La52/13	R. (I?)	Richard Johnson (2)	1693	London	139
		Richard Jones (1)	1696	London	139
17	R. T.	*Robert Tippett* (2)	1678-1713	Bristol	158
22	R. T.	*Robert Tippett* (2)	1678-1713	Bristol	158
22	R. T.	*Robert Tippett* (2)	1678-1713	Bristol	158
35	R. Tippet	*Robert Tippett* (3)	1713-1720	Bristol	158
81	R. T. R. T.	*Robert Tippett* (3)	1713-1720	Bristol	158
21	I. Lewis	John Lewis	1669-1696	Bristol	155
62	S. H.	several in Bristol	1722-1739		154
65	C. (H?)	*Charles Hicks*	1721-1746	Bristol	153
31	C. (H?)	*Charles Hicks*	1721-1746	Bristol	153
65	GE	*George Ebbery*	1721-1781	Bristol	152
72	I. H.	*John Hunt*	1694-1715	Bristol	154
		(numerous other possibilities in Bristol and London)			
Witmer coll.	IA(IA?)	*John Arthur*	1707-1723	Bristol	150
Witmer coll.	IA(?)	(several other possibilities in Bristol)			

The popularity of kaolin pipes was much higher at Conestoga than at any other site in the sequence. Over 50% of the graves had kaolin pipe offerings. The percentages of graves with either kaolin, pewter or native clay pipes is about 70%. These figures may be indicative of the popularity of smoking and the general availability of pipes at this time. This is also reflective of the Susquehannock and Seneca custom of placing pipes with their dead.

At Conoy Town the percentage of graves with pipes drops markedly. Only four kaolin and four pewter pipes were recovered from the Conoy cemetery. In fact, three of the kaolin pipes came from one burial. This is not an indication that smoking was less popular among the Conoy, but probably reflects a difference in burial customs. Pipe fragments were quite abundant in the village of Conoy Town.

Two of the Conoy cemetery pipes (La40/31) were marked *R. T.*, probably Robert Tippet(2), 1678-1713. One other (La40/24) was marked *R. T.* on the back of the bowl and *R. Tippett* on the side. This may be Robert Tippett(3), 1713-1720. The fourth pipe (La40/31) from the cemetery is marked *I. Jenkins* and could be either John Jenkins (1739) or James Jenkins (1707-1739). Both were known Bristol exporters to America (Oswald 1975: 154). One fragmentary bowl from a pit in the village site (La 57/27) is marked (?) *W*.

Eighteenth-century sites of Algonquian-speaking peoples in Pennsylvania generally show less use of pipes as grave offerings. The Delaware site (36Bk450) near Kutztown, in Berks County, produced four kaolin pipes, all of which were found in a child's grave (Deisher notes and collections, William Penn Memorial Museum). All four pipes were marked *E. R.* on the backs of their bowls. At least six graves, for which the contents have been described, were excavated at this site (see also Brunner 1897: 113-14). Oswald (1975: 143, 157) lists two likely candidates for the manufacturer of these pipes: Edward Randal, 1719, an exporter in London, and Edward Reed, 1706-1723, of Bristol.

Two *R. T.* pipes were found in one grave, among six excavated and described, at North Brook (36Ch61) in Chester County (Weslager 1953: 128). Of the 15 graves excavated at the Montgomery site (36Ch60), two produced pipes. Weslager (1953: xvii) recovered three pipes from one grave, one of which is clearly marked *L. R.* Becker (1978a) found one pewter pipe in the 14 graves which he excavated. Oswald (1975: 144) lists one *L. R.* pipe maker, Lancelot Roeculon, who signed the oath of allegiance in 1696 as a journeyman in London.

Three kaolin pipes, all fragmentary, were recovered from the 22 graves excavated at the Delaware Indian site of Wapwallopen (36Lu43). One of these bears the mark *WN* on the back of the bowl, facing the smoker. In Oswald (1975: 142) there is one London maker with these initials listed—William Newell, 1721. For Bristol, Oswald (1975: 156) lists two

Figure 80, opposite. Types of kaolin smoking pipes arranged in approximate chronological order. From bottom (earliest) to top: (36La6); marked E.B. at base of bowl (36Yo170); (36La3); (36Yo170); marked L.E. (36Yo170); next two (36La52); long pipe (36La52).

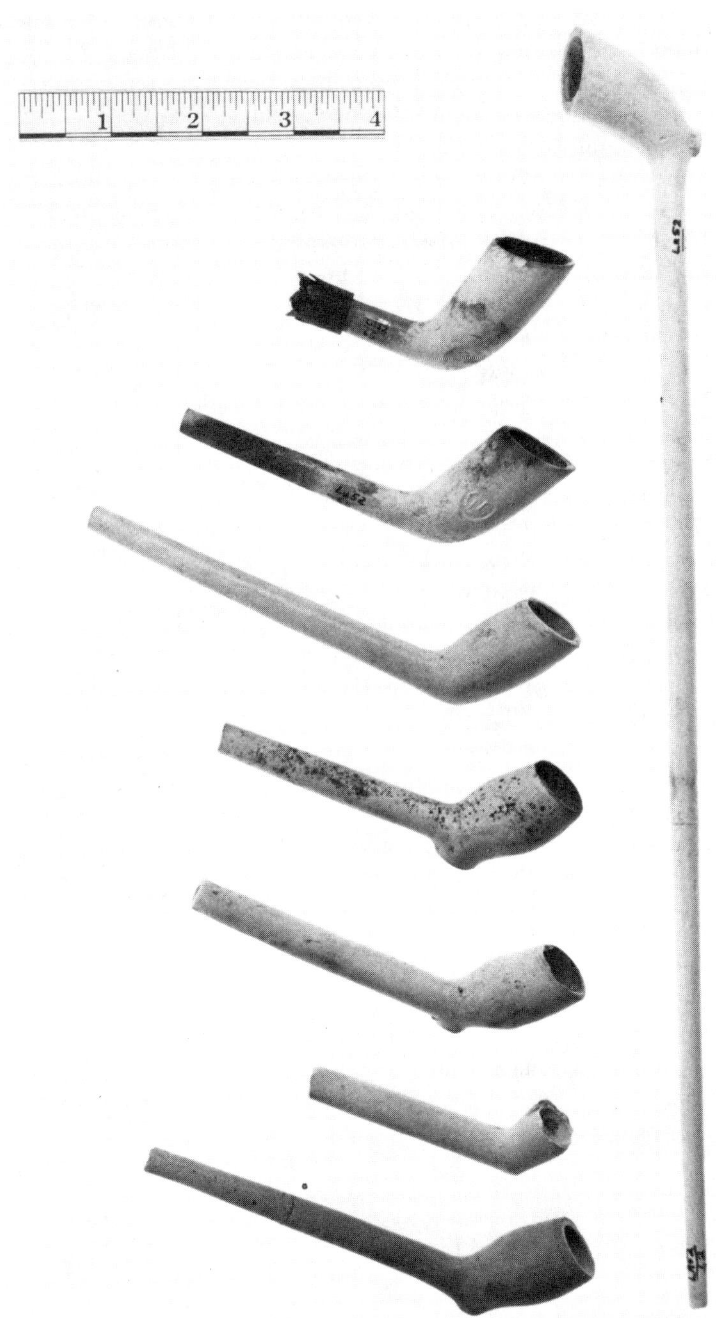
1
2
3
4

WN makers. One, William Naylor, worked between 1722 and 1735. The other, William Nicholas, manufactured pipes between 1730 and 1775, but was also the only one of the three known to have been exporters to North America. For that reason we conclude in favor of Nicholas as the manufacturer of the pipe found at Wapwallopen.

Kinsey and Custer (1982: 42) report three kaolin pipes from the Park site (36La96) near Lancaster which have makers' marks: "Lewis," "I. A.," and "R. Tippet." The first of these is probably the previously discussed John Lewis of Bristol, England (see list of pipes from Conestoga). In this same list we have suggested that *I. A.* is John Arthur. The Tippet pipes have also been discussed above.

During his 1931 excavations at the Brennan site (36Br42), on Tioga Point at Athens, Pennsylvania, James B. Griffin (1931b) found a single kaolin pipe with an *I. B.* mark. This interment probably relates to the eighteenth-century Indian town of Tioga (Kent et al. 1981). The maker of the pipe is perhaps John Frederick Bryant of Bristol, who was registered between 1747 and 1774 (Oswald 1975: 150). Bryant is one of 80 *I. B.* makers listed by Oswald (1975) for London and Bristol, but he is the only one known to have been an exporter to North America.

At Kuskuskies (36Lr11), where Zakucia (1960, and William Penn Memorial Museum files) excavated 70 burials, there were no kaolin pipes as grave offerings, and only one pewter pipe. However, kaolin pipe fragments were recovered with other village debris.

While realizing that our pipestem samples are too small to generate statistically valid dates with the pipestem-dating formula, we have nonetheless computed dates for the samples at hand. By way of very weak justification for this we might point out that many of our samples consist primarily of whole pipes which, had they been broken into the usual one- to

Table 13

PIPESTEM DATES

Formula: Y = 1931.85-38.26x (Binford 1962)

Y = date of sample

X = average bore diameter in 64ths of an inch

Site	*sample*	*average (x)*	*date (y)*
Frey-Haverstick (36La6)	3	11.0	1511
Roberts (36La1)	1	8.0	1635
Strickler (36La3)	37	7.51	1645
O. Leibhart (36Yo9)	3	7.0	1652
B. Leibhart (36Yo170)	34	7.29	1653
Conestoga (36La52)	31	5.28	1729
Conoy (36La57)	78	5.1	1737
Kutztown (36Bk450)	4	5.0	1740

two-inch-long fragments, would have produced a number of rather large samples. Several of the samples were so small as to render the use of the formula ridiculous. However, out of curiosity, dates were computed for these also, and they are presented here (Table 13). The earliest sample, from the Frey-Haverstick site, generated a date of 1511—quite a few years before the invention of kaolin pipes in Europe!

Perhaps fortuitously, the site dates resulting from these mathematical gymnastics fall in the same chronological order that we have, by other means, suggested for these sites. We note also that with the exception of the dates for the pipes from Frey-Haverstick, and the two Leibhart sites, they are very close to, or within the range of, dates which we have assigned to these sites.

As a summary of the marked kaolin pipes reported here, the following list is presented to show the marks, number of occurrences, and the sites at which they occur.

Table 14

DISTRIBUTION OF PIPES WITH MAKERS' MARKS

Site	*mark*	*occurrences*
Strickler (36La3)	EB	7
Strickler	IH	1
Strickler	PE	1
Strickler	ID	1
Oscar Leibhart (36Yo9)	EB	1
Oscar Leibhart	rosette	1
Byrd Leibhart (36Yo170)	EB	2
Byrd Leibhart	rosette	1
Byrd Leibhart	LE	2
Byrd Leibhart	DV	2
Conestoga (36La52)	RT	4
Conestoga	R Tippet	1
Conestoga	IA (A?)	2
Conestoga	I Lewis	1
Conestoga	SH	1
Conestoga	CH (?)	2
Conestoga	GE	1
Conestoga	IH	1
Conoy Cemetery (36La40)	RT	2
Conoy Cemetery	R Tippet	1
Conoy Cemetery	I Jenkins	1
Conoy Town (36La57)	?W	1
Kutztown (38Bk450)	ER	4
North Brook (36Ch61)	RT	2
Montgomery (36Ch60)	LR	1
Wapwallopen (36Lu43)	WN	1
Tioga (36Br42)	IB	1
Park (36La96)	R Tippet	1
Park	Lewis	1
Park	IA	1

SILVER

A silver coin the size of a modern dime had in 1750 the approximate value of a hard day's work by an ordinary free laborer. That coin, when used in that form or when fashioned into a silver crucifix and given in exchange for Indian furs, might have purchased two days of effort at the hunt and in processing the furs.

Today that same cross in the hands of a collector, depending on how well it was made and by whom, might be worth five thousand times the original face value of the coin from which it was made, or a week of physical labor at current average values.

Until we make these comparisons between the seemingly ridiculous prices of such objects today and their original values, we often tend to suppose that the first owner attributed to the object our own inflated values.

The fact that the survivors of a deceased Indian buried a piece or two of silver with him does not imply that his social or political status in life was higher than the person buried next to him who departed life with no furnishings for his grave. Similarly, these conditions say nothing of the personal wealth of either; rather they reflect the attitudes and affections of their surviving relatives. We can well assume that all parties involved had a fairly good appreciation for the current value of silver.

If, in a particular society, we encounter a single individual with whom truly large quantities of silver, etc., had been interred, we might well ascribe to him a special status. But it would also be necessary for us to posit a highly evolved socio-political system for the whole society of which he was a part.

This kind of social system, in which a few individuals were accorded special treatment and to whom an important place in society also meant a disproportionate acquisition of goods and services, was never the situation for any individual or society of the Susquehanna's Indians. To be certain, the tribal folk who lived throughout this area did recognize a degree of authority and leadership in a few individuals. However, this rarely gave those individuals any sumptuary rights. These were egalitarian tribal societies of the sort described by Elman Service (1962) or Julian Steward (1955), and they continued to function even for a while after being severely disrupted by European values, because each individual could largely expect equal rights and equal treatment.

This discourse might have been inserted in a number of places in this volume. However, it is perhaps most appropriate here in the discussion of objects which are, by our own standards, most precious and most indicative of social standing. Anthropological studies, such as that by Service (1962), which summarize the various evolutionary stages of society, show us

Figure 81. King Charles II silver medal. Obverse (1 1/4 inches wide) and reverse, Strickler site (36La3).

that we cannot capriciously attribute special socio-political status to an individual on the basis of the type or quantity of objects with which his relations buried him.

In fact we might note that had all the silver from all the sites in all the known collections from the Susquehanna Valley come from one interment, we would still not be induced to posit high individual status or the chiefdom or state level of society which anthropology tells us must accompany such status.

Perhaps the most graphic arguments in favor of our position lie in the fact that it was generally the children, in our local Indian sites, who were sent to the afterworld with large quantities of "offerings." Again, this did not represent special treatment for special individuals by a society; nor does it indicate the wealth of the survivors of the deceased. Rather, it reflects the varying emotions between kindred, and probably emotions as basically conditioned by prevailing religious belief.

It is our opinion that the use or non-use of burial offerings is culturally prescribed. In some societies they are never used, in some their occurrence is occasional, but in few are they used consistently. A society which at one time included burial offerings with some of its dead, and later lessened the number or quality of such offerings, may have changed its religious (cultural) attitudes or it may have become impoverished.

Strickler was the earliest site in the sequence to produce silver. Two objects of this metal are known. One is a gold and silver alloy (electrum) in the shape of a cicada. This casting (described in Witthoft and Kinsey 1959: 141) is possibly of Mesoamerican or South American origin and for that reason of great curiosity. The second piece is perhaps only slightly less a curiosity in terms of how and why it came to this Susquehannock town. It is, however, of much greater significance as a time marker for the site. This piece, a silver medallion (La3/450a), bears on one face the bust of King Charles II of Great Britain. The reverse side is engraved with the British coat of arms surrounded with the familiar HONI SOIT QUE MAL Y PENSE (Evil to him who evil thinks), and surmounted by the letters C. R. (Carolus Rex: Charles King) and the Crown (Figure 81).

This medallion was recovered during the 1974 excavations in the northeast cemetery at Strickler, where it was found apparently on a thin cord around the neck of an old male, who had been interred in the same grave pit with an infant. Other objects in the grave were typical of Strickler interments: a badly deteriorated pewter porringer, a Strickler Cord-marked pot, two native clay pipes, an iron knife and a brass kettle.

Photographs of the medal were sent to the British Museum for identification. It responded by saying that the medal was similar to a Charles II medal illustrated in Hawkins (1885: 444). Confirmation of this came when Ivor Noël Hume, who was also asked to examine the medal, sent the author a copy of the Hawkins article. The specimens are in fact *very similar*, if not identical, and if Hawkins' identification is correct, the "badge" does pertain to Charles II, who reigned from 1660 to 1685.

We have previously proposed a terminal date of 1665 for the Strickler site. The Charles II medallion rather nicely confirms that the site was occupied at least as late as 1660.

Following Strickler, as we have suggested, the Susquehannocks moved to the Oscar Leibhart site. To the best of our knowledge there is only one silver item from this site, the silver spoon bowl in the Donald Leibhart collection, which is described under Spoons.

The next occurrence of silver items is at Conestoga Town. One grave excavated here by a private individual contained the poorly preserved remains of a child in association with two silver arm bands (actually worn as such) bearing the touchmark *I. L.*; two silver brooches; a pair of cuff links (each unit consisting of two matched octagonal engraved pieces joined by a silver loop); and a silver cross with the mark *S. M.*

A second child's grave excavated by the Museum during the 1972 season was located very close to that previously described. It contained 10 circular silver brooches, a silver cross with a *B. P.* touchmark, and a pair of cuff links virtually identical to those described above (Figure 82).

Both of these sets of cuff links were associated closely enough to the

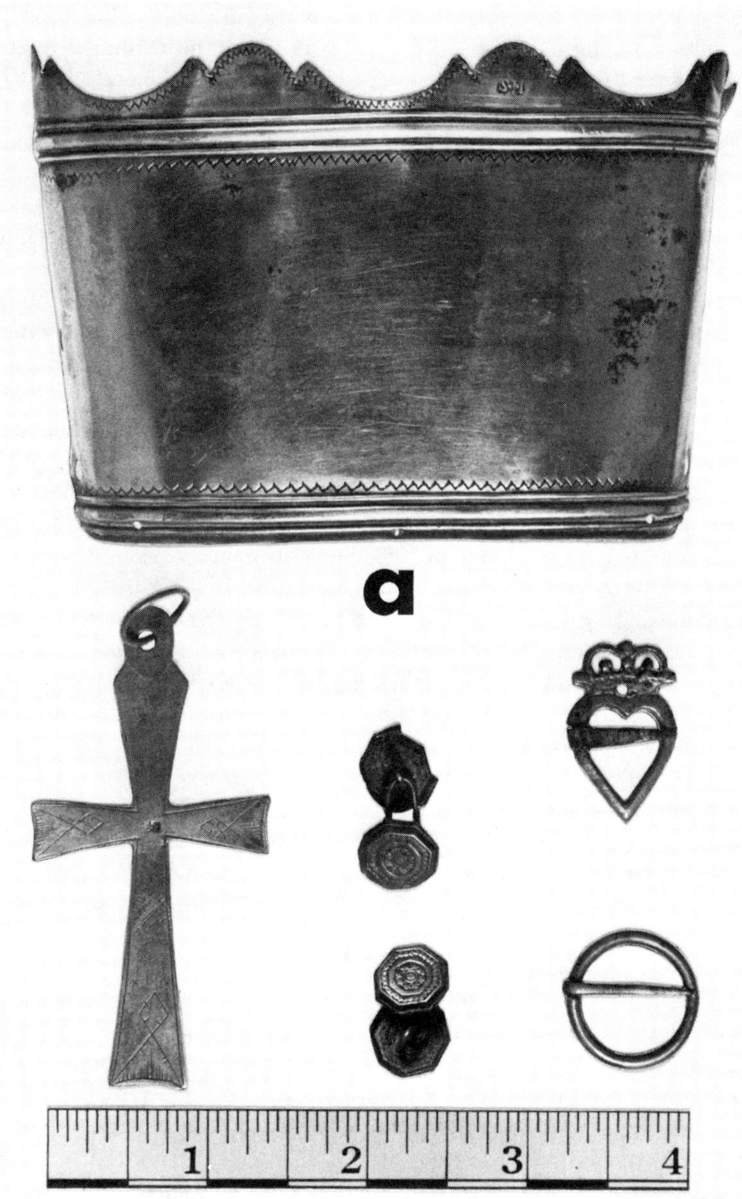

Figure 82. Silver objects from Conestoga Town (36La52).

wrists of each child to suggest their actual use on shirt cuffs. The brooches were found in the chest areas, and may also have been pinned to shirt fronts, or used to close such. Both crosses were also on the chest and were probably suspended from the neck on a cord.

Other silver items from Conestoga Town include a heart-shaped brooch associated with an adult. With another individual of undetermined (but post-adolescent) age was another circular brooch, and an unidentified object which was probably used as a gorget. Originally this object (Figure 82a) was rolled together to form a cylinder. There are three holes on each lateral edge which, if the object was rolled, would align perfectly. In all likelihood there once were rivets through these holes to hold the cylinder together. Around what would be the bottom of the cylinder are three very tiny holes, through which three silver nails were probably driven into a wooden plug in the base of the cylinder. The piece, like the cross mentioned above, is marked *S. M.* (Figure 82a). Although the shape of the piece as it was originally intended to be used is known, its function is still not clear. Its unrolling and partial flattening, presumably by an Indian, suggests its final use as an item of personal adornment.

None of the three silversmiths' marks on the above-described objects has been identified with any degree of certainty. Registries of American silversmiths for Lancaster, Philadelphia, New York, etc., include persons with these initials, but none whose mark is precisely identical, nor does any show a date of registered activity which seems appropriate for Conestoga Town (for comparative materials see Beauchamp 1903; Van Horn 1971; and Carter 1971, 1973).

No silver was found at Conoy Town, and there are only a few poorly reported finds at other later sites farther up the Susquehanna Valley. This is rather surprising, considering the high level of popularity which Indian trade silver attained after about 1740. We know of only one extant silver object from Shamokin, a small crude cross (Nb71/110) found during the Pennsylvania Historical and Museum Commission excavations at the smithy in 1979 (Nichols 1980).

The larger amount of silver recovered from the excavations by Zakucia (1960; also WPMM files) at Kuskuski, near New Castle, Pennsylvania, is typical of the increased use of silver by Indians in the second half of the eighteenth century. Among the identified artifacts from this site are three pieces of marked silver. One of these is a bracelet attributed to Philip Synge, Jr., another is a large circular disc with an engraved deer and a New York stamping. The third is a "hair ornament" with, interestingly, the mark of Benjamin Price 1767 (Zakucia 1960); this is almost certainly not the *B. P.* of the silver cross from Conestoga Town. (See Quimby 1966: 197-202, for a list which includes these silversmiths.)

Coins, Jettons, Medallions and Crosses

With but one exception, all of the coins recovered from these sites are English. The earliest coin, and the only one known from the Strickler site, is French—a Louis XIII double tournois, dated 1621. Cadzow found this coin in a burial in the southwest cemetery.

All of the remaining coins in the Museum's collection come from Conestoga Town, and they are listed here by catalogue lots.

Table 15

COINS FROM CONESTOGA TOWN (36La52)

La52/282:		
1 George I halfpenny	1721	
1 Charles II halfpenny	?	reigned 1660-1685
1 William III halfpenny	?	reigned 1689-1702
La52/27:		
1 James II halfpenny	?	reigned 1685-1688
La52/62:		
1 George I halfpenny	1724	
La52/76:		
1 George I halfpenny	1721	
2 unidentifiable copper coins		
La52/46b:		
1 William III (?) halfpenny	?	reigned 1689-1702
La52/48a:		
1 William III shilling	1697	
Ditchburn collection		
1 George I Irish halfpenny	1723	("Hibernia")

Coinage at Conestoga was of little value to the Indians, not that they were ignorant of its worth if they happened to go to Philadelphia. Several of the coins from Conestoga, and most notably the shilling, were drilled for suspension, suggesting the Indians' greater appreciation of such pieces as necklace ornaments.

According to Noël Hume (1976: 171), jettons or casting counters were originally used as mathematical aids, but frequently they were mistaken for, or passed off as, European coins. He states that the majority of them were made in Germany. In America they were often given or traded to Indians who drilled them for suspension on necklaces or elsewhere on the body.

Six jettons were found at Conestoga and one was recovered at Conoy Town. We are not aware of any from earlier sites. Four of the Conestoga jettons measure 26 mm. in diameter (all seven specimens are of thin brass and because of critical size differences all measurements are given in metric). Another measures 19 mm., and the one example from Conoy Town is

Figure 83. *Recip* counters from Conestoga Town (36La52). Note Queen Anne third from left.

23 mm. in diameter. Six of the above pieces have the bust of King George of Great Britain (facing right—probably George I), surrounded by the inscription 'GEORG. LVD. D.G.M. BRIT. FR. REX" (Georgius Ludovicus Dei Gratia Magnae Brittaniae [et] Franciae Rex = George Louis, by the Grace of God, of Great Britain and France, King) stamped on their obverse surfaces. Their reverses bear the arms of England, Scotland, Ireland and France, surrounded by the legend of their German maker—IACOB DIETZEL RECIP COUNTERS.

The remaining piece is partially deteriorated. It measures 20 mm. in diameter and its reverse is the same as those above. The obverse bears the bust of Queen Anne and the partial inscription "ANNA D. G. ANG. S.F.E.H. REG . . . " (Anna Dei Gratia Angliae Scotiae Franciae et Hiberniae Regina = Anne, by the Grace of God, of England, Scotland, France and Ireland, Queen).

Noël Hume (1976: 173) mentions one of these which he found along the river Thames, and another from the excavations at Pemaquid, Maine (see Camp 1975: 82).

All of the above described jettons were drilled. However, most were found in positions which suggest that they were not on necklaces around the necks of individuals with which they were buried. Some were with caches of other objects placed in various locations within the grave pits.

The earliest known medallion from a Susquenhanna Valley Indian site was found by the Museum's field crew during the 1974 excavations of the northeast cemetery at the Strickler site. Apparently suspended on a thin cord around the neck of an old male was a silver medal with the stamped bust of King Charles II of England (1660-1685) on its obverse side. This medallion is more fully described under silver objects.

During the 1970 excavations at Conoy Town, the field crew recovered three George I "Indian medals." Examination of the literature disclosed a number of similar examples from Pennsylvania sites, and particularly from the Susquehanna Valley. The only illustrated piece was that of Miner (1845; also shown by Beauchamp 1903: Figure 289). At least two additional George I medals from the Susquehanna Valley are described by Betts (1894: 82-84). These specimens are also mentioned by Beauchamp (1903: 56-57). Hayden (1886: 228-29) describes another medal of this sort from Wrightsville in York County (previously cited under our discussion of the Shawnee). We have previously mentioned the probable George I medal from the "Shikellamy" grave at Sunbury.

Figure 84. Medallions. Top: small version (obverse and reverse) of a George II-Caroline Medal. Middle: larger version of George II-Caroline medal. Bottom: George I medal (obverse and reverse).

Doris Freyermuth (personal communication 1977) reported another George I medal, found by a private collector in 1936 at a site along the Delaware River.

The Zakucia collection from the Kuskuskies site in Lawrence County, Pennsylvania, also includes one of these medals. This specimen is now part of the William Penn Memorial Museum collections on exhibit at the Fort Pitt Museum.

Eight more of these medals were found by the Museum's field crew during excavations at Conestoga Town in 1972.

The 12 examples which have been examined firsthand show five different varieties struck during the reign of King George I (1714-1727). They range in size from 38 to 42 mm. in diameter, and 1 to 2 mm. in thickness. They are of copper, or some copper composition, and each was originally tin-washed to give it a silver appearance. All of them have since lost most of their tinned surfaces. All originally had a soldered-on suspension loop.

Basically, there are two types, but with five distinguishable varieties thereof. The obverse side of each medal bears the bust of King George and the inscription "GEORGE KING OF GREAT BRITAIN."

Table 16

TYPES OF GEORGE I MEDALS

Type I: Examples measure 38-39 mm. in diameter and about 1 mm. in thickness.

Type Ia

Obverse: Draped and laureated bust wearing chain mail vest

Reverse: Figure holding a bow in the left hand, an arrow in the right which is pointing downward at a stag or deer on the right side of a tree, with a sunburst (with a human face) overhead.

Catalogue numbers: La40/19, La52/8c, La52/48c, La52/48c.

Type Ib

Obverse: Same as above

Reverse: Figure with a slightly different posture and draped garment and armor, holding a bow in its left hand, and pointing the arrow more horizontally (than above) at the deer.

Catalogue numbers: La52/26, La52/35.

Type II: Examples measure approximately 40-42 mm. in diameter and 2 mm. thick.

Type IIa

Obverse: Bust not wearing a chain mail vest, figure more robust than above.

Reverse: Figure shooting an arrow at a deer to the left of a tree with four branches, sunburst overhead with human face and wriggled radiating lines.

Catalogue numbers: La52/37, La40/12.

Type IIb

Obverse: Slightly different details of hair, wreath, and vestments.

Reverse: Slightly different figure, shooting an arrow at a deer to the left of a tree with four branches; sunburst with human face and straight rays overhead.

Catalogue numbers: La52/32.

Type IIc

Obverse: Same as Type IIb.

Reverse: Same as Type IIb, but tree has six branches.

Catalogue numbers: La40/9, La52/78.

It has generally been assumed that the figure on the reverse side of these medals is that of an Indian. On those examples where the figure is holding an arrow in his right hand, the wearing apparel is decidedly European. He is adorned in a flowing cloak which hangs to the ankles and is pinned at the waist. Underneath he is wearing a skirt which reaches almost to the knees. He is also wearing high-heeled shoes.

The other figure (shooting the arrow) is wearing a loose-fitting garment gathered at the waist by a belt.

This is not to say that Indians of the period would not be depicted wearing European-style clothing, but in neither case are these figures shown in anything like traditional Indian attire.

George II (1727-1760) medals, of a type previously unreported, were also found at both Conestoga and Conoy Town. These medals can be separated into three types. They are also copper or a composition thereof. None of the specimens shows any really clear evidence of tin-washing, but all may have been treated in this manner.

The basic features of all of these medals, and there are 26 of them in the Museum's collection, are the draped and laureated bust of George II facing left, and on the reverse the bust of Queen Caroline facing left. Her death in 1737 suggests that these medals were probably struck on or before that date. Major differences among the three types of these medals are in the sizes and inscriptions.

Table 17

TYPES OF GEORGE II MEDALS

Type I (George II): 26 mm. in diameter, all are approximately 1 mm. thick.

Obverse: King's bust surrounded by the inscription GEORGIUS II D. GRATIA R.

Reverse: Queen's bust surrounded by the inscription CAROLINA REGINA.

Type II: Examples measure 24 mm. in diameter.

Obverse: King's bust surrounded by the inscription GEORGIUS II D.G. MAG. BR. FR. ET HIB. REX.

Reverse: Queen's bust surrounded by the inscription CAROLINA D.G. MAG. BR. FR. ET HIB. REGINA.

Type III: 21 mm. in diameter.

Obverse: King's bust surrounded by the inscription GEORGIUS II D. GRATIA R.

Reverse: Queen's bust surrounded by the inscription CAROLINA REGINA.

Actually only two (and a possible third) George II medals were found at Conoy Town. Both of these were recovered, about 1910, from a plowed-out grave (La57/11) on the village site. A third specimen in the Museum's collection (J.611) is without provenience, but it may have come from the Conoy Town village site.

No George II medals were found in the nearby Conoy cemetery (36La40). This may be an indication of the date on which these medals were struck. It cannot be earlier than 1727. If, as we have suggested, the medals arc as late as the Queen's death (1737), we would expect to find very few of them here, since the Conoy had abandoned this place by 1743.

Witthoft (n.d.b) who had earlier examined the two specimens from Conoy Town (La57/11) and two others from the Wyandotte Town (36Lrl) at West Pittsburg, Lawrence County, Pennsylvania (which he dates to 1748-1751) has suggested that these medals may date from 1738.

In view of their paucity at Conoy Town, we can probably safely assume that they date from the 1730's and very possibly from the latter part of that decade. As such they would become the latest datable items at both Conoy Town and Conestoga.

Table 18

DISTRIBUTION OF GEORGE II MEDALS BY TYPE

Catalogue numbers	Types I	II	III
J. 611			1
La57/11			2
La52/7	1		1
La52/12			1
La52/27	2		1
La52/32	1		
La52/39	1	1	1
La52/60			3
La52/74c	2	1	
La52/76	1		1
La52/78			5
Totals	8	2	16

Figure 85. Religious medals and crosses.

Top row left to right:

La40/44 oval, 17 × 20mm.
Obverse: Christ
Reverse: religious symbols

La52/36b circular; 22mm.
Obverse: cross with letters
Reverse: I.H.S. surrounded by
S?OLIVB?VRSNSM?

Lu43/18 (two other uncleaned specimens not shown)
round, 34mm. dia.
Obverse: bust (Christ?) surrounded by
SOLE. CLARIOR
Reverse: bust (female) surrounded by
MATER CHRI. ORA PRO

Religious Medals

Twelve religious medals were found at Conestoga and Conoy Town (three at Conestoga and nine at Conoy). For the most part these are badly eroded and undatable, except to say that they are from the first half of the eighteenth century. All are of copper-base metal. Three additional religious medals were found at Wapwallopen (36Lu43). A sample of the medals is illustrated here (Figure 85) and briefly described.

Crosses

A total of 14 copper crosses was found at Conestoga and Conoy Town. These can be separated into six types. All five specimens found at Conestoga fall into one type (as illustrated by Figure 85).

The Witmer collection from Conestoga includes one wooden cross, from which the crossbar is missing and on which is mounted a copper or bronze figure of Christ.

La40/44 oval, 22 × 27mm.
Obverse: DE PAUL figure
Reverse: figure (Virgin Mary?), inscription illegible

La40/44 oval, 17 × 19mm.
Obverse: Christ
Reverse: religious symbols

Second row left to right:

La52/29 oval, 18 × 21mm.
Obverse: figure surrounded by CLAIRE and illegible word
Reverse: figure surrounded by illegible words

La40/68 oval, 16 × 20mm.
Obverse: figure
Reverse: completely eroded

La40/35 circular, 24 mm., drilled for suspension
Obverse: bust of Queen Anne (r. 1702-1714) surrounded by ANNA D.G. MAG. BR. FR. ET HIB. R.
Reverse: church over ECCLES. ANGL., surrounded by FUNDAMENTUM QUIETIS NOSTRAE

La52/37 uncleaned specimen

La40/44 oval, 17 × 20mm.
Obverse: two kneeling figures
Reverse: two figures, inscription illegible

Bottom row left to right: (crosses)

La40/30; La40/11; La40/44; La52/36b (with leather thong, see La40/11 for reverse form); La40/21; La40/24.

Pewter

Spoons made of pewter have been described under the chapter dealing with spoons. A large number of other objects made of this metal have been found on Susquehanna Valley sites and are described here. For the most part, things made of pewter do not survive well in the ground. Many such items found during excavation could be recognized in the field, but not collected because of their almost total disintegration. In no case have we been able to recognize any touch marks on the pieces which have been recovered.

The earliest occurrences of pewter are at the Strickler site, and the most common items of this metal are spoons, which as already stated, are barely identifiable beyond the fact that they were spoons. Next in order of frequency are the pewter pipes. Probably several dozen could be accounted for in the numerous excavations which have taken place here. Generally these pipes have some animal or other effigy attached to the part of the bowl away from the smoker (Figure 86).

Pewter mugs or tankards were probably the next most common items of this metal at Strickler, but none was in recoverable condition. Porringers, in similar condition, have also been noted.

This same range of objects has also been noted for the Lower Leibhart site. The porringer shown in Figure 86 is, relatively speaking, in good condition. A remarkably well-preserved chamber pot (Figure 86) from the E. Bowser collection, now in the William Penn Memorial Museum collections, was also found at Lower Leibhart.

Other pewter items include buttons, animal effigies, and a very occasional pewter stem on a native-made pipe.

Pewter objects, on a per-grave basis, were more common at Conestoga (and to a lesser extent at Conoy) than in the earlier sites. The range of objects is pretty much the same, although plain pipes were more popular than those with effigies or other decorations.

Spoons

There is very little which is unusual about the metal spoons from the Susquehannock sites. Most of those which have been found are similar to ones described elsewhere or known through antique collections. However, the collection is rather large and certainly warrants some brief description.

The majority of these spoons are either latten (copper 73%, zinc 25%, iron 2%—actual proportions probably varied considerably) or of pewter (tin 97%, lead 2%, copper 1%). Iron ladles, not actual spoons, have also been found, and some spoons may be of solid brass.

Only one spoon, and apparently a brass one, is known from the Washington Boro site. This is the earliest site in the sequence to have produced

Figure 86. Pewter objects. Chamber pot and porringer (36Yo170); spoons (36La52); smoking pipe (36La3).

any metal spoons. We have previously noted an iron trigger guard from this site which *may* have served as a spoon.

The brass spoon from Washington Boro (actually the Keller cemetery 36La4) has a cloven hoof at the top of the handle (Figure 87a). There is no seal or maker's cartouche on the bowl. According to Price (1908), this type may be of sixteenth- or early seventeenth-century manufacture.

One "seal-top" latten spoon was found at the Frey-Haverstick site, and in the same grave which produced the Rhenish jug dated 1630. This spoon has a rose-like cartouche in the bowl, which is similar to one illustrated by Price (1908: 37, bottom row, fifth from left). Frey-Haverstick was the earliest site in the sequence to have produced any of the "seal-top" spoons.

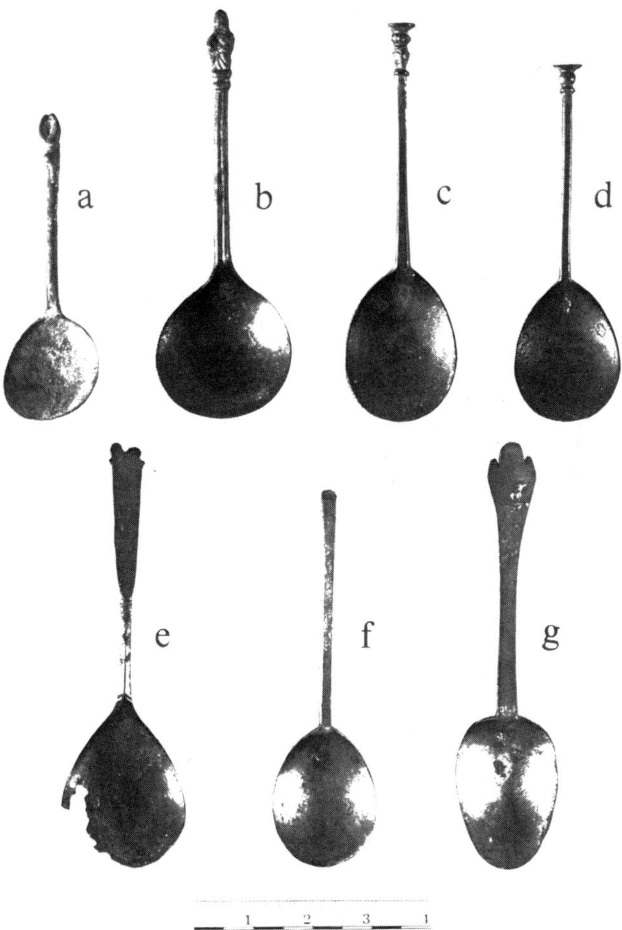

Figure 87. Latten spoons. Top left to right: (36La4); next three (36La3). Bottom row: (36La3); (36Yo170); (36La52).

The Museum's collection from the Strickler site includes two seal-top spoons, one of which has a cartouche like that from Frey-Haverstick. The other has a somewhat different rose stamp, which is like that illustrated by Price (1908: 37, second row, fourth from left). At least a dozen similar seal-top spoons from Strickler exist in other private or museum collections.

One of the Museum's seal-top spoons from this site is quite different in shape, particularly its baluster (according to Peal 1970, this is a sixteenth-century form). This specimen has a fleur-de-lis stamped on the inside of its bowl. Simmons (1970: 77) shows three similarly shaped spoons from the West Ferry site in Rhode Island.

Two apostle spoons (Figure 87b) were excavated from the northeast cemetery at the Strickler site in 1974. At least three others from the site are known from private collections. The one illustrated here has a rose stamp in its bowl. This particular mark is not included among those shown by Price for apostle spoons (Price 1908: 32). He dates spoons of this form up to about 1650.

Figure 87e shows a form of the latten spoon from Strickler which we have not seen elsewhere from Indian sites. It bears no touch mark and its bowl is extremely thin as compared to the others.

At least one "strawberry"-top latten spoon (in a private collection) was found at Strickler. According to Price (1908), these also have a long time range, which covers the first three quarters of the seventeenth century.

Two seal-top spoons were excavated in 1970 by the Museum's field crew at the Byrd Leibhart site. One of these had a rose stamp; the other has a "three-spoon" cartouche (two with bowls up and one in the center with its bowl pointing downward), flanked by the letters *I* and *G*. The grave which produced the latter spoon also contained the bowl (handle cut off) of one with an identical mark.

In 1978 the Museum purchased at auction two plain-end latten spoons (Figure 87f) from the George Keller collection from the Byrd Leibhart site. Both of these have the "three spoon" stamp, one with the letters *I.G.*, the other with *R.S.*

At the York County Historical Society there are two additional seal-top spoons and one bowl without a handle from this site. This collection represents about half of the old Byrd Leibhart-Graham collection. The remainder is in a private collection in Lancaster, and includes five additional spoons from the site. Two of these are seal tops, and one of them has the three-spoon mark with the letters *R.B.* (possibly *R.S.*). There is also one apostle spoon with a three-spoon mark (no visible letters), and a plain-end spoon which also has the three-spoon touchmark. The fifth spoon is an entirely different shape. It is similar in form to that illustrated in Figure 87g from Conestoga Town. It also bears the three-spoon touchmark.

A few seal-top spoons were apparently found at the Oscar Leibhart site, but again we have no accurate counts or descriptions. Our suggestion is that they are far less common than at Strickler or Byrd Leibhart's. The Donald Leibhart collection from the Oscar Leibhart site includes a well-preserved bowl of a silver spoon, with a cartouche in the bowl exhibiting three spoons and the letters *H.G.* One apostle spoon is reported in the Charles Leibhart collection from the Oscar Leibhart site.

Pewter spoons have been found at Strickler and the Leibhart sites, but as yet none has been recovered in good enough condition to allow us to say anything more about them, other than the fact that they are spoons.

Not until the period of Conestoga and Conoy Town do we encounter any pewter spoon in any real state of preservation. A number of spoons made of this material occurred at both sites. The three examples shown (Figure 86) are the best preserved of these, and none was in good enough condition to exhibit any maker's mark.

All of these pewter spoons have rattail reinforcements on the backs of the bowls. Figure 86a is similar to late seventeenth-century forms illustrated by Price (1908); the other two are probably of the early eighteenth century.

Two latten spoons from Conestoga Town, of the type which Price (1908: 42) calls split-ends or *pied de biche*, are of the late seventeenth century. One of these (Figure 87g) bears a mark similar to that shown by Price (1908: 45, first mark for latten spoons). The mark on this spoon clearly shows an *I* at the top margin of the cartouche, rather than the squiggled lines illustrated by Price. The other spoon has a mark resembling the arms of an asterisk radiating from a circle. This mark is not illustrated by Price.

One very worn-out spoon with the top of its handle broken off was also found at Conestoga. This specimen has the three-spoon mark, but the accompanying letters are not distinguishable.

A silver spoon, cut from some other piece of decorated silver, was found on the surface at Conoy Town. This spoon has the letters *L.M.W.*

The Museum collection also includes a small silver spoon from the eighteenth-century Delaware cemetery near Kutztown in Berks County. The letter *L* is engraved on the back of the stem at the top. At the base of the back of the stem is the maker's mark *I.B.*

The earliest spoon in the sequences, the hoof knob from the Washington Boro site, was probably not tinned. However, the remainder of the latten spoons in the sequence were probably all tinned, or "whited" as it was called. Many of these spoons retain varying amounts of their original tin wash. Some show none of it at all, but this is probably the result of erosion in the various places where they were buried.

Generally speaking, these spoons are not very instructive in terms of helping to date the sites at which they were found. By and large, they seem to be slightly earlier than what we would suggest are the actual dates of

Table 19

DISTRIBUTION OF NATIVE AND EUROPEAN OBJECTS BY GRAVE AND SITE

Time	*Site*	*No. Graves*	*stone celts*	*iron axes*	*iron knives*	*iron hoes*	*stone points*	*brass points*	*whole guns*	*native pots*	*brass kettles*	*native pipes*	*metal pipes*	*kaolin pipes*
ca.1550	Engelbert	15	2 (13)				2 (13)			17 (100)				
1575-1600	Schultz	222		5 (2)	7 (3)	1 (x)	68 (31)			210 (95)	1 (x)	2 (1)	1 (x)	
1600-1625	Washington Boro	108	7 (6)	24 (22)	8 (7)	5 (5)	75 (69)	?		200 (100)	4 (4)	4 (4)	4 (4)	
ca.1630	Haverstick	28		3 (11)	7 (25)	4 (14)	10 (36)	1 (4)	2 (7)	23 (82)	3 (11)	4 (14)	1 (4)	3 (11)
1630-1645	Roberts	9	1 (11)	2 (22)	4 (44)	1 (11)	7 (78)	?	?	6 (67)	1 (11)	1 (11)		1 (11)
1645-1665	Strickler	307	1 (x)	53 (17)	136 (44)	41 (13)	68 (22)	102 (33)	36 (12)	169 (55)	145 (47)	130 (42)	9 (3)	12 (4)
1665-1674	Oscar Leibhart	142		6 (4)	13 (9)	3 (2)	?	25 (18)	4 (3)	28 (20)	10 (7)	12 (8)	3 (2)	9 (6)
1676-1680	Byrd Leibhart	130		9 (7)	28 (22)	20 (15)	19 (15)	48 (37)	3 (2)	45 (35)	25 (19)	48 (37)		20 (15)
1690-1750	Conestoga Town	69		24 (35)	74 (100)	3 (4)	3 (4)	11 (16)	9 (13)		42 (61)	9 (13)	5 (7)	37 (54)
1718-1743	Conoy Town	71			6 (8)				2 (3)		3 (4)		4 (6)	4 (6)

Note: Numbers in parentheses indicate percentages (numbers of items divided by numbers of interments)
? = present, number undetermined
x = less than 1 per cent.

occupation for the sites at which they were recovered. Those with the three-spoon marks from the Byrd Leibhart site come closer than any others to being current with the dates for that site.

Many of these spoons were found in brass kettles, and these are generally the ones which are best preserved. Wooden spoons of native manufacture also frequently occur in kettles or native pots. These far outnumber the European base-metal spoons right through the Conestoga period.

A Summary of Changes in Material Culture

The preceding discussions of Susquehannock (and other Indian) material culture were intended to describe the quantity and changing nature thereof, and to point out the shifting patterns in the use of native-made items and their various replacements by European-made equivalents. In anthropological terms the causal factor underlying these replacements is that phenomenon known as culture contact. More specifically, it involves the exposure of one society to the more advanced technology of another. The rate and manner in which the recessive culture adopts the individual technological items of the more advanced and dominant culture may vary from one culture contact situation to another.

Any item of material culture in a static socio-cultural setting (i.e., without the acculturation effects of contact between societies of different technological advancements) will show a curve of popularity over time. Some items will reach a peak of popularity in relatively short time periods. Others may grow slowly but steadily to a peak and then perhaps just as slowly decline in use and popularity.

The measurement and display of these various popularity curves are very basic to anthropological understandings of material culture. In order to depict or diagram these patterns it is necessary to compare the counts of distinguishable types of items at various points in time. If, for example, we are dealing with several types of pottery, let us say types A and B, we may find that at a certain time period (site) only type A occurs. In another site we might find equal amounts of types A and B. In a third site we may discover only type B. These conditions can be expressed as percentages of occurrence at the various sites, and the curves which they generate express shifts in popularity, perhaps due to evolution of a new and better type, or perhaps due to culture contact which introduces a better or more acceptable new type. These diagrams show in a very graphic way what has happened to the popularity of specific items of technology over time, but it becomes the responsibility of the researcher to explain the causal factors which underlie the changes depicted by the chart.

Culture contact and its results—acculturation and culture change—can cause very abrupt changes in popularity curves, especially as compared to curves of evolving forms with no outside influences.

In an acculturation situation such as that presented by the contact between Susquehannock and European cultures, the effect or impact of one technology upon the other is perhaps best shown by the occurrence of all the major technological items at the various recognizable and critical time periods. In a chart of this sort we would have to identify various functional equivalents, for example brass kettles to native pots, arrowheads to guns, or celts to iron axes. We would need to determine the percentage of occurrence of pots against that of brass kettles at each site or time period. However, it may also be useful to express the occurrence of pots against arrowheads or iron axes, etc. The complexities of doing so for each item and for each site and of placing them in a single diagram are enormous.

Table 19 shows the relative popularity or abundance of each of 12 categories of artifacts at 10 excavated sites. In order to make the varying number of samples from the different sites comparable to one another, they have been expressed in terms of their frequency of occurrence as burial furniture. Having done so, it is possible to express on a single diagram the varying popularity of each item through the different time periods represented by the sites, and at the same time we are able to show the changing popularity of all other categories over time or at any given site.

For each site and in each vertical column there are two numbers given. The upper number indicates the number of occurrences of that item at that site; the lower number represents the percentage of graves at that site which produce that item (i.e., the number of items in a category divided by the number of interments).

To some extent, the diagram shows changing burial customs with regard to grave offerings. For example, iron axes were quite abundant during the period of Conoy Town, but they were not an acceptable burial offering. Actually, because of the cultural differences involved, it might be best not to consider Conoy Town in this otherwise Susquehannock diagram.

The diagram exhibits a number of obvious trends, such as guns which replace bows and arrows, or pots which decrease in popularity as brass kettles increase. However, we note certain apparent discrepancies, e.g., brass kettles which seem disproportionately abundant at the Strickler site; or native pipes which have a longevity despite European equivalents. Some of these differences may reflect conscious efforts to retain something of the "old way," or perhaps shifting political circumstances of the Susquehannocks, and therefore varying accumulations of societal wealth. A diagram of this sort can be useful to point out regularities and/or irregularities in trends involving material items of culture. But again, the various factors which influenced these trends or changes and their impact upon the total fabric of Susquehannock culture are what we should be striving to explain.

Evidence from Excavations

Archeology of the Sites

RESULTS which stem from the meticulous archeological investigation of ancient human occupation sites are often exciting discoveries about former ways of life. However, the detailed account of how the archeology was accomplished, of the raw data that were recovered, and of how the material was analyzed are often quite dull. Nevertheless, in order for the results or interpretations of the data to have any credibility, they must be presented so that others can evaluate the methods of excavation and procedures of analysis.

Recognizing this, the present writer has elected to extract the results of the archeological investigations and to use them in the foregoing portrayal of the general culture history of the Susquehanna's Indians. The more detailed descriptions of the history of archeological excavations and the analysis of their products follow herewith as an appendix for those who may care to more critically examine them. The ordering of these site reports largely follows the site chronologies, from earliest to latest.

Sites on the North Branch of the Susquehanna

Properly speaking, the North Branch of the Susquehanna River begins in Lake Otsego at Cooperstown, New York, and ends in the forks of the Susquehanna at Northumberland, Pennsylvania. Considering its source, there is little wonder that so much Susquehanna Valley archeology is closely related to that of central New York State. The present overview of the archeology of this portion of the Susquehanna Valley, again primarily concerned with the Susquehannock Indians, will move upstream from the Northumberland-Sunbury area.

Pottery is the key, in fact the only identifiable archeological remain by which we can confidently recognize the occupation sites and trace the movements of our Susquehannocks. Such evidence at the terminus of the North Branch is quite sparse, and consists of a few sherds of Schultz Incised (and perhaps some related pottery) in various collections from the Northumberland area (see Wren 1914: Plate 8, Figure 1; Plate 19, Figures 8-11).

With the exception of a few strange pots of poorly understood Susquehannock affiliations, the pottery of these people throughout the North Branch is that which we have been calling Proto-Susquehannock and

Schultz Incised. Virtually all of the former comes from the upper reaches of the North Branch, and *most* of the latter also occurs there.

Scattered sherds and occasional whole rockshelter pots of Schultz Incised are found along the route to the Wyoming Valley. Several sites in the vicinity of Wilkes-Barre have produced fair quantities of shell-tempered pottery which practically all previous authorities have attributed to the Susquehannocks. These examples are actually minority types in the otherwise distinctive pottery samples from the stockaded towns of the Wyoming Valley, such as Parker (36Lu14) and Schacht (36Lu1). The major ceramics here are the grit-tempered, Chance Horizon-influenced wares which Sweeney (1966) and Smith (1973) have called the Wyoming Valley complex. Smith recognized that the minority shell-tempered pottery from the Wyoming Valley sites was somewhat different from good Schultz Incised, but he still equated it with Susquehannock. He did indicate that it had its closest affinities to the shell-tempered, so-called Susquehannock pottery from the Quiggle site and from elsewhere in the West Branch Valley. We have previously stated our own case for concluding that these shell-tempered ceramics of the West Branch and the Wyoming Valley are not directly related to Susquehannock.

Figure 88. Parker site (36Lu14) staked out for excavation.

This is not to say that there is no Susquehannock shell tempered pottery in the Wyoming Valley. Wren (1914: Plate 4; Plate 18, no. 2) illustrates a few of the very rare examples from the general area.

Northward from the Wyoming Valley, evidence for Susquehannock sites and pottery is still very thin. Not until we are well into Bradford County, Pennsylvania, do we encounter any quantity of this pottery. Even here, the sites are small and scattered, but there is clearly a concentration of them along the Susquehanna in the northern half of the county.

Elsewhere in this volume we have stated that we favor Witthoft's (1959: 39, 58) hypothesis that Richmond Mills Incised and its local derivative, Proto-Susquehannock, evolved into Schultz Incised. That this happened in Bradford County (and adjacent New York) seems an acceptable theory, particularly in view of the fact that this is the only area where all of the pottery types occur together in any number. We hasten to add, however, that there are still very few discovered instances of positive intrasite associations of Proto-Susquehannock and Schultz Incised. Even though the physical archeological evidence of their relationship is not yet well identified, the stylistic and genetic connections between the two seem reasonably well established.

Witthoft (1959: 28, 30, 42-51) noted that the Schultz Incised pottery from the North Branch, and particularly from Bradford County, is slightly different from the later, more abundant expressions of the type in Lancaster County. North Branch Schultz Incised is generally better made, with more neatly and crisply incised decorations. Only rarely is this pottery found in association with trade goods—but the fact that this does occasionally occur is what is most important. That fact enables a chronometric assignment to upper North Branch Schultz Incised of somewhere between 1525 and 1550. As Witthoft (1959: 29) has indicated, sites in this area generally produce only a few scraps of brass or an occasional glass bead, which are often badly deteriorated.

Susquehannock sites, as presently understood from limited archeology in this area, portray a settlement pattern of scattered small farmsteads or hamlets. This pattern is certainly not unknown elsewhere in Iroquoia, but it was by this time becoming an archaic form. Most contemporary Iroquois settlements were characterized by a shift toward larger clusters of dwellings, often enclosed by palisades. People in the Wyoming Valley and at places like Quiggle on the West Branch, whose occupations there date at least to 1500 A.D., were definitely living in fortified towns. By contrast with these living arrangements, the apparent hamlet settlement style of the early Bradford County Susquehannocks seems very curious. If this is indeed an accurate picture, then clearly there were marked social and political differences between these Susquehannocks and most of their neighbors.

Many facets of developing Susquehannock culture history in the upper reaches of the Susquehanna River valley still need to be worked out. The need for more archeology here *may* be tainting our understanding of settlement patterns, trade good associations, and the evolution of Schultz Incised from Proto-Susquehannock. Even more mundane questions, such as the relationships of the strange vessels with elaborate faces and rim and body decorations from the Athens area of Bradford County (see Witthoft 1959: 48; and illustrations in Wren 1914: Plate 6, Figures 1-8; Plate 8, Figures 1-4), can perhaps be answered through more intensive archeology.

It is not our intention to imply that no archeology of merit has been done here; indeed it should be obvious that a fair amount of work has been accomplished. In keeping with our efforts to summarize the history of archeological investigations relating primarily to the Susquehannocks, we present the following overview of such studies in the region of emerging Susquehannock culture.

As in many other areas of Pennsylvania, there has been an awareness of Indian remains in Bradford County for a long time. And as elsewhere, there has been observation in a historical vein, but an unevenness of sound archeological research until relatively recent times.

One of the earliest recorded observations of Indian remains is that by General Sullivan's troops of Indian burials in 1779 near Fort Sullivan at Tioga Point (Murray 1908: 196).

By at least 1850 Indian graves had been encountered on the Murray farm (36Br5) at the upper end of Queen Esther's Flats (Moorehead 1938: 49). General John S. Clark reported (see Murray 1931: 34) that in about 1860 numerous burials were found when the canal was dug through the area above the mouth of Sugar Creek, where the Indian town of Ogehage (see also Oscalui and Newtychanning, 36Br44) was situated.

Clark (Murray 1931) was one of the first persons to record any careful observations of Indian sites in Bradford County. During the 1870's he and Rev. David Craft visited and corresponded about their thoughts on sites which included the above-mentioned Ogehage; a place which they referred to as Gahontoto, near present Wyalusing (36Br80, 81), and several others). They paid particular attention to Spanish Hill (36Br27) north of Athens, Pennsylvania, which Clark thought was the site of Carantouan, as reported by Ètienne Brulé to Champlain in 1618 (see Murray 1931: 22, 25-28).

The Tioga Point Museum at Athens has a variety of old collections from the area, one of which was gathered below Wyalusing Bridge and other places after the flood of 1865, and which was in the Maynard Bixby collection in the basement of the Museum in 1982. A complete record of this collection was made by Charles Lucy of Athens (see Lucy n.d.).

Figure 89. Tioga Point in Bradford County looking north. Chemung River on the left, Susquehanna on the right.

The first real efforts at digging sites in Bradford County are those reported by Harrison Wright (1885) on the work in 1883 at the so-called Murray Garden site (36Br2) in Athens. Wright represented the Wyoming Historical and Geological Society of Wilkes-Barre, and most of the objects, including several pots which were recovered at Murray Garden, were returned to the society's museum at Wilkes-Barre, where they still reside.

These discoveries stimulated a considerable amount of local interest in Indian artifacts from the Athens-Tioga Point area, particularly on the part of Louise Welles Murray, daughter of the owner of the above-mentioned Murray Garden site (Murray 1908: 201).

These interests in local Indian lore were instrumental in the establishment of the Tioga Point Museum, which was founded in 1895, and which occupied its present headquarters in the Spaulding Memorial Library in 1898 (J. W. Murray 1933: 12). The site of the Library is just a short distance north of the Murray Garden site. When the basement for the building was dug in 1897, additional burials (36Br1) were encountered (Murray 1921: 188). Subsequent artifact recoveries by local persons at the Murray Garden site and elsewhere in the Tioga Point area are also discussed by Murray (1921).

In 1914, Christopher Wren of the Wyoming Historical and Geological Society published his account of North Appalachian Indian pottery (Wren 1914). Shown therein are a number of photographs of North Branch Valley Indian pots, including several from the Tioga Point area of Bradford County. Those recovered for the society by Harrison Wright are illustrated by Wren (1914: Plate 7, Figures 2 and 3, and Plate 8, Figures 2 and 3).

The year 1916 saw the beginning of excavations in Bradford County by trained archeologists (Moorehead 1938). One of the stated goals of the Heye Museum's so-called Susquehanna River Expedition was the investigation of Andaste or Susquehannock remains. The project began along the Susquehanna River in New York State and ended at its mouth in Maryland. Even before the expedition reached Bradford County, its members knew that Andaste sites and artifacts could be found there. Alanson Skinner, a member of the expedition, was the first to identify specific pottery types as being Andaste, and he did so based upon samples from Bradford County (see Skinner in Moorehead 1918: 121-22). Unfortunately, the complete results of the expedition, and Skinner's more thorough report, were not published until over 20 years later (Moorehead 1938). By that time, someone else had already become the first to publish comprehensive examples of pottery from sites identified as Susquehannock (Cadzow 1936). As we have seen, Cadzow's report was based upon his work in Lancaster County, virtually at the other end of the Susquehanna Valley. It is to the credit of Skinner that one of the types which he had much earlier attributed to Andaste sites in Bradford County was almost identical to that which Cadzow (1936) labeled as early Susquehannock from the Schultz site in Lancaster County.

Moorehead (1938) and company conducted rather extensive excavations at the cemetery on the Murray Farm site (36Br5), not to be confused with the Murray Garden site (36Br2). Here the expedition discovered 57 interments (Moorehead 1938: 50) associated with a wide variety of pottery types, but including some which were Susquehannock, and a few that were associated with trade goods.

Before leaving Bradford County, the expedition undertook extensive test excavations at Spanish Hill (36Br27), where very little was found; brief tests and/or surface inspections were also made at Oscalui (36Br44), Sheshequin, Towanda, Wysox and Wyalusing. They reported very little from the 50-mile stretch of river between Wyalusing and Plymouth, Pennsylvania (see also Moorehead 1918 and Donehoo 1918).

By this time considerable interest had been aroused concerning the archeology of Bradford County, particularly in the area of Andaste (or Susquehannock) studies, and identification of the occupants of Spanish Hill (36Br27). Investigations into these matters were continued on a formal basis by the Tioga Point Museum in 1931, when, with the aid of a grant from the National Research Council, they employed James B. Griffin and a field crew to conduct excavations at the Ahbe-Brennan site (36Br42), the Thurston farm (south of 36Br5), Spanish Hill (36Br27), and some re-excavations at the Murray Farm site (36Br5). Griffin's unpublished reports (1931a, b) indicate a wide variety of material from these sites, including an eighteenth-century Indian interment with a koalin pipe at the Ahbe-Brennan site. Griffin's work confirmed the presence of a few Indian artifacts on top of Spanish Hill (36Br27), but had his report been published, it would have put to rest any further concerns about its being the site of Carantouan, or its having Indian earthworks around its top margins.

Immediately following Griffin's work, Mr. Elsworth Cowles began additional excavations at some of these same sites, most of which are unpublished. Cowles (1932, 1933a, 1933b) did report upon a site on the west bank of the Susquehanna north of Sayre, which was designated 36Br38. During this same period, and for some years afterwards, Cowles also conducted investigations in the vicinity of Spanish Hill. As a result, the Carantouan myth continued to have at least some local perpetuation. A short distance south of the foot of Spanish Hill, Cowles discovered a small (approximately 160 by 80 feet) rectangular stockade with rounded corners (Cowles n.d.). Immediately south of the stockade he found what he labeled an effigy hearth, in the shape of a "mammoth" (Cowles 1933b: 20). The so-called effigy site stockade was interpreted as a refuge for the Carantouan.

Test excavations at this site (36Br28) in 1967 by the Pennsylvania Historical and Museum Commission, together with a re-examination of Cowles' collection from the site, plus highway salvage excavations adjacent to the site in 1972 (also by the PHMC), produced evidence of its Owasco affiliations. Indeed, the size and shape of its stockade and the pottery it produces are very similar to those reported by Ritchie (1965: 284-85; Ritchie and Funk 1973: 226-52) for the Bates site in Chenango County, New York.

Archeological research in the upper Susquehanna Valley of Pennsylvania had reached another peak of activity in 1948. This time it was at the hands of the Pennsylvania State Museum, under the field direction of John Witthoft. Again, the major emphasis was on finding out more about the Susquehannocks of the region. Excavations by Witthoft were concentrated at two sites in the vicinity of Towanda: Sick (36Br50) and Cass (36Br57). Collections were examined and limited tests were again conducted at other sites. Witthoft's remarks concerning these sites (in Witthoft and Kinsey 1959: 31-32) seem worth reproducing here:

The site on the Naegle Farm at Sheshequin is unusual because it has only two components, Susquehannock and Transitional (soapstone-bowl culture). This site has been almost entirely destroyed by the river and by several decades of amateur excavation. Graves were sprinkled along the edge of the site nearest the river. We have notes on seventeen of these graves, dug by local amateurs in my time; and several pots are known to have come from here more than thirty years ago. Of the seventeen graves, four contained pots, one double grave contained a celt, and one burial had a tubular brass bead at its breast; the rest had no mortuary goods; and all were flexed.

At Ulster, three flexed burials by the river edge (with pots) and a couple of saucer-shaped pits back of them marked a Susquehannock hamlet, probably a single house. At Ellis Creek, Lucy explored a single large grave with five burials, four of them as one pile of disarticulated bones, the fifth flexed, with five pots and other grave goods (Lucy, 1950). Small bones had been dropped inside the skulls when the bones had been gathered up before burial, and a brass bead had been placed inside one of the skulls along with finger and toe bones. At Wysox, the bottoms of five cache pits were all that the bulldozer left of a Susquehannock site on a terrace-delta. They must have been within a house because they were filled with ash and midden. One of these pits had a Shenk's Ferry rim sherd with the Susquehannock pottery. These are all the single-component Susquehannock sites I have seen in that area, sites which do not have pits from several late prehistoric horizons dug in the same area and where the surface collections do not include a great variety of other pottery types.

The average site is much more confused than this. The Murray Garden Site and the Ahbe-Brennan Site at Athens had graves and pits from every major cultural horizon of Late Woodland times, as well as Susquehannock and eighteenth-century pits and graves (Murray 1908, pp. 198-200; 1896; 1921; Griffin, 1931). The Murray Farm Site, dug by Skinner, is a confusion of Owasco, Proto-Susquehannock, and Susquehannock pits (Moorehead 1927, pp. 43-44, 47-69). At Homet's Ferry, we found a single Susquehannock pit of saucer form, filled with ash and midden, in an area where Castle Creek potsherds and pits were concentrated, and we could find no other trace of this Susquehannock settlement. At the Sick Site at South Towanda, we found only three pits of the Susquehannock occupation in a five-component Late Woodland site. Our posthole patterns here are quite fragmentary as a result of erosion and are confused by the overlapping of five separate periods of building, but a large rectangular house twenty-five feet wide was of the Susquehannock component. Here as elsewhere the quantity of artifacts and potsherds left by a single household is really slight, and a large sample implies a great deal of living on a site.

(Witthoft 1959: 31-32)

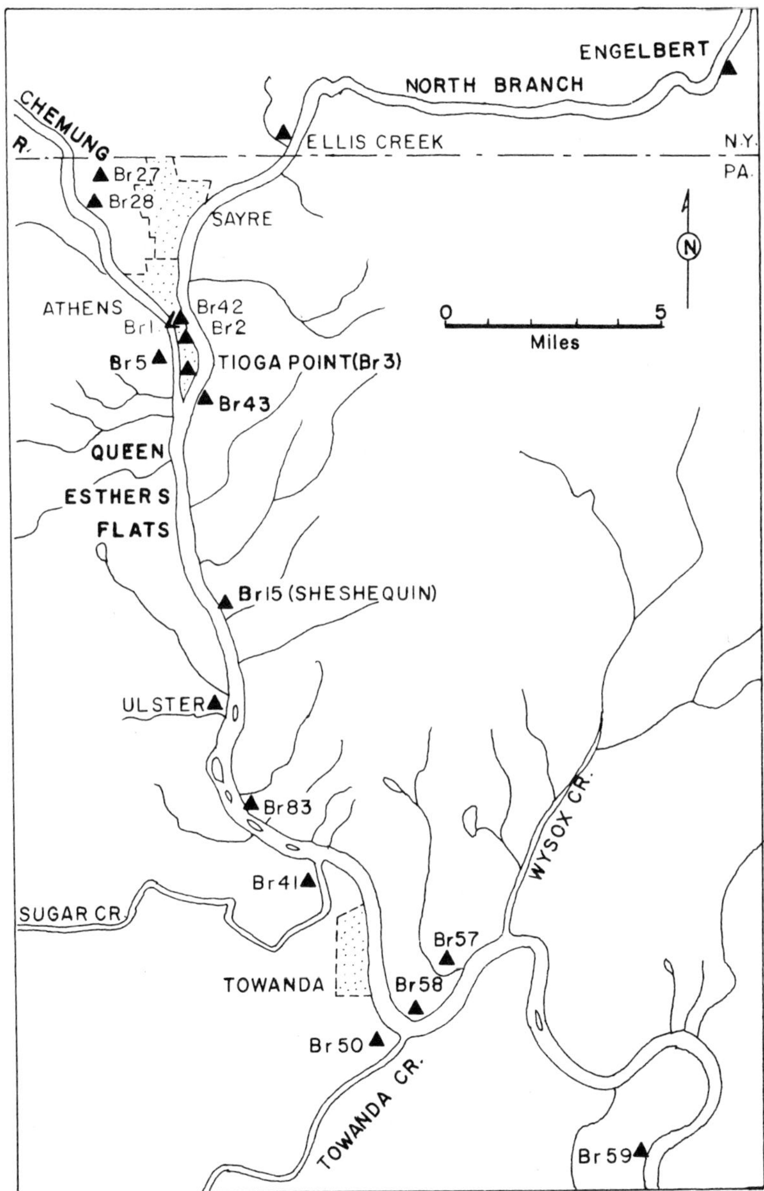

Figure 90. Map of archeological sites in Bradford County.

As we have seen from the above, Witthoft did not publish any of the results of his 1948 Bradford County studies for over 10 years. However, in the interim his colleague Chuck Lucy, of Athens, was conducting his own research on the prehistory of the area (Lucy 1950, 1952). Finally, in 1959, he published (Lucy 1959) his important contribution to the study of pottery types from the upper Susquehanna.

In 1957 and 1958, members of the Bradford County-based Andaste Chapter of the Society for Pennsylvania Archaeology excavated the Wilson site (36Br58) at the East Towanda Fairgrounds. Among other things, it too produced evidence of a small Susquehannock occupation (McCann 1962). Andaste Chapter members also excavated at the Wells site (36Br59) near Asylum, Pennsylvania (Lucy and McCann n.d.).

At this point in the history of archeological investigations in Bradford County, over 60 sites had been more or less officially recorded. Still, it was not possible to point to anything but small hamlets in which the Susquehannocks once lived; and most of these sites were severely mixed with other earlier (and a few later) components. The largest concentration of clearly identifiable Susquehannock remains was eventually found, not in Bradford County, but a short distance over the line in Tioga County, New York. This location, known as the Engelbert site, was just northeast of Nichols, New York, along the Susquehanna River. It was discovered in 1967 during the course of a gravel-quarrying operation, but fortunately, these operations were temporarily halted while excavations were conducted. Work here was undertaken by various persons and organizations (see Elliot and Lipe 1970; and Crannel 1970: 27-30). In 1968 quarrying was resumed and the site was completely destroyed.

Crannel's (1970: 27-30) analysis of the Susquehannock component from the site represents the most extensive description of such materials, primarily ceramics, for the upper Susquehanna Valley. In addition to at least 13 Schultz Incised pots, some of which were recovered in association with copper and other trade items (including one glass bead), there were also two associated Monongahela-like vessels, and one thought to be of Fort Ancient origin. Crannel (1970: 50-51) described several other probable Susquehannock pots from two nearby sites (Kuhlman and River Street), which also included a few trade goods. The latter site, at River Street in Owego, New York, produced an iron axe in apparent association with a shell-tempered pot.

As part of its most recent efforts to study Susquehannock origins, the Pennsylvania Historical and Museum Commission in 1975 undertook excavations at two more sites in Bradford County known (from local collections) to have produced Susquehannock pottery. This time the work was under the direction of Commission staff archeologist Ira F. Smith III, who, with a crew of four, excavated at the Blackman (36Br83) and Kennedy (36Br43) sites.

Results of these 1975 excavations at the Kennedy site included the postmold pattern of a 65- by 25-foot longhouse of indeterminate cultural affiliation, about 60 other features, a predominance of Owasco pottery types, and four burials. One of the burials contained shell-tempered pottery (probably Schultz Incised), together with two tubes of rolled thin copper sheet. These tubes were found at the back of the skull, and each contained the shaft of a feather (see Smith 1981b).

Mr. Elwin Gillette of Towanda, Pennsylvania, had previously found two Susquehannock burials at the Blackman site. Both graves contained a shell-tempered Susquehannock pot. One of these, that of a flexed adolescent, also included two copper beads. Smith's work there in 1975 produced a large number of pits, several of which contained Richmond Incised and Proto-Susquehannock sherds. However, he found no shell-tempered Susquehannock ceramics. Also discovered at that time was what appears to be about half of an elliptical stockade, with evidence of an enlargement. Again, the affiliations of these postmolds cannot be ascertained. In general shape and size, this stockade structure seems reminiscent of that discovered by Cowles at 36Br28, which we have suggested is of Owasco provenience.

We should note here in our general survey of archeological investigation in the upper Susquehanna that Mr. Leslie Delaney, formerly of Kings College in Wilkes-Barre, has also undertaken various excavations there. In 1974, he conducted a few brief tests at the Kennedy site in an area where the 1972 flood (Agnes) had washed out a Susquehannock pot. Delaney (1973) also directed rather extensive excavations at Wyalusing (36Br80, 81), where he discovered evidence of both Late Woodland occupations, and the location of the Moravian Indian Town of Friedenshuetten (1763-1772) (see also Kent et al. 1981).

Another project in Bradford County, little concerned with the Indian history and prehistory of the area, was the PHMC project at the site of French Azilum (36Br134) in 1976 to locate structures and remains of the French refugee occupation of that place in the late eighteenth century.

Considerable digging has continued to occur at various places throughout the county, and isolated Susquehannock remains continue to be discovered. Throughout most of the period covered in this overview, there has been considerable digging on Tioga Point. This peninsula, at the confluence of the Chemung River and the Susquehanna, was occupied by Indians from the very earliest times up through the last Indian settlement in the eighteenth century. The Point has been assigned the general site number 36Br3, but it includes at least six distinct and separately numbered sites. A very useful report on the Tioga Point farm by Lucy and Vanderpoel (1979) illustrates and describes many of the important objects which have been recovered there over the years.

Clearly, additional archeology can be productively pursued along the North Branch of the Susquehanna in Pennsylvania. In recent years a great deal of work has been going on along the Susquehanna in New York State, and most of this is soon to be described by Dr. Robert Funk of the New York State Museum and Science Service.

From our own point of view there is still much which needs to be done to answer the questions concerning the evolution from Proto-Susquehannock to early Schultz-period Susquehannock; the impact (and sources) of early trade materials on emerging Susquehannock culture; and the reasons for their apparent coalition and migration southward.

When we count the number of separate sites (or isolated finds) where early Schultz Incised pottery has been found in Bradford County and adjacent areas of New York State, we find approximately 20 such places. If we assume, for the moment, that these were more or less contemporaneous hamlets, each containing one or two small longhouses of, say, 25 persons, then we might project a population of five hundred Susquehannocks in this area prior to about 1550 A.D. Intuitively this seems too small for the total Susquehannock tribe. In order to account for the sites which are obviously yet to be discovered, or already destroyed, we might reasonably double this figure. A population of one thousand persons, although completely unsubstantiated, is commensurate with the population estimate for them at the Schultz site in Lancaster County, their next place of residence.

Whatever it was that brought these scattered farmsteads together into a more cohesive socio-political group is not clear. Political pressures—specifically outright aggression—from the Iroquoian peoples to the north have frequently been postulated as major causal factors. We know that they had by this time experienced a taste of European trade goods. Even though their appetites for such things had barely been whetted, it may be that this was enough to stimulate their need to have and control their own direct access to the trade. This could only come about through their residential proximity to a coastal area, or through their hegemony over other peoples on the coast or seaports. Their forays down the Delaware, as marked by scattered occurrences of Schultz Incised pottery there, may have been precisely to seek such access or control in that area. In any event, it does appear that they did band together and move rather quickly into the lower Susquehanna Valley. We also know that other indigenous cultures along their route ceased to exist at about this time. The peoples of the Wyoming Valley, the Quiggle site and elsewhere on the West Branch, and the Shenks Ferry did not survive into the contact period of the second half of the sixteenth century. Again, we can only guess at the role of the migrating Susquehannocks in this disappearance.

SITES ON THE WEST BRANCH OF THE SUSQUEHANNA RIVER

Otzinachson, the delightfully written history of the West Branch Valley, by J. F. Meginness (1889), gives the location of numerous Indian sites between Sunbury and Sinnemahoning. To be certain, there are many other areas reached by this drainage system and considerably more archeological sites than have been reported. The geography of the West Branch drainage is quite important to the history of Indian cultures in the Susquehanna Valley, largely because this branch reaches so far to the west—in some places its headwaters are separated by only a few miles from the drainage of the upper Ohio Valley—and because of the varied Indian cultures found there.

Meginness (1889: 53-56) quotes extensively from a report written by the collector, J. H. McMinn of Williamsport. McMinn had prepared these comments at the request of Spencer F. Baird, secretary of the Smithsonian Institution, who expressed surprise at the variety and quantity of such remains in the West Branch. Numerous other collectors, notably M. L. Hendricks of Sunbury, J. M. M. Gernerd of Muncy, D. A. Martin of DuBoistown, J. C. McClosky of Lock Haven, and more recently, T. B. Stewart of Lock Haven, all gathered large collections representing a great diversity of both indigenous and introduced Indian cultures in the West Branch Valley.

During the 1916 Susquehanna River Expedition of the Heye Museum, Warren King Moorehead interviewed T. B. Stewart concerning his collection and his knowledge of sites in this portion of the Susquehanna Valley. In the subsequently published account of the expedition (Moorehead 1938), there is a brief chapter on the West Branch prepared by T. B. Stewart, in which he enumerated certain sites and described various objects from the region. Most of what remains of the T. B. Stewart collection is presently housed at Waynesburg College at Waynesburg, Pennsylvania.

The first recorded excavations in the West Branch Valley were those conducted in 1929 at the Quiggle site, near Pine in Clinton County, by the University of Pennsylvania under the direction of J. Alden Mason. They were joined by several representatives from the Rochester Museum, including William A. Ritchie (see Davidson 1929).

Witthoft (1954) reported on the Shenks Ferry pottery excavated in 1934 by T. B. Stewart at the farm of his parents on the north bank of the river opposite McElhatton, in Clinton County. It was this sample upon which Witthoft (1954) based his definition of the Stewart phase of Shenks Ferry pottery.

Figure 91. Aerial view of excavations at the Quiggle site (36Cn6).

In 1936 the WPA and the Lycoming County Historical Society undertook a number of small-scale excavations, including the Mound- and Clemsons Island-period village at Muncy (see Carpenter 1949; Schoff 1937: b, e), and several historic (eighteenth-century) Indian sites at Montoursville (Schoff 1937d) and at Williamsport (Schoff 1937c); see also Turnbaugh 1975: 12-13.

Various sites throughout the West Branch have been excavated over the years by members of the North Central Chapter of the Society for Pennsylvania Archaeology. Most of these projects are listed by Turnbaugh (1975: 13). A good example of such work is that by Bressler (1978, 1980: 31-63), which describes the excavation of a stockaded Shenks Ferry Village at Bull Run (36Ly119) in Lycoming County. Materials from this site and many other important collections from the West Branch Valley are at the Lycoming County Historical Society Museum at Williamsport.

Based upon his analysis of the pottery excavated at the Quiggle site in 1929 (in the collections of the University Museum, University of Pennsylvania), John Witthoft (in Witthoft and Kinsey 1959: 26-27) felt that this was a Shenks Ferry site with intrusive Susquehannock (Schultz Incised) pottery. He noted that this shell-tempered Susquehannock pottery was nowhere very common in the West Branch Valley, but that small amounts of it had been found by T. B. Stewart as far west as Shawville in Clearfield County.

It was because of this presumed presence of Susquehannock pottery that the PHMC, in the course of its Susquehannock project, sent Ira Smith and a field crew back to the Quiggle site in 1971. Smith's work at the site disclosed a palisaded village and a predominance of shell-tempered pottery and little or no identifiable Shenks Ferry ceramics (Smith 1976: 1-12). Smith continued to identify the shell-tempered pottery from Quiggle and elsewhere in the West Branch as Susquehannock. He did note that it was somewhat different from the Schultz Incised from either Bradford County or the type site in Lancaster County. He also noted its very close similarity to the shell-tempered pottery at the Schacht and Parker sites in the Wyoming Valley of the North Branch.

Elsewhere in the present volume (see the chapter on Ceramics), the present writer has proposed that the shell-tempered pottery of the Quiggle site, and most other places where it has been reported in the West Branch Valley, is not Susquehannock at all, but rather is a vaguely similar-looking, high-collared pottery which has its ancestral ties in the McFate and other cultures of northwestern Pennsylvania.

Work currently under way at the Kalgren site in Clearfield County is producing large amounts of what the present writer has called McFate Quiggle Incised. The final report on the Kalgren site by its excavator,

James T. Herbstritt, should resolve once and for all the ancestral affiliations and the descendants of this West Branch Valley shell-tempered pottery, and perhaps its relationships to the later phases of Shenks Ferry pottery.

Assuming that we are correct in not assigning out so-called McFate-Quiggle pottery to a Susquehannock provenience, we can say that there was almost no Susquehannock occupation (or at least very little pottery) in the West Branch Valley of the Susquehanna River. Since the shell-tempered, so-called Susquehannock pottery from the Sheep Rock Shelter is also entirely of our McFate-Quiggle Incised form, we can also dismiss the use of the term Susquehannock for that site.

In these terms, the only true example of a Schultz Incised shell-tempered Susquehannock pot from the West Branch Valley above Northumberland (or, for that matter, the Juniata Valley) of which we are aware is the single vessel, illustrated by Wren (1914: Plate 10, Figure 1), found at the junction of the Big Moshannon Creek and the Susquehanna in Clearfield County.

Witthoft, Schoff and Wray (1953: 94) refer to an "early seventeenth century Andaste" site at the mouth of the Tangascootack Creek in Clinton County. Although we have not seen any ceramics from this site (see Stewart collection at Waynesburg College), it is our guess that they are more examples of McFate-Quiggle Incised than of Susquehannock.

Without question, Susquehannock Indians did travel throughout the West Branch Valley, but in view of presently known collections, there is no evidence that they settled there for any length of time. A curious reference is that to "a Conestoga Ind. F." located at the mouth of Lycoming (Diadaxton) Creek, at Williamsport, as shown on the Lewis Evans map of 1755 (Pennsylvania Archives, 3d series, appendix i-x, no. 18). Evans' source for this information is uncertain; and because of the apparent lack of any other historical mention of a Conestoga fort in this area, we are inclined to view its inclusion on his map as an error of interpretation. It may be that Evans had seen at this location an abandoned Indian fort similar to that described by Conrad Weiser in 1737, a few miles farther downstream. The place described by Weiser (1854) *may* have been the stockaded Shenks Ferry site at the mouth of Wolf Creek (36Ly110, see Bressler 1980: 36).

According to Weiser (1854: 326), it was a place

> where the Indians, in former times, had a strong fortification on a height. It was surrounded by a deep ditch; the earth was thrown up in the shape of a wall, about nine or ten feet high, and as many broad. But it is now in decay, as, from appearance, it had been deserted beyond the memory of man.

In all previously discussed portions of the Susquehanna Valley, it was indicated that there are many other kinds of Indian remains; the West

Branch of this drainage system is no exception. Once more, we emphasize that the major focus of this volume is the Susquehannocks and those Indians with whom they interacted. As we have seen, the Susquehannocks did not leave an abundant record of their presence in the West Branch. Students of the other Indians of this area are referred to the useful summary of the subject by Turnbaugh (1975) or the more specialized reports by Hatch (1980), and Smith (1981a, b).

Other Susquehannock Sites

Thus far there has been a brief discussion of the archeological investigations of Susquehannock (and other) sites in the North Branch and the general paucity of such sites in the West Branch of the Susquehanna Valley. At this point all of the "major" Susquehannock sites throughout the entire valley have at least been mentioned (the more detailed archeology of those in the lower valley is yet to be discussed). These can be considered "major" sites in the sense that they are archeologically known villages of some size and/or duration. Elsewhere in this volume it has been implied that for several time periods in the Susquehannock sequence, there appear to be at least some "minor" sites which are missing. The purpose of the present chapter is to summarize extant information about, and/or allusions to, some other very obscure sites, particularly in the lower valley, which *may* fill some of these gaps.

During the interim between the time of the scattered Susquehannock settlements on the upper reaches of the North Branch and their coalescence at the Schultz site, there were almost certainly some other places at which they resided.

In our discussion of the North Branch we saw that there were a few isolated pieces of Susquehannock pottery (or pots) in the Wyoming Valley and at Sunbury-Northumberland, but again nothing which indicates a settlement of any size or duration. The same seems to be true for the West Branch Valley. Southward along the main stem of the river toward Harrisburg, we know of only one site which has produced any amount of Susquehannock pottery. This was the Kline site, located a short distance north of Liverpool in Perry County. The single known collection from this site (WPMM collection Pe17/2) includes about 80 potsherds, of which 10 are Clemsons Island rim sherds, 7 Shenks Ferry rims (including one of Funk Incised), and 18 shell-tempered sherds, of which at least three may be Schultz Incised rims. These three rims clearly represent separate pots. Such evidence does not warrant our postulating a major Susquehannock town at this location, but without question there was some sort of Susquehannock occupation there, possibly during the period when Schultz Incised pottery was being made, and perhaps before the Schultz site was occupied.

Moving southward again, the next site of which we are aware that has produced probable early Schultz Incised pottery is the place which Witthoft (in Witthoft and Kinsey 1959: 24) called the Smith site. The site is located in the first saddle on the ridge along the river just south of the mouth of the Conodoguinet Creek in Cumberland County. Witthoft (personal communications) collected the site a few times in the 1950's; since then it has been largely destroyed by an apartment complex. No collections from this site are presently known.

In 1936 construction workers who were building a house for Mr. Paul Porter on North 25th Street in Camp Hill, Pennsylvania, discovered in the wall of cellar excavations a bell-shaped cache pit which contained a large quantity of charred corn (see Cumberland County misc. files and catalogue no. A36.6, WPMM files). Nothing else was recovered from the pit, and no other artifacts have been reported from the area since the original discovery. The presence of a bell-shaped pit is suggestive of Susquehannock origins, but is certainly not conclusive. This location is about one mile west of the previously mentioned Smith site, and is on a ridge which marks the divide between the drainages of the Conodoguinet and Yellow Breeches creeks. At least one spring still issues from the southern side of the ridge. Obviously, at some time in the past another flowed from the north side of the ridge.

Recently, the writer found, on a shelf in the attic closet at the Dauphin County Historical Society, a small box containing several potsherds and a note from their discoverer to Mr. William Kelker of the society dated 1901. The note indicates that the sherds were from an Indian grave found during railroad construction in the vicinity of Lemoyne, Cumberland County, generally known as the "bottleneck." At least one of these sherds is identifiable as having come from the rim of a Schultz Incised pot. The Kelker files at the society include a photograph of a vertically bisected grave with a caption indicating that it was "one of eleven graves discovered August 16, 1901 on the Cumberland County shore of the Susquehanna near the western terminus of the C.V. [Cumberland Valley] Railroad Bridge." Accompanying this photo is another of a map made by Kelker showing the horizontal distribution of the graves, together with a note that only one grave contained any artifacts. Presumably this is the same grave which produced the above-mentioned sherds. If all 11 of these graves were Susquehannock, it would appear that a site of some size and importance was destroyed by railroad and other construction at this place (see WPMM Cu. Co. files).

Again, our evidence is inconclusive, but it is sufficient to point to some sort of Susquehannock occupation of the Harrisburg West Shore area, probably during early Schultz times.

As we continue downriver, the next place at which early Schultz pottery (pre-Schultz site) has been encountered is at the type site for the Shenks Ferry culture. The site of Shenks Ferry is on a remote high point of land between two branches of Grubb Creek (36La2) in Conestoga Township, Lancaster County. Here, in 1931, Cadzow (1936) excavated 13 burials and 43 storage and/or refuse pits. At least five of these pits contained Susquehannock pottery—early Schultz Incised. One of these also yielded two fragmentary antler combs. In practically every case, the pits which produced Susquehannock objects also included Shenks Ferry pottery types. Pit no. 4 at the site contained two small brass scraps and Shenks Ferry pottery. Pit no. 36 contained two brass tubular beads and Funk Incised pottery. Burial 12, an extended male burial in typical Shenks Ferry orientation, had a spiraled brass-wire earring at the left side of the skull.

Much of the pottery from Shenks Ferry shows evidence of experimentation on the part of the potters. There are typical examples of Funk Incised, but there are also strange variants of this type. Witthoft and Farver (1952) have previously commented upon the various hybrids from the site, e.g., Susquehannock-like pots in Shenks Ferry paste. Evidence for the contact and contemporaneity here between Shenks Ferry people and Susquehannocks seems irrefutable. Shenks Ferry remains are by far the most common, which might lead us to pose the question, "Who was in charge here?"

If we compare the quantity of trade items at Shenks Ferry with those from the Seneca sites (Wray and Schoff 1953; Wray 1973), we find that they are probably most comparable to those from the Adams or Tram sites. An acceptable median date between these two early Seneca sites might be 1575.

Until more work is done at the important Shenks Ferry site, the date of 1575 will stand as a guess for its terminal chronological position; but a plus or minus factor of 10 years is certainly to be anticipated.

The Shenks Ferry site, because of the presence, albeit modest, of trade goods there (and the apparent absence of such items on all other sites of the Shenks Ferry people), would seem to be the most recent place occupied by these folk. At this point we have no idea whether the Shenks Ferry site on Grubb Creek was stockaded; it certainly is in a defensible location. The major Lancaster and Funk-phase Shenks Ferry towns, which seem to precede the namesake or type site on Grubb Creek, were all located within a few hundred yards of the Susquehanna River. Defensive works have not been demonstrated for the rather widely scattered Lancaster-phase Shenks Ferry remains within the modern village of Washington Boro (see 36La186, 36La6, 36La54). However, stockades have been discovered around all of the other major river towns, including the Lancaster-phase villages at Mohr (36La39, see Gruber 1971: 64-75) and Locust Grove (36La90, see Kent 1974); and the Funk-phase sites at Murry (36La183, see

Kinsey and Graybill 1971) and Funk (36La9, see Smith and Graybill 1977). Each of these towns may have had companion or satellite villages farther removed from the river, a factor which could account for the plethora of seemingly contemporary, smaller Shenks Ferry villages throughout the more remote areas of Lancaster County.

Witthoft and Farver (1952: 5) attributed a small quantity of European trade material to several features at the Funk site. However, in our opinion, these occurrences result from an admixture of such items into abandoned Funk features caused by the subsequent Susquehannock occupation of the Schultz site, which overlapped the slightly earlier Funk site.

Something caused the Funk-phase Shenks Ferry peoples of the lower Susquehanna Valley to disappear at what would appear to be almost exactly the time of arrival of the Susquehannocks (1550-1575). In light of this it is compelling to suggest that the Susquehannocks destroyed their towns, adopted or captured some of the Shenks Ferry, and eventually established their own town in the vicinity of the destroyed Shenks Ferry stockades.

How a place and situation like the Shenks Ferry site fits into this scenario is not yet clear. Possibly the few Susquehannock remains here were left by several Susquehannock captives among some surviving Shenks Ferry refugees; or perhaps they represent an avante-garde of the Susquehannocks. In any event, there seems to have been a short period of time (probably centered around 1575) when there were some Shenks Ferry and Susquehannocks living together in the same sites. Shenks Ferry, is the most important of these, but others include several rockshelters where the potteries of both people occur. One of the characteristic features of this period, at least at Shenks Ferry, is the hybridizations of the two pottery traditions, again suggesting the face-to-face contemporaneity of the two peoples.

Other notable, scattered occurrences of early Schultz Incised pottery are those from sites in the Delaware Valley. Quite a number of high-collared, shell-tempered sherds have been excavated by various collectors at the Overpeck site (36Bu5) near Kintnersville, along the Delaware in Bucks County (see Forks of the Delaware, Chapter 14, 1980: 27-29). These include classic (but early) Schultz Incised and what can probably best be described as shell-tempered McFate-Quiggle Incised. As such, this represents one of the few intra-site associations of these two shell-tempered pottery types. Cross (1956: 157) reports 44 sherds of what is probably inappropriately labeled proto-Andaste ceramic from the Abbott Farm site near Trenton, New Jersey. The same site produced 23 sherds which she (Cross 1956: 159, Plate 41c) classified more convincingly as Andaste (or Schultz Incised). A few additional examples of probable early Schultz have been recovered from the Eelskin rockshelter on the Neshaminy Creek in Bucks County (36Bu59 WPMM collections). Kinsey et al. 1972: 45-46, 475 and

Kraft 1976: 94 have reported shell-tempered "Susquehannock" pottery from the Pahaquarra and the Miller Field sites along the upper Delaware Valley in New Jersey.

The significance of this pottery in the territory of the Delaware and Munsee Indians is not well understood. Perhaps we are seeing a situation tantamount to the Susquehannock pottery among that of Shenks Ferry.

In our more or less chronologically ordered scenario of "other Susquehannock sites," we now arrive at the point of time wherein fits the Schultz site. Its period of occupation is rather certainly between 1575 and 1600, but in all likelihood its duration was only 15 to 20 years within that quarter century. The year 1590 probably represents an actual year during which the site was occupied, but how much before or after that date the Susquehannocks were in residence there is very moot.

It has rarely been considered that the Susquehannocks moved to any place other than the Washington Boro site after their occupation of the Schultz site. Among our list of "other Susquehannock sites" there are no likely candidates, but perhaps such should be considered. If we look at the total array of material culture for each Schultz and Washington Boro interment, we see that there are marked differences. On the other hand if we could examine the latest grave and its furnishings at Schultz and the earliest at Washington Boro, we *might* see no discernible differences. This we would expect if they had moved from Schultz directly to Washington Boro. Since we cannot do this, we are left with a nagging curiosity about a possible missing town of some 10 to 15 years' duration between these two. Such could easily be hidden or destroyed by one of the modern cities or industrial complexes at Columbia, Wrightsville, Marietta, Bainbridge or even higher up toward Harrisburg.

The Susquehannock village at Washington Boro fits into the period from about 1600 to 1625. Again, in all probability, it was not inhabited for this entire quarter of a century. The year 1610 is probably a good guess for a specific point in time at which it was actually occupied. We can be rather certain that both the Roberts site and the Billmyer site follow Washington Boro in time. It is during this overall period (1600-1645), which we have called the Washington Boro and Transitional stages, that we seem to have a number of hints of "other Susquehannock sites." We have previously mentioned several such pieces of evidence for the Columbia area. The S. S. Haldeman collection at the University of Pennsylvania seems to point toward a few Washington Boro-period sherds and straw beads, possibly from Columbia. Similarly, the newspaper account (see Hazard 1931) which mentions clay pots with moulded faces from an Indian grave in the vicinity of Columbia might also imply a settlement of this period. However, as previously stated, "the vicinity of Columbia" might refer to an area as far away as Washington Boro!

Another hint of a Susquehannock site of this period is found in the J. Haldeman O'Connor collection at the William Penn Museum. This small collection of objects labeled "Middletown Up" (presumably above Middletown in Dauphin County, Da13/6) was wrapped in a newspaper dated April 8, 1891. Our guess is that it may have been found by O'Connor in the area now covered by the Harrisburg International Airport. It consists of a mixture of Archaic and Early Woodland projectile points and some colonial material of the eighteenth century, including kaolin pipestems, redware, a large wrought-iron tire nail, a wrought knife blade, a seventeenth-century glass button like those from the Strickler site, and two glass bottle fragments, possibly of mid-eighteenth-century origin. Objects more germane to the present discussion are seven shell-tempered potsherds, two of which have design elements most characteristic of Washington Boro Incised; seven pieces of scrap brass, a kettle lug, a thin brass tube, two brass triangular arrow points, four quartz triangular points, a blank for a steatite pipe and a broken steatite pipestem, and nine fragments of animal bone.

Obviously there is a mixture of components in this area, but one of them is very suggestive of a Washington Boro-Transitional-stage occupation. Possibilities for a major Susquehannock town of this period in the Middletown to Harrisburg area might well be considered, but proving such seems beyond our range of capabilities. Some interesting, and yet frustrating, observations in this regard were made by Bashore, Kelker and O'Connor (1898: 51-52):

> The town of Middletown was laid out in 1755 in the centre of a large tract of land, bounded by the Swatara and Susquehanna. The site was that of an ancient Indian village founded by the Susquehannocks. At the time of the location of John Harris at Peshtank, Indian towns were existing on the opposite side of the river at the mouth of the Conedoguinet and Yellow Breeches. At the mouth of the Paxtang Creek there was at an early period a considerable village, *and on what is now the site of the Chesapeake nail works was an extensive Indian burial ground*.

The site of the Chesapeake nail works was just south of the present South Bridge, which carries Interstate route 83 over the Susquehanna. The entire area north of the mouth of Paxton Creek has been built over and leveled several times. At present there are no buildings there, but it is covered with great quantities of fill. Unfortunately, we know of no collections from this area, nor do we have independent evidence for the above-cited statement about Indian burials. Could this be a Susquehannock cemetery, or might it be the lost Indian village of Paxtang?

Another interesting discovery from the general area was made by a Mr. McCleary (see WPMM files). In an exposed burial in the bank on the east side and upper third of Three Mile Island, he found the following beads (in the Kidd and Kidd 1970, typology):

4b33	24 beads
4k4	1 "
4a3	9 "
4a11	70 "
2a53	10 "
2g1	4 "

This total assemblage suggests a bead sequence that might fall somewhere between the Schultz and Washington Boro stages. In all probability this represents a very chance discovery of an isolated Susquehannock interment. We know of no other Susquehannock material reported from the island.

At some time, probably during the early years of occupation at the Washington Boro village site, some Susquehannocks traveled to the upper Potomac Valley in the area of Romney, West Virginia. Remains of their sojourn here, at the place called the Herriot Farm site, have been recorded by Manson and MacCord (1941; 1944), MacCord (1952, including an appendix by John Witthoft), and McMichael (1968). The pottery from the site (see MacCord 1952: Figure 1) is primarily Schultz Incised. Spherical blue-glass beads from Herriot Farm are forms which occur at both Schultz and Washington Boro, but more commonly at the latter. Brass ornaments and at least one iron axe from the site (MacCord 1952: Figures 2 and 3) are also identical to forms which occur at both Schultz and Washington Boro, but these too are more common at Washington Boro.

Once again, the historical significance and causes for this Susquehannock presence, so far from their homeland, can only be speculated upon. Trading, hunting and war parties have of course all been postulated.

During the first half of the period which we have labeled the Strickler stage, the Susquehannocks reached what can be considered the height of their political, economic and numerical strength. Their major and probably only town during the first part of this stage was the enormous Strickler site. Unquestionably, many groups of Susquehannocks, for many reasons, traveled from this town to other areas on all points of the compass. But, the presence of a Susquehannock pot or a pipe of this period in the sites of other peoples, or as isolated finds, need not imply anything more than the confirmation of their travels to trade, make war, visit, etc.

What is perhaps an isolated burial of this period was discovered in 1947 at the site of the John Lynn butcher shop in Bainbridge, Pennsylvania. Glass beads and a few skeletal remains of a child were recovered while a trench was being excavated at the northeast corner of the building here. Many of the beads were found in the backdirt of the trench, and therefore cannot positively be associated with the child interment. The entire collection of beads, several brass objects, buttons, and teeth caps from the child were subsequently acquired by S. S. Farver, whose collection is now in the WPMM. Witthoft (n.d.b) described these beads in some detail. Except for one large, opaque white, wire-wound bead, all of the others from this lot can be attributed to the mid-seventeenth century and earlier. It was Witthoft's opinion, because of the presence of the one, possibly intrusive, wire-wound bead, that this interment was made at the time of occupation of the nearby Conoy Town, and that the more ancient beads were evidence of Indian looting of earlier graves. Such Indian looting certainly did occur occasionally; and indeed, in this case, there are beads which occur from Schultz times up to and including Strickler.

The vast majority of these beads, including 30 black-glass buttons with brass wire-loop shanks, and red and blue tubular beads (these latter beads are of a different construction than those blue tubular beads found by Witthoft in a grave at the Conoy site), are identical to those most common at the Strickler site. In light of this and other accounts cited below, one might be tempted to overlook the foregoing admonition about interpreting "isolated finds," and to at least wonder about the possibility of a Strickler-stage site beneath the houses and streets of Bainbridge.

D. H. Landis' notes (Landis n.d.) recorded that, in about 1890, Erb Brinzer of Bainbridge, while digging out the foundation trench for his summer house, found six Indian skeletons and a brass kettle. We have frequently heard collectors tell of finding shell-tempered pottery on and in the vicinity of the Mohr (36La39) or Brandt sites (36La5). Most people have interpreted this as being Susquehannock. It is our opinion that most of the illustrated (see Holmes 1903) or exhibited (Landis collection at Hershey) pottery which was labeled Bainbridge was derived from the Billmyer site. Most of the shell-tempered pottery which we have seen from the Mohr site is of the type which Kent (1974) has described as Locust Grove Cordmarked, possibly having Monongahela and/or McFate-Quiggle affinities, but not Susquehannock. This is not to say that there was no Susquehannock settlement elsewhere in Bainbridge!

Another apparent isolated Strickler-stage grave was found by Rev. Wilmer Wever across the road from his house, located one mile north of the Strickler site on Route 441. This contained a flintlock mechanism of the 1640's to 50's and at least one iron axe.

What may represent other isolated graves of this stage are the occasional tubular beads found near the site of the old Cresswell railroad station about a quarter-mile south of the Strickler site (Henry Heisey, personal communication; see also Landis' notes, n.d. catalogue entry no. 855).

The North Museum collections at Franklin and Marshall College include a string of red straw beads from the "Rawlinsville area," but this site is unsubstantiated and may only refer to the location of the residence of the unknown collector/donor of these beads.

Other Susquehannock sites, not mentioned or even guessed about here, may exist. Their discovery, if ever, will almost certainly be accidental, and due to our continuing need to disturb the earth for our own modern purposes. We can only hope that someone may notice the fragile and inconspicuous remains and call them to the attention of someone who will care enough to work them into the story of the Susquehanna's Indians.

The Schultz Site and General Excavation Techniques

Situated on a gravel knoll overlooking the Susquehanna River in Manor Township, Lancaster County, Pennsylvania, is the Susquehannock Indian village known as the Schultz site (sometimes misspelled Shultz). The soil overlying the knoll is Wheeling silt loam, characterized as moderate to high in fertility, which supported a native forest of oak, hickory, maple and walnut (Carey 1959: 71). From the center of the site to the present western edge of the Susquehanna River, a distance of some nine hundred feet, all of the soils are classed as Wheeling silt loam, of various degrees of slope. In aboriginal times the river's edge was much farther out, and those beach or flood-plain terraces which were arable supported native forests of willow, ash, birch and cherry (Carey 1959: 17). These alluvial lands, when cleared by the natives for agricultural use, also provided the small, straight, pliable timbers necessary for their house building and palisade construction.

About one hundred feet north of the site, the knoll drops sharply into present Witmers Run. To the south and east the land falls very gently. To the eastward, some five hundred feet away, the terrain rises again to form a second knoll. Here was situated a second, earlier site, known as the Funk Shenks Ferry village. Scattered over the entire area are the remains of numerous Archaic through Woodland-period occupations.

Some years ago this site complex was considered by collectors as the best place in Lancaster County to gather triangular arrowheads. The earliest recorded excavations here were those conducted by Donald A. Cadzow (1936) for the Pennsylvania Historical Commission in 1931.

Cadzow's (1936) excavation methods involved "chaining" a horse-drawn plow so that it cut a little deeper and therefore turned out, in the furrows, some of the darker fill of the storage pits and other features. Those areas in which the dark pit fill could be seen were expanded with a shovel and the pit fill was excavated. Using this process Cadzow's field crew recorded 270 pits and 13 burials (see Cadzow 1936: maps 7, 7a). Descriptions of these features and their contents are given in Cadzow (1936: 156-200). He and

James B. Griffin (in Cadzow 1936: 188-90) recognized the Iroquoian affiliations of most of the pottery from the site. Griffin equated it with a type which was previously called Andaste (Skinner 1921), and Cadzow clearly attributed it to the Susquehannocks, thus marking the first identification of the Schultz site as a Susquehannock village.

In 1934 an expedition from the Museum of the American Indian, Heye Foundation, under the field direction of Samuel W. Pennypacker II, spent about three months investigating the site. A few burials and storage pits were excavated, but "nothing very unusual was found" (Heye 1935: 130).

Additional "digging" occurred here in subsequent years, but most of that is not recorded. Arthur Futer of New Holland, Pennsylvania, recovered a Funk Incised burial pot from the site in 1946 (WPMM slide catalogue A.3.30), and the following year John Witthoft and Samuel Farver excavated a single large storage pit (Witthoft and Farver 1952: 3-32). It was at this time that the Susquehannock portion of the site, on the western hillock, was labeled 36La7, and the Shenks Ferry section of the site (36La9), on the eastern knoll, was designated the Funk (misspelled Funck by Witthoft) site for the then owners.

It was Witthoft's contention (Witthoft and Farver 1952: 5; Witthoft and Kinsey 1959: 24) that the Funk-phase Shenks Ferry village here was a contemporary of the Schultz Susquehannock town, and that the two groups actually lived there in separate villages, the Shenks Ferry being captives of the Susquehannocks. Two primary factors suggested this condition to Witthoft: (1) apparent Susquehannock influence on Shenks Ferry ceramics and the resulting hybrid or acculturated Funk Incised pottery; (2) the admixture of Shenks Ferry and Susquehannock features and artifacts at this site.

No cemetery *per se*, in association with the Schultz village, was known prior to 1960. In that year Henry Heisey (Heisey and Witmer 1962) identified a small Susquehannock cemetery of that provenience across Witmers Run, northwest of the village. Sometime around 1950, John Witthoft and Samuel Farver excavated what they thought was an isolated Schultz-period Susquehannock grave in this same area (see WPMM Catalogue no. La37/1). As a result of Heisey's work at this location, known as the Blue Rock site, particularly with regard to a Shenks Ferry component which also existed there, he (Heisey and Witmer 1964: 9; see also Heisey in Kinsey and Graybill 1971: 44-68) began to question the captive or adoptive role of the Shenks Ferry during the time of the Schultz-site occupation.

Confirmation of this situation seemed to lie in a more careful and complete excavation of the Schultz and Funk sites. An opportunity to do so arose in 1967 when it was discovered that the Pennsylvania Power and Light Company was going to purchase this and other lands in the vicinity, and that their future activities there might adversely affect the archeological remains.

In the summer of 1968, a joint operation involving Pennsylvania State University, Franklin and Marshall College, and the Pennsylvania Historical and Museum Commission, using their own resources and a grant from P.P.&L., began excavations at three sites which could potentially be impacted. Pennsylvania State University, under the field direction of Samuel Casselberry (1971), began excavations at the Schultz site. The following year, 1969, Penn State and the Pennsylvania Historical and Museum Commission continued excavations at this site. This time the work was under the field direction of Commission staff archeologist Ira Smith III.

Casselberry (1971) wrote a Ph.D. dissertation based upon his analysis of the 1968, 1969, and the earlier Cadzow excavations at the Schultz site. Among other things, it was Casselberry's conclusion that the Shenks Ferry and Susquehannock occupations at this place were not contemporaneous.

Smith (1970) published his account of the excavations at Schultz in 1969, including a map of the excavations showing pits, and house patterns and stockade lines as delineated by postmolds. Likewise, it was his contention that the Schultz and Funk sites were not contemporaries. However, he did illustrate and discuss additional evidence for Shenks Ferry Funk Incised and Susquehannock ceramic hybridizations, thus implying a contact between the two peoples at some point in time.

Nineteen hundred sixty-eight marked the beginning of a large-scale excavation project by the Pennsylvania Historical and Museum Commission to investigate Susquehannock and related Indian sites. During the summer of that year, the Commission undertook excavations at the Strickler site, about five hundred yards south of the Schultz site, and at the Parker site in Luzerne County (see Smith 1973). This project and the various excavations conducted over the next 10 years had as a primary goal the investigation of Susquehannock (and related groups) culture history, with major emphases on culture change, acculturation and settlement pattern. It was the opinion of the Commission's staff that a better undertaking of the latter could only be achieved through expeditious and massive exposure of the sites being studied. The undertaking of this project at this time was largely conditioned by the fact that many sites, particularly those of Susquehannock provenience, were threatened by eventual or immediate destruction. This factor also warranted, to a large degree, the methods employed. Specifically, those methods involved large-scale exposure of the subsoil underlying the disturbed topsoil on the various sites. This meant bulldozer-stripping.

Naturally we are aware of the comments of the critics of bulldozer archeology, and indeed the actual site surfaces, albeit plow-disturbed, which

Figure 92. Flatshoveling subsoil after removal of topsoil by a bulldozer.

contained most of the artifactual contents of the sites, were pushed to the sides and largely disregarded. A poignant comparison of bulldozer archeology vs. traditional hand excavation was forthcoming from the Commission's 1968 work at the Strickler site and that undertaken by Penn State at Schultz. Using essentially the same-size field crew for the same amount of time, the Penn State crew laboriously cleared approximately ten thousand square feet of an area which had largely been previously excavated by Cadzow. By contrast, the Commission's Strickler site project cleared and mapped over sixty thousand square feet of a Susquehannock village which had been previously undisturbed, and which included hundreds of pits, numerous longhouse patterns and portions of the stockade.

In 1969 these techniques were also employed at the Schultz site. A basic discussion of them here will serve as a general description of the methods employed at the other sites dealt with in this volume.

Topsoil removal was accomplished with the aid of various-size treaded bulldozers, generally with blade rather than bucket attachments. Strips, the width of the blade and usually 75 to 100 feet long, were cut just to subsoil level. Subsequent trenches, usually four or five of them, were cut about

18 inches away from, and parallel to, thc preceding trenches. The remaining baulks were removed after all the trenches were opened. In many cases, depending upon the weather, some or all of the exposed area (usually enough for about two days' work) was covered with black plastic. Generally, the plastic was removed just ahead of the flatshovelers. This operation involved four to five crew members using well-sharpened footer shovels. The crew would work at right angles to the path of the bulldozer, cutting just enough to remove the dozer tread marks and to expose any features. Dirt, so generated, was generally moved to a row 15 to 20 feet ahead. The resulting "wind row" of flatshoveled dirt was then removed by the bulldozer with a side-cocked (or angled) blade setting, or by the use of a tractor with a drawblade. These operations were repeated until the entire bulldozed area was planed down to clean subsoil. Features were outlined or incised with a trowel and marked with short wooden stakes as they were exposed by the flatshoveling. The reader who is unfamiliar with the origins of archeological stains or features or postmolds may want to consult Kent (1980b: 11-13).

Using these techniques, and under the best of conditions, a crew of four to five flatshovelers, one of whom was also the dozer operator, could clear a maximum of five thousand square feet (.11 acre) in one day. At the end of each day of flatshoveling the newly exposed area was surveyed into 10-foot squares. The corners of each square were marked by the white side of a mason-jar lid, held in place with a gutter spike. Key corners were marked with an adhesive plastic tape embossed with the appropriate grid designations, e.g., so many feet north and so many feet east or west of the 0-0 point. This system obviates the need for the traditional wooden corner stakes. As a result, it makes possible three important things: faster and more accurate grid survey and layout, and the ability to set an overlay grid frame directly on the ground over each square, which greatly facilitates square sheet mapping. Figure 93 shows a mapper using the aluminum grid frame with strings at 12-inch intervals to record the features in a 10-foot square.

North 0-East 0 base points are generally indicated on each site map presented in this volume. Specific survey instructions to relocate those points are kept with the field record files for each site at the William Penn Memorial Museum.

Another significant result of this approach to archeological sites of the type dealt with here is that in one field season (usually 10 weeks) a crew of four or five persons could clear and map an area of one and a half to two acres and still have time to adequately investigate the features which were exposed, generally for a total cost of about ten thousand dollars. Substantial savings were effected by renting and operating our own bulldozers. In that regard, the Funk Brothers Construction Co., of the family who owned the Schultz-Funk site and portions of the Strickler site, is to be thanked for its generous rentals of equipment over the many years of this project.

The Schultz site has not been, and possibly never will be, entirely excavated. Our estimate is that as a result of the 1968 and 1969 excavations approximately 40% of the village proper was thoroughly examined and mapped.

This area contained at least 12 longhouses (Figure 94). Casselberry (1971: 180) states that, in his opinion, parts of 26 longhouses could be delineated in these excavated areas. Smith (1970: 30) says that the longhouses vary from 50 to 70 feet in length and are consistently 20 feet wide. His own published maps (Smith 1970: 29; Smith and Graybill 1977: 51) show some houses which exceed 80 feet in length. Casselberry's (1971: 185) report indicates a range of 60 to 95 feet and a mean length of 77.5 feet. The present writer has perhaps added to the discrepancies by rounding off the average longhouse size to 80 by 20 feet. The fifty-seven thousand-square-foot area within the village proper excavated in 1969 contained a possible 12 houses (more or less completely within that area). This would mean, on the average, 57,000 ÷ 12 = one longhouse in every 4,750 square feet (rounded to 4,800 square feet).

Figure 93. Using a grid frame to map a 10-foot square. Note mason-jar lids at corners of squares.

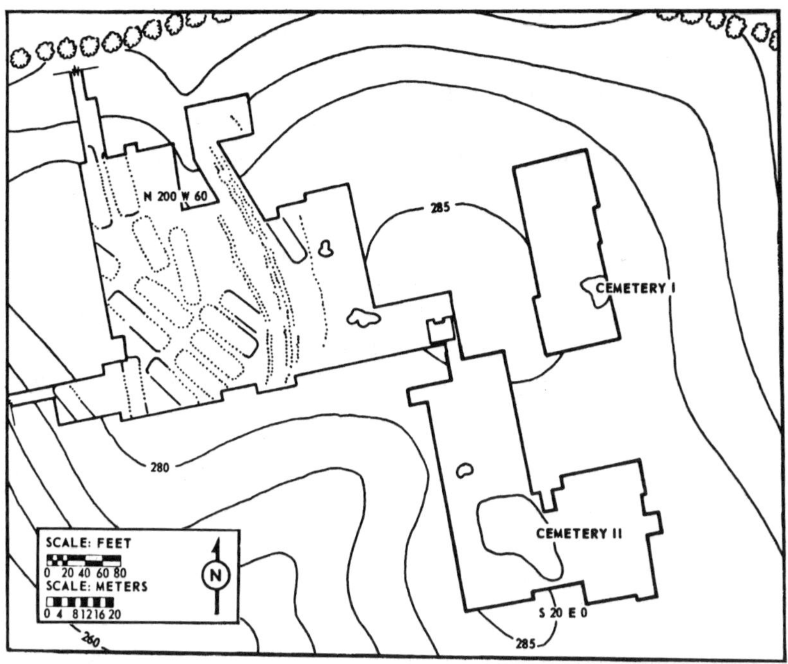

Figure 94. Map of excavations at the Schultz site (36La7) and Schultz-Funk cemeteries (36La9).

Based upon the excavations that have been conducted (as mapped) and upon the topography of the area in which the site is located, it is possible to project the total outline of the stockade. Doing so generates a potential enclosure of about 132,000 square feet. Our figure of 4,800 square feet per longhouse would produce (132,000 ÷ 4,800) an estimated 27 houses. Elsewhere in this volume (see the chapter on the Strickler site), we have developed a formula for determining the average number of longhouse occupants, depending upon the length of the average house in a particular village. In the case of the Schultz-site longhouses (80 feet), the result is 47 people per house. This, times the postulated 27 houses, yields a total population of 1,269.

Casselberry (1971: 188), using somewhat different estimating techniques, concluded that the village could have held between one thousand and fifteen hundred Susquehannocks.

Smith (1970) has proposed that the three apparently separate stockade constructions (actually as many as seven individual lines of posts, see Figure 94) represent three separate stages of village expansion and/or repair of the palisades. In all probability this is true. That being the case, our population estimation technique, assuming that the newly enclosed space was filled with new longhouses, would need to be adjusted in accordance with each successive enlargement. These variables seem too large for us to control, and for the moment our population estimates will stand as an average for the total period during which the site was occupied, in spite of what appear to be successive enlargments of the living area.

Smith (1970) reports that, in the area excavated in 1969, both within and outside the stockades (seventy-two thousand square feet), there were 450 "Indian features," primarily storage pits, but including 13 burials. A very large percentage of the so-called storage pits was aligned just inside the walls of the various longhouses, a pattern which had changed by the time of the Strickler site. Pits at the Schultz site are basically of three shapes, bell, saucer and silo (or sometimes U-shaped in profile). Smith (1970: 30) notes that they averaged three feet in diameter at the point of their subsoil exposure, and were anywhere from very shallow saucer-shapes to silo pits of up to five feet in depth. Although probably food-storage holes initially, Smith (1970: 30) suggests that their secondary use was as refuse pits; they generally contained enormous quantities of garbage and household droppings. The vast majority of these artifacts were of native manufacture, or native-generated garbage. However, there were a few occurrences of European objects, including iron knives, axes, awls, brass ornaments, brass scrap, and occasional glass beads. If one were to look only at the village sample of beads, it would appear that they were very rare at this site. However, the cemetery samples present a somewhat different picture. Glass trade beads were in use at this site, but they were generally not carelessly lost or discarded as in later Susquehannock sites.

The larger quantities of food refuse in the pits at Schultz, as compared with some subsequent Susquehannock sites, might lead one to consider that there were more foodstuffs available at Schultz. However, the lesser amounts of food refuse in the pits of the later sites may reflect different refuse-disposal patterns, including large middens for such waste located at the margins of, or outside of, the villages.

In 1974 Commission field crews returned to the Schultz-Funk site, again with the aid of a P.P.&L. grant. This time the intent was to fully investigate the Shenks Ferry component located on the eastern hillock. Results of this work are described by Smith and Graybill (1977). Two apparently separate Shenks Ferry occupations of the Funk phase were discovered. Somewhat unexpectedly, the project also encountered a major (perhaps *the* major) and a minor Susquehannock cemetery, both of which clearly relate to the Susquehannocks living and dying at the Schultz-site village (see Figure 94).

Smith's and Graybill's (1977: 55-56, 61) description of the excavation results for the two cemeteries is reproduced here in its entirety. We have retained their spelling of the site name (Shultz).

Cemetery I

The smaller of the two cemeteries, containing 18 graves, was only partially exposed along its western perimeter. Soil discolorations in this cemetery were indistinct and the oval-shaped graves were barely distinguishable from the surrounding subsoil. Twelve graves contained a few fragmented bones and a variable number of enamel teeth caps. The remainder contained no skeletal remains whatsoever. Where age assessments were possible, the composition was as follows: 0-5 years (3 ind.), 5-10 years (3 ind.), 20-30 years (2 ind.), 30 plus years (1 ind.).

A flexed posture was noted in three or four instances when sufficient bone remained to make this determination. Enamel teeth caps and/or ceramic burial offerings located in the western portion of a number of graves indicated that the dead were interred with the head oriented in a westerly direction. Flexed inhumations oriented to the west are typical of Susquehannock burial practices (Witthoft and Kinsey 1959; Heisey and Witmer 1962).

Two cremations in this cemetery were not representative of the normal mode of Susquehannock burial. One oval-shaped pit contained the partially cremated remains of an adult and a child deposited beneath three large sandstone slabs that had been transported onto the site. A variety of artifacts—an iron chisel, 2 triangular stone projectile points, red ochre, specular hematite, 3 unmodified flint pebbles, 2 beaver incisor chisels and 7 antler punches—were cached in close proximity to each other and might originally have been contained within a leather or bark pouch. A second cremation was more completely consumed. Four triangular stone points and an iron knife accompanied this interment.

The numbers and types of European trade objects, which began to increase in popularity and availability at about this time, and artifacts of native manufacture are presented in Fig. 4. Shell-tempered, incised-collared pottery characteristic of what is herein referred to as the Shultz phase (AD 1550-1600) of Susquehannock cultural development was the most universal offering. Several graves contained more than one pot, often one packed inside another, while many pots contained fish remains or occasionally the bones of larger mammals. Artifacts of bone, stone or shell occurred with surprising infrequency relative to the rich inventory of native-made tools and ornaments found in 1969 at the nearby Shultz village site. Most native-made objects of these materials in the cemetery were deposited with one or the other of two caches.

Thirteen of the 18 graves had burial offerings. Ten of these contained either iron or brass artifacts or glass beads. This means that 77 percent of the graves with artifacts contained objects of European origin. Iron cutting tools were recovered from both cremations and a third iron artifact was found in another grave. It is significant to note that very little iron was previously found in the Shultz village. It was a valuable commodity that received intense utilization and then was carefully saved to accompany the dead. Brass was more plentiful than iron in the cemetery and in the village and was used mostly for ornamental purposes. Glass beads, typed and tabulated in Fig. 5, were virtually nonexistent in the more than 450 refuse pits excavated in the Shultz village, but were numerically the most common European object deposited in the graves.

Cemetery II

The second cemetery is the larger of the two and represents the single most completely documented, undisturbed Susquehannock cemetery excavated in Pennsylvania (Pl. IV). This cemetery, situated like the first one along the edge of a local high relief topographic feature, consisted of an elongated cluster of graves oriented in a general east-west direction. The discolorations of 166 pits, 121 of which contained material culture remains, were generally darker and more readily visible than in the smaller cemetery.

Located at the center of this cluster was an open area measuring 20 feet (6.09 m) by 30 feet (9.14 m). There were no interments here or subsoil indications of distinctive surface structures. Since a scattering of postmolds from the earlier Shenks Ferry component was visible, it can be assumed that Susquehannock postmolds would also have been preserved had they been present. The area appears to have been devoid of Susquehannock features.

Bone preservation in this cemetery was poor, but better than in the smaller one. Many graves contained only enamel caps, fragments of bone preserved by verdigris, and/or ceramic offerings in the western end of the pit. The following ages of 102 individuals were noted: 0-5 years (31 ind.), 5-10 years (23 ind.), 10-15 years (6 ind.), 15-20 years (5 ind.), 20-30 years (14 ind.), 30 plus years (23 ind.). This breakdown is not particularly reliable because of the disintegrated nature of the remains. At best, it indicates a high infant-juvenile mortality rate and a low mortality among individuals ages 10 to 30. The many small, sterile pits that could only have been used to bury infants or juveniles increases even more the abnormally high percentage of young people interred in this cemetery.

There was a sufficient amount of preserved bone to determine that 71 inhumations were flexed with the head oriented to the west (Pl. III). Burials varied from those that were tightly flexed to others that were more loosely flexed. A case might possibly be made to show a general change in Susquehannock burial character from tightly flexed, to loosely flexed, to extended through time, and in response to the increase in European material culture influence and accompanying social and religious changes.

Four cremation burials were found in this cemetery. Two were especially significant. The first contained a large quantity of partially burned bone together with a burial pot and a cache of objects which included a triangular iron projectile point, fragment of a large glass chevron bead, potters clay, 8 triangular stone projectile points (2 rock crystal), 5 scrapers, 1 honing stone, red ochre clumps, chips and pebble raw material of flint, quartz and jasper corresponding to the finished points, 6 beaver incisor chisels, 2 antler punches, 3 bone awls, 10 shell beads, 2 shell pendants, and various rodent incisors. The other cremation might be classified as an urn burial. One pottery vessel made especially for burial purposes and two larger village pots were placed in the grave. The largest of the pots contained the partially cremated remains of an adult and a modified iron axe. No other remains were discovered.

One hundred and fifty ceramic vessels or portions of vessels were recovered. Most represent variations of early Susquehannock pottery types: Shultz Incised (Witthoft and Kinsey 1959: 68-77) and Blue Rock Valanced (Heisey and Witmer 1962: 111). Five of the Shultz Incised vessels have raised curvilinear human heads modeled on high incised collars. This embellishment is reminiscent of very early Susquehannock pottery in northern Pennsylvania, and undoubtedly represents the motif for the stylized geometric heads that characterize the later pottery of the succeeding Washington Boro phase (ca. AD 1600-1640). Two Susquehannock Washington Boro Incised pots were also found.

Bone and shell artifacts were better represented in the tool inventory of this cemetery than in Cemetery I. Seven turtle-shell rattles were found. Three graves contained the remains of dogs. The lower left mandible of an adult animal was found in one, while in another a complete and well-preserved dog skeleton, two turtle shell rattles, a pot, and miscellaneous brass and glass items accompanied a poorly preserved human infant. Most of the bone and shell tools and ornaments and, for that matter, most of the lithic artifacts were contained in six caches in five different graves.

Sixty-two stone projectile points were recovered. Forty-five of these were associated with six caches. One flint projectile point tip was embedded in the lower mandible of an adult male skeleton and nine complete points were found in the body cavities of various other individuals. The remaining seven projectile points were found in the grave fill and are probably associated with the earlier Shenks Ferry component. Most of the scrapers and honing stones were also included in the caches.

Seventy-six (63%) graves containing material-culture remains contained either brass or iron artifacts or glass beads. Twenty-one iron artifacts were distributed in 17 graves. An iron axe and an iron knife accompanied two of the cremations. No iron gun parts, which were to become prevalent in later Susquehannock cemeteries, were present. Much of the brass was either wire brass modeled into ear spirals, rings, or bracelets or fragments of worn-out and discarded brass kettles cut, drilled and reused as

> ornamental beads and pendants. With one exception, surviving whole brass kettles are nonexistent at this time period.
>
> More important, verdigris, a greenish-blue pigment that results from the action of acetic acid on copper buried in the ground, in many cases created a micro-environment favorable to the preservation of normally perishable organic remains. Fragments of matting, skin, and fur adhering to brass on the floors of various graves suggested that the earthen coffins were lined prior to interment. Occasionally large village utility pots were intentionally smashed and spread over and around the body tc form a lining or covering.
>
> Nearly 3000 glass beads were recovered. They were found as components of necklaces, as belts about the waists of infants, scattered around the body, or loose in the fill of graves as though sprinkled there as a last farewell gesture. One unusual beaded belt consisted of four parallel rows of nile green ovoid beads. Lacking a sufficient number of glass beads to complete the belt, the maker produced replicas in shell and substituted these in place of glass beads.
>
> Several factors suggest that this cemetery postdates Cemetery I. The organic-deficient stains in Cemetery I possibly indicate a longer period of leaching activity. The presence in Cemetery II of a complete brass kettle and a kettle lug, two Washington Boro Incised pots, an iron dagger, and a variety of additional objects that characterize the Washington Boro phase support this contention. More important, however, is the number of bead types in Cemetery II that become more popular and characteristic in the succeeding Washington Boro phase. Tubular beads, increasingly more common as one approaches the latter part of the 17th century, are absent in Cemetery I, but make up 13.7 percent of the bead sample in Cemetery II. Subspherical bead types (small and medium sized) and especially the larger subspherical multicolored varieties that characterize the Washington Boro phase are found principally in Cemetery II. Chevron beads, star beads and nile green ovoid beads are good indicators of the Shultz phase and occur in both cemeteries.

Smith and Graybill (1977) also describe in detail, and with good drawings, the various glass-bead types which they encountered. These have been converted into, or added to, the Kidd and Kidd (1970) types as presented in the chapter in the present volume on glass beads.

Smith's and Graybill's (1977) Figure 4 is also reproduced here because it provides a most useful summary of the types and quantities of other trade materials and native manufactures which were used here as burial furniture.

Absolutely nothing in the list of European materials found here is precisely datable. Many of the bead types are identical to forms found on Seneca sites of western New York which Wray and Schoff (1953) and Wray (1973) have attributed to the period before A.D. 1600. The general "flavor"

Table 20

DISTRIBUTION OF ARTIFACTS AT THE SCHULTZ SITE CEMETERIES
(36La9, after Smith and Graybill 1977: 54, Figure 4)

	ARTIFACT	CEMETERY II	CEMETERY I
Iron	Axe (Complete)	3	1
	Axe (Incomplete)	1	
	Adze	1	
	Dagger	1	
	Knives (Fragmentary)	4	1
	Triangular Point	1	
	Bracelet	1	
	Chisel	1	1
	Miscellaneous	8	
Brass	Beads	138	8
	Ear Spirals	23	2
	Cones	25	1
	Kettle Lug	1	
	Kettle (Minature)	1	
	Bracelets	12	
	Pendants	34	17
	Rings	11	
	Tubes	5	
	Sheet Ring	1	
	Button		1
	Miscellaneous	10	1
Glass Beads		2920	104
Lithic (Functional)	Triangular Points	62	6
	Scrapers	12	
	Honing Stones	6	
	Hammerstones	4	
	Boiling Stones	6	
	Paint Stone	1	
	Pebble Flints, Quartz and Chips	x	x
Lithic (Ornamental)	Coal Beads	26	
	Coal Fragments	11	
	Catlinite Beads	12	
	Catlinite Effigy Head	1	
	Catlinite Effigy Turtle	1	
	Steatite Effigy Turtle	1	
	Steatite Beads	2	
	Ochre & Specular Hematite	55	13
Bone & Antler	Dog Remains	3	
	Turtle Shell Rattles	7	
	Beaver Incisor Chisels	7	2
	Antler Punches	2	7
	Awls	3	
	Combs	2	1
	Antler Ladles	1	
	Bear Teeth	3 +	
	Raccoon Baculi (Polished)		1
	Antler Human Effigy	1	
	Antler Beaver Effigy	2	
	Drilled Animal Teeth	4	
Shell	Beads	1348	
	Pendants	4	
	Miscellaneous	7	
Ceramic	Pots	150	12
	Pipes	1	1
	Potters Clay	x	

of the other European materials—iron tools and brass objects—is also similar to forms from other sites which have been attributed to this time period. As another line of evidence for this chronological positioning we can cite the relative paucity of European manufactures and/or the complete absence of certain things, as compared with what we have "come to expect" for colonial and other Indian sites which date to immediately after 1600. Wolstenholme in Virginia should prove to be a useful example in this regard (Noël Hume 1979; 1982). Similarly, the excavation reports on Jamestown, Virginia (Cotter and Hudson 1957; Cotter 1958), although they deal with a less tightly dated sequence, also provide important comparative materials in our efforts to characterize late sixteenth-century Indian sites.

Elsewhere in this volume we have suggested what we hope is a logically reasoned pre-1600 dating for the Schultz site. In the sense that the evidence for this has derived from both comparisons with other sites and a direct historical approach, i.e., working backward from some known point in time, the dating for the Schultz site between 1575 and 1600 A.D. seems reasonable, if not entirely demonstrable.

As stated above, the primary reason for the 1974 excavation was to investigate the Funk-phase Shenks Ferry component of this site and its relationships, if any, to the Susquehannock settlement there. The archeological evidence overwhelmingly supports the fact that *both* Shenks Ferry occupations found here predate the Susquehannock town. One of the Shenks Ferry settlements actually seems to be overlapped by the Susquehannock stockade, further confirming the stockade's later dating. The best evidence for the antecedence of the Shenks Ferry occupations is that there is no clear evidence of any trade goods with any purely Shenks Ferry feature in this site, an unlikely situation if indeed there were contemporaneous Shenks Ferry and Susquehannock settlements here.

It is quite apparent, however, that some Shenks Ferry people (but not a whole separate village of captives) were living with the Susquehannocks at the Schultz site. These would indeed have been adopted persons. Evidence for this is in the mixing of the pottery styles and technologies of the two peoples and the resulting hybrids (see Smith 1970: 31). The best evidence is perhaps the placement of a Funk Incised Shenks Ferry pot in an otherwise Susquehannock grave (see WPMM field notes 36La7 N12W12, Burial 11). The continuation of a minor undercurrent of Shenks Ferry peoples in Susquehannock sites, as reflected by ceramics, is dealt with at greater length in the chapter of this volume dealing with pottery.

It is very possible that the clearing, perhaps partially overgrown, around the abandoned Shenks Ferry village at this location, is what attracted the first Susquehannocks in this territory to establish their own village. There is some evidence for, and considerable reason to speculate upon, a violent initial contact between the early Susquehannocks and the indigenous Shenks Ferry peoples of the Lancaster and Funk phases. Kinsey and Graybill (1971: 13) reported an unusual mass burial at the Shenks Ferry Murry site in which some of the skeletons have associated or embedded triangular arrowpoints; at least one of these (because it is made of New York chert) may be of Susquehannock origin. There were also several Shenks Ferry burials at the Funk site with embedded triangular points (Smith and Graybill 1977: plate II, the vertebrae of both skeletons have embedded points).

The most logical source of this violence is, again, the invading Susquehannocks. In that light it could well be that the Susquehannocks forceably removed and/or adopted some of the Shenks Ferry people from the Funk site—just prior to building their own town at that place.

The number of pits and burials which the Susquehannocks dug at the Schultz site, together with the number of buildings erected and repaired, plus the stockade enlargements, clearly imply that they lived here for at least 15, if not 25 years as has been postulated. The reasons for their abandonment of the town can probably be traced to their own overuse of local resources, resulting in soil exhaustion and depletion of wood supplies, and perhaps can be coupled with a general dilapidated condition and overcrowding of the town. Archeological evidence points to their next town within present-day Washington Boro.

WASHINGTON BORO SITE

Problems involved in locating the five *supposed* Susquehannock towns shown on Captain John Smith's map of 1612 (drafted in 1608, see Fite and Freeman 1969: 116-19) have been previously discussed. Our own interpretation of these five names on Smith's map is that they represent errors of interpretation or of translation from Iroquois (Susquehannock) to Algonquian to English. These names on the map are associated with Smith's symbols for kings' houses. Nevertheless, there is no other historical or archeological evidence for five Susquehannock towns at this time. There is little doubt that at the time Smith made his map, the Susquehannocks were living on what is presently known as the Washington Boro village site. Smith's town of Susquesahanough (a term used by the English to refer to other Susquehannock towns throughout the seventeenth century) is placed on his map in a position which would coincide with present-day Lancaster County, Pennsylvania. It does, therefore, probably correlate with the Washington Boro village site of ca. 1600-1625 A.D.

The area of the Washington Boro village site has been known to local (and other) collectors since at least the middle of the nineteenth century. Various neighborhood residents excavated burials there from about 1875 onward. A large number of graves were opened by John Keller between 1925 and 1927 in the area about the foundation for his new house on Elizabeth Street. Other graves were subsequently excavated in the immediate vicinity by various individuals. Some of the major surviving collections from this period include the John Stone collection in private hands at Columbia, items purchased by David Landis and now with his collection at the Hershey Museum, and much of the John Keller collection purchased by Gerald B. Fenstermaker of Lancaster and later (1929) sold to the Pennsylvania State Museum. The purchase of this collection by the State Museum attracted the attention of Donald Cadzow to the site in 1931. Cadzow (1936) excavated 79 burials on a plot adjacent to the Keller property. The Keller site, including the adjacent areas excavated by Cadzow, was later assigned the site number 36La4.

During that same field season (1963), Cadzow also undertook excavations in the Washington Boro village site (an area which he also called the Frey Farm village and which was later assigned the number 36La8). Here, Cadzow exposed 17 storage pits and tested a midden area on the eastern slope of the village. This same midden was the site of limited testing by students from Franklin and Marshall College in the mid 70's (see Kinsey 1977: 103).

The next professional excavations here were conducted by John Witthoft of the Pennsylvania Historical and Museum Commission in 1949. His excavations were in the northwest portion of the village in a lot owned by Abraham Eschelman. This site was designated 36La12. Witthoft uncovered 22 pits and numerous postmolds, but none of the latter formed any recognizable house or stockade patterns. According to Witthoft's field notes (WPMM files), much of this area was covered with a recent topsoil, underlaid by a Susquehannock midden deposit and then old topsoil. These excavations yielded an enormous quantity of animal bone and pottery. The faunal materials were analyzed by Guilday, Parmalee and Tanner (1962: 59-83). In the sample of over twenty-three thousand identifiable bone fragments, 73 vertebrate species were recognized. Their analysis of cut marks on the bone disclosed the butchering and skinning techniques of the Susquehannocks.

In 1955 Albert Ibaugh of Washington Boro discovered a number of human skeletons while excavating a cellar for a new house. This was brought to the attention of Franklin and Marshall College and the Pennsylvania State Museum. Excavations were carried out jointly by these two institutions in 1955 and 1957 and again by the Pennsylvania State Museum (William Penn Memorial Museum) in 1958. Considerable digging was also done here at various times after 1955 by individuals. A good portion of the materials from the private digging are included in the George Boyd collec-

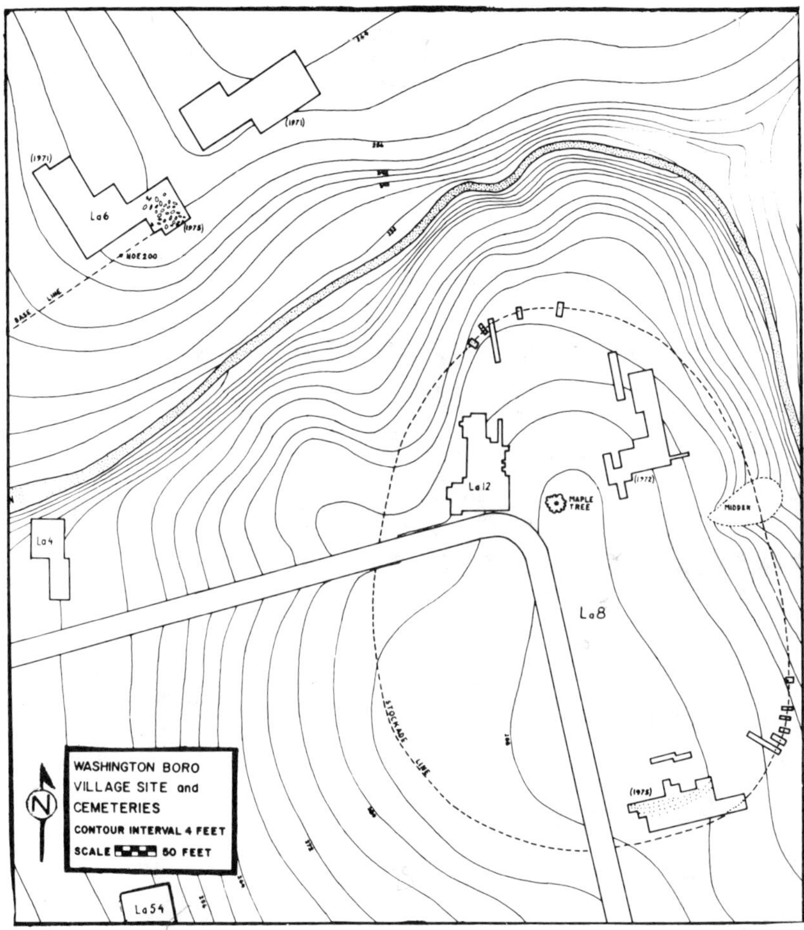

Figure 95. Map of excavations in and around the Washington Boro village site (36La8): Eschelman (36La12); Keller cemetery (36La4); Ibaugh cemetery (36La54); Frey-Haverstick (36La6). Reitz (36La92), not shown, is to the east of the village.

tion, now in the William Penn Memorial Museum, and in the Elwood Walbert collection, subsequently purchased by Gerald B. Fenstermaker of Lancaster (see WPMM photo files B1241-1280).

Results of the major excavations and the precise locations are reported in Witthoft and Kinsey (1959: 99-119) and Kinsey (1960: 81-105). Based upon these published analyses, there is no doubt as to the relationship of this cemetery and its material contents to that at the Keller site, and of both of these to the Washington Boro village site. The Ibaugh site was designated 36La54.

A few years after the discoveries at the Ibaugh site, Mr. Leroy Reitz plowed out several burials on his farm to the east of the village site. Subsequent excavations were done at this site by Charles Holzinger of Franklin and Marshall College. Artifacts from these excavations now at Franklin and Marshall and in the Reitz collection are of the same type and vintage as those from Keller and Ibaugh.

Sometime prior to 1970, several burials were excavated by a local collector on the south end of the village area. Although these materials have not been examined, a reliable source reports that they included Washington Boro Incised pottery.

Figure 96. Excavating and recording the stockade lines on the south edge of the Washington Boro village site (36La8).

John Witthoft's field map (WPMM files) accompanying his notes on the Eschelman site indicates a small cemetery on the south center of the village.

Neither Cadzow's (1931) nor Witthoft's (1949) excavations had done much to delimit the boundaries of the village site. It was apparent that it covered most of the flat hilltop and that it did not extend beyond the major cemeteries or across Stamans Run (see Figure 95). As an effort to determine some of the village boundaries, excavations were conducted in 1972 on property owned by Mr. and Mrs. Scott Haverstick. The work here was done by the author with the assistance of Henry Heisey. At that time this was the only portion of the village area on which permission to excavate could be obtained. This was the same general area tested by Cadzow in 1931.

Approximately fifty-eight hundred square feet of topsoil were removed to subsoil with the use of a bulldozer. After flatshoveling, the subsoil revealed over 30 pits (of both saucer- and bell-shaped profiles) and numerous postmolds. Two east-west parallel rows of postmolds were traced for a lineal distance of about 40 feet. It was noted that a number of pits were located along and just inside the two rows. Neither end of this pattern was exposed, but it is interpreted as a portion of a longhouse (approximately 21 feet in width) in which storage pits were located just inside and along both walls. This arrangement is similar to that noted at the Schultz site.

The excavated area also discloses two north-south lines of posts of 30 to 40 feet in extent. These may have been parts of adjacent longhouses; the two lines were too close to represent a single house.

No evidence of any stockade line was discovered by this work, but it was our general feeling at that time that the nearest line must lie either to the north or east of the excavations.

In the three years which followed these excavations much of the remaining undisturbed surface of the Washington Boro village area was purchased by a housing developer. By the time the developer finally agreed to permit any salvage excavations, only one house lot remained unbuilt upon, and that had had its topsoil stripped away in preparation for building. In the few days alloted to the WPMM field crew by the builder to work in this lot, we were exceedingly fortunate in uncovering what we soon determined to be the south wall of the Washington Boro village stockade. The map (Figure 95) indicates the area exposed and shows the location of four lines of closely paralleled (averaging two to three feet apart) or concentric lines of stockade posts. The posts in any one of the lines were generally about six inches in diameter, with an average of eight inches between posts; average depth into the subsoil was about six inches.

About 35 feet from the outermost of these four lines was found a fifth (and apparently single line) of palisade posts. This line probably reflects an enlargement of the village, since storage pits and other evidence of habitation were found in the area between the four lines and outermost single line. As indicated on the map, the single line was traced, through test-trenching, at a number of points along its circumference on the south, east and north side of the village. Its western configuration was projected along the break between the flat top of the hill and the relatively abrupt slope on that side of the village. Other areas in which the stockade might still exist could not be tested because of houses and buildings on the site.

Using the outermost stockade line and its various projected or anticipated locations, we find that it encompasses approximately 250,000 square feet of village area. Employing the population estimation scheme discussed elsewhere in this volume (see Strickler site), this village area would imply approximately seventeen hundred people. Captain John Smith (Smith 1907: 51) recorded in 1606 that the Susquehannocks "can make neare 600 able men, and are pallisadoed in their Townes." Using our (Mook 1944: 193-208) multiplier of three warriors per ten (1-3.3), Smith's figure would suggest two thousand persons.

Artifacts and features and their general complexion at the Washington Boro village and its four or more attending cemeteries and, indeed, its promontory location and adjoining stream make it more like the Schultz site than like Strickler. This is not a revelation, for as we have suggested elsewhere, the Roberts and Billmyer sites fall chronologically between Washington Boro and Strickler.

Storage pits at Washington Boro, of which we can count several hundred excavated by Cadzow, Witthoft and the writer, are much more like those at Schultz than anything else. Large straight-sided or undercut pits, frequently "loaded" with debris, are typical of both Schultz and Washington Boro. Later pits, particularly at Strickler and the Leibhart sites, are more often shallower and saucer-shaped and contain far less garbage. The paucity of longhouse patterns at Washington Boro is a result of our inability, for one reason or another, to open large areas within the stockades. A seemingly unique feature of this stockade is that it encloses two large hillside midden or refuse dumps (see map). Generalized midden areas are known at Schultz and Strickler, but the size of these and the amount of debris in them is insignificant by comparison with those at Washington Boro.

One final unique character of the Washington Boro site is the presence of two so-called shaft-scraper sites in the bed of Stamans Run, which courses along the base of the hill on the east and north side of the village. These grooves, approximately one-half inch in diameter and two to ten inches long, have been interpreted as shaft-scrapers or polishers. In point of fact their use and their makers are unknown.

ROBERTS SITE

Presently available evidence would suggest that following the abandonment of the Washington Boro village, some of the Susquehannocks moved to the considerably more secluded spot above the Conestoga Creek now referred to as the Roberts site (36La1). Others, as we have previously indicated, may have moved up the Susquehanna River to the place known as the Billmyer Quarry.

One possible reason for occupying the Roberts site is in complete contrast to anything relating to its isolated location, in fact quite the contrary. It may be that this place was closer or more convenient to the Swedish (and other) trade outlets on the Delaware River. We have previously suggested that the Swedish account of ca. 1645 may have been in reference to the Roberts site.

> These Indians lived at the distance of twelve miles from New Sweden, where they daily came to trade with us. . . . They live on a high mountain . . . there they have a fort, or square building, surrounded with palisades. . . . There they have guns, and small iron cannon. . . . (Holm 1834: 157-58)

The Roberts site is situated on a three-sided point of land about 90 feet above Conestoga Creek. Whether or not it is the place mentioned in the Swedish account cited above will remain a moot point. It is, however, indicated on the rough and smaller copy of the Chambers survey of 1688 (Pennsylvania Archives collections). This map shows both the Fort Demolished at the end of the survey line (the Strickler site) and a second Fort Demolished, where a line crosses the Conestoga. A plotting of the Chambers Survey on the modern topographic map would seem to run the line right through the present Roberts site at the point marked "Fort Demolished." The surveyor's notation of a demolished Indian fort could well have referred to the overgrown clearing in which the town once stood. The warrant (Old Rights, D65-106, Division of Land Records, Bureau of Archives; see also Landis 1933: 128) for a piece of patented land at this place by Robert Hodgson and James Hendricks in 1714 mentions "Indian field." This must represent the same place noted on the Chambers survey. We admit that the major problem with this interpretation is that by 1714 this place, if indeed it referred to the Roberts Susquehannock town, was a field which by our reckoning had been abandoned for almost 70 years.

This fact did not pose a problem for David Landis (1933), who thought that the Roberts site was the location of the Shawnee town of Pequehan, which he dated to about the first decade of the eighteenth century.

None of the examined collections from this site, including Landis' material at the Hershey Museum, contains any objects which can be attributed to the late seventeenth or early eighteenth centuries. One of the earliest

Figure 97. Bracelet of red and blue glass straw beads from the Roberts site (36La1).

known collections from this site is that gathered by John Stone (see Landis n.d.). Landis purchased various items found by others on the site. In 1930 Donald Cadzow (1936: 39, 43) conducted test excavations at the Roberts, which resulted in the discovery of two storage pits. Cadzow's field notes for this work indicate that the materials recovered from Pit #1 included a brass wire, three kaolin pipestems and an iron hoe; only the hoe still survives in his collections. He also recovered a restorable Strickler Cord-marked pot and 70 other sherds, of which five are identifiable as Strickler Cord-marked, and five as Washington Boro Incised.

Sometime prior to 1968 the owner of the site plowed out a grave near the top of the four hundred-foot-elevation hill about fifteen hundred feet due west of the site discussed here. This grave produced red-glass straw beads, a Strickler-period clay pipe, and an iron axe. Landis' notes (Landis n.d.) include the following entry concerning this locality:

> Charles Roberts told me, April, 1935, that up on the hill on the west side of Pequehan site (Roberts site) he plowed up some ashes (Charcoal) . . . he also found some glass beads on the east and west side of (the) hill near the top. Dan Witmer about 20 years ago, said that he found iron tomahawks there. Might there have been a fort there? The fort the Swedes mention ("on top of the hill").

The relationship of this site to the Roberts site is uncertain at best. Our own efforts at surface collecting the hilltop produced nothing.

In an effort to learn more about the Roberts site, the Pennsylvania Historical and Museum Commission sought permission to undertake further excavations there in 1971. This work was severely limited by the then tenants (now owners) of the site. However, a small cemetery was located and completely excavated on what is probably the northern margin of the village.

The seven burials in this group produced the following ceramics: a small-spouted vessel (Figure 22), probably of Seneca origin; two Washington Boro Incised-"style" pots with leached shell-tempered paste; one very degenerate Washington Boro-like pot; and a curious heavily cord-marked, very un-Susquehannock pot (Figure 22). Because of the small size of the total collection, a complete inventory does not seem inappropriate here: Burial #1—iron knife blade; Burial #2—small brass ring, iron vanity box with a mirror, steel chisel, large piece of brass, three stone triangular points, paint pigments, one Washington Boro Incised pot; Burial #3—small (Seneca) pot, one Washington Boro Incised pot, iron bracelet, red straw beads, black and white seed beads, one kaolin pipe; Burial #4—three shell-tempered sherds from the grave fill; Burial #5—a bracelet of red and blue straw beads (recovered in a manner which allows the reconstruction of the decorative pattern, see Figure 97), miscellaneous red and black straw beads from the neck area, a cache consisting of a hone-stone, two iron knives, two stone triangular points, frizzen from a flintlock, a bifacial gunflint, an iron screw and a flintlock mechanism; Burial #6—a flintlock mechanism minus its frizzen and pan, a loose frizzen and a pan but not for the foregoing, brass strips, a metal (latten?) bracelet, an iron axe, miscellaneous iron fragments, iron pipe tongs or tweezers, a Washington Boro Incised pot, iron screws and a green-glass case-bottle fragment; Burial #7—a small heavily cord-marked vessel and one iron knife blade; and one quartz bifacial gunflint from the surface.

The Landis collection from the site, at the Hershey Museum, includes three iron axes, a brass pistol barrel, a stone masquette or face broken from a pipe bowl, two clay faces from Washington Boro Incised pots, one glass bottle fragment, plus a variety of glass beads common to both the Washington Boro and Strickler sites.

Several characteristics of the artifacts from this site give it a chronological complexion of a Washington Boro to Strickler-period transition. This is apparent in the rather even distribution of Washington Boro and Strickler pottery types and the glass-bead types at Roberts. The presence of guns, i.e., conventional flintlocks, at Roberts would imply a date of perhaps 1630. This evidence would suggest that Roberts was a contemporary of the Frey-Haverstick site, and, as suggested elsewhere, of the Billmyer site.

Three sides of the point of land on which the Roberts site is situated drop rapidly enough to preclude any Susquehannock houses being built thereon. The fourth or north side of the point slopes gradually upward, and therefore there is no logical topographic barrier to house-building or for a site boundary. Exceedingly limited excavations at Roberts have simply not made possible the determination of village boundaries through the discovery of house or stockade postmold patterns. However, the demonstrated existence of a cemetery on the back or north portion of this point of land would suggest, based upon comparisons with other sites, that that specific locality is outside the stockade.

If we draw an imaginary stockade line just south of this cemetery, across the point of land, and then completely around the top of the three slopes, the area thus enclosed is approximately three acres. (For what should be obvious reasons, no map of this site and the excavations is included here. A finished map is available in the WPMM files for this site.) Using the house (and people) per-acre figures implied for sites between Schultz and Strickler, we arrive at a very crude population estimate for Roberts, viz., nine hundred people. This represents an approximately 50% reduction from our estimate for the Washington Boro site. However, since we have proposed that the Roberts is one of two contemporary Susquehannock towns, this population figure may be very much in order.

Except for the fact that the Roberts site was a Susquehannock settlement, our understanding of this place and its history is very speculative. This is one case where the common archeological lament, "more work needs to be done," is certainly appropriate. At this point we can suggest that this was one of two Susquehannock towns occupied after the abandonment of Washington Boro (ca. 1625-1630) and before the Susquehannocks coalesced at the Strickler site about 1645.

In reality, the significant questions about the reasons for its rather unusual location, its diminutive size, and its cultural-historical position with regard to other contemporary sites are at this point beyond the reach of the information at hand.

BILLMYER SITE

The Susquehannock site at the Billmyer Quarry south of Bainbridge in Lancaster County is the most poorly known of their towns. The widely scattered, but rather sizable, amount of material reported from here suggests that it was a major town site.

One of the earliest references to this site appeared in the *Columbia Spy*, July 16, 1831, when

> workmen on section #18 of the canal, about two miles on this side [south] of Bainbridge, came upon an end of an Old Indian burial. . . . A great many articles of use and ornament were discovered. These were crocks, hatchets, tomahawks, arrowheads, bullets, buck shot, thimbles, beads, pipes, etc.

One of the pipes is described as being clay with the head of a fox engraved on the bowl.

Mombert (1869: 612-13) cites several accounts of discoveries in the Bainbridge area which would appear to relate to a Susquehannock occupation there. From an article in the *Lancaster Gazette*, he (Mombert 1869: 612) notes that a Mr. Landis had received from John Hamilton, Esq., who resided near Bainbridge, "an ornamented tobacco pipe, which has a human head rudely carved upon it." Mombert (1869: 612) also notes that

> In the fall of 1868 while workmen were engaged at the quarries of Messrs. J. L. Kerr and Co., on the farm of Jacob Haldeman, Esq., near Bainbridge, Lancaster County, in clearing the clay from off the limestone, they dug up the larger bones of six fully developed bodies, besides a collection of trinkets consisting of beads, necklace, pipes and several hatchets.

Mombert (1869: 612) further notes that

> whilst digging the Pennsylvania Canal near Bainbridge . . . beads were found . . . about an eighth of an inch in diameter and an inch and a half long, of the red color of the celebrated pipe-stone of Minnesota, when this is wet.

This fully describes the red-glass straw beads which Kidd and Kidd (1970: 58) have designated *IIIa1-3*, and which we have shown first occur about 1625 (see chapter on glass beads). In the same paragraph Mombert also describes a large star bead from Bainbridge (items then in the S. S. Haldeman collection). Although Mombert does not call this a star bead, he equates it to one of this type illustrated in Schoolcraft (1851 I: facing 10), which clearly is the type which Kidd and Kidd (1970: 59) have labeled *IIIml.*

From another quote by Mombert (1869: 612) we read that workmen employed on the Pennsylvania Canal at Bainbridge had found a number of relics, "among which are a stone tobacco pipe, very neatly formed, a rude tomahawk, a small brass basin, two keys, a small globular bell, and some broken pieces of Indian pottery."

In his notes on his own and other Lancaster County collections, David Landis (n.d.) says that he had found many trade beads near the mouth of Conoy Creek (location of Conoy Town), but that these are of a different type from those found a mile south along the river ("now Billmyer and a little farther down the river"). He notes that these beads (from Billmyer) were like those found at Washington Boro, Stehman's (Frey-Haverstick), Harry Witmer's (Strickler) and Dr. Heistand's Binkley Farm (Roberts).

Landis examined a number of collections from this area, and among the identifiable materials which he mentions in his notes are a large number of red and blue straw beads in the Gordon Geistweit collection. Landis further identified the location of the Billmyer site as being "occupied" by the J. E. Baker Company plant, specifically in the field between the "Princess Quarry" and the superintendent's dwelling. Recent investigations would suggest that this area has been totally destroyed by quarrying operations.

The Sam Farver collection in the William Penn Memorial Museum includes three brass arrowheads "found when 35 Christian burials were relocated by the J. E. Baker Company."

Artifacts in the David Landis collection at the Hershey Museum which are attributed in his catalogue to the Billmyer site or the immediate vicinity include at least a dozen sherds of Washington Boro Incised pottery. Other specimens to which Landis refers, specifically those of Rev. Peter Nissley, may have been found at Billmyer, but some were also found elsewhere in the Locust Grove and Bainbridge areas. The distinctions were not always clear.

Locust Grove properly refers to the estate of S. S. Haldeman, located just south of Conoy Creek. Haldeman was a noted scholar, collector and antiquarian of his time. A portion of his collection of archeological materials from the Locust Grove "vicinity" went to the Academy of Natural Sciences of Philadelphia and was later turned over to the University Museum of the University of Pennsylvania. This collection includes two seventeenth-century iron axes marked as being from Billmyer. A third axe of the same style is labeled "Locust Grove area." Three Strickler-period pipes (at least in style) are simply marked "Bainbridge," which may or may not indicate the Billmyer site. Another pipe (catalogue #14030) is identified as being from the canal excavations above Columbia. The pipe is of clay with a canine figure facing the smoker. This may be the pipe referred to in the above-cited account from section 18 of the canal, or it may actually have been found nearer to ("above") Columbia. Haldeman's collection at the University Museum also includes a Washington Boro Incised pot marked "Locust Grove," and eight sherds of the same type listed as "Bainbridge." In addition, there is a large section of a strap-handled Mississippian or Fort Ancient pot.

A small collection of Washington Boro Incised sherds at the North Museum of Franklin and Marshall College is listed as coming from the quarry area at Billmyer. As mentioned elsewhere in this volume, Holmes (1903: Plate CXLIV) illustrated a number of what we now designate as Washington Boro Incised sherds from a "village site at Bainbridge."

Materials in the WPMM collected around the turn of the century by S. Haldeman O'Connor include one lot (now catalogued as PA O/10) marked as being found at Locust Grove on June 6, 1896. In all probability these items came from the Billmyer Quarry site: They include one brass arrowhead, six pieces of cut brass, four pieces of scrap brass, three triangular points of Onondaga chert and one of black chert, one native gunflint of Onondaga chert, one kaolin pipe bowl fragment with a protruding heel and the mark EB in a circle, two pieces of wrought iron, and three shell-tempered incised Susquehannock sherds.

Various other unsubstantiated oral accounts suggested scattered finds of Susquehannock artifacts throughout the Bainbridge area. Many of the accounts cited here also imply a rather wide scattering of Susquehannock materials in this general area. However, the only repeatedly specific locality for the discovery of Susquehannock remains is at the place now destroyed by the Billmyer limestone quarries. Many of the finds reported here were made by workmen on the canal, which at this point along the river is now covered by the railroad and/or J. E. Baker plant.

Our present survey of the few extant collections from the Billmyer Quarry site does not really permit an accurate assessment of the age of the Susquehannock settlement there. Without doubt the Susquehannocks did have a town there, and probably of considerable size. The predominance of Washington Boro Incised pottery and heavy iron axes clearly suggests a Washington Boro time period for the occupation here. References to gun parts, straw beads, brass arrowheads, brass kettles, and animal-figure, clay smoking pipes are suggestive of material items more commonly found at the Strickler site. Obviously, the Washington Boro Incised pottery and the glass straw beads are the key dating factors, and they suggest something between the Washington Boro village and the Strickler site. Our guess is that Billmyer was occupied toward the end, or completely after, the abandonment of the Washington Boro village, and as such is the contemporary of the Roberts site, dating somewhere between 1625 and 1645.

FREY-HAVERSTICK SITE

In 1873 John B. Staman excavated an unusual burial on his property just north across Stamans Run from the Keller site (36La4). This grave, located about 20 feet east of the present dwelling (the old Hiestand Frey house), according to David Landis' notes (Landis n.d., also Landis 1925: 101-104), contained an *iron helmet*, a pike, cutlass, iron axe, iron hoe, several two and one-fourth inch cannonballs and a ceramic vessel. The helmet was subsequently illustrated in Egle's (1883a: 818) history of Pennsylvania.

For a while the helmet was on exhibit in the Museum of Independence Hall in Philadelphia, but later it was transferred to the Historical Society of Pennsylvania, which has kindly provided the photograph of it shown in Figure 62. The specimen, while on exhibit at the historical society, carried with it a label suggesting that it is of Swedish origin from the reign of King Gustavus Adolphus (1611-1632).

The Stamans excavated a number of additional graves in this general area until about 1911. Most of the artifacts from these graves were recorded by Landis and the few which survive were purchased by him for his own collection, now at the Hershey Museum. His notes list four hundred small, round, blue and red beads; red ochre; an iron spike; a sword; a flintlock (a "Schnapphan," according to Landis 1925: 103); a bone (antler) comb, etc.

Landis (1925: 101-104) propounded the notion that at least some of the material recovered by Staman related to a Shawnee town and to the trading post established a short distance north of this area by Martin Chartier in about 1710. In fact, Landis (1925: 104) suggested that the skeleton found with the helmet, etc., might be "the remains of Martin Chartier," who died in 1718 (see inventory of his estate in chapter on Conestoga). However, as we now view the total artifact assemblage from this site, little if any pertains to the eighteenth century. Practically all of it can be assigned to the first half of the seventeenth century. The one exception is a silver coin found by Staman on his property, which according to Landis' notes was a French coin dated 1729 (eleven years after Chartier's death).

Donald Cadzow of the Pennsylvania Historical and Museum Commission was aware of the Staman discoveries and he probably thought that they related to the nearby Keller site, which he excavated in 1931. That same year, Cadzow obtained permission to excavate at Staman's (the property was then owned by Hiestand Frey, who also owned that portion of the Washington Boro village site investigated by Cadzow). Cadzow (1936: 153-55) recovered the contents of two Shenks Ferry interments. Since then these have been identified as belonging to the Lancaster Incised phase of Shenks Ferry culture. Interest in this phase of Shenks was the primary reason for the excavations conducted by the Pennsylvania Historical and Museum Commission at this site in 1971. At the time, and until the present, the property was owned by Mr. and Mrs. Scott Haverstick, who kindly permitted the work there. The site was assigned number 36La6. The 1971 excavations did disclose a Shenks Ferry occupation. In one rather concentrated area (see map) of the excavation, 11 burial pits were encountered. Two or three of those were Shenks Ferry, but the remainder were clearly Susquehannock interments. Ten pots, or fragments thereof, were recovered from these grave pits, all of which were Washington Boro Incised vessels and indistinguishable from those found elsewhere on the Washington Boro site.

Some of the trade items recovered from these graves, particularly the glass beads, were also like those characteristic of the Washington Boro period. However, the remainder of the artifacts were not common to this period. The "atypical" objects include various gun parts, a seal-top latten spoon, a metal vanity case with a mirror, etc., none of which has ever been reported in association with the Washington Boro site. Cadzow (1936: 99) did find one grave at the *edge* of the Keller cemetery which produced a sword and a flintlock, but which he himself attributed to a later interment.

A small percentage, about 8% (see Table 8), of the beads from Frey-Haverstick were blue or red straw beads. These types are far less common at Washington Boro, but are in fact the hallmark type at Strickler.

The overall impression one gets from these materials at Frey-Haverstick is that they are slightly later than those from Washington Boro. Elsewhere, we have proposed a date range for Washington Boro of 1600 to 1625. The *pièce de résistance* from Frey-Haverstick is a Rhenish jug with three seals of the city of Amsterdam, each with the date 1630 (Figure 73). Even if this piece had gone into the ground the year it was made, which is most unlikely, it would still be after our presently conceived terminal date for the Washington Boro site.

No village debris, pits or postmolds, etc., indicative of a Susquehannock town have been found in the extensively tested field in which the Frey-Haverstick site is located. The later dating (post-1630) of the Frey-Haverstick Susquehannock cemetery clearly implies that it is not associated with the Washington Boro village. However, the lack of any village association for this cemetery leaves us in a quandry regarding its presence at this time and place.

About two hundred yards to the north of the Frey-Haverstick Susquehannock cemetery, there is another of the same time period. This one is located in the modern Church of God Cemetery, and most of the Indian materials found there have resulted from the excavation of modern grave pits. All of the known objects from this site are recorded in Landis' (n.d.) notes, having been derived from at least four separate Susquehannock interments and including a string of star beads, two small brass kettles, an iron knife, a brass bracelet, a large cut section of a brass kettle, and two native ceramic vessels, at least one of which has been examined and is Washington Boro Incised. The most impressive piece from this cemetery is, once again, a Rhenish jug, in this case an elaborately paneled vessel of blue on grey salt-glazed stoneware of a style typical of the first half of the seventeenth century. This jug is also described elsewhere in the present volume (see Figure 74).

Once again, there is no evidence of a Susquehannock village between or otherwise associated with these two cemeteries; and the Washington Boro village almost certainly predates them.

With these problems in mind, and in an effort to solve them, a crew from the William Penn Memorial Museum returned to the Frey-Haverstick site in 1975, during which time more work was done on the Susquehannock cemetery (see Figure 95). Material recovered at that time is described and discussed elsewhere in this volume. The general conclusions are that the items found in this cemetery are indeed post-1630 (but also pre-1645) in origin and therefore clearly buried there after the abandonment of the Washington Boro village.

A possible explanation for these "cemeteries without a village" is suggested in the ethnohistorical literature. Wallace (1970: 94) cites a number of examples of the strong religious urge of the Iroquois to be buried near the "old ones." This being the case for the Iroquois of New York, particularly the Seneca, there is no reason to believe that the same custom would not prevail among the "Iroquois" of the Susquehanna. And so we are suggesting that certain, perhaps the more conservative, Susquehannocks carried their dead back to the ancient village at Washington Boro to bury them near the old people. The new villages from which such burial parties would have come may be those which we call Billmyer and Roberts.

STRICKLER (AND POPULATION ESTIMATES FOR OTHER SITES)

Most of the persons who have looked into the matter agree that the Indian village on the banks of the "broad crystall" Susquehanna River, a place now called the Strickler site, was the place shown as the "Fort Demolished" on the Benjamin Chambers survey (Figure 8) of 1688. It follows that it is also the same location indicated "Fort" on Jacob Taylor's 1717 survey of Conestoga Manor (Pennsylvania Archives, 3d series IV: Map 11, Conestoga 1).

It is our opinion that this is the location at which the Susquehannocks coalesced in about 1645, and where they continued to prosper and grow in population until about 1660. By the time Chambers saw the ruins of the village, in 1688, its houses and stockades must have very nearly crumbled to the earth; and yet, enough remained to distinguish it as a demolished, and probably burned, Indian fort.

The first patents for the area in which the Strickler site is located are not recorded in the Division of Land Records of the Pennsylvania Historical and Museum Commission. The connected draft of patent lands for this area in Manor Township, Lancaster County, refers the researcher to the Penn Deeds DGG 545.

In all probability the site has been farmed continuously since at least the 1740's. Unquestionably, numerous artifacts were exposed by the first and subsequent plowings of the site. Even in the beginning, some of these artifacts were picked up, especially metal items which could be reused or forged. Perhaps even some digging was done to secure metal for forging. Landis' (n.d.) book of notes and catalogue information indicates, according to Theodore Urban, a curio collector from Columbia, that "bushels of beads were found here" during his time (1850-1870).

Older descriptions of sites in Lancaster County, particularly those by Landis (1910), refer to this location as the H. G. Witmer farm. In his catalogue (Landis n.d.) he says that, according to H. G. Witmer, "there was no sale for Indian articles prior to about 1875, and it was only after that period that the boys and others began to gather the Indian articles." Landis goes on to say that "the Indian site in the vicinity of the H. G. Witmer farm, was probably the most prolific spot for Indian curios in this county."

Witthoft (n.d.c) says that during the 1860's and 1870's graves were dug here for curios, and that E. A. Barber of the Philadelphia Art Museum purchased a bellarmine jug there in 1878. Recent inquiries to the Philadelphia Art Museum failed to turn up any evidence of the jug. However, Barber (1907: 24) does illustrate a bellarmine taken from a "Conestoga Indian Grave" in Lancaster County.

Landis (n.d.) mentions various individuals who opened graves here after 1900; many of the contents were purchased by him for his own collection and are now at the Hershey Museum.

In 1931 the Pennsylvania Historical Commission began excavations on the Charles Strickler property, where Gerald B. Fenstermaker of Lancaster had indicated that burials could be found (Cadzow 1936). These excavations, on what Cadzow (1936) designated the Strickler site, were in the area marked Cemetery #1 (Figure 98). Although Mr. Strickler did not own the major portion of the village and the other cemeteries, the entire site has since become known as the Strickler site (36La3).

Since the time of Cadzow's work an uncounted number of graves have been disturbed by curio collectors at various locations throughout the site. In 1959 the Conestoga Chapter of the Society for Pennsylvania Archaeology excavated a trench on the east side of the site (see Figure 98), 190 feet east of NO-EO). This work resulted in the discovery of several burials and a 70-foot line of postmolds which was interpreted as a wall of a longhouse (see Heisey and Witmer 1962: 118, fn. 11). During the 1950's systematic and recorded excavations were undertaken on the Funk property to the north of the village (Cemetery #2, Figure 98) by Art Futer of New Holland, Pennsylvania (Futer 1959). More recently, Henry Heisey, owner of the main village area until 1972, excavated in Cemetery #3 (Figure 98). These investigations were reported upon by Heisey and Witmer (1962). Subsequent to his report, Heisey excavated a number of additional graves in this cemetery. The notes pertaining to these excavations and the majority of Heisey's collection from the site are now in the collection of the North Museum at Franklin and Marshall College, Lancaster.

Other materials from the site are scattered in numerous private collections throughout the county, and as a result of sales and auctions they are scattered throughout the country.

In 1967 it was discovered that a major industrial concern, subsequently identified as the Pennsylvania Power and Light Company, was going to purchase a large area of land which would include the Strickler site, and that its activities would eventually destroy the site. As a mitigation effort, salvage archeology was undertaken at the site in 1968, 1969 and 1974, and was fully supported by the power company.

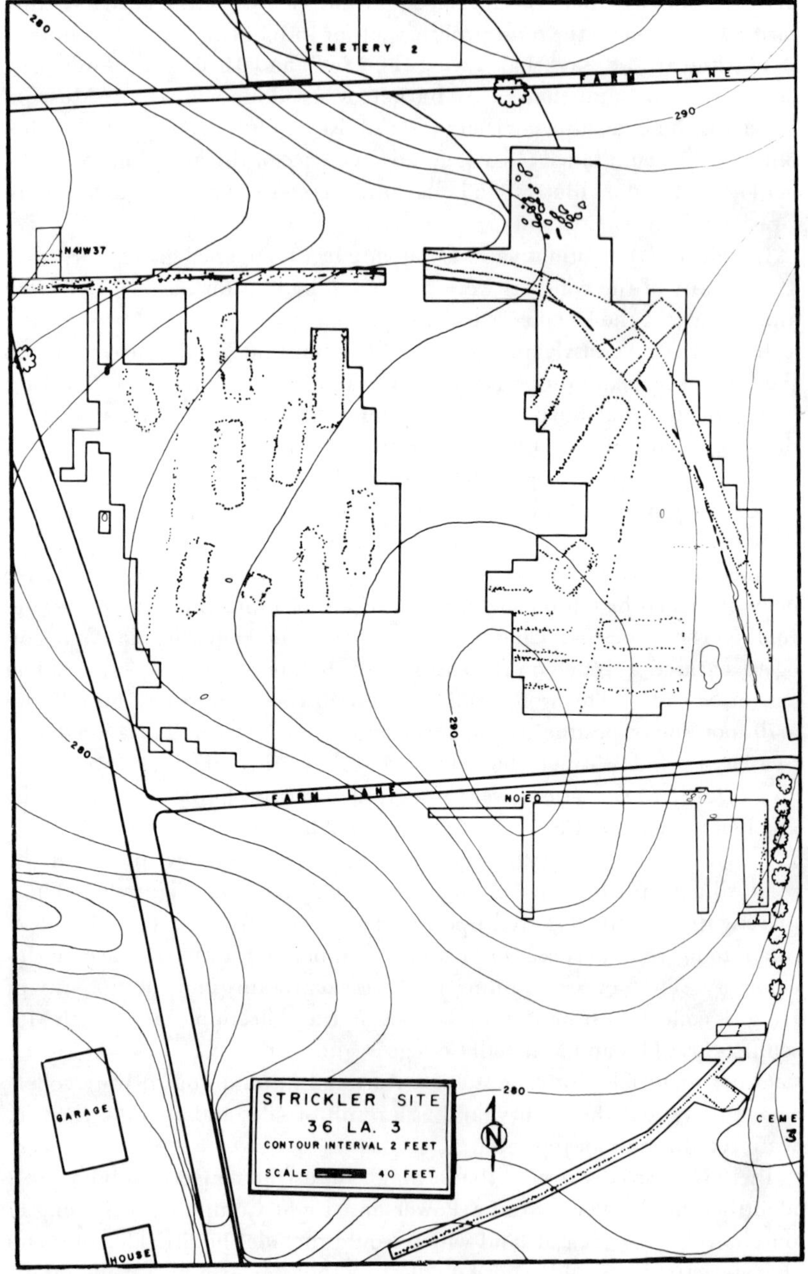

Figure 98. Excavations at the Strickler site. Note longhouses and two bastions. Cemetery 1 is just off map to southwest.

Inasmuch as no Susquehannock site had previously been excavated on the scale proposed for this one, there was no basis for guessing what might be expected. Other archeologists had suggested that very little would be encountered, due to years of erosion and plowing. Earlier testing had indicated that some postmolds and pits could be found, and of course numerous burials had already been excavated.

Preliminary tests in the fall of 1967, including a three hundred foot-long trench running due north from the NO-EO point (Figure 98), exposed a large number of pits and postmolds. It was clear from these tests that sub-plow-zone features did exist, and that the loss of features due to erosion or plowing was at a minimum.

Work began in earnest in June, 1968, when a crew of six men, with the aid of a D-4 Caterpillar bulldozer, started excavations in the general northwest quadrant of the site. During the ensuing 10 weeks sixty thousand square feet of topsoil were pushed off the site, to an average depth of ten inches, and the entire area was flatshoveled and mapped.

Over 350 pits were excavated and recorded, and as Figure 98 indicates, a number of longhouse patterns, as defined by postmolds, were noted. Thousands of other postmolds were recorded in this area, but when plotted on an overall map, many of them were not clearly parts of any discernible structure. Only those postmolds which are obviously parts of longhouse construction are shown on Figure 98.

At the northern boundary of the 1968 excavations, a "ragged line of postmolds" was encountered. This east-west line of posts and narrow associated trench were interpreted as the north wall of the stockade. Before the completion of that season's fieldwork, a number of bulldozer trenches were run at the supposed southeast corner of the village, just inside Cemetery #3. Once again stockade posts were encountered, but this time the arrangement of the posts was far more linear, with very close and regular spacing. It was soon apparent that these stockade posts lined up with the so-called longhouse wall discovered by the Conestoga Chapter in 1959, and thus the stockade alignment could be extended toward the north. Over a long-exposed stretch it could be seen that the stockade line was curving, as though it was making a rounded corner. At the southeasternmost point of that curve a rectangular structure 25 by 18 feet, as marked by postmolds generally more than six inches in diameter, was found attached to the stockade line. This was immediately interpreted as one of the bastions which contemporary English (1661) and French (1663) documents imply for this place.

Excavations were continued at the Strickler site in the summer of 1969. Again, a bulldozer and a crew of six fieldworkers were employed to remove the topsoil and to flatshovel the exposed subsoil. These excavations were largely concentrated in the northeast quadrant of the village. This time, approximately sixty-five thousand square feet were cleared and mapped. Again, a profusion of pits and postmolds was uncovered. A stockade line, curving around the northeast corner of the village, was discovered just beyond the terminus of the village pits. Another rectangular bastion was attached to this curved corner of the stockade. The bastion was apparently enlarged (Figure 98), and at a later time the stockade at this corner was itself enlarged and another bastion was added to this new line. On the east side of the village this new or outermost line of stockade merged with the inner line approximately 220 feet south of the latest bastion. Along the north wall it was not determined (at least not in 1969) where, if at all, the two lines merged. In 1974 excavations in the area of N41-W37 did reveal the inner and outer line paralleling the ragged line and continuing westward for an undetermined distance beyond that point (see Figure 98, in area of N41-W37).

The "ragged stockade" line discovered in 1968 continued into the northeast quadrant excavated in 1969. It shows up on the map (Figure 98) as a narrow, and occasionally discontinuous, trench. In this area the trench was associated with far fewer postmolds on either side of it. It can be seen on the map (Figure 98) that the trench of the "ragged line" passes outside the innermost regular line at the northeast corner, and then comes back inside along the east side of the village.

The function of the "ragged line" is not entirely clear. It seems to represent a stockade, but an apparently irregular variant thereof. At some places within the narrow trench there was some evidence of posts having been set into it. In other words, it may be that the ditch served as a footer trench for the stockade, and because of its dark fill very few postmolds could be distinguished in it. The scattered and irregular placement of posts on either side of the trench could represent repairs. The "inner" regular line of postmolds and the "outer" regular line would seem to represent successive stages of rebuilding and enlargement of the stockades.

To the west of the northeast bastion the three lines of palisades are transected by a gate-like arrangement of posts. The fact that all three lines are cut by this "gate" suggests that, for a time at least, all three lines of palisades were standing coevally.

A short distance outside this gate was the edge of Cemetery #2. In 1969 over 20 burials were excavated in that portion of Cemetery #2 between the gate and the farm lane (see Figure 98).

Inside that portion of the village excavated in 1969, a number of longhouse outlines were discernible, at least on the final map of the excavations. Two house outlines were quite clear in the field. One of these was partially restored by placing posts in the original holes and then tying them to posts on the opposite wall (Figure 98). The rather crude appearance of the resulting frame was in part due to the fact that locust and sumac were the only trees available in quantity for the reconstruction; neither of these bends very well.

In this particular house and the one immediately south of it, the ends of the buildings were rather clearly defined by extant postmolds. Both of these structures and most of the others in this quadrant have their long axes along an east-west line, whereas all those found in the 1968 excavations were oriented north and south.

On the map (Figure 98) there is a long line of postmolds running from the northeast bastion in a southerly direction across the excavated plot. This has the appearance of a stockade line, but neither its northern terminus nor its relationship to the other stockade lines could be established. There is a noticeable difference in the number of postmolds and pits on either side of this line. The fewer such features east of this line suggest a shorter or less intensive occupation. This area also contains the only amorphous midden deposit (in a dug-out depression) encountered at this site.

Earlier tests (1967) south of the NO-EO point (Figure 98) did not pick up an extension of the north-south line mentioned above, suggesting that it stops or turns before reaching those test trenches. Toward the west side of the section excavated in 1968, there is a rather discontinuous line of postmolds which can be more or less traced for over two hundred feet. Originally, our thought was that this (or these) line(s) represented a longhouse wall for which the matching wall simply was not discernible. However, after the 1969 excavation, it was noted that this line and that found in 1969 were pretty much parallel to one another. This raises the possibility that they are opposing sides of an earlier and smaller stockade on the Strickler site. The distance between these two lines is about 350 feet. If they did represent sides of a stockade, say 350 feet on a side, it would have enclosed an area of about three acres! We note, almost parenthetically, that outside what *could be* the southeast corner of this hypothesized stockade (but inside the larger confirmed stockade), there was a small cluster of burials (see area 140 feet east of NO-EO on Figure 98).

Pits

Over 550 pits were recorded and excavated within the Strickler site village during the 1968 and 1969 field seasons. These range in depth from 13 inches to 52 inches below the orginal surface, and in diameter from 12 inches to 110 inches. The most common were between 12 and 36 inches in diameter. Observed colors of the pit fill included tan, mottled brown, dark brown, and black. The latter were the most likely to produce artifacts. About 40% of the black-colored pits contained artifactual material. Over-

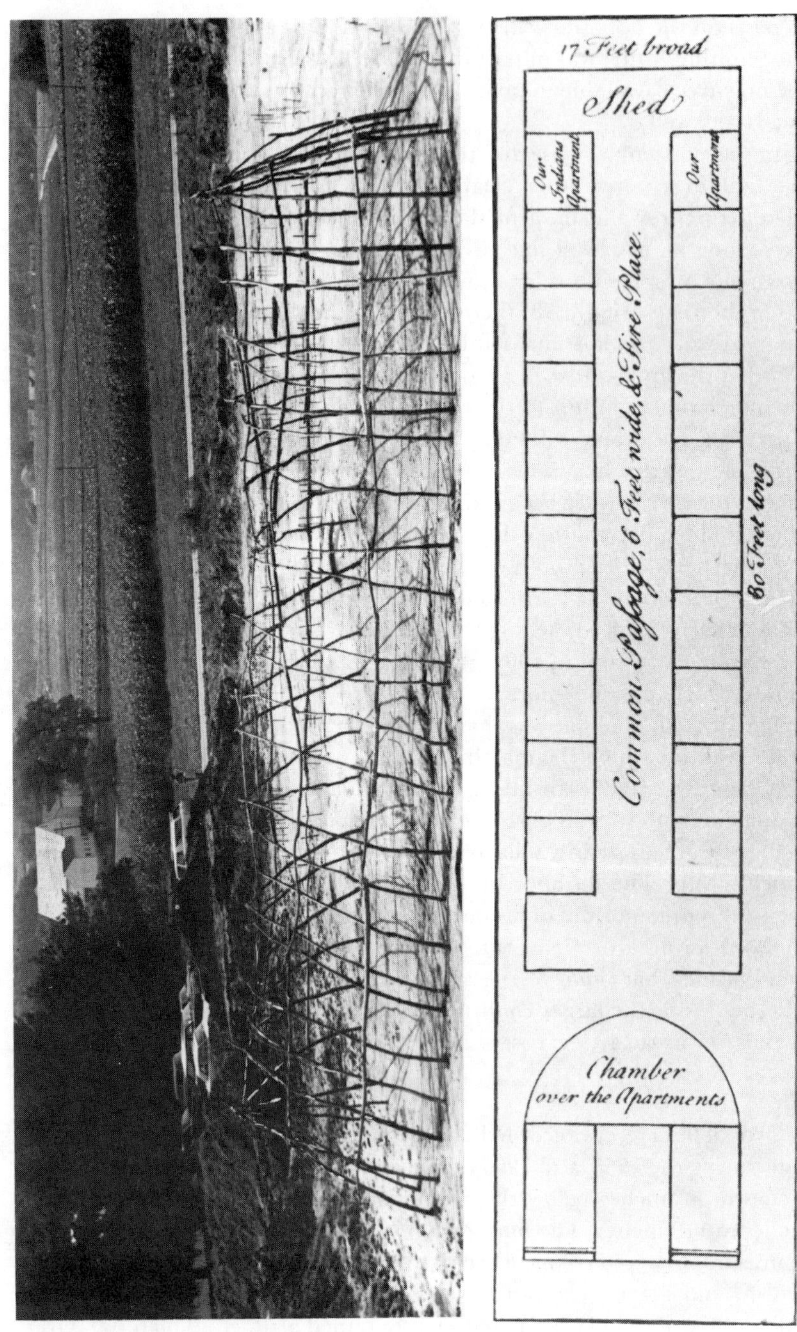
17 Feet broad
Shed
Our Indians Apartment
Our Apartment
Common Paſsage, 6 Feet wide, & Fire Place.
80 Feet long
Chamber over the Apartments

all, about 73% of the pits excavated contained some artifactual material, the remainder being devoid of any macro-artifacts (unfortunately, very little flotation was done).

Table 21 shows the distribution of various shapes of pits at Strickler.

Table 21
PIT SHAPES

Profile	*plan*	*% of total*	*% with artifacts*
saucer	round	43	60
U-shaped	round	25	26
bell-shaped	round	5	99
U-shaped	oblong	7	87
irregular	irregular	9	84
misc.	—	11	97

Since the topsoil on the site was stripped away (by bulldozer), and not sifted (because of the incredible volume), most of the artifacts came from the pits. Although the number of artifacts from the excavations (pits) is relatively large, the actual quantity of artifacts per pit, as compared to earlier Susquehannock sites, is quite small. It is very apparent that the pits from earlier Susquehannock sites are generally deeper, with straighter (or bell-shaped) sides, and that they contain greater quantities of cultural debris. Pits at Strickler were less frequently found along the inside walls of the houses. Very rarely do we find any pits whose contents have been carefully or even purposely placed there. Rather, the artifacts in the pits represent garbage which was thrown into them, or was thrown on the ground near them and eventually washed or swept in. In any event the contents that are usually found, viz., garbage, do not bespeak the function of the pits. Although this cannot be archeologically verified, we can say in all probability that the numerous pits on these sites were places for food storage which were ultimately abandoned and closed with debris or other fill. The cultural and/or functional reason for the various shapes and sizes of pits at any given site are simply not known to us. A few pits had postmolds encircling their orifices; a few others had raised-bottom centers, i.e., a sort of trench around the outside bottom edges. But again, their functions are very much an enigma.

Postmolds

Far too many postmolds were found within the palisades at Strickler for all of them to represent house construction. Many of them must represent racks, frames and other miscellaneous structures, as well as various periods

Figure 99, opposite. Reconstructed framework of a longhouse at the Strickler site (36La3) and Bartram's (1751) sketch of a longhouse at Onondaga showing size and apartments.

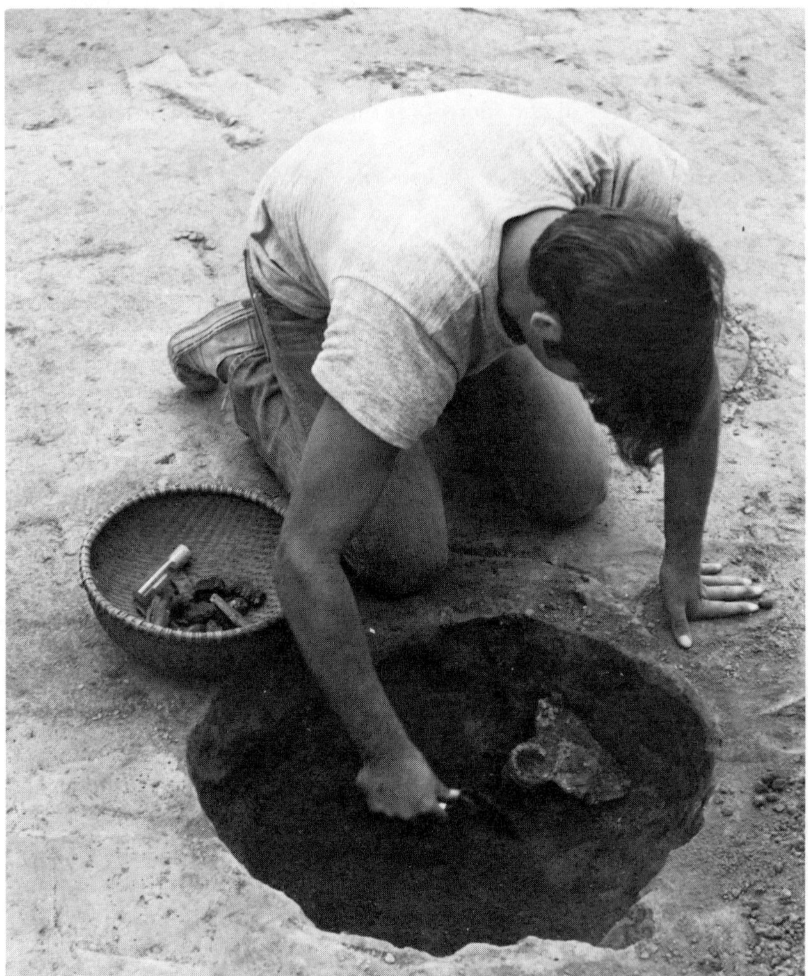

Figure 100. Excavating a saucer-shaped pit at the Strickler site (36La3).

of building. If all these postmolds had held posts at the same time, it would have been almost impossible to walk through the village.

Postmolds which were clearly part of house construction ranged from about one and a half inches to four inches in diameter. Average depth into the subsoil was about eight inches, or 18 inches below the original surface. Generally they were set in vertically, but an occasional slanted post was recorded.

Posts in the house walls were rarely in a perfectly straight line, and frequently there were matched pairs a few inches apart. In all likelihood these represent repairs to an existing wall. On the line of a house wall, the posts varied from being adjacent to each other to being over two feet apart. The average distances between such posts were about 18 inches.

Occasionally there was a vague central aisle, and sometimes partition walls seem to appear, but in no case are these very clear. Where ends of the houses could be determined, or guessed at, they delineated houses of about 60 feet in length, and there was little apparent deviation from this. In addition, the width of the houses was consistently between 18 and 22 feet. In the northwest quadrant of the village, the houses were on parallel alignments running north and south. There is no evidence of any arrangement into rows. In the northeast quadrant the alignment shifts to northeast-southwest, and then on the east side of the village it shifts to east-west. This would suggest that the houses were aligned on a radial plan, i.e., like the spokes of a wheel around a point (or plaza?) at the center of the village.

The previously mentioned experiment in rebuilding the framework of one of these houses was quite instructive with regard to certain practical matters of longhouse construction. As indicated, a variety of trees, including some birch, box elder, sycamore, locust and sumac, were used in the reconstruction. The latter two were most unsatisfactory, but were, unfortunately, the only species available in any quantity. The diameters of the trees used coincided very closely with those of the postmolds into which they were placed, i.e., two to three inches. They provided usable lengths of between 15 and 22 feet. When they were overlapped with posts on the opposite side of the house, they produced an arch which was nine feet above the ground at its apex. A digging stick with a pointed end and greatest diameter of three and a half inches, and a length of eight feet, was used to punch holes into the ground (in this case into the original postmolds). This readily produced a hole which would receive the pointed end of a house post. When the posts were bent over, it was noted that they produced an oval outline to at least eight to ten inches into the ground. This may well account for the oval appearance of many postmolds. If the post hole was not at least 12 inches deep, the leverage produced by bending the post inward would cause the ground on the outward side to bulge, or in some cases pry the post completely out of the ground.

Even though the alignment of the original post holes was not straight, the sides of the house framework, as reconstructed and tied with stringers, was actually quite uniform.

After reconstruction it was noticed that there were slightly larger gaps between the posts in the middle of the long sides of the house. These may have been doorways. There is some historical evidence for this kind of door placement, although contemporary accounts of Iroquoian longhouses usually place the doors at the ends of the house.

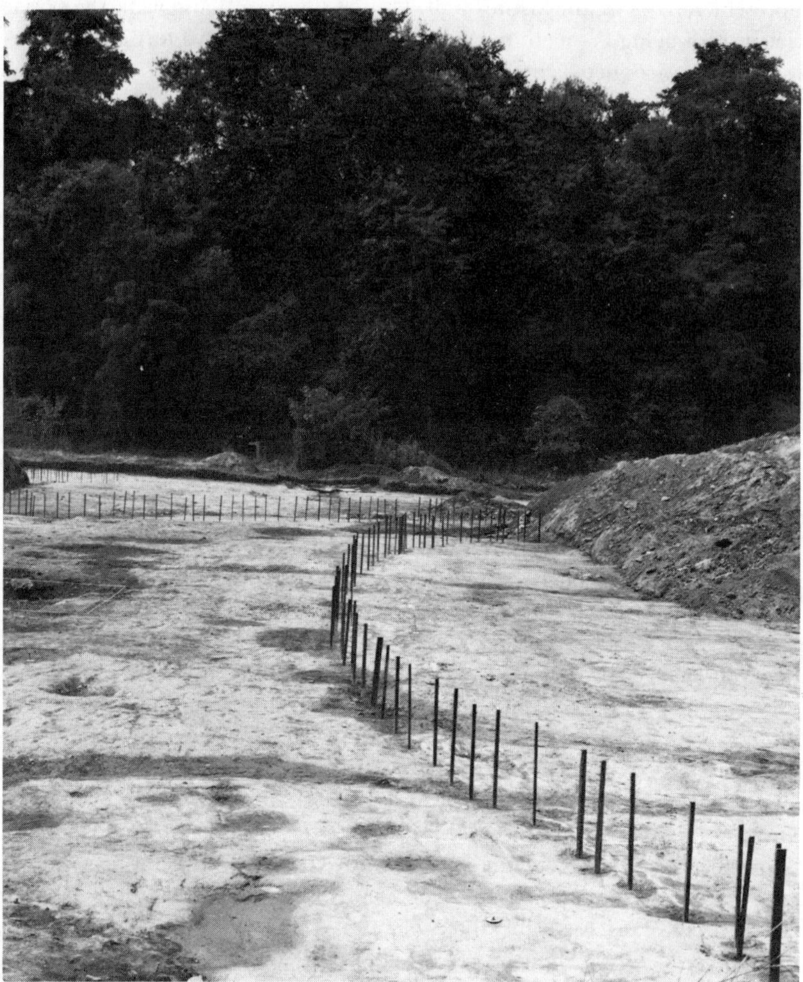

Figure 101. Stakes marking stockade lines (36Cn6).

Largely due to inaccessibility to the land, we were not able to undertake any extensive testing on the west side of Route 441. One bulldozer trench was cut there in hope of finding the west wall of the stockade, but unfortunately the area available for these tests seems to have been severely eroded. Two factors, one cultural and one topographic, would seem to make possible a prediction about the position of the west wall of the Strickler village stockade. The cultural factor is the frequently noted Susquehannock custom of placing cemeteries at varying distances outside some of the corners of the village stockades. And, in no case have we seen a stockade line run through a cemetery. The south wall of the Strickler stockade was heading directly for Cemetery #1. The above observations suggest that the stockade must have turned before it reached the cemetery. Secondly, its turn at this point would have enabled it to run along the top of the rather steep break in the contour on the west side of the site.

Given these conditions we might very well predict that the west wall of the stockade ran parallel to and about two hundred feet west of present-day Route 441. Based upon extant information about the stockade shape and size on its eastern side and the projected location of its western wall, we can rather confidently describe it as a rectangle with rounded corners, measuring approximately eight hundred by seven hundred and enclosing about 550,000 square feet (allowing for the rounded corners), or just over 12.5 acres. Parenthetically, we might note that this was one of the largest contact-period Indian towns in the eastern United States. The slightly later (1670-1687) Seneca town of Totiakton in Monroe County, New York, may have covered as much as 20 acres. Historical accounts indicate that it consisted of 120 houses. Gandagaro, another contemporary Seneca town in nearby Ontario County, New York, may have been equally as large (see Beauchamp 1900 and Wray 1973).

The previously lamented inability to examine the western side of the village (and that stockade) has also made it impossible to determine the exist-

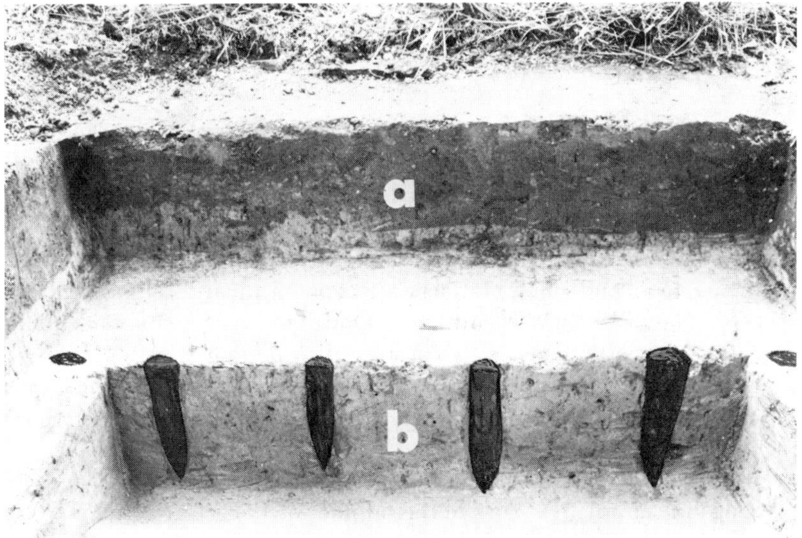

Figure 102. Cross section and horizontal view of postmolds in subsoil (b), and overlying topsoil (a) at the Strickler site (36La3).

ence of bastions on the southwest and northwest corners. It would seem, however, that we might rely upon the ethnohistoric accounts for an answer to this question. Jerome Lalemont in 1663 (Thwaites 1959: 77) recorded a reference, to what we believe to be this village, stating that it "was defended on one side by the stream, on whose banks it was situated and on the opposite by a double curtain of large trees, flanked by two bastions erected in the European manner." All of our evidence would point to the Strickler site as the place described by the Iroquois account given to Lalemont, which he transcribed in the *Jesuit Relations* for 1662-1663. A good case can easily be made for its coincidence with the archeological remains at this site. We leave it to our readers to draw their own conclusions about these relations.

Population Estimates for the Strickler Site

Based upon the two major excavations at the Strickler site, the density of discernible longhouses is about 17 in 106,000 square feeet excavated inside the stockade, or one house per approximately 6,250 square feet. The resulting quotient would round off to about 90 longhouses for the entire village inside the (projected) stockade.

The most critical figures here are those concerning the number of houses in a given area of the village. Again, based upon our several excavations, we have determined and/or proposed one house in every 6,250 square feet of village area. However, this figure does not take into account the rebuilding of houses or, more specifically, the fact that not all of the houses may have stood coevally. This is a factor for which we can probably never account.

In order to estimate the total population for the village we would need to determine the approximate number of persons in the average house. It was previously stated that the average size for the dwellings at Strickler was 60 by 20 feet. There have been numerous attempts made to calculate prehistoric populations (cf. Cook 1972). Many of these are based upon ethnographic analogs concerning numbers of people in square feet of dwelling spaces (cf. Naroll 1962; MacCord 1971). One of the most useful models for population estimates is generally considered to be that which is derived from ethnographic data for the area and general time period in which the estimates are to be applied. In that light, we have gone to a little-cited but potentially very useful ethnohistoric account by John Bartram (1751) of his trip from the Schuylkill River in eastern Pennsylvania to the village of Onondaga in central New York in the summer of 1743. During his stay at Onondaga, Bartram was lodged in an apartment of the village Council House with two other persons—Conrad Weiser and the cartographer Lewis Evans. Bartram (1751) described this longhouse in great detail and included a plan and elevation view of the structure. The apartment in which he and his companions slept was one of 20 similar partitioned areas within the house (see Figure 99). The house measured 80 by 17 feet with *a door at one end*, storage compartments at both ends, and a common passageway six feet wide. The apartments measured 5 by 6.7 feet (33.5 square feet!) and by Bartram's (1751) account slept three of his party in one apartment and two in the one opposite.

From these data we can readily project a house population size: an 80- by 17-foot Iroquois longhouse in the middle of the eighteenth century *could* have accommodated, in 20 compartments, 60 people.

Utilizing a sleeping space of 33 square feet (about the size of a modern queen-size bed) for three people is of course not impossible. However, it does seem to be rather parsimonious use of the space under the general uncrowded conditions that seem to have prevailed at Onondaga. An *average* of two and a half persons per compartment seems to be a somewhat more comfortable, albeit difficult to visualize, number of people.

Scaling these figures down to a 60-foot longhouse (of the same approximate width) like those at Strickler, by removing four apartments, we have 16 spaces times 2.5 persons, or 40 people per house.

Six years before the trip to Onondaga described by Bartram, Conrad Weiser, in the company of "Shikelima" and another white man, made the same trip to that Indian town. Weiser's journal (Weiser 1854: 324-41) states the following concerning the "Onon-tagers":

> They live in huts made of bark, which are very convenient; some of them are 50, 60, to a 100 feet long, generally about 12 or 13 feet wide. In this length there are generally four to five fires, and as many families, who are looked upon as one.

Anthropologists generally consider the average nuclear family to consist of five persons. It is implied (but not explicitly stated) in Weiser's account that a 50-foot longhouse usually contained four families, and that one of 60 feet would house five families; accordingly, a 100-foot house might contain eight families. Using the five-person-per-family average, we might posit 20 persons in a 50-foot house, 25 in a 60-foot house, or 40 in a 100-foot longhouse. These figures do not jibe with those derived from the Bartram account for the same town. We also note a discrepancy in the stated widths of the houses. Bartram reported 17 feet, while Weiser indicated 12 to 13 feet.

Lewis Henry Morgan (1881), who summarized various sources of information about Iroquois longhouses, including the above-cited Bartram account, notes that historic records are quite variable on the subject. He illustrates (Morgan 1881: 120) a 17 by 97 foot longhouse floor plan which contained 24 apartments (12 on each side of a central aisle in which six fireplaces were located). He notes that some of the apartments may have been reserved for storage. The Bartram (1951) account clearly suggests that the equivalent of four compartments was used for storage in the house in which he was lodged.

Morgan's (1881) data on the number of compartments necessary to house the average family are quite varied. For his 97-foot longhouse he posits 24 families (each, in a roughly 40-square-foot area). Again, this seems too small, particularly if we consider the family to average five persons. It seems far more likely that a family (average: five persons) would have occupied two compartments, one on either side of the aisle. This would place two and one-half persons in either compartment, on the average!

Let us assume then the average of two and one-half persons per compartment. It only remains for us to determine the average number of compartments in a longhouse. Once again the accounts vary on this. In Morgan's (1881: 120) 97-foot-long house, each compartment consisted of 8.08 linear feet (i.e., the space along the long wall occupied by each compartment). In Bartram's longhouse each compartment consisted of 6.7 linear feet. Conrad Weiser's (1854: 120) account of four families, plus a presumed two compartments for storage on each side of a 50-foot longhouse, should translate to 8.3 linear feet per compartment. An account from 1677 by Wentworth Greenhalgh, as given in Morgan (1881: 119-20; see also O'Callaghan 1849) implies 12 fires or 12 separate units (compartments?) in a 50-foot house, or 4.16 linear feet per compartment. Even though this is certainly too small, we have included the Greenhalgh data in the average which has been computed here, viz., 6.81 (rounded to seven feet) of linear distance along one wall of a longhouse for each compartment therein.

We have noted above, as did Morgan and Bartram, that some compartments or the ends of the longhouses were used for storage purposes and not as residences. Bartram is rather specific in indicating four such storage areas in the house in which he stayed at Onondago. For that reason we have employed the number four as the number of compartments which must be subtracted in order to derive actual numbers of living compartments. From all of this we have derived the following formula for *estimating* numbers of living compartments in a given length of longhouse:

$$\text{no. of compartments} = \frac{\text{length of house}}{\text{7 feet}} \times \text{(2 sides of the house)}$$

minus 4 storage compartments

House population, then, is derived by multiplying the number of compartments times two and one-half persons/compartment (or five persons per family apartment consisting of two compartments).

The formula can be somewhat more simply expressed as:

$$\text{persons/house} = \left(\frac{2 \times \text{length} - 4\,(\text{storage areas}) \times 7)}{7} \right) \times 2.5$$

—or—

$$\text{persons/house} = \left(\frac{2 \times (\text{length}) - 28}{7} \right) \times 2.5$$

We hasten to add that we fully recognize the problems inherent in creating a formula of this sort, and we place no credence in it above the fact that it allows us to mathematically illustrate our intuition that the ordinary Iroquois longhouse of 50 feet probably housed five families of five people.

Assuming that we can apply these, by and large, eighteenth-century data for Iroquois longhouses to those in a mid-seventeenth-century Susquehannock village, we might generate some population estimates for the Strickler site. Using the above formula for a 60-foot-long longhouse, we arrive at a per-house figure of 32 people. That, times the proposed 90 houses at Strickler, yields a total population estimate of 2,880 persons.

Historical corroboration for this figure is not forthcoming. The *Jesuit Relations* for 1647 (Thwaites 1959 XLII: 129) states that the Susquehannocks (Andastoe) "are very warlike, and in a *single* village they count *thirteen hundred* men capable of bearing arms" (italics mine). Elsewhere in the present study we have employed a ratio of three warriors to ten other persons (1 to 3.3) for calculating total population from cited military strength (Mook 1944: 193-208). Thirteen hundred warriors times 3.3 (1,300 × 3.3) yields a total population of 4,290 people—a discrepancy of some 1,400 souls!

It is our opinion that estimates of military strength for any time period (including the seventeenth century) are very much subject to the expediency of prevailing politics. In the case of the Jesuit estimate of thirteen hundred Susquehannock warriors, we submit that it was to their political advantage to considerably overestimate their numbers.

Based upon the data presented here for the Strickler site, and that discussed elsewhere for the Schultz site, we are proposing to average our population estimation figures once more (we realize that we can average the figures *ad nauseam*, until they seem to suit our purpose). At Schultz we found larger houses and somewhat more densely clustered arrangements of them, as compared to Strickler. Our population figures for the Schultz site were based upon one 80-foot house of 47 people (using the above formula) in approximately five thousand square feet, in a village which encompassed an estimated 132,000 square feet. This yields 27 houses of 47 occupants each, or a total of 1,269 people. This can also be expressed as one person per 104 square feet of stockaded village area.

TABLE 22

SUSQUEHANNOCK POPULATION ACCOUNTS AND ESTIMATES

	Excavation data			Documentary sources			
Site	*Village size in square feet*	*Persons per square feet*	*Population estimate*	*Warriors*	*Total**	*Date*	*References*
Schultz	132,000	1/104	1300				
Washington Boro	250,000	1/147	1700				
Washington Boro				600	2000	1608	Smith 1907: 51
Roberts	130,000	1/147	900				
Billmyer		?	900				
Strickler	550,000	1/190	2900				
Strickler				1300	4329	1647	Thwaites 1959 XXXIII: 129
Oscar Leibhart	221,000	1/190	1200				
Oscar Leibhart				300	1000	1671	Thwaites 1959 LVI: 57
Piscataway				75	250	1675	Hanna 1911: 51
Byrd Leibhart	163,000	1/190	900				
Iroquois towns (captives)				100	333	1681	Maryland Archives XVII: 5
Conestoga				40	132	1697	Maryland Archives XIX: 519-20
Conestoga				20	67	1729	Colonial Records III: 365
Conestoga					39	1756	Pennsylvania Archives 1 II: 242
Conestoga					43	1757	Pennsylvania Archives 8 VI: 4874
Conestoga					22	1763	Colonial Records IX: 101-3

* Note: Total, when based upon warrior counts, is computed by using a multiplier of 3.3.

For the Strickler site we found that the ratio of persons per square foot of village area could have been up to 190 square feet. Assuming that the degree of housing density decreased between Schultz and Strickler times, we have taken it upon ourselves to compute one more average—one person to 147 square feet density for those Susquehannock towns which existed between Schultz and Strickler. It was this formula which was used to estimate populations at the Washington Boro village site and the Roberts site (see Table 22 for a summary of population estimates).

We realize and admit to the highly subjective nature of the estimating techniques used here. They are dependent upon quite variable and uncertain numbers, including village size (which has *only been estimated* for all sites discussed), numbers of houses per area of enclosed village, sizes of houses, and concomitantly, numbers of families in each and numbers of persons per family. Given all these variables, the estimated totals can be exceedingly variable. We leave it to the reader to decide the utility of these population estimates.

A highly representative portion of the population which once inhabited the village at the Strickler site was interred there. Three separate cemeteries are known to exist at three corners of the village, as shown on Figure 98. A few vague reports of burials encountered through farming activities suggest the possible existence of a fourth cemetery at the northwest corner of the village.

Death rates for primitive societies are variously defined, depending upon a wide variety of factors. Cook (1972: 37), for example, suggests that a figure of 25 deaths per thousand per year might be used in some instances. If we apply this death rate to our approximately three thousand population at Strickler, it would mean perhaps 75 deaths per year. Over the 20-year occupation (1645-1665) which we have posited for Strickler, this would mean fifteen hundred deaths. It is not possible to account for that number of interments at Strickler. However, half that number may well have been encountered by the various excavations, professional and otherwise, at the site.

Burials

The typical burial at Strickler was approximately 25 inches deep (from the topsoil surface). Pit shapes can generally be likened to that of a bathtub, the average horizontal dimensions being 65 inches in length and 30 inches in width. Overall, the largest number of interments were flexed, lying on either the right side, left side, or in a position of supine flexure. In the introduction to this volume, we noted a *possible* contemporary account of burials at this site by George Alsop (Hall 1910: 370) which *may* account for those few flexed or collapsed burials which seem to be crowded into one end of the pit. The suggestion was that some persons were placed in a sitting, upright posture, in a grave pit which was not immediately filled, and that the decay and collapse of the skeleton caused the crowding at one end of the pit. In Cemetery #2, at least (Heisey and Witmer [1962] reported none for Cemetery #3), 23% of the interments were supine extended. One or two percent can be described as "placed bone" or bundle burials. The vast majority in all cemeteries were oriented in a westerly (between southwest and northwest) direction, i.e., with the head at the west end of the grave pit. Multiple burials of two to three bodies are recorded for the site, but again the vast majority are single interments. One gets the impression that the burials had some sort of markers, because of the high density of grave pits in the cemeteries and the general paucity of burials interrupted by subsequent interments.

For Cemetery #2 the following age and sex data were recorded, where such determinations could be made on the skeletal material: male, 10; female, 13; child, 27; adolescent, 12; adult, 94. Very few pathologies of any consequence were noted; this is definitely a function of the generally poor bone preservation at this site.

Grave offerings at Stricker consist of virtually every kind of material item made by, or which came into the hands of, the Susquehannocks. These items can be found almost anywhere within the grave pit. There are certain general tendencies, such as kettles at the knees or lower legs, but there were no hard-and-fast rules governing the placement of anything. The specific kinds of objects found here have been described elsewhere in this volume, as has the cultural significance of these material items.

Differences among the three major cemeteries at Strickler are difficult to quantify. Cemetery #2 is clearly the largest, and *apparently* the richest in terms of the variety and amount of trade material and native-made burial furniture. Although we cannot document it, it seems unlikely that the interment of a deceased person in one or the other of the cemeteries was a matter of random choice. Factors influencing the choice of a cemetery *may* relate to clan affiliation. The use of the cemeteries may also be a factor of time, e.g., one may be early and the others later; but again, this has not been discernible, only speculated upon.

Very few burials were made inside the village stockade. A small cluster of graves was previously noted east of the NO-EO point. All of the burial pits encountered by excavation in 1968 and 1969 inside the stockade are shown on Figure 98. The most unusual of these was located in square N21-E10, and consisted of an adult skeleton minus its skull, its lower arms, and its lower legs. On the floor of the grave, under the left femural head, was an iron axe. The pit was filled with village midden. Clearly this individual had been dismembered, with, it is tempting to say, the axe that accompanied the remains!

Overview

Excavations at Strickler, and examination of historic documents relating to the place, give us a fairly good picture of death, as well as life, at this Susquehannock town. We have previously suggested, based upon types of trade goods and the historic records, that the site was probably occupied from about 1645 to 1665. It would appear that it was the sole village of the Susquehannocks during that period. This was clearly the period of the height of Susquehannock political and economic power. Effects of acculturation were becoming much stronger at this time, and indeed, changes in native culture were occurring at an increasing rate.

A general picture of day-to-day life in this very large (for its time and place) and very crowded village is not too difficult to paint. Trading parties and war parties were constantly coming and going. Almost every day some men would leave the village to hunt or fish, just as women would travel to and from the agricultural fields, the berry patches or the wood lots. One might expect to see a funeral procession every four or five days. People ate, slept, worked and played in and about their dark, smokey, crowded longhouses. The by-products of these activities were frequently dropped, where they became waste. Dogs, children and the shuffling feet of hundreds of Indians would crush and scatter the debris; much of it, one way or another, wound up in the abandoned food-storage pits.

On a few rare occasions white men came to the village, and on at least one occasion, in 1663, it was unsuccessfully attacked by eight hundred or more Iroquois warriors. By about 1665 sickness and warfare had substantially reduced the Susquehannock population. The town and its buildings were literally worn out. Its corn, bean and squash fields were exhausted. The wood lots were far from the village. Clearly it was time to establish a new, smaller town in the hope of commencing a better life for the community.

Oscar Leibhart Site

The Oscar Leibhart (or Upper Leibhart) site (36Yo9) is located in Lower Windsor Township, York County, Pennsylvania. It is situated on a hilltop from which all sides slope sharply downward. To the north and south are streams which empty into the Susquehanna River. The hilltop is approximately nine hundred feet west of the river, and some one hundred feet above it. Soil on the site is classified as Conestoga silt loam, a moderately productive soil (Hersh 1963).

During the first quarter of the present century, the site was owned by John Haines (see Landis 1910: 114), who did a limited amount of digging there. After about 1929 Oscar Leibhart, the next owner (until 1975), did considerable digging on the site.

According to Landis' notes (Landis n.d.), Charles Leibhart, a brother of Oscar, dug 26 graves on the south side of the "fence line" at the Oscar Leibhart site. Landis made notes on the materials in both Leibhart collections. Charles unfortunately also dug on the Byrd Leibhart site; it is possible therefore that Landis could not tell the provenience of all the material which he saw in Charles's collection. Digging was sporadic during the 1940's and early 1950's. In 1956 Fred Kinsey and the Lower Susquehanna Chapter of the Society for Pennsylvania Archaeology were given permission by Oscar Leibhart to undertake limited excavations on the site to search for the stockade (Kinsey 1957: 180-81).

Kinsey's work apparently stimulated renewed interest in digging among the Leibhart family. This time it was Oscar's son, Donald Leibhart. He removed and kept some minimal records on the contents of at least one hundred graves, during and after the period when Kinsey was working at the site. We note parenthetically that the area churned over by Donald Leibhart at that time is visible on the York County Soil Survey map (Hersh 1963: sheet no. 21).

Kinsey's excavations were limited by the Leibharts to the complete exposure of a single longhouse. This structure (Kinsey 1957: 180-81; see also Figure 103) measured 24 by 92 feet. Its floor plan shows that there were several pits located just inside the long walls of the house. As noted earlier, this arrangement was more characteristic of Washington Boro- or Schultz-period houses, and less common at Strickler.

Materials recovered by Kinsey in the topsoil and from postmolds and pits include three kaolin pipestems (all of which are impressed with the fleur-de-lis and have stem hole measurements of $\frac{7}{64}$ inch), four gunflints (three native and one Clactonian), two musket balls (.61 and .65 caliber), two brass triangular points, two native pipestems, about a dozen glass beads (primarily red straw beads), some iron and brass scraps, several side-notched projectile points, and about one hundred potsherds, some of which are Strickler Cord-marked, but the majority of which are local Early Woodland types.

During this period Donald Leibhart dug a burial pit which contained a complete (reconstructable) Point Peninsula Early Woodland pot (about 18 inches high); a tubular (tapered) pipe of serpentine (measuring eight and one-half inches in length), with its pebble plug inside; a pop-eyed birdstone of banded slate (measuring seven inches); two slate gorgets, one with two holes and one with three holes; several side-notched points of Onondaga chert; five cache blades or blanks of unweathered rhyolite; and, according to Leibhart, several disc shell beads. This unusual burial, together with the rather abundant interior-exterior cord-marked pottery scattered over the site, is ample evidence of the significant Early Woodland occupa-

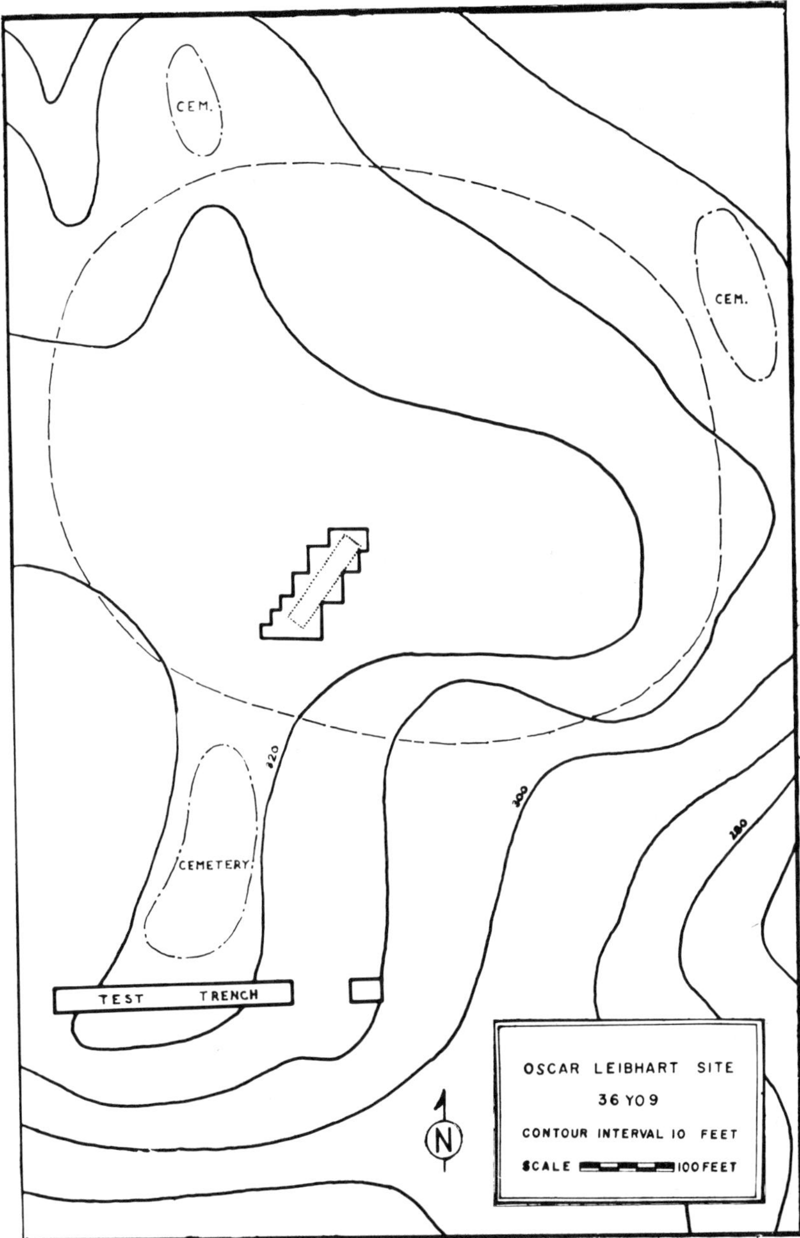

Figure 103. Oscar Leibhart site. Note longhouse excavated by Kinsey (1957), and assumed line of stockade.

tion there. Archaic projectile points are also very much in evidence from the surface collections.

The major collections from this site, all gathered by members of the Leibhart family, have been examined and recorded by several observers. As previously indicated, D. H. Landis (n.d.) recorded items in both the Oscar and Charles Leibhart collections. In 1956 Kinsey (WPMM photo files) photographed and made notes on what then remained of the Oscar Leibhart collection. Sometime during the 1950's John Witthoft (n.d.a) examined Oscar's collection and that of his brother, whom Witthoft mistakenly called Horace Leibhart. Both the Charles and Oscar Leibhart collections have since been dispersed; a few of Oscar's specimens are in the Donald Leibhart collection. Portions of the Donald Leibhart collection were shown to the writer in July, 1979; all of the items seen were recorded and photographed.

There are some discrepancies between the Landis, Kinsey and Witthoft descriptions of the Oscar and Charles Leibhart collections. Landis, for example, mentions a native-made pot with five legs, and apparently with strap handles, which he observed in the Charles Leibhart collection in 1933. He also mentions an apostle spoon. Neither of these specimens was noted by other observers. Witthoft (n.d.a) mentions a bellarmine jug and several case bottles; these were not recorded by the other observers. Kinsey (Witthoft and Kinsey 1959: 95) records that, of the 21 pots which he saw in the Oscar Leibhart collection, 33% were Washington Boro Incised, and 62% were Strickler Cord-marked. The remaining 5% he called Schultz Incised. Witthoft's notes list only Strickler Cord-marked. Donald Leibhart claims to have about 25 pots in his collection; however, we were not able to examine them and thus no percentage counts are possible. Kinsey and Landis both illustrate a brass candlestick from the "Chief's grave" near the south side of the site. This specimen is currently at the York County Historical Society. It may well be that the differences recorded by the various observers reflect the periods during which the collections were examined as well as the various sales of items by the Leibharts.

The notes of Landis, Witthoft and Kinsey all indicate that the Leibharts had dug graves on the south side of the site on property presently owned by the Safe Harbor Water and Power Company. The William Penn Memorial Museum was granted permission to conduct excavations in that area in the summer of 1973. A 220-foot by 10-foot trench and several lateral trenches were excavated, but not a single feature was discovered (see Figure 103). If nothing else, these test trenches demonstrated that the site did not extend that far south. It is clear, however, that the southern margin of the cemetery excavated by the Leibharts was only a few feet farther north across the property line.

Using the reconstructed notes of various persons, it would appear that the Susquehannock burials here were arranged in the same general fashion as those observed on other Susquehannock sites—basically with the head to the west-northwest, and generally in a flexed position. According to a personal communication from Donald Leibhart, he observed 10 bundle, 30 extended, and 60 flexed burials.

Based largely upon information received from Oscar Leibhart, Kinsey was able to develop a map of the site showing the various cemetery locations. Assuming that this site follows the same general pattern observed in other Susquehannock towns, its cemeteries were located *outside* the rounded corners of its stockade. Since nowhere have we found a longhouse outside a Susquehannock stockade, we can also assume such for this site. No stockade was actually recorded by any of the excavators at this site. However, Oscar Leibhart told Landis that the stockade holes and "charred posts" were found during plowing at several localities on the slopes surrounding the hill on which the site is situated. By interpolation, using the positions of the recorded cemeteries, the longhouse excavated by Kinsey, and the topography of the site, we have drawn a hypothetical stockade line. The area which it encloses is approximately 221,000 square feet. Using the persons-per-square-foot-of-village-area ratio developed elsewhere in this volume, we obtain a population guess of twelve hundred persons. We have previously noted that the Jesuit account (Thwaites 1959 LVI: 57) of 1671 which records three hundred warriors (or one thousand people) probably pertains to this site. It has also been postulated that this was the site shown on the Herrman map of 1670, which depicts a stockade surrounding eight longhouses with north-south axes, arranged in two rows.

That the Susquehannocks, at this time and place, had fallen on hard times, both politically and economically, is clearly recorded by contemporary accounts. In fact conditions seem to have been so bad as to become manifest in a rather substantial decimation of their population. These declining conditions also seem to be reflected by the reduced size of this site and the lesser quantities of trade materials interred with the dead.

Except perhaps for glass beads, there is a noticeable decline, as compared to Strickler, in all items of European manufacture. This almost certainly is symptomatic of their increased conflict with the Europeans and the Iroquois, the loss of the control which they had exercised in the fur trade, and the epidemics of disease which they suffered.

The final historical event involving the Susquehannocks at this town was their abandonment of the place in 1674, due apparently to a military defeat suffered at the hands of the Iroquois.

BYRD LEIBHART SITE

Four thousand feet due south of the Oscar Leibhart site lies the Lower or Byrd Leibhart Susquehannock town. It too is on a hilltop some one hundred feet above the Susquehanna and about eight hundred feet from the river's present western shore. Before construction of the Safe Harbor Dam, the distance to the river's edge here at Long Level may have been several hundred feet greater. That additional area of once-fertile alluvial soils, now inundated by the Safe Harbor backwater, was probably the location of some of the land farmed by the Susquehannocks.

Witthoft and Kinsey (1959) mistakenly called this the *Bert* Leibhart site; and for reasons which are not entirely clear, they accepted as its official trinomial number 36Yo170. This number had been arbitrarily and unofficially assigned to the site by George Boyd, an amateur archeologist from York, Pennsylvania.

In our opinion, and it is hardly more than that, the earliest possible historical reference to this Susquehannock town is in the *Maryland Archives* (XV: 126) for 1676, wherein the Council mentions the *new fort* which the Susquehannocks had built.

During the course of William Penn's petition to King Charles II for a grant of land in American north of Lord Bȧltimore's Maryland province, agents for Lord Baltimore issued a statement in 1680 which referred to what should have been this same Susquehannock fort: Mr. Penn's land "shall lie North of Sasquehannah Fort . . . for that Fort is the boundary of Maryland Northward" (Pennsylvania Archives, 8th series I: xiii-xiv). This statement became a major issue in the dispute over the boundary line between Pennsylvania and Maryland, and was not resolved for almost 75 years. Testimony from expert witnesses produced by the Penns placed a Susquehannock fort at the mouth of Octoraro Creek. Maryland witnesses generally spoke of a fort much higher up on the west side of the River.

With the advantage of three hundred years of historical and archeological hindsight, it is our opinion that the *new fort* or the 1680 fort, which marked the boundary as stated by Maryland officials, was at the location which we now call the Byrd Leibhart site. Obviously, the Penns and their attorneys, who in essence won the dispute, did not agree, for the Mason-Dixon line, established in 1765 (Russ 1966: 21), was 16 miles south of this Indian fort.

During the height of the Penn-Calvert disputes over the boundary in the 1720's, Maryland issued a number of patents for land up to a point a short distance above the Byrd Leibhart site. It was certainly no accident that the first of these patents, issued to one Thomas Cresap for a tract called Pleasant Garden, included most of the fertile Long Level river shore and the adjacent hills *on which the Byrd Leibhart site is located.* It is probably

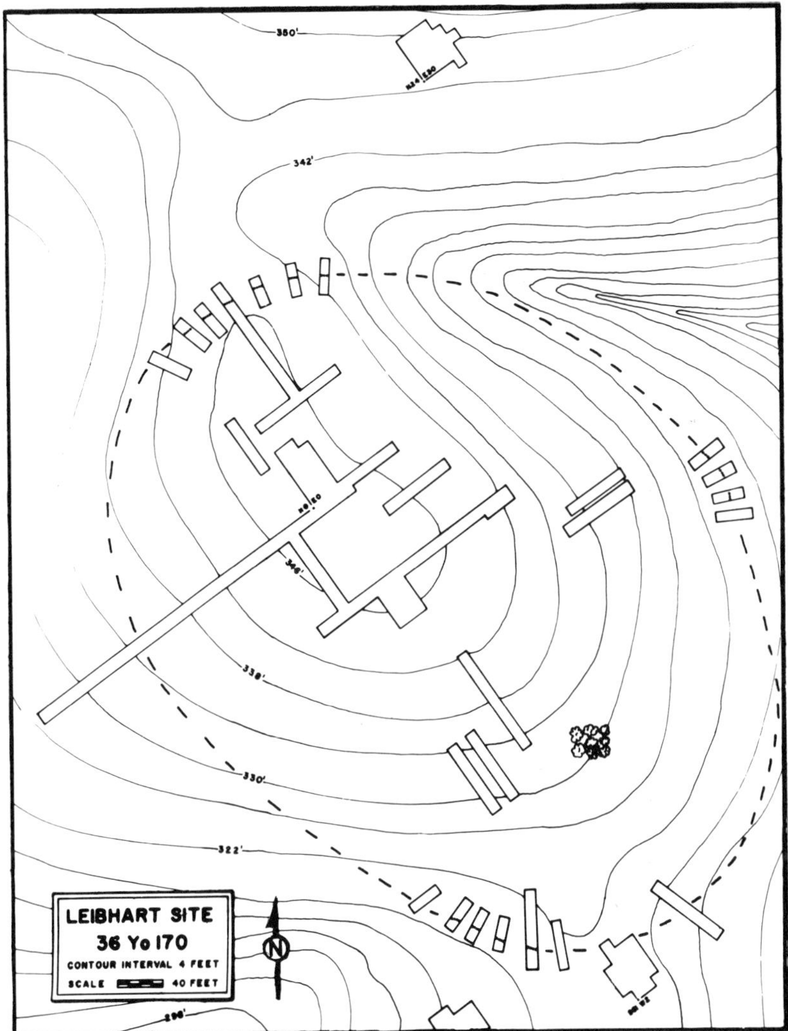

Figure 104. Map of the Byrd Leibhart site showing projected line of the stockade.

also no accident that one of the next patents issued was to Stephen Onion in 1729 for a tract called "Canhodah" that included the Upper or Oscar Leibhart site (see Maryland Hall of Records, Vol. PL#8, folio 93-94, Annapolis). Perhaps not so curiously, *Canhodah* is the Iroquois word for "town." All of this would seem to reflect very definite efforts on the part of Maryland to prove rights to lands as far north as the seventeenth-century Susquehannock towns on the west side of the river.

Earliest references, of which we are aware, to any collecting at the Byrd Leibhart site come, once again, from the D. H. Landis notes (n.d.). According to these notes, he and Albert Cook Myers visited the site in 1921, at which time Myers purchased a number of "trader articles" which a local boy had gathered on the fields about one hundred yards west of Byrd Leibhart's buildings. By at least 1930, various local persons were occasionally digging up graves at this site. According to Landis, David Graham of Craley, Pennsylvania, and Charles Leibhart dug two graves about "200 or 300 yards south of the old grave yard west of Byrd Leibhart's house." Then in October, 1933, Byrd plowed up some "Indian remains" just a few yards south of the old (Dritt) cemetery west of his house. In the month that followed, Byrd and David Graham started "digging Indian graves in partnership and they dug up about 80 graves." Byrd kept a map of sorts showing the grave-pit locations and orientations, together with a list of the "important" objects in each of 90 graves. Thanks to Landis (n.d.), a copy of the map and list made by Leibhart does survive. Landis (n.d.) also made some detailed drawings and descriptions of many of the objects.

Graham's portion of the collection eventually wound up in the Lauck's Farm Museum at Red Lion, Pennsylvania, and ultimately became the property of the York County Historical Society, where it is currently on exhibit and/or in storage. Byrd Leibhart's portion was eventually sold at auction, and most of it was purchased by E. Tshudy of Lancaster, Pennsylvania, in whose collection most of it still resides.

Prior to the time when Graham and Leibhart divided their findings, a newspaper photograph was taken of the entire collection. A copy of that photograph was found by the author with the original Landis notes and catalogues at the Hershey Museum. Figure 63 is a copy of that photograph made in 1973.

Occasional diggings continued at the site and various collections were sold and moved about. Gerald B. Fenstermaker, of Lancaster, photographed two of the three European ceramic vessels shown in Figure 78 while they were still in the possession of Byrd Leibhart. His original photograph appeared on the cover of the *Pennsylvania Archaeologist* (Vol. VII, no. 2, 1937). The largest vessel is most unusual, and unfortunately its present whereabouts is unknown.

In subsequent years Mr. George Keller of Long Level, who lived adjacent to the site, did a considerable amount of digging there. His collection was examined and partially photographed by the writer in August, 1970. As the result of a public sale in June, 1978, the Keller collection became widely dispersed. A large bear pipe was purchased by E. Bowser, of York, Pennsylvania. Most of the kaolin pipes, two latten spoons, and a brass vanity case dated 1634 were secured by the William Penn Memorial Museum.

The only formal excavations ever conducted at this site were those undertaken during July and August, 1970, by the Pennsylvania Historical and Museum Commission. Work here was done with the permission of Mrs. George T. Pack, then owner of the Lauxmont farms estate, on which the site was located. Five weeks were spent there with a bulldozer and a crew of four. Mr. Joseph Wallace, of Craley, Pennsylvania, and Mr. George Keller both provided useful information about areas of the site which might be most productively excavated.

Areas exposed in 1970 are shown on Figure 104. A major discovery was a single-line palisade composed of generally five- to six-inch diameter posts, set between four and twelve inches apart. On the south side of the village only, the palisade posts were set into a narrow trench. It was in this area where the postmolds were best preserved. No evidence of the stockade was found on the west side of the village, perhaps due to more severe erosion there. The various locations and alignments of stockade posts as recorded during these excavations, and as shown on Figure 104, suggest an oval outline for the total stockade, and an encompassed area of approximately 163,000 square feet. Using the population-estimating procedure developed elsewhere in this volume (see Table 22), we arrive at a figure of nine hundred persons for a Susquehannock village of this period and of these dimensions.

Storage pits were primarily saucer-shape in profile, although most of the other shapes observed at the Strickler site did occur at Byrd Leibhart's. Pits were most abundant in the center of the site and at its point of highest elevation. However, by comparison with the Strickler site, pits at Leibhart's could be considered to be relatively infrequent. A vast majority of those found in 1970 had been previously dug by local collectors. Those which were undisturbed generally did not contain very much bone or other artifactual refuse, although a few did. A number of burials were reported by local informants within the village proper. Several previously disturbed burial pits were encountered in 1970 near the center of the village.

There was also a paucity of postmolds within the village, especially as seen against the profusion of such features at the Strickler site. Undoubtedly there were longhouse patterns represented in the clusters of postmolds found in the larger excavations at the center of the site. Unfortunately none was readily discernible. Walls of at least two houses were recorded in trenches in the area of S15-E21 and in the parallel trenches around S24-EO. Again, no complete house outline was traceable. There was good evidence that houses had been erected toward the outer margins of the village (inside the palisades). It was noted that storage pits were less common toward margins of the village. These areas were also characterized by what *we* might consider an uncomfortable grade for housing of this sort. Interestingly, the alignment of the few identified house walls was east and west on the east side of the village and north and south on the south side. This is very suggestive of the radial arrangement observed at the Strickler site.

Outside the stockade there were at least four associated cemeteries. Locations of three of these are shown on Figure 104, as excavation plots. A fourth cemetery, reported by informants as being completely "dug out," was located in the area of N50-EO. The excavated area at N24-E30 was the cemetery excavated by Leibhart and Graham in 1933.

Body orientation could be established for at least 35 interments, even though many had been previously disturbed. All of these had a north to northwest head orientation, and the vast majority were northwest. Only four of the previously disturbed grave pits (in which no body orientation could be reconstructed) had pit alignments other than northwest. All four were northeast-southwest. Based on these data, the Byrd Leibhart site had the lowest percentage (4%) of any investigated Susquehannock site of grave alignments not in the northwest quadrant. This site also seems to exhibit the greatest tendency to arrange graves in rows. Depths and shapes of the grave pits are similar to those recorded at Strickler.

As in the other seventeenth-century Susquehannock sites, flexed burials were the most common form. Of the 34 interments for which observations could be made, only 8% were extended (and one of those three may be a Shenks Ferry burial). Six graves (or 17%) contained bundles or rearranged collections of human bones. The remaining 25 were flexed, although generally not very tightly. Many were supine, with knees bent to one side or the other. Approximately 23% of the interments for which determinations could be made were classed as adolescents.

From the various records of excavation at this site, it is possible to account for approximately two hundred interments. This would appear to be close to the total number. Elsewhere in this volume it was indicated (Cook 1972: 37) that a normal death rate is about 2.5% per year. The rates, of course, vary considerably, depending on a variety of other factors, not the least of which are economic conditions and the prevalence of disease. Our historical and archeological impressions are that these and other death-rate-increasing factors were *quite* prevalent at this time and place. Consequently, it seems reasonable for us to posit a much higher death rate for the occupants of this site. A 5% rate for the postulated nine hundred people here, over a period of four years, would mean 180 deaths. Our point is simply that as many as two hundred individuals could have died and been buried at his town during the proposed period of its occupation (1676-1680).

Graves at the Byrd Leibhart site contained noticeably fewer offerings as compared with Strickler, but perhaps somewhat more than those at Oscar

Leibhart's. Guns, now a hard-to-come-by item of necessity to the Indians, were very uncommon in the graves. As noted in our chapter on guns, votive offerings consisting of gun parts (and often pairs of parts) were placed in a fair number of graves at Byrd Leibhart's.

Only four types of items occur here with a noticeably greater frequency than at Strickler. These include European ceramics, kaolin pipes, miscellaneous iron tools (but not axes or knives), and gun parts. The relatively large quantity of the latter may be largely accounted for by the contents of a single grave excavated by Leibhart and Graham. Latten and pewter spoons were also relatively abundant, but not quite so numerous as at Strickler. These increases may well reflect the generally greater availability at this time of such relatively common—or even worthless—items to Indians and colonials alike. More expensive and more useful items, such as guns, axes, knives and liquor (bottles), although readily available at this time, were far more precious (difficult to acquire) to these Susquehannocks in their vastly declined economic and political state. In other words, their ability to control or even to participate in the trade with the Europeans had been markedly reduced.

One item of native manufacture in which this site also seems to have exceeded the others is foreign Indian-made ceramic vessels. At least two Madisonville-like vessels (at least upper Ohio Valley types), one with loop handles, were illustrated by Landis (n.d.). Another was found by the Museum's field crew during 1970 in the southeast cemetery (Figure 105). This latter vessel was in a grave with a very rare black-flint, French blade-style gunflint. This grave also exhibited the earliest recorded use of a coffin (or wooden box without nails) at a Susquehannock site; wooden planks were found above and below the skeleton. The pedestaled pot (also from the southeast cemetery) illustrated in Figure 105 may also have Ohio Valley (Madisonville) relationships (see Hooton 1920: plate 24).

We are tempted to equate the occurrence of these foreign (western Indian) pottery types with the statement in the *Maryland Archives* (XV: 122) for 1676

> that they [the Susquehannocks] shortly expect the remainder of their troopes, and so many of the *Western Indians neer or beyond the Mountaines* as they have been able to persuade to come to live with them.

Totally unrelated to the Susquehannock occupation of this site is a wide scattering over the area of Shenks Ferry Incised and Cord-marked pottery. A fairly large quantity of these potteries was recovered from a long, irregular, rather deep, trench-like midden in the southwestern cemetery. Three separate grave pits had been dug into this earlier feature, two of which were positively of Susquehannock derivation. The third, an extended interment without grave furniture, was probably a product of the Shenks Ferry occupation on this hill.

Figure 105. Pedestaled pot and Madisonville-like vessel, Byrd Leibhart site (36Yo170).

The *specific* character of certain trade items recovered from the Susquehannock component of the Byrd Leibhart site (e.g., kaolin pipes, a globular glass bottle, certain of the Rhenish stonewares, and some of the iron hardware) suggests a date of between 1660 and 1680. The *general* character of the cultural material found here is suggestive of a period of economic and political decline (e.g., the inability to properly furnish the graves of the deceased). Through the interpretation of the meager historical accounts pertaining to Susquehannocks of this period, coupled with the *general* and *specific* nature of the artifacts from this town, we have postulated that they coincide with the Susquehannock reoccupation of the area two years after their defeat in 1674. Unfortunately, all of the digging of which we are aware at this site has not produced a precisely dated object which would enable us to place it in the period 1676 to 1680.

What became of the Susquehannocks in the 10-year period after 1680 is historically rather uncertain, and archeologically unknown. We do know that during this period many of them were living among the Iroquois in New York. In May, 1680, it was recorded that about three hundred Sinniquo (Seneca) and Susquehannocks had built a fort some five hundred yards from a Piscataway Indian fort in Maryland (Maryland Archives XV: 280). Clearly this fort was not intended as a residence, but rather a place from which the Seneca and Susquehannocks could harass their old enemies, the Piscataway, an endeavor which they variously pursued for some time.

An actual place at which we can study the archeological remains of the Susquehannocks after about 1680 and prior to 1690 has not yet been identified. Investigation of their place of residence after that date is the subject of our next site report.

CONESTOGA TOWN

Conestoga (Quanistagua), as a village name in the lower Susquehanna Valley, first appears among the colonial records in 1696. The first mention of its specific location (Carristauga) is in the deposition given to the Maryland authorities by the trader John Hans Tillman in 1697. As previously indicated, the Augustine Herrman map of 1670 shows the word *Onestoga R.* as the name of the river which has since become known as the Conestoga. We have suggested elsewhere that it was considerably after 1670, but before 1696, when the Indian town of Conestoga was established in Lancaster County. We have arbitrarily set the date of its inception at 1690.

William Penn's journey to Conestoga Town in 1700 was the first official visit to the place. In the years following, the location of the town was well known to the many governmental officials and traders who traveled there. In 1717 the Pennsylvania Land Commissioners ordered the Surveyor Gen-

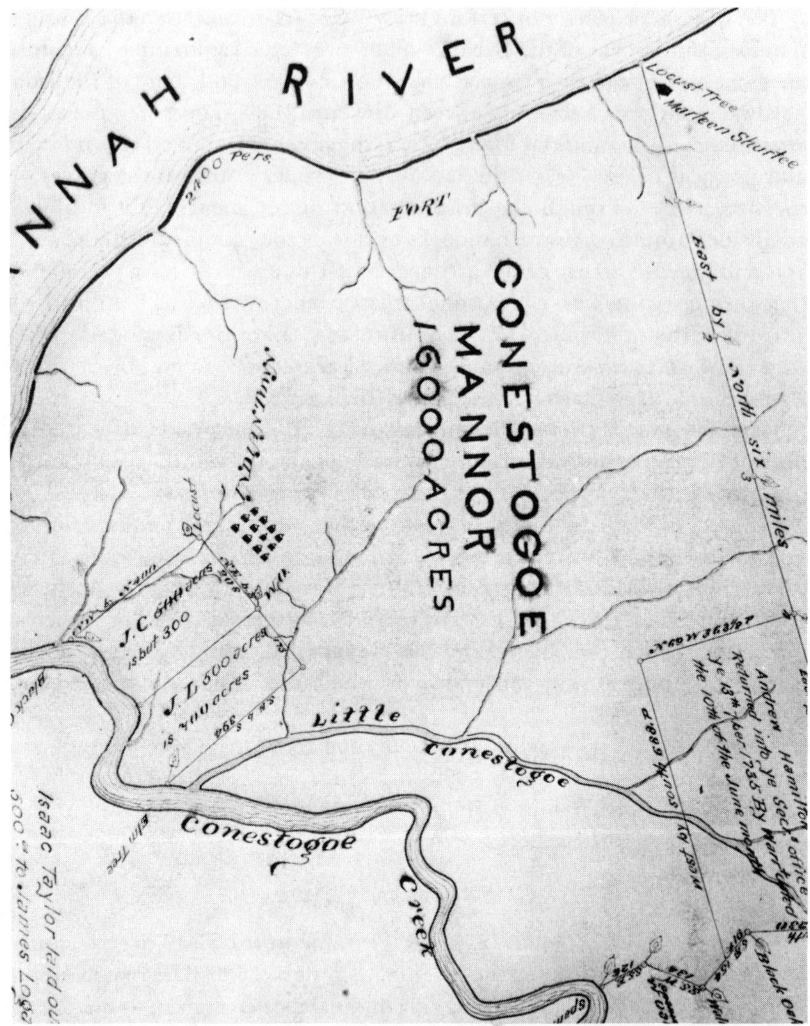

Figure 106. Survey of Conestogoe Mannor from the original done in 1717, showing "Indian Town" (Conestoga); "Marteen Shurtee" (Chartier's place); and "Fort" (Strickler site). North is to the right.

eral to lay out, for the Proprietors, a manor in the area of Conestoga Town. The Jacob Taylor map (Figure 106) of the surveyed Manor of Conestoga (Pennsylvania Archives, 3d series IV: Conestoga No. 1) clearly shows, for the first time, the location of the Indian town situated therein. Today the area of Conestoga Manor falls within what is defined as Manor Township, Lancaster County. Historians have not forgotten that the manor included the Indian town, but its precise location was largely a matter of conjecture.

Shortly after the turn of the present century, David H. Landis (n.d.) discovered the scattered remains of several collections of artifacts gathered from graves which were exposed by farming activities on what he called the Dr. Hiestand (Breneman) farm. Landis' description of the materials which he saw (and some which he purchased for his own collection) is clearly of eighteenth-century items, and would therefore seem to confirm their association with Conestoga Town.

In 1924 the Pennsylvania Historical Commission and the Lancaster County Historical Society erected a monument near the site of Conestoga. The plaque on the massive native-stone marker reads:

> THE CONESTOGA INDIANS IN ORIGIN LARGELY THE SURVIVORS OF THE DEFEATED ANCIENT SUSQUEHANNAS OR MINQUAS OF IROQUOIAN STOCK LOCATED THEIR VILLAGE VARIOUSLY ON THESE LANDS IN THE PENN PROPRIETARY MANOR OF CONESTOGA CHIEFLY WEST OF THIS POINT. THEY WERE VISITED HERE IN 1701 [*sic*] BY WILLIAM PENN WHO MADE TREATIES WITH THEM. THE TRIBE WAS EXTERMINATED BY THE PAXTON BOYS IN 1763.

In his address at the dedication ceremony for the marker, D. H. Landis (1924: 132-36) noted the locations of three Indian sites, each of which he thought represented a different phase of occupation at Conestoga. One of these, located about four hundred yards west of the marker, is the only confirmed Conestoga settlement. Others probably do exist.

Following the placement of the marker near the site, very little attention was paid to the place, until it was literally rediscovered in 1950 by Sam Farver and John Witthoft. It was at this time that the site was labeled 36La52. Farver excavated one grave at the site which contained so little in the way of burial furniture that it led Witthoft to postulate that the Conestoga were so impoverished as to be unable to afford any burial offerings for their dead.

Once again activity at the site subsided, and it was not until 1967 that there was any renewed interest in the remains of Conestoga Town. At that time, an amateur archeologist from Gettysburg, Pennsylvania, with the permission of the site owners, Mr. and Mrs. L. Witmer, excavated five burials. Subsequently, and continuing into 1968, the owners of the site excavated an additional eight burials. The notes, photographs, and an examination of the artifacts from these excavations are all summarized or included in the present volume. Locations for the previously mentioned 13 interments are shown as empty pits on Figure 107.

It was not until the summer of 1972 that arrangements could be made for the Pennsylvania Historical and Museum Commission to undertake a major excavation here. Unlike the other known Susquehannock sites, Conestoga is far removed from any major (or minor) waterway (see Figure 4). It is curiously situated on a small hilltop some one thousand feet south of Indian Run and east of the promontory locally known as the Indian Round Top. The nearest water is a spring on the west slope of the site. Its soil is Pequea silt loam, which is shallow, well drained, and formed from dark calcareous schist. It grades into the underlying subsoil in such a subtle manner that it makes features or disturbances very difficult to distinguish. Between June and August, 1972, with the aid of a bulldozer and a crew of four, an area of approximately thirty-two thousand square feet was cleared of topsoil, flatshoveled, and mapped (see Figure 107). The resulting discoveries were about a half-dozen storage pits, three houses, as defined by postmold patterns, and five separate small cemeteries.

Total plan dimensions of two of the houses at Conestoga could be determined. The larger measured 15 feet by 50 feet, and the other was 15 feet by 35 feet. Both ends of a third house could not be precisely determined, but it was 20 feet wide by at least 40 feet long. Postmolds in all three houses averaged five inches in diameter (somewhat larger than at earlier sites), and usually extended four inches into the subsoil. The average distance between the post holes was about 20 inches. Corners of the houses were very neat right angles.

Obviously the floor plan and the construction (size and spacing of post holes) had changed since the last major Susquehannock town had been built in the lower Susquehanna Valley. Houses at Conestoga were more cabin-like, and probably within the range of those descriptions given by Bartram (1751), Weiser in 1745 (Schoolcraft 1854 IV: 324-41), or perhaps even like those mentioned by Christian Frederick Post at Wyalusing in 1760, which were of frame construction covered with vertical planks planted upright in the ground (A. F. C. Wallace 1949: 228).

Similarly, the spacing of houses had also changed by Conestoga times. According to the journals of such observers as Bartram and Weiser, mid-eighteenth-century Indians not only had considerable space between individual houses, but clusters of houses were often scattered over many miles. Whether or not this was the case in the Conestoga vicinity is uncertain. The archeology would indicate that the interval between houses was greatly increased, as compared with seventeenth-century towns. We probably cannot place much credence in the sketch of the town on the Taylor map (Figure 106), but it shows a town of peak-roofed houses in regular rows. Typically, eighteenth-century Indian towns of Pennsylvania and New York were not surrounded by palisades; and none was found at Conestoga (see Kent et al. 1981: 3-4).

Only one or two of the storage pits discovered at Conestoga could definitely be attributed to that occupation. These contained a rare bead or iron scrap of the period. None of the pits had more than a few fragments of bone, an occasional kernel of charred corn, or other garbage; and some contained only a sherd or two of earlier Shenks Ferry pottery, which leaves considerable question as to their cultural affiliations. Several of the storage pits, albeit without identifiable artifacts, were deep (three to four feet into the subsoil), cone-shaped features, quite unlike any seen on earlier Susquehannock (or Shenks Ferry) sites.

It should come as no surprise that the Indians at Conestoga engaged in hunting and trapping, and that they raised corn and other crops in their nearby fields. The colonial records contain many lists of animal skins which the Indians sold, traded or gave to various parties. For example, at a council held at Philadelphia in 1729 (D. Kent 1979: 321-22) the Conestogas were given, among other items, "Rum, Bread, Cheese, Bacon, Tobacco and Pipes." The Indians in return gave the Lieutenant Governor, Patrick Gordon,

72 fall Deer skins, Weighing			287 pounds
79 Summer	Do. —	—	142
108 Drest	Do. —	—	119
3 Beavers	Do. —		
17 Raccoons, 3 Foxes, and 6 Catts			

We note, as this list underscores, that the flourishing beaver trade was a thing of the past.

An historic document relating to the Indian cornfields at Conestoga is of itself not unusual, except that in this case it refers to a fence erected around their cornfields by John Cartledge, whose tract adjoined the Indian Town in 1717, presumably to keep out the cattle of local white settlers (Pennsylvania Archives 1852, III: 48). That the Conestogas occasionally ate beef is recorded in the archival documents and by the archeology relating to this place: the only large fragment of bone recovered from a pit at the site is from a cow.

Based upon the distribution of artifacts on the surface, and as a result of test-trenching over the hill on which the site is situated, it would seem that this particular Conestoga settlement was confined to an area of less than ninety thousand square feet. The archeological data from within this area are not sufficient to warrant our making any population estimates. However, we might guess a figure of somewhere between one and two hundred souls for this Conestoga town "area" at the peak of population.

In 1697 John Hans Tillman (Maryland Archives XIX: 519-20) reported to the Maryland Assembly that there were "40" lusty young men besides women and children" living at Conestoga. Using the Mook (1944: 193-208) and the Feest (1973: 66-79) ratio of three warriors ("lusty young men") to

10 other persons in the community, we would derive a 1697 population at Conestoga of about 130 people.

Other historical indications of Conestoga's population are rather few and far between. In 1728 (Pennsylvania Archives 1852 III: 302), two Conestoga Indians were killed by Shawnees. Shortly thereafter, John Wright, who lived in what is now the Columbia area, wrote to James Logan to report that the Conestogas were greatly incensed by these murders and that he met 17 or 18 Conestoga men "painted for war" and apparently going against the Shawnee. This is not necessarily the total number of warriors at Conestoga; however, it seems likely that most would have joined this war party.

In 1729 (Pennsylvania Archives 1852 I: 240), the Conestoga Chief Civility reported that "we have sent *all* our young brisk men accompanied with some Delawares and Conoys in all near *thirty* men in order to Look outt and see if they can find any of the Southern Indians." This more clearly implies a warrior population at Conestoga of less than 30.

A treaty of 1730 was consummated with presentations by the Provincial government to the Conestoga of 20 matchcoats and 20 shirts (Pennsylvania

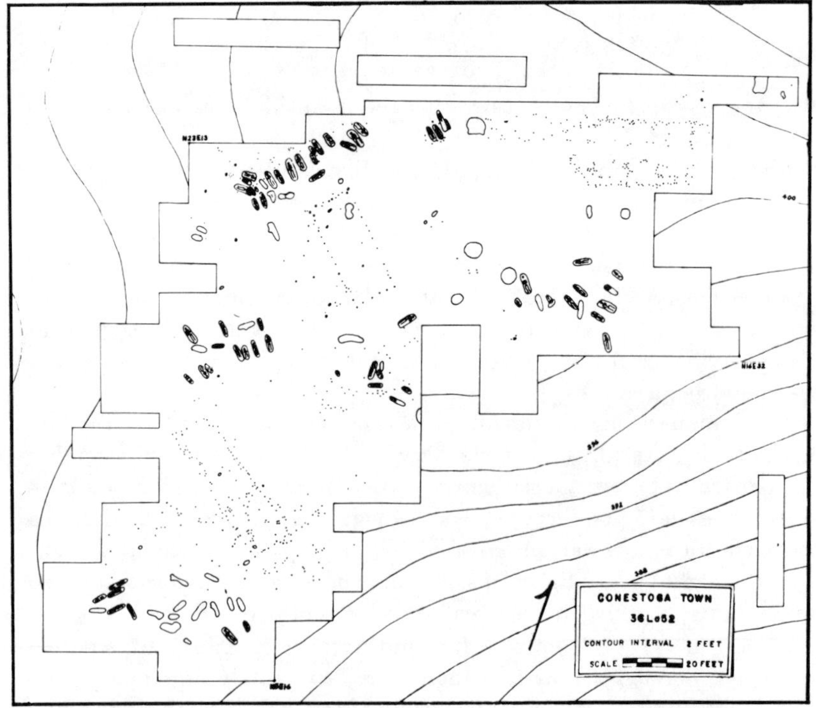

Figure 107. Map of excavations at Conestoga Town (36La52). Note houses and clusters of graves.

Archives 1852 III: 361). Similarly, in 1728 a treaty was confirmed with the presentation of 20 matchcoats, 20 duffels, 20 blankets, and 20 shirts (see D. Kent 1979: 287). It is most tempting to suggest that one of each item was given to each warrior at Conestoga.

The indication is that, during this period (1728-1730), Conestoga comprised about 20 warriors. Using the Mook ratio, this would translate to about 60 people in the community (see Table 22).

The *Pennsylvania Archives* (1852 VII: 507) notes that in 1757 Captain "Sahays" and 29 men, women and children of Conestoga were present at the meeting of the Six Nations at Harris' Ferry. Eshleman (1909: 368) states that he believed this was practically the whole tribe at this time. We find (thanks to William A. Hunter) in the *Pennsylvania Archives* for 1755 (1st series 1852 II: 242; see also unpublished archives, PHMC, Papers of the Provincial Council, card 1062, 1063, dated March 2, 1756) the names of 39 Indians of "Connestogoe":

Present at the Treaty in Lancaster	*Indians of Conestogoe Town not at the Treaty*
Jo: Hays	Old Peggy
John	old Molly
Billy Sock	Peggy Tillehanzey
Peter	Jammy Wright
Billy Sam	Young Mary
Will: James	Young Margaret
Young Peter	Wawahnah
Will John	Kawnonsah
Geo: William	Serzy
Young Warriour	Sawateah
Isaac	Tuahahuhn
Harry	Quahawey Children
Jemmy Harris	Whaney
Billy Taylor	Kintasa
Betty	Hayenehs
Sally	Kaquaungush
Margaret	
Jemmy Sam (a child)	
Nancy	
Peggy	
Mary	
Young Billy	
Young Jo:	

It is interesting to note that only the children had their Indian, or non-Christian, names recorded in this instance.

On July 5, 1757 (Pennsylvania Archives, 8th series IV: 4874), there is mention of 43 Indians at Conestoga by John Ross, who was charging the Provincial government for support of these Indians for whom he had provided.

Approximately 90 separate interments can be accounted for as a result of various excavations at 36La52. Considering the amount of exposure here, it is unlikely that more than a hundred interments were made at this particular location. Given the usual Iroquoian proclivity for moving villages every 15 to 20 years or so, it is most unlikely that this village site (36La52) was occupied for the full 73 years during which the Conestoga lived in the general area. It is our intuitive feeling that this was the location first settled in about 1690. The latest datable objects recovered from the site are from about 1730. It is very probable that it was actually occupied, or at least used as a place of burial until about 1740.

In all probability the village was located, after 1740, at a springhead in some other nearby field. Landis (1924: 132-36), without any good evidence, felt that the site of the 1763 Conestoga town was on the (in 1924) Doerstler property, about three-fourths mile southeast of the 36La52 location.

On December 14, 1763, the site of the Conestoga's cabins was visited by two separate parties of white men. The first was a group of men later identified as the Paxton Boys. These persons ruthlessly murdered the six Indians who were at that time present in the Indian town, and then burned their cabins. The second party was led by the Lancaster County Coroner, Mathias Slough, who, in the company of 14 other men, went there to conduct an inquest into the "manner in which the same Six Indians came to their Death" (Pennsylvania Archives 1852 IV: 147-48). Presumably, the Coroner and his party buried the six Indians in a common grave near the place where their bodies were found. On December 27, 1763, the Lancaster County Sheriff, John Hay, wrote to Governor John Penn, indicating that Messrs. John Miller and Robert Beatty were holding in trust for the surviving Conestogas, then lodged in the Lancaster Work House, their personal belongings,

> to Witt: Three horses; two writings on parchment, one of which was the 1701 agreement between William Penn and the Indians inhabiting in or about Susquehanna River; three letters; a paper dated 1708, requesting the apprehension of Nicole Godin; and two wampum belts.

On that same day (December 27, 1763) Sheriff Hay, much to his dismay, found it necessary to send a second letter to the Governor, this time relating the murder of the 14 Conestogas *lodged in the workhouse for protection against the Paxton Boys* (Pennsylvania Archives 1852 IX: 101-103). The ultimate disposition of the material possessions of the Conestogas, held in trust for them, is not disclosed by the records. Those 14 who died in the workhouse were buried in the Lancaster potter's field.

Sheriff Hay (Colonial Records IX: 103-104) also recorded the names of the Conestogas killed at the town and in the workhouse at Lancaster.

at the town:	Their Indian Names:
Sheehays	Sheehays,
George	Wa-a-shen,
Harry	Tee-Kau-ley,
A son of Sheehays,	Ess-canesh,
Sally, an Old Woman,	Tea-wonsha-i-ong,
A Woman,	Kannenquas.
at the work House:	
Captain John	Kyunqueagoah,
Betty, his Wife	Koweenasee,
Bill Sack	Tenseedaagua,
Molly, his Wife	Kanianguas,
John Smith	Saquies-hat-tah,
Peggy, his Wife	Chee-na-wan,
little John, Capt. John's Son	Quaachow,
Jacob, a Boy	Shae-e-kah,
Young Sheehays, a Boy	Ex-undas
Chrisly, a Boy	Tong-quas
little Peter, a Boy	Hy-ye-naes
Molly, a little Girl	Ko-qoa-e-un-quas
a little Girl	Karen-do-uah
Peggy, a little Girl	Canu-kie-sung.

Probably none of the burials at 36La52 relates to the first massacre, and indeed, it is unlikely that this was the place where it occurred. The five separate clusters of graves show minor differences. That which is easternmost on Figure 107 contained objects which were generally, but not unequivocally, earlier than the rest. Several of the clusters seem to exhibit a spatial relationship to a nearby house. Perhaps such a relationship did exist, since the various grave clusters are scattered throughout the living area, rather than being confined to prescribed areas at the margins of the village.

Most of the interments were in a supine extended position. A few were rolled more or less to one side, with the knees slightly bent. Eleven bundle burials were recovered, probably representing persons who died away from the village and whose remains were later collected and transported to the village for burial near their relatives. Most of the burial pits were dug just large enough to accommodate the body, although a few did show evidence of a coffin burial. Depths below the original surface averaged about 24 inches. Sixty-nine percent were oriented with the head to the west-northwest. Six percent were southwest, 8% were southeast, and the remainder (17%) were between east and northeast. Age and sex distributions observed in 1972 were as follows: adult-8, adult female-10, adult male-13, undetermined-7, adolescent-16, infant-6, bundle-11.

Every previously undisturbed burial excavated had some sort of grave offering. This ranged from a few beads or a knife to thousands of glass beads and a great variety of other objects. Generally it was the adolescents who had the largest quantities of objects interred with them.

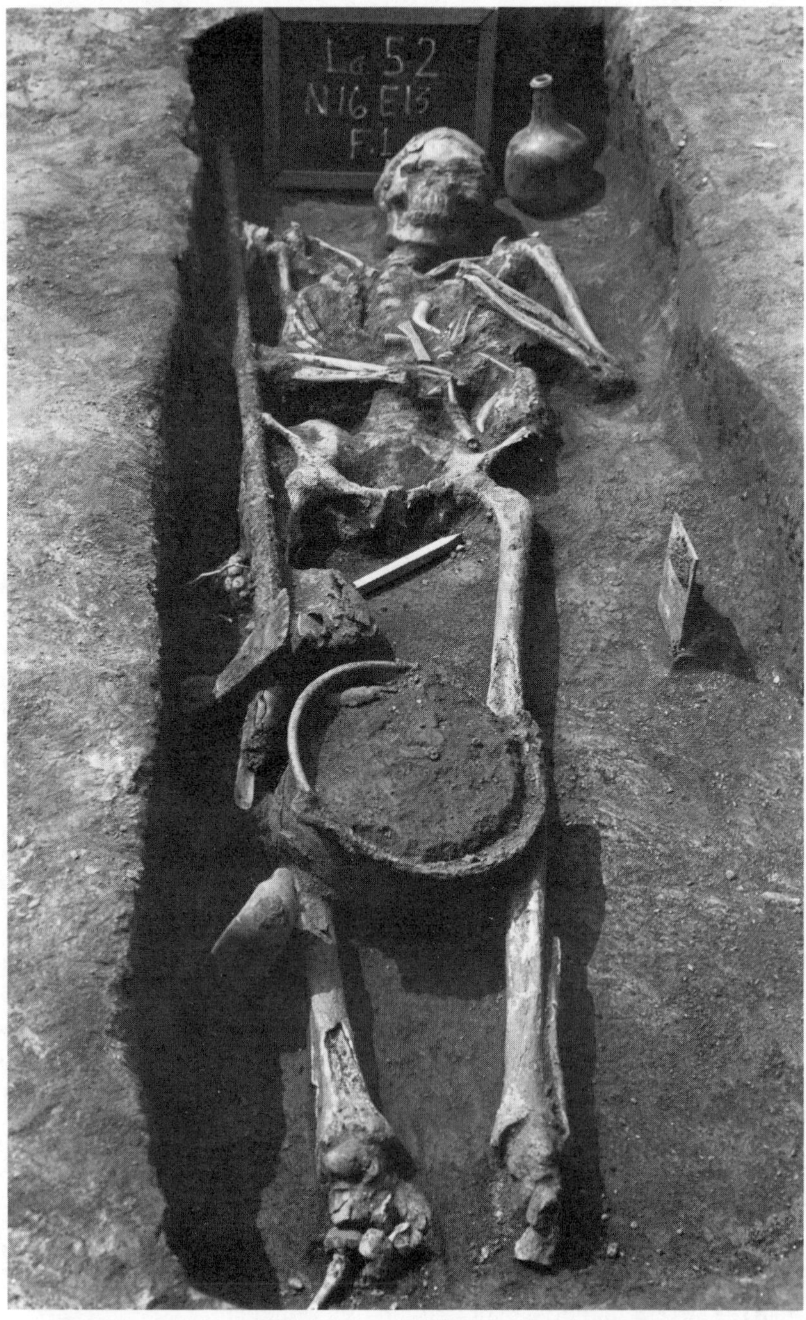

Figure 108. Typical extended burial at Conestoga Town (36La52).

Other than beads, iron knives were the most common items in the graves. These were both clasp and straight knives. Among the most common items were brass kettles, which were generally placed at or below the knees. Frequently, the kettles served as repositories for caches of other materials, but occasionally they contained food offerings, in which case they generally also included a wooden ladle or spoon.

Wooden spoons, and a few elaborate antler combs, were the most notable items of local Indian manufacture. Other Indian-made objects included shell beads, and perhaps runtees, although many of these may have been of colonial manufacture, as were the wampum beads. Obviously there was some woodwork (other than spoons), little of which survives. A few fragments of splint baskets or mats were found. Several small caches of stone projectile points appear to have been curios, since they included Archaic types as well as Seneca triangular points.

Some of the most outstanding Indian-made objects were pipes, beads, and pendants fashioned from red and orange Minnesota catlinite. There was little evidence that this material was worked locally. Instead, most of it appears to have come east in a flourishing trade of such items.

Probably the only locally made pieces in catlinite are four Iroquois false-face-like masquettes (Figure 38). Six Great Lakes area-made, catlinite calumet pipes were recovered at Conestoga. These bespeak the importance, and the widespread nature, of the calumet ceremony.

The balance of the material found at Conestoga, and by far the majority, was of European or colonial manufacture. Most of these items have been separately discussed in earlier chapters. However, a list of them seems pertinent here, since it reflects an accurate inventory of the nature of eighteenth-century Indian material culture:

glass beads
buttons
coins
medallions
metal spoons
kaolin pipes
gunflints
strike-a-lights
guns
gun parts
wampum
mirrors
glass bottles
bracelets
buckles
ceramics
cloth
shoes
metal crosses
metal rings
brooches
brass kettles
vanity boxes
tobacco boxes
wooden boxes
brass coils
silver ornaments
parchment
paint pigments
iron:
  knives
  axes
  pipe tongs
  scissors
  misc. tools
  hardware
leather items
pewter pipes
brass chains
gunpowder
bullets
lead bars

Not so surprisingly, this list of archeologically recovered materials reads very much like those colonial documents which account the items given to the Indians at the numerous treaties or land purchases, a good example of which is the list of materials given to the Delaware Indians in 1732 in exchange for their lands on either side of the Schuylkill River to the heads of its tributaries, and lying between Keekachtanemin Hills (Blue Mountain) and Lechaig Hills (South Mountain):

> . . . for and in consideration of twenty brass Kettles, one Hundred Strowdwater Matchcoats of two Yards each, One Hundred Duffel Ditto, One Hundred Blankets, One Hundred Yards of half Thicks, Sixty linnen Shirts, Twenty Hatts, Six made Coats, twelve pair of Shoos and buckles, Thirty pair of Stockings, three Hundred pounds of Gun Powder, Six Hundred pounds of Lead, Twenty fine Guns, twelve Gun Locks, fifty Tommyhocks or hatchets, fifty planting houghs, one Hundred and twenty Knives, Sixty pair of Scissars, one Hundred Tobacco Tongs, Twenty four looking Glasses, forty Tobacco Boxes, one Thousand Flints, five pounds of paint, Twenty four dozen of Gartering, Six dozen of Ribbon, twelve dozen of Rings, two Hundred Awl Blades, one Hundred pounds of Tobacco, four Hundred Tobacco Pipes, Twenty Gallons of Rum and Fifty Pounds in Money, to us in hand paid or secured to be paid by Thomas Penn, Esquire, one of the Proprietors of the said Province. . . . (Pennsylvania Archives, 1st series 1852 I: 344-47)

The various kinds of objects and their quantities found buried with the dead at Conestoga Town are indicative of the retention of certain old native beliefs, together with a cumbersome admixture of ideas borrowed from Christianity. In our opinion the kinds or quantities of objects do not reflect anything about individual status or economic condition of the community. A letter written by Bishop Cammerhof to Count Zinzendorf about his observations of an Indian funeral at Shamokin in 1748 describes very poignantly these conditions and the Indian meaning of burial offerings:

> Our brethren attend the funeral of the [Indian] child. Its mother showed them the child in the coffin with its presents viz: a blanket, several pairs of moccasins, buckskins for new ones, needle and thread, a kettle, two hatchets—one large and one smaller—to cut kindling wood, flint, steel and tinder, so that on its arrival in the *new country*, it could at once go to housekeeping. Besides, it was beautifully painted and had a supply of beans, corn and a calabash. The Indians thought it was cruel in us not to have supplied Hagen [a white man who died at Shamokin the year before] with all these things. . . . After the funeral she [the mother] came to our house with a quart tin which she gave to Sr. Mack, saying: "This had been my daughter's—keep it in remembrance of her." It is an Indian custom, that when one dies, not all of the effects are buried with it, but that some are reserved for distribution among the deceased ones friends. (Wallace 1945: 272-73)

Conestoga Town began largely as a refugee relocation center. During its heyday (if the relatively better years between 1700 and 1725 can be construed as such), there was some wealth which changed hands or passed through Conestoga Town as a result of the so-called Indian trade. Access to this trade was one of the reasons why some Seneca and Susquehannocks settled and continued to occupy this place. However, it was simply not Indian for any one individual to accumulate or control large amounts of goods.

During its first 30 years or so Conestoga Town was a place of considerable political importance. In essence, Conestoga was an Iroquoian town, and as such it was the nearest settlement of this important nation to the seat of Pennsylvania government. That, plus its considerable longevity of settlement, made Conestoga a convenient and popular place of meeting between the Provincial government and the various Indians with whom it *had* to deal.

As the colonial frontiers shifted, so did the significance of Conestoga Town as a trade and treaty center. After the first quarter of the eighteenth century, it fell into a state of rapid decline. Yet, in spite of the impoverished condition which overcame the place, some Indians continued to live there. The fact that it had become their home, protected, as it were, from the encroachments of white settlers by virtue of its location within one of the Proprietary manors, gave the Indians some reason to stay. An even better reason was the fact that the Proprietors encouraged them to remain at Conestoga through a program of government-financed welfare. Ostensibly this was an effort to maintain the Quaker tradition of fair play with the Indians—to keep the "Covenant Chain bright"—but covertly it was an attempt to maintain order and good relations with the more powerful Iroquois and western Indians through a token offering to the indigent local Conestogas.

Conoy Town and Cemetery

Conoy Town (36La57) is located on a prominent point of land on the south side of Conoy Creek a short distance from its mouth, in Conoy Township, Lancaster County. At the time of the most recent archeological investigations there (1970), parts of the site were separately owned by Vernon Hixon and the J. E. Baker Company. Both property owners kindly granted permission for the Pennsylvnia Historical and Museum Commission to conduct excavations on their land during the summer of that year.

Historical accounts and oral traditions pertaining to the site were accurate enough and sufficiently well known so that over the years many collectors have been aware of its location. S. S. Haldeman, who lived literally on one corner of the Conoy cemetery, collected on the village area in the mid-nineteenth century. Numerous collectors since that time have referred to the site as the bead patch.

Landis (1933) published the location of the site and as he notes, there is no doubt that this is the historically documented Conoy (or Piscataway) Indian town occupied from about 1718 to 1743. These dates for the occupation of Conoy Town are fairly well established by contemporary documents relating to these people and this place; these sources were fully discussed in our chapter dealing with the history of the Conoy Indians.

Sam Farver, a collector from Palmyra, Pennsylvania, was a frequent visitor to this site as his collection from there (now in the WPMM) attests. His knowledge of the site and relationship with its owner were instrumental in setting up the small-scale excavation conducted by John Witthoft of the Pennsylvania State Museum. Witthoft excavated several pits and one burial here, at what he called the Hixon site, in 1951. A broken bottle (Figure 59), broken animal bone, pipestems, and a number of Archaic and Woodland chipped-stone tools were recovered from the pits. The latter items were quite abundant on the site and they seem to have gotten into the fill of most of the pits dug there by later Indians. The burial produced a large quantity of blue tubular glass beads (over four hundred) and some of white (about fifty). According to Witthoft's notes (WPMM files), these tubular beads were part of a bracelet on the left wrist and were also from a necklace. The beads in the bracelet were strung four beads wide, with their long axis on the axis of the band (the opposite of a wampum belt).

Scattered burials which seem to have been contemporaries of the site have been found in various places throughout the nearby town of Bainbridge. A construction trench at John Lynn's butcher shop in Bainbridge produced a number of beads characteristic of the first half of the seventeenth century, a few teeth from an adolescent burial, and at least one large white, wire-wound bead like those known to occur on early eighteenth-century sites. As discussed under "Other Sites" in this volume, the association of this bead and the earlier types and the burial is uncertain.

Other isolated burials which are more clearly of the Conoy period and more likely to be of Conoy origins have been found on the nearby Mohr site (36La39, see collections at Temple University), and on the high field directly west across the creek from Conoy Town; the latter is according to unsubstantiated local tradition.

Conoy Cemetery (36La40)

On the second day of the museum's excavation at Conoy Town, in 1970, a local farmer reported that he had plowed out a number of burials in a field two hundred yards south of the Conoy village. Operations were temporarily shifted to this site (36La40) in the hope that it might prove to be a cemetery for the nearby Billmyer Susquehannock site. No Susquehannock material was found here; instead the museum's field crew located a small

Figure 109. A partially disarticulated burial (the skull is as found) at the Conoy cemetery (36La40).

stockaded Shenks Ferry village and at least seven Shenks Ferry burials. This site was subsequently reported upon as the Locust Grove Shenks Ferry site by Kinsey and Graybill (1971: 37-38) and Kent (1974: 1-5). A second component which overlapped the southern portion of this Shenks Ferry settlement turned out to be the major cemetery for Conoy Town. The portion of the site attributed to the Conoy consisted of 71 interred packages or bundles of more or less disarticulated human skeletal remains.

Burial pits ranged from circular to oval to rectangular. The latter were rarely more than five feet long; the circular and oval forms ranged between two and one-half feet and five feet in greatest dimension. These ranged in depth from a few inches into the subsoil up to almost two feet in a few instances. Average depth was about 10 inches below the subsoil. Depth of the topsoil here was approximately 10 inches. In almost every case, the brown pit fill was very discernible against a background of bright yellow subsoil.

Some of these burial pits contained as many as five bundles or packages of human bones. In several cases there were preserved remains of woven fabric or skin bags or wrappings in which the bones had been collected. Osteological remains varied from the inclusion of just a mandible or skull, or long bones and skull, to complete and only partially disarticulated skeletons. There was no consistent orientation of the packages, but a majority had the long axis of the bones and the skull toward the southwest.

The bodies of these deceased individuals were obviously allowed to decompose somewhere prior to their final interment in this cemetery. Groups of bundles representing various stages of decomposition were occasionally deposited in the same hole at one time. The evidence for this is the *general* lack of any subsequent disturbance of any of the packages, which certainly would have occurred if these pits were reopened to deposit additional bundles. A number of the pits, almost always more than large enough, contained only one bundle. As indicated above, the degree of decomposition and disarticulation varied considerably. At least two burials can be described as very tightly flexed. Several others were in a supine position, with the upper portions of the bodies fully articulated but with lower legs folded back parallel with the femurs. In one instance, an old male was buried at a stage when it was obviously difficult to wrap him in a tight bundle or flexure. However, his cranium was removed from its anatomical position and placed by his knees.

The burials which showed lesser degrees of disarticulation were all older (generally with highly worn or no teeth), and all had few or no grave offerings with them. In some cases bodies that were collected for final burial were so completely decomposed that the bones were quite loose, and in fact many were not even picked up and placed in the bundle. Others, however, were obviously still quite well articulated and were subjected to drastic wrenching or twisting to separate, especially the leg bones at their joints.

Pits at the Conoy cemetery with as many as five individual bundles are really not ossuaries in the sense that that term applied to the more ancient cemeteries of the Conoy, such as that on Piscataway Creek in Maryland (Ferguson and Stewart 1940), or at the nearby Accokeek Creek site (Stephenson et al. 1963). The ossuaries at those sites contained hundreds of individuals, which generally were not neatly placed as individual packages, but were rather unceremoniously thrown into the pit. Captain John Smith (Stephenson et al. 1963: 68) mentioned individual pit burials for certain commoners in Virginia Indian society. Among the Piscataway, as reported archeologically by Stevenson et al. (1963: 59-74), there were a number of individual pit burials (56), but by far the greatest number (over one thousand individuals) were in ossuaries. Stevenson et al. (1963: 68) postulate, based largely upon contemporary descriptions, that among the Piscataway the initial burial or deposition of the body was on a rack or in a charnel

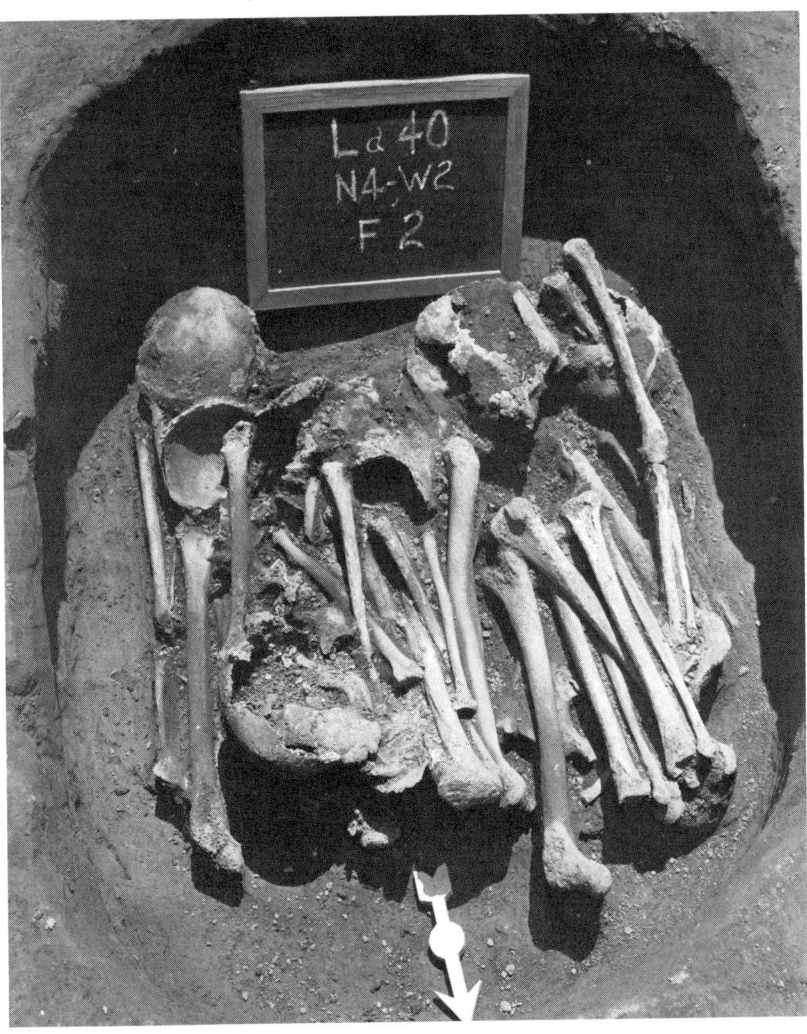

Figure 110. Five bundle burials in one grave pit at the Conoy cemetery (36La40).

house, not as an individual interment in the ground. Placement in the charnel house in many cases seems to have involved prior disembowelment, but probably not complete removal of the flesh (see Bushnell 1920: 27, or Smith 1907 I: 72). At some special ceremony the bones in the charnel house were cleaned of any remaining flesh and gathered up in packages, or in some cases a skull was used as a receptacle for certain smaller bones (sometimes even of a child), and then they were casually tossed into the ossuary pit.

Heckewelder (1819: 75-76) remarked concerning the Nanticoke Indians that they had the

> custom of removing the bones of their deceased friends from the burial place to the place of deposit in the country they dwell in. In earlier times they were known to go from Wyoming to Chemenk to fetch the bones of their dead from the eastern shore of Maryland, even when the bodies were in a putrid state so that they had to take off the flesh and scrape the bones clean before they could carry them along. I well remember having seen them between the years 1750 and 1760, loaded with such bones, which, being fresh, caused a disagreeable stench, as they passed through the town of Bethlehem.

Zeisberger (1910: 90) said of the Naticoke that

> about three or four months after the funeral they open up the grave, take out the bones, clean them of the flesh and dry them, wrap them up in new linen and inter them again. A feast is usually provided for the occasion, consisting of the best they can afford. Only the bones of the arms and legs of the corpse are thus treated. All the rest is buried or burned.

Weslager (1948: 103-107), who carefully reviewed most of the contemporary accounts concerning Nanticoke burial practices, said that he was unwilling to accept the statements that they dug up the bones merely for sentimental reasons. It was his opinion that the dead were initially placed in a *Chiacason* house (charnel house), and after a lapse of time the bones were collected and reburied in an ossuary, and that this reburial was final. Furthermore, he felt that those bones of the Nanticoke which were transported north into Pennsylvania came not from the ground or ossuary, but from a *Chiacason* house.

Weslager's (1948) statements to the contrary do not necessarily negate all possibility (as suggested for example by Zeisberger) of some in-ground burial immediately following death for a period during which most of the flesh would decay. After that, "scraping the bone" might have been somewhat easier (but perhaps just as odious) than doing so after decomposition on the charnel house rack.

An exceeding germane ethnohistoric account of what was apparently a mixed population of Conoy and Nanticoke Indians living at the mouth of the Juniata River in 1745 was provided by David Brainerd (Styles 1821: 235-38).

> They do not bury their dead in a common form, but let the flesh consume above the ground in close cribs made for that purpose. At the end of a year or sometimes a longer space of time they take the bones when the flesh is all consumed and wash and scrape them and afterwards bury them with some ceremony. (See a fuller quotation from Brainerd's account in the chapter of the present volume dealing with the history of Conoy.)

Grave offerings are referred to in some seventeenth-century accounts of Tidewater Algonquian charnel house burials, e.g., Captain John Smith (1907 I: 75-76) noted that

> about the most of the jointes and neck they hang bracelets or chaines of copper, pearle, and such like as they use to weare: their inwards they stuff with copper beads and cover with a skin, hatchets and such trash.

Offerings of any sort were generally uncommon in the burial pits or ossuaries of the Tidewater Algonquian peoples which have thus far been excavated. Indeed there were a few artifacts found in the ossuaries at Accokeek Creek, particularly shell beads, which were sometimes inside of skulls (Stephenson et al. 1963: 74). Similarly there were some artifacts in the ossuary at Piscataway Creek, including first-quarter seventeenth-century glass beads and brass objects (Ferguson and Stewart 1940). However, considering the large numbers of individuals represented in these ossuaries, the ratio of artifacts is quite low. As we will see, the Piscataway or Conoy custom regarding grave offerings seems to have changed considerably by the time they migrated into the Susquehanna Valley.

Age and sex for the interments at the Conoy cemetery, as they could be determined included: 23 adolescents (under 15 years of age) and 29 adults. There were 19 individuals whose remains were so poorly preserved that no determinations could be made. Again, where identification was possible, there were 15 females and 9 males.

Grave offerings of local manufacture were quite rare in these burials. Pendants and beads of red to orange catlinite were fairly abundant, but these were probably imported as finished items made by midwestern Indians.

There is some question as to how much, if any, wampum was Indian-made during the eighteenth century. Shell wampum of blue and white was quite abundant in these burials. It was employed in making necklaces, strings, bracelets and conventional belts. In at least one case a belt had been placed underneath a bundle. Portions of this and other belts from the site were collected intact. Unfortunately the colors of the beads were generally so faded that the designs on the belts cannot be discerned.

Shell runtees and various zoomorphic forms in carved white shells and large shell beads were fairly numerous. This may be a reflection of the earlier Piscataway burial custom involving an apparent penchant for shell beads.

A few fragments of splint basketry are most likely Indian products, but virtually everything else in these graves was of European or colonial origin and had been sold to or otherwise acquired by the Indians.

Glass beads and wampum were by far the most numerous items in the cemetery (over twenty-five thousand glass beads). Distributions of the glass-bead types (by percentages) are shown in Table 8. These were essentially like those for Conestoga Town. Notable differences between these two sites are the far greater quantity of medium-size black-seed beads at Conoy Town and the lack of blue-seed beads, which were so common at Conestoga.

Items of brass were the next most common grave offering at the Conoy cemetery. These have been more fully enumerated under the chapter entitled "Items Made of Brass," but in general these included rings (worn as such and on glass-bead necklaces), religious medals, crosses, bells, thimbles, jinglers, coils, spirals, tubes and miscellaneous objects or containers. Most of these things served as decorations on necklaces or as other clothing or body adornment. Another significant group of objects made of a copper alloy are the three George I medals (Figure 84). Kinsey (1977: 120) illustrates a fourth example from the surface of the village site. These are among the most tightly dated objects from the site, having been struck during the reign of King George I of Great Britain (1714-1727). There were no George II-Caroline medals in the Conoy cemetery. The S. Farver collection at the WPMM includes two such medals from the surface of the Conoy village area, which had been recovered by a former landowner from a plowed-into grave about 1910. A far greater number of the George II medals were found at Conestoga Town.

Iron objects at the Conoy cemetery consisted of knives (primarily clasp knives), a few iron snuff or vanity boxes, a bracelet and two pistols. Pewter items, such as spoons, buttons, and pipes had a minimal occurrence and all items of this material were very poorly preserved. Four complete kaolin pipes were found. Three of these are marked R. T. or R. Tippet, and one is marked I. Jenkins. Jenkins pipes do not appear to have been made later than 1739. Two bottles were found in the grave pits (Figure 59). One of these bears the initials I.B. and the date 1716.

Objects which were conspiciously absent or infrequent, as compared to Conestoga Town, were brass kettles (only three small ones were found at the Conoy cemetery); no iron axes or hoes were recovered; there were no colonial or European ceramics and of course no native ceramics. In general there were very few utilitarian items or things of any real value.

The use of the skull as a receptacle for small bones or even burial furniture, as reported among certain of the Tidewater Algonquians (see Stephenson et al. 1963: 69), was not a readily apparent custom of the Conoy by the time they buried their dead at the Conoy cemetery. Occasionally bones or beads or other objects were discovered in the eye sockets, but this seems more likely to have been a fortuitous accumulation of such items rather than intentional placements.

In some cases it was fairly obvious that burial furnishings had been placed inside the package with the bones. However, it would also appear that some things were placed on or next to the package. In several of those pits containing multiple bundles, a few grave goods were placed in such a manner that it was not possible to clearly determine the intended associations.

Frequently it was possible to recover exact necklace or other bead patterns in these graves. This is due to the fact that the bundles included little or no flesh at the time of interment. Consequently a necklace in or on the package settled very little due to decomposition. In some cases necklaces were laid directly on the floor of the grave—a condition which also enhanced preservation of necklace patterns. Unfortunately, most of the intact necklaces were comprised of monochrome (or single-bead types). A few necklaces of multiple-bead types showed a random or non-patterned arrangement of colors on the necklace. Necklaces composed of one bead type and color were in fact the most common. Several necklaces of catlinite beads were also recovered intact. One of these consisted of squares of catlinite with large central holes in which red seed beads were strung (Figure 37). In several cases it was possible to see that triangular catlinite beads were strung continuously (with their narrow ends all pointed in the same direction).

The distribution of grave goods according to the age of individuals showed a marked tendency to place something, and more often a greater quantity of objects, with the young, viz., from infancy to about 15 years of age. Ninety-two percent of these individuals had some sort of associated grave offering, and 52% of them had what can be considered abundant offerings. Only 8% had nothing with them. For those individuals over 15, only 62% had any grave goods and only 34% had abundant grave furniture.

The excavation here in 1970 involved the use of a bulldozer to remove the topsoil. Areas cleared with the bulldozer were then carefully flat-shoveled to the subsoil at which point burials and other features were easily discerned. In this manner, an area of more than sixty-five hundred square feet was exposed over and around the cemetery. These excavations were broad enough in all directions to uncover the entire cemetery. Upon completion of this work the field crew returned to the village site.

Conoy Town (36La57)

Excavation methods in the village area were the same as those employed at the cemetery. Here the crew exposed approximately eight thousand square feet of subsoil. At least a dozen storage or refuse pits were mapped and excavated. These were generally bowl-shaped and ranged in size from 12 inches in diameter and six inches deep (into the subsoil) to 50 inches in diameter and 25 inches deep. Only a few of these produced any material which clearly related to the Conoy occupation. One of the pits contained a fair amount of animal bone which had been broken for the soup kettle. Another yielded numerous charred corncobs. Pits were more abundant here than at Conestoga Town, but they produced little more in the way of village debris. Most of that, as at Conestoga, was in the topsoil, where it was actually quite prevalent.

A single, partial house pattern of postmolds was exposed at Conoy Town. The area in which it appeared contained a profusion of postmolds, but there were two distinguishable parallel lines some 15 feet apart. No ends of the structure could be traced.

Five burials were found on the southern margin of the site. All of these were extended interments. Grave goods were found with three of these individuals, and although these items were rather sparse, they were not unlike those encountered in the main cemetery. The major difference is that all of these and at least three other burials previously reported from the village site were extended.

Evidence cited above from Piscataway and Nanticoke sites in Maryland, and elsewhere, would suggest that these extended inhumations in the village area at Conoy Town do not represent primary burials which were to be exhumed later and reinterred as bundle burials in the larger cemetery. There were two empty burial pits in the village, but this evidence does not go very far toward accounting for the number of bundle burials at the cemetery. Conoy burial practices had changed somewhat at this period as compared to those at the Picataway sites in Maryland. For one thing there were no large ossuaries at Conoy Town. This might be accounted for by virtue of their then smaller population and the shorter occupation and, therefore, lesser number of dead to bury on the appropriate ceremonial occasions. Perhaps burial practices had changed for some Conoy to the point where it was acceptable to bury one's dead relatives in an extended primary interment. However, it is more likely that we could explain the burials of this form at the edge of the village as being those of some other Indians who were living, and dying, among the Conoy at Conoy Town. The orientation and body position of these graves is not unlike that at Conestoga Town. Could they represent a few Iroquoian folk living among the Conoy?

At least 80 deaths can be accounted for by various excavations at Conoy Town and the cemetery. Whether or not the Conoy moved some of their dead to this place from an earlier site, as did the Nanticoke, is not known. Perhaps that possibility should be considered, but any number of such occurrences are unaccountable.

If Conoy Town and its environs were occupied by these Indians for about 25 years (1718-1743) and if we assume a normal death rate of about two and a half percent per year, then the 80 burials over a period of 25 years would *imply* an average population of about 130 persons.

Archeology at Conoy Town and its major cemetery gives us a few more insights into the pattern (and changes) of culture of eighteenth-century refugee Piscataway Indians along the Susquehanna River. History, with something of an archeological confirmation, sets this stage of their culture history between about 1718 and 1743. Following this, historic accounts place them at the mouth of the Juniata with the Nanticoke and later perhaps with the Nanticoke at the Wyoming Valley, and finally in New York State. Nowhere after Conoy Town have we been able to discover them archeologically.

KNOUSE SITE

The Knouse site (36Lu43), also designated the Smith Farm site (Gardner 1939) and the Wapwallopen Village site, is located on the flood plain of the Susquehanna River's North Branch upstream from the modern village of Wapwallopen in Conyngham Township, Luzerne County, Pennsylvania. The entire site appears to extend over several properties (Gardner 1939: 23), and has produced a variety of cultural remains.

Testing at the site occurred as early as the summer of 1936, at which time 13 test pits were excavated by Gardner, who encountered therein six "fire pits" or hearths, five apparent storage pits, and one each of postmolds, burials and caches. Gardner noted that the burial was sterile of artifacts, and that the skeletal remains were too badly disintegrated to measure, although parts, at least, of the skeleton were identifiable (Gardner 1939: 25). Gardner further noted a post-contact provenience for some of these features at the site, as manifested by the presence of certain "trade articles." It was his suggestion that these materials resulted from an occupation by a "small band or tribe of Nanticoke Indians" from about "1730 to the late 1790's" (Gardner 1939: 26). One of the features which his crew excavated measured 10 feet by 6 feet by 25 inches deep and contained "a quantity of fire burned stone," underlain by a five-inch-thick lens of wood ash, and with charcoal and animal bone throughout. The "trade articles" from this feature included glazed pottery, a small tin or iron cup, a broken knife blade, "two pieces of white clay trade pipe," and a copper coin "struck by King George of England, dated 1774. . . . Another pit, also with a large quantity of burned stones and a six-inch layer of ash produced glazed pottery and one small fragment of clear window glass. A third pit, as noted by Gardner (1939: 24), produced "a two-tyned table fork, the stag horn handle badly decomposed. . . . Owing to the inexperience of the workmen excavating this pit, accurate measurements were impossible to determine"! In view of this latter statement, it seems prudent to question the association of these features and artifacts, and persons responsible. Do they relate to an eighteenth-century Indian occupation of the area, or are they the result of a slightly later colonial house on the site, which may have been burned? Unfortunately, Gardner's brand of archeology leaves us with these doubts, and therefore a decided uncertainty about the dating significance of the 1774 coin.

In the early 1970's, the Pennsylvania Power and Light company was informed that the construction of transmission lines from their nearby Susquehanna Steam Electric plant might adversely affect archeological remains at the Knouse site. At that time the company indicated its willingness to fund any archeological investigations necessary to avoid the adverse impact of their activities on local archeological resources. In 1978, with the aid of a grant from the company, the Pennsylvania Historical and Museum Commission undertook excavations at the Knouse site. The excavations were superimposed on the general area investigated by Gardner in 1936. The 1978 project was under the supervision of Ira Smith and the field direction of Jamie McIntyre (McIntyre 1979).

Thirteen refuse and other pits and 21 burials were excavated by the Commission's field team that season. Two of the pit features produced objects (redware sherds and a kaolin pipestem) of European or colonial manufacture.

Interments at the site were in an established and fairly concentrated cemetery area. Grave orientation was almost without exception southwest-northeast, with the head at either end of the grave, but favoring an arrangement with the head at the southwest end of the pit. Bodies were placed in flexed, flexed supine, or extended positions; the last of these appears to have been the most common. Several of these burials were clearly in wooden coffins, some of which were held together with nails. Generally, the interments were quite shallow and some had been previously disturbed by agriculture or by looting.

None of the burials was accompanied by any large quantity of grave furniture, at least by comparison with other eighteenth-century sites. The laboratory count (as opposed to the field count) of glass beads from the site is 13,355. The vast majority (58%) are white-seed beads (see Table 8). Others include black-seed beads (12%), dark-blue-seed beads (3%), light-

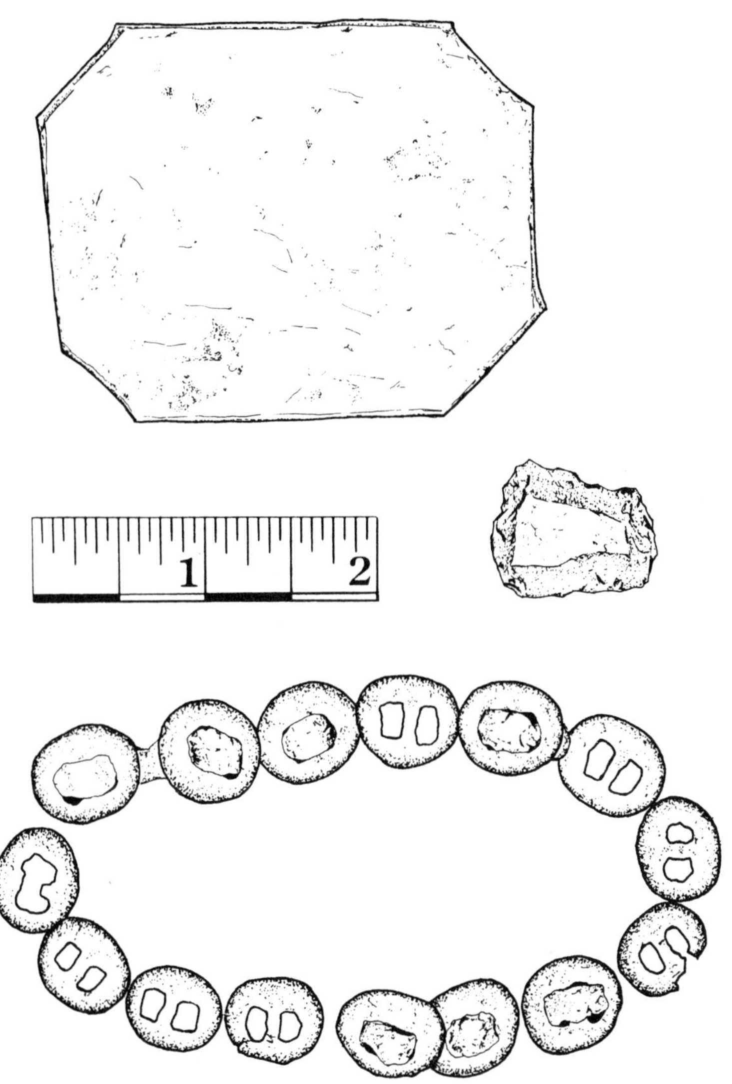

Figure 111. Glass mirror, gunflint, and choker of brass ovals, Wapwallopen (36Lu43).

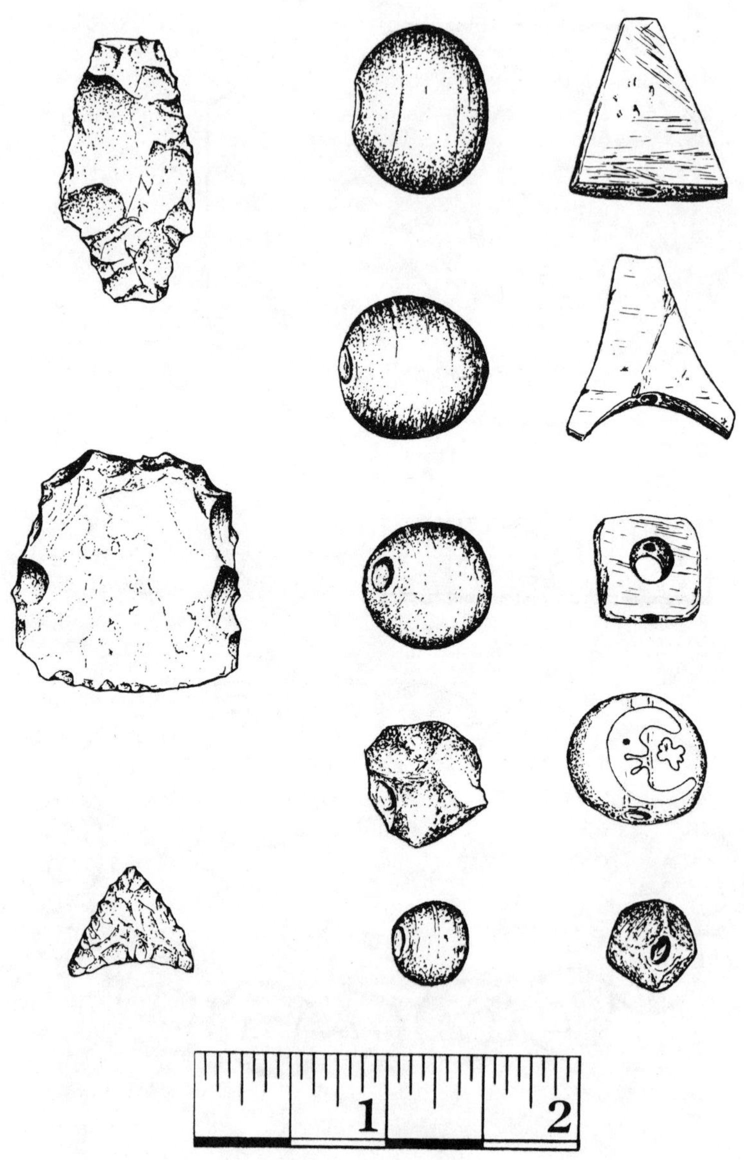

Figure 112. Objects from Wapwallopen (36Lu43). Note "moon" bead (second row from bottom, right).

blue-seed beads (18%), and green-seed beads (5%). There was a presence (less than 1% [130 beads]) of wire-wound beads, including the characteristic blue-faceted; large opaque white; spherical and donut-shaped, root-beer-colored beads; and others identical (and in similar ratios) to those from Conoy Town or Conestoga. However, the overall complexion of this bead sample as viewed against those from other sites (See Figure 56) is most like that from the 1760's Kuskuski site in western Pennsylvania, and therefore may call for a date later than the 1740's suggested in Table 8.

Most of the other objects recovered in 1978 are less datable than the beads. The one exception may be the W. N. kaolin pipe found in Burial 19. Previously (see chapter on kaolin pipes), we have suggested that this may have been made by William Nicholas, the Bristol pipe maker and exporter during the period 1730-1775. Also recovered were three religious medallions (Burial 5), which may, upon further research, prove to be more precisely datable.

Burial 3, an adult male wrapped in a cloth or blanket and placed in a coffin, produced a choker of 15 perforated, oval brass ornaments strung on a thin strap of rawhide (see Figure 111), and numerous seed beads, particularly in the pelvic area (where they were probably sewn on a garment). There was also a necklace of large, wire-wound beads; a brass vanity case by the left arm; as well as a thimble; a possible pewter pipe; a circular iron container, under which was a glass mirror; and nine brass jinglers at the ankles. This grave also produced two brass triangular arrowheads with central perforations, and a smoker's companion (tweezers).

Burial 14 was also in a coffin, and was an adult, possibly female. In the vicinity of the right arm was a cache (perhaps in a bag containing red paint pigment), which included a greystone calumet pipe (Figure 31), coiled brass wire, two gunflints, six brass jinglers, a whetstone, and an iron vanity box. On the fingers of the right hand were several brass rings, with and without paste settings. At the pelvis were other brass jinglers and white seed beads. A brass bell was found at the left knee together with a large quantity of white seed beads. Seed beads were also scattered over the lower legs and feet, suggesting ornamentation of a garment and perhaps moccasins.

The total gunflints from the excavations include one French and four of Clactonian style. Also found was a silver brooch, brass bracelets (worn as such on the right arm of Burial 6), a chert triangular point (Burial 19; see Figure 112), and various triangular and square catlinite pendants (see Figure 112). Grave 22, excavated after the close of the field season by local persons, produced, among other things, 15 blue-glass beads with imbedded white quarter moons and stars (see Figure 112).

The village location for those Indians responsible for the burials discussed above may have been partially touched upon by Gardner's test pits and those of the PHMC to the south of the cemetery. Features in this area produced redware, a nondescript white ware, kaolin pipestems, a few iron objects, and the coin dated 1774. If these objects were indeed the result of a mid-eighteenth-century Indian occupation, they may well have been in the area of a house site of such folk. It is very likely that the 12 houses reported by Brainerd in 1744 (Styles 1821: 85-86) were widely scattered over the broad flood-plain area which the Indians called Wapwallopen.

It is also very possible that eighteenth-century Indians of various ethnic or tribal backgrounds lived in the two-mile stretch of flat lands between the Big and Little Wapwallopen creeks. However, it is our opinion that the Moravian records (Fliegel 1970: 879) which label the Indian settlement of Wapwallopen as a Delaware Indian town correctly identify the major residents of the area and the persons responsible for the burials at the Knouse site.

Conclusions

THROUGH the special, but often cloudy, vision of archeology and history, we have looked at ways of life and change in late prehistoric and historic-period Indian cultures of the Susquehanna Valley. For reasons stated early in the book, the major focus has been upon those people whom we now call the Susquehannocks. Consequently, the majority of conclusions drawn here should relate to them. As we have seen, they interacted with a variety of native and European cultures; and as a result, some investigation of those other ways of life was a necessary part of our efforts to unravel the culture history of the Susquehannocks.

The term culture history as used here means a chronological ordering of whatever behavioral patterns, and changes in those patterns, can be identified as part of a particular culture through the techniques of archeology. For the most part, these patterns are indicated by preserved artifacts such as tools, or refuse. There can also be evidence for things like postmolds or pits, which may imply, for example, village sizes, house shapes, various activities, etc. In addition, when all of the discovered artifactual materials and evidence are compared to other anthropological studies of culture patterns, it may be possible to surmise certain less tangible aspects of a society's way of life, such as its basic social organization or even some of its religious concepts.

The fact that any or all of these patterns of culture, especially those represented by tangible artifacts, *may* change their form as time passes is precisely what enables archeologists to trace a culture's history. If nothing had changed it would be impossible to identify any reference points along the historical path of an ancient culture by which its remains could be chronologically organized.

This is not a history in the sense which historians use that term. Historians work with written documents about finite events involving specific times, places, and even individuals. History can in a very fascinating way show that various societies had different cultures and that those cultures changed over time. However, rarely have historians attempted to explain the causes or mechanisms of these differences or changes. For those answers, at least theoretical answers, we have generally had to turn to anthropology. Archeologists and anthropologists would certainly take advantage of any contemporary accounts about specific times, places, events and individuals. Unfortunately, there are very few such documents pertaining to the Susquehannocks. The same is true for most societies dealt with by archeologists. Because of the nature of the resource materials with which archeologists must work — primarily artifactual remains of a way of life — they have generally had to content themselves with the search for and analysis of things which can only reveal in a general way the patterns of human behavior in a particular society and the causes and nature of change in those patterns through time. That is culture history.

It is not our intention here to summarize all of the bits and pieces of things which have been identified as being part of the Susquehannock way of life. This is primarily what the book has been about. We can, however, recapitulate some of the most salient features of their culture history.

Susquehannock material culture, social organization, religion and language had roots with those of the Iroquois. The Susquehannock way of life is first recognizable as a separate entity about 1500 A.D. in the area now known as the north branch of the Susquehanna Valley.

Some 50 years later the Susquehannocks made a rather quick descent of the river to the Washington Boro area of Lancaster County, Pennsylvania. There they erected, perhaps for the first time in their history, a defensive stockade around their compactly arranged bark-covered longhouses. In or about this village, and those which followed, the inhabitants hunted, fished, farmed, made things, lost things, interacted with one another, fought, traded, played, lived and died. Their population prospered in both general health and numbers, reaching a peak of about three thousand persons around 1650 A.D.

At several points in their history they found it necessary to relocate and enlarge their villages. For a while, only certain aspects of their culture underwent noticeable change; but gradually a new force, with which they had to reckon, caused accelerating modifications of their way of life. Such was the impact of growing contact with the Europeans. Indeed, these interactions became paramount in directing the course of Susquehannock culture, eventually causing its extinction. By December 27, 1763, the Susquehannock way of life was officially and completely a thing of the past, relegated, as it were, to a few largely forgotten passages of contemporary accounts.

The full understanding and appreciation of Susquehannock culture history requires that we literally and figuratively dig into its sparse remains. The steps which have been taken in this direction through the present volume, when compared to similar endeavors for other areas and other cultures, show that there are many widespread patterns of cause and effect with regard to change and stability of the world's cultures. Restated, we might say that the lessons to be learned from the study of the Susquehanna's Indians are applicable in a general or theoretical way to a better understanding of mankind. It is within this purview that the author finds the greatest social value of archeological studies, and not that they may stand simply as an esoteric chronicle of the bits and pieces of some former way of life.

Patterns for any specific culture are carried in the minds of the participants of that culture. Individuals learn the rules or customs for their particular way of life by growing up in that cultural surrounding—a process known as enculturation. The unique patterns of a culture are exhibited by its individual carriers in their speech, dress, tools, housing, social customs, beliefs, likes, dislikes, etc. The form of each of these is (or can be) conditioned by what the majority of a group or society has found most acceptable.

There is always the potential for some individuals to do certain things outside what anthropologists consider the cultural norm or pattern (the average behavior of a culture). Even though it is individuals who actually do the things peculiar to a given culture, it is the overall, average group behavior which we perceive as comprising or distinguishing a culture.

A culture—actually the majority of human participants in it—tends to hold very tightly to all of its customary patterns or traditions for doing things. Among the technologically less complex cultures of the world, and maybe only because it is more obvious among them, there is usually a strong resistance to any impetus for change. Infrequent or occasional variations on the part of a few members of a society may be overlooked. In those rare instances when they are accepted they are called inventions; but generally they are sternly renounced. How then, we may ask, does a culture ever change? For as we have seen, it does change.

Anthropologists have theorized that a culture which exists in a stable environment (meaning its physical, natural and other cultural surroundings), where its particular patterns of life can continue without interference or competition, may go unaltered for long periods of time. Such cultures are considered to be ecologically well-adapted or stabilized and, therefore, seem to have no reason to accept or undergo any modifications of their pattern.

A related theory suggests that certain things *within* a culture may tend to drift very slowly toward a new form. For example, styles, as in clothing or pottery decorations, manners of speech, etc., may gradually change despite strong cultural traditions to the contrary, and without any environmental disruptions which might otherwise render such new forms useful or adaptive.

Anthropologists have demonstrated that most changes, particularly those which are sudden or drastic, are clearly in response to shifts in environment which upset the stable balance of a way of life. Environmental changes which might cause such severe disruptions could include, for example, shifts in climate; decreases in food supplies or other natural resources; or, particularly, new cultural surroundings, viz., human societies, with which a group suddenly finds itself interacting.

The direction or form of the changes which a society selects in these situations is what it *hopes* will enable it to regain its stability, comfort, or at least some measure of predictability about its existence. The choices it makes may or may not be rational or functional; indeed they may prove to be very wrong. Newly adopted patterns could be derived from the timely innovation of a single member of the society, or they might be drawn from that unsanctioned "outside the culural norm" area of behavior. Another important source of change lies entirely outside the culture, in the form of things which may be borrowed from the cultural behavior of some foreign society. The results of interactions with other societies (culture contact) have been the spread (diffusion) and often the curious admixtures (acculturation) of many culture traits among numerous societies of the world.

Sometimes it might seem that one culture borrows or readapts things from another without being under any environmentally disruptive pressures to do so. For example, glass beads or brass kettles which eventually replace native equivalents may appear to have been accepted simply because they were obviously more functional or attractive. But is this really the case? Does it not contradict the notion that societies do not easily or without readaptive necessity accept new things or changes? Indeed, when we examined this particular situation among the Susquehannocks, we saw that it was not that simple. Brass kettles were not at first used as such, but rather were cut up to make other things. Likewise, some of the earliest glass trade beads had portions of their surfaces ground away by the Indians to make them appear more like their own native forms!

The key factor really seems to be the *attempt* to maintain the well-established, the traditional, the stable, the good old comfortable way of doing things—even though the efforts to do so may seem very awkward, backward or impractical to another society.

Perhaps the classic example of a seemingly well adjusted, stable existence was that which we now call the Paleolithic culture of the Old World. This general way of life, involving hunting and gathering of wild foods, continued basically unchanged for hundreds of thousands of years. About ten thousand years ago, certain groups of these Paleolithic hunters and gatherers seem to have found themselves in an environment which no longer yielded the accustomed food resources. As the story goes, at least in anthropological theory, some of those groups changed their way of life to one involving horticulture and, eventually, agriculture. These food-producing technological modifications quickly brought on the need to alter other aspects of their cultural behavior. For example, resulting increases in population density would have created a need to readjust social organization, i.e., how the members of a group related to one another. Other technological innovations would have followed, just as did changes in religion.

Eventually these alterations posed new environmental settings to which neighboring cultures found it necessary to adapt. Their readaptations created backlashing situations to which the original group had to adjust—and so on. The pace for cultural dynamics was set—at a constantly accelerating rate—back and forth, with increasing geographic expansion and complexity of cultural patterns. Cultures which could not, or would not, readapt remained backward by comparison, or in many cases ceased to exist.

Today, the rate of interaction and adjustment of one culture to another is such that many, like our own, are changing literally at a daily rate.

Obviously these examples have strayed somewhat from the culture history of the Susquehanna's Indians, but the general principles of culture change nevertheless apply very well.

The specific mechanisms or causes of change in the cultural patterns of Susquehannock, or any other, society are exceedingly difficult to pinpoint. However, it can be said that such change took place in response to new or disruptive environmental situations, and to what were, primarily, new cultural environments created when two or more differing cultures came into contact with one another.

One of the usually predictable results of such contact, as confirmed by the present study of the Susquehanna's Indians and through many other examinations of the world's cultures, is that the dominant or technologically more advanced culture will suppress, absorb, or even exterminate the less advanced culture.

Some modern-day observers may be moved to view the results of such culture contact with emotions of distaste, pity, and even outrage. On the other hand, history and anthropology have shown competition and extinction to be so common and widespread as to imply that they are natural, albeit ugly, processes in the evolution of human societies. We might well equate such with the Darwinian concept of survival of the fittest. These processes seem less odious when they involve non-human species which have undergone biological evolution in the face of life-threatening environmental change or competition.

An animal life form, or that conceptual thing which we call culture, when it has undergone a survival-of-the-fittest kind of evolution in response to environmental adversity, can certainly be characterized as more fit than some form which did not survive. However, this may not automatically call for the description of the evolved, surviving form as better. Better as compared to what? Better as compared to the old life; better because it is now more complex, or more populous; because it moves faster, is bigger or smaller, consumes more or consumes more efficiently, etc.?

The myriad of culture changes throughout the history of the world, and especially since the development of agriculture, make it impossible for most persons to be concerned about those which did not survive, or to understand anything more than the basics of evolution. But perhaps that is all that is necessary.

Anthropologists, who do attempt to understand a wide variety of culture dynamics, find that there are certain recurring patterns. Knowledge of these patterns has rendered much of past cultural evolution more comprehensible. Perhaps someday that same knowledge may actually permit a few social scientists to predict the course of the world's mega-culture(s).

In the present examination of the history of culture in that tiny part of the world known as the Susquehanna Valley, we have seen some drastic, but certainly not unique, changes in the way of life of its native inhabitants.

Can it be that our only conclusion is that we recognize that these examples are nothing more than a confirmation of world-wide and continuing processes of cultural evolution—leading either to some form of change or extinction? As viewed from the perspective of a presumably enlightened modern society, which repeatedly exhibits its inability to cope with culture change or evolution, it seems unlikely that enough people will ever understand the processes well enough to influence their future directions. We can only hope, therefore, that the natural course of cultural evolution will not lead our own way of life down the same path of extinction followed by the Susquehanna's Indians.

BIBLIOGRAPHY

Barber, Edwin Atlee
1907 *Salt glazed stoneware.* Doubleday, New York.

Bartram, John
1751 *Observations on the inhabitants, climate, soil, rivers, productions, animals, and other matters worthy of notice made by Mr. John Bartram. . . .* J. Whiston and B. White, London.

Bashore, Harvey B., William A. Kelker and J. Haldeman O'Connor
1898 *Contributions to the Indian history of the Lower Susquehanna Valley:* Annual Report of the Committee on Archaeology of The Dauphin County Historical Society, Harrisburg.

Beauchamp, William M.
1900 Aboriginal Occupation of New York. New York State Museum *Bulletin* 32 (7).
1902 Horn and bone implements of the New York Indians. New York State Museum *Bulletin* 50: 243-343.
1903 Metallic Ornaments of the New York Indians. New York State Museum *Bulletin* 73(8): 1-120
1906 Civil, religious & mourning councils and ceremonies of adoption of the New York Indians. New York State Museum *Bulletin* 113.
1922 *Iroquois folk lore.* Dehler Press, Syracuse.

Becker, Marshall J.
1975 The Okehocking tract: An early Indian "reservation" in Pennsylvania. Ms. #9, on file, Division of Archaeology, William Penn Memorial Museum, Harrisburg.
1976 The Okehocking: A remnant band of Delaware. *Pennsylvania Archaeologist* 46(3):24-61.
1978a Montgomery site, 36Ch60: Late contact Lenape (Delaware) site in Wallace Township, Chester County. Ms. #7, on file, Division of Archaeology, William Penn Memorial Museum, Harrisburg.
1978b Lenape archaeology: Ethnohistoric and archaeological data on Lenape sites as revealed by the 1978 field project. Ms. #4, on file, Division of Archaeology, William Penn Memorial Museum, Harrisburg.
1980 Lenape archaeology: Archaeological and ethnohistoric considerations in light of recent excavations. *Pennsylvania Archaeologist* 50(4):19-30.

Bender, Harry E.
1929 The Nanticoke Indians in Lancaster County. Lancaster County Historical Society *Papers* 33(7):121-131.

Benson, Evelyn
1958 *The story of the Susquehannocks.* Conestoga Chapter no. 4, Society for Pennsylvania Archaeology, Lancaster.

Betts, Charles W.
1894 *American colonial history illustrated by contemporary medals.* Quarterman Publications (reprint 1972), Boston.

Biggar, Henry P.
1901 *The early trading companies of New France.* University of Toronto Library, Toronto.

Binford, Lewis R.
1962a A new method of calculating dates from kaolin pipe stem samples. *Southeastern Archaeological Conference Newsletter* 9(1):19-21.
1962b Archaeology as anthropology. *American Antiquity* 28:221-225.
Black, Glenn A.
1954 Archaeological consideration of the Walam Olum, in *Walam Olum, or Red Score: The migration legend of the Lenni Lenape or Delaware Indians*, pp. 292-348. Indiana Historical Society, Indianapolis.
Blaker, Margaret C.
1963 Aboriginal ceramics, in H. Geiger Omwake and T. D. Stewart, eds., The Townsend site, near Lewes, Delaware. *The Sussex Society of Archaeology and History* 15(1):14-39.
Blakeslee, Donald J.
1981 The origin and spread of the calumet ceremony. *American Antiquity* 46(4):759-768.
Brackbill, Martin H.
1938 The Manor of Conestoga in the the colonial period. Lancaster County Historical Society *Papers* 42(2).
Bradley, James W.
1979 *The Onondaga Iroquois: 1500-1655.* PhD dissertation, Department of Anthropology, Syracuse University, Syracuse.
Bradley, James W., and Gordon DeAngelo
1981 European clay pipe marks from 17th century Onondaga Iroquois sites. *Archaeology of Eastern North America* 9:109-133.
Brasser, T. J.
1978 Mahican, in Bruce G. Trigger, ed., *Handbook of North American Indians* 15(Northeast):198-212. Smithsonian Institution, Washington, D.C.
Braun, E. Lucy
1964 *Deciduous forests of Eastern North America.* Hafner Publishing Co., New York.
Bressler, James
1978 Excavation of the Bull Run site in Loyalsock Township, Lycoming County, Pennsylvania. Ms. #3, on file, Division of Archaeology, William Penn Memorial Museum, Harrisburg.
1980 Excavation of the Bull Run site 36Ly119. *Pennsylvania Archaeologist* 50(4):31-63.
Brinton, Daniel G.
1885 *The Lenape and their legends.* . . . Daniel G. Brinton, Philadelphia.
British Public Records Office
n.d. Colonial office 5/1233 (Pennsylvania material, 1689-1707), Foreign office 353/59, 353/60. Microfilm in Bureau of Archives and History, Pennsylvania Historical and Museum Commission, Harrisburg.
Brunner, D. B.
1897 *Indians of Berks County, Pa.* . . . Spirit of Berks Book Printing Office, Reading, Pa.
Bushnell, David I.
1920 Native cemeteries and forms of burial east of the Mississippi. Smithsonian Institution, Bureau of American Ethnology, *Bulletin* 71.
Butler, Mary
1947 Two Lenape rock shelters near Philadelphia. *American Antiquity* 12:246-255.
Cadzow, Donald A.
1931a Report of Donald A. Cadzow on work at Safe Harbor. *Fifth Report of the Pennsylvania Historical Commission*, pp. 115-124. Harrisburg.
1931b Safe Harbor. *Pennsylvania Archaeologist* 2(2):3-4.

1934 *Petroglyphs in the Susquehanna River near Safe Harbor, Pennsylvania.* Safe Harbor Report no. 1. Pennsylvania Historical Commission, Harrisburg.

1936 *Archeaological studies of the Susquehannock Indians of Pennsylvania.* Safe Harbor Report no. 2. Pennsylvania Historical Commission, Harrisburg.

Callender, Charles

1978 Shawnee, in Bruce G. Trigger, ed., *Handbook of North American Indians* 15(Northeast):622-635. Smithsonian Institution, Washington, D.C.

Camp, Helen B.

1975 *Archaeological excavations at Pemaquid, Maine, 1965-1974.* Maine State Museum, Augusta.

Carey, John Breniser

1959 *Soil survey, Lancaster County, Pennsylvania.* U.S. Department of Agriculture, Soil Conservation Services, Series 1956, no. 4, Washington, D.C.

Carpenter, Edmund S.

1949 The Brock site. *Pennsylvania Archaeologist* 19(3-4):69-77.

Carter, John H.

1931 Shikellamy: The Indian vice king at Shamokin. *Proceedings and Addresses* of the Northumberland County Historical Society 3:28-53.

1937 The Moravians at Shamokin. *Proceedings and Addresses* of the Northumberland County Historical Society 9:52-72.

Carter, William H.

1971 *North American Indian trade silver.* Engel Printing, London, Ontario.

1973 *North American Indian medical practices and burial customs.* Namind Printers and Publishers, London, Ontario.

Casselberry, Samuel Emerson

1971 The Schultz-Funk site (36La7): Its role in the culture history of the Susquehannock and Shenk's Ferry Indians. Doctoral thesis submitted to the Department of Anthropology, Pennsylvania State University, University Park, Pa. Ms. #1, on file, Division of Archaeology, William Penn Memorial Museum, Harrisburg.

Chambers, Benjamin

1688 Manuscript map of line survey, Pennsylvania State Archives, RG26: Charters, Proprietary and Indian Deeds . . . , 1681-1838, no. 18. Pennsylvania Historical and Museum Commission, Harrisburg.

Champlain, Samuel de

1632 *Les voyages de la Nouvelle France Occidentale, dicte Canada. . . .* Claude Collet, Paris. Reprinted in W. L. Grant, ed., *Voyages of Samuel de Champlain, 1604-1618.* Barnes and Noble, Inc., New York (1952).

1882 Voyages of Samuel de Champlain (trans. C. P. Otis). *Publications of the Prince Society* 13.

Clark, John S.

1931 *Selected manuscripts of General John S. Clark relating to the aboriginal history of the Susquehanna*, ed. by Louise Welles Murray. Society for Pennsylvania Archaeology, Athens, Pa.

Clark, Wayne E.

1980 The origins of the Piscataway and related Indian cultures. Ms. #1 on file, Division of Archaeology, William Penn Memorial Museum, Harrisburg.

Cleland, Charles E.

1971 *The Lasanen site: An historic burial locality in Mackinac County, Michigan.* Publications of the Museum, Michigan State University.

1972 From sacred to profane: Style drift in the decoration of Jesuit finger rings. *American Antiquity* 37(2):202-210.

Colonial Records
1838 Minutes of the Provincial Council of Pennsylvania. Theophilus Fenn, Harrisburg.

Columbia Spy
1831 Article reprinted in *Hazard's Register* 8(3):33-48, for July 16, 1831. William F. Geddes, Philadelphia.

Cook, Sherburne F.
1972 Prehistoric demography. *McCaleb Module in Anthropology* 16.

Cornplanter, Jesse J.
1938 *Legends of the longhouse*. J. B. Lippincott Co., Philadelphia.

Cotter, John L.
1958 Archaeological excavations at Jamestown. United States Department of the Interior, National Park Service, *Archaeological Research Series* 4. Washington, D.C.

Cotter, John L., and J. Paul Hudson
1957 *New discoveries at Jamestown*. U.S. Department of the Interior, National Park Service, Washington, D.C.

Cowles, Ellsworth C.
1932 Excavating an Indian site near Sayre, Pa. *Pennsylvania Archaeologist* 3(2):14-15.
1933a Excavating an Indian site near Sayre, Pa. *Pennsylvania Archaeologist* 3(3):12-15.
1933b Excavating an Indian site near Sayre, Pa. *Pennsylvania Archaeologist* 3(4):1, 16-21.
1933c Effigy site, Bradford County no. 43. Ms #1, on file, Division of Archaeology, William Penn Memorial Museum, Harrisburg.

Cox, Warren Earle
1944 *The book of pottery and porcelain*. Crown Publishers, New York.

Crannell, Marilyn A. (Stewart)
1970 *Shell-tempered pottery vessels from the Englebert site, Nichols, New York*. MA thesis, State University of New York at Binghamton.

Cross, Dorothy
1941 *Archaeology of New Jersey*, Vol. I. Archaeological Society of New Jersey; New Jersey State Museum, Trenton.
1956 *Archaeology of New Jersey*, Vol. II. Archaeological Society of New Jersey; New Jersey State Museum, Trenton.

Danckaerts, Jasper, and Peter Sluyter
1913 Journal of Jasper Danckaerts, 1679-1680, edited by B. B. James and J. F. Jameson. *Original narratives of early American history*. Charles Scribner's Sons, New York.

Davidson, D. S.
1929 The Lock Haven expedition. *The Museum Journal* 20(3-4):307-317. University of Pennsylvania Museum, Philadelphia.

Delaney, Leslie L., Jr.
1973 *Search for Friedenshutten, 1772-1972*. Cro Woods, Wyoming, Pa.

DeLotbiniere, Seymour
1980 English gunflint making in the seventeenth and eighteenth centuries, in T. M. Hamilton, *Colonial frontier guns*, pp. 154-160. The Fur-Press, Chadron, Neb.

Dice, Lee R.
1943 *The biotic provinces of North America*. The University of Michigan Press, Ann Arbor.

Diderot, Denis

1959 A Diderot pictorial encyclopedia of trades and industry: Manufacturing and the technical arts in plates selected from "L'Encyclopedie ou Dictionnaire Raisonne des Sciences, des Arts et des Metiers" of Denis Diderot, ed. by Charles C. Gillispie. Dover Publications, Inc., New York.

Donehoo, George P.

1918 Brief summary of the archaeology of the Susquehanna, in *Second Report of the Pennsylvania Historical Commission*, pp. 126-151. Pennsylvania Historical Commission, Harrisburg.

1928 *A history of the Indian villages and place names in Pennsylvania*. Pennsylvania Historical Commission, Harrisburg.

Dunbar, Helen R., and Katharine C. Ruhl

1974 Copper artifacts from the Engelbert site. New York State Archeological Association *Bulletin* 61:1-10.

Du Ponceau, Peter S.

1834 *A short description of the province of New Sweden, translated from the Swedish of Thomas Campanius Holm*. McCarty and Davis, Philadelphia.

Durant, P. A., and J. Fraise Richard

1886 History of Cumberland County, in *History of Cumberland and Adams Counties, Pennsylvania*. Warner, Beers, & and Co., Chicago.

Eckert, Allan W.

1967 *The frontiersmen*. Little, Brown and Co., Boston.

Egle, William Henry

1883a *History of the Commonwealth of Pennsylvania*. E. M. Gardner, Philadelphia.

1883b *History of the counties of Dauphin and Lebanon. . . .* Everts and Peck, Philadelphia.

Egle, William Henry, ed.

1894 *Pennsylvania Archives*, third series, IV. Clarence M. Busch, Harrisburg.

Elliott, Delores

1977 Otsiningo, an example of an eighteenth century settlement pattern, *in* Robert E. Funk and Charles F. Hayes III, eds., Current perspectives in Northeastern archeology: Essays in honor of William A. Ritchie. New York State Archeological Association *Transactions* 17(1):93-105.

Elliott, Delores N., and William D. Lipe

1970 *The Engelbert site*. Triple Cities Chapter, New York State Archeological Association, Binghamton, N.Y.

Ellis, Franklin, and Samuel Evans

1883 *History of Lancaster County, Pennsylvania. . . .* Everts and Peck, Philadelphia.

Eshleman, H. Frank

1909 *Lancaster County Indians: Annals of the Susquehannocks and other Indian tribes of the Susquehanna territory from about the year 1500 to 1763*. Lancaster.

Feest, Christian F.

1973 Seventeenth century Virginia Algonquian population estimates. *Quarterly Bulletin* of the Archaeological Society of Virginia 28(2):66-79.

1978 Virginia Algonquians, in Burce G. Trigger, ed., *Handbook of North American Indians* 15(Northeast):253-270. Smithsonian Institution, Washington, D.C.

Fenneman, Nevin M.

1938 *Physiography of eastern United States*. McGraw-Hill Book Co., New York.

Ferguson, Alice L. L.
1941 The Susquehannock fort on Piscataway Creek. *Maryland Historical Magazine* 36(1):1-9.

Ferguson, Alice L. L., and Henry G. Ferguson
1960 *The Piscataway Indians of southern Maryland*. Alice Ferguson Foundation, Accokeek, Md.

Ferguson, Alice L. L., and T. Dale Stewart
1940 An ossuary near Piscataway Creek. *American Antiquity* 6(1):4-18.

Fite, Emerson D., and Archibald Freeman, comps. and eds.
1969 *A book of old maps delineating American history*. Dover Publications, Inc., New York.

Fliegel, Carl John
1970 *Index to the records of the Moravian mission among the Indians of North America*. Research Publications, Inc., New Haven, Conn.

Force, Peter, comp.
1836 *Tracts and other papers, relating principally to the origin, settlement, and progress of the colonies in North America*. . . . Reprinted 1947, Peter Smith, New York.

Forks of the Delaware Chapter (Elinor Fehr and F. Dayton Staats)
1980 The Overpeck site (36Bu5). *Pennsylvania Archaeologist* 50(3).

Futer, Arthur A.
1958 *European trade materials from historical periods on Susquehannock sites*. Conestoga Chapter no. 4, Society for Pennsylvania Archaeology, Lancaster, Pa.
1959 The Strickler site, in Witthoft and Kinsey, eds., *Susquehannock Miscellany*, pp. 136-147. Pennsylvania Historical and Museum Commission, Harrisburg.

Futhey, J. Smith, and Gilbert Cope
1881 *History of Chester County, Pennsylvania*. . . . Louis H. Everts, Philadelphia.

Gardner, Eugene M.
1939 An archaeological study of Indian village sites in the lower Wyoming Valley. *Pennsylvania Archaeologist* 9(2):21-34.

Goddard, Ives
1978 Delaware, in Bruce G. Trigger, ed., *Handbook of North American Indians* 15(Northeast):213-219. Smithsonian Institution, Washington, D.C.

Griffin, James B.
1931a Griffin excavation: Spanish Hill. Ms. #1, on file, Division of Archaeology, William Penn Memorial Museum, Harrisburg.
1931b The Tioga Point Museum Expedition for 1931. Ms. #4, on file. Division of Archaeology, William Penn Memorial Museum, Harrisburg.
1943 *The Fort Ancient aspect: Its cultural and chronological position in Mississippi Valley archaeology*. University of Michigan Press, Ann Arbor.

Gruber, Jacob W.
1967 Ethnological needs for archaeological reconstruction: A Late Woodland example, in Elisabeth Tooker, ed., *Iroquois culture history and prehistory: Proceedings of the 1965 Conference on Iroquois Research*. New York State Museum and Science Service, Albany, N.Y.
1969 Excavations at the Mohr site. *Yearbook of the American Philosophical Society*, 1968.
1971 Patterning in death in a late prehistoric village in Pennsylvania. *American Antiquity* 36(1):64-76.

Guilday, John, Paul W. Parmalee, and Donald P. Tanner
1962 Aboriginal butchering techniques at the Eschelman site (36La12), Lancaster County, Pennsylvania. *Pennsylvania Archaeologist* 32(2): 59-83.
Guilland, Harold F.
1971 *Early American folk pottery*. Chilton Book Co., Philadelphia.
Guthe, Alfred K.
1958 The late prehistoric occupation in southwestern New York: An interpretive analysis. Rochester Museum of Arts and Sciences *Research Records* 11.
Haggerty, Gilbert
1963 The iron trade-knife in Oneida territory. *Pennsylvania Archaeologist* 33(1-2):93-114.
Hall, Clayton Colman, ed.
1910 *Narratives of early Maryland, 1633-1684*. Charles Scribner's Sons, New York.
Hamell, George R.
1979 Untitled working paper on Iroquois symbolism on artifacts. Ms. #1, on file, Division of Archaeology, William Penn Memorial Museum, Harrisburg.
Hamilton, T. M.
1968 Early Indian trade guns: 1625-1775. *Contributions of the Museum of the Great Plains* 3. Lawton, Oklahoma.
1980 *Colonial frontier guns*. The Fur Press, Chadron, Neb.
Hamilton, T. M., comp.
1960 Indian trade guns. *The Missouri Archaeologist* 22.
Hanna, Charles A.
1911 *The wilderness trail*, two vols. Ames Press, Inc., New York.
Harrington, Jean C.
1954 Dating stem fragments of seventeenth century clay tobacco pipes. Archaeological Society of Virginia *Quarterly Bulletin* 9(1):10-14.
Harrington, Mark R.
1913 A preliminary sketch of Lenape culture. *American Antiquity* 15:208-235.
1921 Religion and ceremonies of the Lenape. Museum of the American Indian, Heye Foundation *Indian Notes and Monographs* 19.
Hatch, James M.
1980 The Fisher farm site. The Pennsylvania State University, Department of Anthropology. *Occasional Papers* 12.
Hawkins, E.
1885 *Medallic illustrations of the history of Great Britain & Ireland*, ed. by A. W. Franks and H. A. Gruber, London. Reprinted 1969, Spink & Son, Ltd., London.
Hayden, Horace E.
1886 Various silver and copper medals. *Proceedings and Collections* of the Wyoming Historical and Geological Society 2(2):217-238.
Hazard, Samuel, ed.
1831 *The register of Pennsylvania* 7. Wm. F. Geddes, Philadelphia.
1835 *Hazards's register of Pennsylvania* 15. Wm. F. Geddes, Philadelphia.
Heckewelder, John
1819 *An account of the history, manners, and customs, of the Indian nations. . . .* Abraham Small, Philadelphia.
Heisey, Henry
1971 An interpretation of Shenks Ferry ceramics. *Pennsylvania Archaeologist* 41(4):44-70.

Heisey, Henry W., and J. Paul Witmer

1962 Of historic Susquehannock cemeteries. *Pennsylvania Archaeologist* 32(3-4):99-130.

1964 The Shenks Ferry people: A site and some generalities. *Pennsylvania Archaeologist* 34(1):8-34.

Held, Robert

1970 *The age of firearms*. The Gun Digest Co., Northfield, Ill.

Henry, Susan L.

1979 Terra-cotta tobacco pipes in 17th century Maryland and Virginia: A preliminary study. *American Antiquity* 13:14-37.

Herrman, Augustine

1673 *Virginia and Maryland . . . 1670, . . . by Augustine Herrman. . . .* J. Seller, London. Reprint 1963, John Carter Brown Library, Providence, R.I.

Hersh, Donald M.

1963 *Soil survey of York County, Pennsylvania*. U.S. Department of Agriculture, series 1959, no. 3.

Heye, George

1935 Untitled communication in field work in North America. *American Antiquity* 1(2):130.

Heye, George G., and George H. Pepper

1915 *Exploration of a Munsee cemetery near Montague, New Jersey*. The Museum of the American Indian, Heye Foundation, New York.

Hodge, Frederick W., ed.

1910 Handbook of American Indians north of Mexico. Bureau of Indian Affairs, Smithsonian Institution, *Bulletin* 30, part 2.

1912 Handbook of American Indians north of Mexico. U.S. Government Printing Office, *Bulletin* 30, part 1.

Holm, Thomas Campanius

1834 *Description of the province of New Sweden. . . .* Historical Society of Pennsylvania *Memoirs* 3, part 1.

Holmes, William H.

1903 Aboriginal pottery of the eastern United States. Smithsonian Institution, Bureau of American Ethnology, 20th *Annual Report*.

Hooton, Earnest A.

1920 Indian village site and cemetery near Madisonville, Ohio, *Papers* of the Peabody Museum of American Archaeology and Ethnology, Harvard University 8(1):1-137.

Hunt, George P.

1940 *The wars of the Iroquois: A study in intertribal trade relations*. University of Wisconsin Press, Madison.

Hunter, William A.

1959 The historic role of the Susquehannocks, in Witthoft and Kinsey, eds., *Susquehannock Miscellany*, pp. 8-18. Pennsylvania Historical and Museum Commission, Harrisburg.

1978 Documented subdivisions of the Delaware. *Bulletin* of the Archaeological Society of New Jersey 35:20-40.

Jennings, Francis P.

1966 The Indian trade of the Susquehanna Valley. *Proceedings* of the American Philosophical Society 110(6):406-424.

1968 Glory, death, and transfiguration: The Susquehannock Indians in the seventeenth century. *Proceedings* of the American Philosophical Society 112(1):15-53.

1978 Susquehannock, in Bruce G. Trigger, ed., *Handbook of North American Indians* 15(Northeast):362-367. Smithsonian Institution, Washington, D.C.

Johnson, Amandus
1911 *The Swedish settlements on the Delaware, 1632-1664*, Vol. I. New Era Printing Co., Lancaster.
1925 *Geographia Americae . . .* , in P. M. Lindeström Swedish Colonial Society. Philadelphia.
Johnson, William C.
1972 The Late Woodland in Northwestern Pennsylvania. Ms. #1, on file, Division of Archaeology, William Penn Memorial Museum, Harrisburg.
Johnston, George
1881 *History of Cecil County, Maryland. . . .* Elkton, Md. (reprinted Regional Publishing Co., Baltimore 1972).
Kellock, Katharine A.
1962 *Colonial Piscataway in Maryland.* The Alice Ferguson Foundation, Accokeek, Md.
Kent, Barry C.
1970 An unusual cache from the Wyoming Valley, Pennsylvania. *American Antiquity* 35(2):185-193.
1974 Locust Grove pottery: A new Late Woodland variety. *Pennsylvania Archaeologist* 44(4):1-5.
1980a An update on Susquehanna Iroquoian pottery. *Proceedings* of the 1979 Iroquois Pottery Conference. Rochester Museum and Science Center *Research Records* 13:99-103.
1980b *Discovering Pennsylvania's archeological heritage.* Pennsylvania Historical and Museum Commission, Harrisburg.
1983 More on gunflints. *Historical Archaeology* 17(2).
Kent, Barry C., and Vance P. Packard
1969 The Erb rockshelter. *Pennsylvania Archaeologist* 39(1-4):29-39.
Kent, Barry C., Janet Rice, and Kakuko Ota
1981 A map of 18th century Indian towns in Pennsylvania. *Pennsylvania Archaeologist* 51(4):1-18.
Kent, Barry C., Ira F. Smith III, and Catherine McCann, comps.
1971 *Foundations of Pennsylvania prehistory.* Pennsylvania Historical and Museum Commission, Harrisburg.
Kent, Donald H., ed.
1979 *Early American Indian documents: Treaties and laws, 1607-1789*, Vol. I: Pennsylvania and Delaware treaties, 1629-1737. University Publications of America, Inc., Washington, D.C.
Kidd, Kenneth E., and Martha Ann Kidd
1970 A classification system for glass beads for the use of field archaeologists. *Canadian Historic Sites: Occasional papers in Archaeology and History* 1:45-89. National Historic Sites Service, National and Historic Park Branch, Department of Indian Affairs and Northern Development.
Kinietz, Vernon
1946 Delaware cultural chronology. Indiana Historical Society *Prehistory Research Series* 3(1), April. Indianapolis.
Kinsey, W. Fred, III
1957 A Susquehannock longhouse. *American Antiquity* 23(2):180-181.
1958 An Indian pipe chronology. *Journal for 1958* of the Lower Susquehanna Chapter no. 9 of the Society for Pennsylvania Archaeology.
1959a Recent excavations on Bare Island in Pennsylvania: The Kent-Hally site. *Pennsylvania Archaeologist* 29(3-4):109-133.
1959b Historic Susquehannock pottery, in Witthoft and Kinsey, eds., *Susquehannock Miscellany*, pp. 61-98. Pennsylvania Historical and Museum Commission, Harrisburg.

1960 Additional notes on the Albert Ibaugh site. *Pennsylvania Archaeologist* 30(3-4):81-105.

1977 *Lower Susquehanna prehistoric Indians.* Science Press, Ephrata.

1981 Catlinite and red pipestone: A preliminary report. Paper presented at the meeting of the Eastern States Archaeological Federation, 1981. Ms. #12, on file, Division of Archaeology, William Penn Memorial Museum, Harrisburg.

Kinsey, W. Fred III, and Jay F. Custer

1982 Lancaster County Park site (36La96): Conestoga phase. *Pennsylvania Archaeologist* 52(3-4):17-56.

Kinsey, W. Fred III, and Jeffrey R. Graybill

1971 Murry site and its role in Lancaster and Funk phases of Shenks Ferry culture. *Pennsylvania Archaeologist* 41(4):7-44.

Kinsey, W. Fred III, *et al.*

1972 Archaeology of the upper Delaware Valley. *Anthropological Series no. 2.* Pennsylvania Historical and Museum Commission, Harrisburg.

Klein, Philip S., and Ari Hoogenboom

1973 *A History of Pennsylvania.* McGraw-Hill Book Company, New York.

Kraft, Herbert

1976 *Archaeology of the Pahaquarra site.* Archaeological Research Center, Seton Hall University.

Kraft, Herbert C., ed.

1974 A Delaware Indian symposium. *Anthropological Series no. 4.* Pennsylvania Historical and Museum Commission, Harrisburg.

Kroeber, Alfred L.

1939 *Cultural and natural areas of native North America.* University of California Press, Berkeley.

Lancaster County Court House

n.d. Deed Book BB, p. 28. Lancaster, Pa.

Landis, David H.

1910 The location of Susquehannock fort. Lancaster County Historical Society *Papers* 14(3):81-113.

1919 The location of Pequehan. Lancaster County Historical Society *Papers* 23(4):69-77.

1924 Historical address. Lancaster County Historical Society *Papers* 28(9): 132-138.

1925 The Indian town site at Washington Boro. Lancaster County Historical Society *Papers* 29(8):101-104.

1929 A brief description of Indian life and Indian trade of the Susquehannock Indians. Lancaster (Pa.) *Intelligencer-Journal,* June 22, 1929.

1933 Conoy Indian town and Peter Bezaillion. Lancaster County Historical Society *Papers* 37(3):113-136.

n.d. Catalogue of my collection of Indian curios. Ms. #1, on file, Division of Archaeology, William Penn Memorial Museum, Harrisburg.

Landy, David

1978 Tuscarora among the Iroquois, in Bruce G. Trigger, ed., *Handbook of North American Indians* 15(Northeast):198-212. Smithsonian Institution, Washington, D.C.

Leder, Lawrence H., ed.

1956 The Livingston Indian records, 1666-1723. *Pennsylvania History* 23(1):5-240.

Lenig, Donald

1965 The Oak Hill horizon. . . . *Researches and Transactions* of the New York State Archeological Association 15(1). Buffalo.

Lenk, Torsten

1965 *The flintlock: Its origin and development.* Holland Press, London.

Lorant, Stefan, ed.
1946 *The New World: The first pictures of America.* Duell, Sloan & Pearce, Inc., New York.

Lucy, Charles L.
1950 Notes on a small Andaste burial site and Andaste archaeology. *Pennsylvania Archaeologist* 20(3-4):55-62.
1952 An upper Susquehanna mixed site. *Pennsylvania Archaeologist* 22(3-4):95-97.
1959 Pottery types of the upper Susquehanna. *Pennsylvania Archaeologist* 29(1):28-37.

Lucy, Charles L., and Catherine McCann
n.d. The Wells site, Asylum Township, Bradford County. *Pennsylvania Archaeologist*, in press.

Lucy, Charles L., and Leroy Vanderpoel
1979 The Tioga Point farm. *Pennsylvania Archaeologist* 49(1-2):1-12.

MacCord, Howard A., Sr.
1952 The Susquehannock Indians in West Virginia, 1630-77. *West Virginia History* 13(4):239-253.
1971 The Brown Johnson site, Bland County, Virginia. Archaeological Society of Virginia *Quarterly Bulletin* 25(4):230-272.

MacNeish, Richard S.
1952 Iroquois pottery types: A technique for the study of Iroquois prehistory. National Museum of Canada *Bulletin* no. 124; Anthropological series no. 31.

Magee, D. F.
1924 Address of D. F. Magee, Esq. *Historical Papers and Addresses* of the Lancaster County Historical Society 28:139-144.
1925 The location and boundaries of the Martin Chartier tract, together with the site of the original residence of Martin Chartier. Lancaster County Historical Society *Papers* 29(8):97-100.

Manson, Carl P. and Howard A. MacCord
1941 An historic Iroquois site near Romney, West Virginia. *West Virginia History* 2:290-293.
1944 Additional notes on the Herriot farm site. *West Virginia History* 5:201-211.

Margry, Pierre, ed.
1876-1886 Decouvertes et establissements des Francais dans l'ouest et dans le sud de l'Amerique septentrionale, 1614-1754. *Memoires et documents originaux*. 6 Vols. D. Jouaust, Paris.

Martin, C. H.
1930 Two Delaware Indians who lived on farm of Christian Hershey. Lancaster County Historical Society *Papers* 34(10):217-220. Lancaster

Maryland Archives
1899 *Proceedings and acts of the General Assembly of Maryland*, edited by William Hand Browne. Maryland Historical Society, Baltimore.

Maryland Hall of Records
1776 Hall of Records Vol. PL#8, folio 92-3, Annapolis, Md.

Mayer, J. R.
1943 Flintlocks of the Iroquois, 1620-1687. *Researches and Transactions* of the New York State Archeological Association 10(6).

Mayer-Oakes, William J.
1955 Prehistory of the upper Ohio Valley. *Annals* of Carnegie Museum 34(2). Pittsburgh.

McCann, Catherine
1962 The Wilson site, Bradford Co., Penna. *Pennsylvania Archaeologist* 32(2):43-55.

McCary, Ben C.
1957a *John Smith's map of Virginia, with a brief account of its history*. Virginia 350th Anniversary Celebration Corporation, Williamsburg
1957b *Indians in seventeenth-century Virginia*. Virginia 350th Anniversary Celebration Corporation, Williamsburg.
McCashion, John H.
1975 The clay tobacco pipes of New York State—Part one: Caughnawaga. New York State Archeological Association *Bulletin* 65:1-19.
1979 A preliminary chronology and discussion of seventeenth and early eighteenth century clay pipes from New York State sites. *British Archaeological Reports*, International Series 60(2):63-149.
McCashion, John H., and Theodore Robinson
1977 The clay tobacco pipes of New York State, under the sidewalks of New York: Archaeological investigations near the U.S. customs house on Manhattan Island, New York. New York State Archeological Association *Bulletin* 71:2-19.
McIntyre, Jamie
1979 The Knouse site: An historical site in Luzerne County, Pennsylvania. Ms. #1, on file, Division of Archaeology, William Penn Memorial Museum, Harrisburg.
McKearin, George S., and Helen McKearin
1941 *American glass*. Crown Publishers, New York.
McMichael, Edward V.
1968 Introduction to West Virginia archeology. *Educational Series*, West Virginia Geological and Economic Survey, Morgantown.
Meginness, J. F.
1889 *History of the West Branch*. Gazette and Bulletin Printing House, Williamsport, Pa.
Michels, Joseph, and Ira F. Smith III
1967 *Archaeological investigations of Sheep Rock shelter, Huntingdon County, Pennsylvania* (2 Vols.). Pennsylvania State University, Department of Sociology and Anthropology, University Park.
Miner, Charles
1845 *History of Wyoming*. . . . J. Crissey, Philadelphia.
Minutes of the Provincial Council (1838 ed.)
1838 *Minutes of the Provincial Council of Pennsylvania*, 1683-1776. 3 Vols. Theophilus Fenn. (Vol. I: 1683-1700; Vol. II: 1700-1717).
Mitchell, Vivienne
1976 Decorated brown clay pipe bowls from Nominy plantation: Progress report. Archaeological Society of Virginia *Quarterly Bulletin* 31(2): 83-87.
Mithun, Marianne
n.d. Stalking the Susquehannocks. Ms. #1, on file, Division of Archeology, William Penn Memorial Museum, Harrisburg.
Mombert, J. I.
1869 *An authentic history of Lancaster County in the State of Pennsylvania*. J. E. Barr & Co., Lancaster.
Mook, Maurice
1944 The aboriginal population of tidewater Virginia. *American Anthropologist* 46(2):193-208.
Moorehead, Warren K.
1918 *A brief summary of the archaeology of the Susquehanna*. Second Report of the Pennsylvania Historical Commission, pp. 117-126.
1938 *A report of the Susquehanna river expedition*. Andover Press, Andover, Mass.

Morgan, Lewis Henry
1881 Houses and house-life of the American Aborigines. *U.S. Geological and Geographical Survey of the Rocky Mountain Region, Contributions to North American Ethnology* 4.
1901 League of the Ho-de-no-sau-nee or Iroquois (2 Vols.). Dodd, Mead and Company, New York.
Murphy, Henry C., ed.
1867 Journal of a voyage to New York and a tour in several of the American colonies in 1679-80, by Jasper Dankers and Peter Sluyter of Wiewerd in Friesland. Long Island Historical Society *Memoirs*, 1.
Murphy, James L.
1973 "Five vessels from the McFate site, Crawford County, Pennsylvania." *Pennsylvania Archaeologist* 43(2):51-57.
Murray, Jessie Welles
1933 Depression aids archaeology at Athens, Pa. *Pennsylvania Archaeologist* 3(5):17-19.
Murray, Louise Welles
1908 *A History of old Tioga Point and early Athens, Pennsylvania. . . .* Athens, Pa.
1921 Aboriginal sites in and near Teaoga, now Athens, Penna. *American Anthropologist* 23:183-214.
Murray, Louise Welles, ed.
1931 Selected manuscripts of General John S. Clark, relating to the aboriginal history of the Susquehanna. Society for Pennsylvania Archaeology, *Publication* no. 1.
Myers, Albert Cook
1925 Substance of the address of Dr. Albert Cook Myers, delivered at the unveiling exercises of the Martin Chartier marker. . . . Lancaster County Historical Society *Papers* 29(10):127-133.
Myers, Albert Cook, ed.
1912 *Narratives of early Pennsylvania, West New Jersey, and Delaware, 1630-1707*. Reprinted 1953 Barnes & Noble, Inc, New York.
Naroll, Raoul
1962 Floor area and settlement population. *American Antiquity* 27(4):587-589.
Neill, Edward D.
1876 *The founders of Maryland, as portrayed in manuscripts*. J. Munsell, Albany, N.Y.
Newcomb, William W., Jr.
1956 The culture and acculturation of the Delaware Indians. University of Michigan Museum of Anthropology, *Anthropology Papers* 10.
Nichols, Deborah L.
1979 Field report on the 1979 excavations at 36Nb71, Fort Augusta, Sunbury, Pennsylvania. Ms. #1, on file, Division of Archaeology, William Penn Memorial Museum, Harrisburg.
1980 Field report on the 1979 excavations at 36Nb71, Fort Augusta, Sunbury, Pennsylvania. Northumberland County Historical Society *Proceedings and Addresses* 28:101-129.
Noël Hume, Ivor
1961 The glass wine bottle in colonial Virginia. *Journal of Glass Studies* 3:90-117.
1976 *A guide to artifacts of colonial America*. Alfred A. Knopf, New York.
1979 First look at a lost Virginia settlement. *National Geographic* 155(6):737-767.
1982 New clues to an old mystery. *National Geographic* 161(1):53-77.

O'Callaghan, E. B., ed.
1849 *Documentary history of the State of New York* 1. Weed, Parsons & Co., Albany.
1855 *Documentary history of the State of New York* 9. Weed, Parsons & Co., Albany.
Omwake, H. Geiger
1959 White kaolin pipes from the Oscar Leibhart site, in Witthoft and Kinsey, eds., *Susquehannock Miscellany*, pp. 126-135. Pennsylvania Historical and Museum Commission, Harrisburg.
Omwake, H. Geiger, and T. D. Stewart, eds.
1963 The Townsend site near Lewes, Delaware. The Sussex County Society of Archeology and History, *Publication* 15(1).
Oswald, Adrian
1975 Clay pipes for the archaeologist. *British Archaeological Reports*, Oxford, England.
Parker, Arthur C.
1923 *Seneca myths and folk tales.* Tribune Publishing Co., Meadville, Pa.
Peal, Christopher
1970 English knopped latten spoons. Part I: *The Connoisseur* 173(698): 254-257, April; Part II: *The Connoisseur* 174(701):196-200, July.
Pennsylvania Archaeologist
1937 *Pennsylvania Archaeologist* 7(2), July, 1937.
Pennsylvania Archives
1664-1776 *Pennsylvania Archives.* Joseph Severns & Co., Philadelphia.
1852 *Pennsylvania Archives*, first series, edited by Samuel Hazard. Joseph Severns & Co., Philadelphia
1895 *Pennsylvania Archives*, third series, ed. by William Henry Egle. Volume IV: Draughts of the Proprietary Manors in the Province of Pennsylvania: Appendix I-X (binder's title). Harrisburg: Clarence M. Busch, State Printer.
1931-1935 *Pennsylvania Archives*, eighth series, edited by Gertrude MacKinney. Pennsylvania Department of Property and Supplies, Harrisburg.
1890 *Pennsylvania Archives*, second series, Vol. 16. E. K. Myers, State Printer, Harrisburg.
Pennsylvania Division of Land Records (Record Group 26: Records of the Department of State), Harrisburg, Pa.

a.	PA DLR P.B. A6	Patent Book A6 (Old Rights)
b.	PA DLR P.B. BB2	Copied Surveys, Book BB-2
c.	PA DLR P.B. BB3	Copied Surveys, Book BB-3
d.	PA DLR P.B. BB4	Copied Surveys, Book BB-4
e.	PA DLR P.B. BB23	Copied Surveys, Book BB-23
f.	PA DLR P.B. BB65	Copied Surveys, Book BB-65
g.	PA DLR S.B. A1	Survey Book A-1
h.	PA DLR S.B. B6	Copied Surveys, Book B-6
i.	PA DLR S.B. D80	Copied Surveys, Book D-80
j.	PA DLR S.B. D113	Copied Surveys, Book D-113

Pennsylvania State Archives
n.d. MG11: Map Collection, 1681-1973. Harrisburg (no. 150).
Peterson, Harold L.
1956 *Arms and armor in colonial America, 1526-1783.* Stackpole Co., Harrisburg.
Plantagenet, Beauchamp (alias)
1648 A description of the Province of New Albion . . ., reprinted in John E. Pomfret, *The Province of West New Jersey, 1609-1702: A history of the origins of an American colony*. Princeton University Press, Princeton.

Pratt, Peter P.
1961 *Oneida Iroquois glass trade bead sequence, 1585-1745*. Fort Stanwix Museum, Rome, N.Y.
1976 Archaeology of the Oneida Iroquois, 1. *Occasional Papers in Northeastern Anthropology* 1. Man in the Northeast, Inc.

Price, G. Hilton
1908 *Old base metal spoons*. London.

Proud, Robert
1797 *The history of Pennsylvania, in North America. . . .* Zachariah Poulson, Philadelphia.

Prowell, George R.
1907 *History of York County, Pennsylvania*. J. H. Beers & Co., Chicago.

Quimby, George Irving
1966 *Indian culture and European trade goods*. University of Wisconsin Press, Madison.

Reichel, William C., ed.
1870 *Memorials of the Moravian Church*. J. B. Lippincott & Co., Philadelphia.

Ritchie, William A.
1949 The Bell-Philhower site, Sussex County, New Jersey. Indiana Historical Society *Prehistory Research Series* 3(2).
1954 Dutch Hollow, an early historic period Seneca site in Livingston County, New York. *Researches and Transactions* of the New York State Archeological Association 13(1).
1965 *The archaeology of New York State*. Natural History Press, Garden City, N.Y.

Ritchie, William A., and Robert E. Funk
1973 Aboriginal settlement patterns in the northeast. New York State Museum and Science Service, *Memoir* 20.

Rochester Museum and Science Center
1975 *Newsletter*. 12(1).

Rupp, I. Daniel
1844 *History of Lancaster County, Pennsylvania. . . .* Gilbert Hills, Lancaster.

Russ, William A.
1966 How Pennsylvania acquired its present boundaries. *Pennsylvania Historical Studies* 8. Pennsylvania Historical Association, Pennsylvania State University, University Park.

Russell, Carl P.
1957 *Guns on the early frontiers. . . .* University of California Press, Berkeley.

Rutsch, Edward S.
1973 *Smoking technology of the aborigines of the Iroquois area of New York State*. Fairleigh Dickinson University Press, Rutherford, N.J.

Salwen, Bert
1978 Indians of southern New England and Long Island: Early period, in Bruce G. Trigger, ed., *Handbook of North American Indians* 15(Northeast):160-176. Smithsonian Institution, Washington, D.C.

Schaeffer, Claude E.
1942 The Tutelo Indians in Pennsylvania history, in Frank G. Speck, *The Tutelo spirit adoption ceremony*, pp. v-xix. Pennsylvania Historical Commission, Harrisburg.

Schoff, Harry L.
1937a The excavation of the site of Provincial Fort Muncy. *Pennsylvania Archaeologist* 7(1):9-11.
1937b Excavation of the village area near the burial mound of the H. G. Brock property, Muncy, Pa. *Pennsylvania Archaeologist* 7(1):6-7.

1937c Excavations of the Indian burial ground on the Updegraff property, Reach Road, Newberry, Lycoming County, Pennsylvania. *Pennsylvania Archaeologist* 7(1):11-12.

1937d Report on archaeological investigations carried on at the J. T. Roberts property, Montoursville, Lycoming County, Pennsylvania. *Pennsylvania Archaeologist* 7(1):8.

1937e A report of the excavation of the ancient Indian burial mound near Muncy, Lycoming County, Penna. *Pennsylvania Archaeologist* 7(1)3-5.

n.d. McFate site: Report on archaeological excavations conducted in northwestern Pennsylvania by the Works Progress Administration. Ms. #2, on file, Division of Archaeology, William Penn Memorial Museum, Harrisburg.

Schoolcraft, Henry R.

1851 *The American Indians, their history, condition and prospects, from original notes and manuscripts*. Wanzer, Foot, N.Y.

1854 *Information respecting the history, condition and prospects of the Indian tribes of the United States. . . .* Part IV. Lippincott, Grambo & Company, Rochester, N.Y.

Scull, G. D.

1881 *The Evelyns in America, 1608-1805*. Parker and Co., Oxford.

Semmes, Raphael

1937 *Captains and mariners of early Maryland*. Johns Hopkins Press, Baltimore.

Service, Elman R.

1962 *Primitive social organization*. Random House, Inc., New York.

Simmons, W. S.

1970 *Cantantowwit's house: An Indian burial ground on the Island of Conanicut in Narragansett Bay*. Brown University Press, Providence.

Sipe, C. Hale

1927 *The Indian chiefs of Pennsylvania*. Ziegler Printing Co., Butler, Pa.

1929 *The Indian wars of Pennsylvania*. The Telegraph Press, Harrisburg.

Skinner, A. Alanson

1921 Notes on Iroquois archaeology. Museum of the American Indian, Heye Foundation, *Miscellaneous Indian Notes and Monographs* 18.

1938 The Andaste, in W. K. Moorehead, ed., *A report of the Susquehanna River expedition* . . ., pp. 45-67. Andover Press, Andover, Mass.

Smith, Carlyle S.

1950 The archaeology of coastal New York. American Museum of Natural History *Anthropological Papers* 43:91-200.

Smith, Ira F. III

1970 Schultz site settlement patterns and external relations: A preliminary discussion and possible interpretation. New York State Archeological Association *Bulletin* 50(Nov. 1970):27-34.

1973 The Parker site: A manifestation of the Wyoming Valley culture. *Pennsylvania Archaeologist* 43(3-4):1-56.

1976 A functional interpretation of "keyhole" structures in the northeast. *Pennsylvania Archaeologist* 46(1-2):1-12.

1981a A late woodland village site in north central Pennsylvania: Its role in Susquehannock culture history. Ms. #5, on file, Division of Archaeology, William Penn Memorial Museum, Harrisburg.

1981b Clemson Island culture in Pennsylvania. Ms. #6, on file, Division of Archaeology, William Penn Memorial Museum, Harrisburg.

Smith, Ira F. III, and Jeffrey C. Graybill

1977 A report on the Shenks Ferry and Susquehannock components at the Funk site, Lancaster County, Pennsylvania. *Man in the Northeast* 11:45-65, Spring, 1977.

Smith, Ira F. III, and James T. Herbstritt
1976 Preliminary investigations of the prehistoric earthworks in Elk County, Pa. Pennsylvania Historical and Museum Commission, Harrisburg.
1977 *A status report on the Pennsylvania Archaeological Site Survey.* Pennsylvania Historical and Museum Commission, Harrisburg.

Smith, John.
1624 *The generall historie of Virginia New England and the Summer Isles. . . .* Michael Sparkes, London.
1907 *The generall historie of Virginia. . . .*, two vols. James Maclehose & Sons, Glasgow.

Smith, Joseph
1816 *Explanation or key to the various manufactories of Sheffield. . . .* H. A. Bacon, Sheffield. Reprint 1975 by the Early American Industries Association, South Burlington, Vt.

Speck, Frank G.
1931 *A study of the Delaware Indian big house ceremony.* Pennsylvania Historical Commission Publications 2.
1942 *The Tutelo spirit adoption ceremony.* Pennsylvania Historical Commission, Harrisburg.

Stephenson, Robert L., Alice L. L. Ferguson, and Henry G. Ferguson
1963 The Accokeek Creek site: A Middle Atlantic seaboard culture sequence. Museum of Anthropology, University of Michigan, *Anthropological Papers* 20.

Stewart, Julian H.
1955 *Theory of culture change: The methodology of multilinear evolution.* University of Illinois Press, Urbana.

Stewart, Marilyn C.
1973 A Proto-historic Susquehannock cemetery near Nichols, New York. New York State Archeological Association *Bulletin* 58:1-21.

Stewart, T. B.
1930 Andaste camp site at Pine, Clinton County, Pennsylvania. *Now and Then* 4:76-78.

Stewart, T. D.
1952 Report on the human skeletal material from the Herriot Site, West Virginia. Pp. 246-248 of Howard A. MacCord, The Susquehannock Indians in West Virginia, 1630-77. *West Virginia History* 13(4):246-248.

Streeter, S. F.
1857 The fall of the Susquehannocks: A chapter from the Indian history of Maryland. *Historical Magazine* . . . 1(3):65-73.

Styles, John
1821 *The life of David Brainerd, missionary to the Indians. . . .* Samuel T. Armstrong, and Crocker and Brewster, Boston

Sweeney, Jeanne W.
1966 The Wyoming Valley complex: A ceramic analysis and some cultural associations. M.S. thesis, University of Pennsylvania, Philadelphia; Ms. #1, on file, Division of Archaeology, William Penn Memorial Museum, Harrisburg.

Talbot, Sir William
1966 *The discoveries of John Lederer, in . . . Virginia, to the west of Carolina. . . .* J. C. for Samuel Heyrick; reprinted 1966, Readex Microprint Corporation, London.

Taylor, Jacob
n.d. Abstracts of warrants of survey. Taylor papers, Historical Society of Pennsylvania, Philadelphia.

Thornton, John
1681 A map of Pennsylvania in America, being partly inhabited. . . . John Thornton, London. Reproduced 1923: Albert Cook Myers, Philadelphia.
Thwaites, Reuben Gold, ed.
1959 *The Jesuit relations and allied documents: Travels and explorations of the Jesuit missionaries in New France, 1610-1791.* Pageant Book Company, New York.
Tooker, Elisabeth
1982 The demise of the Susquehannocks: A seventeenth century mystery. Ms. #1, on file, Division of Archaeology, William Penn Memorial Museum, Harrisburg.
Tooley, R. V.
1980 *The mapping of America.* Holland Press, Ltd., London.
Tuck, James A.
1971 *Onondaga Iroquois prehistory.* Syracuse University Press, Syracuse.
Turnbaugh, William A.
1975 *Man, land, and time: The cultural prehistory and demographic patterns of north-central Pennsylvania.* Lycoming County Historical Society, Williamsport, Pa.
1979 Calumet ceremonialism as a nativistic response. *American Antiquity* 44(4):685-691.
Tyler, Lyon G., ed.
1907 *Narratives of early Virginia, 1606-1625.* Barnes & Noble, Inc., New York.
Van der Donck, Adrian
1841 A description of the New Netherlands, translated from the original of 1656 by Jeremiah Johnson. *Collections* of the New-York Historical Society, second series 1:125-242.
Van Horn, Elizabeth H.
1971 *Iroquois silver brooches (As-ne-as-gih) in the Rochester Museum.* Rochester Museum and Science Center, Rochester.
Wallace, Anthony F. C.
1949 *King of the Delawares: Teedyuscung, 1700-1763.* University of Pennsylvania Press, Philadelphia.
1970 *The death and rebirth of the Seneca.* Alfred A. Knopf, New York.
Wallace, Paul A. W.
1945 *Conrad Weiser: Friend of colonist and Mohawk.* University of Pennsylvania Press, Philadelphia.
1964 *Indians in Pennsylvania.* Pennsylvania Historical and Museum Commission, Harrisburg.
1965 *Indian paths of Pennsylvania.* Pennsylvania Historical and Museum Commission, Harrisburg.
1981 *Indians in Pennsylvania* (revised edition). Pennsylvania Historical and Museum Commission, Harrisburg.
Washburn, Wilcomb E.
1957 *The governor and the rebel.* University of North Carolina Press, Chapel Hill.
Watkins, C. Malcolm
1960 North Devon pottery and its export to America in the seventeenth century. United States National Museum *Bulletin* 225, paper 13. Washington, D.C.
Webster, Gary S.
1983 Northern Iroquoian hunting: An optimization approach. Ph.D. thesis, Department of Anthropology, The Pennsylvania State University.

Weiser, Conrad
1854 Narrative of a journey from Tulpehocken, Pennsylvania, to Onondaga, in 1737. Translated from the German by Hiester H. Muhlenberg, M.D., communicated by F. A. Hiester, Esq. in Henry R. Schoolcraft, *Information respecting the history, condition and prospects of the Indian tribes of the United States. . . .*, part IV. Lippincott, Grambo & Company, Philadelphia.

Weslager, C. A.
1948 *The Nanticoke Indians: A refugee tribal group of Pennsylvania.* Pennsylvania Historical and Museum Commission, Harrisburg.
1967 *The English on the Delaware, 1610-1682.* Rutgers University Press, New Brunswick, N.J.
1972 *The Delaware Indians: A history.* Rutgers University Press, New Brunswick, N.J.
1976 *Red men on the Brandywine.* Hambleton Company, Inc. (originally published 1953), Wilmington, Del.

Weslager, C. A. and A. R. Dunlap
1961 *Dutch explorers, traders and settlers in the Delaware Valley, 1609-1644.* University of Pennsylvania Press, Philadelphia.

White, Marian E.
1978 Erie, in Bruce G. Trigger, ed., *Handbook of North American Indians* 15(Northeast):412-417. Smithsonian Institution, Washington, D.C.

White, Stephen W.
1975 On the origins of gunspalls. *Historical Archaeology* 9:65-73.

Willey, Lorraine M.
1974 A functional analysis of perishable artifacts during the late woodland period in the northeastern United States. M.A. thesis, Pennsylvania State University.

Witthoft, John
1952 Comments on the cultural position of the Herriot farm site, in Howard A. MacCord, The Susquehannock Indians in West Virginia, 1630-77. *West Virginia History* 13(4):249-253.
1954 Pottery from the Stewart site, Clinton County, Pennsylvania. *Pennsylvania Archaeologist* 24(1):22-29.
1959a Ancestry of the Susquehannocks, in John Witthoft and W. Fred Kinsey III, eds., *Susquehannock miscellany*, pp. 19-60. Pennsylvania Historical and Museum Commission, Harrisburg.
1959b Susquehannock shaft polishers and the Indian sundial, in Witthoft and Kinsey, eds., *Susquehannock miscellany*, pp. 120-125. Pennsylvania Historical and Museum Commission, Harrisburg.
1966 A history of gunflints. *Pennsylvania Archaeologist* 36(1-2):12-49.
n.d.a The Conestoga towns. Ms. #4,7b, on file, Division of Archaeology, William Penn Memorial Museum, Harrisburg.
n.d.b Notes on medals, beads, etc., found in 18th century Indian sites, including Conoytown (Hixon site). Ms. #6, on file, Division of Archaeology, William Penn Memorial Museum, Harrisburg.
n.d.c The Susquehannock and Conestoga towns of 1640-1763. Ms. #7,7a on file, Division of Archaeology, William Penn Memorial Museum, Harrisburg.
n.d.d Ceramic sequences in eastern Pennsylvania. Ms. #12 on file, Division of Archaeology, William Penn Memorial Museum, Harrisburg.

Witthoft, John, and S. S. Farver
1952 Two Shenk's Ferry sites in Lebanon County, Pennsylvania. *Pennsylvania Archaeologist* 22(1):3-32.

Witthoft, John, and William A. Hunter
1955 The seventeenth-century origin of the Shawnee. *Ethnohistory* 2(1):42-57.
Witthoft, John, and W. Fred Kinsey III, eds.
1959 *Susquehannock miscellany*. Pennsylvania Historical and Museum Commission, Harrisburg.
Witthoft, John, Harry Schoff, and Charles F. Wray
1953 Micmac pipes, vase-shaped pipes, and calumets. *Pennsylvania Archaeologist* 23(3-4):89-107.
Woodward, Arthur
1933 Wampum and its uses. *Pennsylvania Archaeologist* 3(5):1, 11-16.
Wray, Charles F.
1963 Ornamental hair combs of the Seneca Iroquois. *Pennsylvania Archaeologist* 33(1-2):35-50.
1964 The bird in Seneca archeology. *Proceedings* of the Rochester Academy of Science 11(1):1-28.
1973 *Manual for Seneca Iroquois archeology*. Cultures Primitive, Inc., Rochester, N.Y.
Wray, Charles F., and Harry L. Schoff
1953 A preliminary report on the Seneca sequence in western New York, 1550-1627. *Pennsylvania Archaeologist* 23(2):53-63.
Wren, Christopher
1908 Turtle shell rattles and other implements from Indian graves at Athens, Penna. *Proceedings and Collections* of the Wyoming Historical and Geological Society 10:195-210..
1912 Some Indian graves at Plymouth, Pa. *Proceedings and Collections* of the Wyoming Historical and Geological Society 12:199-204.
1914 A study of north Appalachian Indian pottery. *Proceedings and Collections* of the Wyoming Historical and Geological Society 13:131-222.
Wright, Harrison
1883 A memorandum description of the finer specimens of Indian earthenware pots in the collection of the Wyoming Historical and Geological Society. *Proceedings and Collections* of the Wyoming Historical and Geological Society 1(4).
1885 Report of the special archaeological committee on the Athens locality. *Proceedings and Collections* of the Wyoming Historical and Geological Society 2(1):55-67.
York County Deed Book G114
1776 Deed book G, on file, Office of the Recorder of Deeds, York, Pa.
Zakucia, John A.
1960 The Chambers site, an historical burial ground of 1750-75. Eastern States Archaeological Federation *Bulletin* 19:12.
Zeisberger, David
1910 History of the North American Indian, ed. by A. B. Hulbert and W. N. Schwarze. Ohio Archaeological and Historical Society *Publications* 19:1-189.

Appendix

Site Numbers and Counties

Armstrong (Ar)
36Ar12 - Molbucteetam

Berks (Bk)
36Bk450 - Kutztown (near; also Maxatawny)

Bradford (Br)
36Br1 - Tioga Point Museum
36Br2 - Murray Garden
36Br3 - Tioga Point
36Br5 - Murray Farm
36Br15 - Sheshequin
36Br27 - Spanish Hill (Carantouan)
36Br28 - Spanish Hill (south of)
36Br38 - Sayre (NE of)
36Br41 - Ogehage
36Br42 - Ahbe-Brennan
36Br43 - Kennedy
36Br44 - Oscalui (Newtychanning)
36Br50 - Sick
36Br57 - Cass
36Br58 - Wilson
36Br59 - Wells
36Br80, 81 - Wyalusing (Gohontoto, Friedenshuetten)
36Br83 - Blackman
36Br134 - French Azilum

Bucks (Bu)
36Bu5 - Overpeck
36Bu19 - Pennsbury Manor
36Bu59 - Eelskin Rock Shelter

Chester (Ch)
36Ch3 - Minguhanan
36Ch60 - Montgomery
36Ch61 - North Brook
36Ch121 - Okehocking

Clearfield (Cd)
36Cd7 - Kalgren

Clinton (Cn)
36Cn6 - Quiggle
36Cn10 - Stewart Farm

Crawford (Cw)
36Cw1 - McFate

Dauphin (Da)
36Da13 - Middletown "Up"

Delaware (De)
36De3 - Printzhof
36De6 - Queonemysing (Big Bend)

Huntingdon (Hu)
36Hu1 - Sheep Rock Shelter

Lancaster (La)
36La1 - Roberts
36La2 - Shenks Ferry
36La3 - Strickler
36La4 - Keller
36La5 - Brandt
36La6 - Frey-Haverstick
36La7 - Schultz
36La8 - Washington Boro Village
36La9 - Funk (and Schultz-Funk Cemetery)
36La10 - Billmyer
36La11 - Erb Rock Shelter
36La12 - Eschelman
36La36 - Blue Rock (Nace)
36La37 - Blue Rock (Witmer)
36La39 - Mohr
36La40 - Conoy Cemetery
36La52 - Conestoga Town
36La54 - Ibaugh
36La57 - Conoy Town
36La90 - Locust Grove
36La92 - Reitz
36La96 - County Park
36La183 - Murry
36La186 - Firehouse
36La185 - Little Indian Rock

Lawrence (Lr)
36Lr1 - Wyandotte Town (also West Pittsburg)
36Lr11 - Kuskuski

Lebanon (Le)
36Le2 - Miller
36Le198 - Tulpehocken

Luzerne (Lu)
36Lu1 - Schacht
36Lu2 - Wermuth
36Lu3 - Sarf
36Lu14 - Parker
36Lu43 - Knouse (Smith Farm, Wapwallopen)
36Lu54 - Bead Hill

Lycoming (Ly)
36Ly110 - Wolf Creek
36Ly119 - Bull Run

Montgomery (Mg)
36Mg19 - Unami Creek Rock Shelter

Northumberland (Nb)
36Nb71 - Fort Augusta

Perry (Pe)
36Pe17 - Kline

Philadelphia (Ph)
36Ph1 - Market Street

York (Yo)
36Yo9 - Leibhart (Oscar, Upper)
36Yo170 - Leibhart (Byrd, Lower)

Index

Site Names and Locations